Vital Problems for American Society

Vital Problems for

CONSULTING EDITOR / Marvin Bressler / PRINCETON UNIVERSITY

RANDOM HOUSE ∾ NEW YORK

American Society

Meanings and Means

EDITED WITH INTRODUCTIONS BY

J. Alan Winter / TEMPLE UNIVERSITY

Jerome Rabow / UNIVERSITY OF CALIFORNIA, LOS ANGELES

Mark Chesler / THE UNIVERSITY OF MICHIGAN

∽

TO
Gail, Thelma, and Joan,
Wendy, Joshua, David, and Deborah

PREFACE

This book examines problems encountered in attempts to define and implement a particular statement of the goals and values of American society: that found in the Preamble to its Constitution. Specifically, the book examines both problems encountered in specifying the referents or *meanings* of the Preamble terms "We the People of the United States," "Justice," "domestic Tranquility," "the common defence," "the general Welfare," "the Blessings of Liberty," and "ourselves and our Posterity," and problems encountered in creating and maintaining the social conditions or *means* by which they are achieved. We have, of course, found the Preamble terms to be vague and overlapping in meaning. Using the insights of sociology, our aim has been to reduce the vagueness and overlap while retaining meanings that are both common and reasonable.

The rationale for the use of the Preamble in a study of American social problems is discussed in the Introduction. The Introduction also discusses the relationship between the approach that led to the Preamble's use and that found in more traditional social problems texts. Each of the succeeding chapters deals with the problems of meaning—defining a particular Preamble phrase —and the problems of means—implementing whatever definition is offered. A chapter consists of an introductory statement by the editors followed by several selected readings. The introductory statement is designed to provide a framework within which to consider the specific issues raised in the readings and within which additional subjects can be pursued.

This preface first alerts the reader to two important features of our use of the Preamble and then discusses the effect that its use has on the study of American social problems.

As the reader will soon discover, our study of the problems of defining

and implementing Preamble goals and values is not restricted to a consideration of the issues of interests to the framers of the Constitution. They were
primarily concerned with the operations of government and its relationship
to the people. However, such problems as promoting the general welfare or
insuring the domestic tranquillity are only partly matters of government and
politics. Hence, the subject matter of this book, while it deals with government and politics, extends beyond their boundaries to a consideration of other
social structures and processes.

We want also to draw attention to our treatment of the phrases "We the
People of the United States," and "ourselves and our Posterity." Each is regarded as referring to social facts or conditions which are deemed desirable
and which Americans can seek to create and maintain. That is, they are regarded as referring to a value or goal in much the same sense as does a term
such as "Justice." In the case of "We the People," the reference is taken to
be to the norms and practices that define one as an "American," as one of
"We the People" with all the rights and privileges thereof. "Ourselves and our
Posterity" is taken to refer to the particular relationships among generations
which Americans value and seek to maintain.

The use of the Preamble as a guide to the study of American social
problems draws attention to the more basic dimensions of concrete and
specific problems. For example, it views the present racial problems as part of
a continuing debate over what constitutes justice and of how an individual
member of a minority group is to attain full membership as one of "We the
People of the United States." Indeed, we often found that concrete problems
could and should be analyzed in terms of more than one Preamble value or
goal. Problems involving pluralism, for example, are first discussed as an aspect
of the more perfect union and then as part of the process of securing the
blessings of liberty. The question of whether or not an effective pluralism
exists on matters of defense is also raised. In short, the concrete and specific
issues which fall under the rubric of "pluralism" are discussed in not one but
three chapters.

The tendency to deal with different aspects of familiar problems under
different rubrics and in separate chapters will undoubtedly prove disturbing to
some. We hope, however, that the depth of understanding that results will
compensate for the intellectual efforts required to master newly discovered
issues and a new approach to familiar problems.

We hope too that the reader will join us as we express our gratitude to
those who helped make this book possible: to Gail Winter, Helene Conticchio,

and Emily Kosobucki, who typed various early drafts; to Joanne Hesslink, who did a magnificent job of typing the final manuscript; to Marta Greenwald for her work on the index; to June Fischbein, whose copyediting did much to improve our work; and to Marvin Bressler, our consulting editor, and Theodore Caris of Random House whose combined faith in us was a prerequisite for the completion of this work.

New Brunswick, New Jersey   J. A. W.
Los Angeles, California   J. R.
Ann Arbor, Michigan   M. C.
May, 1967

CONTENTS

Vital Problems for American Society

We the People of the United
States, in Order to form a
more perfect Union, establish
Justice, insure domestic
Tranquility, provide for the
common defence, promote the

general Welfare, and secure

the Blessings of Liberty to

ourselves and our Posterity,

do ordain and establish

this Constitution for the

United States of America.

The Preamble and American Social Problems

This book uses the Preamble to the Constitution of the United States of America to give order and coherence to a study of American social problems. The use of the Preamble as a guide stems from a desire to focus upon the dominant problems of American society, problems that involve America's dominant values and goals and that are described in terms of its most important common symbols. The Preamble can serve as such a guide because it is a list of dominant American values and goals expressed in terms of important common symbols.

This book examines two kinds of problems: the problems of *meanings* —the problems of defining the key values and goals of American society and the problems of *means*—the problems of implementing whatever definition is offered. Specifically, it deals with the problems of defining what is meant by a more perfect union with justice, tranquillity, defense, welfare, and the blessings of liberty for the people of the United States and their posterity and the problems of forming, establishing, insuring, providing, promoting, and securing this set of goals.

This approach to the study of the problems of American society represents a departure from the traditional sociological approach to the subject, which focuses on failures to follow or implement widely accepted definitions of what is normal or desirable. The first section of this Introduction discusses the more traditional perspective. The second section discusses the approach taken in this book, which focuses on the problems of meanings and means, the problems of defining and implementing societal goals, and then compares the two approaches.

The Traditional Study of Social Problems

The traditional sociological approach to the study of a society's problems may be called the *discrepancy approach*, to emphasize the fact that it takes the existence of a discrepancy between societal standards and actual conditions as the basic feature of social problems. Robert K. Merton and Robert A. Nisbet's definition of "social problems" is typical of this approach. They regard social problems as

problems in the sense that they represent interruptions in the socially expected or morally desired scheme of things. They are violations of the good and the right, as a society defines these moral attributes; dislocations of the social patterns and relationships that a society approves or takes for granted.[1]

Other sociologists add the requirement that the discrepancy be one about which at least some people believe collective action can or should be taken. For example, Edward C. McDonagh and Jon E. Simpson view social problems as "the significant discrepancies between cultural prescriptions and present-day conditions that influential leaders and involved persons believe should be ameliorated through appropriate social action."[2] While Paul B. Horton and Gerald R. Leslie, in a similar vein, define social problems as "conditions affecting a significant number of people in ways considered undesirable, about which it is felt something be done through collective action."[3]

Still other sociologists, who employ the traditional approach, focus on particular types of undesirable conditions. Earl Raab and Gertrude Jaeger Selznick assert,

A social problem exists (1) where prevailing relationships among people frustrate the important goals of a substantial number of people, or (2) where organized society appears to be seriously threatened by an inability to order relationships among people.[4]

[1] Robert K. Merton and Robert A. Nisbet, ed., *Contemporary Social Problems,* 2nd ed. (New York: Harcourt, Brace & World, 1966), p. 5.

[2] Edward C. McDonagh and Jon E. Simpson, *Social Problems: Persistent Challenges* (New York: Holt, Rinehart & Winston, 1965), p. v.

[3] Paul B. Horton and Gerald R. Leslie, *The Sociology of Social Problems,* 3rd ed. (New York: Appleton-Century-Crofts, 1965), p. 4. A similar definition is offered in S. Kirson Weinberg, *Social Problems in Our Time: A Sociological Analysis* (Englewood Cliffs, N.J.: Prentice-Hall, 1960), p. 4. It reads: "Social problems are behavior patterns or conditions that are considered objectionable or undesirable by many members of society. These members recognize that corrective policies, programs and services are necessary to cope with and reduce the scope of these problems."

[4] Earl Raab and Gertrude Jaeger Selznick, *Major Social Problems,* 2nd ed. (New York: Harper & Row, 1964), p. 3. A similar definition is offered by Judson R. Landis, ed., *Current Perspectives on Social Problems* (Belmont, Cal.: Wadsworth,

Russell R. Dynes, Alfred C. Clarke, Simon Dinitz, and Iwao Ishino view the existence of either dissensus or deviation as constituting the social problems that "transform the ideal of a trouble-free society into the reality of a society with social problems."[5]

The discrepancy approach focuses attention on situations which are: (1) considered immoral in that they violate cultural prescriptions or other definitions of what is right and good; (2) regarded as abnormal in that they represent dislocations or departures from what is taken for granted; or (3) otherwise undesirable. Thus, the discrepancy approach has led to the study of such problems as illegitimacy, where it is regarded as immoral; homosexuality, where heterosexuality is taken for granted; and poverty, where it is deemed undesirable on humanitarian or other grounds. The discrepancy approach may also lead to the study of conditions which are not thought of as immoral, abnormal, or undesirable, per se, but in which a difference exists between what is accepted as good and what is thought to be better. For example, a literacy rate as high as 80 or 90 per cent may be regarded as a problem if it is seen as "good, but not good enough." Conversely, the unemployment rate may be viewed as a problem if it is considered "low, but not low enough."

The labeling of a condition as a social problem in the discrepancy sense of the term is, of course, relative to the standards or norms which define what is taken as desirable or normal. Where individuals or groups differ with respect to such standards, their lists of problems will differ. What is seen as a problem in one culture or society may be regarded as normal or desirable in another. Moreover, the problems studied need not be the dominant ones of the society in which they occur; they need not be problems which involve the society's dominant values and goals, and need not be described in terms of the society's important common symbols.

Harry C. Bredemeier and Jackson Toby's *Social Problems in America*[6] uses the traditional discrepancy approach, but still examines conditions that could be regarded as dominant American problems. These conditions involve values that define and govern the pursuit of material, secular success. They include self-reliance, competition, and the nego-

---

1966), p. 1. It reads: "A social problem exists (1) when the important personal goals of a number of people are blocked or frustrated, or (2) when the organization of society appears to be seriously threatened."

[5] Russell R. Dynes, Alfred C. Clarke, Simon Dinitz, and Iwao Ishino, *Social Problems: Dissensus and Deviation in an Industrial Society* (New York: Oxford University Press, 1964), p. 7.

[6] Harry C. Bredemeier and Jackson Toby, eds., *Social Problems in America: Costs and Casualties in an Acquisitive Society* (New York: Wiley, 1960).

tiated exchange of goods and services for profit or wages. However, in the years since Bredemeier and Toby elected to study problems involving the failure to attain personal success as defined by these values, the degree to which these values characterize the pursuit of success in the United States has declined. As America becomes more bureaucratized, corporatized, and unionized, self-reliance and competition are replaced by cooperative interdependence as the major path to success.[7] The Lone Eagle, Charles A. Lindbergh, who flew solo across the Atlantic, is replaced as a cultural hero by the astronaut who flies with the aid of a team of thousands. Similarly, the widespread acceptance of private and public welfare systems that provide payments upon retirement, illness, or other forced withdrawals from the marketplace represent an acceptance of means of maintaining a position of personal material wealth other than that of negotiated exchanges for profit or wages. In short, the values and symbols which guided the Bredemeier and Toby selection of problems, while still prevalent and widely accepted in the United States, no longer dominate the activities of the individual and collectivities within it as they once did. Another guide to America's dominant problems, values, and goals seems to be needed.

The Preamble and
America's Vital Social Problems

This study takes the Preamble as a meaningful list of America's dominant goals and values expressed in terms of its important common symbols. The Preamble may be so regarded because it lists the objectives that the Constitution is designed to ordain and establish. The Constitution is the source or referent of basic definitions of the legitimate aims and activities of the individuals and collectivities which comprise American society. This is not to say that everybody agrees on how to interpret the Constitution and its Preamble, but it is to say that interpreting the Constitution is a crucial enterprise in America and that *interpretations* of the Constitution constitute definitions of what is and is not deemed desirable. To call something unconstitutional is tantamount to calling it un-American. Insofar as the United States requires a statement of loyalty from its officials and citizens, it is the Constitution with its Preamble that is used to legitimate the request and to define the commitment. All public officials and all naturalized citizens must swear allegiance to abide by the pro-

---

[7] Changes related to the shift from an emphasis on self-reliance to a stress on cooperative interdependence are dealt with in Chapter Seven in the discussion of changing conceptions of the blessings of liberty.

visions of the Constitution, as must many employees in government and other public institutions.

There are, of course, other documents that could be reasonably viewed as stating the dominant American goals and values. The Pledge of Allegiance, the Gettysburg Address, and the Declaration of Independence may be said to list goals and values as fundamental as those mentioned in the Preamble. However, the essential items in these other lists are included in or implied by the Preamble. For example, Americans pledge allegiance to a "republic . . . with liberty and justice for all." The Preamble refers to establishing justice and securing the blessings of liberty for the people of the United States and their posterity. The Pledge aks of "one nation, indivisible"; the Preamble, of "a more perfect Union." Lincoln's reference to "government of the people, by the people, and for the people" may also be thought of as one way of defining the character of the union mentioned in the Preamble. Finally, the life, liberty, and pursuit of happiness to which the Declaration of Independence asserts all men are entitled may be subsumed under the phrases "the general Welfare" and "the Blessings of Liberty" used in the Preamble.

Still other lists of important American values and goals may be drawn on the basis of general observations of the workings of American society. Such a list might include the doctrines of fair play, political democracy, equal opportunity, and individual initiative to which Kingsley Davis, Harry C. Bredemeier, and Marion Levy refer.[8] It might also include the values that John F. Cuber, William F. Kenkel, and Robert A. Harper[9] cite in their study of the problems of American society; namely, education, monogamy, acquisitiveness, technology and science, freedom, democracy, and monotheism.[10]

It is our belief, however, that any list drawn from observations of

---

[8] Kingsley Davis, Harry C. Bredemeier, and Marion Levy, *Modern American Society: Readings in the Problems of Order and Change* (New York: Rinehart, 1949), see p. 6.

[9] John F. Cuber, William F. Kenkel, and Robert A. Harper, *Problems of American Society*, 4th ed. (New York: Holt, Rinehart & Winston, 1964), p. 396.

[10] It should be noted that studies have raised questions about the extent to which there is a consensus on the meaning of some of the values referred to by Davis, Bredemeier, and Levy, *op. cit.*, and by Cuber, Kenkel, and Harper, *op. cit.* The values in question include political democracy, freedom, and equality of opportunity. The studies are: Samuel A. Stouffer, *Communism, Conformity and Civil Liberties* (Garden City, N.Y.: Doubleday, 1955); Raymond Mack, "Do We Really Believe in the Bill of Rights?" *Social Problems*, III (April, 1956), 264–269; James W. Prothro and Charles W. Grigg, "Fundamental Principles of Democracy: Basis of Agreement and Disagreement," *Journal of Politics*, XXII (May, 1960), 276–294; Herbert McCloskey, "Consensus and Ideology in American Politics," *American Political Science Review*, LXIII (June, 1964), 361–382; and Frank R. Westie, "The American Dilemma: An Empirical Test," *American Sociological Review*, XXX (August, 1965), 527–538.

American society will generally constitute alternative interpretations of the values and goals mentioned in the Preamble or strategies of how to implement them. The doctrine of fair play, for example, to which Davis, Bredemeier, and Levy refer can be seen as a specification of what constitutes justice; the doctrine of political democracy as a statement of how to secure the blessings of liberty. Similarly, education, acquisitiveness, and science and technology to which Cuber, Kenkel, and Harper refer, all play their role in promoting the general welfare.

Conditions which represent significant discrepancies between present-day conditions and the provisions of the Preamble constitute problems in the discrepancy sense of the term. They are not, however, the problems to which this book draws attention. The problems discussed here are central in an alternate approach, the *vital problems approach*.

The vital problems approach to the study of social problems examines the problems involved in defining and actualizing a society's preferred way of life—its desired patterns of social interaction and forms of social organization. It is the ways in which the individuals and collectivities within the society believe they ought to relate to and interact with each other. The preferred ways are defined and delimited by the society's dominant goals and values. In terms of the Preamble to the Constitution, the preferred American way of life is one which forms a more perfect union, establishes justice, insures the domestic tranquillity, provides for the common defense, promotes the general welfare, and secures the blessings of liberty to its people and their posterity.

We call the problems of defining a society's important common symbols and of actualizing its goals and values *vital social problems*, or *vital societal problems* because they affect the viability of a society's preferred way of life. The vital problems that a particular society faces may or may not be those facing other societies. For example, while insuring the domestic tranquillity and providing for the common defense are vital problems for all societies, establishing justice, promoting the general welfare, and securing the blessings of liberty are not. In a society where the rulers are not responsible to the people, such as a medieval feudal society or its modern counterpart in underdeveloped nations, justice, the general welfare, and the blessings of liberty are often not the dominant values. But America must be concerned with their definition and implementation if it is to survive in a form that is recognizably "American." The attainment and maintenance of the way of life outlined by the Preamble may not be requisite to the continued functioning of all societies, but it is requisite to the continued functioning of a society that can properly call itself America.

There is, of course, no guarantee that the United States can insure the survival of its way of life. Changes may occur within it that are so great as to warrant claiming that the American way has not survived and that a new way of life has taken its place. Even the mightiest empires have fallen and their demise is testimony to the problematic nature of societal survival. On the other hand, the changes that take place within a society need not be so great as to represent the end of a way of life. Since the definition of a way of life is usually made in general and vague terms, many changes can and do occur within a society without going beyond its limits. For example, the blessings of liberty sought by one generation may not be identical to those sought by later generations. However, the difference need not be so great as to warrant calling it an entirely new goal or a preference for a new way of life.

Changes may also occur in a society because the priorities among its various goals are altered. The emphasis may be shifted, for example, from promoting the general welfare to providing for the common defense. Such shifting of priorities may result in massive changes. The composition of the work force may change as more people join the armed forces and take jobs in defense industries and fewer become involved in social work. It may mean the growth of industries that produce war materials and a decline in those concerned with consumer goods. However, a change in the priorities of a society's immediate objectives need not be taken as a change in its way of life. The basic patterns of interaction and fundamental forms of social organization may remain; no completely new goals rise to dominance; no presently dominant goals are discarded.

Whatever the fate of a society's preferred way of life, the problems involved in defining and actualizing it differ in three ways from those to which the discrepancy approach calls attention. First, the vital problems approach defines problems in terms of basic social processes, while the discrepancy approach does so in terms of specific, concrete situations. The former, for example, refers to the process of perfecting the union; the latter to the existence of specific imperfections.

Second, vital problems cannot be ignored if the preferred way of life is to remain viable; discrepancies can be ignored. That is, some minimal solution to a vital problem must be attempted if the prevailing way is to survive. Discrepancies, however, may be of such a minor nature or so contained as to constitute no threat to the viability of the preferred way of life. America, if it is to remain America, must do something to establish justice. Minor injustices, however, may be ignored without undermining the viability of the society or its way of life.

Third, vital problems are rarely completely solved, but discrepancies can be eliminated. A way of life can seldom, if ever, be secured for all times. Some activity is generally required on a continuous or at least periodic basis; definitions accepted by one generation need not suit another; and what is presently done need not suffice in all the situations which can be encountered. For example, what is done to insure the domestic tranquillity in one era may not suffice in another as conditions change within the society. Tensions that may once have been released by migration from the cities to the frontier wilderness may have to be dealt with in the cities when the frontiers are settled. On the other hand, a specific disturbance or breach of the domestic tranquillity, such as a riot, can be eliminated.

To summarize, the vital problems approach focuses attention on processes which must be undertaken if the preferred ways are to remain viable. The discrepancy approach focuses on situations viewed as undesirable or abnormal, but which need not threaten the viability of preferred ways and may be completely ameliorated. Despite the differences between these two approaches, the problems each focuses upon may be related. The failure to secure some aspect of the preferred way of life may create a state that is openly regarded as abnormal or undesirable. Failure to provide for the common defense, for example, can lead to an undesired war. Conversely, the persistence of a discrepancy may lead to the death or destruction of an important aspect of the dominant ways. Persistent poverty or oppression may precede a bitter civil strife which destroys the society or changes its way of life; such was the fate of Czarist Russia, Bourbon France, and British colonial America. The adoption of the Constitution whose Preamble guides this study of America's social problems signified the emergence of a new society with a new way of life. This book now turns to the vital problems of meanings and means —the problems of defining and actualizing the way of life to which America committed itself nearly two centuries ago.

We the People of

Any social organization, whether it is a society, university, corporation, or even a criminal syndicate, must deal with the problem of deciding who is and who is not to be considered a member of that organization. Similarly, all organizations specify what conditions, if any, limit the kind and degree of participation permitted various members. Finally, organizations set criteria and establish policy regarding the recruitment of new members.

This chapter examines America's experience with the issues of membership: the problems of defining who are "We the People of the United States" and of specifying the grounds on which participation is to be limited; and American policies concerning sources of potential new members.

The definitions of membership, the kind and degree of participation permitted different groups of members, and a society's recruitment policy are important not only in their own right but because their solution affects the size and composition of its population, which, in turn, affects such vital factors as the division of labor, the amount and nature of communication, the number of status hierarchies and social classes, the type of social control relied on, and the amount of deviance tolerated

the United States . . .

within the society.[1] Moreover, the size and composition of a society's population have important effects on its ability to promote the general welfare, as Philip M. Hauser shows in his article "The United States Population Explosion: Consequences and Implications."

Who Are "We the People"?

This section focuses on two components of the problem of defining membership in American society. The first problem involves the establishment of criteria for deciding who is and who is not an American. The second involves deciding on what grounds, if any, to limit the kind and amount of participation in American society to be permitted its various members.

[1] This list of factors affected by population size and composition is based on Paul E. Mott, *The Organization of Society* (Englewood Cliffs, N.J.: Prentice-Hall, 1965), pp. 48–66. For other discussions of the role of population factors, see Robert C. Angell, "The Moral Integration of American Cities," in Paul K. Hatt and Albert J. Reiss, Jr. (eds.), *Cities and Society*, rev. ed. (New York: Free Press, 1957), pp. 617–630; and William F. Ogburn and O. D. Duncan, "City Size as a Sociological Variable," in Ernest W. Burgess and Donald Bogue (eds.), *Contributions to Urban Sociology* (Chicago: University of Chicago Press, 1964), pp. 129–147.

The first question to be raised in the process of setting criteria for membership in American society is whether or not mere residence within its territory should suffice. The framers of the Constitution faced this question. Their answer was that Indians and slaves, even though living in the United States, were not part of "the People" or citizenry. Indians were not counted at all in the census that determined the size of a state's congressional representation; slaves counted as only three-fifths of a person.[2] The Supreme Court, in the Dred Scott decision of 1857, decided that the phrase "We the People" was not intended to refer to slaves and their descendants. It read, in part:

The words "people of the United States," and "citizens" are synonomous terms. . . . We think they [slaves and their descendants] . . . are not included and were not intended to be included, under the word "citizen," in the Constitution. . . . On the contrary, they were at the time considered as a subordinate and inferior class of being . . .[3]

This decision was, of course, reversed after the Civil War by the Fourteenth, Fifteenth, and Sixteenth Amendments.

The question of whether or not all who lived within the borders of the United States were to be regarded as "truly" Americans was again raised in the late nineteenth and early twentieth centuries with the great influx of non-Protestant immigrants from Southern and Eastern Europe. More recently, the status of Negroes has been highlighted, as has that of Americans of Mexican or Puerto Rican descent. Throughout its history America has answered the question of whether residence was a sufficient criterion for regarding one as an American with a definite, although sometimes hesitant and contested, "No."

Agreement that residence is not a sufficient criterion for inclusion among "the People of the United States" has not resulted in agreement on just what does define a person as an American. For some, an American is defined by what he does: by how he performs such citizenship roles as voting, paying taxes, and serving in the military. Persons who deny or evade these obligations of citizenship may be regarded as un-American or non-American. It is also possible to define an American by what he believes. Although there is much disagreement over just what beliefs an American must hold, belief in freedom, democracy, and free enterprise are standard points of reference.

[2] Staughton Lynd, "A Constitution Divided," *Columbia University Forum*, VIII (Spring, 1965), 17–22, analyzes the nature of the compromise between North and South and offers a rationale for the South's acceptance of it.
[3] *Dred Scott* v. *Sanford*, 19 How. 393, 404–405 (1857).

The selection "Assimilation in America: Theory and Reality," by Milton M. Gordon, discusses three alternative definitions of what an American is. Two of Gordon's definitions, the Anglo-conformist and the melting pot versions, hold that an American is one whose primary allegiance is to some distinctly American way of life. For the Anglo-conformist, that way of life is defined by the English-oriented, Anglo-Saxon Protestant traditions of the founders of American society. For those who stress the concept of the "melting pot," an American's primary allegiance is not to the original American traditions, but to a new and distinctive set of standards created by the amalgamation of the traditions of all who have resided in the United States. The third definition, that offered by the cultural pluralists, rejects both the stress of conformity to the Anglo-Saxon model of the past and the attempt to create a new, amalgamated uniformity. The cultural pluralists argue that adherence to a non-American tradition should not preclude one's being regarded as an American if he also adheres to the essential American values. In short, cultural pluralists believe that "We the People" should include individuals and groups with widely different beliefs and practices.

Just as all social organizations must decide upon the criteria for membership, they must also decide on the kinds and amount of participation permissible to various groups of members. All may be granted first-class or full membership. However, not all Americans are granted full membership. There are, in general, three criteria used to deny a person full membership: age, criminality, and insanity. The young do not vote for the officials who shape and mold their futures. Despite competence and skill, an older person may be forced to retire from a lifelong position or career. Persons judged criminal or insane can lose their voting rights and be forced to enter a prison or a mental hospital.

Criteria besides age, criminality, and insanity have sometimes been used to limit participation in American society. Femininity was and, to some extent, still is a basis for denying full membership. The participation of women in American society is further discussed in Chapter Three on establishing justice.

Poverty and educational deficiencies also prevent individuals from being full participants in American society and all the more so when they are correlated with "undesirable" ethnic or racial group membership. However, it has been the general American position that all who are now denied full membership in American society be encouraged to seek it.

There is, however, considerable disagreement over just how full membership is to be attained. As David Danzig notes, in "The Meaning of Negro Strategy," the traditional theory is that each individual proves his worthiness and seeks full membership by himself and on the basis of his own merits. Danzig, however, claims that such was not always the practice, that members of various ethnic groups have banded together and sought membership on a group basis. In any case, he asserts, such is the meaning or implication of the strategy of the Negro civil rights movement. That is, as Danzig views it, this movement has challenged the idea that the barriers to full membership created by poverty, ignorance, ethnicity, and race be overcome on an individual, one-at-a-time basis.

Recruiting Members of "We the People"

We have thus far noted that criteria are developed by all social organizations for identifying their members (Who are Americans?) and for limiting the areas of legitimate participation for the various members of the society (Who may or may not vote? for example). Organizations and societies also develop policies concerning potential new members. How are they to be recruited? How are non-Americans to become Americans?

Many non-Americans became members of American society following their own immigration; others, after their native land was acquired by the United States. Until the 1880s, America's policy regarding immigration was that anyone who wished to enter the country was welcome as a potential member of the society. In the 1880s, Chinese immigration was all but halted. Later, in the 1920s, the National Origins Quota System was established to reduce and regulate immigration. This system applied only to immigrants from countries outside the Western Hemisphere. Each country was given a quota of no less than 100 immigrants a year based on the proportion in the 1920 census who were originally from that country. In practice, the system favored immigration from Great Britain and Northern Europe over that from Southern and Eastern Europe, Asia, and Africa. The National Origins Quota System was replaced in 1965 by a system based not on national origin but on the skills of the potential immigrant and his familial relationship to citizens or resident aliens in the United States. A limit of 170,000 was placed on the number of immigrants per year. Moreover, for the first time in its history the United States established a quota for immigration from Western Hemisphere nations. As President Johnson has observed, "The days of unlimited immigration are past. But those who come will come because of what they are—not because of the land from which they sprung."[4] However,

[4] From the President's speech upon signing the new immigration bill into law as quoted by *The New York Times*, Supplement, October 4, 1965. See also Edward P. Hutchinson (ed.), "The New Immigration," *Annals of the American Academy of Political and Social Science*, CCCLXIII (September, 1966), 1–149.

all quotas may be waived in the cases of refugees from totalitarian regimes.

Over the years the United States has tightened the standards for the recruitment of new members via immigration. However, immigration is not the only source of new members. Historically, new members have been added by granting membership to the inhabitants of newly acquired territory. Some of the new lands have been acquired through peaceful annexation, as in the case of the Louisiana Purchase and Alaska; others by conquest, as in the case of much of the Southwestern territory and Hawaii. However, the United States has not always decided to include the inhabitants of newly acquired land among the American people. The Philippine territory and people, originally acquired by conquest, have been given their independence; the Virgin Islands and Puerto Rico have been given a status between that of independence and statehood.

Immigration and territorial acquisition are, then, two possible sources of additions to "We the People." However, the main source of new members now is, of course, the children born to present citizens. And with a population in excess of 200 million, some have urged that even this source be limited or controlled by the three means available: contraception, sterilization, and abortion. At present, decisions concerning contraception and sterilization are primarily matters for the individuals and families concerned. But the questions of contraception and sterilization have entered the arena of public debate, albeit softly. Some states have sought to limit the use of contraceptives,[5] while others have attempted to encourage their use, and in some cases have even urged the sterilization of underprivileged and promiscuous individuals.[6]

Abortion, in contrast to contraception and sterilization, is not primarily a matter to be decided by the individuals and families concerned. States have asserted their authority and forbid abortions except where the life of the mother is threatened or if the pregnancy was induced by rape. Nevertheless, many individual Americans have resorted to abortions to prevent unwanted births and have, thus, privately prevented an unborn

---

[5] A discussion of laws that seek to limit use of contraceptives is found in H. Frank Way, Jr., "Birth Control: A New Consensus," in J. Landis (ed.), *Current Perspectives on Social Problems* (Belmont, Cal.: Wadsworth, 1966), pp. 147–150. The legitimacy of birth control is discussed in William Petersen and David Matza (eds.), *Social Controversy* (Belmont, Cal.: Wadsworth, 1963), pp. 14–35.

[6] Some twenty-eight states have laws allowing involuntary sterilization. They are: Alabama, Arizona, California, Connecticut, Delaware, Georgia, Idaho, Indiana, Iowa, Kentucky, Maine, Michigan, Minnesota, Mississippi, Montana, Nebraska, New Hampshire, North Carolina, North Dakota, Oklahoma, Oregon, South Carolina,

child from becoming one of "We the People."[7] In the future, America may, as Sweden and Japan now do, allow abortions as one means for controlling the number of unwanted members of "We the People of the United States."

South Dakota, Utah, Vermont, Virginia, West Virginia, and Wisconsin (*The New York Times,* April 4, 1965, p. 78). Sterilization laws are discussed in Alan W. Sullowy, "The Legal and Political Aspects of Population Control," *Law and Contemporary Problems,* XXV (Summer, 1960), 593–613.

[7] America's abortion laws and the violations of them are discussed in Edwin Schur, *Crimes Without Victims* (Englewood Cliffs, N.J.: Prentice-Hall, 1965), pp. 11–64; and in Alice S. Rossi, "Abortion Laws and Their Victims," *Trans-action,* III (September–October, 1966), 7–12.

The United States Population Explosion:
Consequences and Implications

Philip M. Hauser

I

Increased and widespread attention to the world population explosion and its implications has tended to obscure the fact that the United States is also experiencing a population explosion that is producing severe national problems. Blinded by the short run gains of national resurgence in population growth, we fail to see its short range deleterious effects, and ignore its insidious consequences for the longer run.

As a result of the postwar, cold war boom in marriages and babies and continued progress in death control, the United States is now approximating the growth rate it had at the end of the nineteenth century. In the period between 1950 and 1980, the most important impact of our national resurgence in population growth undoubtedly lies in the thrust it has given and will continue to give to the maintenance of a high level of economic activity and economic growth. In the short run, our increased rate of population growth spells expanded market, greater labor input, and larger gross national product.

In 1957, for example, the population of the United States included a labor force averaging 65 million workers. They worked a 30 hour week, produced a product worth $3.29 per man-hour, and generated a Gross National Product of $434 billion. By 1975, drawing on projections by the McGraw-Hill Department of Economics,[1] we could have a labor force, reflecting population increase, averaging about 88 million workers. They are likely, with present trends, to be working a 35½ hour week, to be producing a product worth $5.14 per man-hour (in 1957 dollars), and to

Reprinted from *Population Perspectives* (New Brunswick, N.J.: Rutgers University Press, 1960, pp. 65–91, by permission of Rutgers University Press.

be generating a Gross National Product of $835 billion (also in 1957 dollars).

In the course of a single human generation, we could double our Gross National Product. This would be adding to the national product of the United States in one generation an amount greater than the national product of any nation on the face of the earth other than the United States itself. This could follow not only from our rapid population growth but also from continued increase in productivity. The projections, as a matter of fact, indicate a gain by 1975 of some 40 per cent in personal income after taxes (in 1957 dollars).

The businessman is, in general, heartened by considerations such as these, for a fast growing population accompanied by increased productivity, and therefore income, means rapidly expanding markets. This prospect opens up new fields of investment opportunity for expanded plant and facilities. But this analysis, even while probably reflecting the proper perspective for the short run, ignores other factors operating to produce longer range adverse effects, some of which are evident even in the short run.[2]

For example, greatly increased population means, all other things being equal, greatly reduced non-renewable natural resources per head, and operation of the law of diminishing returns as an offset to economics of scale. It also means higher densities of population with accompanying gains in potential of interaction, range, and intensity of contacts, increased frictions, and greater tension and frustration in daily living. Growing population density, especially when accompanied by the increasing metropolitanization of population, has been accompanied irresistibly by greater governmental intervention into the economic and social spheres—expanded government functions on the national, state, and local levels. These accompaniments of rapid population increase are operative even in the short run, as are the deleterious consequences resulting from changes in population composition discussed below.

II

Changes in age structure of the magnitude indicated over successive decades (Figure 1) will necessarily have a profound effect upon many sectors of the American social, economic, and political scene. The differential rates of growth of the various population age groupings will mean differential rates of market expansion to the business community. To business and industry the relatively large increases in the late teenage population during the sixties mean greatly expanded markets for such

Figure 1 / *Population of United States by Age, 1880 to 1960 and Projected to 1980*

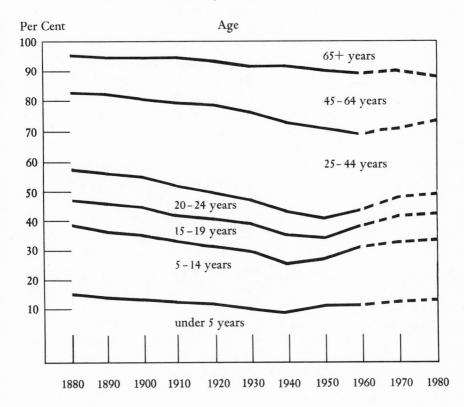

source: U.S. Bureau of the Census.

things as high school textbooks and other educational equipment, sport clothes, food and drink in teenage eating places, dance records, jazz bands, and various forms of commercial recreation.

The great boom in young adults, 20 to 24 years of age, means a great rise in the number of marriages, and therefore in the demand for the goods and services required in the early years of family formation. Young couples tend to form the basic core of the market for consumer durable goods, including automobiles, major appliances, furniture, and the vast assortment of goods and services associated with the coming of first and second children. Further discussion of the boom effects on the economy of the increase in young adults will be found below in our consideration of household formation.

The explosive growth of teenage and young adult population which means expanding markets to business will not necessarily benefit other sectors of the social order. For example, even if delinquency rates remain the same, the volume of juvenile delinquency during the sixties will rise by 44 per cent by reason of the increase in the number of persons of this age. This, of course, means a larger clientele for reform schools, reformatories, jails, and penitentiaries, and an expansion in the work loads of the police force, the court system, probation officers, and social workers.

The great impetus to purchases of automobiles resulting from the more than 50 per cent increase in young adults will be accompanied by further frustrations as highways, despite new construction, become even more congested and parking spaces even scarcer. The explosive rise in marriages will create pressures on virtually all public services: the physical services such as water supply, sanitation, and drainage; the health and welfare services; the recreational services, and so forth. The explosive increase in young adults will make present shortages in housing supply more acute in many communities.

Similarly, the continued steep rise in the number of older persons requires rapid expansion of services for the aged. Gerontological services must almost double in less than a generation if even present relatively low levels are to be maintained. Pressures on obstetrical services, public and private, may be expected to rise again as the boom of newly married couples produces a new surge in the birth rate, approximately 20 years after the beginning of the postwar boom in 1946.

One of the most important effects of the changing age structure of the United States as the result of the postwar resurgence in national growth is the changing dependency ratio—that is, the number of young persons under 20 and older persons 65 and over per 100 persons of working age, 20 to 64. Throughout the course of the history of this nation until 1940, the dependency ratio had been declining (Table 1). In 1820, for example, for each 100 persons of working age there were 153 dependents, 146 of whom were under 20 and about 7 of whom were 65 and over. By 1900, as the result of the aging of the population, the number of dependents had declined to 94, of whom 86 were young dependents and 8 were old dependents. By 1940, the total number of dependents had declined to 71, of whom 59 were young and 12 were old.

As the result of the combination of the rising birth rate during the forties and the continued aging of the population, dependents had increased to 72 by 1950, of whom 58 were young and 14 were older dependents. By 1980, if the postwar birth rate continues, the dependency ratio will have risen to 95. Of the 104 dependents in 1980, younger dependents would number 85, a number approximately the 1900 level of 86, whereas older dependents would number 19, twice as many as in 1900 (Figure 2).

Thus the resurgent birth rate during the forties and fifties has introduced changes in the age structure which, all other things being

TABLE 1 / *Dependency Ratios for Population of the Continental United States, Selected Dates, 1820–1980*

Year	Dependents Per 100 Persons of Working Age*		
	YOUNG† AND OLD‡	YOUNG ONLY	OLD ONLY
Census			
1820	153	146	7
1850	123	117	6
1900	94	86	8
1940	71	59	12
Estimate			
1950	72	58	14
Projection			
1960	91	74	17
1970	98	80	18
1980	104	85	19

* Working age: persons 20 to 64 years of age.
† Young: persons under 20 years of age.
‡ Old: persons 65 years of age and over.
SOURCE: Computed from data in U.S. Bureau of the Census, *Current Population Reports,* Series P-25, No. 187 (November 10, 1958), p. 16, using projections based upon the assumption 1955–1957 level of fertility would continue and *Historical Statistics of the United States, 1789–1945,* Washington, D.C., 1949, Series B81–94. Also, 1820, and, in part, 1850 age distributions based upon interpolations.

equal, would bring about the first decrease in product per head in our history. That is, prior to World War II the combination of forces affecting the age structure of the population of the United States produced "hands" faster than "mouths." As the result of the sharp upturn in birth rate in the postwar period, mouths began to be generated more rapidly than hands. The increase in dependency rates is also attributable in part to the rise in the number and proportion of older persons, which reflects past demographic behavior.

FIGURE 2 / *Dependency Ratios for the United States, 1820 to 1960 and Projected to 1980*

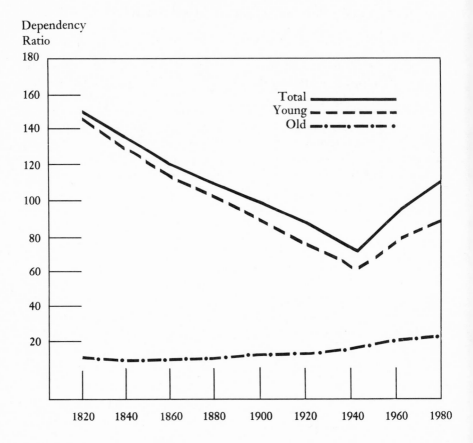

SOURCE: U.S. Bureau of the Census.

Another consequence of the changing dependency ratio will be found in its adverse effects on claims against savings. An increase in younger dependents requires a larger allocation of savings for purposes of "social investment," that is, investment in the rearing and education of the young. This is achieved only at the expense, in some measure, of decreased savings allocated to "productive investment," or investment designed specifically to increase product per head. A rise in the number of older dependents increases the claims on current production of that part of the population which tends no longer to contribute to increased product. Thus, apart from raising the ratio of dependents to workers, increased dependency, all other things being equal, operates in these other ways to reduce product per head and therefore to affect level of living adversely.

Without question the most visible consequence of our changing age structure during the fifties was the tremendous pressure on elementary school facilities throughout the nation. The grade schools of the United States were inundated by the tidal wave of postwar babies who reached school entrance age early in the fifties, many of whom flowed through the eight years of elementary schooling within the decade (Figure 3). During the sixties, pressure on elementary schools will level off, reflecting the plateau in the postwar birth rate. But the tidal wave will continue its relentless surge through the high schools of the United States in the early sixties, and, later in the decade, through the colleges.

Enrollment increases . . . have not been, nor are they likely to be, accompanied by adequate expansion in school plant, facilities, and teachers. The present explosive rise in school population has undoubtedly had an adverse effect on the quality of education at the elementary and high school levels during the fifties. It will further deleteriously affect the quality of high school education, and begin the erosion of that of college education during the sixties. During the seventies the colleges and professional schools will still be reeling under the impact of rapidly increasing student enrollment. Part of the upturn in enrollment especially in high school and college arises from increases in rates of enrollment rather than the population explosion. Gains in enrollment rate are, of course, indicative of the rising level of living. The expansion of educational facilities that would be necessary to accommodate increased enrollment alone would, however, be but a fraction of the present and prospective need arising both from higher rates of enrollment and rapid population growth.

Although the exceedingly rapid rates of increase in school age population together with higher rates of enrollment have created serious problems for the schools, the increases in enrollment rates mean higher levels of education. What are the implications of the American people's rising level of formal education (Figure 4)?

First of all, it should be noted that increased education opens up new vistas of intellectual, emotional, and aesthetic experience to the population. It means that the level of living of the people of the United States will be raised culturally as well as materially. It may also mean modifications of many present practices. For example, the increased educational level of the American people could change the character of American politics and perhaps that of political campaigns. The kinds of appeals

FIGURE 3 / *School Enrollment for the United States by Type of School, 1950, and Projected to 1980*

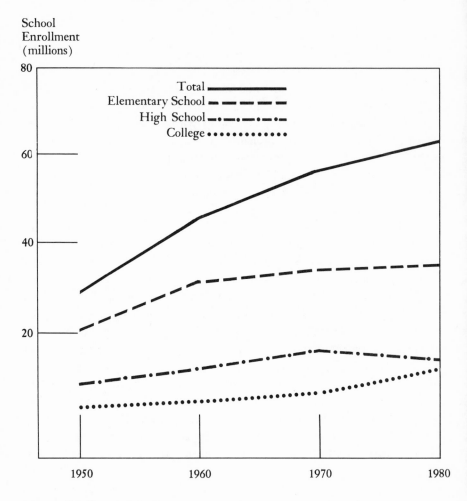

School
Enrollment
(millions)

SOURCE: U.S. Bureau of the Census.

candidates can make to an electorate are undoubtedly of a different order when the average voter has not progressed beyond grade school, than when he has at least a high school education. Similarly, the increasing educational level of the population may bring about important changes in the patterns of consumption of goods and services. There could conceivably be greater demand for the types of goods and services associated with the "egghead"—more good magazines, books, music, art, museums, and travel—and decreased demand for other goods and services such as

FIGURE 4 / *Educational Attainment for the United States, 1950*
and Projected to 1980

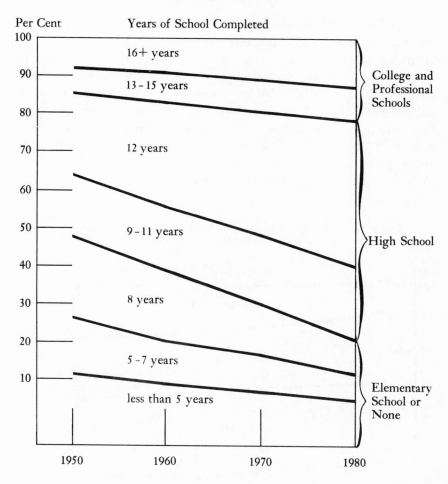

SOURCE: U.S. Bureau of the Census.

lurid and sensational publications, honky-tonk amusements, and fraudu-
lent sucker products ranging from false cures for arthritis and cancer to
astrological guides to behavior. Further, it may be anticipated that the
rising educational level of the American people will have an important
impact upon the advertising profession, since both the form and the
substance of advertising appeals will very likely require considerable
modification.

Predictions as to the consequences of the increased educational level
of the American people are necessarily speculative, but we can expect

that it will alter many present aspects of life in these United States, possibly even the caliber of TV programs.

The increase in national population growth and changes in the age structure of the population, together with changes in trends in education, in retirement, and in the role of women, have markedly affected and will continue to make great changes in the composition of the nation's labor force. While the proportion of the population working or seeking work should remain relatively constant over the next two decades, the labor force will expand tremendously and undergo important changes in composition (Figure 5). The labor supply will have growing proportions of young and old workers, and fewer workers of intermediate age. It is likely to become more female in the next two decades. The changes in

FIGURE 5 / *Labor Force of the United States by Sex and Broad Age Groups, 1950 and Projected to 1975*

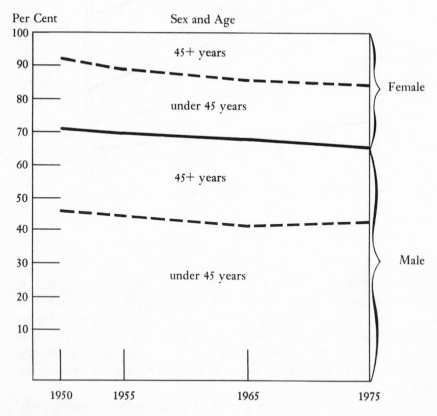

SOURCE: U.S. Bureau of the Census.

prospect have important implications for workers, employers, and the economy at large.

From the standpoint of the individual worker, it was the astute youngster who managed to be born during the depression and so entered the labor force when the new entrant group was relatively small. This favorable market situation—a seller's market from the standpoint of labor—meant relatively high entrance wage rates and opportunity for promotion. In contrast, the youngster who contrived to be born during the postwar baby boom, as part of a much larger new entrant group, is faced with a much more competitive situation. Workers seeking their first jobs will, during the sixties and seventies, encounter stiffer competition and probably relatively lower entrance wages than the smaller cohort of new workers during the fifties. They will have stiffer competition, also, all other things being equal, throughout their work careers in respect to such things as promotion and retention or layoff.

The increased number of new entrant workers could conceivably affect adversely some types of opportunities for the expanding supply of female workers. The prospective increase in new entrant workers could depress the trend toward greater labor force participation of women. Changes in this trend could, of course, markedly influence family income, and thereby consumption patterns. The economic contribution of women, and especially of wives, has been an important factor in home ownership, in the second TV set or car, and, in general, in the expanded market for household appliances, clothing, and a higher quality diet. Any dip in the trend toward greater labor force activity of women could have serious consequences for the American market. If the present trend continues, however, household consumption standards will continue to rise and to swell the growing United States market for goods and services.

Increases in the proportion of working wives and mothers are bound to have social as well as economic repercussions. For example, with larger proportions of children having little or no daytime parental supervision, the school, the day nursery, the church, family welfare agencies, and various recreational facilities will be confronted with an increasing and more diversified clientele.

From the employer's standpoint, the sixties will herald a new era in providing a relatively large reservoir of new employees. The change in the relative supply of new workers may ease his problems in the recruitment, training, placement, supervision, and development of workers. On the other hand, the employer will be more and more faced with the necessity of using older workers, as larger proportions of the labor supply become 45 years of age and over.

The great increase in the size of the labor force in prospect as a consequence of national resurgent population growth has significant implications for the economy as a whole. On the one hand, it spells economic opportunity in heralding the continued growth of the economy. On the other hand, it spells challenge, in that the expansion of entrepreneurial enterprise will be needed to create enough jobs to absorb the swelling supply of labor.

As recently as the late forties, Henry Wallace's insistence that the United States economy must expand to provide 60 million jobs[3] was greeted by many business and political leaders, as well as by some economists, with considerable dismay. They believed such a program to be visionary, unrealistic, and designed to embarrass business leadership. Yet Wallace's program was founded on census projections of the labor force based on anticipated growth of the total population.

As the result of the resumption of explosive national growth, the United States economy is now faced, not with the need to provide 60 million jobs, a task accomplished by the civilian economy by 1950, but with the goal of about 90 million jobs by 1975. To reach it, the economy must create about 20 million additional jobs between 1960 and 1975. Even with our fabulous history of economic growth, this will be a formidable task, particularly in view of the trend toward increased automation. There is no reason to regard the achievement of such an objective as impossible. But there can be little doubt that the rapid growth of the labor force deriving from the population explosion, involving as it does disproportionately great increases in younger, in older, and in female workers, will pose many problems in the years ahead—problems that will challenge the ingenuity of the nation.

The difference between rates of growth of total population and households, respectively, has important implications for all sectors of American life (Figure 6). For example, business institutions or health and welfare agencies primarily concerned with the household as a unit must follow the pattern of household rather than of total population changes. During the fifties, while total population was rising explosively, annual increments to the number of households declined appreciably. During the sixties, in contrast, net household formations will turn upward in an increase approximating a million a year or more.

The way in which shifts in the relative numbers of young, old, and intermediate households can affect different sectors of the economic and social order is illustrated by differences among such households in their home ownership. About half of the total household growth in the period

FIGURE 6 / *Growth of Households, 1890 to 1950 and Projected to 1980*

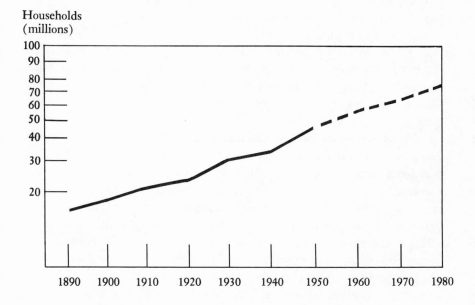

Households
(millions)

SOURCE: U.S. Bureau of the Census.

from 1958 to 1965 will be accounted for by an increase in older households and about a fourth by a rise in younger households. The increase in
young households will have relatively little effect on the demand for new
home ownership. In fact, young home-owners with mortgages constituted only 3 per cent of total borrowers in a recent study.[4] Older
households with mortgaged homes accounted for only 8 per cent of
borrowers. Eighty-nine per cent of borrowers were in households with
heads 25 to 54 years of age. The relatively great percentage rise in
younger and older households may point to increased demand for apartments rather than houses during the sixties—a fact of both economic and
sociological significance.

In similar fashion, all sectors of the economy in which the household
is the basic consumer unit will be affected by the changes in household
rather than total population growth. This consideration is of vital importance to manufacturers and distributors of durable products such as the
automobile, the refrigerator, the television and the home laundry. The
number of sets of encyclopaedias and hi-fi and stereo sets will also be
affected, not to mention the work loads on family service organizations,
magazine salesmen, domestic employment, and obstetrical services.

So we see that the changing age structure accompanying the population explosion, together with factors affecting the transition from the large to the small family system, is greatly influencing the rate of net household formation. The rapid increase in the number of households, like the rise in total population, will mean expanded markets and higher levels of economic activity in the short run. Even in the short run, however, explosive rates of household growth also produce frictions and maladjustments in the economy by necessitating spurts of expansion after periods of decelerated growth.

Rapid household increase also means rapid change in the number and composition of families, the basic social institutions, and, therefore, in the social and cultural context in which children are reared. While the exact consequences of such changes cannot be accurately traced in the present stage of knowledge, they certainly influence the character of inter-personal relations in the family—of spouses, of parents and children, of siblings—and affect the relations of the family to the community and its various sub-units. In the vortex of rapid family growth and fundamental changes in family size and composition, both the character of human nature and the mechanisms and processes by which it is formed are altered. Such modifications undoubtedly add to the frictions of social change manifest in various forms of social and personal disorganization. These short run problems are, of course, augmented by the longer run consequences of the population explosion.

III

It has been indicated that the Negro population explosion is of much greater magnitude than that of the white. The implications of present rates of growth of the Negro may be grasped by examination of projections of population by color beyond 1980. The continuation of present trends of white and nonwhite (mainly Negro) growth, respectively, would result in over 50 million nonwhites by the year 2000, about 14 per cent of total population. By 2050, the trend would increase the proportion of nonwhites to about the same level as at the beginning of our national history—approximately one-fifth. That is, present growth rates indicate that of a possible total of 1 billion persons in 2050, about 200 million would be nonwhite.[5] Thus in less than a century the present growth rate of the Negro could give the United States a much larger Negro population than Africa had in 1950, and almost as many Negroes as there were in the entire world at mid-century.[6]

The magnitude of the explosive growth of the Negro population will undoubtedly make the problems of inter-group relations even more difficult in the coming years. That is, the complex problems of adjustment created by the great streams of Negro out-migrants from the South to the North and West, involving transition from a rural folk culture to urbanism as a way of life, will undoubtedly be aggravated by the exceedingly rapid expansion of the Negro population. This explosive growth will intensify the already acute problems facing both the communities of destination and the Negro in-migrant in respect to housing, employment, prejudice, and discriminatory practices. Without question the transition would be much easier both for the Negro and the communities to which he is migrating if the tempo of growth were dampened.

The high fertility of the Negro, actually increased in recent years by his access to better health facilities and care, undoubtedly contributes to his relatively low level of living by decreasing per capita income in the Negro family. Moreover, large families combined with relatively low income mean fewer Negro children who can acquire an adequate education. Thus the Negro worker, who has a relatively low income partly because of his lack of education and skill, is handicapped in his effort to improve the educational and skill levels of his children by his high birth rate.

The foreign-born population is, of course, not experiencing explosive growth. The size of this population is entirely dependent on the aging and mortality of the foreign-born already here and on the volume of net immigration . . . with present trends the foreign-born population will remain about the same size over the next several decades but become a smaller proportion of the total population (Figure 7). It can safely be predicted that the process of assimilation of the foreign-born and their general acceptability will be furthered by the relative stability of their numbers. In contrast, problems in white-Negro inter-group relations are likely to be aggravated by the explosive growth of both the Negro and white populations. Certainly this prospect must be reckoned among the costs of the resurgence we have experienced in national population growth.

IV

In the course of our national history the frictions of rapid population growth have shifted across the nation as each section has in turn experienced great economic development. At present, and for at least several decades into the future, the opportunities afforded by rapid growth of the West Coast, the Gulf area, and the Great Lakes areas, will be accompanied by the same deleterious consequences as the nation as a

FIGURE 7 / *Population of the United States by Race and Nativity,*
1850 to 1950 and Projected to 1980

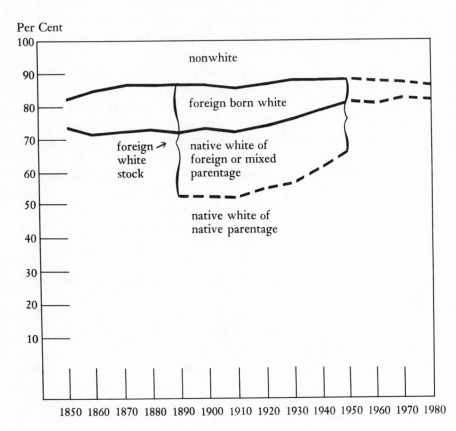

SOURCE: U.S. Bureau of the Census.

whole. Moreover, the areas of greatest growth will also be the areas of
greatest in-migration. Many social and personal problems will be most
acute in areas subject to heavy in-migration, because such change of
residence means not only adjustment to life in a new area but often
adjustment from a rural to an urban pattern of living as well.

Needless to say the great differentials in past and prospective population growth and the great inequalities in internal migratory flows point to
important differences in problems in the various parts of the United
States (Figure 8). The frictions of explosive growth will, of course, be
most acute in the more rapidly expansive areas. On the other hand, the
regions of the nation which are experiencing relatively little population
increase or even some decline may in this, their period of demographic

Figure 8 / *Population of the United States by Regions, 1790 to 1960 and Projected to 1970*

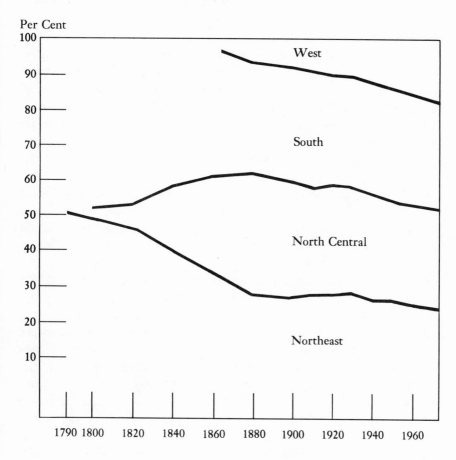

source: U.S. Bureau of the Census.

maturity, have the opportunity to consolidate earlier gains and to concentrate on the qualitative rather than the quantitative aspects of living.

V

In the long run, present rates of population increase in the United States confront the same limit of space as those in prospect for the world as a whole. For the United States, with approximately the same population density as that of the world (56 persons per square mile as compared with 52 for the world) and with about the same rate of increase (1.7 to 1.8 per cent per year), is faced with the same outlook of a density of one person per square foot of land surface in less than 200 years. Such a period is only twice as long as that which has elapsed since the landing at Plymouth Rock.

Because of the limited human life-span, it is difficult for the average person to become concerned about potential problems several centuries in the future even though in the perspective of human evolution they are almost upon us. It is impossible, however, to avoid facing the consequences of the present rate of growth of the United States to the year 2050—a date less than a century away—a date many persons now alive are destined to reach.

The continuation of our present birth rate could, by 2050, produce a population of over 1 billion (Figure 9)!

What impact would a population of a billion have on the United States? To begin with, such a population, if ever attained, would greatly accelerate the dependence of the United States upon the rest of the world as a deficit nation in respect to many essential raw materials. Prior to 1940, the United States was a surplus nation, producing more raw materials than it consumed. During the forties this position changed.[7] At the beginning of the century the United States produced some 15 per cent more raw materials than it consumed (except for food). By the middle of the century, however, this nation was consuming about 10 per cent more raw materials than it produced. In 1952, the President's Materials Policy Commission pointed to 33 separate minerals on the "critical" list at that time. Nor can the United States indefinitely depend on the rest of the world for its mineral needs at present and increasing rates of consumption. Explosive population growth in this country and in the world as a whole would have profound effects upon the utilization of natural resources. Denudation of non-renewable resources and greatly increased costs for renewable materials could seriously lower levels of living.

In respect to food supply, the United States is not likely to be in a bad way during the second half of the century, even with a population of 1 billion. But the ratio of population to acreage under cultivation would be greatly decreased. From a level of 2.1 cultivated acres per capita in 1950, a population of 1 billion would produce a mere 0.35 of a cultivated acre per capita by 2050—a ratio below that in contemporary China.[8] In 1950 there were 509 million acres under cultivation. Despite probable rises in production costs, heavy population pressure might expand this to include all the land available for crops. But the days of huge United States agricultural surpluses will have passed. A population increase of this

FIGURE 9 / *Population of United States 1950 and 1960 and Projected to 2050 Assuming Continuation of Post War Birth Rate*

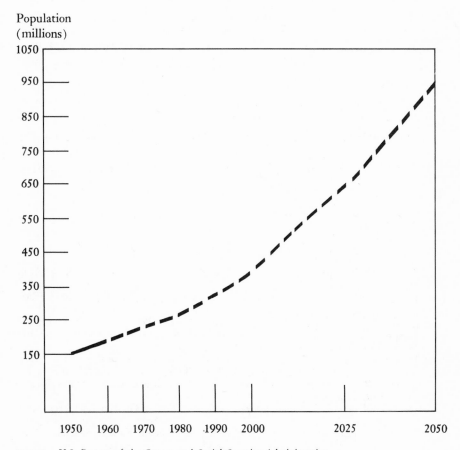

SOURCE: U.S. Bureau of the Census and Social Security Administration.

magnitude, however, is not likely to be universally acclaimed as the most desirable solution to our problem of agricultural surplus.

After reviewing our potential consumption in relation to supply for a number of raw materials, Ordway, in disagreeing with the relatively optimistic conclusions of the President's Materials Policy Commission, develops a theory of "the limit of growth."[9] The theory is based on two premises: (1) levels of human living are constantly rising with mounting use of natural resources, and (2) despite technological progress we are spending each year more resource capital than is created. The theory maintains: "If this cycle continues long enough basic resources will come into such short supply that rising cost will make their use for additional production unprofitable, industrial expansion will cease, and we shall have reached the limit of growth."

It is not possible to fix the precise date for such an eventuality as Ordway describes. It is clear, however, that with a population of a billion such a situation, if not already reached by this nation, would not be far in the future.

In the short run, then, explosive population growth contributes to economic growth and to continued prosperity. In the longer run, however, it will become clear that these gains may have been achieved at the expense of levels of living of future generations, even in a country as fabulously wealthy and rich in resources as the United States of America.

Notes

1) McGraw-Hill Department of Economics, *The American Economy* (New York: McGraw-Hill, 1958).
2) For general discussion of population as a factor in the level of United States economy, see conflicting views of J. J. Spengler, "Population Threatens Prosperity," *Harvard Business Review*, XXXIV (January–February, 1956), 85–94, and Joseph S. Davis, "The Population Upsurge and the American Economy, 1945–80," *Journal of Political Economy*, LXI (October, 1953), 369–88.
3) Henry A. Wallace, *Sixty Million Jobs* (New York: Simon and Schuster, 1945).
4) Miles L. Colean and Leon T. Kendall, *Who Buys the Homes: A Report on the Characteristics of Single Family Home Buyers* (Chicago: United States Savings and Loan League, 1959).
5) Donald J. Bogue, *The Population of the United States* (Glencoe, Ill.: Free Press 1959), p. 761.
6) W. S. Woytinsky and E. S. Woytinsky, *World Population and Production* (New York: Twentieth Century Fund, 1953), p. 51.
7) Samuel H. Ordway, Jr., "Possible Limits of Raw Material Consumption," in William L. Thomas, Jr., *Man's Role in Changing the Face of the Earth* (Chicago: University of Chicago Press, 1956).
8) Chauncy D. Harris, "Agricultural Production in the United States: The Past Fifty Years and the Next," *The Geographical Review*, XLVII, 2 (1957), 175–93; J. Frederick Dewhurst and Associates, *America's Needs and Resources, a New Survey* (New York: Twentieth Century Fund, 1955), Chap. 22.
9) Samuel H. Ordway, *op. cit.*, pp. 990–92.

Assimilation in America: Theory and Reality

❧

Milton M. Gordon

Three ideologies or conceptual models have competed for attention on the American scene as explanations of the way in which a nation, in the beginning largely white, Anglo-Saxon, and Protestant, has absorbed over 41 million immigrants and their descendants from variegated sources and welded them into the contemporary American people. These ideologies are Anglo-conformity, the melting pot, and cultural pluralism. They have served at various times, and often simultaneously, as explanations of what has happened—descriptive models—and of what should happen—goal models. Not infrequently they have been used in such a fashion that it is difficult to tell which of these two usages the writer has had in mind. In fact, one of the more remarkable omissions in the history of American intellectual thought is the relative lack of close analytical attention given to the theory of immigrant adjustment in the United States by its social scientists.

The result has been that this field of discussion—an overridingly important one since it has significant implications for the more familiar problems of prejudice, discrimination, and majority-minority group relations generally—has been largely preempted by laymen, representatives of belles lettres, philosophers, and apologists of various persuasions. Even from these sources the amount of attention devoted to ideologies of assimilation is hardly extensive. Consequently, the work of improving intergroup relations in America is carried out by dedicated professional agencies and individuals who deal as best they can with day-to-day problems of discriminatory behavior, but who for the most part are

Reprinted from "Assimilation in America: Theory and Reality," *Daedalus*, 90 (Spring, 1961), 263–285, by permission of the author and *Daedalus*, published by the American Academy of Arts and Sciences, Boston, Massachusetts.

unable to relate their efforts to an adequate conceptual apparatus. Such an apparatus would, at one and the same time, accurately describe the present structure of American society with respect to its ethnic groups (I shall use the term "ethnic group" to refer to any racial, religious, or national-origins collectivity), and allow for a considered formulation of its assimilation or integration goals for the foreseeable future. One is reminded of Alice's distraught question in her travels in Wonderland: "Would you tell me, please, which way I ought to go from here?" "That depends a good deal," replied the Cat with irrefutable logic, "on where you want to get to."

The story of America's immigration can be quickly told for our present purposes. The white American population at the time of the Revolution was largely English and Protestant in origin, but had already absorbed substantial groups of Germans and Scotch-Irish and smaller contingents of Frenchmen, Dutchmen, Swedes, Swiss, South Irish, Poles, and a handful of migrants from other European nations. Catholics were represented in modest numbers, particularly in the middle colonies, and a small number of Jews were residents of the incipient nation. With the exception of the Quakers and a few missionaries, the colonists had generally treated the Indians and their cultures with contempt and hostility, driving them from the coastal plains and making the western frontier a bloody battleground where eternal vigilance was the price of survival.

Although the Negro at that time made up nearly one-fifth of the total population, his predominantly slave status, together with racial and cultural prejudice, barred him from serious consideration as an assimilable element of the society. And while many groups of European origin started out as determined ethnic enclaves, eventually, most historians believe, considerable ethnic intermixture within the white population took place. "People of different blood" [sic]—write two American historians about the colonial period, "English, Irish, German, Huguenot, Dutch, Swedish—mingled and intermarried with little thought of any difference."[1] In such a society, its people predominantly English, its white immigrants of other ethnic origins either English-speaking or derived largely from countries of northern and western Europe whose cultural divergences from the English were not great, and its dominant white population excluding by fiat the claims and considerations of welfare of the non-Caucasian minorities, the problem of assimilation understandably did not loom unduly large or complex.

The unfolding events of the next century and a half with increasing momentum dispelled the complacency which rested upon the relative simplicity of colonial and immediate post-Revolutionary conditions. The large-scale immigration to America of the famine-fleeing Irish, the Germans, and later the Scandinavians (along with additional Englishmen and other peoples of northern and western Europe) in the middle of the nineteenth century (the so-called "old immigration"), the emancipation of the Negro slaves and the problems created by post-Civil War reconstruction, the placing of the conquered Indian with his broken culture on government reservations, the arrival of the Oriental, first attracted by the discovery of gold and other opportunities in the West, and finally, beginning in the last quarter of the nineteenth century and continuing to the early 1920's, the swelling to proportions hitherto unimagined of the tide of immigration from the peasantries and "pales" of southern and eastern Europe—the Italians, Jews, and Slavs of the so-called "new immigration," fleeing the persecutions and industrial dislocations of the day—all these events constitute the background against which we may consider the rise of the theories of assimilation mentioned above. After a necessarily foreshortened description of each of these theories and their historical emergence, we shall suggest analytical distinctions designed to aid in clarifying the nature of the assimilation process, and then conclude by focusing on the American scene.

Anglo-Conformity

"Anglo-conformity"[2] is a broad term used to cover a variety of viewpoints about assimilation and immigration; they all assume the desirability of maintaining English institutions (as modified by the American Revolution), the English language, and English-oriented cultural patterns as dominant and standard in American life. However, bound up with this assumption are related attitudes. These may range from discredited notions about race and "Nordic" and "Aryan" racial superiority, together with the nativist political programs and exclusionist immigration policies which such notions entail, through an intermediate position of favoring immigration from northern and western Europe on amorphous, unreflective grounds ("They are more like us"), to a lack of opposition to any source of immigration, as long as these immigrants and their descendants duly adopt the standard Anglo-Saxon cultural patterns. There is by no means any necessary equation between Anglo-conformity and racist attitudes.

It is quite likely that "Anglo-conformity" in its more moderate aspects, however explicit its formulation, has been the most prevalent ideology of assimilation goals in America throughout the nation's history. As far back as colonial times, Benjamin Franklin recorded concern about the clannishness of the Germans in Pennsylvania, their slowness in learning English, and the establishment of their own native-language press.[3] Others of the founding fathers had similar reservations about large-scale immigration from Europe. In the context of their times they were unable to foresee the role such immigration was to play in creating the later greatness of the nation. They were not at all men of unthinking prejudices. The disestablishment of religion and the separation of church and state (so that no religious group—whether New England Congregationalists, Virginian Anglicans, or even all Protestants combined—could call upon the federal government for special favors or support, and so that man's religious conscience should be free) were cardinal points of the new national policy they fostered. "The Government of the United States," George Washington had written to the Jewish congregation of Newport during his first term as president, "gives to bigotry no sanction, to persecution no assistance."

Political differences with ancestral England had just been written in blood; but there is no reason to suppose that these men looked upon their fledgling country as an impartial melting pot for the merging of the various cultures of Europe, or as a new "nation of nations," or as anything but a society in which, with important political modifications, Anglo-Saxon speech and institutional forms would be standard. Indeed, their newly won victory for democracy and republicanism made them especially anxious that these still precarious fruits of revolution should not be threatened by a large influx of European peoples whose life experiences had accustomed them to the bonds of despotic monarchy. Thus, although they explicitly conceived of the new United States of America as a haven for those unfortunates of Europe who were persecuted and oppressed, they had characteristic reservations about the effects of too free a policy. "My opinion, with respect to immigration," Washington wrote to John Adams in 1794, "is that except of useful mechanics and some particular descriptions of men or professions, there is no need of encouragement, while the policy or advantage of its taking place in a body (I mean the settling of them in a body) may be much questioned; for, by so doing, they retain the language, habits and principles (good or bad) which they bring with them."[4] Thomas Jefferson, whose views on race and attitudes towards slavery were notably liberal and advanced for his time, had similar doubts concerning the effects of mass immigration on American institutions, while conceding that immigrants, "if they come of themselves . . . are entitled to all the rights of citizenship."[5]

The attitudes of Americans toward foreign immigration in the first three-quarters of the nineteenth century may correctly be described as ambiguous. On the one hand, immigrants were much desired, so as to swell the population and importance of states and territories, to man the farms of expanding prairie settlement, to work the mines, build the railroads and canals, and take their place in expanding industry. This was a period in which no federal legislation of any consequence prevented the entry of aliens, and such state legislation as existed attempted to bar on an individual basis only those who were likely to become a burden on the community, such as convicts and paupers. On the other hand, the arrival in an overwhelmingly Protestant society of large numbers of poverty-stricken Irish Catholics, who settled in groups in the slums of Eastern cities, roused dormant fears of "Popery" and Rome. Another source of anxiety was the substantial influx of Germans, who made their way to the cities and farms of the mid-West and whose different language, separate communal life, and freer ideas on temperance and sabbath observance brought them into conflict with the Anglo-Saxon bearers of the Puritan and Evangelical traditions. Fear of foreign "radicals" and suspicion of the economic demands of the occasionally aroused workingmen added fuel to the nativist fires. In their extreme form these fears resulted in the Native-American movement of the 1830's and 1840's and the "American" or "Know-Nothing" party of the 1850's, with their anti-Catholic campaigns and their demands for restrictive laws on naturalization procedures and for keeping the foreign-born out of political office. While these movements scored local political successes and their turbulences so rent the national social fabric that the patches are not yet entirely invisible, they failed to influence national legislative policy on immigration and immigrants; and their fulminations inevitably provoked the expected reactions from thoughtful observers.

The flood of newcomers to the westward expanding nation grew larger, reaching over one and two-thirds million between 1841 and 1850 and over two and one-half million in the decade before the Civil War. Throughout the entire period, quite apart from the excesses of the Know-Nothings, the predominant (though not exclusive) conception of what the ideal immigrant adjustment should be was probably summed up in a letter written in 1818 by John Quincy Adams, then Secretary of State, in answer to the inquiries of the Baron von Fürstenwaerther. If not the earliest, it is certainly the most elegant version of the sentiment, "If they don't like it here, they can go back where they came from." Adams declared:[6]

> They [immigrants to America] come to a life of independence, but to a life of labor—and, if they cannot accommodate themselves to the character, moral, political and physical, of this country with all its compensating balances of good and evil, the Atlantic is always open to them to return to the land of their nativity and their fathers. To one thing they must make up their minds, or they will be disappointed in every expectation of happiness as Americans. They must cast off the European skin, never to resume it. They must look forward to their posterity rather than backward to their ancestors; they must be sure that whatever their own feelings may be, those of their children will cling to the prejudices of this country.

The events that followed the Civil War created their own ambiguities in attitude toward the immigrant. A nation undergoing wholesale industrial expansion and not yet finished with the march of westward settlement could make good use of the never faltering waves of newcomers. But sporadic bursts of labor unrest, attributed to foreign radicals, the growth of Catholic institutions and the rise of Catholics to municipal political power, and the continuing association of immigrant settlement with urban slums revived familiar fears. The first federal selective law restricting immigration was passed in 1882, and Chinese immigration was cut off in the same year. The most significant development of all, barely recognized at first, was the change in the source of European migrants. Beginning in the 1880's, the countries of southern and eastern Europe began to be represented in substantial numbers for the first time, and in the next decade immigrants from these sources became numerically dominant. Now the notes of a new, or at least hitherto unemphasized, chord from the nativist lyre began to sound—the ugly chord, or discord, of racism. Previously vague and romantic notions of Anglo-Saxon peoplehood, combined with general ethnocentrism, rudimentary wisps of genetics, selected tidbits of evolutionary theory, and naive assumptions from an early and crude imported anthropology produced the doctrine that the English, Germans, and others of the "old immigration" constituted a superior race of tall, blonde, blue-eyed "Nordics" or "Aryans," whereas the peoples of eastern and southern Europe made up the darker Alpines or Mediterraneans—both "inferior" breeds whose presence in America threatened, either by intermixture or supplementation, the traditional American stock and culture. The obvious corollary to this doctrine was to exclude the allegedly inferior breeds; but if the new type of immigrant could not be excluded, then everything must be done to instill Anglo-

Saxon virtues in these benighted creatures. Thus, one educator writing in 1909 could state:[7]

> These southern and eastern Europeans are of a very different type from the north Europeans who preceded them. Illiterate, docile, lacking in self-reliance and initiative, and not possessing the Anglo-Teutonic conceptions of law, order, and government, their coming has served to dilute tremendously our national stock, and to corrupt our civic life. . . . Everywhere these people tend to settle in groups or settlements, and to set up here their national manners, customs, and observances. Our task is to break up these groups or settlements, to assimilate and amalgamate these people as a part of our American race, and to implant in their children, so far as can be done, the Anglo-Saxon conception of righteousness, law and order, and popular government, and to awaken in them a reverence for our democratic institutions and for those things in our national life which we as a people hold to be of abiding worth.

Anglo-conformity received its fullest expression in the so-called Americanization movement which gripped the nation during World War I. While "Americanization" in its various stages had more than one emphasis, it was essentially a consciously articulated movement to strip the immigrant of his native culture and attachments and make him over into an American along Anglo-Saxon lines—all this to be accomplished with great rapidity. To use an image of a later day, it was an attempt at "pressure-cooking assimilation." It had prewar antecedents, but it was during the height of the world conflict that federal agencies, state governments, municipalities, and a host of private organizations joined in the effort to persuade the immigrant to learn English, take out naturalization papers, buy war bonds, forget his former origins and culture, and give himself over to patriotic hysteria.

After the war and the "Red scare" which followed, the excesses of the Americanization movement subsided. In its place, however, came the restriction of immigration through federal law. Foiled at first by presidential vetoes, and later by the failure of the 1917 literacy test to halt the immigrant tide, the proponents of restriction finally put through in the early 1920's a series of acts culminating in the well-known national-origins formula for immigrant quotas which went into effect in 1929. Whatever the merits of a quantitative limit on the number of immigrants to be admitted to the United States, the provisions of the formula, which discriminated sharply against the countries of southern and eastern Europe, in effect institutionalized the assumptions of the rightful dominance of Anglo-Saxon patterns in the land. Reaffirmed with only slight modifications in the McCarran-Walter Act of 1952, these laws, then, stand as a legal monument to the creed of Anglo-conformity and a telling reminder that this ideological system still has numerous and powerful adherents on the American scene.

The Melting Pot

While Anglo-conformity in various guises has probably been the most prevalent ideology of assimilation in the American historical experience, a competing viewpoint with more generous and idealistic overtones has had its adherents and exponents from the eighteenth century onward. Conditions in the virgin continent, it was clear, were modifying the institutions which the English colonists brought with them from the mother country. Arrivals from non-English homelands such as Germany, Sweden, and France were similarly exposed to this fresh environment. Was it not possible, then, to think of the evolving American society not as a slightly modified England but rather as a totally new blend, culturally and biologically, in which the stocks and folkways of Europe, figuratively speaking, were indiscriminately mixed in the political pot of the emerging nation and fused by the fires of American influence and interaction into a distinctly new type?

Such, at any rate, was the conception of the new society which motivated that eighteenth-century French-born writer and agriculturalist, J. Hector St. John Crèvecoeur, who, after many years of American residence, published his reflections and observations in *Letters from an American Farmer*.[8] Who, he asks, is the American?

He is either an European, or the descendant of an European, hence that strange mixture of blood, which you will find in no other country. I could point out to you a family whose grandfather was an Englishman, whose wife was Dutch, whose son married a French woman, and whose present four sons have now four wives of different nations. *He* is an American, who leaving behind him all his ancient prejudices and manners, receives new ones from the new mode of life he has embraced, the new government he obeys, and the new rank he holds. He becomes an American by being received in the broad lap of our great *Alma Mater*. Here individuals of all nations are melted into a new race of men, whose labours and posterity will one day cause great changes in the world.

Some observers have interpreted the open-door policy on immigration of the first three-quarters of the nineteenth century as reflecting an underlying faith in the effectiveness of the American melting pot, in the belief "that all could be absorbed and that all could contribute to an emerging national character."[9] No doubt many who observed with dismay the nativist agitation of the times felt as did Ralph Waldo

Emerson that such conformity-demanding and immigrant-hating forces represented a perversion of the best American ideals. In 1845, Emerson wrote in his Journal:[10]

I hate the narrowness of the Native American Party. It is the dog in the manger. It is precisely opposite to all the dictates of love and magnanimity; and therefore, of course, opposite to true wisdom. . . . Man is the most composite of all creatures. . . . Well, as in the old burning of the Temple at Corinth, by the melting and intermixture of silver and gold and other metals a new compound more precious than any, called Corinthian brass, was formed; so in this continent,—asylum of all nations,—the energy of Irish, Germans, Swedes, Poles, and Cossacks, and all the European tribes,—of the Africans, and of the Polynesians,—will construct a new race, a new religion, a new state, a new literature, which will be as vigorous as the new Europe which came out of the smelting-pot of the Dark Ages, or that which earlier emerged from the Pelasgic and Etruscan barbarism. *La Nature aime les croisements.*

Eventually, the melting-pot hypothesis found its way into historical scholarship and interpretation. While many American historians of the late nineteenth century, some fresh from graduate study at German universities, tended to adopt the view that American institutions derived in essence from Anglo-Saxon (and ultimately Teutonic) sources, others were not so sure.[11] One of these was Frederick Jackson Turner, a young historian from Wisconsin, not long emerged from his graduate training at Johns Hopkins. Turner presented a paper to the American Historical Association, meeting in Chicago in 1893. Called "The Significance of the Frontier in American History," this paper proved to be one of the most influential essays in the history of American scholarship, and its point of view, supported by Turner's subsequent writings and his teaching, pervaded the field of American historical interpretation for at least a generation. Turner's thesis was that the dominant influence in the shaping of American institutions and American democracy was not this nation's European heritage in any of its forms, nor the forces emanating from the eastern seaboard cities, but rather the experiences created by a moving and variegated western frontier. Among the many effects attributed to the frontier environment and the challenges it presented was that it acted as a solvent for the national heritages and the separatist tendencies of the many nationality groups which had joined the trek westward, including the Germans and Scotch-Irish of the eighteenth century and the Scandinavians and Germans of the nineteenth. "The frontier," asserted Turner, "promoted the formation of a composite nationality for the American people. . . . In the crucible of the frontier the immigrants were Americanized, liberated, and fused into a mixed race, English in neither nationality nor characteristics. The process has gone on from the early days to our own." And later, in an essay on the role of the Mississippi Valley, he refers to "the tide of foreign immigration which has risen so steadily that it has made a composite American people whose amalgamation is destined to produce a new national stock."[12]

Thus far, the proponents of the melting-pot idea has dealt largely with the diversity produced by the sizeable immigration from the countries of northern and western Europe alone—the "old immigration," consisting of peoples with cultures and physical appearance not greatly different from those of the Anglo-Saxon stock. Emerson, it is true, had impartially included Africans, Polynesians, and Cossacks in his conception of the mixture; but it was only in the last two decades of the nineteenth century that a large-scale influx of peoples from the countries of southern and eastern Europe imperatively posed the question of whether these uprooted newcomers who were crowding into the large cities of the nation and the industrial sector of the economy could also be successfully "melted." Would the "urban melting pot" work as well as the "frontier melting pot" of an essentially rural society was alleged to have done?

It remained for an English-Jewish writer with strong social convictions, moved by his observation of the role of the United States as a haven for the poor and oppressed of Europe, to give utterance to the broader view of the American melting pot in a way which attracted public attention. In 1908, Israel Zangwill's drama, *The Melting Pot*, was produced in this country and became a popular success. It is a play dominated by the dream of its protagonist, a young Russian-Jewish immigrant to America, a composer, whose goal is the completion of a vast "American" symphony which will express his deeply felt conception of his adopted country as a divinely appointed crucible in which all the ethnic divisions of mankind will divest themselves of their ancient animosities and differences and become fused into one group, signifying the brotherhood of man. In the process he falls in love with a beautiful and cultured Gentile girl. The play ends with the performance of the symphony and, after numerous vicissitudes and traditional family opposition from both sides, with the approaching marriage of David Quixano and his beloved. During the course of these developments, David, in the rhetoric of the time, delivers himself of such sentiments as these:[13]

America is God's crucible, the great Melting Pot where all the races of Europe are melting and re-forming! Here you stand, good folk, think I, when I see them at Ellis Island, here you stand in your fifty groups, with your fifty languages and histories, and your fifty blood hatreds and rivalries. But you

won't be long like that, brothers, for these are the fires of God you've come to—
these are the fires of God. A fig for your feuds and vendettas! Germans and
Frenchmen, Irishmen and Englishmen, Jews and Russians—into the Crucible
with you all! God is making the American.

Here we have a conception of a melting pot which admits of no
exceptions or qualifications with regard to the ethnic stocks which will
fuse in the great crucible. Englishmen, Germans, Frenchmen, Slavs,
Greeks, Syrians, Jews, Gentiles, even the black and yellow races, were
specifically mentioned in Zangwill's rhapsodic enumeration. And this pot
patently was to boil in the great cities of America.

Thus around the turn of the century the melting-pot idea became
embedded in the ideals of the age as one response to the immigrant
receiving experience of the nation. Soon to be challenged by a new
philosophy of group adjustment (to be discussed below) and always
competing with the more pervasive adherence to Anglo-conformity, the
melting-pot image, however, continued to draw a portion of the attention
consciously directed toward this aspect of the American scene in the first
half of the twentieth century. In the mid-1940's a sociologist who had
carried out an investigation of intermarriage trends in New Haven,
Connecticut, described a revised conception of the melting process in that
city and suggested a basic modification of the theory of that process. In
New Haven, Ruby Jo Reeves Kennedy[14] reported from a study of
intermarriages from 1870 to 1940 that there was a distinct tendency for
the British-Americans, Germans, and Scandinavians to marry among
themselves—that is, within a Protestant "pool"; for the Irish, Italians,
and Poles to marry among themselves—a Catholic "pool"; and for the
Jews to marry other Jews. In other words, intermarriage was taking place
across lines of nationality background, but there was a strong tendency
for it to stay confined within one or the other of the three major religious
groups, Protestants, Catholics, and Jews. Thus, declared Mrs. Kennedy,
the picture in New Haven resembled a "triple melting pot" based on
religious divisions, rather than a "single melting pot." Her study indicated, she stated, that "while strict endogamy is loosening, religious
endogamy is persisting and the future cleavages will be along religious
lines rather than along nationality lines as in the past. If this is the case,
then the traditional 'single-melting-pot' idea must be abandoned, and a
new conception, which we term the 'triple-melting-pot' theory of American assimilation, will take its place as the true expression of what is
happening to the various nationality groups in the United States."[15] The
triple melting-pot thesis was later taken up by the theologian, Will

Herberg, and formed an important sociological frame of reference for his analysis of religious trends in American society, *Protestant-Catholic-Jew*.[16] But the triple melting-pot hypothesis patently takes us into the realm of a society pluralistically conceived. We turn now to the rise of an ideology which attempts to justify such a conception.

Cultural Pluralism

Probably all the non-English immigrants who came to American shores in any significant numbers from colonial times onward—settling either in the forbidding wilderness, the lonely prairie, or in some accessible urban slum—created ethnic enclaves and looked forward to the preservation of at least some of their native cultural patterns. Such a development, natural as breathing, was supported by the later accretion of friends, relatives, and countrymen seeking out oases of familiarity in a strange land, by the desire of the settlers to rebuild (necessarily in miniature) a society in which they could communicate in the familiar tongue and maintain familiar institutions, and, finally, by the necessity to band together for mutual aid and mutual protection against the uncertainties of a strange and frequently hostile environment. This was as true of the "old" immigrants as of the "new." In fact, some of the liberal intellectuals who fled to America from an inhospitable political climate in Germany in the 1830's, 1840's, and 1850's looked forward to the creation of an all-German state within the union, or, even more hopefully, to the eventual formation of a separate German nation, as soon as the expected dissolution of the union under the impact of the slavery controversy should have taken place.[17] Oscar Handlin, writing of the sons of Erin in mid-nineteenth-century Boston, recent refugees from famine and economic degradation in their homeland, points out: "Unable to participate in the normal associational affairs of the community, the Irish felt obliged to erect a society within a society, to act together in their own way. In every contact therefore the group, acting apart from other sections of the community, became intensely aware of its peculiar and exclusive identity."[18] Thus cultural pluralism was a fact in American society before it became a theory—a theory with explicit relevance for the nation as a whole, and articulated and discussed in the English-speaking circles of American intellectual life.

Eventually, the cultural enclaves of the Germans (and the later arriving Scandinavians) were to decline in scope and significance as succeeding generations of their native-born attended public schools, left the farms and villages to strike out as individuals for the Americanizing city, and generally became subject to the influences of a standardizing industrial civilization. The German-American community, too, was struck a powerful blow by the accumulated passions generated by World War I—a blow from which it never fully recovered. The Irish were to be the dominant and pervasive element in the gradual emergence of a pan-Catholic group in America, but these developments would reveal themselves only in the twentieth century. In the meantime, in the last two decades of the nineteenth, the influx of immigrants from southern and eastern Europe had begun. These groups were all the more sociologically visible because the closing of the frontier, the occupational demands of an expanding industrial economy, and their own poverty made it inevitable that they would remain in the urban areas of the nation. In the swirling fires of controversy and the steadier flame of experience created by these new events, the ideology of cultural pluralism as a philosophy for the nation was forged.

The first manifestations of an ideological counterattack against draconic Americanization came not from the beleaguered newcomers (who were, after all, more concerned with survival than with theories of adjustment), but from those idealistic members of the middle class who, in the decade or so before the turn of the century, had followed the example of their English predecessors and "settled" in the slums to "learn to sup sorrow with the poor."[19] Immediately, these workers in the "settlement houses" were forced to come to grips with the realities of immigrant life and adjustment. Not all reacted in the same way, but on the whole the settlements developed an approach to the immigrant which was sympathetic to his native cultural heritage and to his newly created ethnic institutions.[20] For one thing, their workers, necessarily in intimate contact with the lives of these often pathetic and bewildered newcomers and their daily problems, could see how unfortunate were the effects of those forces which impelled rapid Americanization in their impact on the immigrants' children, who not infrequently became alienated from their parents and the restraining influence of family authority. Were not their parents ignorant and uneducated "Hunkies," "Sheenies," or "Dagoes," as that limited portion of the American environment in which they moved defined the matter? Ethnic "self-hatred" with its debilitating psychological consequences, family disorganization, and juvenile delinquency, were not unusual results of this state of affairs. Furthermore, the immigrants themselves were adversely affected by the incessant attacks on their culture, their language, their institutions, their very conception of themselves. How were they to maintain their self-respect when all that they knew, felt, and dreamed, beyond their sheer capacity for manual labor—in other words, all that they *were*—was despised or scoffed at in America? And—unkindest cut of all—their own children had begun to adopt the contemptuous attitude of the "Americans." Jane Addams relates in a moving chapter of her *Twenty Years at Hull House* how, after coming to have some conception of the extent and depth of these problems, she created at the settlement a "Labor Museum," in which the immigrant women of the various nationalities crowded together in the slums of Chicago could illustrate their native methods of spinning and weaving, and in which the relation of these earlier techniques to contemporary factory methods could be graphically shown. For the first time these peasant women were made to feel by some part of their American environment that they possessed valuable and interesting skills —that they too had something to offer—and for the first time, the daughters of these women who, after a long day's work at their dank "needletrade" sweatshops, came to Hull House to observe, began to appreciate the fact that their mothers, too, had a "culture," that this culture possessed its own merit, and that it was related to their own contemporary lives. How aptly Jane Addams concludes her chapter with the hope that "our American citizenship might be built without disturbing these foundations which were laid of old time."[21]

This appreciative view of the immigrant's cultural heritage and of its distinctive usefulness both to himself and his adopted country received additional sustenance from another source: those intellectual currents of the day which, however overborne by their currently more powerful opposites, emphasized liberalism, internationalism, and tolerance. From time to time, an occasional educator or publicist protested the demands of the "Americanizers," arguing that the immigrant, too, had an ancient and honorable culture, and that this culture had much to offer an America whose character and destiny were still in the process of formation, an America which must serve as an example of the harmonious cooperation of various heritages to a world inflamed by nationalism and war. In 1916 John Dewey, Norman Hapgood, and the young literary critic, Randolph Bourne, published articles or addresses elaborating various aspects of this theme.

The classic statement of the cultural pluralist position, however, had been made over a year before. Early in 1915 there appeared in the pages of *The Nation* two articles under the title "Democracy *versus* the Melting-Pot." Their author was Horace Kallen, a Harvard-educated philosopher with a concern for the application of philosophy to societal affairs, and, as an American Jew, himself derivative of an ethnic background which was subject to the contemporary pressures for dissolution implicit in the "Americanization," or Anglo-conformity, and the melting-pot theories. In these articles Kallen vigorously rejected the usefulness of these theories as models of what was actually transpiring in American life or as ideals for the future. Rather he was impressed by the way in which the various ethnic groups in America were coincident with particular areas and regions, and with the tendency for each group to preserve its own language, religion, communal institutions, and ancestral culture. All the while, he pointed out, the immigrant has been learning to speak English as the language of general communication, and has participated in the over-all economic and political life of the nation. These developments in which "the United States are in the process of becoming a federal state not merely as a union of geographical and administrative unities, but also as a cooperation of cultural diversities, as a federation or commonwealth of national cultures,"[22] the author argued, far from constituting a violation of historic American political principles, as the "Americanizers" claimed, actually represented the inevitable consequences of democratic ideals, since individuals are implicated in groups, and since democracy for the individual must by extension also mean democracy for his group.

The processes just described, however, as Kallen develops his argument, are far from having been thoroughly realized. They are menaced by "Americanization" programs, assumptions of Anglo-Saxon superiority, and misguided attempts to promote "racial" amalgamation. Thus America stands at a kind of cultural crossroads. It can attempt to impose by force an artificial, Anglo-Saxon oriented uniformity on its peoples, or it can consciously allow and encourage its ethnic groups to develop democratically, each emphasizing its particular cultural heritage. If the latter course is followed, as Kallen puts it at the close of his essay, then,[23]

The outlines of a possible great and truly democratic commonwealth become discernible. Its form would be that of the federal republic; its substance a democracy of nationalities, cooperating voluntarily and autonomously through common institutions in the enterprise of self-realization through the perfection of men according to their kind. The common language of the commonwealth, the language of its great tradition, would be English, but each nationality would have for its emotional and involuntary life its own peculiar dialect or speech, its own individual and inevitable esthetic and intellectual forms. The political and economic life of the commonwealth is a single unit and serves as the foundation and background for the realization of the distinctive individuality of each *nation* that composes it and of the pooling of these in a harmony above them all. Thus "American civilization" may come to mean the perfection of the cooperative harmonies of "European civilization"—the waste, the squalor and the distress of Europe being eliminated—a multiplicity in a unity, an orchestration of mankind.

Within the next decade Kallen published more essays dealing with the theme of American multiple-group life, later collected in a volume.[24] In the introductory note to this book he used for the first time the term "cultural pluralism" to refer to his position. These essays reflect both his increasingly sharp rejection of the onslaughts on the immigrant and his culture which the coming of World War I and its attendant fears, the "Red scare," the projection of themes of racial superiority, the continued exploitation of the newcomers, and the rise of the Ku Klux Klan all served to increase in intensity, and also his emphasis on cultural pluralism as the democratic antidote to these ills. He has since published other essays elaborating or annotating the theme of cultural pluralism. Thus, for at least forty-five years, most of them spent teaching at the New School for Social Research, Kallen has been acknowledged as the originator and leading philosophical exponent of the idea of cultural pluralism.

In the late 1930's and early 1940's the late Louis Adamic, the Yugoslav immigrant who had become an American writer, took up the theme of America's multicultural heritage and the role of these groups in forging the country's national character. Borrowing Walt Whitman's phrase, he described America as "a nation of nations," and while his ultimate goal was closer to the melting-pot idea than to cultural pluralism, he saw the immediate task as that of making America conscious of what it owed to all its ethnic groups, not just to the Anglo-Saxons. The children and grandchildren of immigrants of non-English origins, he was convinced, must be taught to be proud of the cultural heritage of their ancestral ethnic group and of its role in building the American nation; otherwise, they would not lose their sense of ethnic inferiority and the feeling of rootlessness he claimed to find in them.

Thus in the twentieth century, particularly since World War II, "cultural pluralism" has become a concept which has worked its way into the vocabulary and imagery of specialists in intergroup relations and leaders of ethnic communal groups. In view of this new pluralistic emphasis, some writers now prefer to speak of the "integration" of immigrants rather than of their "assimilation."[25] However, with a few exceptions,[26] no close analytical attention has been given either by social scientists or practitioners of intergroup relations to the meaning of cultural pluralism, its nature and relevance for a modern industrialized

society, and its implications for problems of prejudice and discrimination
—a point to which we referred at the outset of this discussion.

Conclusions

In the remaining pages I can make only a few analytical comments which
I shall apply in context to the American scene, historical and current. My
view of the American situation will not be documented here, but may be
considered as a series of hypotheses in which I shall attempt to outline the
American assimilation process.

First of all, it must be realized that "assimilation" is a blanket term
which in reality covers a multitude of subprocesses. The most crucial
distinction is one often ignored—the distinction between what I elsewhere called "behavioral assimilation" and "structural assimilation."[27]
The first refers to the absorption of the cultural behavior patterns of the
"host" society. (At the same time, there is frequently some modification
of the cultural patterns of the immigrant-receiving country, as well.)
There is a special term for this process of cultural modification or "behavioral assimilation"—namely, "acculturation." "Structural assimilation," on the other hand, refers to the entrance of the immigrants and
their descendants into the social cliques, organizations, institutional activities, and general civic life of the receiving society. If this process takes
place on a large enough scale, then a high frequency of intermarriage
must result. A further distinction must be made between, on the one
hand, those activities of the general civic life which involve earning a
living, carrying out political responsibilities, and engaging in the instrumental affairs of the larger community, and, on the other hand, activities
which create personal friendship patterns, frequent home intervisiting,
communal worship, and communal recreation. The first type usually
develops so-called "secondary relationships," which tend to be relatively
impersonal and segmental; the latter type leads to "primary relationships," which are warm, intimate, and personal.

With these various distinctions in mind, we may then proceed.

Built on the base of the original immigrant "colony" but frequently
extending into the life of successive generations, the characteristic ethnic
group experience is this: within the ethnic group there develops a
network of organizations and informal social relationships which permits
and encourages the members of the ethnic group to remain within the
confines of the group for all of their primary relationships and some of
their secondary relationships throughout all the stages of the life cycle.
From the cradle in the sectarian hospital to the child's play group, the

social clique in high school, the fraternity and religious center in college, the dating group within which he searches for a spouse, the marriage partner, the neighborhood of his residence, the church affiliation and the church clubs, the men's and the women's social and service organizations, the adult clique of "marrieds," the vacation resort, and then, as the age cycle nears completion, the rest home for the elderly and, finally, the sectarian cemetery—in all these activities and relationships which are close to the core of personality and selfhood—the member of the ethnic group may if he wishes follow a path which never takes him across the boundaries of his ethnic structural network.

The picture is made more complex by the existence of social class divisions which cut across ethnic group lines just as they do those of the white Protestant population in America. As each ethnic group which has been here for the requisite time has developed second, third, or in some cases, succeeding generations, it has produced a college-educated group which composes an upper middle class (and sometimes upper class, as well) segment of the larger groups. Such class divisions tend to restrict primary group relations even further, for although the ethnic-group member feels a general sense of identification with all the bearers of his ethnic heritage, he feels comfortable in intimate social relations only with those who also share his own class background or attainment.

In short, my point is that, while *behavioral assimilation* or acculturation has taken place in America to a considerable degree, *structural assimilation*, with some important exceptions, has not been extensive.[28] The exceptions are of two types. The first brings us back to the "triple melting pot" thesis of Ruby Jo Reeves Kennedy and Will Herberg. The "nationality" ethnic groups have tended to merge within each of the three major religious groups. This has been particularly true of the Protestant and Jewish communities. Those descendants of the "old" immigration of the nineteenth century, who were Protestant (many of the Germans and all the Scandinavians), have in considerable part gradually merged into the white Protestant "subsociety." Jews of Sephardic, German, and eastern-European origins have similarly tended to come together in their communal life. The process of absorbing the various Catholic nationalities, such as the Italians, Poles, and French Canadians, into an American Catholic community hitherto dominated by the Irish has begun, although I do not believe that it is by any means close to completion. Racial and quasi-racial groups such as the Negroes, Indians, Mexican-Americans, and Puerto Ricans still retain their separate sociological structures. The outcome of all this in contemporary American life is thus pluralism—but it is more than "triple" and it is more accurately described as *structural pluralism* than as cultural pluralism, although some of the latter also remains.

My second exception refers to the social structures which implicate intellectuals. There is no space to develop the issue here, but I would argue that there is a social world or subsociety of the intellectuals in America in which true structural intermixture among persons of various ethnic backgrounds, including the religious, has markedly taken place.

My final point deals with the reasons for these developments. If structural assimilation has been retarded in America by religious and racial lines, we must ask why. The answer lies in the attitudes of both the majority and the minority groups and in the way these attitudes have interacted. A saying of the current day is, "It takes two to tango." To apply the analogy, there is no good reason to believe that white Protestant America has ever extended a firm and cordial invitation to its minorities to dance. Furthermore, the attitudes of the minority-group members themselves on the matter have been divided and ambiguous. Particularly for the minority religious groups, there is a certain logic in ethnic communality, since there is a commitment to the perpetuation of the religious ideology and since structural intermixture leads to inter-marriage and the possible loss to the group of the intermarried family. Let us, then, examine the situation serially for various types of minorities.

With regard to the immigrant, in his characteristic numbers and socioeconomic background, structural assimilation was out of the question. He did not want it, and he had a positive need for the comfort of his own communal institutions. The native American, moreover, whatever the implications of his public pronouncements, had no intention of opening up his primary group life to entrance by these hordes of alien newcomers. The situation was a functionally complementary standoff.

The second generation found a much more complex situation. Many believed they heard the siren call of welcome to the social cliques, clubs, and institutions of white Protestant America. After all, it was simply a matter of learning American ways, was it not? Had they not grown up as Americans, and were they not culturally different from their parents, the "greenhorns?" Or perhaps an especially eager one reasoned (like the Jewish protagonist of Myron Kaufmann's novel, *Remember Me To God*, aspiring to membership in the prestigious club system of Harvard under-graduate social life) "If only I can go the last few steps in Ivy League man-ners and behavior, they will surely recognize that I am one of them and take me in." But, alas, Brooks Brothers suit notwithstanding, the doors of the fraternity house, the city men's club, and the country club were slammed in the face of the immigrant's offspring. That invitation was not really there in the first place; or, to the extent it was, in Joshua Fishman's phrase, it was a " 'look me over but don't touch me' invitation to the American minority group child."[29] And so the rebuffed one returned to the homelier but dependable comfort of the communal institutions of his ancestral group. There he found his fellows of the same generation who had never stirred from the home fires. Some of these had been too timid to stray; others were ethnic ideologists committed to the group's survival; still others had never really believed in the authenticity of the siren call or were simply too passive to do more than go along the familiar way. All could now join in the task that was well within the realm of the sociologically possible—the build-up of social institutions and organizations within the ethnic enclave, manned increasingly by members of the second generation and suitably separated by social class.

Those who had for a time ventured out gingerly or confidently, as the case might be, had been lured by the vision of an "American" social structure that was somehow larger than all subgroups and was ethnically neutral. Were they, too, not Americans? But they found to their dismay that at the primary group level a neutral American social structure was a mirage. What at a distance seemed to be a quasi-public edifice flying only the all-inclusive flag of American nationality turned out on closer inspection to be the clubhouse of a particular ethnic group—the white Anglo-Saxon Protestants, its operation shot through with the premises and expectations of its parental ethnicity. In these terms, the desirability of whatever invitation was grudgingly extended to those of other ethnic backgrounds could only become a considerably attenuated one.

With the racial minorities, there was not even the pretense of an invitation. Negroes, to take the most salient example, have for the most part been determinedly barred from the cliques, social clubs, and churches of white America. Consequently, with due allowance for internal class differences, they have constructed their own network of organizations and institutions, their own "social world." There are now many vested interests served by the preservation of this separate communal life, and doubtless many Negroes are psychologically comfortable in it, even though at the same time they keenly desire that discrimination in such areas as employment, education, housing, and public accommodations be eliminated. However, the ideological attachment of Negroes to their communal separation is not conspicuous. Their sense of identification with ancestral African national cultures is virtually nonexistent, although Pan-Africanism engages the interest of some intellectuals and although "black nationalist" and "black racist" fringe groups have recently made an appearance at the other end of the communal spectrum. As for their religion, they are either

Protestant or Catholic (overwhelmingly the former). Thus, there are no "logical" ideological reasons for their separate communality; dual social structures are created solely by the dynamics of prejudice and discrimination, rather than being reinforced by the ideological commitments of the minority itself.

Structural assimilation, then, has turned out to be the rock on which the ships of Anglo-conformity and the melting pot have foundered. To understand that behavioral assimilation (or acculturation) without massive structural intermingling in primary relationships has been the dominant motif in the American experience of creating and developing a nation out of diverse peoples is to comprehend the most essential sociological fact of that experience. It is against the background of "structural pluralism" that strategies of strengthening intergroup harmony, reducing ethnic discrimination and prejudice, and maintaining the rights of both those who stay within and those who venture beyond their ethnic boundaries must be thoughtfully devised.

Notes

1) Allan Nevins and Henry Steele Commager, *America: The Story of a Free People* (Boston, Little, Brown, 1942), p. 58.
2) The phrase is the Coles's. See Stewart G. Cole and Mildred Wiese Cole, *Minorities and the American Promise* (New York, Harper & Brothers, 1954), ch. 6.
3) Maurice R. Davie, *World Immigration* (New York, Macmillan, 1936), p. 36, and (cited therein) "Letter of Benjamin Franklin to Peter Collinson, 9th May, 1753, on the condition and character of the Germans in Pennsylvania," in *The Works of Benjamin Franklin, with notes and a life of the author,* by Jared Sparks (Boston, 1828), vol. 7, pp. 71–73.
4) *The Writings of George Washington,* collected and edited by W. C. Ford (New York, G. P. Putnam's Sons, 1889), vol. 12, p. 489.
5) Thomas Jefferson, "Notes on Virginia, Query 8;" in *The Writings of Thomas Jefferson,* edited by A. E. Bergh (Washington, The Thomas Jefferson Memorial Association, 1907), vol. 2, p. 121.
6) *Niles' Weekly Register,* vol. 18, April 29, 1820, pp. 157–158; also, Marcus L. Hansen, *The Atlantic Migration, 1607–1860* (Cambridge, Harvard University Press, 1940), pp. 96–97.
7) Ellwood P. Cubberly, *Changing Conceptions of Education* (Boston, Houghton Mifflin, 1909), pp. 15–16.
8) J. Hector St. John Crèvecoeur, *Letters from an American Farmer* (New York, Albert and Charles Boni, 1925; reprinted from the 1st edn., London, 1782), pp. 54–55.
9) Oscar Handlin, ed., *Immigration as a Factor in American History* (Englewood, Prentice-Hall, 1959), p. 146.
10) Quoted by Stuart P. Sherman in his Introduction to *Essays and Poems of Emerson* (New York, Harcourt, Brace, 1921), p. xxxiv.
11) See Edward N. Saveth, *American Historians and European Immigrants, 1875–1925* (New York, Columbia University Press, 1948).

12) Frederick Jackson Turner, *The Frontier in American History* (New York, Holt, 1920), pp. 22–23, 190.
13) Israel Zangwill, *The Melting Pot* (New York, Macmillan, 1909), p. 37.
14) Ruby Jo Reeves Kennedy, "Single or Triple Melting-Pot? Intermarriage Trends in New Haven, 1870–1940," *American Journal of Sociology*, 1944, *49:* 331–339. See also her "Single or Triple Melting-Pot? Intermarriage in New Haven, 1870–1950," *ibid.*, 1952, *58:* 56–59.
15) Ruby Jo Reeves Kennedy, "Single or Triple Melting-Pot? . . . 1870–1940," p. 332 (author's italics omitted).
16) Will Herberg, *Protestant-Catholic-Jew* (Garden City, Doubleday, 1955).
17) Nathan Glazer, "Ethnic Groups in America: From National Culture to Ideology," in Morroe Berger, Theodore Abel, and Charles H. Page, eds., *Freedom and Control in Modern Society* (New York, D. Van Nostrand, 1954), p. 161; Marcus Lee Hansen, *The Immigrant in American History* (Cambridge, Harvard University Press, 1940), pp. 129–140; John A. Hawgood, *The Tragedy of German-America* (New York, Putnam's, 1940), *passim.*
18) Oscar Handlin, *Boston's Immigrants* (Cambridge, Harvard University Press, 1959; rev. edn.), p. 176.
19) From a letter (1883) by Samuel A. Barnett; quoted in Arthur C. Holden, *The Settlement Idea* (New York, Macmillan, 1922), p. 12.
20) Jane Addams, *Twenty Years at Hull House* (New York, Macmillan, 1914), pp. 231–258; Arthur C. Holden, *op. cit.*, pp. 109–131, 182–189; John Higham, *Strangers in the Land* (New Brunswick, Rutgers University Press, 1955), p. 236.
21) Jane Addams, *op. cit.*, p. 258.
22) Horace M. Kallen, "Democracy *versus* the Melting-Pot," *The Nation*, February 18 and 25, 1915; reprinted in his *Culture and Democracy in the United States* (New York, Boni & Liveright, 1924); the quotation is on p. 116.
23) Horace M. Kallen, *Culture and Democracy* . . . , p. 124.
24) *Ibid.*
25) See W. D. Borrie *et al.*, *The Cultural Integration of Immigrants* (a survey based on the papers and proceedings of the UNESCO Conference in Havana, April 1956; Paris, UNESCO, 1959); and William S. Bernard, "The Integration of Immigrants in the United States" (mimeographed), one of the papers for this conference.
26) See particularly Milton M. Gordon, "Social Structure and Goals in Group Relations"; and Nathan Glazer, "Ethnic Groups in America: From National Culture to Ideology," both articles in Berger, Abel, and Page, *op. cit.*; S. N. Eisenstadt, *The Absorption of Immigrants* (London, Routledge & Kegan Paul, 1954); and W. D. Borrie *et al.*, *op. cit.*
27) Milton M. Gordon, "Social Structure and Goals in Group Relations," *op. cit.*, p. 151.
28) See Erich Rosenthal, "Acculturation without Assimilation?" *American Journal of Sociology*, 1960, *66:* 275–288.
29) Joshua A. Fishman, "Childhood Indoctrination for Minority-Group Membership and the Quest for Minority-Group Biculturism in America," in Oscar Handlin, ed., *Group Life in America* (Cambridge, Harvard University Press, forthcoming).

The Meaning of Negro Strategy

‿ᴈᴈ‿

David Danzig

In May of 1963, the world was abruptly made aware that a new minority
community had emerged as a significant and self-conscious force in American society. The evidence was clear, eloquent, and disturbing. In Birmingham, Alabama during the week of May 13, the formerly dispersed and
demoralized masses of Negroes suddenly became a well-organized, resolute
body of citizens, marching forward to their daily encounter with the city's
police force and fire department. The following week in Nashville,
Tennessee, students of Fisk University led a protest march of their fellow
Negroes through the main avenues of the city as part of a new campaign
for complete desegregation. In Raleigh, North Carolina, five hundred college students broke three years of relative racial peace that had followed
the desegregation of lunch counters, and launched a similar drive for total
equality by a demonstration at the Governor's mansion. In Greensboro,
North Carolina, a thousand Negroes attempted to sit-in at two movie
houses and a public cafeteria. In Cambridge, Maryland, as in Albany,
Georgia, the long, desperate struggle was joined again, while in Selma,
Alabama, the first stage of a new one was initiated by Negro leaders in a
campaign to register voters. But it was not only in the South that the
presence and pressure of a coherent movement were unmistakably apparent. Immediately following "Birmingham," the groundwave of protest
began to swell in the Negro ghettos of New York, Chicago, and Detroit, as
well as in pleasant suburbs like Orange and Englewood in New Jersey.
Following these two weeks in May the tide of Negro group action continued to grow through the late spring and summer, rolling across the
Eastern half of the nation and culminating in the great demonstration in
Washington on August 28.

Reprinted from "The Meaning of Negro Strategy," *Commentary*, 37 (February,
1964), 41–46, by permission of the author and publisher. Copyright © 1964 by the
American Jewish Committee.

The most immediate and dramatic reaction of the white community was that of resentment and resistance. Nothing was quite to match that long Saturday night of May 18 in Birmingham when the motel where Martin Luther King had set up headquarters and the home of King's brother were both bombed, and when for some hours Negroes and police struggled amid the havoc and terror of an incipient race war. But almost everywhere that Negroes protested there was violence or the threat of it. The demonstrations in Nashville ended in knife-fighting between Negroes and whites; in Greensboro 241 marchers were arrested while a mob of whites swirled about them under the banners of "Blacks, Go Home," and "Go Back to Africa." And the mood of white resistance was to continue making itself felt in the infamous church bombing in Birmingham, and in the chain of assaults and police harassment that eventually extended from Jackson, Mississippi, to New York.

This outcropping of violence and intransigence, bombings and imprisonment, however, tended to obscure the less dramatic but more significant development of a new stage in Negro-white relations. For example, even as the Birmingham police were packing the marchers off to jail, an unprecedented series of negotiations was taking place between the leading businessmen of the city—six white and six Negro—which culminated in an agreement providing for a phased integration of lunch counters and the opening of job opportunities to Negroes. So, too, the Negro demonstrations in Nashville, Raleigh, and Greensboro were promptly followed by the establishment of new bi-racial committees to plan further desegregation, backed by statements from the white business leaders of both cities calling for the removal of all public and business policies that denied rights and services on racial grounds. And similarly, in Orange, New Jersey, the efforts of the Negro community resulted in an order from the State Commissioner of Education to present a plan for integrating a segregated elementary school in that town.

In other words, what underlay the specific conflicts both in the South and in the North during this two-week period in May was the emergence of an organized Negro community in each town representing the interests of its members and able to negotiate for them. Even the agreement reached in Birmingham—though it was soon to be repudiated by the business community of the city, not to mention the city government, the state police, and the fanatical terrorists—is an illustration of this development. Written in the spirit of civic pragmatism that has been displacing the rabid intransigence of the racists, the Birmingham agreement reads like what it essentially is: a pact between two distinct political bodies:

Responsible leaders of both Negro and white communities of Birmingham, being desirous of promoting conditions which will ensure sound moral, economic and political growth of their city, in the interest of all citizens of Birmingham, after mutual consideration and discussion of the issues relating to the recent demonstrations in the city, have agreed to . . .

What we have here, in effect, is a radical departure from the traditional conception of civil rights as the rights of individuals. This departure lies at the heart of the "Negro Revolution," and may, indeed, almost be said to *be* that revolution. Today, in America as elsewhere, the Negro has made us forcefully aware that the rights and privileges of an individual rest upon the status attained by the group to which he belongs—that is to say, by the power it controls and can use. That this fact determined race relations in the 19th century is clear enough: Hillaire Belloc, disdaining to rationalize colonialism as "the white man's burden," put the matter very simply: "When all is said and done, we have the Gatling gun and they have none." To the extent that power is available to him, the Negro is now responding in kind. And in the American pluralistic pattern, where social power is distributed by group, the Negro has perforce come to recognize that he can achieve equal opportunities only through the concerted action of the Negro community. No longer addressing himself exclusively to the white man's attitudes of prejudice, to effecting changes in "the hearts and minds of men"—an approach that dooms him to gradualism—the Negro now confronts the white society on the issue of his rights with all the political and economic strength that his group is able to wield.

The Negro bloc of yesterday, in short, has become the mass movement of today. The speed with which this change has occurred, as well as its tendency to become identified with specific personalities like Martin Luther King and with specific incidents like those in Birmingham or Jackson or Albany, have deflected attention from the more general meaning of what has been happening. First of all, it is clear that the upsurge of Negro action is not merely a matter of temporary fervor; it is rather a profound response to a number of pressures which have been generated by the Negro's changing relation to American society and which, taken together, constitute a social upheaval of major significance. Among the more salient of these pressures is the accelerated migration of Negroes from the South to the North and from rural areas to the cities. While the state of Mississippi has been losing over 30 per cent of its Negro population in each of the past two decades, cities like Chicago, Detroit, and Los Angeles have been experiencing an equally phenomenal rise in their Negro populations. Within the deprived and impacted Negro ghettos, the demands steadily grow for improved housing, education, and other public services. At the same time, the mounting population and its concentration in big cities provide Negro leaders with an increasingly strong base of political power. For example, in the Woodlawn neighborhood of Chicago's Black Belt, whose Negro population has increased by 80 per cent since the war, a grass-roots political movement has sprung up recently which has been agitating effectively for better police protection, school facilities, and housing, and which has forged a new spirit of group solidarity and communal responsibility that has enabled its leaders to oppose the acquisition of the best sections of the neighborhood by the powerful University of Chicago.

In the economic sphere, similarly, the advent of automation and other technological advances has produced a growing unemployment rate among Negroes and a widening split between Negro and white incomes. As the pressures of Negro poverty and frustration mount, the barriers of job discrimination become that much more unendurable; the result has been a concerted effort to breach them through mass demonstrations against labor and management alike, as well as through boycotts, selective buying, and other pressure tactics.

Given all these tensions within the Negro population, it is not surprising that they should be pressing for action. What is surprising, however, is the solidarity and skill which have characterized Negro action during the past year. The March on Washington presented an especially conclusive example of Negro unity. Such unity—indeed, unity of any kind —is new in Negro life; one of the important effects of the strategy of mass demonstrations has been to create a sense of community among a people whose group ties were deliberately and persistently shattered during the period of slavery and whose subsequent social history has produced, for the most part, no larger unit of community than the church congregation. The spectacle of 200,000 people marching [in 1963] through Washington, along with the other group demonstrations in the North and South and the innumerable acts of individual heroism, have produced a new feeling of collective self-awareness, of peoplehood. The March on Washington, moreover, was a testimony to the rapid progress that the Negro has been making in wielding power. The organizational feat involved in planning and carrying through the huge demonstration, and the discipline of the marchers themselves, most of them Negro, marked an impressive stage in the maturing of the community. And it showed that a new Negro bureaucracy had come to the fore whose political sophistication and organizational talent were comparable to those of the best leadership found among the other ethnic and religious groups.

Thus, within a very short time, the Negro has developed the rudimentary group coherence and indigenous leadership that enables him to speak for his own rights and interests. Lacking these strengths, the Negro has in the past necessarily been dependent upon whites to represent him in American society. Both the Urban League, his main social agency, and the NAACP, his main political action group, were founded by whites and until recently have functioned within the ambience of the white community. Similarly with the Negro's political power, which has been mortgaged to the liberal coalition of the big-city political machines and the CIO that was created a generation ago under the New Deal. While the Negro has not as yet withdrawn from this coalition, he is no longer willing to accept the theory that what is good for the Democratic party is necessarily good for him. Nor is he any more patient with the "trickle-down" concept of prosperity when it is advanced to him by Big Labor than was the union man himself when he heard it expressed by Big Business during the Hoover years. Having taken into his own hands the reins of his destiny in American society, the Negro has found that the gradualism to which so many Northern liberals are committed can be as pressing an obstacle as the intransigence of the Southern conservatives, and consequently he has been forced to assert specific Negro demands in the North through his attacks upon the unions, upon de facto school and housing segregation, and through his drive for greater political patronage and a more independent use of the vote. What is now perceived as the "revolt of the Negro" amounts to this: the solitary Negro seeking admission into the white world through unusual achievement has been replaced by the organized Negro insisting upon a legitimate share for his group of the goods of American society. The white liberal, in turn, who—whether or not he has been fully conscious of it—has generally conceived of progress in race relations as the one-by-one assimilation of deserving Negroes into the larger society, finds himself confused and threatened by suddenly having to come to terms with an aggressive Negro community that wishes to enter it *en masse*.

Accordingly, in the arena of civil rights the Negro Revolution has tended to take the struggle out of the courts and bring it to the streets and the negotiating tables. Granting the potential for unprecedented violence that exists here, it must also be borne in mind that what the Negro people are now beginning to do, other ethnic minorities—who brought to America their strong traditions of communal solidarity—did before them. With this powerful asset the Irish rapidly acquired political strength and the Jews succeeded in raising virtually an entire immigrant population into the middle class within the span of two generations. Viewed in this perspective, the Negroes are merely the last of America's significant ethnic minorities to achieve communal solidarity and to grasp the role of the informal group power structure in protecting the rights and advancing the opportunities of the individual members of the community.

Indeed, ethnic groups (including of course the White Anglo-Saxon Protestant group) have played a much more significant role in American society than is commonly recognized or at least admitted. Except in the realm of politics, where the backing of a given ethnic group is often the primary qualification for office, we tend to maintain the fiction that American society is made up of isolated individuals who depend mainly upon their own talents for the position they achieve in it. The truth is, however, that the economic structure of the nation has been no less strongly influenced by ethnic factors than political ones. Wherever we look—whether at heavy industry or dairy farming, public utilities or banking, the building or the garment trades, organized crime or law enforcement—we find clearly marked ethnic patterns of occupation opportunities. Though these patterns have been breaking down in recent decades, in many of the older industries and vocations it still makes a difference whether one's forebears came from Ireland or Italy or whether one's first name or last name is Milton.

The converse of the fiction of social individualism has been the idea that minority organization hinders assimilation and perpetuates the disabilities of minority status. In the light of this idea, the immigrants pouring into America at the turn of the century were repeatedly advised that naturalization was an individual—and not a group—process and were admonished to shed their group identities and organizations as rapidly as possible. Today, Negro solidarity and its forms of collective self-assertion are provoking a similar anxiety and counsel from the dominant group. Disapproval by the majority, however, is unlikely to have much influence on the new Negro movement. The traditional approach to civil rights and equal opportunities as the slow but continuous expansion of democracy on an individual basis means little to a group which is demanding the immediate rectification of a severe and continuous injustice to it. Moreover, when the authority of state governments and the power of most social and economic institutions have been used to deny the individual Negro his rights and opportunities merely because of his membership in the Negro group, it seems only fitting that he should muster the power he possesses to establish his rights and opportunities on a group basis.

But Negro action has not only turned the civil rights program into a conflict between groups, it has also extended this conflict to employment, housing, and education. Looking beyond the demand for civil rights, Negro leaders see that the "open society" of 1964 is in many areas even more closed to their community than was the ethnocentric WASP society of 1900 to the waves of new immigrants, and that the inequities suffered by Negroes are more extreme. Even in jobs, residential neighborhoods, and schools where Negroes are not excluded by explicit policy, their absence in significant numbers is rightly seen as proof of discrimination. The sad and brutal truth is that de facto segregation permeates our institutions and exerts a cumulative force: like a tropism beyond the reach of law, it impels the white man to identify with his race and to turn his back on the Negro.

The real issue, then, is not that of giving special considerations to Negroes to compensate for past injustices, but that of adopting realistic measures which will begin to correct a profound tendency in our society to exclude and penalize the Negro. So profound is this tendency that even where the formula "regardless of race, creed, or color" has been taken seriously, the Negro has found himself excluded on the ground of inadequate qualifications. The present anxiety about "maintaining standards" is far from new: it is a traditional ethnocentric reaction to any serious threat from outsiders, and it is as often a rationalization for prejudice as a concern for quality. Certainly the recently expressed determination of the building trades unions to maintain the "standards" of their craft must seem unconvincing to any occupant of a modern New York apartment. Where there is good will, the problem of equipping Negroes would seem to be no more difficult than that faced by American industry during World War II when it created virtually a whole new skilled work force through on-the-job training. After all, no one is suggesting that Negro laborers should immediately be sent to medical school, though no doubt a good many more Negro college students with good grades in biology should be.

To deal with this form of institutional prejudice the Negro activists have adopted the new strategy of attempting to fix responsibility on the management level—housing authorities, trade-union officials, corporation executives, boards of education, and so forth. Such an approach to the objective of increasing vocational, housing, and educational opportunities must sooner or later involve a discussion of numbers. However, insistence that the number of Negroes in some industries, housing projects, and schools be increased to a proportion reasonably related to Negro incidence in the population has been misrepresented, sometimes intentionally, as a demand for a rigid quota that would be imposed for the benefit of Negroes and at the expense of whites. Both Governor Rockefeller and President Kennedy received strong support from the white community when they condemned quotas. The President did so on practical grounds: "We are too mixed, this society of ours, to begin to divide ourselves on the basis of race or color." The governor made his opposition a matter of doctrine, arguing that such quotas were both unlawful and counter to American principles. The New York *Times*, having acknowledged that Negroes are justified in being impatient about the rate of unemployment in their community, went on to observe that "this impatience often finds expression in suggestions for a conscious system of reverse discrimination in favor of Negroes." Trade unions have also found reasons for strongly condemning quotas. So has President Eisenhower who fears that we may be in danger of "over-compensating" the Negro.

In general, white opposition to the Negro movement has crystallized around the issues of "quotas" and "preferential treatment." But to the Negro seeking a radical improvement in his situation, the issues are jobs and decent living conditions, not quotas; improved education, not school-busing privileges. Due to the lack of white support of any large-scale measures to aid the Negro, progress in these basic areas has been pitifully small. After being subjected to immense pressure, for example, the building trades agreed to add Negro apprentices; three thousand applicants were screened and 14 accepted! And in the other areas of the Negro plight, the advances have been no less meager.

Liberal opinion, in the North and in the South, thus continues to stand upon its traditions of gradualism—the one-by-one admission of deserving Negroes into the larger society—and to reject the idea that to help the Negro it must help the Negro community. Yet the fact is that the Negro belongs to an economic as well as a racial group. Certainly a child born in East Harlem is as much bound by economic limitations as a coal miner's child in eastern Kentucky. Given the conditions in a region like eastern Kentucky, we recognize that opportunity is in good part socially determined: if unemployment goes over 7 per cent, the town qualifies as a "depressed area" and the community as a whole receives federal aid. But the Negro, who by virtue of his color belongs to an economic community which suffers almost constantly from an unemployment rate of more than 12 per cent, is expected to find resources and opportunities by himself and on his own.

Secretary of Labor Wirtz recently remarked that machines can now do more cheaply and effectively most work done by the high-school graduate. Obviously the resources needed for earning an acceptable place in our society are far different from what they were a century ago when a grant of three acres and the ability to farm it provided a sufficient start. However, we still tend to accept the American frontier ideology of resourceful individualism in positing the requirements for success in our society, just as we still accept the classical liberal ideology of laissez-faire as the backbone of our economic system. The truth is that this frontier ideology has as little relation to the actual routes to advancement in our highly developed technocracy as the laissez-faire ideology has to the actual operation of our federally subsidized and highly integrated economy. The individual who is adequately equipped to meet its demands usually has the backing of community and family achievement, which motivates him to seek a college education and orients him in making use of it.

Why then should we still insist upon holding the Negro to an extreme and outmoded doctrine of individual merit? More than half of all Negro men have not even graduated from primary school, and the continuing process of discrimination makes a bad situation increasingly worse. Between 1952 and 1962, the average Negro income dropped from 57 per cent to 53 per cent of the average white income, and the future looks even darker than the present. Negroes are heavily over-represented in unskilled labor, where jobs are decreasing daily, and heavily under-represented in the white-collar fields, which accounts for nearly all new jobs nowadays and where the rate of Negro unemployment is already about twice as high as the white rate.

The number of Americans living on a minimal subsistence level has been variously estimated as ranging between 36 and 50 million. Let us accept the mid-point figure of 44 million. It has been pointed out that 11 million of these people—that is, *only* one out of four—are Negroes. But looked at from another point of view, nearly two-thirds of all Negroes are impoverished. As Michael Harrington has demonstrated, poverty, like wealth, is inherited. Within the larger perspective of American society as a whole, the inherited poverty of whites, though far from negligible, is still a minority phenomenon; from the Negro's perspective, inherited poverty is a majority phenomenon, indeed an endemic one. In the generally accepted notion that America is an affluent society, we merely confirm our exclusion of the Negro from it.

This prolonged, virtually systematic exclusion of the Negro group from American life and the growing desperation of his position explain why the Negro is making such radical demands for freedom and opportunity—"now." But along with objecting to the Negro's impatient and militantly self-interested demands as "racism in reverse," white liberals have also questioned the efficacy of his strategy. The position expressed by Professor Eli Ginzberg is typical:

In the past the Negro has made significant gains when he has been included in important national efforts—the Revolutionary War, the Civil War, the New Deal, the C.I.O., World War II, the expansion of public programs for health, education, and welfare. There is little prospect that white America will do much for the handicapped Negro group. But we *can* expect our democracy to attend to its less fortunate citizens, Negroes included. All America needs a higher level of employment, more and better education, a closer approximation to true equality. To the extent that we move energetically towards these national goals, to that extent will the status of the Negro be improved.

One need hardly argue the superior value, to say nothing of the political advantage, of a national program supported by a wide variety of groups for the benefit of all deprived members of the society. But what allows us to "expect our democracy to attend to its less fortunate citizens, Negroes included" when doing so to any real effect would require major structural changes in the economy as well as in our institutional patterns? What political force will generate such a program? For there is very little political action today that does not have its source in one or another organized and powerful group—and (as was amply demonstrated during the battle for medicare) our forty to fifty million citizens who live in poverty are far too heterogeneous to constitute themselves into an effective political bloc. In general, Professor Ginzberg's analysis reduces to the moral rhetoric that contemporary liberals tend to substitute for political insight. Professor Andrew Hacker has described the situation of the underprivileged in far more realistic and relevant terms:

It may well be that two Americas are emerging, one a society protected by the corporate umbrella and the other a society whose members have failed to affiliate themselves with the dominant institutions. . . . more importantly, it [the "second America"] will be comprised of the unemployed, the ill-educated and the entire residue of human beings who are not needed by the corporate machine.

One might expect organized labor to begin to concern itself with the economic needs of this second America. But for the most part the unions in practice act as a conservative establishment that is mainly worried about maintaining its prerogatives against the sweeping changes of automation. During the Depression, the AFL denied its support to the unemployed and to those in the mass-production industries. Today, with one-fourth of the nation still ill-housed, ill-fed, and ill-clothed (about the same absolute number of individuals as in the Depression), the AFL-CIO is hardly more interested in speaking for the unorganized worker than the AFL was then. And just as the failure of the AFL in the thirties necessitated the organization of the CIO, so the inadequacy of the trade-union movement today forces the Negro group into acting to mitigate its own economic plight. Thus the sectarian character of the Negro's economic and political demands can be understood as a consequence of the absence of any political movement in the United States that speaks for the new American proletariat in general.

In the postwar period, the emergence of a highly integrated mass society has forced the politics of sectionalism to give way to the politics of groups. More than ever before, the key to political power is group interest. And as often as not, the group interest in question is ethnic, religious, or racial. Such special interests are not necessarily antagonistic to the general good; indeed, they have often helped to advance the general interest by strengthening our democracy and by promoting programs of social welfare. Today the special interest of the Negro involves the burdens of poverty, inadequate training, and other social disabilities that afflict the entire "under-class" of the society, though they fall most heavily upon him. And it is already becoming evident that the Negro's militancy on behalf of his own cause may well serve the cause of the new American proletariat as a whole. The March on Washington, though primarily concerned with civil rights, also included among its ten points a request for a massive federal program to train unemployed workers—Negro and white; a national Minimum Wage Act that would give to all a decent living; and a broad Federal Labor Standards Act covering all areas of employment which are presently excluded. More generally, the Negro movement today provides the only likely center around which a new coalition might be created to fill the current political vacuum.

A. Philip Randolph, the Negroes' leading spokesman in the councils of labor, is keenly aware of the strategic role of the Negro movement at this juncture of history. Addressing the AFL-CIO Convention in November, he argued for an alliance between labor and the Negro:

> Let our alliance be strengthened. It is in labor's own interest. For the Negro's protest today is but the first rumbling of the *"under-class."* As the Negro has taken to the streets, so will the unemployed of all races take to the streets. . . . To discuss the civil rights revolution is therefore to write the agenda of labor's unfinished revolution. The labor movement cannot ignore this underclass. It cannot degenerate into a mere protective association, insulating the "haves" from the "have-nots" in the working class . . .

The implications of such an alliance were graphically spelled out in a subsequent speech at the same convention by Hank Brown, President of the Texas AFL-CIO:

> There are a half-million Negroes in our state working for less than fifty cents an hour. There are nearly a million unorganized Latin Americans in our state working for less than fifty cents an hour. . . . Civil rights means more

than just doing something for the Negro . . . we can't win in Texas against the money changers that run the temple, called the state government, with just organized labor. We formed, Brother Randolph, the alliance you speak of a year ago then known as the coalition . . . and we would like for other states to take the hand of the Negro, the Latin American, the Indian, whatever he is, if he is a worker, and he is not making at least $2.00 an hour. Then that is the brother that we need to get with and win the kind of progress we are talking about.

It is still too early to say whether local coalitions like the one in Texas are the grass-roots beginnings of a new national coalition. Certainly any such coalition would have to be formed in the teeth of the apathy toward the unorganized poor that currently prevails among many of labor's statesmen as well as much of the rank-and-file. Be that as it may, it is becoming evident that only the new proletariat speaking for itself can join the issues of the day. The social planners who have analyzed the problems, the liberals who have moralized them, and the politicians who have articulated them can help in a new progressive coalition, but they lack the energy to initiate it. Group self-interest provides the very core of real politics, and Negro solidarity will have a large role to play if our democracy is once again to find its way to those humane values which were so important in shaping the original conception of America.

to form a

The American motto E Pluribus Unum, one out of many, points to one of two central issues in a discussion of the nature and perfection of the American union, namely, the issue of the *degree* to which its many and varied components constitute a single, integrated unit. The second issue is the *way* the various components of American society and their activities are "put together" or structured. Concern for this latter issue was demonstrated by the framers of the Constitution who sought to change the structure of the American political union from a decentralized confederacy to a more centralized federal system. The latter was deemed a more perfect union in that it was a better way to structure or organize the activities of the states and the central government. In short, both the *degree* and the *kind* of union are of central concern to a discussion of the American union.[1] Both are discussed in the first of this chapter's three sections. The second section examines factors that shape or form the union, while the third deals with the relationship between the perfecting of the social structure or union and the attainment of other Preamble goals.

[1] The perfection of the union may also be judged in terms of a society's ability to attain its goals. We do not discuss this aspect of the problem of forming a more perfect union in the present chapter, since each of the subsequent chapters discusses the problems of attaining a specific goal of American society.

more perfect Union . . .

What Is the More Perfect Union?

The structure or union of a complex society can be described in two ways: in terms of its normative integration, and in terms of its functional integration. Normative integration refers to the adherence of individuals and collectivities to a common value system and code of behavior; functional integration refers to the interdependence and coordination among the activities performed in and by the society.[2] The degree of normative and functional integration reflects the extent to which the many and varied components of a society constitute a single, integrated moral and functional unit or union.

The degree of normative integration is first of all a matter of the number of people and organizations who adhere to a common value system and a common code of behavior. However, the degree of normative integration is also a matter of the content of the common values and

[2] Our discussion of normative and functional integration draws upon Ronald Freedman, Amos H. Hawley, Werner S. Landecker, Gerhard E. Lenski, and Horace M. Miner, *Principles of Sociology,* 2nd ed. (New York: Holt, Rinehart & Winston, 1956), pp. 170–230. For an alternate view on the aspects of societal unity or integration, see Werner S. Landecker, "Types of Integration and Their Measurement," *American Journal of Sociology,* LVI (January, 1951), 332–340.

codes. In particular, it reflects the degree of internal consistency and mutual compatibility of the rules of the common code and the range of activities covered by them. That is, normative integration increases as the internal consistency among the parts of the common code increases, and as the range or number of activities covered increases. Thus, a society with complete normative integration is one in which all individuals and organizations conform to a consistent set of rules dealing with all of their activities.

The degree of normative integration regarded as perfect need not be complete. Some departures from a common code may be deemed acceptable as evidence or symbols of the American tradition of individual liberty or cultural pluralism. The deviance of some people may be useful in that it occasions punishments that deter others from violating the rules.[3] However, many Americans do feel that the normative integration of the perfect union ought to be complete insofar as the degree of adherence is concerned, and even as to the internal consistency of the common code, but not with respect to the range of activities covered. They see the perfect union as one in which everybody adheres to a common code, but in which the code itself is not exhaustive.

The reading "Shared Values in Complex Societies," by David F. Aberle, examines the problems of what areas need to be covered by the common value system of a complex society. He suggests that only values pertaining to interaction among individuals and organizations with different beliefs and practices need be common. He notes, for example, that religious beliefs and practices vary greatly in the United States and that religious tolerance is highly valued. The common value system does not pertain to the individual's mode of prayer, but it does enjoin him from interfering with those who pray in a manner different from his. That is, the common value system need pertain to religious tolerance only and not to religion per se.

Whatever the content of the common values and norms in a perfect union, it is clear that not everybody can perform the same tasks: there will be a division of labor. The degree to which all the separate and distinct activities performed in and by the society are dependent upon or coordinated with each other is the degree to which the union is functionally integrated. The greater the dependence and coordination, the more the society constitutes a single functional unit or union.

The degree of functional unity regarded as desirable has varied widely in American history. Some early thinkers, including Thomas

---

[3] The utility of punishing deviants for deterring others from doing likewise is discussed further by Jackson Toby in Chapter Three.

Jefferson, preferred a low degree of functional integration. They preferred a society in which all or most members were self-reliant and self-sufficient, able to go their own ways without the help of others, and without the fear that they would hinder others or be hindered by them. Such a society existed when most Americans were either farmers or frontiersmen whose activities were not highly dependent upon or coordinated with those of individuals outside their own immediate families. More recently, Americans have come to prefer the quality of life that results from the specialization in an urbanized, industrial society. The specialist, however, is dependent upon others and must coordinate his work with theirs. The modern farmer depends on the manufacturer to produce the machinery he needs; the manufacturer depends on miners for raw materials; and the miners, in turn, are nourished by the food grown on distant farms. Those who wish to enjoy the benefits of an urbanized, industrial society have generally come to regard the high degree of functional integration that it requires as characteristic of the more perfect union.

A high degree of functional integration is not, of course, without its own risks. In particular, there is the risk that should the operation of any one part or special sector of the society be interrupted, the work of other sectors is endangered. This risk becomes evident when a strike in one industry leads to layoffs in related industries; or, for example, as on November 9, 1965, when the failure of one electrical plant plunges virtually all of the Northeastern United States into total darkness. The relatively unintegrated state of American society during the Revolutionary War and the War of 1812 helped it to withstand the loss of such major cities as New York and Washington, D.C. Similar losses in a modern war would be far more harmful, if not actually fatal.

There are, then, some reasons for preferring a low degree of functional integration and some for preferring a high degree. But whatever the degree of integration, there remains the question of content, the question of just who is to be responsible for performing or regulating any given set of activities. The remainder of this section discusses American thinking on three aspects of this question, namely, the division of responsibility in the areas of government, economics, and religion.

Throughout its history, America has paid a great deal of attention to the problem of specifying the proper division of influence and responsibility between state and federal agencies, that is, delineating the proper activities of the federal government and each of the state governments. As Daniel J. Elazar shows in "The Shaping of Intergovernmental Relations in the Twentieth Century," the relationship between the states and the federal government has been changing throughout the twentieth century.[4] The meaning of state sovereignty has been clouded by federal attempts to persuade states to accept federal or national norms and by the attempts of the states themselves to secure and defend regional interstate authorities. The concern for noncentralized government and maximum local control, however, has not abated. Despite the extension of federal influence to many new areas, from the racial composition of schools to automotive safety, there is no immediate danger that the powers of the states will wither away. States can still initiate programs of their own and refuse programs initiated by the federal government. They are often responsible for administering the federal programs that they do allow in their jurisdiction.

The division of labor among governmental agencies does not exhaust American interest in the question of who is responsible for governing the people. The ultimate responsibility for government in the perfect American union is generally thought to rest with the electorate, issues being decided in accord with the will of the majority. Still, the people are rarely called upon to decide specific issues and then only on state or municipal matters. Federal laws, for example, are never submitted for evaluation by direct vote of the people. In general, whatever the level of government, the electorate is called upon only to choose the men who either make the decisions on specific issues or appoint those who do. The elected officials, in turn, have usually taken a stance on not one, but a multiplicity of issues. As Robert A. Dahl argues in "The Ambiguity of Elections," a system of voting for men who take stances on many issues rather than voting on each issue by itself can make it difficult to know just what the electorate wants done on a given issue. Consequently, elections are an imperfect means of communicating what the people want done. Furthermore, sole reliance on elections deprives the electorate of a means of communicating their desires during the period between elections. Fortunately, there are various ways of compensating for the defects of the electoral system including petitions and letters to elected officials and the activities of special interest or pressure groups.

Special interest groups inform elected officials of what those most concerned with a specific issue want done and they can do so during the inter-election period. Thus, as V. O. Key, Jr., argues in "Interest Groups

[4] See also Harry W. Reynolds (ed.), "Intergovernmental Relations in the United States," *Annals of the American Academy of Political and Social Science,* CCCLIX (May, 1965), 1–156; Roscoe C. Martin, *The Cities and the Federal System* (New York: Atherton, 1965); and William V. D'Antonio, "Community Leadership in an Economic Crisis: Testing Ground for Ideological Cleavage," *American Journal of Sociology,* LXXI (May, 1966), 688–700.

and the Governing Process," they become an important part of the American political union. This is not to say that such groups are an unblemished good; they often do not serve the national or collective interest. They are, however, one means by which organized private citizens participate in government and they implement the American desire to divide responsibility between public and private organizations. A similar desire is now found in the arena of economics, although such a desire was not as popular in the past.

Early American political and social thinkers argued that government should neither engage in economic activities on its own nor attempt to regulate the economic activities of others. It was assumed that good products and fair prices were guaranteed as a result of consumer selection in the open, private market. Moreover, it was believed that the market itself would adjust for any temporary aberrances, such as inflation or deflation, and would eliminate any harmful or unscrupulous practices. Recently, however, government has come to regulate a variety of economic activities in order to protect the consumer and to safeguard the system of private enterprise itself. Various unsafe products and un-informative packages have been eliminated by governmental actions rather than by the operation of the competitive marketplace. Price fixing, interlocking directorates, and monopolizing mergers have come under government scrutiny in the interest of maintaining effective competition. Moreover, as Adolph A. Berle, Jr., notes in "Of Statist and Non-Statist Economic Power," such specific enterprises as public utilities, banks, railroads, airlines, stock markets, and insurance companies are regulated by various government agencies as are the food and drug industries, radio and television. The essential question in disputes over the composition of the perfect economic union is whether free enterprise is more severely threatened by private subversion or public regulation.

Government activity in regulating relationships among private economic organizations is also evident in attempts to mediate labor-management disputes. Presidents or their cabinets have often cajoled, persuaded, and even threatened major business and labor interests into cooperating in some way with them. Standards of collective bargaining have been set by federal authorities, and government officials often exert pressures to induce labor and management to sit down together. In some cases, they may also act as arbiters who determine the content or outline of an agreement.

Despite the prevailing rhetoric on the virtues of private enterprise, government has been given the responsibility not only to regulate certain economic activities, but to perform certain supportive tasks as well. The government coins money, carries the mail, and builds highways so that business may proceed effectively. Government may even subsidize a new industry by direct monetary aid or through special tax relief. Other governmental activities benefit or support private enterprise even though this is not their primary function. Government research in aeronautics, agriculture, atomic energy, and communication satellites has provided the basis for developments in private industry. Public education provides at least the rudiments of knowledge required of employees in private industry. Even the largest corporation would be greatly handicapped if it had to teach all its employees to read and write. Local governments provide the benefits of police, fire, and sanitation departments. Thus, despite the prestige and predominance of private enterprise, the total American economy is a joint endeavor of the public and private sectors.

The economy is, of course, only one of many areas in which there is considerable debate as to the division of labor appropriate to the American union; religion is another. Two aspects of the problem in the division of labor on religious matters are: (1) What religious activities may a government official participate in or be favorable to in his capacity as an official and toward which must he be neutral? and (2) What influence may religious groups exert on government?

The Supreme Court has recognized that while church and state are to be separate, government officials may, in their official capacities, engage in some religious practices. The Court itself cited examples of

prayers in our legislative halls; the appeals to the Almighty in the messages of the Chief Executive; the proclamation making Thanksgiving a holiday; . . . the supplication with which the Court opens each session: "God save the United States and this Honorable Court."[5]

Nevertheless, while recognizing that government officials may legitimately ask in public for divine guidance, the Court has ruled that a schoolboard cannot compose a prayer for use in the classroom nor allow school grounds to be used for religious instruction.[6]

In addition to the question of what religious activities may be sponsored by or actually participated in by government officials, there is the question of how government should relate to religious organizations. One aspect of this question is whether the government has the right, in the interest of secular aims, to forbid a group from engaging in practices that the group regards as important to its religious faith. The Amish in

[5] *Zorach* v. *Clausen* (1952) as abridged in Earl Raab (ed.), *Religious Conflict in America* (Garden City, N.Y.: Doubleday, 1964), p. 186.

[6] See *Engel* v. *Vatale,* and *McCollum* v. *Board of Education,* both in Raab, *op. cit.,* pp. 183–192, and 182–184, respectively. For an historical review of state-church relations in the United States, see William H. Marnell, *The First Amendment: The History of Religious Freedom in America* (Garden City, N.Y.: Doubleday, 1964).

Michigan and Iowa, for example, have been told by state officials to hire non-Amish school teachers for their community schools despite the Amish belief that doing so would be detrimental to their faith.[7] They prefer to hire members of their own faith, even if they fail to meet state standards. State officials argue that a qualified teacher is essential if the children are to get a proper secular education. The Amish are more concerned with the status of their children's religious faith and fear that a non-Amish teacher will, even if inadvertently, challenge and undermine their children's beliefs.

Another issue in the relationship of government to religious organizations is the problem of financial aid to religious organizations. Some claim that present rules that exempt religious organizations from taxes represent an unwarranted, indirect subsidy of their activities. Others object to financial aid to parochial schools as illegitimate cooperation between church and state. Earl Raab in "Church-State Problems" discusses issues raised in attempts to delineate the role of government in religious affairs. Not all the questions dealing with the division of labor between church and state, however, deal with how the state is to treat religious groups. There is the parallel question of how religious groups are to respond to government action or inaction on secular issues. This question becomes especially important when a religious group believes it must advocate passage of some law in order that God's moral code be implemented. In the last hundred and fifty years, religious groups have called for the abolition of slavery, the establishment of Prohibition, an end to war, and the passage of civil rights legislation.[8] Laws dealing with such matters as birth control, divorce, and abortion have also been sought by religious groups. Nevertheless, some religious groups believe it is improper for them to concern themselves with the secular government's course of action.

The perfection of the union, then, is a matter of establishing the proper division of influence and responsibility between the public and private sectors of the society in such areas as politics, economics, and religion. It is also a matter of the degree of normative and functional integration.

[7] For an account of the events in Michigan, see *The Detroit Free Press*, May 25, 1965; and of those in Iowa, *The New York Times*, November 28, 1965.

[8] For historical background on the involvement of religious groups in social issues, see John R. Bodo, *The Protestant Clergy and Public Issues: 1817–1848* (Princeton, N.J.: Princeton University Press, 1954); Henry F. May, *Protestant Churches and Industrial America* (New York: Octagon Books, 1963); Donald B. Meyer, *The Protestant Search for Political Realism: 1914–1941* (Berkeley: University of California Press, 1960). See also Luke R. Ebersole, *Church Lobbying in the Nation's Capital* (New York: Macmillan, 1951).

Forming a More Perfect Union

The task of forming a more perfect union is basically that of inducing the individuals and organizations within the society to adhere to a common code and to perform their special tasks. Forming a more perfect union requires the institution of social control to bring about the desired kind and degree of normative and functional integration. This section examines three factors which shape or form the nature and extent of union through their influence on the effectiveness of social controls:[9] (1) the system of communication of norms and information; (2) the distribution of rewards and punishments; and (3) appeals to the loyalty of individual Americans.

The first requirement of any system of social control is the existence of the means of communicating what is desired of them to the members of the society. Several different groups and organizations help perform the communicative tasks. Many of the basic common rules are learned in face-to-face primary groups such as the family or peer group. Larger groups such as churches play an important role in the attempt to communicate and support many of the basic American values;[10] schools serve the dual function of providing exposure to the common code of the American Way of Life and of imparting the skills needed for performing specialized tasks; mass media communicate norms of behavior both directly through advice columns and information programs, and indirectly through morality plays in which dilemmas are discussed and solved in a conventional way.

The importance of communication for effective social control is highlighted by the efforts made to control the content and process of communication by groups interested in promoting some specific conception of a perfect union or in increasing the adherence to some specific norm. In totalitarian societies attempts may even be made to include one propagandist in every work group.[11] Similar efforts were made in the United States on a limited scale as a means of increasing the sales of war

9 For other discussions of factors which shape the union, see Paul E. Mott, "Some Sources of Integration," and "The Family as an Integrating Influence," *The Organization of Society* (Englewood Cliffs, N.J.: Prentice-Hall, 1965), pp. 278–304; and Robin Williams, "The Integration of American Society," *American Society*, 2nd ed. (New York: Knopf, 1960), pp. 541–575.

10 Will Herberg in *Protestant, Catholic, Jew* (Garden City, N.Y.: Doubleday, 1960), and Peter L. Berger in *The Noise of Solemn Assemblies* (Garden City, N.Y.: Doubleday, 1961) both discuss the support given to the American Way by the American churches.

11 The Soviet system is described by Alex Inkeles in *Public Opinion in Soviet Russia* (Cambridge: Harvard University Press, 1962), pp. 67–92.

bonds, and are now made by political parties which organize scores of block workers to influence their neighbors.[12]

Attempts may also be made to replace or control a socializing person or group in order to overcome their alleged shortcomings. The federal government, for example, has induced local school systems to get a head start in the education of three- or four-year-olds from underprivileged families. Such a program seeks to counteract or prevent what is seen as defective socialization by underprivileged families. In a different but related vein, periodic campaigns are waged to institute controls on the portrayal of sex and violence in the mass media in the hope of preventing their communicating what are viewed as inappropriate norms regarding sexual and aggressive behavior. Such campaigns assume that audiences, especially young audiences, come to accept as normal or desirable what they see and hear through mass media.

A second component of any system of social control is the punishment of inappropriate or deviant acts and the rewarding of appropriate or conforming acts. Some such system for dispensing punishments and rewards is found in every social organization. For America as a whole, the police and courts bear the main responsibility for meting out punishments; the occupational marketplace is the main mechanism for distributing rewards. (The problem of administering systems of rewards and punishments is discussed further in Chapter Three.)

Individuals who receive sufficient and just rewards are apt to conform to the standards of society. Those who feel they are receiving insufficient rewards or overabundant and undeserved troubles are not as apt to conform. Nonconformity may take any of a number of forms: the active opposition of a political protest, the patterned evasion of crime, or the withdrawal from responsibility of alcoholism or drug addiction.[13]

A third factor in establishing effective social controls is the appeal to the loyalty of group members. This type of appeal is most frequent and effective during such extreme crises as wars. However, such an appeal may also be made during less intense crises such as those occasioned by racial tensions. For example, in the name of patriotism, President Kennedy appealed to white Mississippians to end the rioting which

[12] The importance of influencing informal groups in order to maximize control of public opinion is stressed by Elihu Katz, "The Two-Step Flow of Communication," in Wilbur Schramm (ed.), *Mass Communications* (Urbana: University of Illinois Press, 1960), pp. 346–365.

[13] For a discussion of the general relationship between access to societal rewards and deviance, see Robert K. Merton, "Social Structure and Amonie," *Social Theory and Social Structure*, 2nd ed. (New York: Free Press, 1957), pp. 131–160.

followed James Meredith's attempts to enroll in the University of Mississippi in September, 1962.

Appeals to loyalty assume, of course, that such loyalty exists and is strong enough to induce people to forego or channel their individual desires for the good of the society. The creation of such loyalty, then, is part of the process of social control. Group loyalty is heightened by the existence of a person who can serve as a symbol of the society as a whole and with whom the people can identify. European monarchs now serve such a function. In the United States, an especially dynamic president such as Franklin D. Roosevelt or John F. Kennedy may serve as a rallying point or national symbol. Group loyalty is also advanced by the activities on holidays such as the Fourth of July and Veteran's Day when people are reminded of the glory of their society and the value of its tradition. Pride in accomplishments which in some sense belong to the whole nation may enhance loyalty. These accomplishments may range from military victory to sending a man to the moon or even to winning an international sports event. Lastly, some Americans suggest that national loyalty will be increased by periodically requiring people to pledge their allegiance to the flag and to sign an oath of allegiance before taking a job in government.[14]

Perfecting the Union and Other Preamble Goals

The goal of forming a more perfect union, of forming a better social structure, is perhaps the most general and pervasive of the Preamble goals. The organization or structure of the individual and collective components of American society limits and directs efforts to attain other goals. The existing structure of society represents both the means by which Preamble goals are attained and the environment in which they are to be gotten. Americans who are unsuccessful in their efforts to obtain some goal may seek changes in the present degree and form of union. Those, for example, who seek to promote the general welfare by making automobiles safer have sought some government standards for automobile manufacturers because they believe efforts at voluntary controls will not succeed. Others have sought federal involvement in setting standards for the apportionment of state legislatures as a means of circumventing the resistance of local politicians. Both are seeking changes in federal-state or public-private relationships, that is, changes in the political union.

[14] For a discussion of the problem of maintaining loyalty in America, see Morton Grodzins, *The Loyal and the Disloyal* (Chicago: University of Chicago Press, 1956).

There is, of course, no clear and simple answer to the question of just what form and degree of union is needed to simultaneously "establish Justice, insure domestic Tranquility, provide for the common defence, promote the general Welfare, and secure the Blessings of Liberty to ourselves and our Posterity." It may well be that no one form of union can provide all these goals equally well. Perhaps this is why the framers of the Constitution decided merely to seek improvement rather than perfection, to seek a *more* perfect union rather than a perfect one.

Shared Values in Complex Societies

୧୮৯

David F. Aberle

There is a significant trend in contemporary social theory which strongly emphasizes the crucial importance of a shared system of ultimate values as an element in any society.[1] . . . Though the concept of a shared system of ultimate values is of great importance for social analysis, there is occasionally a danger that it may gloss over significant problems. Particularly when we examine complex societies we are likely to stress those qualifications which we always introduce in asserting the general proposition regarding shared value-systems. Thus we ordinarily note that the system of values is only "shared to a certain extent" by the members of a society, or that it is only integrated "to some degree." Such qualifications are usually introduced to prevent quibbling empirical exceptions from inhibiting a significant theoretical development. After all, even in speaking of a simple homogeneous society we would be little disposed to insist either that the value-system is perfectly integrated, or that it is shared in all its parts to the same degree by all members of the society. Yet when we turn to a complex society such as that of the United States, these qualifications do not seem to exhaust the statements we would like to make about American values in all their diversity. We can find significant and systematized values that are shared by a very large sector of the population, but there are a large number of values which do *not* seem to be shared by the total population, or even by a considerable part of it. In what sense do the Western cowboy and the Eastern dairy farmer, the upper-upper of Yankee City and the lower-lower of Chicago, the Negro and the White in the South, the Irish Catholic, the Swedish Lutheran and the Polish Jew share a common value-system? Are we to take the total value-systems current in these groups and reduce them to a lowest

Abridged and reprinted from "Shared Values in Complex Societies," *American Sociological Review*, 15 (August, 1950), 495–502, by permission of the author and The American Sociological Association.

common denominator and call this rather thin product the common value-element of American society?[2] Or are we to assert that each of these diversified value-systems is logically implied in the most general value-system of the society—in which case it is hard to see why they should be diversified? Or are we to refer to all cases of divergence as evidences of malintegration in the society? There are, of course, important elements of malintegration in American society which involve, among other things, value-conflicts. The tension surrounding the American Negro's status can be profitably analyzed in part by reference to value-conflicts. But not every case of value-differences is to be understood in terms of mal-integration.

It would seem, therefore, that a greater richness might be available to us in our analyses of value-systems in complex societies if we were to use other approaches than the search for the most general or the most universal values, important though that search undoubtedly is. While this paper cannot set forth the systematic tools for another type of analysis, it can, perhaps, by example, foreshadow such a systematic approach.

(The general focus of this paper will be on the integration of sub-systems with diverse values, within the total social system.[3] Let us take as given the fact of our own complex, industrialized society, with its highly diversified roles and role-systems, with all its regional, ethnic, and religious diversity. For our purposes there are two salient features of this society: first, that any individual actor occupies several roles in several role-systems, and second that any actor participates in only a few of the role-systems of the total society. Given these circumstances, under what conditions does social integration demand the sharing of values, and under what conditions does it permit the diversification of values which in fact exists? . . .)

Perhaps no general useful answer to these questions can be provided. But the analysis of a somewhat simplified and idealized example may be of utility. Let us take the case of the Catholic, Protestant and Jewish faiths in this country, and try to examine the ways in which their diverse value-systems may co-exist in our particular kind of society. In doing so we shall have to simplify the case greatly, and also overlook certain malinte-grations which in fact exist.

Let us begin with the churches themselves as social systems. The members of these churches, in their roles as church members, must share, within each faith, a common set of values (with the usual qualifications), or the organizations in question will be seriously unstable. Thus we have groups of people who share value-systems which differ from group to group. We must now ask, first, in what sense must the churches as organizations share common values in order to engage in coordinated action; second, in what sense the members of each church must share values with members of the others, in order for them to engage as individuals in coordinated action in extra-religious roles; and last, whether the values which must be shared for such coordinated action to occur set limits on the value-systems which these churches can conceivably hold.

It is possible that the churches might not engage in joint action, in which case we would have other problems for analysis than those which in fact confront us. But they do actually join for many purposes, including charitable programs, organized reform, and others. In addition, they meet in the context of the "interfaith" or "tolerance" meeting, a practice directly related to the very heterogeneity of our society, though by no means arising solely out of differences in religious orientation. When individuals acting in their roles as representatives of their respective church organizations gather for these or other joint action purposes, they must, at least overtly, share the value of religious toleration. They need not have marked enthusiasm for the values and beliefs of churches other than their own; indeed an overvaluation in this direction would raise problems of recruitment and perpetuation for each church as an organization. Should a church militantly oppose toleration in this sense as a value, it could not operate in joint action with other churches—and certainly could not engage in "interfaith" or "tolerance" activities. (This is by no means to say that *therefore* tolerance will necessarily be found in our society. Its total absence, however, would create very serious problems of integration.) But if tolerance is to be sustained as a value, and joint action is to be carried out, this value has implications for the values of the component churches. Thus, if a central value of one church were an abomination to another, they could not engage in joint activities as organizations. The bounds of such abominations are somewhat difficult to determine. Priapic rites and their associated sexual attitudes, cannibalism, polytheism as it is found in primitive societies, gods endowed with all-too-human frailties—these behaviors, beliefs and values would certainly clash seriously with the values of Catholics, Protestants and Jews, and it is, to say the least, unlikely that religious groups which practiced and believed along these lines could conceivably share in interfaith meetings with our churches. Yet the Jewish denial that Jesus was the Messiah does not preclude Jewish participation in such groups, for many and complex reasons.

This last problem cannot be gone into at length, but certain lines of inquiry that might prove profitable can be pointed out. The value of tolerance has its place not only in the context which we have been examining, but in the central values of the sociopolitical system in which we live. Even if a particular faith did consider the Jewish attitude toward Jesus reprehensible, the complex of forces and balance of power is such as to render it inexpedient to profess out-and-out opposition to the Jewish church. The possibility that members of a church may only profess tolerance, but may act for expedient reasons must remind us that shared values are only *one* factor which permits action to be integrated. It is true that a society in which individuals pursue their ends in ways governed *only* by norms of expediency is unthinkable; nevertheless, expedient action can be a *part* of the action-system of a viable society. Lastly, of course, the effect of secularization, and the *intensity* with which sacred values are adhered to is of importance.[4]

Our analysis thus far would indicate, then, that if the churches, or rather their members acting in their roles as representatives of the churches, engage in joint action, they must at least profess a minimum value of tolerance. On the one hand, this value permits a considerable diversification of the value-systems of these churches, but on the other, it sets limits, however indefinite, on the nature of the value-systems of the participating church organizations.

Church members, however, do not meet one another only in religious roles. There are many other role-systems in which they engage. Our society has a political, a market, and an occupational system in which universalistic criteria play an important part. It has an open class system and its patterns of marital choice are based on romantic love. Members of diverse religious membership are involved in political, market, job, social (in the non-technical sense of the word) and marital relationships. Marriage and "social" life involve primary relationships; in the other cases there may be more ramified and remote organizational ties.

Under these circumstances, the values of the individual in his role as a member of the church must not be such as (a) to exclude him from all these spheres of secular activity, or such as (b) to create serious problems of integration with members of other churches with whom he participates in non-religious role-systems. If a man belonged to a religion that looked with horror on profits, he could not comfortably occupy the role of entrepreneur. If he were a caste Hindu, he could not comfortably act as a butcher. The non-religious role-systems which he could share with members of other churches would be correspondingly reduced. While it is not necessary that he be free to engage in every conceivable role in the society with members of other religious sects, his total exclusion from such role-systems would, if carried to its logical conclusion, result in the disintegration of the social system into a series of theocratic states.

Carried rather less far, it would result in a kind of compartmentalized system rather different from the present one.

But even if the value-system of a particular church permits its members to participate in a variety of secular role-systems, there may still arise problems of integration. For example, if one church were to take the value-position that solidarity with members of that church was overwhelmingly more important than any other obligation, then a variety of non-religious role-systems would be thrown into an intolerable state of indeterminacy. In the sphere of market activities, members of such a church might feel free to cancel contracts or break verbal agreements with members of another church. These considerations, like those introduced earlier, set limits on the kinds of value-systems which can be held in two role-systems with overlapping membership. Since in our society individuals are involved with one another in religious and secular roles, the prescriptions for life in this world which are afforded by the value-systems of the various churches must be to some degree compatible with the other roles in which individuals are engaged, and with the value-systems that govern those role-systems. (It is, of course, possible for secular values to outweigh religious values, but if this tendency is carried to its logical conclusion, the churches will be faced with problems of integration and perpetuation, and the social system under analysis will be correspondingly altered.) There is thus a range within which the value-systems of the churches and those of the occupational sphere may vary, but that range is not infinite if the social system is to remain integrated. The same type of analysis might be carried out with respect to martial, "social" and other role-systems. In these instances, the absence of such phenomena as hypergamy and the importance of commensality would serve to remind us that other types of integration than those of our own society are conceivable and possible—for example, in a caste system such as that of India. Still, the type of analysis would be similar in other cases.

Before turning to further considerations, we may sum up the conclusions thus far arrived at. The churches involved need not at all have a total value-system in common. Their members, whether acting as representatives of the church in interfaith activities, or acting in non-religious roles in ways that are compatible with their total definition of "the whole duty of man," must share certain crucial values with one another. The values of each system of roles set limits on the other. But even these limits permit a rather looser integration of the total social system and a greater diversity of sub-system values than would be implied if we were to seek only for the common values shared by all the component individuals in all of their roles. It must be pointed out that this analysis has focused *only* on the integrative aspects of the picture and has deliberately ignored large-scale problems of strain. It is by no means clear, however, that the strains arise out of heterogeneity alone. They may arise out of the *kinds* of values in the various sub-systems, and out of a variety of other factors.

The fact that individuals participate in several role-systems raises the possibility of still other modes of integration than those already mentioned. Certain individuals stand as "middle-men" in the system, sharing, without particular strain, certain values in each of two role-systems in which they act as an articulating link. A Western ranch owner may share a set of values with respect to appropriate masculine behavior with his ranch hands, who may have a dislike for the "market mentality," and share another set of values with respect to the market, with cattle buyers in Chicago, with whom he also maintains periodic face-to-face relationships. The cattle buyer and the cowboy may have little in common in many ways, but their activities can be articulated, nevertheless, without unendurable tensions for the ranch owner. The roles he plays are separated in time and space. Were the buyers to visit him on the ranch, he might feel quite uncomfortable for a time, but this is not a necessary feature of his situation. There are, of course, thousands of such "middle-men" in the total society, plus thousands of situations where the links are so much more attenuated that individuals who could not interact without serious stress are so insulated from one another as to create no problems.

It is also well worth mentioning that the "mediator," who occupies a rather different position from that of the "middle-man," may be a potent force in integration. Such a person may serve to interpret the values of one group to another, or to arrange compromises. He may hold a standard position in one or more of the potentially opposed groups, or may have a rather special role which is said to be "outside" the traditional role-system. Examples are those representatives of science who mediate between universities and foundations, various types of public relations representatives, labor mediators, whether government employed, hired by labor and management, or—as in some cases—clergymen and hence "outside" the system, and a variety of others.

This is by no means to deny that individuals who are spatially remote from one another may be involved in an institutional complex which does definitely require subscription to the same value-system. An example is participation in the political system. This system can tolerate a large number of apathetic individuals, but not a large number of individuals who believe that installation of a candidate in office is to be accomplished by storming the White House. Another example which potentially involves large numbers of people, though it may actually involve fairly small numbers at any given time, is that of universalistic values[5] in the treatment of strangers.

In our society physical and social mobility are exceedingly important. Furthermore, individuals are continually interacting with others who are anonymous prior to or even during and after a specific contact. Consequently the sharing of universalistic manners and morals as values governing conduct toward strangers is of great significance. If people could not travel or engage in commercial and other transactions with strangers, without some confidence that they would be accorded (roughly speaking) the same treatment as that which prevails among acquaintances, and not subjected to force or fraud, the structure of the society would be seriously impaired. It would be possible to indicate other respects in which very large numbers of people must share the same set of values if the system is to remain integrated.

· · ·

Finally, then, we see that in addition to the common value-elements of the total social system, there can be a considerable diversification of value-systems in parts of that total system, and that such diversification can occur without malintegration as an inevitable result. Sub-systems are themselves internally integrated by adherence to shared bodies of values which differ from system to system. These sub-systems may be integrated with one another by sharing certain values relative to the kinds of joint action in which they are engaged. The sharing of such values in action which integrates these parts of the total society sets limits on the kinds of value-systems possible in each part. Furthermore, every individual participates in several role-systems. Though the value-systems of each role-system may not at all be identical, there are problems of compatibility which similarly set limits on the range of possible diversification. The existence of "middle-men" as articulations between two role-systems permits an increasing degree of diversification of the values of the two role-systems. The more extended the links, the greater the degree to which the value-systems may vary. "Mediators" as interpreters and peacemakers reduce the possibility of serious tensions arising from value-heterogeneity. Nevertheless, the existence of actual or potential situations which involve large numbers of people in the same situation of action—though by no means always in face-to-face relationships (we have used the cases of voting and of "anonymous" contacts)—does necessitate the sharing of a common value-system for large numbers of people. But none of these considerations permits us to dispense with the concept of a shared system of values for the total society. This is essential both in setting limits upon the types of value-systems that can exist in the sub-systems, and in establishing the nature of the articulations between the sub-systems . . .

.   .   .

The analysis of value-systems alone, whether value-systems of total societies or of sub-systems, is insufficient for social analysis. Value-considerations must be related to roles, role-systems, and role-behavior, and to individual values and deviant motivations. They must be related to the analysis of the amount of latitude for apathy, expediency, and conflict which can exist with a tolerable degree of integration. Furthermore, we have here omitted a variety of exceedingly pertinent questions which must be asked in any adequately described empirical situation: the "cruciality" of the values, roles, etc., under consideration vis-à-vis the total society or sub-system under consideration; the extensive or limited character of the value-prescriptions—that is, they may bind a man to a set of obligations regarding "the whole duty of man" or they may bind a man to a set of obligations regarding a small sector of his total existence; the degree to which lip-service vs. "internalization" of values exists; the relative weight of two value-commitments when there is conflict, with the possibility that one commitment may be greatly attenuated. Lastly, it may be crucial for the system, the sub-system or the articulation of two sub-systems, that certain values be held by individuals or groups in particular *positions*—rather than that they be held by a certain *number* of persons. Problems of power and influence enter here. All these questions are of the utmost significance but would require great scope and empirical material for development.

By no means asserting that a complex society has no common values, and in fact insisting that a core of common values is an integrational principle of any viable social system, this approach asks for further analysis of the value-systems or sub-systems of the society, in close connection with the recognition that these sub-systems themselves must be integrated with one another, and that every individual participates in a number of sub-systems. It asks for the functional analysis of these various interactional situations to see *what* values must be shared in each situation, and how this impinges on the value-systems shared in other situations. Rather than assuming that heterogeneity inevitably results in malintegration, or attempting to reduce heterogeneity to exiguous common values, it looks toward a more precise formulation of role-systems and their component value-elements, and their integration with one another through certain common value-elements from one system to the next, as essential for the continued functioning of the society.

Notes

1) By a value is meant an effectively charged idea or attitude in terms of which objects, events, actions, individuals, etc., are judged on a scale of approval-disapproval, whether the approval and disapproval are moral, aesthetic, hedonic, or in terms of some other dimension. By a *shared* value is meant—for present purposes—one held in common by a plurality of individuals. By a *system* of values is meant a set of such ideas or attitudes which have a logical, meaningful, or affective consistency. The question of "internalized" vs. "simply verbalized" values is largely left untreated.

2) There is also the possibility that a number of value-systems which are in many respects heterogeneous may nevertheless fall within a particular type of "cultural orientation" typical of the Western world and not of other societies. Cf. Florence Kluckhohn, "Dominant and Substitutive Profiles of Cultural Orientations: Their Significance for the Analysis of Social Stratification," *Social Forces*, May, 1949.

3) It must be noted that the role of shared values as an integrational principle within each sub-system is identical with the role of shared values within the total social system. There is no intent to attack the general proposition that one essential element in integrating the action of a plurality of individuals is a shared value-system.

4) It must be noted that tolerance on the one hand requires a certain degree of secularization, and on the other furthers the process of secularization—or at any rate reduces the possibility of extremism in religious matters.

5) Cf. Talcott Parsons, *Essays in Sociological Theory*, Glencoe, Illinois, 1949, *passim*, for discussion of "universalism" and "particularism."

The Shaping of Intergovernmental Relations in the Twentieth Century

Daniel J. Elazar

One very practical manifestation of the political changes that have characterized the twentieth century has been the great increase in government activity, much of it in the form of new intergovernmental programs. Despite popular views to the contrary, intergovernmental collaboration is not a new phenomenon. Co-operative federalism—the patterned sharing of governmental activities by all levels of government —has been characteristic of the American federal system since its establishment. American governments have traditionally assumed responsibilities only in response to public demands but, where governments have acted, federal, state, and local governments usually have acted in concert. Whether this "co-operative federalism" was intended by the founders of the Union or not, it was quickly demonstrated to be necessary. Governments operating in the same territory, serving the same people, generally sharing the same goals, and faced with the same demands could not maintain a posture of "dual federalism" (the separation of functions by levels of government).[1]

The American Partnership

By the mid-twentieth century, certain basic principles and mechanisms for intergovernmental collaboration have become part of the American governmental tradition, most of which came into existence a century ago and persist to color the character of American federalism today. Among the principles are: national supremacy, broad national legislative and

Reprinted from "The Shaping of Intergovernmental Relations in the Twentieth Century," *The Annals,* 359 (May, 1965), 11–22, by permission of the author and The American Academy of Political and Social Science.

appropriation powers, noncentralized government, and maximum local control. Among the mechanisms are: a nondisciplined, noncentralized party system; routinized legislative "interference" in administration; regular intergovernmental consultation; and a system of grants-in-aid from higher to lower levels of government.

From the very first, Congress has acquired the authority to legislate very broadly under the Constitution. Although this authority was frequently diluted by the Supreme Court and by Congress itself until the 1930's, it was nonetheless apparent in the general expansion of federal activities in the intervening years. Also demonstrated from the first was the inherent superiority of the federal government as a raiser of revenue because of the tax sources available to it and the reluctance of the people to allow equally substantial state and local tax levies. For these reasons, federal funds provided the stimulus for new programs in a majority of the states throughout the nineteenth century.[2]

These two trends, coupled with the great political decisions of the nineteenth century, firmly established the principle of national supremacy. Along with it, however, the equally important principle of non-centralized government was also established. If the general government was early cast in the role of stimulator and partial supporter of such major governmental functions as education, internal improvements, and public welfare, the states—either directly or through their local subdivisions—were simultaneously cast in the role of managers and administrators of these functions. Policy-making for these programs became a joint state-federal activity.

This arrangement is often mislabeled decentralization. Decentralization implies the existence of a central authority having a legitimate monopoly of governmental power which can concentrate, devolve, or reconcentrate functions more or less as it pleases. Noncentralization—on the other hand, the keystone of every true federal system—implies the constitutional coexistence of a general government and governments with more particularized authority which share governmental power. In the American case, the basic authority of the states is delineated in the Constitution and cannot be withdrawn except with their consent thus making dynamic federal action possible without concomitant reduction of local self-government by protecting the less formal institutions that deconcentrate power.

The American commitment to noncentralization has forced federal authorities to seek ways to develop nationwide programs with minimum national requirements within the framework of the co-operative system and has enabled the states to secure federal assistance without fearing any real loss of their integrity.

Thus it has always been the prerogative of the states to decide whether or not to accept any federal aid proffered under formal grant programs. And, despite the prevalent idea that no state can resist federal subsidies, few, if any, states have ever taken advantage of every grant offered them. The strong record of state participation, particularly in the major programs in any given period, is really a reflection of the nation-wide consensus as to their value and necessity. Such programs represent only a few of the over a hundred available to the states and localities today. Moreover, many states do not take advantage of all the funds available to them under grants they have accepted. In both cases, state policy-decisions rule.[3]

Even more important, noncentralization means that the states, as of right, share in the initial development of most co-operative programs before they are written into law. They share in the shaping of policies from the first and throughout the existence of each program, and develop their own patterns of program implementation within the framework of agreed-upon guidelines.[4]

The sharing process has worked both ways. The states have become involved in the fields of foreign affairs, interstate commerce, defense, and monetary policy just as the federal government has become involved in the fields of education, health and welfare, agriculture, and urban development.[5]

Moreover, local governments, public nongovernmental agencies, and private interests have acquired roles of their own as partners in the process because they have made an effort to become involved and have found ways to "pay the ante" required to sit in on the great game of government in the United States.[6]

The Forms of the Partnership

Intergovernmental co-operation has taken on a variety of forms, all of which have histories as old as the sharing system itself.[7] Among the most common and recurring are those of *informal co-operation* through conferences, the provision of advisory and training services, the exchange of general services, the lending of equipment and personnel, and the performance of services by one government in place of another. Such collaboration is barely visible to the general public except when a conference is sponsored by the White House or when a public-health team moves into a community on the heels of an epidemic. The informal luncheon meeting, no matter how important, attracts no attention whatsoever.

Formal co-operation activities, on the other hand, are based on *contracts and compacts for co-operative action.* In the largest sense, contractual relationships are basic to a federal system which is founded upon a fundamental compact to begin with. In essence, it is the contractual relationship that makes possible large-scale intergovernmental co-operation to achieve common ends. Every formal co-operative relationship involves some form of contractual tie. The flexibility of the contract as a device enhances its usefulness and allows it to be adapted for many purposes. There are contractual relationships for co-operative research, for the division of costs to support shared activities, for provision or exchange of services, to prevent conflict or misunderstanding, for exchange of personnel, for joint enforcement of laws, for sharing revenues, and for lending agreements.

Recurring informal contracts are often formalized to the point of receiving statutory recognition and contractual ratification through *contracts for simple sharing.* These are relationships that involve nothing more than a formal agreement to share resources without formal transfers of funds or personnel from one government to another. They are often used to prevent needless duplication of time, money, and effort or to enhance the possibilities for more comprehensive execution of particular programs. State-federal crop reports, Bureau of Labor Statistics calculations, state regulation of nuclear installations, formal agreements for the exchange of tax information or co-operative inspections of public utilities are examples of this type of relationship.

Another form of co-operation involves the interchange of *personnel.* This includes the provision of "services-in-aid," that is, arrangements by one government to lend its personnel to assist another; jointly paid agents; joint inspections by personnel of more than one government; and the deputization of personnel of one government by another for co-operative purposes. Under this type of co-operative activity, federal engineers are lent to states and localities to plan projects; county sanitarians are paid with federal, state, and local funds and have special obligations to all three governments; banks are jointly inspected by state and federal officers; and state hospital guards are deputized by the local police.

The pervasiveness of the partnership has led to the development of *interdependent activities* in which one government depends upon another (or both depend upon each other) for the enforcement of laws or the administration of programs otherwise not apparently "shared." The administration of elections is one good example of this. The election of national officials is contingent upon state implementation of the constitutional requirements. In this case, there is federal dependence upon state action. States, on the other hand, may depend upon federal authorities to exclude the transportation of prohibited goods (liquor, oleo, firecrackers) across their boundaries.

First in importance among the forms of intergovernmental cooperation are the grants-in-aid: federal transfers of funds to the states and federal or state transfers to local governments for specified purposes usually subject to a measure of supervision and review by the granting government. They are particularly distinctive because they involve the transfer of funds from one government to another in order to attain certain agreed-upon ends. The first grants-in-aid were generally transfers of land to be sold to finance specific programs. Supervision of these grants was relatively loose by today's standards but still significant; conditions attached to them governed disposition of the lands and use of the proceeds earned.

Cash grants-in-aid, like land grants, date from the nineteenth century —six were established before 1900—but did not flower until the twentieth. Since 1911 some sixty-five new federal grant-in-aid programs have been established, fourteen of which have since been discontinued. In general, they have been more rigorously administered by all governments concerned.

Grants-in-aid are of three kinds: (1) flat grants, which provide each recipient government with an equal sum regardless of local conditions or deviations from the national means, and without requiring formal matching of funds by the recipient governments—although recipients may have to shoulder administrative costs; (2) proportionate grants, as with road-building, made to recipient governments in proportion to their own contributions to the program or project in question, and often allocated on the basis of preset formulas which take the need and capabilities of the recipient into account; and (3) percentage grants, allocated like proportionate grants but with the granter's contribution fixed as a set percentage of the cost to the grantee for maintaining a particular program. Among the best known of these are the federal public welfare grants and some state grants to local school districts. Grants-in-aid may also include grants in kind, which generally resemble flat grants and are rarely subject to extensive supervision.

Other forms of intergovernmental sharing include tax offsets (used when nationwide compliance is necessary as in the unemployment compensation program), shared revenues (such as timber and mineral royalties and shared license fees), and grants or contracts awarded on similar terms to public and private applicants (such as federal research grants to universities). These all represent variations of the grant-in-aid principle, developed to meet conditions which would frustrate simpler grant mechanisms.

Supplementing the regular channels of co-operative control, the sharing system is strengthened through the maintenance of a nondisciplined, noncentralized party system which encourages elected representatives to follow the interest of their districts—from wards through states—rather than maintain party responsibility. This system encourages them to frame programs in such a way as to guarantee the maintenance of local control, thereby increasing their own power. One of the consequences of this has been the development of routinized mechanisms for continuous legislative "interference" (used in the neutral sense) in the administration of government programs, further enhancing local control over program execution as well as policy-making.[8]

The Course of the Twentieth-Century Partnership

The record of the partnership since approximately 1913 has been one of maintaining and appropriately modifying the patterns established earlier, in the face of a continually increasing "velocity of government"—the amount of total government activity in relation to the total activity of society—through the formal institutionalization of the co-operative system.[9]

This has meant (1) the development of more complex and sophisticated techniques for administering co-operative programs to secure better financial control by the granting government, (2) improved sharing of policy formation by all participants, including the panoply of interest groups that contribute so much to policy-making in the United States, (3) expansion of the range and variety of shared activities so that today one is hard-pressed to find any area of public concern that does not somehow involve government and in turn, federal-state-local collaboration, and (4) the adjustment of the theories and mechanisms of federalism to meet new times, situations, and demands. This, in turn, has led to growing public recognition of the co-operative system for what it is and an increased interest on the part of public officials and scholars in understanding how American federalism really functions.

The course of intergovernmental relations in this century can be traced through four periods and into a fifth. Understandably, the trends in intergovernmental relations are closely tied to the larger political and economic movements on the American political scene.

By 1913 the era of virtually unregulated enterprise capitalism was coming to an end. During the next generation, government regulation was progressively extended over an even more complex corporate economy while an ideological battle over the legitimacy of government's new role was being fought.

The first period may be characterized as one of *progressive agrarianism*. It was actually inaugurated when the Republican party, whose national majority status had been consolidated in the critical elections of 1892 and 1896, briefly gave way to a progressive and activist Democratic administration in 1913.[10] It reflected the first concerted national response to the Populist-Progressive-Liberal agitation for positive government action to meet the problems of an industrialized society, and laid the foundations for co-operation in the subsequent periods. Growing government activism, begun in part under Theodore Roosevelt, brought with it revival of large scale co-operative activity. The magnitude of this revival is seen in the more than sixfold increase in federal grant expenditures and the near doubling of the number of formal grant programs between 1912 and 1920 (see tables)[11] and the development of "many other forms of formal and informal co-operative activities as government at all levels took on expanded roles in American life."

This period saw three important developments that were to influence the course of intergovernmental relations thereafter: (1) the beginning of clear public recognition of the possibilities inherent in an intergovernmental partnership to meet the nation's new governmental needs, (2) the inauguration of modernized forms of federal-state collaboration particularly through the grant-in-aid system, and (3) the first efforts to develop a more sophisticated understanding of the functioning of the American federal system. Woodrow Wilson set the tone for all three. Concerned simultaneously with expanding the federal role and with preserving the federal-state relationship, his public expressions and the programs enacted during his administration reflected the idea that the federal government was to assist the states in developing and maintaining programs already approved or requested by a substantial number of them.[12] The agricultural-extension, highway-construction, and vocational-education grant programs—the major ones inaugurated in Wilson's administration—all reflect this. In the case of the first two, and of the forest-protection program expanded under Wilson, formal co-operative relationships were actually established to replace or prevent unilateral federal action. These new grant programs betrayed the agrarian bent of Wilsonian Progres-

TABLE 1 / *Twentieth-Century Patterns of American Federalism*

YEAR	PERIOD	ECONOMIC ERA	POLITICAL CONDITION	STATE OF INTERGOVERNMENTAL RELATIONS
1900 ⋮ 1910	Transition (1895–1911)*	Concentrated Enterprise Capitalism (1877–1913)* ↓	GOP majority party ↓	Passing of nineteenth-century co-operative programs. New experiments in collaboration under T. Roosevelt. Widespread state experimentation has important influence on public.
1920	Progressive Agrarianism (1911–1921)*	Transition Era (1913–1933)*	(Democratic Administration, 1913–1921)*	Wilson's "New Freedom" lays foundation for twentieth-century co-operative federalism.
1930	Normalized Entrenchment (1921–1931)*		↓ 1928 Critical Elections 1932	GOP restoration starts second period. Existing co-operative programs continued and improved but no significant new federal starts. State experimentation again significant.
1940	Crisis-oriented Centralism (1931–1945)*	↓	Democrats forge majority coalition, become majority party	New Deal "explosion" in federal-state co-operation, heading off centralization through temporary concentration of power in Washington. Expansion of federal-local and unilateral programs along with co-operative ones.
1950 ⋮ 1960	Noncentralist Restoration (1946–1961)*	Regulated Capitalism (1946–)*	(GOP Administration, 1953–1961)* 1956 Critical Elections 1960	Fourth period brings great expansion of small co-operative programs, great expansion of state government expenditures, and increased concern with states' role.
	Concentrated Co-operation (1961–)*	↓	Democratic Majority coalition reforged	Fifth period brings new emphasis on federal stimulatory action and new threat of centralization from outside of the co-operative system.

* Dating of periods is approximate.

TABLE 2 / *Federal Grants to State and Local Governments,*
1902–1964 (selected years) *

YEAR	TOTAL IN $ '000s	NUMBER OF GRANT PROGRAMS IN OPERATION
1902	3,001	5†
1912	5,255	7†
1920	33,886	11
1925	113,746	12
1933	192,966	12
1937	2,663,828	26
1942	1,819,574	27
1946	894,625	28
1953	2,762,912	38
1957	3,816,404	45
1961	7,103,983	46
1964	9,864,000	51

* SOURCES: Advisory Commission on Intergovernmental Relations, Statistical Abstract of the United States, 1964.
† Exclusive of fifteen land grant programs.

sivism, being specifically designed to benefit the declining rural American majority.[13]

As both federal and state governments became involved in the same general areas of activity, it became profitable for them to work out appropriate co-operative relations, even for apparently unilateral programs. This was particularly true in matters involving government regulation. Bank regulation had been a co-operative activity since 1865; regulation of railroads became increasingly co-operative as it became more meaningful. There was even some co-operation in the administration of anti-trust legislation. Law enforcement had always led to a great deal of co-operative activity which was intensified after passage of the spate of federal criminal legislation to assist in handling interstate crimes, in this period. Perhaps the foremost "temporary" co-operative program of the period was selective service for World War I.[14] In some cases federal-state collaboration was explicitly authorized by law. In others, collaboration just grew informally because it was mutually advantageous.

The second period was one of *normalized entrenchment.* It began when the Republicans resumed power in Washington in 1921, and was characterized by a general reluctance to increase the role of government coupled with a negative attitude toward intergovernmental collaboration. Despite the hostile political climate, this period saw the expansion of existing programs and refinements in their co-operative administration. Actual expenditures for co-operative programs increased six-and-a-half times between 1920 and 1932. After an initial period of intensive federal supervisory activity to get the new programs under way, administrative arrangements began to take on a significantly noncentralized character.

At the same time, the number and scope of administrative decisions required to implement complex grant programs gave those who made the programs work substantial influence in shaping the character of inter-governmental co-operation. The professional associations of state and federal officials engaged in the same tasks, and national associations of state officials, such as the American Association of State Highway Officials and the Association of Land Grant Colleges and Universities, whose memberships cut across all levels of government and all jurisdictions, began to assume important policy-making duties. These developments further limited the potential role of the federal bureaus to set policy unilaterally.[15]

The second period was one of considerable activity in the states, activity that would later win the period designation as the "seedtime of reform." Whereas federal expenditures rose by only $503 million between 1922 and 1932, state-local expenditures rose by $2,752 million. The expansion of state activity invariably meant an increase in state involvement in previously "local" problems. The expenditure figures are revealing. State transfers of payments to localities rose from $312 million in 1922 to $801 million in 1932, exceeding the growth of all federal transfers in the same period both proportionately and absolutely. Increases in established federal-aid programs in the 1920's and new state-initiated programs in the welfare field precipitated this growth.[16]

The third period, characterized by *crisis-oriented centralism*, coincided with Democratic achievement of majority party status. Their inauguration of the New Deal as a governmental response to the massive depression problems of a society by then over 56 per cent urban, and later a global war, brought great expansion of new federal programs, co-operative and otherwise. Some of these were in response to state and local pressures; others were developed by reformers eager to stimulate state and local action. The great acceleration of the velocity of government made co-operative federalism all-pervasive. The crisis broke down much of the resistance to federal aid. As a result, existing co-operative programs were made more national in scope, and new ones were broadly oriented from the first.

The co-operative system was subtly reoriented toward Washington, as that city became the nation's unrivaled center of political excitement, if not of governmental inventiveness. "Bright young men" of all ages were brought into the federal government to plan new schemes to meet the problems of the day, many of whom had no particular attachment to the principles of federalism, *per se*. The sheer fact of state and local dependence on federal aid meant that they were willing to tolerate pressures from Washington which they might have rejected forcefully in other times.

Yet the most significant fact that stands out in all this is the way in which the application of accepted techniques and principles of co-operative federalism prevented the tremendous growth in national government activity from becoming an excuse for an equivalent centralization of power. Regardless of the growth of federal influence, the unwillingness of some New Deal planners to develop co-operative programs rather than unilateral ones, and the notions of some political theorists popular in that day that federalism was obsolete, the entrenched forces of American politics directed most new federal programs into co-operative channels. Thus, all but one of the great public welfare programs originally designed by Roosevelt's "brain trust" to be directly administered by federal officials, were reshaped by other administration leaders and by Congress into shared programs in which state and local roles were central. So it was with virtually all the other programs inaugurated in this period that did not absolutely have to be centrally administered.

Indeed, while the New Deal brought formerly unilateral state programs into the sharing system, it also brought in several initially unilateral federal programs as well.[17] Often, experienced public servants (among them FDR himself) were plucked from successful agencies in progressive states and brought to Washington to manage new programs. Their understanding of state and local needs helped maintain the sharing system. Within the states themselves, new co-operative programs were generally subject to modification to meet special local needs.[18] In many cases of erstwhile "centralization," first appearances are deceiving. Consider the Hatch Act requiring states to establish merit systems for federal-aided programs. While this law was greeted by many as a serious limitation of state autonomy, its requirement that states adopt a single merit system of their own design in lieu of federally-imposed program-by-program controls (common in earlier grants-in-aid) helped maintain their integrity as political systems.[19]

The third period featured an expansion of direct federal-local relationships. Partly through urban assistance programs, partly through emergency relief activities, and partly through expanded agricultural programs, the federal government undertook formally to assist local communities in the same spirit of partnership that had animated other forms of intergovernmental relations.[20] This, of course, exacerbated the already complex problems of the states' co-ordination of their internal affairs, even while bringing local relief in a time of crisis.

The growing institutionalization of the intergovernmental partnership was reflected in the development of new institutions to enhance the ability of the states and localities to participate in the development of policy and the improvement of administrative procedures. The Council of State Governments and the complex of "conferences" of state officials connected with it came into being. Headquartered in Chicago, they provided the states with an able instrument to use in negotiating with Washington and a means to further interstate co-operation, providing a measure of "federalism-without-Washington." Local officials, similarly organized, were also called upon to help shape the co-operative programs of the new era.[21]

By the end of the third period, the role of government in a mixed economy had been firmly established and generally accepted. With the beginning of the fourth period a new generation of regulated capitalism, in which government played a positive role in the economy, began. But the fourth and fifth periods reflect this new generation. A Republican interlude during most of the fourth period served to consolidate and assimilate the changes of the New Deal; then it gave way to a restoration of the Democratic majority coalition through the critical elections of 1956 and 1960. The Democrats' return to office in 1961 inaugurated the fifth period in a burst of renewed federal activism.

The fourth period was one of *noncentralist restoration*, marked by a resurgence of the states as spenders and policy-makers and great expansion of local government. Its public image was set by Dwight D. Eisenhower, who repeatedly called for increased reliance on state efforts in place of federal "intervention." However, its real tone was not one of federal "retrenchment" or unilateral state assumption of previously shared responsibilities, as the President and his advisors suggested, but of continued expansion of intergovernmental collaboration—some twenty-one new grant programs were established between 1946 and 1960—with the states and localities assuming a stronger position in the federal system.

This took four forms. There was a substantial shift in the balance of government expenditures for domestic purposes, with the states and localities coming to outspend the federal government by a two-to-one margin. There was also a marked relaxation in detailed federal supervision of state handling of established grant programs, a reflection of the increased professionalization of state and local program administrators and the growing willingness of their federal counterparts to trust their judgment. The states and localities, through their representatives in Congress, were responsible for the initiation of most of the new programs, which generally involved small grants to give them greater leverage in expanding their services. Finally, the states and localities again became centers of experimentation, developing "pilot projects" of all sorts, often aided with foundation grants or small doses of federal funds.

The states also began to concern themselves with acquiring some control over the unilateral federal programs carried on within their boundaries and, in some very important cases, a role in the federal-local programs. In some cases, this was a matter of informal intervention to co-ordinate programs or to render supplementary services. In others, it involved the acquisition of very real power over the implementation of programs within the state.

An added impetus to the resurgence of the states was the increased interest in studying the federal system and its functioning by government commissions for the first time in American history and by academic scholars who continued the tradition begun in the Progressive period.[22] The official studies sponsored by the President suffered somewhat from the disability of starting with the mistaken assumption that the ideal federal system demanded maximum separation of government functions by level.[23] Those sponsored by Congress, on the other hand, were directed toward understanding how the existing co-operative system worked without questioning its legitimacy.[24] The most important direct products of these studies were the relatively small but continuing efforts by the federal administration and Congress to smooth over the rough edges of intergovernmental relations, as evidenced by the establishment of the Advisory Commission on Intergovernmental Relations.[25] As the period ended, public discussion turned to consider the problems of co-ordinating diverse federal assistance programs within the state and metropolitan areas so as to allow both to better maintain their governmental and social integrity.

With the return of the Democrats to power in 1961, a fifth period of *concentrated co-operation* was inaugurated. Increased federal activity in a number of fields was coupled with an intensification of the debate over "states rights" on one hand and widespread acknowledgment of intergovernmental collaboration on the other. While this period is not yet sufficiently advanced to be fully characterized, it seems clear that it will be one of considerable governmental expansion, particularly at the federal level, to deal with the problems of a metropolitan society. Part of this represents federal "picking up the slack" after the fourth period and part, the extension of government in new ways.

Most of the new federal domestic programs have been resurrected from New Deal days, but recently some potentially new departures have been proposed. They are of two different kinds. There is a movement underway to raise federal minimum requirements in some programs unilaterally in a way that would seriously limit state discretion to adjust them to local needs. At the same time, serious proposals have been made to provide some federal aid through block grants and shared revenues to be used as needed at the states' discretion, thus widening their policy-making powers. However, most of the new programs enacted as of this writing, including the two most revolutionary ones (the Civil Rights Act of 1964 and the anti-poverty program) are being implemented so as to continue the established traditions of intergovernmental collaboration. Both provide for substantial state and local participation and maximum possible local control. The anti-poverty program, for example, is designed to provide federal money for locally sponsored projects and gives the states veto power over most projects proposed for within their limits.

The Maintenance of the Partnership

The foregoing description of the successful maintenance of the traditional system of noncentralized co-operation to date should not obscure the great centralizing pressures operating within the American political system today which may have a decisive impact before the century's end. Nor should it obscure the rough edges within the co-operative system itself that could contribute to a drastic change in the character of the American partnership. The need for managing a national economy, meeting foreign pressures, and securing the constitutional rights of all citizens, as well as the pressures toward elimination of diversity within the country—all these operate to centralize governmental power even when steps to prevent centralization are taken within specific programs. With the constitutional barriers to centralization lowered, the pressures of reformers to secure their reforms and of politicians to secure their rewards wherever it is easiest, without regard for the principles of federalism, further complicate the situation. Finally, the great growth of direct federal relations with private parties through defense and veterans' expenditures, agricultural subsidies, and loan guarantees, none of which are susceptible to organization along traditional co-operative lines, cuts into the old patterns even when they are brought into the co-operative system by the back door.

Within the co-operative system, there are problems—for example, weak state and local governments unwilling or unable to uphold their share of the partnership and proliferating "red tape" required by federal administrators to meet federal requirements. There is another problem in that the public information system, as it is presently constituted, tends to focus public attention on Washington to the exclusion of the states and localities.

Logic tells us that noncentralized co-operative federalism is not an easy system to maintain, particularly in a nation that prides itself on being pragmatic—less concerned with form than with function and willing to try anything if it "works." Yet the system has been maintained despite the pressures and in the face of all logic because it has continued to satisfy most of the particular interests in this country more often than not. If not one of them gets everything he wants, each gets something, re-enforcing their attachments to a system they feel they can hope to influence.

Notes

1) For a discussion of federal-state co-operation before 1913, see Daniel J. Elazar, *The American Partnership* (Chicago: University of Chicago Press, 1962).
2) Adequate statistical data for most of the nineteenth century is lacking, but the author's sampling based on the available data confirms this. The figures usually cited show state-local expenditures as exceeding federal expenditures by an approximately two-to-one margin until 1933. However, when the value of federal land grants to states, localities, corporations, and individuals is included in the calculations of federal expenditures and the share of state and local expenditures derived from federal endowments is eliminated, the result is quite different.
3) As of April 1964, 115 programs were available as listed in the *Catalog of Federal Aids to State and Local Governments*, prepared for the Subcommittee on Intergovernmental Relations of the Senate Committee on Government Operations (Washington, D.C., 1964). The most current and comprehensive published information on the extent of state participation in federal grant programs is available from the Advisory Commission on Intergovernmental Relations.
4) For a brief, yet thorough discussion of this aspect of American federalism, see Morton Grodzins, "Centralization and Decentralization in the American Federal System," *A Nation of States*, ed. Robert A. Goldwin (Chicago: Rand, McNally, 1963).
5) See, for example, Dennis J. Palumbo, "The States and American Foreign Relations" (Unpublished doctoral dissertation, Department of Political Science, University of Chicago, 1960); Morton Grodzins, "The Federal System," *Goals for Americans*, ed. President's Commission on National Goals (Englewood Cliffs, N.J.: Prentice-Hall, 1960); and Edward C. Banfield (ed.), *Urban Government* (New York: Free Press of Glencoe, 1961).

6) For further elucidation of the role of local and private interests, see Daniel J. Elazar, "Local Government in Intergovernmental Perspective," *Illinois Local Government*, ed. Lois Pelakoudas (Urbana: University of Illinois, 1960) and Morton Grodzins, "Local Strength in the American Federal System: The Mobilization of Public-Private Influence," *Continuing Crisis in American Politics*, ed. Marian D. Irish (Englewood Cliffs, N.J.: Prentice-Hall, 1963).

7) The following outline was suggested in part by Jane Perry Clark's important study, *The Rise of a New Federalism* (New York: Columbia University Press, 1938) which, as the first work to attempt to catalog the entire range of federal co-operative activities, established some essential guidelines that are still quite relevant.

8) See Grodzins, in *Goals for Americans, op. cit.*, for a discussion of this and Kenneth E. Gray, "Congressional Interference in the Executive Branch" (Paper delivered at the annual meeting of the American Political Science Association, September 1962) for a detailed analysis of its operation at the federal level.

9) While no single date for the real beginning of the "twentieth century" is precisely accurate, 1913 is chosen as the most appropriate, since it was the first year of Woodrow Wilson's "New Freedom," which represented the first great and co-ordinated nationwide response to the problems of the new century and the beginning of a five-year period of great changes in American life.

10) A "critical election" has been defined as one in which substantial shifts occur in the voting behavior of major electoral blocs, shifts which become sufficiently "permanent" to set the voting patterns for a generation. The United States has experienced critical elections at the national level in pairs every twenty-four to thirty-two years. Every two generations, they have reflected a shift of the voting majority from one political party to the other.

11) The figures cited here and subsequently—unless otherwise indicated—are from the report of the Advisory Commission on Intergovernmental Relations, "Periodic Congressional Assessment of Federal Grants-in-Aid to State and Local Government" (June 1961).

12) See John Wells Davidson (ed.), *A Crossroads of Freedom* (New Haven: Yale University Press, 1956), the most complete edition of Wilson's campaign addresses available.

13) For a comprehensive review of federal-state relations under the formal grant-in-aid programs in this period and a discussion of the sectional bases for their support, see Austin F. Macdonald, *Federal Aid* (New York: The Macmillan Company, 1928). Statutes restricting these programs to rural areas have been progressively modified, since 1921, reflecting the increased urbanization of American society. These first programs were primarily supported by the representatives of the generally rural and relatively poor Southern and Western states as a means for partial redistribution of the national wealth concentrated in the Northeast.

14) The story of how the draft was made a co-operative activity is told by Hugh Johnson in his autobiography, *The Blue Eagle from Egg to Earth* (Garden City, N.Y.: Doubleday, 1935). It is a highly significant illustration of the utility of the sharing system in a time of crisis.

15) See MacDonald, *op. cit.*; V. O. Key, *The Administration of Federal Grants to States* (Chicago: University of Chicago Press, 1937) for discussions of the development of these programs in the second period.

16) See Clarke Chambers, *Seedtime of Reform* (Minneapolis: University of Minnesota Press, 1963); U.S. Census Bureau, *Historical Statistics of the United States* (Washington, D.C., 1960).

17) Morton Grodzins discusses this in "American Political Parties and the American System," *Western Political Quarterly*, Vol. XII (December 1960), pp. 974–998.

18) A study of one such case which has become classic is Paul Ylvisaker's *The Battle of Blue Earth County* (Washington, D.C., 1950).

19) See George C. S. Benson, "Federal-State Personnel Relations," *The Annals*, Vol. 207 (January 1940), pp. 38–43.

20) Raymond S. Short, "Municipalities and the Federal Government," *The Annals*, Vol. 207 (January 1940), pp. 44–53; Robert H. Connery and Richard H. Leach, *The Federal Government and Metropolitan Areas* (Cambridge, Mass.: Harvard University Press, 1960).

21) See Clark, *op. cit.*; Key, *op. cit.*, for discussion of these developments.

22) A list of even the important publications on the subject of intergovernmental relations would be prohibitively long. There are, however, several good bibliographies that may be consulted, among them: *Intergovernmental Relations in the United States: A Selected Bibliography*, prepared for the Intergovernmental Relations Subcommittee of the Senate Committee on Government Operations (Washington, D.C., 1956); Glen L. Bachelder and Paul C. Shaw, *Federalism: A Selected Bibliography*, Michigan State University Institute for Community Development and Services, Bibliographic Series No. 1 (March 1964).

23) These studies included: The [Kestnbaum] Commission on Intergovernmental Relations, *A Report to the President*, with attachments (Washington, D.C., 1955) and Joint Federal-State Action Committee, *Progress Reports* (Washington, D.C., 1957, 1959). An excellent critique of the first study commission can be found in William Anderson, *The Nation and the States: Rivals or Partners?* (Minneapolis: University of Minnesota Press, 1955). The second is equally well treated in Grodzins, "Centralization and Decentralization in the American Federal System," *op. cit.* The first [Hoover] Commission on Reorganization of the Executive Branch of the Government also sponsored a study of federal-state relations by Mr. Hoover's own decision. The study report was prepared by Grodzins for the Council of State Governments and set forth the outlines of his later work on federalism, but the Commission's recommendations ignored his conclusions and called for a restoration of dual federalism. See *Federal-State Relations by the Council of State Governments* (Washington, D.C., 1949).

24) These studies included those of the [Fountain] Intergovernmental Relations Subcommittee of the House Committee on Government Operations issued in 1956 and those of the [Muskie] Intergovernmental Relations Subcommittee of the Senate Committee on Government Operations, issued beginning in 1963.

25) The contributions of this body are just now beginning to be felt. They have issued some eighteen reports to date, on a number of phases of intergovernmental relations, available from the Washington, D.C., offices.

The Ambiguity of Elections

Robert A. Dahl

. . . *it is important to notice how little a national election tells us about* the preferences of majorities. Strictly speaking, all an election reveals is the first preferences of some citizens among the candidates standing for office. Let us see what it does not do.

Let us put to one side the fact that because of election machinery the outcome may actually run counter to the expressed preferences of a plurality of voters; for example, in three national elections in the United States, the candidate preferred by the most voters was not made President. Let us also put to one side the fact that when more than two candidates run for office, the winning candidate may have a plurality but not a majority of votes; and it is usually impossible to say what the outcome would have been if there had been a run-off election between the two candidates with the highest number of votes. Thus in nine American presidential elections the winning candidate has had a plurality but not a majority of popular votes. Hence in twelve cases, or more than one-third of the presidential elections since Jackson,[1] the winning candidate has not been the first choice of a majority of voters.

Far more significant is the fact that even when a candidate is evidently a first choice of a majority of voters, we cannot be sure in a national election that he is also a first choice of a majority of adults or eligible voters.[2] Although the American case is extreme, in every nation state where compulsory voting does not exist the basic proposition holds. In any given election we are almost never in a position to know for sure what the outcome would have been if some or all of the non-voters had actually voted. We have slight reason to suppose that the outcome would have been the same. In a close election a small last minute rise in the

Reprinted from *A Preface to Democratic Theory* (Chicago: University of Chicago Press, 1956), pp. 125-130, by permission of the publisher. C. 1956 by The University of Chicago Press.

proportion of voters drawn from those favorable to one of the sides can change the outcome; something like this seems to have happened in the last two weeks of the 1948 campaign.[3] Moreover, one of the sides is often handicapped by non-voting more than the other; for example, when non-voting is inversely related to income, education, and other related factors, in a close division of opinion the candidate of the poor and uneducated is more likely to lose, even when he is the first preference of all the adults or eligible voters, than is the candidate of the educated and the well-to-do. In the 1952 presidential election, it appears that about 20 per cent of those who favored Eisenhower did not vote, whereas about 29 per cent of those who favored Stevenson did not vote.[4] In a close division of opinion, the difference in the proportions of non-voters would have been crucial.[5]

Now if all the non-voters were indifferent as to the outcome, then, their preferences, or lack of them, could be ignored in determining what a majority of adults prefer. But unfortunately it is not true that all non-voters are indifferent; for example, in one national sample studied in 1952, out of 450 persons who said they cared very much which party won the presidential election, 76 (or 17 per cent) evidently did not vote. Of the Stevenson supporters who "cared very much" about the outcome, a much higher percentage (28 per cent) failed to vote than among highly concerned Eisenhower supporters (10 per cent).[6]

Finally, in appraising the significance of elections as an indication of first choices, it must be remembered that a great many voters do not really perceive a choice between candidate A and candidate B; for many people the only perceived alternatives are to vote for one of the candidates or not to vote at all.[7]

Even if we could rule out all these difficulties, it would still be true that we can rarely interpret a majority of first choices among candidates in a national election as being equivalent to a majority of first choices for a specific policy. Some people evidently vote for a candidate although they are quite indifferent about the issues. Others support a candidate who is opposed to them on some issues; in the 1952 sample already referred to, 29 per cent of those who took a Democratic position on the Taft-Hartley Act nonetheless supported Eisenhower. Furthermore, the supporters of a candidate often differ widely in their preferences on issues. In one sample of those who supported Eisenhower in 1952, about 64 per cent thought the United States had gone too far in concerning itself with problems in other parts of the world, about 27 per cent thought it had not, and about 9 per cent were neutral.[8] Thus it becomes possible for a resounding majority of the voters to elect a candidate all of whose policies are the first choices of only a minority.

Imagine, for example, that voters must choose between two candidates who disagree on three policies as set forth in Table 1. Now let us suppose that each of these minorities is a distinct group, so that together the three minorities make up 75 per cent of the voters. Let us suppose that the first minority regards foreign policy as the crucial issue and ranks its choices: *u, x, z, w, y, v.* That is, these voters prefer candidate A because he offers them a foreign policy of which they approve, even though they dislike his farm and fiscal policies. Now suppose that the second minority of voters regards farm policy as crucial and ranks its

TABLE 1

	Candi- date A prefers al- ternative	Supported by	Candi- date B prefers al- ternative	Supported by
Foreign policy	*u*	25 per cent of voters	*v*	75 per cent of voters
Farm policy	*w*	25 per cent of voters	*x*	75 per cent of voters
Fiscal policy	*y*	25 per cent of voters	*z*	75 per cent of voters

choices: *w, z, v, u, y, x.* That is, these voters prefer candidate A because he offers them a farm policy they like, even though they disapprove of his stand on foreign and fiscal policy. Applying the same kind of reasoning to the third minority, it can be readily seen that candidate A might win 75 per cent of the votes, even though each of his policies is opposed by 75 per cent of the voters. This is an instance, not of majority rule or even of minority rule, but of *minorities* rule.

In addition, in so far as voters prefer a candidate because of his policies, frequently the support represents approval or disapproval of a policy already enacted, even if little or nothing can be done to change the consequences of the policy. No doubt many people voted against Stevenson in 1952 because Truman had not stopped the Chinese Communists in 1947.[9] The vote was more of a punishment for past action than a choice of future policy. Political leaders recognize this aspect of elections and frequently seek to avoid a decision until an election is over so that they may then act relatively free from campaign commitments. Thus paradoxically an election may actually prevent rather than facilitate policy choices by the electorate.

Now the unwary student of contemporary democracies may hastily conclude that the deficiencies in elections I have alluded to are characteristic only of the United States, but except for peculiarities that I agree to put to one side as remediable in principle, what I have said applies with equal force, I believe, to the politics of any large nation state. Although political scientists sometimes appear to believe that many of the virtues and few of the vices of American politics are to be found in the English parliamentary system, operating with two highly unified and disciplined parties, I am inclined to think that elections under that system are, if anything, even less controlling than our own.[10] The only important point to stress here is that in no large nation state can elections tell us much about the preferences of majorities and minorities, beyond the bare fact that among those who went to the polls a majority, plurality, or minority indicated their first choices for some particular candidate or group of candidates. What the first choices of this electoral majority are, beyond that for the particular candidates, it is almost impossible to say with much confidence.

.   .   .

Notes

1) Before Jackson, presidential electors were usually chosen by state legislatures. Consequently it is difficult to estimate the number of voters who supported a given candidate; compilations of popular votes in presidential elections usually begin with the election of 1828.
2) However, modern sample surveys of public opinion are now helpful in this respect.
3) See *The Pre-Election Polls of 1948* (New York: Social Science Research Council, 1949); Angus Campbell and R. L. Kahn, *The People Elect a President* (Ann Arbor: Institute for Social Research, 1952); Angus Campbell, Gerald Gurin, and Warren E. Miller, *The Voter Decides* (Evanston: Row, Peterson & Co., 1954).
4) Campbell *et al.*, *op. cit.*, p. 31, Table 3.2.
5) It can easily be shown that in order for the winning candidate to be the first choice of a majority of all eligible voters, he must also be the first choice of a percentage of the non-voters greater than: $(X-2W)/2Z$, where X is the number of eligible voters, W is the number of votes obtained by the winning candidate, and Z is the number of non-voters. For example, in 1948, Mr. Truman was the first choice of a majority of all eligible voters only if he was also the first choice of more than 50.7 per cent of the non-voters; in 1952, on the other hand, Mr. Eisenhower would only have needed the support of more than 41.2 per cent of the non-voters. The estimates are based on data in tables in: *The Political Almanac of 1952* (New York: Forbes & Sons, 1952), p. 22; *Statistics of the Presidential and Congressional Elections of Nov. 4, 1952* (Washington: Government Printing Office, 1953), p. 52; and V. O. Key, *A Primer of Statistics for Political Scientists* (New York: Thomas Y. Crowell & Co., 1953), p. 197.
6) My estimates are based on the data in Table 3.8, Campbell *et al.*, *op. cit.*, p. 37.
7) In the 1948 election, in one sample of voters, 73 per cent said they had never thought of voting for the other candidate at any time during the campaign; in the 1952 election, in another sample of voters, the figure was 78 per cent, *ibid.*, p. 23, Table 2.7. This suggests the upper limit; the data do not indicate how many of these saw non-voting as an alternative to voting for their candidate.

8) My estimates are based upon Table 8.1, *ibid.*
9) 71 per cent of those who thought it "was our government's fault that China went Communistic" supported Eisenhower, *ibid.*
10) Great Britain furnishes an interesting confirmation of the fact that electoral majorities rarely determine specific policy. The British political system has few of the constitutional and political barriers to majority rule characteristic of the American system. Nevertheless, it is comparatively rare for the party in power to have been the first preference of a majority of the voters—much less of the whole electorate—at the preceding election. Since 1923 there have been nine elections. Only two of these indicated a majority of first preferences for the ensuing government. Even the two exceptions are politically aberrant. In the election of 1931, candidates endorsing Ramsay MacDonald's national coalition won a majority of the votes, the Labor party having been badly hit by Mac-Donald's withdrawal. In 1935, the Conservative party candidates won only 47.7 per cent of the votes, but candidates endorsing the National government won 54.7 per cent of the votes. Not since 1945 has any government been the first preference of a majority of the voters. Indeed, in 1945, 10.4 million people eligible to vote either did not vote or voted for candidates other than Labor or Conservative compared with 9.6 million for the Conservatives and 12 million for Labor candidates. In 1950, this group numbered 8.2 million, compared with 12.1 million Conservative voters and 13.2 million Labor voters. Cf. *The Constitutional Year Book, 1938* (London: Harrison, 1938), Vol. LII; D. E. Butler, *The Electoral System in Britain, 1918–1951* (Oxford: Clarendon Press, 1953), p. 173; John Bonham, *The Middle Class Vote* (London: Faber & Faber, 1955), p. 120.

Interest Groups and the Governing Process

V. O. Key, Jr.

. . . *Campaigns and elections . . . are not the totality of politics. Our* conception of the political process is broad enough to cover all sorts of efforts to guide, influence, or affect governmental action. The striving for power, for status, for privilege is never-ending and not restricted to campaigns and elections. Administrators take action every day. Legislators make laws. Organized groups incessantly seek to influence these decisions which are, in a sense, the pay off of the process of politics in which elections are but episodes, albeit significant episodes. The decisions taken between elections constitute the basic stuff of politics, the pelf and glory for which men and groups battle. And the stakes of between-elections politics are great. A conservative estimate, say, of the costs imposed on consumers by the public policies born of the efforts of the sugar lobby would be $100,000,000 annually.[1]

A working conception of the political *process* must take into account the interactions among groups, interests, and governmental institutions that produce such decisions. Moreover, a working conception of the political *system* must make a place for organized interest groups: they not only seek to exert influence; they are a part of the political system—elements quite as integral to the system as are political parties.

Representative Function of Private Groups

Obviously, organized groups, for good or ill, perform a function of representation in the political system. The characterization of the lobby as the "third house" puts the point vividly if somewhat exuberantly. The explanation of the development of this system of spokesmen for specialized segments of society probably rests in part on the shortcomings of geographical representation in a highly differentiated society. Legislators could speak authoritatively for the more or less homogeneous interests of their districts in a less complex society. The relative simplicity of legislative questions permitted easy accommodation of geographical representation to such necessity as existed for functional representation. The growth of the number of specialized interests in society and the increasing complexity of legislative questions created tasks beyond ready performance by spokesmen for geographical areas. No legislator could regularly be relied upon to look out for interests that spread across many districts. Organized groups supplement the system of geographical representation.

Representation does not consist solely in serving as a conduit for sentiments already in existence among the members of a group. Antecedent to the expression of group views is a process of creation of those views. Associations—or their committees—engage in extensive study and discussion in reaching decisions on their program for legislation. By this process differences are ironed out and the association can approach the public and the government with a united front. Reconciliation of differences within interest groups facilitates the work of legislatures and of Congress by reducing the number of conflicts with which they have to deal, as well as by giving the government an authoritative statement of the group position. Government is then left with the task of ironing out conflicts between opposing groups.

The hammering out within private groups of consensus on public policy often produces legislative proposals that both reflect the views of the group and take into account the angularities of the situation with which legislation deals. Legislators, to be sure, could work out the details of policy proposals. On major issues they may do so, but countless lesser legislative schemes evolve within the groups to be concerned, greatly to the relief of legislators and often by no means to the detriment of the public interest.[2] In fact, the most efficacious statutes may well be those enacted at the behest of private groups which advocate measures to protect the group as a whole from the actions of its unethical fringe—or from its competitors.

Representation includes more than advocacy; it extends to the maintenance of close watch on the legislative process to spot threats to the interest of the constituency represented. The staffs of pressure groups perform this intelligence function, an operation that requires skill, for often hidden away in bills are clauses with the most untoward effects, at times not intended by anyone concerned. An alert lobbyist may prevent foolish or uninformed action. Whatever the portent of a bill may be, the group staff sounds the alarm to arouse the membership. One sometimes suspects that the staffs thrive on attempts to panic the members by horrendous accounts of what is in prospect in the way of public regulation. The group bureaucracy prospers as it succeeds in arousing fears, but individuals are likely to be much less well informed on what the legislative trend holds in store for them than are their lobbyists.[3]

To say that pressure groups perform a representative function is not to assert that public officials should not be wary of them. Most groups do not include nearly all persons of the class they purport to represent. The National Association of Manufacturers includes only a small proportion of the manufacturers of the nation. Probably two-thirds of the farmers are not affiliated with any farm organization. Members of pressure groups tend to be the more aggressive, often the more prosperous, or the larger units of the potential membership. Thus, the larger farmers affiliate with farm groups in a higher degree than do others. This greater degree of affiliation from the upper brackets appears to be common to nearly all organized groups.[4] Even among the aged pensioners, it seems that those who are "slightly privileged" are the more active.[5]

Resolutions, programs, and platforms may reflect the views of its leaders and bureaucracy rather than those of the association's membership. At times the controlling oligarchy may, of course, express sentiments widely held within the membership. On other occasions the leadership of a nonparty group may be unfaithful to its trust or may misrepresent the views of the association.[6] Still other situations may by no means be what they seem. An organization with an impressive letterhead and name purports to speak for thousands or hundreds of thousands of persons when it consists of nothing more than an energetic promoter financed by some interest not eager to make its identity known. Or the promoter may simply have seen an opportunity to make a killing by collecting contributions from the gullible. Or perfectly respectable organizations may be used as fronts. A recurring situation is illustrated by the remark of an official of the Association of American Railroads about a bill sponsored in the New Jersey legislature by the Chamber of Commerce of the State of New Jersey: "Mr. Russell thinks it inadvisable to let it be known . . . that this bill was prepared by railroad counsel or is in any sense sponsored by a committee of the Association." Or false-front organizations may be established for short-term tactical advantage.[7]

These observations make clear that groups differ in their performance of the representative function. The spokesmen of some groups may be relied upon to present a case that has been preceded by extensive group deliberation. Others speak only for a small but active minority within the group. Some lobbyists gain reputations as men who will provide legislators with trustworthy information and advice; others follow hit-and-run tactics.

Legislation as Intergroup Negotiation

Another dimension of the role of organized groups in the political process may be seen in the phenomenon of legislation by negotiation. An act of a legislature may be in reality only the ratification of an agreement negotiated by the representatives of those private groups with an interest in a specific question. The legislative body, far from being pressured into conversion of private understandings into the law of the land, may act with an alacrity that comes from the pleasure of avoiding the agony of deciding a dispute between groups.

An illustration of this pattern, drawn from the work of the Vermont legislature, has been recorded in detail by Oliver Garceau and Corinne Silverman.[8] In 1951 the Associated Industries of Vermont found itself faced by a CIO-sponsored proposal to bring silicosis under the Workman's Compensation Act. The Associated Industries, on the other hand, wished to tighten the eligibility requirements for unemployment benefits, while the CIO favored an increase in both the duration and the level of benefits. In the negotiations the CIO, bargaining from a relatively weak position, agreed not to push its bills for more liberal unemployment benefits; the AIV agreed to drop its plea for tightened qualifications for benefits. The AIV conceded an occupational disease bill to deal with the silicosis question in a manner far less unacceptable to it than was the CIO proposal. All these negotiations took place in a situation that limited the demands each group could make. Enactment by the legislature came automatically when sponsors of the legislation announced that both industry and labor thought the bill should pass. The operation involved no buttonholing or pressuring of legislators, only a few of whom knew of the negotiations leading to the agreement.

In Illinois the process of legislation by negotiation has at times been formalized, according to studies by Gilbert Y. Steiner. Early in the century agreements between Illinois miners and operators "stipulated that neither party should introduce bills affecting the industry without previously consulting with the other." Under these arrangements the terms of a good many legislative proposals were fixed by collective bargaining. Labor might yield a point here and the operators concede a point there. An "agreed" bill would then be supported before the legislature by both the union and the operators, a set of circumstances likely to produce legislative results. Negotiation apparently became feasible in part because either group could block within the legislature proposals by the other.[9]

These examples of lawmaking by negotiation among private groups followed by formal legislative ratification raise the question of how frequently this pattern occurs. Does a large proportion of legislation find its way to the statute books by this means? The answer is that nobody knows, but many acts are preceded by negotiation and agreement among private groups. Often, predictable opposition from other groups moves the interest sponsoring legislation to yield a point in advance with or without negotiation. The pattern shades over into one in which members of the legislative committee mediate among affected groups and bring them to agreement.[10] Legislators, rather than undertake the onerous task of negotiating a compromise or the painful responsibility of deciding between conflicting interests, may even postpone action until the groups concerned narrow their differences. . . .

Notes

1) A figure probably nearer to the reality is $666,000,000, an estimate made by Senator Paul Douglas. See *Congressional Record* (daily ed.), March 29, 1961, p. 4826.

2) Illustrative of the legislative attitude is the observation of a publication of the National Lumber Manufacturers' Association that public officials prefer to have "the view of an industry, rather than to listen *ad infinitum* to the variant views of countless individuals." Quoted by Donald Blaisdell, *Economic Power and Political Pressures* (Monograph No. 26, Temporary National Economic Committee, 1941), p. 3. Mmbers of industries, too, prefer to iron out their differences in private. Consider the comment of the president of a life insurance company: "The writer was aghast at the way certain parts of the life insurance business viciously attacked other parts in front of the Senate Finance Committee. All of this bickering should have been conducted on the floor of some meeting room in a hotel, before any representations of any kind were made to Congress." *Congressional Record* (daily ed.), May 1, 1959, p. A3649.

3) Closely akin to legislative intelligence is the function performed by many groups of keeping their members posted on laws and regulations affecting them. Large corporations may keep track of these things themselves, but trade associations perform this service for smaller concerns. The process at times shades over into the explanation of the factors underlying public policies which aids to a degree in obtaining acceptance and consent.

4) See C. R. Wright and H. H. Hyman, "Voluntary Association Memberships of American Adults: Evidence from National Sample Surveys," *American Sociological Review*, 23 (1958), 284–94.

5) See F. A. Pinner, *et al.*, *Old Age and Political Behavior* (Berkeley: University of California Press, 1959).

6) Perhaps, too, it is in the nature of organization for the leadership echelon to adhere in special degree to the pure and undefiled group doctrine. We expect the

clergy to be more pious than the laity; perhaps we should expect a pattern no different in other organizations.

7) Such hoaxes can become fairly subtle. Thus, in 1958 the "Association of First Class Mailers" ran large ads in the *Washington Post* against a proposed increase in first class mail rates. It turned out that the Association's president was a printer and mailer for big users of third class mail and that some of the financial support came from the Mail Advertising Service Association. The supposition was that if first class rates were increased, the low rates enjoyed by "junk" mailers would become less defensible. See *Congressional Record* (daily ed.), March 27, 1958, p. 4930.

8) "A Pressure Group and the Pressured: A Case Report," *American Political Science Review*, 48 (1954), 672–91.

9) For Professor Steiner's insightful analysis, see his *Legislation by Collective Bargaining* (Urbana: University of Illinois, 1951).

10) The following interchange between Representatives illustrates the point:

"*Mr. Gavin.* I am tremendously interested in the bill also and I wanted to state that the bill as amended has been approved by the Izaak Walton League, the Outdoor Writers Association, the National Parks Association, the Wilderness Society, and the Wildlife Management Association.

"*Mr. Bonner.* The gentleman is correct; and I wish to advise him and the other Members of the House that we, and the committee, have had a difficult time working this bill out so that it would receive unanimous support of both the commercial fishing interests and the sportsmen of the Nation, which the amendment I have added to the Senate bill does." *Congressional Record* (daily ed.), July 7, 1956, p. 10911.

Of Statist and Non-Statist Economic Power

Adolph A. Berle, Jr.

It would be an absurd caricature of the American economic power structure to suggest that all economic power, and with it corresponding responsibility, is lodged in private (that is to say, non-Statist) corporations. Chiefly due to repeated political intervention, the American political State today exercises a great deal. It regulates the price of practically all forms of public transportation. It controls, through the indirect management of the banking system, both long-term and short-term interest rates. It outlaws a whole range of trade practices, such as private price-fixing agreements, arrangements not to compete in given territories, and (less successfully) abuse of financial strength permitting cut-throat price competition and price discrimination. In a newer and steadily growing range of specific situations, the State intervenes to provide or require production (as in the case of the Rural Electrification Authority) or to adjust current supply of product to current demand (as in the case of the oil and refined sugar industries). It fixes minimum wages for most of nonagricultural industry and attempts a roughly equivalent operation in farming by establishing prices for staple agricultural commodities. It assists in providing credit, which is the greatest single element in the housing industry. Were it possible to draw a map of the extent of American economic power, it would be found that a very substantial, though minority, proportion of such power was exercised by one or another instrumentality of the United States Government or, locally, by the governments of the various States.

Yet, I think on fair analysis two conclusions are justified. Most, though by no means all, governmental power is negatively exercised: it takes the form of prohibiting certain uses of economic power by non-

Reprinted from *Power Without Property* (New York: Harcourt, Brace & World, 1959), pp. 93–98, by permission of the author, Harcourt, Brace & World, Inc., and Sidgwick & Jackson, Ltd. © 1959 by A. A. Berle, Jr.

Statist organizations. Direct insistence on, or requirement of, positive action is relatively rare. Second, it leaves to private organizations the main task of production, supply, and distribution, and certainly the main initiative in developing new economic areas, geographic or technical. It assumes that the profit motive will be adequate to cause performance of these functions. In most fields it does not object when the profits are generous. This last is possibly due to unconscious realization that the profit mechanism is also the capital-gathering mechanism. In result, the driving force of the American system is non-Statist, and to non-Statist institutions like corporations primarily falls the power of initiative and action. The guiding and limiting power is that primarily used by the State, though in extreme cases the American State occasionally initiates, as it did in the case of Tennessee Valley Authority and, more recently, in the fields of activity opened by atomic fission and fusion, and advanced electronics.

It is appropriate here to clear up a major dispute which befogs the pages of much contemporary writing. Private corporations steadily assert that they do not want the government in business. They mean by this that they do not wish the area of their economic power diminished. The same corporations are nevertheless frequently the first to demand that the government get into business when they feel their power position threatened by forces they themselves are unable to control. They have invoked Statist economic power to keep out foreign competition through tariffs; to supply credit through government or government-guaranteed financing; sometimes (as in the oil industry) to keep production in line with demand, and so forth. Their objection therefore cannot be that exercise of economic power by the State is *per se* wrong. Equally it would be wrong to dismiss the objections of private corporations to government intervention as merely expression of self-interest. The reason they commonly give for wishing government "out of business" is abbreviated into the phrase that if the government enters into business, politics also enters. Analyzed, the real objection is not that the State must not exercise economic power, but that where economic power is exercised by the State there is danger that this power may be badly exercised or, worse still, combined with other forms of Statist power—for example, the power of the police system or of a military system.

This last objection certainly has merit. We noted some of the built-in limitations which place boundaries on economic power as such. These limitations frequently cease to apply when economic power is joined to some other form. The State might undertake to operate the American Telephone & Telegraph Company, or the National Broadcasting Company. Many governments in various parts of the world do own and operate communications, and both Britain and Canada own and operate broadcasting systems—operate them, in fact, far better than similar American systems. But there is always the inherent danger that the Federal government might wish to use the telephone and telegraph system as a means for detecting crime or ascertaining the political plans of individuals. There is always the possibility that the political State might undertake to use its broadcasting system for political propaganda. That is, there is danger that the purely economic function will be used for ends foreign to its economic purpose. This is a blueprint of the road to tyranny, as Stalin, Mussolini, and Hitler have forcefully demonstrated.

But, it seems, the nub of this objection is not exercise of economic power by the State, but rather danger of combining disparate power functions. This is a problem the American State has met before in another connection and which it tolerably well solved. It is the old constitutional problem of "separation of powers." Jeremy Bentham laid down, the Massachussets Constitution states, and Federal constitutional thinking accepts, the principle that legislative, judicial, and executive functions and power shall not be combined. The Congress cannot judge. The Supreme Court is not empowered to legislate. The President can neither judge nor legislate. We have insisted on this system (with only occasional controversies about it) during our entire national life.

What we may be seeing in this controversy over "government in business" is the emergence of a fourth category in this doctrine of constitutional separation of powers. This is that economic power, Statist or private, must not be joined to or controlled by—nor may it control—any other form of power. Violation of this principle would be a nail in the coffin of individual freedom. The principle applies quite as much to the Interstate Commerce Commission or the Securities and Exchange Commission (both of which have economic power) as to the American Telephone & Telegraph Company or the Columbia Broadcasting System. It is a principle which must be controlling within the State, as well as between the State and private organizations endowed with economic power.

For, if the political State could decree in any fashion that the American Telephone & Telegraph Company should employ only good Republicans or good Democrats, or that none but commentators approved by the United States Army should perform over National or Columbia Broadcasting Systems, democracy as we know it would rapidly cease to exist. In Great Britain the government-owned British Broadcasting Corporation enjoys a "constitutional" separation from British government control. Its officers can (and on occasion do) tell British Cabinet officers to keep their hands off their programs. Americans prefer to do this at second remove by keeping our broadcasting companies in private hands and constitutionally limiting the government from interfering with their freedom of speech.

But the doctrine must surely apply with no less force when the State is not involved at all. If the Standard Oil Company of New Jersey were ever (it has not) to indulge the inconceivable folly of decreeing that no Negro should buy its gasoline at any of its stations—adding to its economic function of supplying oil the quite different function of regulating race relations—it would violate just this same principle. Probably it would promptly be prevented from doing so by political intervention in the form of law.

The point need not be labored. The primary consideration is not that the State shall not have economic power. It is that economic power exercised either by the State or by non-Statist organizations shall not be combined with any other form of power, or used for other than economic ends. Otherwise, there is inherent danger to individuality, which our government and our economic system are designed to serve. There is also the fact that combinations of power have no visible limit; they are capable of being extended over huge areas and huge masses of men. If the State can carry on economic functions more efficiently than corporations, there is no reason why it should not fulfill them; but there are powerful reasons why, in doing so, the exercise of the function should not be mixed with or perverted by other functions of government.

Church-State Problems

⌒⌇⌒

Earl Raab

Defining the relationship between religion and human society is a generic problem; defining the relationship between church and state is a special- ized aspect of that problem, resulting from the intervention of political rather than religious considerations. In America, the intervening political considerations are those of the modern democratic state and are suggested in two tantalizingly sparse clauses contained in the First Amendment to the Constitution.

The first clause directs Congress "to make no law respecting an establishment of religion." Behind this prescription lies the political concept of the "secular state."

The history of political states during a dozen centuries of Western Christian civilization had been a history of ecclesiastical rule and imperial rule "by divine origin." The concept of the modern democratic state was developed not only in revolt against older absolutist forms of powers, but in a period when philosophies of naturalism and rationalism were as- cendant.

Jefferson wrote:

Reading, reflection and time have convinced me that the interests of society require observation of those moral principles only in which all religions agree . . . The practice of morality being necessary for the well-being of society, He (the Creator) has taken care to impress its precepts so indelibly on our hearts that they shall not be effaced by the subtleties of our brain.[1]

Not without its own subtleties, this statement suggests that God had already so sufficiently endowed man that any further intrusion of religious dogma would be not only unnecessary but harmful. The dis- position of men's public affairs was to be left to men and to the rational faculties which they could bring to these affairs. Jefferson wrote that "truth is great and will prevail if left to herself (and unless) disarmed of her natural weapons, free argument and debate . . ."[2] Revelation and religious dogma were not subject to debate, and were therefore not to be directly imposed on the political process. The state was to be secular.

The second constitutional clause directs Congress to make no law "prohibiting the free exercise" of religion. This clause emphasizes the concept of religious liberty. Religious affiliation was to be voluntary, and religious conscience was not to be interfered with by the political state.

Together, these two clauses comprise the constitutional principle which has been called "separation of church and state." It has been said that Jefferson was interested in this principle in order to protect the state from religion, and that Roger Williams had been interested in the same principle in order to protect religion from the state. The two concerns may not be finally divisible. But it can similarly be said that the establishment clause approaches the "separation" principle by a stress on the inviolability of the secular state; the free-exercise clause approaches the "separation" principle by a stress on the inviolability of religious freedom. If a Catholic school child were somehow forced to participate in a Protestant religious exercise, the free-exercise clause could clearly be invoked. But even if all the children were willing and even if they were all of the same denomination, a religious exercise in the schools could run afoul of the establishment clause.

But the concepts of the secular state and of religious liberty are complicated by a third political principle of a more general nature: the state exists to serve the prevailing aspirations of the population at large, within the limitations prescribed by the Constitution. The question then becomes one of determining the precise limitations on majority will prescribed by the two relevant clauses of the First Amendment. In both cases, there are problems of interpretation.

The establishment clause reflects an inevitable tension between the concept of the secular state and the thrust of the American religious culture. No one has questioned that "separation" in this case certainly means separation between *church* and state. But to what extent is separation between *religion* and state required? At what point does an official religious invocation, reference, or exercise begin to seriously curb the secular nature of the state or hamper the Jeffersonian debate?

The free-exercise clause reflects an ongoing tension between the majority religious will and the individual religious conscience. At what point does government's accommodation to the prevailing religious culture violate the religious rights of deviant individuals?

There clearly is no absolute answer to either of these questions, and no blueprint that can be applied. The Supreme Court has said that this problem, "like many problems in constitutional law, is one of degree." Judge Learned Hand said that the canons of the First Amendment "are not jural concepts at all in the ordinary sense; and in application they turn out to be no more than admonitions of moderation."

There is, at the least, a constitutional *direction* in these admonitions. The old saw has it that a man is free to swing his fist up to the point of another man's nose—*not* that a man's nose has a right to be unbroken up to the point where it interferes with the swinging of another man's fist. At the least, the First Amendment prescription would hold that the religious culture can be expressed up to the point where the secular state is endangered; not that the secular state is to be maintained up to the point where it interferes with the prevailing religious culture. It would hold that the religious aspirations of the majority can be served up to the point where they interfere with the religious rights of an individual; not that the individual's religious rights are sacrosanct up to the point where they interfere with the religious aspirations of the majority. If a balance is to be struck between these tensions, it is to be struck within these directional limits.

Some hold that the only limits that are feasible are absolute limits which preclude any official state consideration of majority religious will or culture, and therefore eliminate the necessity of "balancing" these tensions at all. According to this view, the only safe way to safeguard the basic secular state and the religious rights of the individual is to operate a state which is stone blind to religion.

The practicality of such a course has been questioned, but further, it has been pointed out that the extension of such a "blindness" doctrine could finally serve to strip the majority of their "free exercise of religion." One of the functions of the democratic state, presumably, is to further the major aspirations of the population at large. If there is absolute separation of religion and state, beyond the limits required to guarantee a fundamentally secular state and the deviant religious conscience, then the majority's religious aspirations may be under certain circumstances unnecessarily curtailed. In 1962, when the U. S. Supreme Court found unconstitutional the recitation in public schools of a highly generalized prayer devised by the New York State Board of Regents on grounds that it violated the "establishment clause," one Justice dissented, saying: "I cannot see how an 'official religion' is established by letting those who want to say a prayer say it." The converse implication was that if the establishment clause was not being violated (and, of course, if no student was being forced to say the prayer), then the banishing of the prayer was a violation of the religious rights of those who did want to pray.

In other words, the tension between the secular state and the religious culture, as reflected in the establishment clause, was translated as a tension between the establishment clause and the free-exercise clause.

The Supreme Court has wrestled with these tensions and balances in a number of recent cases.

In two cases, the court ruled on "released-time" programs, whereby students who so desired were released from class an hour or two a week to attend religious classes under the auspices of their own church or synagogue. In 1948, the court ruled that such programs were unconstitutional when held on school grounds. In 1952, the court found that such programs were constitutional when held off of school grounds, since they only "accommodated to religious needs," even though some administrative assistance from the school system was involved. In 1962, the court ruled that the New York State Regents prayer was unconstitutional, even though students could be exempted upon request. In 1963, the court found that Bible-reading and the recitation of the Lord's Prayer in the schools were also unconstitutional.

These Supreme Court decisions have typically created a ferment of national excitement; indeed a ferment which the specific practices involved in these cases have not clearly warranted. Released-time programs provide an hour or two of "weekday Sunday school" to that small band— perhaps 5 per cent—of America's schoolchildren who elect it. Many communities have discontinued the program because of slim attendance. One prominent Protestant theologian, Reinhold Niebuhr, objected strenuously to the court's prohibition of the New York Regents prayer, but acknowledged: "I do not think religion in our culture will stand or fall by the presence or absence of the Regent's prayer . . ."[3] Bible-reading would also seem to be included in the admonition of another Protestant author, Edwin O. Miller, that "meaningful prayer takes place within an appropriate context, not as classroom routine along with the salute to the flag."[4] There is much evidence that biblical recitation or knowledge, by itself, without a deeper religious discussion and commitment, has limited religious effect. However, religious tokenism is a dull knife that cuts neither way. If religion is not seriously advanced by such shallow exercises, then neither is the secular state nor the deviant individual conscience seriously threatened by them.

There is always, of course, the "principle of the thing." If the integrity of a principle is violated under any circumstances, it is presumably weakened for all circumstances. It is the business of the Supreme Court to clarify these principles for their own sake. But the kind of public asperity which has surrounded these cases suggests that there is more at stake than an abstract debate on church-state relations. The legalistic welter tends to hide the fact that church-state questions, in addition to having their own intrinsic importance, are surrogates for more comprehensive issues actively stirring in American society: one reflecting a basic tension in America's political life; the other reflecting a basic tension in America's religious life.

The Political Issue: Populism vs. Constitutionalism

That aspect of the church-state debate which emphasizes majority will vs. minority rights reflects a recurrent and often critical tug between populist impulses and constitutional limitations. As defined generically by Edward A. Shils,

> populism proclaims that the will of the people as such is supreme over every other standard, over the standards of traditional institutions, over the autonomy of institutions and over the will of other strata. Populism identifies the will of the people with justice and morality.[5]

At its most extreme, populism can be used to simulate and pervert the democratic concept, as it has typically done in modern totalitarian societies. At its best, the populist tendency is a check against the use of constitutional forms to prevent social change. Populism is a highly volatile but necessary ingredient in modern social revolutions.

The American Revolution, more legal than social, did not start with a burst of populism, but the populist tendency has been a constant strand in American history. It has often been the case that widespread discontent has manifested itself in impatience with constitutional procedures. The Supreme Court as a final arbiter of constitutional limitations has frequently been the symbolic target of these frustrations. In the depth of the Great Depression, when the Supreme Court was ruling out a number of the economic measures of the New Deal, there was a strong populist move to evade the court by "packing it" with additional members.

Many of the current changes in American society and in the world have created some apparently insoluble problems and new veins of discontent and frustration, e.g.: The knotty interracial problems of both the North and the South, America's cramped style on the new international scene. More generally, from these and other problems related to the cities, the youth, and the economy, there has developed a widespread feeling that traditional controls are somehow irretrievably slipping away.

These frustrations have often drawn taut the natural tension between populist and constitutional tendencies in American life. Some of this tension has been conveniently displaced on church-state questions.

Southern legislators, still restive under the 1954 decision of the court ordering desegregation of the schools, were markedly vehement in their denunciation of the New York Regents prayer decision in 1962. "They put the Negroes in the schools and now they've driven God out of them," commented one representative from Alabama.[6] A senator from Georgia said: "For some years now the members of the Supreme Court have persisted in reading alien meanings into the Constitution. . . ."[7] A senator from Mississippi used the occasion to sponsor an amendment to the Constitution which would allow each state substantially to by-pass the Constitution in its enactment of legislation "based on its own public policy based on decency and morality."[8]

Other legislators had been frustrated by limitations which the court had placed on some subversive-control legislation. The chairman of the House Unamerican Activities Committee said about the New York Regents Prayer decision: "This is just one more decision in line with the philosophy guiding the group of men sitting there as justices of our court of last resort."[9] Among the thousands of organizational and individual expressions of dissatisfaction with the 1962 and 1963 Supreme Court decisions, there was a constant repetition of this theme as expressed in one public letter: "Don't the wishes of the majority in this country mean anything anymore?"[10]

The Religious Issue: The Search for Values

Religion, as traditionally conceived, was at low ebb at the country's birth. "The new nation," writes one church historian, "was a heathen nation."[11] It is estimated that in 1776 only about 5 per cent of the American people were church members. The churches were able to exert little influence. The mass of people were, at the least, religiously indifferent. Many of the Revolution's leaders and intellectuals, the Founding Fathers, were guilty of the "French infidelity"; an explicit rejection of revealed religion in favor of deism. None of the first four presidents of the United States belonged to a traditional church. George Washington, Thomas Jefferson, John Adams, and James Madison, as well as many other early American leaders were either deists or Unitarians.

The Constitutional Convention of 1777 made passing mention only of the "Great Governor of the World." The Declaration of Independence included such phrases as "the Supreme Judge of the World" and "Divine Providence." Thomas C. Hall commented that such documents were "as completely secular as the by-laws of an insurance company."[12] Thomas Paine expressed a widespread intellectual sentiment when he found "an adequate revelation of God in the constitution of nature." In his very first general order, George Washington instructed each of his men to "live and act as becomes a Christian soldier," but his context was a Christian civilization rather than a formal Christian religion. Insofar as the concepts of morality and God were separated from any commitment to revelation or theology, the "religion" that remained was by definition secularized.

Secularism is not, of course, a synonym for atheism. The term "secular" itself merely describes those aspects of man's life which are "of the world," finite, civil, nonecclesiastical. Secularism denotes the relative ascendancy of secular institutions over religious institutions, or, the ascendancy of secular considerations over sacred considerations. Even at its more aggressive, secularism does not necessarily deny the existence of God, although it does tend to hold that man rather than God is the measure of social behavior.

In fact, religious tendencies and secularist tendencies have flourished side by side in America. By 1850, more than 15 per cent of the American people were church-affiliated; by 1900 more than a third of the American people were affiliated. By 1963, when there seemed to be a "leveling off," two thirds of the nation were affiliated. History had never recorded such a spectacular religious growth. The United States now led the world in voluntary church membership.

But religious life had changed character as it grew. The growth had been characterized in the nineteenth century by a series of great revival movements which swept the country. These were missionary movements, in effect, and addressed in large part to America's rapidly moving frontiers. But they were also shaped by the nature and needs of these frontiers. Traditional forms of organization, ritual, and theological dogma were de-emphasized. Personal religious experience was emphasized. The over-all effect of this frontier experience was to generalize the mainstream of American religion. Religious complexities gave way to common denominators.

Traditional religious doctrine was further eroded by a latter-day mood of naturalism, pragmatism, and secular optimism which accompanied the phenomenal growth of science, industry, and wealth. One

American theologian said: "The new theology seeks to recover spiritual processes from the magical to a moral conception."[13] Another said: "A valid Christianity is to be known not by its roots but by its fruits."[14]

Religion had become part of the American Way of Life, its institutions and rhetoric flourished, but it had itself become secularized. Religion was now often primarily measured by its ability to contribute to the strength of secular life, to democracy, to social well-being. The relationship between man's religious beliefs and his social behavior had been reversed, or at the least, severed in a new version of the French Infidelity.

In various polls, about 96 per cent of the American people say they believe in God, but about 80 per cent indicate that they are more concerned about a comfortable life on earth rather than about any other-worldly considerations, and 54 per cent admit that their religious beliefs do not have any effect on the way they conduct their daily business. Gerhard Lenski's study of religious life in Detroit concluded that at least among Protestants, "despite attending the churches more frequently, their thoughts and values are less often derived from distinctly religious sources and more often derived from secular sources."[15]

Religious leaders worry about the disparity between religious affiliation and religious commitment. They also worry about an American society without religious commitment. According to Rabbi Abraham Joshua Heschel:

> The central problem of this generation is emptiness in the heart, the decreased sensitivity to the imponderable quality of the spirit, the collapse of communication between the realm of tradition and the inner world of the individual.[16]

Many theologians warn that secular moral habits and humanistic values do not automatically replenish themselves and that

> the faith upon which these values were based no longer animate many of those who profess the values. . . . [The values] depend for their propulsion upon sources of power beyond themselves and beyond their own culture.[17]

But there is more involved than a religious-secular tension about sources of value. As American society seems to linger in a kind of limbo between its past and its future, there is a tension between the old and the new. The sociologists worry about the "value-vacuum" in an America in limbo, and point to a rise in a variety of social and personal pathologies. This sense of a loss of values is expressed in less theoretical terms by various sections of the population, many of whom see the religious tradition of America, however secularized it may have become, as symbolic of

America's past, of values lost. And there is no doubt that America's history is intertwined with religious tradition and rhetoric.

President Eisenhower said: "You cannot otherwise explain our government except on the basis of a deeply felt religious faith." And the U. S. Supreme Court has held that "we are a religious people whose institutions presuppose a Supreme Being." There is surely built into the American culture a pervasive "faith in faith," an affinity for religious traditions and institutions.

There are then two levels of conflict: a genuine religious-secular tension and a simulated religious-secular tension, really a tug between traditional America as identified by its religion-culture, and a plastic new America. These concerns and tensions have clearly intruded themselves into the debate on church-state issues.

Evangelist Billy Graham stated about the 1962 Supreme Court decision: "The decision is another step towards secularism . . ."[18] Cardinal Spellman called it another example of the secularists' aim "to strip America of all her religious tradition."[19] In Pittsburgh the Episcopal bishop and the Catholic bishop issued a joint statement attacking the "powerful, aggressive spirit of secularism." And one Protestant theologian who acknowledged that the Regents Prayer was not of much religious value in itself was nevertheless concerned with it as "a symbol of the religious life and tradition of the nation."[20]

These are, to some degree, irrelevant intrusions. The principle of the secular state, for example, is itself essentially a political principle, neither religious nor irreligious. But "church-state questions," under the pressure of these other tensions in American life, cannot be understood or perhaps dealt with forever in a legalistic vacuum. If "balances" are to be struck, they will be struck under these pressures. Nor are the constitutional limitations themselves immutable.

Notes

1) H. A. Washington, editor, *Jefferson Writings* (New York: 1853-4), Vol. V, p. 471.
2) Philip S. Foner, *Basic Writings of Thomas Jefferson* (Garden City, N.Y.: Halcyon House, 1944), p. 49.
3) Quoted in "Religious Reactions to the Regent's Prayer Decision," *Interreligious Newsletter* (New York: Anti-Defamation League).
4) *Ibid.*
5) Edward A. Shils, *The Torment of Secrecy* (Glencoe, Illinois: The Free Press, 1956), p. 98.

6) Representative George Andrews, quoted in the New York *Herald Tribune*, June 26, 1962.
7) Senator Henry Talmadge quoted in "The Supreme Court and the Regents' Prayer, The Dialogue" (New York: National Conference of Christians and Jews, 1962).
8) Senator James O. Eastland, *ibid*.
9) Representative Francis E. Walter, *ibid*.
10) From Letters to the Editor, New York *Daily News*, June 29, 1962.
11) This theme runs through Franklin Hamlin Littell, *From State Church to Pluralism* (Garden City, N.Y.: Doubleday Anchor Books, 1962).
12) Thomas C. Hall, *The Religious Background of American Culture* (New York: Frederick Ungar Publishing Co., 1930), p. 169.
13) From Theodore Munger, *Essays for the Day* (Boston: Houghton Mifflin, 1904), p. 7.
14) Charles D. Williams, *A Valid Christianity for Today* (New York: Macmillan Co., 1909), pp. vii–viii.
15) See Gerhard Lenski, "The Four Socio-Religious Groups," in *Religious Conflict in America*, Earl Raab, ed. (Garden City, N.Y.: Doubleday, 1964), pp. 29–49.
16) Abraham Joshua Heschel, "The Religious Message," in *Religion in America*, John Cogley, ed. (New York: Meridian, 1958), p. 256.
17) See Jaroslav Pelikan, "Religious Responsibility for the Social Order," *Religious Conflict in America*, Earl Raab, ed. (Garden City, N.Y.: Doubleday, 1964), pp. 126–137.
18) New York *Herald Tribune*, June 28, 1962.
19) *Ibid*.
20) Reinhold Niebuhr, *Interreligious Newsletter*, July 9, 1962.

to establish

The task of defining "justice" requires specifying what should be the consequences of committing a given act or of possessing a given characteristic. It is the problem of deciding which acts or characteristics are to be rewarded, which punished, and which ignored; the task, for example, of specifying whether going to college is just ground for a draft deferment.[1] Establishing justice is basically a problem of insuring that what should happen does happen: the problem of insuring that the specified consequences actually follow a given act or accrue to those with a given quality. In more colloquial terms, justice is done when a person gets precisely what is coming to him because of what he has done and of what he is: when virtue and the virtuous are rewarded and evil and the malicious punished.

The definition and establishment of justice are, of course, matters involving lawmaking and law enforcement. Justice may be defined, however, by informal and unwritten codes embodied in a society's customs and mores as well as by formal and written laws. The discussion, therefore, of problems of defining justice contained in the first section of

[1] The question of draft deferments for college youths will be raised in Merriam H. Trytten's article in Chapter Five, where the issue is not the justice of such deferments but their effect on the national interest. That article is concerned with the question of whether the national interest is better served by fostering preparation for contributions in the future or by requiring service to meet immediate dangers.

Justice . . .

this introduction deals with both legal and nonlegal aspects of the meaning of "justice." Similarly, the discussion presented in the second section treats, but is not confined to, the role of law enforcement in determining whether or not justice is done.

What Is Justice?

An agreement on whether or not justice is being done in a given instance is possible only if there is agreement on three issues. First, there must be a common evaluation of the act in question in terms of how good or bad, important or unimportant, it is. Second, there must be agreement that the consequences accruing to a person for his deeds are of a kind and quantity that all think appropriate. Third, there must be agreement that relevant personal characteristics and background factors are being given proper consideration.

Consider, for example, whether or not a person is getting his just rewards at work. There must first be agreement on how well he is doing his job and on how important that job is. (In general, the better the performance and the more important the job, the more one can justly demand.) Second, there must be agreement as to whether only monetary rewards are to be considered or if prestige and personal satisfaction should also be forthcoming. Third, there must be agreement on such questions as whether married men should receive more than bachelors, or ex-criminals as much as those without a record. The present American income tax system, for example, favors married men over bachelors, while ex-criminals may find they cannot get a job unless they accept lower wages than a man with no record.[2] Either or both of these practices may be regarded as a just or unjust treatment of individuals with certain characteristics or background. While agreement on all three issues is necessary if there is to be agreement that justice has been done, the absence of such agreement is not at all uncommon.

Americans often disagree on whether or not justice has been done in a given situation because they disagree on how to evaluate specific acts. For example, laws and moral standards vary greatly with respect to gambling, drinking, and specific sexual practices. There are sweepstakes in New Hampshire and gambling casinos in Nevada; yet off-track betting is generally illegal and some people frown on a poker game at home. There are dry counties and counties in which liquor can be sold to eighteen-year-olds. In some circles, premarital sexual relations and contraception are permitted, if not encouraged; in others, they are regarded as mortal sins.[3] A member of the Playboy set and a religious fundamentalist are not apt to agree on whether a given act is good or bad.

Another area of disagreement is the evaluation of such practices as homosexuality and drug addiction. Some people regard such practices as criminal; others view them as signs of illness. A third group contends that homosexuality and addiction are not necessarily either crimes or signs of illness. They suggest that such practices should only be regarded as bad if done in excess or with consequences detrimental to people involuntarily involved.[4]

Americans who agree on whether a given act is good or bad may differ on what the just consequences of that act should be. They may have different solutions to the problem of fitting the punishment to the crime. One may ask, as Jackson Toby does in "Is Punishment Necessary?," just what is to be gained by punishing wrongdoers. Assuming

[2] Richard D. Schwartz and Jerome H. Skolnick discuss prejudices against hiring ex-criminals in "Two Studies of Legal Stigma," *Social Problems*, X (April, 1962), 133–147.
[3] Recent changes in American sexual mores are discussed in Ira L. Reiss (ed.), "The Sexual Renaissance in America," *Journal of Social Issues*, XXII (April, 1966), 1–137.
[4] See Edwin M. Schur, *Crimes Without Victims* (Englewood Cliffs, N.J.: Prentice-Hall, 1965), which discusses abortion as well as homosexuality and drug addiction, and William Petersen and David Matza (eds.), *Social Controversy* (Belmont, Cal.: Wadsworth, 1963), pp. 125–155, which discusses the pros and cons of legalizing homosexual acts.

punishment is warranted, one may ask what is to be the balance between retribution and rehabilitation, between seeing to it that one pays for his crimes and helping him to return to society.[5] In a related vein, there is debate over what punishments are to be regarded as so cruel and unusual as to be unfit for any crime. Some people and groups argue that the death penalty, like flogging and being placed in stocks, should never be used as punishment for a crime. Eleven states have eliminated the death penalty: Alaska, Hawaii, Iowa, Maine, Michigan, Minnesota, North Dakota, Oregon, Rhode Island, West Virginia, and Wisconsin.[6]

Debate over the just consequences of an act or characteristic may refer to rewards as well as to punishments. The justice of the distribution of salaries and other monetary incomes may be questioned. For example, the justice of having a leading athlete receive a salary higher than that of the President may be examined; the justice of a society in which a popular singer receives more money in a week than a teacher does in a year may be questioned. Not all rewards, of course, come in the form of money or even as material goods. Inequalities in the distribution of money and goods may be justly compensated for by differences in the degree of prestige, status, happiness, security, and opportunity for personal development or service received.

The third aspect of the problem of defining "justice" is the specification of the role of a person's characteristics and background. American society, for example, uses different rules for the treatment of different age groups: many people are required to retire at a given age regardless of their present capabilities; seniority alone may guarantee a promotion which would otherwise have gone to a more qualified, but younger, person; a juvenile lawbreaker may not receive the same sentence as an adult, even if the crime is the same. For some, treating juvenile offenders more leniently than adult offenders is a sign of coddling. Others are dismayed by the fact that youths have not always been provided the same guarantees of civil liberties given adults.[7] Whether the concern is cod-

[5] For a discussion of the American penal system, see Louis B. Schwartz (ed.), "Crime and the American Penal System," *Annals of the American Academy of Political and Social Science*, CCCXXXIX (January, 1962), 1–170; and Hans W. Mattick (ed.), "The Future of Imprisonment in a Free Society," *Key Issues: A Journal of Controversial Issues in Criminology*, II (1965), 4–12.

[6] *The World Almanac and Book of Facts* (New York: World-Telegram and the Sun, 1966), p. 398. The death penalty is discussed in Hugo Adam Bedau (ed.), *The Death Penalty in America* (Garden City, N.Y.: Doubleday Anchor, 1964); and in Thorsten Sellin, *Capital Punishment* (New York: Harper & Row, 1967, forthcoming).

[7] The Supreme Court has supported those who protested the denial of civil liberties to youths appearing in Juvenile Court. In the Matter of Gault, the Court ruled, in the words of Judge Fortas, "Neither the Fourteenth Amendment nor the

dling or civil liberties, the underlying debate is over the role of age in the definition of justice.

Race is another characteristic which occasions serious debate over what constitutes justice. Even those who can agree that "all men are created equal" may argue over whether or not de facto segregation, on the one hand, or the preferential hiring of Negroes, on the other, are examples of injustice. To some extent, the notion of different codes of justice for blacks and whites has been rejected by American society. All three branches of the federal government, and many states, have indicated that race is no longer to be viewed as a legitimate reason for treating otherwise similar people differently. Nevertheless, the place of race in the American conception of justice is still far from a settled issue. For some, the establishment of racial equality and integration takes precedence over most, if not all, other considerations. Such people hold a conception of justice that requires their support of the movement of a Negro into their previously all-white neighborhood. Others, however, may feel justified in opposing such a move, although their grounds may be fear of economic loss rather than simple prejudice. Similarly, some people feel it is just to bus students to schools outside their neighborhood in order to overcome de facto segregation, while others feel the preservation of the concept of the neighborhood school should take precedence over racial integration in deciding what is a just and proper educational policy.[8]

Sex is also a factor in defining what is just, even though we no longer argue over the "mixing" of the sexes in our schools and despite the fact that women can vote and hold political office. Although Americans may no longer believe that a "woman's place is in the kitchen," they generally prefer women to stress family life more than a career in business. Some means that would enable women more easily to combine family life with occupational endeavors, thereby increasing the equality of the sexes, are discussed in "Institutional Levers for Achieving Sex Equality" by Alice Rossi.

Not all of the personal characteristics that are taken into account have a biological component as do sex, age, and race. Whether a person is mentally ill or not is an important, generally nonbiological, factor. For most of its history, the United States has been satisfied to use the M'Naghten rule in determining whether a person is insane. Under this

---

Bill of Rights are for adults only;" and that "under our Constitution, the condition of being a boy does not justify a kangaroo court." *The New York Times*, May 15, 1967. See Petersen and Matza, *op. cit.*, pp. 107–125 for a further discussion of Juvenile Courts.

[8] See J. Michael Ross, Thomas Crawford, and Thomas Pettigrew, "Negro Neighbors—Banned in Boston," *Trans-action*, III (September–October, 1966), 13–18.

rule, a person can be acquitted on grounds of mental incompetence only if it can be proven that as a result of mental illness the accused did not "know the nature and quality of the act he was doing, or, if he did know it, that he did not know what he was doing was wrong." More recently, some states and some federal courts have added the Durham or "irresistible impulse" rule to the M'Naghten criteria.[9] The "irresistible impulse" rule permits acquittal if it can be shown that the defendant could not control his conduct while committing the crime even though he knew it to be wrong.

Occupation is another nonbiological factor that may be considered in determining the just consequences of one's actions. A priest, lawyer, or doctor may refuse to give a court information given to him in confidence. Such refusal would generally result in a fine for contempt of court. Similarly, many people would object to the punishment of a policeman, soldier, or executioner who killed a person in the performance of his duty.

A person's background may also be relevant. A third-time offender is often treated more harshly than a first offender. A history of deprivation and poverty may entitle a person to special treatment. A youth who is poorly educated because he comes from a culturally deprived area with bad schools could conceivably be entitled to a second chance not given a middle-class youth.

The determination of whether or not justice has been done is not solely a matter of distinguishing good acts from bad and rewarding or punishing a person accordingly. A person's background and characteristics may have to be considered as well.

The Establishment of Justice

This section discusses two different sets of problems encountered in the process of establishing justice in American society. The first set is encountered when attempting to establish justice through a system of laws and law enforcement. The second set is involved in implementing that part of the American Dream which defines a just society as one in which the degree of a person's success or failure reflects the extent to

[9] The M'Naghten rule and other issues in defining responsibility for criminal acts are discussed by Herbert Wechsler, "Culpability and Crime: The Treatment of *Mens Rea* in the Model Penal Code," *Annals of the American Academy of Political and Social Science*, CCCXXXIX (January, 1962), 25–41. An attempt to obtain empirical evidence on how juries apply the M'Naghten and Durham rules is found in Rita James Simon, *The American Jury: The Defense of Insanity* (Boston: Little, Brown, 1967).

which he has made achievements through the development and use of his natural talents.

The process of establishing justice through a system of laws and law enforcement consists of four basic steps: (1) the passage of just laws; (2) the gathering of information as to whether a person has or has not followed the law; (3) the evaluation of the information gathered and the determination of what the consequences are to be; and (4) the enforcement of that determination.[10]

The passage of just laws is the first step in the establishment of a system of justice. The injustices perpetrated on the German people by the lawful actions of the Nazi regime are perhaps the most striking example of legalized injustice. More recently, the United States Supreme Court has indicated that many of the laws that supported segregation in the South are unjust. Disagreement over the meaning of justice, as discussed in the previous section, can lead to disagreements over whether a given law is just or not. Those, for example, who disapprove of pre-marital sexual intercourse may regard laws penalizing those who engage in it as perfectly just; those who approve of such intercourse may regard such laws as unjust. Moreover, disagreements over the justness of a law can lead to questions of the propriety of applying a code to somebody who rejects it. Where definitions of justice differ, it is sometimes difficult to distinguish proper law enforcement from unwarranted harassment. Many Southerners, for example, feel harassed by the enforcement of laws which implement the Supreme Court's decisions overruling the legal supports of segregation.

The second step in establishing justice through law is the gathering of information as to whether the law has been broken. In the case of a police investigation of a crime, the information gathering process may be hampered when what is defined as illegal is regarded as desirable by the so-called victims. The buying of liquor during Prohibition is a classic illustration of such a case. The transactions involved in prostitution, gambling, homosexuality, drug addiction, and abortion are generally of this type.[11] Where so-called victims are willing or eager partners in the act, it is very difficult, if not impossible, to get them to cooperate with law enforcement agents. Helping to convict their partners in the illegal transaction will only make it more difficult to repeat the transactions

---

[10] For other discussions of the problems of establishing justice through law and law enforcement, see Talcott Parsons, "The Law and Social Control," in William M. Evan (ed.), *Law and Sociology: Exploratory Essays* (New York: Free Press, 1962), pp. 56–72; and William M. Evan, "Public and Private Legal Systems," in Evan, *op. cit.*, pp. 165–184.

[11] See Schur, *op. cit.*

should they want to do so. Quite a different situation exists, of course, in cases of theft or even discrimination, where the victim is an unwilling party and may sometimes take strenuous efforts to ensure that justice is done.

The gathering of information concerning crimes may also be hampered by the rules of due process of law, as the reading "The Revolution in Criminal Justice," from *Time* notes. The police, for example, may find that by the time they have obtained the necessary search warrant, the evidence they sought has been destroyed. Moreover, evidence which has been gathered may be unusable in court since the rules of due process were violated in obtaining it. Even the most obviously guilty criminal must be freed if the evidence which proves his guilt is barred from court. In recent years, much controversy has centered on the question of whether wiretapping and other modern "bugging" devices represent an unwarranted invasion of privacy and an erosion of the constitutional protections against self-incrimination, and therefore an unacceptable, even if more efficient, means of collecting useful information.

Whatever the information eventually gathered, the next step in the process of establishing justice is that of evaluating the information and judging what the just consequences are. In many instances, the first interpretations and judgments are made by the police. They simply do not arrest everybody they have reason to believe has committed a crime. "Police Discretion" by Sanford H. Kadish discusses some of the basic reasons and factors that guide the discretionary use of the policeman's power to arrest.[12] These reasons include the policeman's belief that the law was not really intended to cover the act in question. He may, for example, decide that while gambling laws are broad enough to cover playing poker at home, they were not intended to make it illegal to do so. The policeman may decide not to make an arrest when he feels justice can best be served otherwise. He may decide that replacing a stolen item or paying cash after attempting to pass a bad check will suffice and that formal charges need not be made.

The decision to make or not make an arrest may also depend, as Irving Piliavin and Scott Briar note in "Police Encounters with Juveniles," on the policeman's evaluation of the suspect's background and criminal potential. Such judgments are more common when dealing with the offenses of juveniles than with adults, and tend to reflect the biases of the community in which the police operate and the influence of their

[12] For further discussions of police practices, see Jerome H. Skolnick, *Justice Without Trial* (New York: Wiley, 1966); and David J. Bordua, *The Police* (New York: Wiley, 1966).

own experiences on the force. In any event, the possibility exists that innocent youths will be harassed more than is just, because the police believe they are potential criminals and that some guilty youths will go unpunished because the police believe they are not likely to become adult offenders.

Where there are disagreements concerning the use of discretionary powers by law enforcement officials, justice may require the creation of a means for appealing their decisions and for reversing their judgments. Thus, the decisions of one court may be appealed to a higher court which is empowered to reverse the original judgment. Appeals systems are one protection against the arbitrary or mistaken use of discretionary power. However, where the decision in question is that of whether or not to use force in making an arrest, the power of appeal may be meaningless. One cannot reverse a policeman's decision to shoot and kill an escaping suspect. However, it may be possible to deter the arbitrary and mistaken use of force through the punishment of those who misuse their power. A board to review the actions of the police and to investigate complaints of "police brutality" may deter the misuse of powers if it is empowered to punish those found guilty of misusing their power.[13]

Once the police have made their arrest and formal charges are filed, the next step is to decide what the just consequences of the act in question are. Such decisions are made in court either by a judge or a jury. The latter system has been criticized by those who question the competence of a jury compared to that of a trained, disciplined, and experienced judge. The jury system, they claim, will not mete out justice as well as trial by judge, even if the jury understands and approves of the law, because the jury is unlikely to have the training, discipline, and experience to wisely and justly apply the law.[14]

Whether the decision is to be made by judge or jury, the American system of law assumes that the merits of the case can be most adequately presented and the truth most fairly arrived at if the parties involved are represented by able lawyers seeking their clients' interests. If poverty deprives a person of an able and interested lawyer, his case may be poorly argued and an unjust verdict reached. This and other problems of providing legal aid for the poor are discussed in "Legal Representation and Class Justice" by Jerome E. Carlin and Jan Howard.

Once a decision has been made, whether by judge or jury, with

[13] See Walter Gellhorn, "Police Review Boards: Hoax or Hope?" *Columbia University Forum*, IX (Summer, 1966), 5–10.

[14] This and other criticisms of the jury system are discussed in Harry Kalven, Jr., and Hans Zeisel, *The American Jury* (Boston: Little, Brown, 1966), pp. 3–11.

adequate legal arguments or without, the next step toward justice by law can be taken—the implementation of the judicial decision. One problem that may be encountered at this juncture is that of providing the facilities for carrying out the decision. A sentence to a term in prison cannot be implemented if the state has not built enough prisons to hold its convicted criminals. Thus, a massive campaign of civil disobedience or even rioting may result in many arrests, but few trials. In general, the ability of society to punish a few assumes it will not have to punish the many. The just implementing of sentences also assumes that no more than the legal punishment is meted out, and, of course, that punishment is not meted out when there is a decision to acquit. However, such is not always the case because of the working of the American bail-bond system.

The size of bail is generally governed by the nature of the suspected crime rather than the nature of the accused. Thus, a bond may be set for a given crime which is excessive for a poor man but "chicken feed" for a rich person. In such cases, the rich man is set free until the trial while the poor man spends time in jail. Should the poor man be found guilty, he may not be given "credit" for time spent in jail before the trial and thus his total time in prison may exceed his sentence. Should he be found innocent, then he has spent time in jail for a crime he did not commit.[15]

Justice may, then, be established by a system of law: (1) if the laws themselves are just; (2) if there is an adequate system of gathering information to determine who does not follow the laws; (3) if this information is properly evaluated and just decisions are made on the basis of it; and (4) if the decisions are justly implemented. Such a legal system, however, does not solve all the problems of establishing justice because the laws alone do not cover all possible instances in which the question of justice arises. For example, the problem of establishing justice as defined by the American Dream is primarily a social and economic matter and only secondarily a legal one.

The American Dream suggests that justice prevails when a person's success or failure is the result of the use and development of his natural talents. Within this view, luck and other factors beyond the individual's control do not, if justice prevails, affect his success to any important degree. If they do, then special treatment, not given to others, may be given an individual on grounds of need rather than achievement. Imple-

15 For further discussion of the bail system and alternatives to it, see Daniel J. Freed and Patricia M. Wald, *Bail in the United States: 1964* (New York: The Vera Foundation, 1964); *Proceedings and Interim Report of the National Conference on Bail and Criminal Justice* (New York: The Vera Foundation, 1964); and Ronald Goldfarb, *Ransom: A Critique of the American Bail System* (New York: Harper & Row, 1965).

menting such a concept of justice calls for the determination of how much of an individual's failure is due to factors which are beyond his control and how much results from his own decisions and efforts. Thus, some Americans consider it just to make allowances for accidents of birth such as blindness or mental retardation, but do not consider an unhappy childhood an excuse for failure in adult life. They note that some people succeed despite such obstacles and see no justice in excusing such failures. Others are willing to make allowances for early experiences such as living in a deprived area or going to bad schools, but hold all adults responsible for what happens to them. That is, they would regard special training or compensation for youths as just, but not allowances for adults who become unemployed because of technological change, depressions, or other changes in society. Adults, they would contend, can justly be expected to fend for themselves, any failure to do so revealing their own faults and not society's.

The American Dream is also the dream of an open-class society; a society in which every person starts out on essentially equal terms. The implementation of this aspect of the Dream implies that the disadvantages of being born into poverty should not be a permanent handicap. An open-class society, however, is also one in which the advantages of being born into a wealthy family are controlled. For example, two young men with equal ability and desire, but whose families have widely different incomes, would in an open-class society have approximately equal chances of going to college. If it is unjust for a poor boy to lose a chance for a higher education solely because his family lacks the necessary funds, it is also unjust for the son of a wealthy family to be admitted simply because his relatives sit on the college's board of trustees. Yet as long as the dignity and sanctity of the family are maintained, it will be difficult to prevent the advantages or disadvantages of family background from being key factors in determining one's access to the rewards America has to offer. Intelligent, informed, and interested parents will generally raise children who have an advantage over others in their generation. The transmission of the knowledge and skills that parents have as a result of their position in society may well be the most important inheritance any family has to offer.[16]

[16] A number of studies have come to the conclusion that a child is apt to have the same general occupational position as his father. See Richard Centers, *The Psychology of Social Classes* (Princeton, N.J.: Princeton University Press, 1949); Seymour M. Lipset and Reinhard Bendix, *Social Mobility in an Industrial Society* (Berkeley: University of California Press, 1959); Albert J. Reiss, Jr., "Occupational Mobility of Professional Workers," *American Sociological Review*, XX (1955), 693–700.

Further, an open-class society is generally regarded as one in which access to food, clothing, shelter, and luxuries is determined by financial resources only. However, when racial prejudice is as prevalent as it is in the United States, those who sell food, clothing, and shelter may prefer not to deal with Negroes. It is just, they believe, for a person to do with his property as he wishes even if he wishes to discriminate on racial grounds. In such instances the conceptions of property rights and the commitment to equal opportunities for men of all races clash. The administration of justice in the United States then requires that the priorities of the property rights of the owner and the rights of the potential consumer be clarified.

In sum, while Americans may believe that "all men are created equal," they also recognize that what one does and what one is soon makes each person unique. The problems of establishing justice are mainly those of specifying how life, liberty, and happiness are to be related to one's unique acts, talents, and background, and of insuring that the specified relationship among them becomes a reality.

Is Punishment Necessary?

Jackson Toby

Of eleven contemporary textbooks in criminology written by sociologists, ten have one or more chapters devoted to the punishment of offenders.[1] All ten include a history of methods of punishment in Western society and, more specifically, a discussion of capital punishment. Seven discuss punishment in pre-literate societies. Seven include theoretical or philosophical discussions of the "justification" of punishment —usually in terms of "retribution," "deterrence," and "reformation." These theoretical analyses are at least as much indebted to law and philosophy as to sociology. Thus, in considering the basis for punishment, three textbooks refer both to Jeremy Bentham and to Emile Durkheim; three textbooks refer to Bentham but not to Durkheim; and one textbook refers to Durkheim but not to Bentham. Several textbook writers express their opposition to punishment, especially to cruel punishment. This opposition is alleged to be based on an incompatibility of punishment with scientific considerations. The following quotation is a case in point:

> We still punish primarily for vengeance, or to deter, or in the interest of a "just" balance of accounts between "deliberate" evildoers on the one hand and an injured and enraged society on the other. We do not yet generally punish or treat as scientific criminology would imply, namely, in order to change antisocial attitudes into social attitudes.[2]

Most of the textbook writers note with satisfaction that "the trend in modern countries has been toward humanizing punishment and toward the reduction of brutalities."[3] They point to the decreased use of capital punishment, the introduction of amenities into the modern prison by enlightened penology, and the increasing emphasis on nonpunitive and individualized methods of dealing with offenders, e.g., probation, parole, psychotherapy. In short, students reading these textbooks might infer that punishment is a vestigial carryover of a barbaric past and will disappear as humanitarianism and rationality spread. Let us examine this inference in terms of the motives underlying punishment and the necessities of social control.

The Urge to Punish

Many crimes have identifiable victims. In the case of crimes against the person, physical or psychic injuries have been visited upon the victim. In the case of crimes against property, someone's property has been stolen or destroyed. In pressing charges against the offender, the victim may express hostility against the person who injured him in a socially acceptable way. Those who identify with the victim—not only his friends and family but those who can imagine the same injury being done to them— may join with him in clamoring for the punishment of the offender. If, as has been argued, the norm of reciprocity is fundamental to human interaction, this hostility of the victim constituency toward offenders is an obstacle to the elimination of punishment from social life.[4] Of course, the size of the group constituted by victims and those who identify with victims may be small. Empirical study would probably show that it varies by offense. Thus, it is possible that nearly everyone identifies with the victim of a murderer but relatively few people with the victim of a blackmailer. The greater the size of the victim constituency, the greater the opposition to a nonpunitive reaction to the offender.

It would be interesting indeed to measure the size and the composition of the victim constituencies for various crimes. Take rape as an illustration. Since the victims of rape are females, we might hypothesize that *women* would express greater punitiveness toward rapists than *men* and that degrees of hostility would correspond to real or imaginary exposure to rape. Thus, pretty young girls might express more punitiveness toward rapists than homely women. Among males, we might predict the greater punitiveness would be expressed by those with more reason to identify with the victims. Thus, males having sisters or daughters in the late teens or early twenties might express more punitiveness toward rapists than males lacking vulnerable "hostages to fortune."

Such a study might throw considerable light on the wellsprings of punitive motivation, particularly if victimization reactions were distinguished from other reasons for punitiveness. One way to explore such motivation would be to ask the same respondents to express their punitive predispositions toward offenses which do not involve victims at all, e.g., gambling, or which involve victims of a quite different kind. Thus, rape might be balanced by an offense the victims of which are largely male. Survey research of this type is capable of ascertaining the opposition to milder penalties for various offenses. It would incidentally throw light on the comparatively gentle societal reaction to white-collar crime. Perhaps the explanation lies in the difficulty of identifying with the victims of patent infringement or watered hams.[5]

The Social Control Functions of Punishment

Conformists who identify with the *victim* are motivated to punish the offender out of some combination of rage and fear. Conformists who identify with the *offender*, albeit unconsciously, may wish to punish him for quite different reasons. Whatever the basis for the motivation to punish, the existence of punitive reactions to deviance is an obstacle to the abolition of punishment. However, it is by no means the sole obstacle. Even though a negligible segment of society felt punitive toward offenders, it might still not be feasible to eliminate punishment if the social control of deviance depended on it. Let us consider, therefore, the consequences of punishing offenders for (a) preventing crime, (b) sustaining the morale of conformists, and (c) rehabilitating offenders.

PUNISHMENT AS A MEANS OF CRIME PREVENTION

Durkheim defined punishment as an act of vengeance. "What we avenge, what the criminal expiates, is the outrage to morality."[6] But why is vengeance necessary? Not because of the need to deter the bulk of the population from doing likewise. The socialization process prevents most deviant behavior. Those who have introjected the moral norms of their society cannot commit crimes because their self-concepts will not permit them to do so. Only the unsocialized (and therefore amoral) individual fits the model of classical criminology and is deterred from expressing deviant impulses by a nice calculation of pleasures and punishments.[7] Other things being equal, the anticipation of punishment would seem to have more deterrent value for inadequately socialized members of the group. It is difficult to investigate this proposition empirically because other motivationally relevant factors are usually varying simultaneously, e.g., the situational temptations confronting various individuals, their optimism about the chances of escaping detection, and the differential impact of the same punishment on individuals of different status.[8]

Clearly, though, the deterrent effect of anticipated punishments is a complex empirical problem, and Durkheim was not interested in it. Feeling as he did that *some* crime is normal in every society, he apparently decided that the crime prevention function of punishment is not crucial. He pointed out that minute gradation in punishment would not be necessary if punishment were simply a means of deterring the potential offender (crime prevention). "Robbers are as strongly inclined to rob as murderers are to murder; the resistance offered by the former is not less than that of the latter, and consequently, to control it, we would have recourse to the same means."[9] Durkheim was factually correct; the offenses punished most severely are not necessarily the ones which present the greatest problem of social defense. Thus, quantitatively speaking, murder is an unimportant cause of death; in the United States it claims only half as many lives annually as does suicide and only one-fifth the toll of automobile accidents. Furthermore, criminologists have been unable to demonstrate a relationship between the murder rate of a community and its use or lack of use of capital punishment.

Most contemporary sociologists would agree with Durkheim that the anticipation of punishment is not the first line of defense against crime. The socialization process keeps most people law abiding, not the police—if for no other reason than the police are not able to catch every offender. This does not mean, however, that the police could be disbanded. During World War II, the Nazis deported all of Denmark's police force, thus providing a natural experiment testing the deterrent efficacy of formal sanctions.[10] Crime increased greatly. Even though punishment is uncertain, especially under contemporary urban conditions, the possibility of punishment keeps some conformists law abiding. The empirical question is: *How many* conformists would become deviants if they did not fear punishment?

PUNISHMENT AS A MEANS OF SUSTAINING THE MORALE OF CONFORMISTS

Durkheim considered punishment indispensable as a means of containing the demoralizing consequences of the crimes that could not be prevented. Punishment was not for Durkheim mere vindictiveness. Without punishment Durkheim anticipated the demoralization of "upright people" in the face of defiance of the collective conscience. He believed that unpunished deviance tends to demoralize the conformist and therefore he talked about punishment as a means of repairing "the wounds made upon collective sentiments."[11] Durkheim was not entirely clear; he expressed his ideas in metaphorical language. Nonetheless, we can identify the hypothesis that the punishment of offenders promotes the solidarity of conformists.

Durkheim anticipated psychoanalytic thinking as the following reformulation of his argument shows: One who resists the temptation to do what the group prohibits, to drive his car at 80 miles per hour, to beat up an enemy, to take what he wants without paying for it, would like to feel that these self-imposed abnegations have some meaning. When he sees others defy rules without untoward consequences, he needs some reassurance that his sacrifices were made in a good cause. If "the good die young and the wicked flourish as the green bay tree," the moral scruples which enable conformists to restrain their own deviant inclinations lack social validation. The social significance of punishing offenders is that deviance is thereby defined as unsuccessful in the eyes of conformists, thus making the inhibition or repression of their own deviant impulses seem worthwhile. Righteous indignation is collectively sanctioned reaction formation. The law-abiding person who unconsciously resents restraining his desire to steal and murder has an opportunity, by identifying with the police and the courts, to affect the precarious balance within his own personality between internal controls and the temptation to deviate. A bizarre example of this psychological mechanism is the man who seeks out homosexuals and beats them up mercilessly. Such pathological hostility toward homosexuals is due to the sadist's anxiety over his own sex-role identification. By "punishing" the homosexual, he denies the latent homosexuality in his own psyche. No doubt, some of the persons involved in the administration of punishment are sadistically motivated. But Durkheim hypothesized that the psychic equilibrium of the *ordinary* member of the group may be threatened by violation of norms; Durkheim was not concerned about psychopathological punitiveness.

Whatever the practical difficulties, Durkheim's hypothesis is, in principle, testable. It should be possible to estimate the demoralizing impact of nonconformity on conformists. Clearly, though, this is no simple matter. The extent of demoralization resulting from the failure to punish may vary with type of crime. The unpunished traffic violator may cause more demoralization than the unpunished exhibitionist—depending on whether or not outwardly conforming members of society are more tempted to exceed the speed limit than to expose themselves. The extent of demoralization may also vary with position in the social structure occupied by the conformist. Thus, Ranulf suggested that the middle class was especially vulnerable:

[T]he disinterested tendency to inflict punishment is a distinctive characteristic of the lower middle class, that is, of a social class living under
conditions which force its members to an extraordinarily high degree of self-
restraint and subject them to much frustration of natural desires. If a
psychological interpretation is to be put on this correlation of facts, it can
hardly be to any other effect than that moral indignation is a kind of
resentment caused by the repression of instincts.[12]

Once the facts on the rate and the incidence of moral indignation are
known, it will become possible to determine whether something must be
done to the offender in order to prevent the demoralization of conformists. Suppose that research revealed that a very large proportion of
conformists react with moral indignation to *most* violations of the
criminal laws. Does this imply that punishment is a functional necessity?
Durkheim apparently thought so, but he might have been less dogmatic in
his approach to punishment had he specified the functional problem more
clearly: making the nonconformist unattractive as a role model. If the
norm violation can be defined as unenviable through some other process
than by inflicting suffering upon him, punishment is not required by the
exigencies of social control.

Punishment can be discussed on three distinct levels: (a) in terms of
the motivations of the societal agents administering it, (b) in terms of the
definition of the situation on the part of the person being punished, and
(c) in terms of its impact on conformists. At this point I am chiefly
concerned with the third level, the impact on conformists. Note that
punishment of offenders sustains the morale of conformists only under
certain conditions. The first has already been discussed, namely that
conformists unconsciously wish to violate the rules themselves. The
second is that conformists implicitly assume that the nonconformity is a
result of *deliberate defiance* of society's norms. For some conformists,
this second condition is not met. Under the guidance of psychiatric
thinking, some conformists assume that norm violation is the result of
illness rather than wickedness.[13] For such conformists, punishment of the
offender does not contribute to their morale. Since they assume that the
nonconformity is an involuntary symptom of a disordered personality,
the offender is automatically unenviable because illness is (by definition)
undesirable. Of course, it is an empirical question as to the relative
proportions of the conforming members of society who make the
"wicked" or the "sick" assumption about the motivation of the offender,
but this can be discovered by investigation.

In Western industrial societies, there is increasing tendency to call
contemporary methods of dealing with offenders "treatment" rather than

"punishment." Perhaps this means that increasing proportions of the population are willing to accept the "sick" theory of nonconformity. Note, however, that the emphasis on "treatment" may be more a matter of symbolism than of substance. Although the definition of the situation as treatment rather than punishment tends to be humanizing—both to the offender and to the persons who must deal with him—there are still kind guards and cruel nurses. Furthermore, it would be an error to suppose that punishment is invariably experienced as painful by the criminal whereas treatment is always experienced as pleasant by the psychopathological offender. Some gang delinquents consider a reformatory sentence an opportunity to renew old acquaintances and to learn new delinquent skills; they resist fiercely the degrading suggestion that they need the services of the "nut doctor." Some mental patients are terrified by shock treatment and embarrassed by group therapy.

What then is the significance of the increasing emphasis on "treatment"? Why call an institution for the criminally insane a "hospital" although it bears a closer resemblance to a prison than to a hospital for the physically ill? In my opinion, the increased emphasis on treatment in penological thinking and practice reflects the existence of a large group of conformists who are undecided as between the "wicked" and the "sick" theories of nonconformity. When they observe that the offender is placed in "treatment," their provisional diagnosis of illness is confirmed, and therefore they do not feel that he has "gotten away with it." Note that "treatment" has the capacity to make the offender unenviable to conformists whether or not it is effective in rehabilitating him and whether or not he experiences it as pleasant. Those old-fashioned conformists who are not persuaded by official diagnoses of illness will not be satisfied by "treatment"; they will prefer to see an attempt made to visit physical suffering or mental anguish on the offender. For them, punishment is necessary to prevent demoralization.

PUNISHMENT AS A MEANS OF REFORMING THE OFFENDER

Rehabilitation of offenders swells the number of conformists and therefore is regarded both by humanitarians and by scientifically minded penologists as more constructive than punishment. Most of the arguments against imprisonment and other forms of punishment in the correctional literature boil down to the assertion that punishment is incompatible with rehabilitation. The high rate of recidivism for prisons and reformatories is cited as evidence of the irrationality of punishment.[14] What sense is there in subjecting offenders to the frustrations of incarceration? If rehabilitative programs are designed to help the offender cope with frustrations in his life situation, which presumably were responsible for his non-conformity, imprisoning him hardly seems a good way to begin. To generalize the argument, the status degradation inherent in punishment makes it more difficult to induce the offender to play a legitimate role instead of a nonconforming one. Whatever the offender's original motivations for nonconformity, punishment adds to them by neutralizing his fear of losing the respect of the community; he has already lost it.

Plausible though this argument is, empirical research has not yet verified it. The superior rehabilitative efficacy of "enlightened" prisons is a humanitarian assumption, but brutal correctional systems have, so far as is known, comparable recidivism rates to "enlightened" systems. True, the recidivism rate of offenders who are fined or placed on probation is less than the recidivism rate of offenders who are incarcerated, but this comparison is not merely one of varying degrees of punishment. Presumably, more severe punishment is meted out to criminals who are more deeply committed to a deviant way of life. Until it is demonstrated that the recidivism rates of strictly comparable populations of deviants differ depending on the degree of punitiveness with which they are treated, the empirical incompatibility of punishment and rehabilitation will remain an open question.

Even on theoretical grounds, however, the incompatibility of punishment and rehabilitation can be questioned once it is recognized that one may precede the other. Perhaps, as Lloyd McCorkle and Richard Korn think, some types of deviants become willing to change only if the bankruptcy of their way of life is conclusively demonstrated to them.[15] On this assumption, punishment may be a necessary preliminary to a rehabilitative program in much the same way that shock treatment makes certain types of psychotics accessible to psychotherapy.

It seems to me that the compatibility of punishment and rehabilitation could be clarified (although not settled) if it were considered from the point of view of the *meaning* of punishment to the offender. Those offenders who regard punishment as a deserved deprivation resulting from their own misbehavior are qualitatively different from offenders who regard punishment as a misfortune bearing no relationship to morality. Thus, a child who is spanked by his father and the member of a bopping gang who is jailed for carrying concealed weapons are both "punished." But one accepts the deprivation as legitimate, and the other bows before superior force. I would hypothesize that punishment has rehabilitative significance only for the former. If this is so, correctional officials must convince the prisoner that his punishment is just before they can motivate him to change. This is no simple task. It is difficult for several reasons:

1) It is obvious to convicted offenders, if not to correctional officials, that *some* so-called "criminals" are being punished disproportionately for trifling offenses whereas *some* predatory business men and politicians enjoy prosperity and freedom. To deny that injustices occur confirms the cynical in their belief that "legitimate" people are not only as predatory as criminals but hypocritical to boot. When correctional officials act as though there were no intermediate position between asserting that perfect justice characterizes our society and that it is a jungle, they make it more difficult to persuade persons undergoing punishment that the best approximation of justice is available that imperfect human beings can manage.[16]

2) Of course, the more cases of injustice known to offenders, the harder it is to argue that the contemporary approximation of justice is the best that can be managed. It is difficult to persuade Negro inmates that their incarceration has moral significance if their life experience has demonstrated to them that the police and the courts are less scrupulous of *their* rights than of the rights of white persons. It is difficult to persuade an indigent inmate that his incarceration has moral significance if his poverty resulted in inadequate legal representation.[17]

3) Finally, the major form of punishment for serious offenders (imprisonment) tends to generate a contraculture which denies that justice has anything to do with legal penalties.[18] That is to say, it is too costly to confine large numbers of people in isolation from one another, yet congregate confinement results in the mutual reinforcement of self-justifications. Even those who enter prison feeling contrite are influenced by the self-righteous inmate climate; this may be part of the reason recidivism rates rise with each successive commitment.[19]

In view of the foregoing considerations, I hypothesize that punishment—as it is now practiced in Western societies—is usually an obstacle to rehabilitation. Some exceptions to this generalization should be noted. A few small treatment institutions have not only prevented the development of a self-righteous contraculture but have managed to establish an inmate climate supportive of changed values.[20] In such institutions punishment has rehabilitative significance for the same reason it has educational significance in the normal family: it is legitimate.

To sum up: The social control functions of punishment include crime prevention, sustaining the morale of conformists, and the rehabilitation of offenders. All of the empirical evidence is not in, but it is quite possible that punishment contributes to some of these and interferes with others. Suppose, for example, that punishment is necessary for crime prevention and to maintain the morale of conformists but is generally an obstacle to the rehabilitation of offenders. Since the proportion of deviants is small in any viable system as compared with the proportion of conformists, the failure to rehabilitate them will not jeopardize the social order. Therefore, under these assumptions, sociological counsel would favor the continued employment of punishment.

Conclusion

A member of a social system who violates its cherished rules threatens the stability of that system. Conformists who identify with the victim are motivated to punish the criminal in order to feel safe. Conformists who unconsciously identify with the criminal fear their own ambivalence. If norm violation is defined by conformists as willful, visiting upon the offender some injury or degradation will make him unenviable. If his behavior is defined by conformists as a symptom of pathology they are delighted not to share, putting him into treatment validates their diagnosis of undesirable illness. Whether he is "punished" or "treated," however, the disruptive consequence of his deviance is contained. Thus, from the viewpoint of social control, the alternative outcomes of the punishment or treatment processes, rehabilitation or recidivism, are less important than the deviant's neutralization as a possible role model. Whether punishment is or is not necessary rests ultimately on empirical questions: (1) the extent to which identification with the victim occurs, (2) the extent to which nonconformity is prevented by the anticipation of punishment, (3) what the consequences are for the morale of conformists of punishing the deviant or of treating his imputed pathology, and (4) the compatibility between punishment and rehabilitation.

Notes

1) Barnes and Teeters, *New Horizons in Criminology* (3d ed. 1959); Caldwell, *Criminology* (1956); Cavan, *Criminology* (1955); Elliot, *Crime in Modern Society* (1952); Korn and McCorkle, *Criminology and Penology* (1959); Reckless, *The Crime Problem* (2d ed. 1955); Sutherland and Cressey, *Principles of Criminology* (5th ed. 1955); Taft, *Criminology* (3d ed. 1956); Tappan, *Crime, Justice and Correction* (1960); von Hentig, *Crime: Causes and Conditions* (1947); Wood and Waite, *Crime and Its Treatment* (1941).
2) Taft, *op. cit. supra* note 1, at 359.
3) Reckless, *op. cit. supra* note 1, at 450.
4) Gouldner, "The Norm of Reciprocity: A Preliminary Statement," 25 *Am. Soc. Rev.* 161 (1960).
5) In this connection, it is well to recall that there is less reluctance to steal from corporations than from humans. See A. W. Jones, *Life, Liberty, and Property* (1941).
6) Durkheim, *The Division of Labor in Society*, 89 (1947).
7) Parsons, *The Structure of Social Action*, 402–03 (1949).
8) Toby, "Social Disorganization and Stake in Conformity: Complementary Factors in the Predatory Behavior of Young Hoodlums," 48 *J. Crim. L., C & P.S.* 12 (1957).
9) *Op. cit. supra* note 6, at 88.
10) Trolle, *Syv Måneder uten politi* (*Seven Months Without Police*) (Copenhagen, 1945), quoted in Christie, "Scandinavian Criminology," 31 *Sociological Inquiry* 101 (1961).
11) Durkheim, *op. cit. supra* note 6, at 108.
12) Ranulf, *Moral Indignation and Middle-Class Psychology*, 198 (Copenhagen, 1938).
13) Talcott Parsons has repeatedly suggested the analogy between illness and criminality. See also Aubert and Messinger, "The Criminal and the Sick," 1 *Inquiry* 137 (1958), and Wootton, *Social Science and Social Pathology*, 203–67 (1959).
14) Vold, "Does the Prison Reform?" 293 *Annals* 42 (1954).
15) McCorkle and Korn, "Resocialization Within Walls," 293 *Annals* 88 (1954).
16) See the interesting discussions of human fallibility in the works of Reinhold Neibuhr—e.g., *The Children of Light and the Children of Darkness* (1950).
17) Trebach, "The Indigent Defendant," 11 *Rutgers L. Rev.* 625 (1957).
18) For a discussion of the concept of contraculture, see Yinger, "Contraculture and Subculture," 25 *Am. Soc. Rev.* 625 (1960).
19) Sellin, "Recidivism and Maturation," 4 *Nat'l Probation and Parole A.J.* 241 (1958).
20) McCorkle, Elias and Bixby, *The Highfields Story* (1958), and Empey and Rabow, "Experiment in Delinquency Rehabilitation," 26 *Am. Soc. Rev.* 679 (1961).

Institutional Levers for Achieving Sex Equality

Alice S. Rossi

In turning to the problem of how equality between the sexes may be implemented as a societal goal, I shall concentrate on the three major areas of child care, residence and education. Institutional change in these areas in no sense exhausts the possible spheres in which institutional change could be effected to facilitate the goal of sex equality. Clearly government and industry, for example, could effect highly significant changes in the relations between the sexes. But one must begin somewhere, and I have chosen these three topics, for they all involve questions of critical significance to the goal of equality between men and women.

1) It is widely assumed that rearing children and maintaining a career is so difficult a combination that except for those few women with an extraordinary amount of physical strength, emotional endurance and a dedicated sense of calling to their work, it is unwise for women to attempt the combination. Women who have successfully combined child-rearing and careers are considered out of the ordinary, although many men with far heavier work responsibilities who yet spend willing loving hours as fathers, and who also contribute to home maintenance, are cause for little comment. We should be wary of the assumption that home and work combinations are necessarily difficult. The simplified contemporary home and smaller sized family of a working mother today probably represent a lesser burden of responsibility than that shouldered by her grandmother.

This does not mean that we should overlook the real difficulties that are involved for women who attempt this combination. Working mothers

Reprinted from "Equality Between the Sexes: An Immodest Proposal," *Daedalus*, 93 (Spring, 1964), 628–649, by permission of the author and the American Academy of Arts and Sciences.

do have primary responsibility for the hundreds of details involved in home maintenance, as planners and managers, even if they have household help to do the actual work. No one could suggest that child-rearing and a career are easy to combine, or even that this is some royal road to greater happiness, but only that the combination would give innumerable intelligent and creative women a degree of satisfaction and fulfillment that they cannot obtain in any other way. Certainly many things have to "give" if a woman works when she also has young children at home. Volunteer and social activities, gardening and entertaining may all have to be curtailed. The important point to recognize is that as children get older, it is far easier to resume these social activities than it is to resume an interrupted career. The major difficulty, and the one most in need of social innovation, is the problem of providing adequate care for the children of working mothers.

If a significant number of American middle-class women wish to work while their children are still young and in need of care and supervision, who are these mother-substitutes to be? In the American experience to date, they have been either relatives or paid domestic helpers. A study conducted by the Children's Bureau in 1958 outlines the types of child-care arrangements made by women working full time who had children under twelve years of age.[1] The study showed that the majority of these children (57 per cent) were cared for by relatives: fathers, older siblings, grandparents and others. About 21 per cent were cared for by nonrelatives, including neighbors as well as domestic helpers. Only 2 per cent of the children were receiving group care—in day nurseries, day-care centers, settlement houses, nursery schools and the like. Of the remainder, 8 per cent were expected to take care of themselves, the majority being the "latchkey" youngsters of ten and twelve years of age about whom we have heard a good deal in the press in recent years.

These figures refer to a national sample of employed mothers and concern women in blue collar jobs and predominantly low-skill white collar jobs. Presumably the proportion of middle-class working mothers who can rely on either relatives or their husbands would be drastically lower than this national average, and will probably decline even further in future years. Many of today's, and more of tomorrow's American grandmothers are going to be wage earners themselves and not babysitters for their grandchildren. In addition, as middle-class women enter the occupational world, they will experience less of a tug to remain close to the kinswomen of their childhood, and hence may contribute further to the pattern of geographic and social separation between young couples and both sets of their parents. Nor can many middle-class husbands care for their children, for their work hours are typically the same as those of their working wives: there can be little dovetailing of the work schedules of wives and husbands in the middle class as there can be in the working class.

At present, the major child-care arrangement for the middle-class woman who plans a return to work has to be hired household help. In the 1920's the professional and business wife-mother had little difficulty securing such domestic help, for there were thousands of first generation immigrant girls and women in our large cities whose first jobs in America were as domestic servants.[2] In the 1960's, the situation is quite different: the major source of domestic help in our large cities is Negro and Puerto Rican women. Assuming the continuation of economic affluence and further success in the American Negro's struggle for equal opportunity in education, jobs and housing, this reservoir will be further diminished in coming decades. The daughters of many present-day Negro domestic servants will be able to secure far better paying and more prestigeful jobs than their mothers can obtain in 1964. There will be increasing difficulty of finding adequate child-care help in future years as a result.

The problem is not merely that there may be decreasing numbers of domestic helpers available at the same time more women require their aid. There is an even more important question involved: are domestic helpers the best qualified persons to leave in charge of young children? Most middle-class families have exacting standards for the kind of teachers and the kind of schools they would like their children to have. But a working mother who searches for a competent woman to leave in charge of her home has to adjust to considerably lower standards than she would tolerate in any nursery school program in which she placed her young son or daughter, either because such competent help is scarce, or because the margin of salary left after paying for good child care and the other expenses associated with employment is very slight.

One solution to the problem of adequate child care would be an attempt to upgrade the status of child-care jobs. I think one productive way would be to develop a course of study which would yield a certificate for practical mothering, along the lines that such courses and certificates have been developed for practical nursing. There would be several important advantages to such a program. There are many older women in American communities whose lives seem empty because their children are grown and their grandchildren far away, yet who have no interest in factory or sales work, for they are deeply committed to life and work within the context of a home. Indeed, there are many older women who now work in factories or as cashiers or salesclerks who would be much more satisfied with child-care jobs, if the status and pay for such jobs were upgraded. These are the women, sometimes painfully lonely for contact with children, who stop young mothers to comment on the baby in the carriage, to talk with the three-year-old and to discuss their own distant grandchildren. I think many of these women would be attracted by a program of "refresher" courses in first aid, child development, books and crafts appropriate for children of various ages, and the special problems of the mother substitute-child relationship. Such a program would build upon their own experiences as mothers but would update and broaden their knowledge, bringing it closer to the values and practices of the middle-class woman who is seeking a practical mother for her family. Substitute motherhood for which she earns a wage, following active motherhood of her own, could provide continuity, meaning and variety to the life-span of those American women who are committed to the traditional conception of woman's role. Such a course of study might be developed in a number of school contexts—a branch of a college department of education, an adult education extension program or a school of nursing.

A longer-range solution to the problem of child care will involve the establishment of a network of child-care centers.[3] Most of the detailed plans for such centers must be left for future discussion, but there are several important advantages to professionally run child-care centers which should be noted. Most important, better care could be provided by such centers than any individual mother can provide by hiring a mother's helper, housekeeper or even the practical mother I have just proposed. In a child-care center, there can be greater specialization of skills, better facilities and equipment and play groups for the children. Second, a child-care center would mean less expense for the individual working mother, and both higher wages and shorter hours for the staff of the center. Third, these centers could operate on a full-time, year-round schedule, something of particular importance for women trained in professional or technical fields, the majority of which can be handled only on a full-time basis. Except for the teaching fields, such women must provide for the afternoon care of their nursery school and kindergarten-age children, after-school hours for older children and three summer months for all their children. Fourth, a child-care center could develop a roster of home-duty practical mothers or practical nurses to care for the ill or convalescent child at home, in much the way school systems now call upon substitute teachers to cover the classes of absent regular teachers.

A major practical problem is where to locate such child-care centers.

During the years of experimentation which would follow acceptance of this idea, they might be in a variety of places, under a variety of organizational auspices, as a service facility offered by an industrial firm, a large insurance company, a university, the federal or a state government. Community groups of women interested in such service might organize small centers of their own much as they have informal pooled baby-sitting services and cooperatively run nursery schools at the present time.

I believe that one of the most likely contexts for early experimentation with such child-care centers is the large urban university. As these universities continue to expand in future years, in terms of the size of the student body, the varied research institutes associated with the university and the expansion of administrative, technical and counseling personnel, there will be increasing opportunity and increasing need for the employment of women. A child-care center established under the auspices of a major university would facilitate the return for training of older women to complete or refresh advanced training, forestall the dropping out of younger graduate married women with infants and young children to care for and attract competent professional women to administrative, teaching or research positions, who would otherwise withdraw from their fields for the child-rearing years. It would also be an excellent context within which to innovate a program of child care, for the university has the specialists in psychology, education and human development on whom to call for the planning, research and evaluation that the establishment of child-care centers would require. If a university-sponsored child-care program were successful and widely publicized, it would then constitute an encouragement and a challenge to extend child-care centers from the auspices of specific organizations to a more inclusive community basis. A logical location for community child-care centers may be as wings of the elementary schools, which have precisely the geographic distribution throughout a city to make for easy access between the homes of very young children and the centers for their daytime care. Since school and center would share a location, it would also facilitate easy supervision of older children during the after-school hours. The costs of such care would also be considerably reduced if the facilities of the school were available for the older children during after-school hours, under the supervision of the staff of the child-care center. There are, of course, numerous problems to be solved in working out the details of any such program under a local educational system, but assuming widespread support for the desirability of community facilities for child care, these are technical and administrative problems well within the competence of school and political officials in our communities.

I have begun this discussion of the institutional changes needed to effect equality between the sexes with the question of child-care provision because it is of central importance in permitting women to enter and remain in the professional, technical and administrative occupations in which they are presently so underrepresented. Unless provision for child care is made, women will continue to find it necessary to withdraw from active occupational involvement during the child-rearing years. However, the professional and scientific fields are all growing in knowledge and skill, and even a practitioner who remains in the field often has difficulty keeping abreast of new developments. A woman who withdraws for a number of years from a professional field has an exceedingly difficult time catching up. The more exacting the occupation, then, the shorter the period of withdrawal should probably be from active participation in the labor force. If a reserve of trained practical mothers were available, a professional woman could return to her field a few months after the birth of a child, leaving the infant under the care of a practical mother until he or she reached the age of two years, at about which age the child could enter a child-care center for daytime care. Assuming a two-child family, this could mean not more than one year of withdrawal from her professional field for the working mother.

2) The preferred residential pattern of the American middle class in the postwar decades has been suburban. In many sections of the country it is difficult to tell where one municipality ends and another begins, for the farm, forest and waste land between towns and cities have been built up with one housing development after another. The American family portrayed in the mass media typically occupies a house in this sprawling suburbia, and here too, are the American women, and sometimes men, whose problems are aired and analyzed with such frequency. We know a good deal about the characteristics and quality of social life in the American suburb[4] and the problems of the men and women who live in them. We hear about the changing political complexion of the American suburbs, the struggle of residents to provide sufficient community facilities to meet their growing needs. But the social and personal difficulties of suburban women are more likely to be attributed to their early family relationships or to the contradictory nature of the socialization of girls in our society than to any characteristic of the environment in which they now live. My focus will be somewhat different: I shall examine the suburban residence pattern for the limitations it imposes on the utilization of women's creative work abilities and the participation of men in family life. Both limitations have important implications for the lives of boys and girls growing up in the suburban home.

The geographic distance between home and work has a number of implications for the role of the father-husband in the family. It reduces the hours of possible contact between children and their fathers. The hour or more men spend in cars, buses or trains may serve a useful decompression function by providing time in which to sort out and assess the experience at home and the events of the work day, but it is questionable whether this outweighs the disadvantage of severely curtailing the early morning and late afternoon hours during which men could be with their children.

The geographic distance also imposes a rigid exclusion of the father from the events which highlight the children's lives. Commuting fathers can rarely participate in any special daytime activities at home or at school, whether a party, a play the child performs in or a conference with a teacher. It is far less rewarding to a child to report to his father at night about such a party or part in a play than to have his father present at these events. If the husband-father must work late or attend an evening function in the city, he cannot sandwich in a few family hours but must remain in the city. This is the pattern which prompted Margaret Mead to characterize the American middle-class father as the "children's mother's husband," and partly why mother looms so oversized in the lives of suburban children.

Any social mixing of family-neighborhood and job associates is reduced or made quite formal: a work colleague cannot drop in for an after-work drink or a Saturday brunch when an hour or more separates the two men and their families. The father-husband's office and work associates have a quality of unreality to both wife and children. All these things sharpen the differences between the lives of men and women—fewer mutual acquaintances, less sharing of the day's events, and perhaps most importantly, less simultaneous filling of their complementary parent roles. The image of parenthood to the child is mostly motherhood, a bit of fatherhood and practically no parenthood as a joint enterprise shared at the same time by father and mother. Many suburban parents, I suspect, spend more time together as verbal parents—discussing their children in the children's absence—than they do actively interacting with their children, the togetherness cult notwithstanding. For couples whose relationship in courtship and early marriage was equalitarian, the pressures are strong in the suburban setting for parenthood to be highly differentiated and skewed to an ascendant position of the mother. Women dominate the family, men the job world.

The geographic distance between home and the center of the city restricts the world of the wife-mother in a complementary fashion. Not only does she have to do and be more things to her children, but she is confined to the limitations of the suburban community for a great many of her extrafamilial experiences. That suburban children are restricted in their social exposure to other young children and relatively young adults, mostly women and all of the same social class, has often been noted. I think the social restriction of the young wife to women of her own age and class is of equal importance: with very few older persons in her immediate environment, she has little first-hand exposure to the problems attending the empty-nest stage of life which lies ahead for herself. It is easy for her to continue to be satisfied to live each day as it comes, with little thought of preparing for the thirty-odd years when her children are no longer dependent upon her. If the suburban wife-mother had more opportunity to become acquainted with older widows and grandmothers, this would be pressed home to her in a way that might encourage a change in her unrealistic expectations of the future, with some preparation for that stage of life while she is young.[5]

If and when the suburban woman awakens from this short-range perspective and wants either to work or to prepare for a return to work when her children are older, how is she to do this, given the suburban pattern of residence? It is all very well to urge that school systems should extend adult education, that colleges and universities must make it possible for older women to complete education interrupted ten or more years previously or to be retrained for new fields; but this is a difficult program for the suburban wife to participate in. She lives far from the center of most large cities, where the educational facilities tend to be concentrated, in a predominantly middle-class community, where domestic help is often difficult to arrange and transportation often erratic during the hours she would be using it.

It is for these reasons that I believe any attempt to draw a significant portion of married women into the mainstream of occupational life must involve a reconsideration of the suburban pattern of living. Decentralization of business and industry has only partly alleviated the problem: a growing proportion of the husbands living in the suburbs also work in the suburbs. There are numerous shops and service businesses providing job opportunities for the suburban wife. Most such jobs, however, are at skill levels far below the ability potential and social status of the suburban middle-class wife. Opportunities for the more exacting professional, welfare and business jobs are still predominantly in the central sections of the city. In addition, since so many young wives and mothers in this generation married very young, before their formal education was completed, they will need more schooling before they can hope to enter the fields in which their talents can be most fruitfully exercised, in jobs which will not be either dull or a status embarrassment to themselves and their husbands. Numerous retail stores have opened suburban branches; colleges and universities have yet to do so. A woman can spend in the suburb, but she can neither learn nor earn.

That some outward expansion of American cities has been necessary is clear, given the population increase in our middle- to large-sized cities. But there are many tracts in American cities between the business center and the outlying suburbs which imaginative planning and architectural design could transform and which would attract the men and women who realize the drawbacks of a suburban residence. Unless there is a shift in this direction in American housing, I do not think there can be any marked increase in the proportion of married middle-class women who will enter the labor force. That Swedish women find work and home easier to combine than American women is closely related to the fact that Sweden avoided the sprawling suburban development in its postwar housing expansion. The emphasis in Swedish housing has been on inner-city housing improvement. With home close to diversified services for schooling, child care, household help and places of work, it has been much easier in Sweden than in the United States to draw married women into the labor force and keep them there.

In contrast, the policy guiding the American federal agencies which affect the housing field, such as the FHA, have stressed the individual home, with the result that mortgage money was readily available to encourage builders to develop the sprawling peripheries of American cities. Luxury high-rise dwellings at the hub of the city and individual homes at the periphery have therefore been the pattern of middle-class housing development in the past twenty years. A shift in policy on the part of the federal government which would embrace buildings with three and four dwelling units and middle-income high-rise apartment buildings in the in-between zones of the city could go a long way to counteract this trend toward greater and greater distance between home and job. Not everyone can or will want to live close to the hub of the city. From spring through early fall, it is undoubtedly easier to rear very young children in a suburban setting with back yards for the exercise of healthy lungs and bodies. But this is at the expense of increased dependence of children on their mothers, of minimization of fathers' time with their youngsters, of restriction of the social environment of women, of drastic separation of family and job worlds and of less opportunity for even part-time schooling or work for married women.

3) Men and women must not only be able to participate equally;

they must want to do so. It is necessary, therefore, to look more closely into their motivations, and the early experiences which mold their self-images and life expectations. A prime example of this point can be seen in the question of occupational choice. The goal of sex equality calls for not only an increase in the extent of women's participation in the occupational system, but a more equitable distribution of men and women in all the occupations which comprise that system. This means more women doctors, lawyers and scientists, more men social workers and school teachers. To change the sex ratio within occupations can only be achieved by altering the sex-typing of such occupations long before young people make a career decision.[6] Many men and women change their career plans during college, but this is usually within a narrow range of relatively homogeneous fields: a student may shift from medicine to a basic science, from journalism to teaching English. Radical shifts such as from nursing to medicine, from kindergarten teaching to the law, are rare indeed. Thus while the problem could be attacked at the college level, any significant change in the career choices men and women make must be attempted when they are young boys and girls. It is during the early years of elementary school education that young people develop their basic views of appropriate characteristics, activities and goals for their sex. It is for this reason that I shall give primary attention to the sources of sex-role stereotypes and what the elementary school system could do to eradicate these stereotypes and to help instead in the development of a more androgynous conception of sex role.[7]

The all-female social atmosphere of the American child has been frequently noted by social scientists, but it has been seen as a problem only in its effect upon boys. It has been claimed, for example, that the American boy must fight against a feminine identification this atmosphere encourages, with the result that he becomes overly aggressive, loudly asserting his maleness. In contrast, it is claimed that the American girl has an easy socialization, for she has an extensive number of feminine models in her environment to facilitate her identification as a female.

There are several important factors which this analysis overlooks. To begin with the boy: while it is certainly true that much of his primary group world is controlled by women, this does not mean that he has no image of the male social and job world as well. The content of the boy's image of man's work has a very special quality to it, however. Although an increasingly smaller proportion of occupations in a complex industrial society relies on sheer physical strength, the young boy's exposure to the work of men remains largely the occupations which do require physical strength. The jobs he can see are those which are socially visible, and these are jobs in which men are reshaping and repairing the physical environment. The young boy sees working class men operating trucks, bulldozers, cranes; paving roads; building houses; planting trees; delivering groceries. This image is further reinforced by his television viewing: the gun-toting cowboy, the bat-swinging ballplayer, the arrow-slinging Indian. Space operas suggest not scientific exploration but military combat, the collision and collusion of other worlds. In short, even if the boy sees little of his father and knows next to nothing of what his father does away from home, there is some content to his image of men's work in the larger society. At least some part of his aggressive active play may be as much acting out similar male roles in response to the cultural cues provided by his environment as it is an over-reaction to his feminine environment or an identification with an aggressor-father.

And what of the girl? What image of the female role is she acquiring during her early years? In her primary group environment, she sees women largely in roles defined in terms that relate to her as a child—as mother, aunt, grandmother, baby-sitter—or in roles relating to the house —the cleaning, cooking, mending activities of mother and domestic helpers. Many mothers work outside the home, but the daughter often knows as little of that work as she does of her father's. Even if her own mother works, the reasons for such working that are given to the child are most often couched in terms of the mother or housewife role. Thus, a girl is seldom told that her mother works because she enjoys it or finds it very important to her own satisfaction in life, but because the money she earns will help pay for the house, a car, the daughter's clothes, dancing lessons or school tuition.[8] In other words, working is something mothers sometimes have to do as mothers, not something mothers do as adult women. This is as misleading and distorted an image of the meaning of work as the father who tells his child he works "to take care of mummy and you" and neglects to mention that he also works because he finds personal satisfaction in doing so, or that he is contributing to knowledge, peace or the comfort of others in the society.

The young girl also learns that it is only in the family that women seem to have an important superordinate position. However high her father's occupational status outside the home, when he returns at night, he is likely to remove his white shirt and become a blue collar Mr. Fixit or mother's helper. The traditional woman's self-esteem would be seriously threatened if her husband were to play a role equal to her own in the lives and affections of her children or in the creative or managerial aspect of home management, precisely because her major sphere in which to acquire the sense of personal worth is her home and children.[9] The lesson is surely not lost on her daughter, who learns that at home father does not know best, though outside the home men are the bosses over women, as she can see only too well in the nurse-doctor, secretary-boss, salesclerk-store manager, space Jane-space John relationships that she has an opportunity to observe.

The view that the socialization of the girl is an easy one compared with the boy depends on the kind of woman one has in mind as an end-product of socialization. Only if the woman is to be the traditional wife-mother is present-day socialization of young girls adequate, for from this point of view the confinement to the kinds of feminine models noted above and the superordinate position of the mother in the family facilitate an easy identification. If a girl sees that women reign only at home or in a history book, whereas outside the home they are Girl Fridays to men, then clearly for many young girls the wife-mother role may appear the best possible goal to have. It should be noted, however, that identification has been viewed primarily as an either-or process—the child identifies either with the mother or the father—and not as a process in which there is a fusion of the two parent models such that identification involves a modeling of the self after mother in some respects, father in others. It is possible that those women who have led exciting, intellectually assertive and creative lives did not identify exclusively with their traditional mothers, but crossed the sex line and looked to their fathers as model sources for ideas and life commitments of their own. This is to suggest that an exclusively same-sex identification between parent and child is no necessary condition for either mentally healthy or creative adults.

If I am correct about the significance of the father in the childhoods of those women who later led creative adult lives, then an increased accessibility of the middle-class father to his daughters and greater sharing of his ideas and interests could help to counteract the narrow confines of the feminine models daughters have. Beyond this, young girls need exposure to female models in professional and scientific occupations and to women with drive and dedication who are playing innovative volunteer roles in community organizations; they need an encouragement to emulate them and a preparation for an equalitarian rather than a dominant role in parenthood. Only if a woman's self-esteem is rooted in an independent life outside her family as well as her roles within the home can she freely welcome her husband to share on an equal basis the most rewarding tasks involved in child-rearing and home maintenance.

What happens when youngsters enter school? Instead of broadening the base on which they are forming their image of male and female roles, the school perpetuates the image children bring from home and their observations in the community. It has been mother who guided their preschool training; now in school it is almost exclusively women teachers who guide their first serious learning experiences. In the boy's first readers, men work at the same jobs with the same tools he has observed in his neighborhood—"T" for truck, "B" for bus, "W" for wagon. His teachers expect him to be rugged, physically strong and aggressive. After a few years he moves into separate classes for gym, woodworking and machine shop. For the girl, women are again the ones in charge of children. Her first readers portray women in aprons, brooms in their hands or babies in their arms. Teachers expect her to be quiet, dependent, with feminine interests in doll and house play and dressing up. In a few years she moves into separate classes for child care, cooking and practical nursing. In excursions into the community, elementary school boys and girls visit airports, bus terminals, construction sites, factories and farms.

What can the schools do to counteract these tendencies to either outmoded or traditional images of the roles of men and women? For one, class excursions into the community are no longer needed to introduce American children to building construction, airports or zoos. Except for those in the most underprivileged areas of our cities, American children have ample exposure to such things with their car- and plane-riding families. There are, after all, only a limited number of such excursions possible in the course of a school year. I think visits to a publishing house, research laboratory, computer firm or art studio would be more enriching than airports and zoos.

Going out into the community in this way, youngsters would observe men and women in their present occupational distribution. By a program of bringing representatives of occupations into the classroom and auditorium, however, the school could broaden the spectrum of occupations young children may link to their own abilities and interests regardless of the present sex-typing of occupations, by making a point of having children see and hear a woman scientist or doctor; a man dancer or artist; both women and men who are business executives, writers and architects.[10]

Another way in which the elementary schools could help is making a concerted effort to attract male teachers to work in the lower grades. This would add a rare and important man to the primary group environment of both boys and girls. This might seem a forlorn hope to some, since elementary school teaching has been such a predominantly feminine field, and it may be harder to attract men to it than to attract women to fields presently considered masculine. It may well be that in the next decade or so the schools could not attract and keep such men as teachers. But it should be possible for graduate schools of education and also school systems to devise ways of incorporating more men teachers in the lower grades, either as part of their teacher training requirements or in the capacity of specialized teachers: the science, art or music teacher who works with children at many grade levels rather than just one or two contiguous grade levels.[11] His presence in the lives of very young children could help dispel their expectation that only women are in charge of children, that nurturance is a female attribute or that strength and an aggressive assault on the physical environment is the predominant attribute of man's work.

The suggestions made thus far relate to a change in the sex-linking of occupations. There is one crucial way in which the schools could effect a change in the traditional division of labor by sex within the family sphere. The claim that boys and girls are reared in their early years without any differentiation by sex is only partially true. There are classes in all elementary schools which boys and girls take separately or which are offered only to one sex. These are precisely the courses most directly relevant to adult family roles: courses in sex and family living (where communities are brave enough to hold them) are typically offered in separate classes for boys and for girls, or for girls only. Courses in shop and craft work are scheduled for boys only; courses in child care, nursing and cooking are for girls only. In departing from completely coeducational programs, the schools are reinforcing the traditional division of labor by sex which most children observe in their homes. Fifteen years later, these girls find that they cannot fix a broken plug, set a furnace pilot light or repair a broken high chair or favorite toy. These things await the return of the child's father and family handyman in the evening. When a child is sick in the middle of the night, his mother takes over; father is only her assistant or helper.

These may seem like minor matters, but I do not think they are. They unwittingly communicate to and reinforce in the child a rigid differentiation of role between men and women in family life. If first aid, the rudiments of child care and of cooking have no place in their early years as sons, brothers and schoolboys, then it is little wonder that as husbands and fathers American men learn these things under their wives' tutelage. Even assuming these wives were actively involved in occupations of their own and hence free of the psychological pressure to assert their ascendancy in the family, it would be far better for all concerned—the married pair and the children as well—if men brought such skills with them to marriage.

This is the point where the schools could effect a change: if boys and girls took child care, nursing, cooking, shop and craft classes together, they would have an opportunity to acquire comparable skills and pave the way for true parental substitutability as adults. They would also be learning something about how to complement each other, not just how to compete with each other.[12] Teamwork should be taught in school in the subjects relevant to adult family roles, not just within each sex on the playground or in the gymnasium. In addition to encouraging more equality in the parental role, such preparation as school children could ease their adjustment to the crises of adult life; illness, separation due to the demands of a job or military service, divorce or death would have far less trauma and panic for the one-parent family—whether mother or father—if such equivalence and substitutability were a part of the general definition of the parental role.

A school curriculum which brought boys and girls into the same classes and trained them in social poise, the healing skills, care of children, handling of interpersonal difficulties and related subjects would also encourage the development of skills which are increasingly needed in our complex economy. Whether the adult job is to be that of a worker in an automated industry, a professional man in law, medicine or scholarship, or an executive in a large bureaucratic organization, the skills which are needed are not physical strength and ruggedness in interpersonal combat but understanding in human dealings, social poise and persuasive skill in interpersonal relations.[13] All too often, neither the family nor the school encourages the development of these skills in boys. Hundreds of large business firms look for these qualities in young male applicants but often end up trying to develop them in their young executives through on-the-job training programs.

I have suggested a number of ways in which the educational system could serve as an important catalyst for change toward sex equality. The schools could reduce sex-role stereotypes of appropriate male and female attributes and activities by broadening the spectrum of occupations youngsters may consider for themselves irrespective of present sex-linked notions of man's work and woman's work, and by providing boys as well as girls with training in the tasks they will have as parents and spouses. The specific suggestions for achieving these ends which I have made should be viewed more as illustrative than as definitive, for educators themselves may have far better suggestions for how to implement the goal in the nation's classrooms than I have offered in these pages. Equality between the sexes cannot be achieved by proclamation or decree but only through a multitude of concrete steps, each of which may seem insignificant by itself, but all of which add up to the social blueprint for attaining the general goal.

Summary Profile

In the course of this essay I have suggested a number of institutional innovations in education, residence and child care which would facilitate equality between the sexes. Instead of a more conventional kind of summary, I shall describe a hypothetical case of a woman who is reared and lives out her life under the changed social conditions proposed in this essay.

She will be reared, as her brother will be reared, with a combination of loving warmth, firm discipline, household responsibility and encouragement of independence and self-reliance. She will not be pampered and indulged, subtly taught to achieve her ends through coquetry and tears, as so many girls are taught today. She will view domestic skills as useful tools to acquire, some of which, like fine cooking or needlework, having their own intrinsic pleasures but most of which are necessary repetitive work best gotten done as quickly and efficiently as possible. She will be able to handle minor mechanical breakdowns in the home as well as her brother can, and he will be able to tend a child, press, sew and cook with the same easy skills and comfortable feeling his sister has.

During their school years, both sister and brother will increasingly assume responsibility for their own decisions, freely experiment with numerous possible fields of study, gradually narrowing to a choice that best suits their interests and abilities rather than what is considered appropriate or prestigeful work for men and women. They will be encouraged by parents and teachers alike to think ahead to a whole life span, viewing marriage and parenthood as one strand among many which will constitute their lives. The girl will not feel the pressure to belittle her accomplishments, lower her aspirations, learn to be a receptive listener in her relations with boys, but will be as true to her growing sense of self as her brother and male friends are. She will not marry before her adolescence and schooling are completed, but will be willing and able to view the college years as a "moratorium" from deeply intense cross-sex commitments, a period of life during which her identity can be "at large and open and various."[14] Her intellectual aggressiveness as well as her brother's tender sentiments will be welcomed and accepted as *human* characteristics, without the self-questioning doubt of latent homosexuality that troubles many college-age men and women in our era when these qualities are sex-linked.[15] She will not cling to her parents, nor they to her, but will establish an increasingly larger sphere of her own independent world in which she moves and works, loves and thinks, as a maturing young person. She will learn to take pleasure in her own body and a man's body and to view sex as a good and wonderful experience, but not as an exclusive basis for an ultimate commitment to another person, and not as a test of her competence as a female or her partner's competence as a male. Because she will have a many-faceted conception of her self and its worth, she will be free to merge and lose herself in the sex act with a lover or a husband.[16]

Marriage for our hypothetical woman will not mark a withdrawal from the life and work pattern that she has established, just as there will be no sharp discontinuity between her early childhood and youthful adult years. Marriage will be an enlargement of her life experiences, the addition of a new dimension to an already established pattern, rather than an abrupt withdrawal to the home and a turning in upon the marital relationship. Marriage will be a "looking outward in the same direction" for both the woman and her husband. She will marry and bear children only if she deeply desires a mate and children, and will not be judged a failure as a person if she decides against either. She will have few children if she does have them, and will view her pregnancies, childbirth and early months of motherhood as one among many equally important highlights in her life, experienced intensely and with joy but not as the exclusive basis for a sense of self-fulfillment and purpose in life. With planning and foresight, her early years of child bearing and rearing can fit a long-range view of all sides of herself. If her children are not to suffer from "paternal deprivation," her husband will also anticipate that the assumption of parenthood will involve a weeding out of nonessential activities either in work, civic or social participation. Both the woman and the man will feel that unless a man can make room in his life for parenthood, he should not become a father. The woman will make sure, even if she remains at home during her child's infancy, that he has ample experience of being with and cared for by other adults besides herself, so that her return to a full-time position in her field will not constitute a drastic change in the life of the child, but a gradual pattern of increasing supplementation by others of the mother. The children will have a less intense involvement with their mother, and she with them, and they will all be the better for it. When they are grown and establish adult lives of their own, our woman will face no retirement twenty years before her husband, for her own independent activities will continue and expand. She will be neither an embittered wife, an interfering mother-in-law nor an idle parasite, but together with her husband she will be able to live an independent, purposeful and satisfying third act in life.

Notes

1) Henry C. Lajewski, *Child Care Arrangements of Full-Time Working Mothers* (Washington, D.C.: U.S. Department of Health, Education and Welfare, Children's Bureau Publication No. 378, 1959); and Herzog, *Children of Working Mothers*.

2) In one study conducted for the Bureau of Vocational Information in 1925, Collier found that 42% of the one hundred professional and business mothers she interviewed had two or more full-time domestic servants to maintain their homes and care for their children during the day; only 9 of these 100 women had no full-time servants, 5 of whom had their mothers living with them. Virginia MacMakin Collier, *Marriage and Careers: A Study of One Hundred Women who are Wives, Mothers, Homemakers and Professional Women* (New York: The Channel Bookshop, 1926), pp. 59 and 74.

3) Child-care centers would not be an entirely new phenomenon in the United States, for there were a number of municipal day-care centers established during World War II when the need for womanpower in factories engaged in war production made them necessary to free women to accept employment. There have also been continuing debates about the provision of child-care centers for other mothers, such as the ADC mother, the problem revolving about whether such women should be given sufficient money from municipal funds to stay at home and care for her children, or to establish child-care centers and thus enable such women to hold down jobs and at least partially support their children. In either case, the focus has been upon working-class women. Child-care centers as an institutional device to facilitate the combination of job and family by women in professional and technical occupations in the middle class are very rare, and are largely confined to small private ventures in the large metropoli.

4) William Whyte, *Organization Man* (New York: Simon and Schuster, 1956); Robert Wood, *Suburbia, Its People and Their Politics* (Boston: Houghton Mifflin, 1959); John Keats, *The Crack in the Picture Window* (Boston: Houghton Mifflin, 1956); A. C. Spectorsky, *The Exurbanites* (Philadelphia: J. B. Lippincott, 1955); and Nanette E. Scofield, "Some Changing Roles of Women in Suburbia: A Social Anthropological Case Study," *Transactions of the New York Academy of Sciences*, 22 (April, 1960), 6.

5) George Gallup and Evan Hill, "The American Woman," *The Saturday Evening Post*, December 22, 1962. One must read this survey very carefully to get behind the gloss of the authors' rosy perspective. Gallup reports that almost half of the married women in the sample claimed that childbirth was the "most thrilling event" in their lives. He gives two quotes to illustrate why these women were so fascinated by childbirth: one stresses the point that it was "the one time in my life when everything was right"; the other points out "you've done something that's recognized as a good thing to do, and you're the center of attention." If these are truly typical, it tells us a good deal about the underlying attitude toward the thousands of days on which no child is born: things are *not* all right, and there must be some sense of being on the sidelines, of having a low level of self-esteem, if childbirth is important because "society views it as good" and it is the only time in her life that she is the important center of attention. In other parts of the article, which generally stresses the central importance of children to women, and their high satisfaction with marriage, we learn that a

large proportion of American women wish the schools would do more of the socializing of these children—teach them good citizenship, how to drive, sex education; and if these women were so satisfied with their lives, why does only 10% of the sample want their daughters to live the same lives they have? Instead, these women say they want their daughters to get more education and to marry later than they did. If marriage is the perfect female state, then why wish to postpone it, unless there are unexpressed sides of the self which have not been fulfilled?

The only strong critical point made is the following: "with early weddings and extended longevity, marriage is now a part-time career for women, and unless they prepare now for the freer years, this period will be a loss. American society will hardly accept millions of ladies of leisure, or female drones, in their 40's" (p. 32). But only 31% of the sample reported they are "taking courses or following a plan to improve themselves," a third of these involving improvement of their physical shape or appearance. The photographs accompanying this article reveal the authors' own focus on the years of youth rather than of maturity: of 29 women appearing in these pictures, only 2 are clearly of women over 45 years of age.

6) The extent of this sex-typing of occupations is shown dramatically in a study of the June, 1961 college graduates conducted by the National Opinion Research Center at the University of Chicago. Although the women in this sample of college graduates showed a superior academic performance during the college years—only 36% of the women in contrast to 50% of the men were in the "bottom half" of their class—their career aspirations differed markedly from those of men. Of those who were going on to graduate and professional schools in the fall of 1961, only 6% of those aspiring to careers in medicine were women; 7% in physics, 7% in pharmacology, 10% in business and administration, 28% in the social sciences. In contrast, women predominated in the following fields: 51% in humanities, 59% in elementary and secondary education, 68% in social work, 78% in health fields such as nursing, medical technology, physical and occupational therapy. In a sample of 33,782 college graduates, there were 11,000 women who expected to follow careers in elementary and secondary education, but only 285 women who hoped to enter the combined fields of medicine, law and engineering. See James A. Davis and Norman Bradburn, "Great Aspirations: Career Plans of America's June 1961 College Graduates," National Opinion Research Center Report No. 82, September, 1961 (mimeographed). Davis and Bradburn report that some 40% of the graduates had changed their career plans during their college years (p. 40).

7) My attention in this section will be largely on the early years of schooling. There is a great need, however, for a return of the spirit that characterized high school and college educators of women in the 1930's. It has seemed to me that there is an insidious trend at this level of education toward discouraging women from aspiring to the most demanding and rewarding fields of work and thought. Dr. Mary Bunting, noteworthy for the imaginative Radcliffe Institute for Independent Study, now urges women to work on the "fringes" of the occupational system, away from the most competitive intellectual market places. In her first public address upon assuming the presidency of Barnard College, Dr. Rosemary Park stated that in her view college education of women in the United States should have as its goal the creation of "enlightened laymen." High school and college counselors give hearty approval if women students show talent and interest in elementary school teaching, nursing, social work; their approval is all too often very lukewarm if not discouraging, if women students show interest in physics, medicine or law.

8) Although her sample was upper-middle-class mothers of girls in progressive schools in New York City, Ruth Hartley reports that the working mothers in her sample told their children they were working out of the home because of financial need: "They express guilt about their working and appear to hold quite traditional concepts of appropriate 'feminine' behavior which they feel they are violating." An example is provided by a well-to-do working mother who

obviously loves her work but told her daughter that she works because of financial necessity. When asked why she doesn't let her daughter know she enjoys her work, she answered, "well, then what excuse would I have for working?" Ruth Hartley and A. Klein, "Sex Role Concepts among Elementary School-Age Girls," *Marriage and Family Living*, 21 (February, 1959), 59–64.

9) Women enhance their own self-esteem when they urge their children to "be good when father gets home" because he is tired and needs to rest. They are not only portraying an image of the father as a fragile person, a "Dresden cup" as Irene Joselyn expresses it, but by expanding their maternalism to include the father, they are symbolically relegating him to the subordinate position of the child in the family structure. See Irene Joselyn, "Cultural Forces, Motherliness and Fatherliness," *American Journal of Orthopsychiatry*, 26 (1956), 264–271.

10) In a large metropolis, resource persons could be invited through the city business and professional organizations, the Chamber of Commerce, art, music and dancing schools, etc. This could constitute a challenging program for PTA groups to handle; or a Community Resources Pool could be formed similar to that the New World Foundation has supported in New York City whereby people from business, the arts and sciences and the professions work with the public schools. Many educators and teachers might hesitate to try such a project in anticipation of parent-resistance. But parent-resistance could be a good opportunity for parent-education, if teachers and school officials were firm and informed about what they are trying to do.

11) Though predominantly a feminine field, there is one man to approximately every two women planning careers in teaching. In the "Great Aspirations" study, there were 11,388 women students planning to teach in elementary and secondary schools, but also 5,038 men. The problem may therefore not be as great as it seems at first: schools of education could surely do more to encourage some of these men to work in the lower grades, in part or for part of their teaching careers.

12) Bruno Bettelheim makes the point that American boys and girls learn to compete with each other, but not how to complement each other. He sees this lack of experience in complementarity as part of the difficulty in achieving a satisfactory sexual adjustment in marriage: the girl is used to "performing with males on equal grounds, but she has little sense of how to complement them. She cannot suddenly learn this in bed." See Bruno Bettelheim, "Growing Up Female," *Harper's*, November, 1962, p. 125.

13) These are the same skills which, when found in women, go by the names of charm, tact, intuition. See Helen Mayer Hacker, "The New Burdens of Masculinity," *Marriage and Family Living*, 19 (August, 1957), 227–233.

14) Eric Erikson, *Childhood and Society* (New York: W. W. Norton, 1950).

15) David Riesman has observed that this latent fear of homosexuality haunts the Ivy League campuses, putting pressure on many young men to be guarded in their relations with each other and with their male teachers, reflecting in part the lag in the cultural image of appropriate sex characteristics. See David Riesman, "Permissiveness and Sex Roles," *Marriage and Family Living*, 21 (August, 1959), 211–217.

16) It goes beyond the intended scope of this essay to discuss the effects of a social pattern of equality between men and women upon their sexual relationship. A few words are, however, necessary, since the defenders of traditional sex roles often claim that full equality would so feminize men and masculinize women that satisfactory sexual adjustments would be impossible and homosexuality would probably increase. If the view of the sex act presupposes a dominant male actor and a passive female subject, then it is indeed the case that full sex equality would probably be the death knell of this traditional sexual relationship. Men and women who participate as equals in their parental and occupational and social roles will complement each other sexually in the same way, as essentially equal partners, and not as an ascendant male and a submissive female. This does not mean, however, that equality in non-sexual roles necessarily de-eroticizes the sexual one. The enlarged base of shared experience can, if anything, heighten

the salience of sex *qua* sex. Sweden, where men and women approach equality more than perhaps any other western society, visitors are struck by the erotic atmosphere of that society. Sexually men and women do after all each lack what the other has and wishes for completion of the self; the salience of sex may be enhanced precisely in the situation of the diminished significance of sex as a differentiating factor in all other areas of life. It has always seemed paradoxical to me that so many psychoanalysts defend the traditional sex roles and warn that drastic warping of the sexual impulses may flow from full sex equality; surely they are underestimating the power and force of the very drive which is in so central a position in their theoretical framework. Maslow is one of the few psychologists who has explored the connections between sex experience and the conception of self among women. With a sample of one hundred and thirty college-educated women in their twenties, he found, contrary to traditional notions of femininity and psychoanalytic theories, that the more "dominant" the woman, the greater her enjoyment of sexuality, the greater her ability to give herself freely in love. Women with dominance feelings were free to be completely themselves, and this was crucial for their full expression in sex. They were not feminine in the traditional sense, but enjoyed sexual fulfillment to a much greater degree than the conventionally feminine women he studied. See A. H. Maslow, "Dominance, Personality and Social Behavior in Women," *Journal of Social Psychology*, 10 (1939), 3–39; and "Self-Esteem (Dominance Feeling) and Sexuality in Women," *Journal of Social Psychology*, 16 (1942), 259–294; or a review of Maslow's studies in Betty Friedan, *The Feminine Mystique* (New York: W. W. Norton, 1963), pp. 316–326.

The Revolution in Criminal Justice

Time Magazine

"We have to choose," said Oliver Wendell Holmes Jr., *"and for my part,*
I think it less evil that some criminals should escape than that the
government should play an ignoble part." Thus, speaking in 1928, Mr.
Justice Holmes not only described one of the most hotly debated social
issues of the '60s, but foreshadowed as well the present-day philosophy of
a Supreme Court that has done more than any other in U.S. history to
bolster the rights of the individual against "ignoble" government power.
In so doing, the court in recent years has wrought a revolution in
criminal justice.

Nonetheless, in an era when the incidence of crime in the U.S. is
increasing at up to five times the rate of population growth, the Supreme
Court—as viewed by its critics—appears to have ignored the urgent
threat to law and order in favor of abstract constitutional principles. Law-
enforcement officers are almost unanimous in deploring a series of
decisions that seem to them to be aimed at "coddling criminals" and
"handcuffing the police." The court's rulings outlawing accepted methods
of arrest and interrogation, protests Chicago Police Superintendent
Orlando W. Wilson, are simply "devices for excluding the truth from
criminal trials." Many legal scholars, while conceding that the court has
redressed some longstanding abuses, are concerned about the enormous
problems of readjustment it has posed for police and prosecutors.

Unlike many constitutional controversies, the debate over crime and
punishment involves the emotions and physical security of every American. City dwellers in particular, for whom parks and streets after dark
bristle with potential danger, would argue that the safety of the innocent
is at least as implicit in the Jeffersonian ideal of "equal and exact justice to
all men" as fair treatment for the accused.

Reprinted from "The Revolution in Criminal Justice," *Time The Weekly News-
magazine*, 86 (July 16, 1965), 22–23, by permission of the publisher. © Time, Inc.,
1965.

The actual effects of recent Supreme Court rulings on crime and police procedures are hard to measure. "Criminal laws," says Yale Law Professor Alexander Bickel, "are blunt, primitive tools of social control. The real trouble is that criminal law doesn't fit what you are trying to do." Narcotics and gambling, Bickel points out, are both primarily social problems for which the law has no real cure. Clearly, police must have effective powers to curb these offenses, as well as more serious crimes. The question that has never been fully answered in the U.S. is what the extent of those powers should be.

The Individual v. the State

Many experts gravely doubt that law-enforcement agencies even now have either the legal or technical weapons needed to combat violence, theft and organized crime at today's intensified levels. At the heart of the controversy over the court lies the danger that the judicial pendulum may have swung too far toward protection of the individual criminal, too far away from protection of society.

The individual's interests seem more than adequately bulwarked by the Bill of Rights—basically the Constitution's first eight amendments—which was specifically designed to limit police power and to protect the citizen from government oppression. In essence, the Bill of Rights commands government to prove its case against the accused beyond reasonable doubt. The state cannot force a defendant to testify against himself; the courts must exclude "confessions" that have been obtained by coercion, even if it means freeing the guilty. As Felix Frankfurter summarized the significance of such provisions: "The history of liberty has largely been the history of the observance of procedural safeguards."

What laymen seldom realize, however, is that in practice the Bill of Rights long gave most defendants no protection whatever. The Supreme Court ruled in 1833 that it safeguarded the individual only against the Federal Government. Out of concern for states' rights, the court also was reluctant to shield nonfederal criminal defendants under the 14th Amendment, which stipulates that "no state shall . . . deprive any person of life, liberty or property without due process of law."

Thus, local police in the U.S. were for generations under no obligation to observe constitutional guarantees in criminal cases. Arrests and searches without warrants were routine; even today, third-degree methods are not unknown. In New York City, former Deputy Police Commissioner Richard Dougherty wrote recently: "It is hardly news that suspects of serious crimes often get 'worked over' in the back rooms of station houses. The truth is that most crimes are not solved by finger-prints and wristwatch radios and the skillful assembling of clues. The suspect confesses, voluntarily or involuntarily."

Interrogation and Trial

Ironically, this is no problem for the big-time crook with an attorney in attendance. For the suspect without a lawyer, however, arrest and detention are the most crucial phases of his entire case. In the intimidating atmosphere of a station house, vigorous police grilling often takes on all the aspects of a star chamber. "The trial," observes one jurist, "is too often merely a review of that interrogation." Even if the defendant later recants a confession in court, it is one man's oath against those of three or four detectives. A distinguished federal judge said recently: "We'll never be fully civilized until we eliminate this from our society."

Even coerced confessions are by no means automatically excluded by the courts. State judges, who are mostly elected, are sometimes subject to strong public pressure to convict in crimes that shock the community. Conversely, the vast majority of criminal defendants plead guilty and waive trial in order to make things easier for themselves. Many prose-cutors, anxious to build their conviction records, engage in "bargain justice," the practice of pressuring defendants to plead guilty to reduced charges. Of some 12% who do stand trial, nearly all are convicted; only a handful ever succeed in having tainted evidence excluded.

The underlying principle of fair trial, that it should be a truth-seeking contest between equal adversaries, has also been undermined by the cost of competent legal aid. Until 1963, when the Supreme Court's celebrated *Gideon* v. *Wainwright* ruling established the absolute right to counsel in serious criminal proceedings under state jurisdictions, the great majority of defendants had no lawyers because they could not afford them (60% still cannot). A disproportionate number of people wound up in jail or on death row largely because they happened to be poor, undefended and ignorant of their rights. In short, criminal justice re-mained, as the highly conservative William Howard Taft—later Chief Justice—described it in 1905, "a disgrace to our civilization."

What is now under way is a concerted effort by the Supreme Court to make the Bill of Rights a reality for all Americans. A landmark in this process occurred in the 1947 case of *Adamson* v. *California*, when the court debated whether state courts should be bound by the Fifth Amend-ment's provision that a defendant may not be forced to testify against himself. Four Justices argued that the 14th Amendment's due-process clause was a form of "shorthand" for all the guarantees spelled out in the first eight amendments, and that the Bill of Rights thus applied to the states. To give the states greater latitude, however, a five-man majority ruled that state courts would violate due-process only by action that "shocks the conscience" or otherwise imperils "ordered liberty."

All the same, on a case-by-case basis, most of the crucial provisions of the Bill of Rights have since been applied to the states as binding standards under the 14th Amendment. In *Mapp* v. *Ohio*, the Supreme Court ruled in 1961 that state courts must enforce the Fourth Amendment's guarantee against "unreasonable searches and seizures" by excluding illegal evidence, thus forcing state and local police to use judge-approved warrants for the first time in U.S. history. The *Gideon* decision invoked the Sixth Amendment to establish the right to counsel of all indigents accused of felonies—a decision that may be held to apply to misdemeanor cases as well. In other recent cases, the Supreme Court has also extended to the states the Fifth Amendment guarantee against self-incrimination and the Sixth Amendment right of the accused to cross-examine his accuser.

These rulings have inevitably stirred cries that the Supreme Court is "opening the jailhouse doors" to hundreds of prisoners whose convictions may be nullified retroactively. In an important decision last month [June, 1965] (*Linkletter* v. *Louisiana*), the court answered much of the criticism by holding that retroactivity depends on each decision's purpose. When a ruling concerns the right to counsel, as in *Gideon*, it is likely to be made retroactive, because it raises new questions about the prisoner's actual guilt. By contrast, the court refused to make *Mapp* retroactive because that decision had what lawyers call the "prophylactic" purpose of deterring lawless police action in the future.

Many implications of the Supreme Court's decisions have yet to be resolved. The *Gideon* ruling raised an infinitely complex question: At what precise moment after his arrest is a suspect entitled to counsel? For federal defendants, this issue has been solved. In *Mallory* v. *U.S.* (1957), the Supreme Court emphasized that anyone under federal arrest must be taken "without unnecessary delay" before a U.S. commissioner for instruction on his rights to silence and counsel; admissions obtained during an excessive delay must be excluded. The 1964 Criminal Justice Act requires as well that all indigents must be assigned lawyers on appearing before the commissioner.

While such safeguards seem like simple justice, in one case at least they have also led to impassioned criticism of the court. As a result of *Mallory*, a Washington, D.C., mailman named James Killough was released from prison even though he had confessed on three occasions to strangling his wife and tossing her body on a dump "like a piece of garbage." An appellate court excluded all three confessions because the police had broken the law by grilling the suspect for 15 hours before taking him before a U.S. commissioner. Forced to free Killough for lack of other evidence, U.S. District Judge George L. Hart Jr. bitterly protested: "We know the man is guilty, but we sit here blind, deaf and dumb, and we can't admit we know."

Search for Rational Standards

Despite the furor over *Mallory*, the Supreme Court last year tackled the interrogation problem at the state level with the now-famous decision in *Escobedo* v. *Illinois*. In its most controversial action yet, the court voided Chicago Laborer Danny Escobedo's murder confession because it was made after the police had refused to let him see his lawyer, who was actually waiting in the station house at the time. Though vaguely worded, the court's ruling indicated that the right to counsel begins when police start grilling a prime suspect—a plainly impractical proposition, declared dissenting Justice Byron White "unless police cars are equipped with public defenders."

Because 75% to 80% of all convictions for serious crimes are based on presumably voluntary confessions, police and prosecutors have been in a tailspin ever since. Does *Escobedo* apply only to precisely similar situations? Or does it mean that police failure to advise a suspect of his rights to counsel and to silence automatically invalidates his confession? If interrogation requires the physical presence of a lawyer, will he not obviously advise his client to say nothing? Worried police officers now fear that as a result even valid confessions will be virtually eliminated. The Supreme Court has let 13 months pass without clarifying *Escobedo*.* Presumably it is waiting to see whether its decision has had the intended effect of forcing police to do more investigating than interrogating. Despite lawmen's bitter criticism of *Escobedo*, it is a powerful reminder

---

* Since the publication of this article, the Supreme Court has clarified the Escobedo ruling. First, in Miranda v. Arizona (384 U.S. 759), the court ruled that confessions are invalid under the Fifth Amendment unless certain protections are provided the suspect. These protections include: (1) being informed of one's right to remain silent; (2) being informed that anything one says can be used against you; (3) being informed of one's right to have a lawyer; and (4) being informed of one's right to have counsel present during interrogation. (See also, *The New York Times*, June 14, 1966.) The Supreme Court later ruled, in Johnson et al. v. New Jersey (384 U.S. 762) that neither the Escobedo nor the Miranda decisions apply retroactively. (See also, *The New York Times*, June 21, 1967.) [Editors' note.]

that U.S. judicial processes are theoretically based on accusation, not inquisition.

The *Escobedo* ruling highlights a critical vacuum in U.S. criminal justice: the lack of a complete set of rational standards to coordinate the thinking of police, judges, lawyers, law professors and informed citizens. The Supreme Court has done the pioneering work—work that it could not constitutionally avoid. But rule making by constitutional interpretation has limits; such rules tend to be confined to the happenstances in particular cases and are often more confusing than clarifying. The burden is now on Congress and state legislatures, which are ideally equipped for the fact finding required in so vast and varied a country as the U.S.

Many states are in fact busily modernizing archaic codes of criminal procedure, and devising new legal weapons to meet contemporary conditions. Under New York's new "no knock" law, for instance, policemen no longer need identify themselves when executing search warrants in certain kinds of cases, such as those involving narcotics, thus reducing the risk that suspects will destroy the evidence. Local authorities have also sought to reform the out-of-date bail system, under which bondsmen grow fat while poor defendants stay in jail, where they cannot build their cases. As a result, 59% of such defendants get convicted, compared with 10% in cases where the accused can afford bail. One hopeful solution to the problem is the four-year-old Manhattan Bail Project, through which indigents are released on their own recognizance; less than 1% later fail to show up in court.

Order and Equal Justice

The prestigious American Law Institute may offer a way out of the *Escobedo* impasse with a model code of prearraignment procedure that is being force-drafted by Harvard Law Professor James Vorenberg and dozens of eminent advisers. The drafters tend to approve police interrogation of suspects under proper safeguards. Though the precise formula is still being debated, one possible answer is that grilling should be made "visible"—if not to outside witnesses, then from the evidence of movie cameras or tape recorders.

The most ambitious of all efforts at reform is the American Bar Association's three-year project to offer state legislatures "minimum standards" of criminal procedure. Started last year, under Chief Judge J. Edward Lumbard of the U.S. Court of Appeals for the Second Circuit, the undertaking is being researched by 80 of the country's top police officers, judges and lawyers. One A.B.A. committee seeks ways to get lawyers for indigents in all 3,100 of the nation's counties; more than two years after *Gideon,* there has been virtually no progress in 2,900 counties handling 70% of U.S. criminal cases. Another committee is investigating sentencing procedures. At present, no courts in the U.S. save in Connecticut and Massachusetts have the power to review sentences, however harsh or inadequate, unless they exceed statutory maximums. A more equable system of criminal justice, most authorities agree, would also demand better training, higher pay and greater public support for the nation's 350,000 policemen.

Such efforts at reform may ultimately rebut the militant argument that crime will decrease only if the cops and courts get tougher. Admittedly, fear of dire punishment is often an effective deterrent. So, for that matter, is torture. But the reformers argue that the hope of an orderly society lies in making "equal and exact justice" more equal and more exact. As Theologian Reinhold Niebuhr has observed, "Man's capacity for justice makes democracy possible, but man's inclination to injustice makes democracy necessary."

What the controversy over crime and punishment tends to overlook is that the Bill of Rights must protect everyone—the unsavory as well as the savory—or it protects no one. The goal of judicial reform should be a system that genuinely safeguards the rights of the accused wrongdoer, yet effectively upholds the innocent citizen's right to be protected from the criminal. If it can achieve both these objectives, the revolution in criminal justice will have been well fought.

Legal Representation and Class Justice

⧫

Jerome E. Carlin / Jan Howard

In 1919, Reginald Heber Smith in his book, Justice and the Poor, indicted the United States legal system as inherently unequal. The rich and the poor, he felt, did not stand on a basis of equality before the law because of the very nature of our legal system which requires the services of trained lawyers but prices such services beyond the means of large numbers of individuals.

Smith also proposed a solution: an expansion of the then newly emerging Legal Aid organizations.

Half a century later, the administration of justice in the United States still results in a radically different quality of justice for the rich and the poor. This class system of justice, as Smith saw, still rests on differences in availability and quality of legal representation. Nor have the Legal Aid organizations proved to be an effective remedy.

The use of lawyers is considerably less prevalent among the poor; about two-thirds of lower-class families have *never* employed a lawyer, compared with about one-third of upper-class families. Even when low-income people do use lawyers, the quality of representation is often not very good. "Lawyers representing lower-class persons tend to be the least competent members of the bar, and those least likely to employ a high level or wide range of technical skills.

"In the highly stratified professional community of the metropolitan bar, for example, the large firms serving wealthy individuals and large corporations claim a lion's share of the best legal talent. Lawyers available to lower-class clients, on the other hand, practice almost exclusively in the smaller firms, and consequently are at the lower end of the bar in terms of quality of training and academic achievement.

Reprinted from "Poverty and the Law," Current, 59 (June, 1965), 37–43, by permission of the publisher and *UCLA Law Review*. This article first appeared in a longer version entitled "Legal Representation and Class Justice," in 12 *UCLA Law Review* 381–437.

"Lawyers available to lower-class clients are not only less competent, but whatever legal talents they have are less likely to be employed in handling matters for their poorer clients. In part this is a direct consequence of the fee." Not only does the size of the fee affect the quality of the service provided, but fees may also dictate the strategy and tactics employed. Sound guidance is useless if the client cannot pay for it.

"A final significant fact about quality of representation is that lower-class clients are most likely to be provided with remedial service only. If a poor person gets to a lawyer it is generally after the fact—after he has been arrested, after his wages have been garnisheed, or after his property has been repossessed.

"The quality of legal service provided the poor, of course, is a far cry from that available to the well-to-do client. In representing these clients lawyers provide a much wider range of services and they are of a more continuous and preventive nature." Such services include clarifying and fashioning the law itself by means of lobbying in legislative and administrative agencies, and by presenting carefully worked out legal arguments before various official bodies.

"In addition to the foregoing, the lawyers available to lower-class clients (those in smaller firms) are less likely to conform to the minimal ethical standards of the bar; which means, among other things, that they are most likely to take advantage of their clients. A study of individual practitioners in Chicago has shown, for example, that lawyers with lower-status clients who become dependent on intermediaries to supply them with a large number of 'one-shot' matters often consider their clients expendable and are apt to exploit them. . . .

Why the Poor Need Legal Help

"Class differences in legal representation need not necessarily constitute a denial of justice to the poor." It could be argued that the poor are less likely to use lawyers because in fact they are less likely to need lawyers, the contention being that they have fewer problems requiring legal representation. Furthermore, it has been suggested that, although private counsel may be inaccessible to the poor, adequate substitutes exist in the form of Legal Aid, court-assigned counsel, public defenders and special tribunals. In our view, both these arguments are false.

It is true, of course, that the poor are less likely to have the kind of property or business interests that require legal services. But "those who pursue this particular argument to show that the poor have fewer legal *problems* generally adopt a quite narrow and somewhat unrealistic definition of property. It is undoubtedly true that lower-class persons are less likely to own or to be involved in transactions concerning the more traditional forms of property such as real estate or corporate securities. These traditional forms of property, however, do not necessarily exhaust the full range of economic interests that already have or may well deserve to be given the protection of property.

"Job rights, social security, unemployment compensation, public assistance, health insurance, retirement funds and a host of similar interests tend to be the characteristic forms of economic wealth for the poor. The fact that these interests may not always be recognized as property may well be the result of the failure of the poor to establish or pursue their legal rights in these areas. Indeed, Charles Reich argues that to insure the dignity of the individual these benefits must be recognized as property and protected as a matter of right."

In fact, there are a number of areas in which the poor encounter at least as many legal problems as do the rich. Crime, for example, is principally a poor man's problem. The poor are the ones most likely to suffer from the effects of injustice or inefficiency in the criminal process; they are almost never socially powerful or sophisticated enough to bring a complaint to the proper authorities and to fight it through successfully.

The need for legal representation arises at every stage of the criminal process, from time of arrest to final appeal. Indeed, the Supreme Court has given increasing recognition to the proposition that legal representation for the accused is itself a fundamental constitutional right.

Less obvious are the legal problems of the poor in the civil area. Poor people ordinarily live in slums or semi-slums and often face a multitude of housing problems that clearly have legal implications. There are many ways in which lawyers might help.

First, they can help make tenants aware of their legal rights, either directly or through social workers. Second, they can make it possible for tenants to exercise existing legal rights which are often so hedged in with technicalities that even lawyers have problems. Most states, for example, have laws requiring the landlord to provide heat, water and electricity, and to keep the premises free of vermin. These laws are often violated; yet without legal counsel, tenants have a particularly difficult time forcing the landlord to fulfill the law. The so-called "rent strikes" in New York City were situations in which tenants who had access to attorneys took advantage of a legal remedy which had rarely before been exercised.

Lawyers can also help clarify and develop the law of landlord-tenant relations itself and bring it into harmony with the realities of modern urban living. For example, the courts usually treat the leasing of apartments as a leasing of real property. But in modern multiple dwelling units, the tenant rents services and facilities as well as physical space. The failure to push through such legal concepts is related to the lack of legal counsel readily available to those most concerned with the problem—the poor tenants.

A third area in which the poor have special legal problems is civil rights. A disproportionate number of the poor are nonwhite, and it is often hard to determine where the legal problems of the poor leave off and those of race and nationality begin. "Through Federal, state, and local legislative acts, executive orders and judicial decisions, a whole new set of rights and remedies for minority persons is being developed and clarified. These rights are applicable to such areas as employment, housing, education, public accommodations and voting. The mere existence of rights, of course, is not sufficient to guarantee their fulfillment. There must be active, aggressive attorneys to employ the legal machinery effectively. This is particularly true in the civil rights area, where there is widespread and organized resistance to change."

Implementation of civil rights is especially difficult without legal help when intimidation comes not only from the citizenry-at-large but from agents of the law as well—judges, lawyers, police and other public officials.

The development of the welfare state has led to the emergence of a whole new set of legal problems for the poor, both for those who are on welfare as well as for those who are not but who are entitled to be. In order to be a welfare recipient, it is necessary to meet certain eligibility standards. Poor people have to prove that they need welfare; that they are not deliberately scheming to get welfare; that they satisfy residence requirements; that they are morally worthy. Unjust rejections appear to be common. If the poor had greater access to legal representation, more rejected applicants might effectively challenge the grounds for their rejection.

Those on welfare are particularly vulnerable to unconstitutional invasions of privacy. Public agencies tend to view welfare as a *privilege* rather than a *right*, and that therefore welfare recipients retain their benefits conditionally, subject to confiscation in the interests of the state. This view permits a great deal of administrative abuse.

Unannounced midnight welfare searches, made without warrants, to determine whether or not a man is sharing the bed of a mother whose children are receiving aid, is one example of such abuse. Charles Reich contends that these searches are unconstitutional invasions of privacy and that the Federal Department of Health, Education and Welfare has a legal responsibility to prohibit them.

Such practices have continued for so long primarily because persons on public assistance are in no position to enforce constitutional rights. They lack the means, they lack the knowledge, and they lack adequate counsel.

There is a whole complex of legal problems in the consumer area. Between 1920 and 1960, installment debt, exclusive of mortgages, rose from $1 billion to $42 billion. By mid-1964, installment debt in the United States stood at $56 billion. Credit buying has a special impact on the poor. To begin with, low-income groups are more likely than high-income groups to have a large proportion of their income tied up in debt payments. Furthermore, the poor are especially vulnerable because they often lack the savings to back up their debts.

Consequently, many poor people experience legal pressure due to missed payments, which often set off a downward spiral of debt. A missed payment can lead to a repossession and/or a deficiency judgment; and the deficiency judgment can lead to a wage attachment; and the wage attachment can lead to a loss of job. In some areas it is common practice for private industry to dismiss employees after three wage attachments. Many employers simply will not bother with garnishments and fire workers whose salaries have been attached.

"Obviously, anyone who is entangled in the debtor spiral needs the services of an attorney—to tell him what his rights may be (*e.g.,* how much of his wages can be attached), and to intervene on his behalf at a number of points along the line (*e.g.,* to work out a 'deal' before the repossession, to challenge the proposed amount of the deficiency judgment). If legal representation were obtained before the signing of the initial contract, missed payments might be avoided altogether."

Many poor people are the victims of fraud and misrepresentation on the part of merchants. Very often, missed payment problems are linked to problems of fraud. Families capable of maintaining payments may stop payment when they discover they have been cheated. Instead of gaining retribution, the cheated person without legal help often finds himself subject to all the legal penalties applicable to one who misses payments.

There are also many problems stemming from inept or biased law enforcement. Judgments against the poor for failing to appear in court are quite common. It may be particularly difficult for a poor person to leave his job, or to travel a long way to court. Or he may be unaware of the legal implications of failing to appear. But many times, the consumer fails to respond to a summons because it was never delivered. Process servers, hired by the plaintiff's lawyer, may shirk their responsibility and simply throw the summons away. This happens with such frequency that a special term, "sewer service," is used to refer to it.

Similarly, collection agents sometimes indulge in questionable practices. In New York City, a defendant's salary can be attached only if his property is insufficient to satisfy the debt. Only as a last resort are wages to be attached. But since the collecting agent's income is totally derived from fees, he is naturally eager to dispose of his cases rapidly. Consequently, he sometimes moves to wage attachment directly without investigating the defendant's property at all.

"Whatever public interest there is in consumer problems seems to be primarily oriented toward those of the middle class, truth in lending, deceptive packaging, misleading advertising, misleading labeling, short weighting and price fixing. Although new laws in these areas might be helpful to the poor, what they really need is protection against the 'debtor spiral.' Thus, low-income consumers may require lawyers to frame and promote laws more directly in their interest. . . .

"Those who argue that the problems of the poor are essentially social or psychological rather than legal tend to conceive of the poor as incapable of comprehending, let alone altering, their predicament. The poor are thus seen as 'human material that will be worked on, helped and hopefully transformed,' as objects to be manipulated or treated by those who claim to know what is good for them—*i.e.*, social workers, psychiatrists, probation officers or marriage counselors. . . .

"We propose that a distinctive characteristic of the poor, and an essential condition of their predicament, is their lack of participation in the legal and governmental process. Thus the answer to the question of whether the poor have legal problems and need lawyers turns ultimately on the strength of our commitment to the extension of citizenship, for enfranchisement necessarily rests on the capacity to participate in and make effective use of the legal order—in our legal system, this means access to competent legal representation."

Is Adequate Legal Help Available?

Whatever class differences exist in legal representation have been defended on the ground that adequate substitutes for private lawyers are available. "Much can and should be said in praise of those who have contributed so much time and energy to the cause of providing legal services to the needy. Although there is tangible evidence of their labors, it is our opinion—shared by a number of Legal Aid workers themselves—that Legal Aid is seriously handicapped both in meeting the vast potential need for legal representation and in dealing with cases that are actually handled. Moreover, we suggest that the effectiveness of Legal Aid is undermined by the way it is organized and financed and the way it conceives of its task."

The principal limitations of Legal Aid seem to be these: 1) Grossly inadequate resources. Over the past 50 years the hoped for growth in Legal Aid has simply not materialized. The fundamental defect in Legal Aid service today is that, from a national point of view, it hardly exists.

2) Vulnerability to the demands of local private lawyers and businessmen. Many people in need of legal help are turned away because they are able to pay a fee. The policy of Legal Aid is to refer those who can pay a fee to a private attorney through the Lawyers Referral Service or the local bar. But this tends to penalize those thrifty and industrious poor who have managed to save a little money. Furthermore, those who are sent to the Lawyers Referral Service must go through yet another step before ending up with a lawyer. How many of those "referred" actually obtain a reasonably responsible and competent attorney? How many of those turned away are soured by the experience and further alienated from the legal system? We suspect that the policy against competition with private practitioners more often serves the local bar than the needy clients. This is the price that is paid for the support of the bar.

3) The tendency of Legal Aid to adopt a social-welfare orientation toward its clients and toward its over-all goals. The policy of many Legal Aid offices, for example, is that divorce is a privilege and not a right and that social need must be determined before the poor can be given legal help in obtaining a divorce. "In making that determination the Legal Aid attorney frequently relies on the judgment or certification of a social worker. This, in turn, may mean that the client will have to submit not only to an investigation by a social worker, but also to some form of marriage counseling as a condition for obtaining a divorce. Such counseling is rarely required of those who can afford a private attorney. . . .

"The underlying attitude here is that the poor person is essentially a welfare client, rather than a citizen capable of having rights and duties and of knowing his own best interests. As a result, Legal Aid is deemed a privilege granted solely within the discretion of the grantor."

Court-assigned counsels and public defender offices are two other methods which theoretically provide the 60 per cent of defendants in criminal actions who are unable to pay for private counsel with adequate legal representation. In our judgment, neither method is effective.

Assigned attorneys are often young and inexperienced, hence no match for the prosecuting attorney. The assigned counsel method may provide valuable training for young lawyers, but it can have dire consequences for the client. This is fundamentally at odds with the concept of effective defense in an adversary system.

Furthermore, assigned counsels rarely have adequate time or money to prepare a good defense. They are not generally reimbursed for out-of-pocket expenses, and are paid very little for their services. Thus the assigned counsel is often under pressure to end the case quickly by pleading his client guilty. Finally, assigned counsel usually enters a case at the stage of arraignment or even sometimes after indictment; by this time, it may be too late to make any real difference. And even with all these defects, a large proportion of accused persons are still never represented.

It has been said that public defender offices, presumably with a full-time staff of experienced attorneys and sufficient funds for investigation, could remedy the inadequacies of the assigned counsel method. But although a few public defender offices seem to have these resources, most do not.

Special tribunals have also been suggested as possible substitutes for private counsel. The Small Claims Court was designed for this purpose. In the view of its founders, it was supposed to provide the poor person with a low-cost forum in which to present his case without the encumbrances of usual procedural rules. Unfortunately, it has not turned out that way.

The actual operation of these courts shows that it is primarily the business community and not the poor that reaps the advantages of the inexpensive and speedy process provided by the Small Claims Court. Thus the initial purpose of the court has been thwarted, not only because the poor cannot afford the costs involved, but also because they do not have the awareness, the capacity or the organizational support to press their claims. They simply cannot cope with the system without extensive help. In sharp contrast, highly organized business firms have precisely what it takes to make effective use of the court, and that is exactly what they have done.

The Preconditions of Equality

It should by now be obvious that the poor do indeed have extensive need for legal help. It should be equally obvious that effective legal services for the poor do not exist. What are the conditions for providing effective legal services to the poor?

First of all, legal services must be subsidized. "It should be quite obvious that lower-income groups simply cannot afford the range and type of legal service that is required for effective solution of their legal problems. Existing expenditures for legal aid to the poor are patently insufficient."

Second, it is essential that legal services take the initiative in going to the people. Lower-class people cannot be reached by middle-class devices. Institutions which sit back and wait for the needy to take the first step only widen the distance between them.

In order to seek out the needy and actively offer help, geographical proximity is an absolute necessity; legal services must be situated as close as possible to those in need of them. But beyond that, social proximity is equally important. Provision of legal services must be tied to informal referral networks; there have to be social links between lawyers and potential clients, as well as informal social support for using lawyers. As of now, the law is frequently viewed by the poor as something that works against them, as an alien device used by their enemies.

Third, organizational support could play a crucial role. "Middle-class persons are more likely to belong to organizations that can inform them of their legal rights, act as watchdogs of agencies, provide resources for seeking legal help, and even initiate legal action on their members' behalf. Labor unions often serve these purposes, but the poor are frequently unemployed or in occupations that are non-unionized. It may be necessary, therefore, to create new types of organizations for the poor." These may take the form of an association of tenants, of recipients of welfare or of consumers. It may even include the incorporation of a block.

Fourth, the legal problems of the poor must be dealt with at an institutional level. This might include bringing about changes in the routine practices of landlords, finance companies and merchants; and reforming administrative regulations and official procedures of welfare agencies, certain courts or police departments that are inconsistent with the standards of due process. These changes could be effected on an individual case-by-case basis or by representation of class interests (like a legally organized rent strike) or by lobbying in appropriate administrative agencies and legislative committees. All this suggests, of course, that lawyers serving the poor must be capable of exercising a high level of technical skill and ingenuity on a continuous basis, as do lawyers serving the rich.

Fifth, legal services for the poor must be independent. As the earlier discussion of Legal Aid showed, it would appear to be essential to avoid excessive involvement with, or dependence upon, those interests that will necessarily be threatened by effective legal representation of the poor.

Sixth, legal representation must be seen as a right and not as a privilege. This does not mean that every poor person has to have a trained lawyer at his side, nor does it mean that adequate legal representation is the panacea for poverty. It does mean, however, that every person should have the right to some form of legal help. Without such a right, the poor cannot possibly make effective use of the legal system.

Police Discretion

✺

Sanford H. Kadish

The ideal of full enforcement by the police is preserved officially in formal law as well as in popular conception.[1] Statutes, mostly of nineteenth century vintage, tend to speak in terms of the duty of the police diligently and faithfully to enforce all the penal laws.[2] Decisions of appellate courts dealing with the legality of arrest commonly assert that the officer had not only the right but the duty to arrest or face charges of recreancy to that duty.[3] A recent decision exemplifies the common hostility to selectivity in police law enforcement.[4] In a proceeding to enjoin police enforcement of the Sunday Blue Law against a large retailing operation, the police department admitted (remarkably) a policy of selective enforcement against the larger retailers because of limitations on police personnel available. While recognizing that "to enforce [the law] . . . against all retail merchants would necessitate the transfer of large numbers of police personnel from other important duties,"[5] the court granted the injunction, concluding that the policy of selective enforcement constituted unconstitutional discrimination.[6] In informal sources as well, one finds a conception of the duty of full enforcement. Thus police manuals, when they address themselves to this question at all, either speak with some ambiguity or expressly instruct the police officer that it is his duty to enforce all the laws against everyone without exception.[7] The common reaction of police chiefs queried by the press concerning their attitude to enforcement of controversial laws is revealing. On the record, it is that the duty of the police is to enforce all the criminal laws of the state; off the record it is that to say otherwise would create hostility in some segments of the public and expose the police to nonfeasance charges by grand juries.

Reprinted from "Police Discretion," in "Legal Norms and Discretion in the Police and Sentencing Processes," 75 *Harvard Law Review* 906 (1962), by permission of the author and publisher. Copyright © 1962 by The Harvard Law Review Association.

In terms of fact, of course, the practice reduces this ideal to a myth, and the need to preserve the existence of the ideal in these mythological terms has tended to divert attention from the nature of the problem presented: Is it subversive of the principle of legality that the police in fact exercise a wide discretion in their enforcement of the criminal law, even though what is involved is the withholding of prosecution? Is this discretion practically inevitable? Is it desirable? Should it be eliminated or controlled? How should it be controlled?

It is not helpful in approaching these problems to insist either that all selective police law enforcement is an intolerable compromise with the principle of legality, or, contrariwise, that it is all a legitimate and necessary means of making the law act soundly and in accordance with common sense.[8] The discretionary judgment to arrest or not is made in a wide variety of circumstances, for a wide variety of reasons, raising considerations which are not the same in all cases.[9] The point of what follows is to select a few of the circumstances in which arrest judgments are made in order to explore the particular kinds of choices called for in evaluating rule and discretion at the police level.

The most obvious kind of discretionary judgment involves the police deployment of forces for patrolling and for investigation.[10] Such judgments clearly affect the persons who will be subject to the criminal process and to some extent the crimes which will be sanctioned. There may nonetheless be some force in the view that such decisions are essentially professional in nature, involving ways of making maximum use of limited men, equipment, and resources, and that the consequences for the principle of legality are not major. In any event the necessity for judgments such as these is created by limitations on the amount of resources a community is prepared to invest in police enforcement and the refusal of the public to accept the consequences of a garrison-type community entailed in a program of saturation law enforcement.

The more difficult cases are those in which the policeman declines to make an arrest of an apparently guilty suspect on the ground that it is better for some reason that the criminal process not be invoked against him. To some extent, of course, every decision of this kind, despite its ameliorative character, is inconsistent with the rule of law in the occasion it creates for inequality in official action, arbitrariness, discrimination, and abuse,[11] let alone in its potential for thwarting the legislative goals of crime prevention usually implicit in the substantive definition of the crime.[12] There are, however, considerable differences in the degree of danger posed and in the desirability and feasibility of eliminating such discretionary judgments.

One kind of systematic nonenforcement by the police is produced by criminal statutes which seem deliberately to overcriminalize, in the sense of encompassing conduct not the target of legislative concern, in order to assure that suitable suspects will be prevented from escaping through legal loopholes as the result of the inability of the prosecution to prove acts which bring the defendants within the scope of the prohibited conduct. A prime example are laws prohibiting gambling. Such laws are frequently drawn by the legislature in deliberately wide terms purporting to make unlawful, without material exception, all kinds of gambling, whether of a commercial character or of a private social character and even where used as part of a charitable or religious fund-raising project. The task then devolves upon the police (and prosecutor, in the second instance) to determine whether a particular violation falls within the real vice with which the legislature was concerned.[13] Therefore, private social gambling among friends in their own homes, church bingo games, and the like are typically left alone. Where however the police believe sufficient elements of commercialization to be present, the decision to arrest is made. There are of course other instances of this deliberate overcriminalization, *e.g.*, automobile homicide and strict liability statutes.[14] In these, however, it is generally the prosecutor who tends to assume primary responsibility for the discriminating judgment through his power to charge, rather than the police through their power to arrest.

Insofar as such laws purport to bring within the condemnation of the criminal statute kinds of activities whose moral neutrality, if not innocence, is widely recognized, they raise basic issues of a morally acceptable criminal code.[15] Moreover, these laws are in effect equivalent to enactments of a broad legislative policy against, for example, undesirable gambling, leaving it to the police to further that policy by such arrests as seem to them compatible with it. From one point of view such statutes invite a danger cognate to that of defining crime by analogy, augmented by the fact that it is the policeman who is defining criminal conduct rather than a court.[16] That no actual abuse has been demonstrated in police administration of an overdrawn statute,[17] such as gambling, would not seem to answer the moral and precedential objections to this tactic, any more than the fact that courts in states where the doctrine of common law crimes exists have not in recent years abused it would answer the objections to this doctrine. Doubts concerning such practices have their source too deep in history to be swept aside because of a fortunate experience. Nor are abuses of these powers likely to be sufficiently visible and demonstrable to permit the inference that all is well from the absence of affirmative evidence of their existence. It may be

concluded of this genre of police discretion, therefore, that it is deliberately created by the legislature, that it holds primary dangers, and that it
is, to a large degree, avoidable by substantive law reform, although with
some loss to law enforcement.

A second category of substantial police discretion is the product of
criminal legislation which, either in practical effect or in actual purpose,
involves the use of the criminal law for social objectives other than crime
prevention. A well known example is legislation prohibiting consenting
extramarital or deviant sexual behavior among adults. That these laws
only rarely result in criminal arrests and prosecutions is well known. And
the studies of Dr. Kinsey have not let us believe the lack of enforcement
is due to an absence of violations.[18] Thurman Arnold has neatly put the
final justification of such unenforced laws: They "survive in order to
satisfy moral objections to established modes of conduct. They are
unenforced because we want to continue our conduct, and unrepealed
because we want to preserve our morals."[19]

Their existence, however, casts the same shadow of potentially
arbitrary and abusive law enforcement as that cast by purposely overdrawn legislation. It has been suggested that here, as in overdrawn
gambling laws, the lack of adequate demonstration that harm results from
this legislation weakens the case against it.[20] The point carries no greater
weight here than there. Moreover, it does not seem convincing to argue,
as it has been argued,[21] that the objection loses further force in view of
the broad discretionary power which exists elsewhere in our legal system,
such as the power to use the income tax penalty against gangsters where
gangster activity can not be proved. If sex legislation and tax legislation
are meant to be enforced equally and are in fact generally enforced
equally, the point is well taken. In that event the problem, if it be one, is
the use by the police or prosecutor of a generally enforced criminal
statute, intended to be enforced, when the authorities are really concerned with the accused because of other criminal conduct. The point is
less convincing, however, if the starting point is that much sex legislation,
unlike criminal tax penalties, is not enforced except for other reasons,
nor, in a sense, meant to be enforced, and that violation is general and
known. In this case the problem is prosecution for conduct which is
criminal in name only, as it were, in order to convict a defendant whom
the police, for reasons sufficient or insufficient, regard as otherwise
worthy of imprisonment.[22]

A group of criminal laws plainly not meant, as well as in practice not
used, for purposes of crime prevention is constituted of those designed to
perform essentially social service functions. The bad-checks laws, insofar

as they include insufficient-funds cases, are an instance of this kind; another are the nonsupport laws. In the former, the criminal law is designed as a means of enforcing payment of debts; in the latter it is used in order to ensure payments by defaulting husbands. The rationale of these laws, therefore, invites, if it does not require, judgments by the police to arrest not simply where there has been a violation, but only where the arrest will tend to serve the end of ensuring that the debt is paid or the payment made. As with sex legislation, the problem to be faced here is a legislative one of determining whether the cost of adding to discretionary judgments by the police is worth the assumed social value of using the criminal law for noncriminal purposes.[23]

A third category of discretionary police nonenforcement differs from the previous two in that the responsibility for its existence is not primarily a legislative choice and it is not amenable to resolution by broad policy formulations. In these cases, the discretionary judgment is the product of the inevitable need for mediation between generally formulated laws and the human values contained in the varieties of particular circumstances in which the law is technically violated. For example, should the police arrest for assault where the dispute which gave rise to the incident occurs in connection with a matrimonial difference and the victim declines to sign a complaint? Should the police arrest where a customer is bilked of his money by a defaulting prostitute? Should they arrest a wife for falsely reporting a felony, where under interrogation she admits to claiming she was raped in order to conceal her infidelity from her husband? Should a respected citizen be arrested for a homosexual accosting when he is already under psychiatric care? In cases of this kind the need for some kind of amelioration is plain. The issue is whether that function should be confined to the sentencing and dismissal powers of the court, where it is normally vested by statute, or on the other hand, whether it is worth the cost of adding to police discretion to save the stigma, embarrassment, and general destructiveness to a man's life often entailed in the very preliminary act of arresting.

The foregoing examples of circumstances calling for free police judgment in the arrest function suggest, as counterbalancing the gains of maintaining the police choice, the potential losses in inequality, arbitrariness, and abuse. That there are losses of subtler dimension even in the conscientious arrest decision is suggested by two kinds of police practice recently brought into sharp focus.[24] At least in one large city with a sizable Negro population the Negro press commonly exploits the charge that the police are harder on Negroes than on whites, a charge that finds apparent support in the far greater percentage of Negroes arrested. The facts, however, suggest a subtler kind of discrimination, insidious rather than invidious. Rather than overly strict enforcement against Negroes, what commonly is involved is a calculated nonenforcement of certain laws against the Negro population, justified on the ground that a lesser standard of morality prevails and that it is therefore unwise to apply the general legal standards to them. On this rationale arrests of Negroes are often not made for such offenses as bigamy, open and notorious cohabitation, and, most strikingly, felonious assault where both the aggressor and the victim are Negroes and the latter declines to complain. This, of course, constitutes a form of discrimination no less significant than the commonly charged overzealous arrest of Negroes, in view of its perpetuation of a lower moral standard in an underprivileged cultural subgroup and by the failure to use the criminal law for one of its central purposes as a solidifier and communalizer of moral values. A practice which gives rise to problems of a related character is the decision not to arrest a minor offender in order to use him as an informer or decoy to detect and arrest persons whom the police regard as major offenders. A dramatic example is the grant of a police "license" to narcotics users to continue their use so long as they cooperate in apprehending larger sellers. Apart from the moral issue of police participation in crime, it may be doubtful that in exhibiting nonenforcement the police contribute to deterring traffic in narcotics; and it would seem clear that in following this pattern of nonenforcement against known users the police are depriving the victims of the opportunity for rehabilitation, presumably one of the ends of the narcotics laws.[25]

What has been said would seem to point to the inevitable selectivity of judgment required in evaluating rule and discretion at the police level. Police discretion owes its existence to a variety of causes and serves varying values and purposes, some weightier and less dispensable than others. Judgments reached out of apprehension of the potential for abuse and discrimination and the subtler kinds of evils, which fail to pass on the case for discretion in particular situations and the relative feasibility of eliminating it, can neither be rounded nor reliable. But there is a further task, which arises after deliberative judgment has decided to retain the discretionary judgment in those situations where its usefulness outweighs its dangers, or to abide with it where it appears ineradicable. This is the task of devising means whereby abusive judgments may be minimized or neutralized and conscientious judgments guided to ensure consistency with the totality of goals of a criminal law system. The traditional means of guiding the exercise of discretionary judgment, through the legislative (or administrative) formulation of criteria for nonenforcement, is probably unsuitable for this purpose in view of the need to avoid weakening the deterrent and moralizing force of the substantive criminal law.[26] Other suggestions have been to provide mechanisms or arrangements whereby the nonarrest decision is shared by the police and some other agency; or to create an "Appraisal and Review Board" in order "to increase visibility and hence reviewability of these police decisions."[27] How far these proposals would constitute improvements in the end over existing allocations of responsibility among police, prosecutors, and trial judges is hard to say.[28] Certainly the challenge of making accountable the policeman's exercise of power not to arrest is formidable. Neither the perpetuation of the myth of full enforcement nor of the myth of the benignity and inevitability of unfettered discretion will move us towards an acceptable accommodation.

Notes

1) See generally Arnold, *The Symbols of Government*, 149–71 (1935). His observation concerning prosecutorial discretion is equally applicable to police discretion:

> The idea that a prosecuting attorney should be permitted to use his discretion concerning the laws which he will enforce and those which he will disregard appears to the ordinary citizen to border on anarchy. The fact that prosecuting attorneys are compelled to do this very thing is generally ignored, or, when attention is called to it, regarded as evidence of some kind of social degeneration which must be preached away in public speech and judicial utterance.

Id. at 151.

2) For a compilation of such statutes see Goldstein, "Police Discretion Not to Invoke the Criminal Process: Low-Visibility Decisions in the Administration of Justice," 69 *Yale L.J.* 543, 557 n.26 (1960).

3) See, *e.g.*, People v. Woodward, 220 Mich. 511, 515, 190 N.W. 721, 723 (1922). The view is that "the lodgment in an officer of the power to enforce a law necessarily implies the duty of enforcement." Gowan v. Smith, 157 Mich. 443, 459, 122 N.W. 286, 291 (1909). See also the cases dealing with mandamus to compel a magistrate to issue an arrest warrant where a proper complaint has been filed. Such proceedings are often upheld on the ground that police enforcement is a compulsory ministerial act. *E.g.*, Marshall v Herndon, 161 Ky. 232, 170 S.W. 623 (1914). Where relief has been denied it is often for the reason that relator lacked a necessary special and personal interest in the arrest sought. See State *ex rel.* Skilton v. Miller, 164 Ohio St. 163, 128 N.E.2d 47 (1955); Annot., 49 A.L.R.2d 1285 (1956).

4) Bargain City U.S.A. Inc. v. Dilworth, The Philadelphia Legal Intelligencer, June 22, 1960, p. 1, col. 1 (Phila. Ct. C.P. 1960).

5) *Id.* at p. 6, col. 2.

6) *But see* Comment, "The Right to Nondiscriminatory Enforcement of State Penal Laws," 61 *Colum. L. Rev.* 1103, 1118 (1961), where it is concluded that United States Supreme Court decisions support the conclusion that "administrative agencies charged with enforcing penal laws possess the power to make reasonable classifications of a legislative nature."

7) See the compilation in Goldstein, *supra* note 2, at 558 n.27.

8) Thoughtful commentators have recently been turning their attention to these problems. For positions generally favorable to a rule-of-law approach, see Goldstein, *supra* note 2; Hall, "Police and Law in a Democratic Society," 28 *Ind. L.J.* 133 (1953). For positions generally favorable to freedom for the discretionary judgment, see . . . Remington and Rosenblum, "The Criminal Law and the Legislative Process," 1960 *U. Ill. L.F.* 481, at 491.

9) Most of the illustrations which follow are based upon or suggested by two of the American Bar Foundation studies in connection with the continuing program of research into the administration of criminal justice in the United States: II *Pilot Project Report—The Administration of Criminal Justice in the United States* (1959), and LaFave, *Arrest in Michigan* (1960). The present confidential status of these preliminary studies precludes further acknowledgment of my indebtedness to them through specific references. None of these arrest situations will be new to those who have read Professor Goldstein's acute analysis based on the data revealed by these studies, *supra* note 2.

10) See Walton, "'Selective Distribution' of Police Patrol Force," 49 *J. Crim. L., C. & P.S.* 165, 379 (1958).

11) But however intelligently this power is used the fundamental question remains, should the police have the recognized right to dispense with the criminal law at will?

   Dicey believed that the rule of law meant that the citizen should be free from arbitrary power. A discretion to withhold a punishment may result in just as much arbitrary power as discretion to use extralegal punishment.

   Hargrove, "Police Discretion," 25 *Sol.* 337 (1958).

12) Goldstein, *supra* note 2, at 562.

13) See Comment on § 3 of the Model Anti-Gambling Act in 2 *American Bar Association Commission on Organized Crime, Organized Crime and Law Enforcement* 75 (1953):

   [A]bout half [of the states] impose penalties for all gambling, apparently leaving the problem of the social gambler to the discretion of enforcement authorities and the courts. . . .

   The Commission has . . . had great difficulty with . . . finding a formula which would exclude the social or casual gambler from prosecution and punishment, yet which would not result in opening a large breach in the statute for the benefit of professional gamblers and their patrons. The Commission recognizes that it is unrealistic to promulgate a law literally aimed at making a criminal offense of the friendly election bet, the private, social card game among friends, etc. Nevertheless, it is imperative to confront the professional gambler with a statutory facade that is wholly devoid of loopholes.

14) *Cf.* James & Son Ltd. v. Smee, [1955] I Q.B. 78, 93: "Where legislation, as here [strict liability statute], throws a wide net it is important that only those should be charged who either deserve punishment or in whose case it can be said that punishment would tend to induce them to keep themselves and their organization up to the mark."

15) Hart, "The Aims of the Criminal Law," 23 *Law & Contemp. Prob.* 401, 424 (1958). See People v. Bunis, 9 N.Y.2d 1, 4, 172 N.E.2d 273, 274, 210 N.Y.S.2d 505, 507 (1961), in which the court of appeals invalidated § 436-d of the N.Y. Penal Law proscribing the sale of coverless magazines, stating: "What is wrong is not the sale of coverless magazines, but rather their sale by a vendor who takes part in a scheme to defraud a magazine publisher. Admittedly by denominating as criminal all sales, section 436-d necessarily tends to prevent corrupt sales. But . . . it is unreasonable and beyond the legitimate exercise of the police power for the Legislature to interdict all sales, permissible and illicit alike, in order to prevent those which are illicit."

16) For attempts to draft more narrowly defined gambling statutes, see *Mont. Rev. Code Ann.* § 94-2403 (1947); *Model Anti-Gambling Act* § 3[(2)], note 13 *supra*.

17) See Remington & Rosenblum, *supra* note 8, at 491, 493.

18) Kinsey, Pomeroy and Martin, *Sexual Behaviour in the Human Male*, 392 (1948): "The persons involved in these activities [illicit sexual activities punishable as

crimes] taken as a whole, constitute more than 95 per cent of the total population."

19) *Symbols of Government,* 160 (1935).
20) See Remington & Rosenblum, *supra* note 8, at 493.
21) See *id.* at 494.
22) *Cf.* Kinsey, Martin and Gebhard, *Sexual Behaviour in the Human Female,* 18 (1953):

> The prodding of some reform group, a newspaper-generated hysteria over some local sex crime, a vice drive which is put on by the local authorities to distract attention from defects in their administration of the city government, or the addition to the law-enforcement group of a sadistic officer who is disturbed over his own sexual problems, may result in a doubling . . . in the number of arrests on sex charges, even though there may have been no change in the actual behaviour of the community, and even though the illicit sex acts that are apprehended and prosecuted may still represent no more than a fantastically minute part of the illicit activity which takes place every day in the community.

23) See Allen, "The Borderland of the Criminal Law: Problems of 'Socializing' Criminal Justice," 32 *Social Service Rev.* 107, 109 (1958).
24) See note 9 *supra.*
25) The problem is carefully examined in Goldstein, *supra* note 2, at 562–73.
26) However, on occasion this has been done. Article 88 of the *Uniform Code of Military Justice* makes it an offense for an officer to use contemptuous words against certain officials of the United States Government. 10 U.S.C. § 888 (1958). The comment upon this provision in the *Manual for Courts-Martial,* however, states that "expressions of opinion made in a purely private conversation should not ordinarily be made the basis for a court martial charge." *Manual for Courts-Martial, United States,* 318 (1951). Another well known example was the detailed OPA guide to price-control enforcement policy during World War II. These are summarized in Schwartz, "Federal Criminal Jurisdiction and Prosecutors' Discretion," 13 *Law & Contemp. Prob.* 64, 84 (1948).
27) Goldstein, *supra* note 2, at 586.
28) While nonenforcement judgments by prosecutors and trial judges may often influence police not to arrest (except where the police motive is other than prosecution, *e.g.,* harassment), they do not reach independent judgments of police not to arrest in the first place. Beyond this, there appears to be little systematic formulation and communication of standards from prosecutors to police. Furthermore, it can not be assumed that prosecutorial discretionary judgments and policies are not generative of cognate dangers themselves.

Police Encounters with Juveniles

Irving Piliavin / Scott Briar

As the first of a series of decisions made in the channeling of youthful offenders through the agencies concerned with juvenile justice and corrections, the disposition decisions made by police officers have potentially profound consequences for apprehended juveniles. Thus arrest, the most severe of the dispositions available to police, may not only lead to confinement of the suspected offender but also bring him loss of social status, restriction of educational and employment opportunities, and future harassment by law-enforcement personnel.[1] According to some criminologists, the stigmatization resulting from police apprehension, arrest, and detention actually reinforces deviant behavior.[2] Other authorities have suggested, in fact, that this stigmatization serves as the catalytic agent initiating delinquent careers.[3] Despite their presumed significance, however, little empirical analysis has been reported regarding the factors influencing, or consequences resulting from, police actions with juvenile offenders. Furthermore, while some studies of police encounters with adult offenders have been reported, the extent to which the findings of these investigations pertain to law-enforcement practices with youthful offenders is not known.[4]

The above considerations have led the writers to undertake a longitudinal study of the conditions influencing, and consequences flowing from, police actions with juveniles. In the present paper findings will be presented indicating the influence of certain factors on police actions. Research data consist primarily of notes and records based on nine months' observation of all juvenile officers in one police department.[5] The officers were observed in the course of their regular tours of duty.[6] While these data do not lend themselves to quantitative assessments of

---

reliability and validity, the candor shown by the officers in their interviews with the investigators and their use of officially frowned-upon practices while under observation provide some assurance that the materials presented below accurately reflect the typical operations and attitudes of the law-enforcement personnel studied.

The setting for the research, a metropolitan police department serving an industrial city with approximately 450,000 inhabitants, was noted within the community it served and among law-enforcement officials elsewhere for the honesty and superior quality of its personnel. Incidents involving criminal activity or brutality by members of the department had been extremely rare during the ten years preceding this study; personnel standards were comparatively high; and an extensive training program was provided to both new and experienced personnel. Juvenile Bureau members, the primary subjects of this investigation, differed somewhat from other members of the department in that they were responsible for delinquency prevention as well as law enforcement, that is, juvenile officers were expected to be knowledgeable about conditions leading to crime and delinquency and to be able to work with community agencies serving known or potential juvenile offenders. Accordingly, in the assignment of personnel to the Juvenile Bureau, consideration was given not only to an officer's devotion to and reliability in law enforcement but also to his commitment to delinquency prevention. Assignment to the Bureau was of advantage to policemen seeking promotions. Consequently, many officers requested transfer to this unit, and its personnel comprised a highly select group of officers.

In the field, juvenile officers operated essentially as patrol officers. They cruised assigned beats and, although concerned primarily with juvenile offenders, frequently had occasion to apprehend and arrest adults. Confrontations between the officers and juveniles occurred in one of the following three ways, in order of increasing frequency: (1) encounters resulting from officers' spotting officially "wanted" youths; (2) encounters taking place at or near the scene of offenses reported to police headquarters; and (3) encounters occurring as the result of officers' directly observing youths either committing offenses or in "suspicious circumstances." However, the probability that a confrontation would take place between officer and juvenile, or that a particular disposition of an identified offender would be made, was only in part determined by the knowledge that an offense had occurred or that a particular juvenile had committed an offense. The bases for and utilization of non-offenses related criteria by police in accosting and disposing of juveniles are the focuses of the following discussion.

Sanctions for Discretion

In each encounter with juveniles, with the minor exception of officially "wanted" youths,[7] a central task confronting the officer was to decide what official action to take against the boys involved. In making these disposition decisions, officers could select any one of five discrete alternatives:

1) outright release
2) release and submission of a "field interrogation report" briefly describing the circumstances initiating the police-juvenile confrontation
3) "official reprimand" and release to parents or guardian
4) citation to juvenile court
5) arrest and confinement in juvenile hall.

Dispositions 3, 4, and 5 differed from the others in two basic respects. First, with rare exceptions, when an officer chose to reprimand, cite, or arrest a boy, he took the youth to the police station. Second, the reprimanded, cited, or arrested boy acquired an official police "record," that is, his name was officially recorded in Bureau files as a juvenile violator.

Analysis of the distribution of police disposition decisions about juveniles revealed that in virtually every category of offense the full range of official disposition alternatives available to officers was employed. This wide range of discretion resulted primarily from two conditions. First, it reflected the reluctance of officers to expose certain youths to the stigmatization presumed to be associated with official police action. Few juvenile officers believed that correctional agencies serving the community could effectively help delinquents. For some officers this attitude reflected a lack of confidence in rehabilitation techniques; for others, a belief that high case loads and lack of professional training among correctional workers vitiated their efforts at treatment. All officers were agreed, however, that juvenile justice and correctional processes were essentially concerned with apprehension and punishment rather than treatment. Furthermore, all officers believed that some aspects of these processes (e.g., judicial definition of youths as delinquents and removal of delinquents from the community), as well as some of the possible consequences of these processes (e.g., intimate institutional contact with "hard-core" delinquents, as well as parental, school, and conventional peer disapproval or rejection), could reinforce what previously might have been only a tentative proclivity toward delinquent values and behavior.

Consequently, when officers found reason to doubt that a youth being confronted was highly committed toward deviance, they were inclined to treat him with leniency.

Second, and more important, the practice of discretion was sanctioned by police-department policy. Training manuals and departmental bulletins stressed that the disposition of each juvenile offender was not to be based solely on the type of infraction he committed. Thus, while it was departmental policy to "arrest and confine all juveniles who have committed a felony or misdemeanor involving theft, sex offense, battery, possession of dangerous weapons, prowling, peeping, intoxication, incorrigibility, and disturbance of the peace," it was acknowledged that "such considerations as age, attitude and prior criminal record might indicate that a different disposition would be more appropriate."[8] The official justification for discretion in processing juvenile offenders, based on the preventive aims of the Juvenile Bureau, was that each juvenile violator should be dealt with solely on the basis of what was best for him.[9] Unofficially, administrative legitimation of discretion was further justified on the grounds that strict enforcement practices would overcrowd court calendars and detention facilities, as well as dramatically increase juvenile crime rates—consequences to be avoided because they would expose the police department to community criticism.[10]

In practice, the official policy justifying use of discretion served as a demand that discretion be exercised. As such, it posed three problems for juvenile officers. First, it represented a departure from the traditional police practice with which the juvenile officers themselves were identified, in the sense that they were expected to justify their juvenile disposition decisions not simply by evidence proving a youth had committed a crime—grounds on which police were officially expected to base their dispositions of non-juvenile offenders[11]—but in the *character* of the youth. Second, in disposing of juvenile offenders, officers were expected, in effect, to make judicial rather than ministerial decisions.[12] Third, the shift from the offense to the offender as the basis for determining the appropriate disposition substantially increased the uncertainty and ambiguity for officers in the situation of apprehension because no explicit rules existed for determining which disposition different types of youths should receive. Despite these problems, officers were constrained to base disposition decisions on the character of the apprehended youth, not only because they wanted to be fair, but because persistent failure to do so could result in judicial criticism, departmental censure, and, they believed, loss of authority with juveniles.[13]

Disposition Criteria

Assessing the character of apprehended offenders posed relatively few difficulties for officers in the case of youths who had committed serious crimes such as robbery, homicide, aggravated assault, grand theft, auto theft, rape, and arson. Officials generally regarded these juveniles as confirmed delinquents simply by virtue of their involvement in offenses of this magnitude.[14] However, the infraction committed did not always suffice to determine the appropriate disposition for some serious offenders;[15] and, in the case of minor offenders, who comprised over 90 per cent of the youths against whom police took action, the violation per se generally played an insignificant role in the choice of disposition. While a number of minor offenders were seen as serious delinquents deserving arrest, many others were perceived either as "good" boys whose offenses were atypical of their customary behavior, as pawns of undesirable associates or, in any case, as boys for whom arrest was regarded as an unwarranted and possibly harmful punishment. Thus, for nearly all minor violators and for some serious delinquents, the assessment of character—the distinction between serious delinquents, "good" boys, misguided youths, and so on—and the dispositions which followed from these assessments were based on youths' personal characteristics and not their offenses.

Despite this dependence of disposition decisions on the personal characteristics of these youths, however, police officers actually had access only to very limited information about boys at the time they had to decide what to do with them. In the field, officers typically had no data concerning the past offense records, school performance, family situation, or personal adjustment of apprehended youths.[16] Furthermore, files at police headquarters provided data only about each boy's prior offense record. Thus both the decision made in the field—whether or not to bring the boy in—and the decision made at the station—which disposition to invoke—were based largely on cues which emerged from the interaction between the officer and the youth, cues from which the officer inferred the youth's character. These cues included the youth's group affiliations, age, race, grooming, dress, and demeanor. Older juveniles, members of known delinquent gangs, Negroes, youths with well-oiled hair, black jackets, and soiled denims or jeans (the presumed uniform of "tough" boys), and boys who in their interactions with officers did not manifest what were considered to be appropriate signs of respect tended to receive the more severe dispositions.

Other than prior record, the most important of the above clues was a

TABLE 1 / *Severity of Police Disposition by Youth's Demeanor*

Severity of police disposition	Youth's demeanor		Total
	CO-OPERATIVE	UNCO-OPERATIVE	
Arrest (most severe)	2	14	16
Citation or official reprimand	4	5	9
Informal reprimand	15	1	16
Admonish and release (least severe)	24	1	25
Total	45	21	66

youth's *demeanor*. In the opinion of juvenile patrolmen themselves the demeanor of apprehended juveniles was a major determinant of their decisions for 50–60 per cent of the juvenile cases they processed.[17] A less subjective indication of the association between a youth's demeanor and police disposition is provided by Table 1, which presents the police dispositions for sixty-six youths whose encounters with police were observed in the course of this study.[18] For purposes of this analysis, each youth's demeanor in the encounter was classified as either co-operative or unco-operative.[19] The results clearly reveal a marked association between youth demeanor and the severity of police dispositions.

The cues used by police to assess demeanor were fairly simple. Juveniles who were contrite about their infractions, respectful to officers, and fearful of the sanctions that might be employed against them tended to be viewed by patrolmen as basically law-abiding or at least "salvage-able." For these youths it was usually assumed that informal or formal reprimand would suffice to guarantee their future conformity. In contrast, youthful offenders who were fractious, obdurate, or who appeared nonchalant in their encounters with patrolmen were likely to be viewed as "would-be tough guys" or "punks" who fully deserved the most severe sanction: arrest. The following excerpts from observation notes illustrate the importance attached to demeanor by police in making disposition decisions.

1. The interrogation of "A" (an eighteen-year-old upper-lower-class white male accused of statutory rape) was assigned to a police sergeant with long experience on the force. As I sat in his office while we waited for the youth to arrive for questioning, the sergeant expressed his uncertainty as to what he should do with this young man. On the one hand, he could not ignore the fact that an offense had been committed; he had been informed, in fact, that the youth was prepared to confess to the offense. Nor could he overlook the continued pressure from the girl's father (an important political figure) for

the police to take severe action against the youth. On the other hand, the sergeant had formed a low opinion of the girl's moral character, and he considered it unfair to charge "A" with statutory rape when the girl was a willing partner to the offense and might even have been the instigator of it. However, his sense of injustice concerning "A" was tempered by his image of the youth as a "punk," based, he explained, on information he had received that the youth belonged to a certain gang, the members of which were well known to, and disliked by, the police. Nevertheless, as we prepared to leave his office to interview "A," the sergeant was still in doubt as to what he should do with him.

As we walked down the corridor to the interrogation room, the sergeant was stopped by a reporter from the local newspaper. In an excited tone of voice, the reporter explained that his editor was pressing him to get further information about this case. The newspaper had printed some of the facts about the girl's disappearance, and as a consequence the girl's father was threatening suit against the paper for defamation of the girl's character. It would strengthen the newspaper's position, the reporter explained, if the police had information indicating that the girl's associates, particularly the youth the sergeant was about to interrogate, were persons of disreputable character. This stimulus seemed to resolve the sergeant's uncertainty. He told the reporter, "unofficially," that the youth was known to be an undesirable person, citing as evidence his membership in the delinquent gang. Furthermore, the sergeant added that he had evidence that this youth had been intimate with the girl over a period of many months. When the reporter asked if the police were planning to do anything to the youth, the sergeant answered that he intended to charge the youth with statutory rape.

In the interrogation, however, three points quickly emerged which profoundly affected the sergeant's judgment of the youth. First, the youth was polite and co-operative; he consistently addressed the officer as "sir," answered all questions quietly, and signed a statement implicating himself in numerous counts of statutory rape. Second, the youth's intentions toward the girl appeared to have been honorable; for example, he said that he wanted to marry her eventually. Third, the youth was not in fact a member of the gang in question. The sergeant's attitude became increasingly sympathetic, and after we left the interrogation room he announced his intention to "get 'A' off the hook," meaning that he wanted to have the charges against "A" reduced or, if possible, dropped.

2. Officers "X" and "Y" brought into the police station a seventeen-year-old white boy who, along with two older companions, had been found in a home having sex relations with a fifteen-year-old girl. The boy responded to police officers' queries slowly and with obvious disregard. It was apparent that his lack of deference toward the officers and his failure to evidence concern about his situation were irritating his questioners. Finally, one of the officers turned to me and, obviously angry, commented that in his view the boy was

simply a "stud" interested only in sex, eating, and sleeping. The policemen conjectured that the boy "probably already had knocked up half a dozen girls." The boy ignored these remarks, except for an occasional impassive stare at the patrolmen. Turning to the boy, the officer remarked, "What the hell am I going to do with you?" And again the boy simply returned the officer's gaze. The latter then said, "Well, I guess we'll just have to put you away for a while." An arrest report was then made out and the boy was taken to Juvenile Hall.

Although anger and disgust frequently characterized officers' attitudes toward recalcitrant and impassive juvenile offenders, their manner while processing these youths was typically routine, restrained, and without rancor. While the officers' restraint may have been due in part to their desire to avoid accusation and censure, it also seemed to reflect their inurement to a frequent experience. By and large, only their occasional "needling" or insulting of a boy gave any hint of the underlying resentment and dislike they felt toward many of these youths.[20]

Prejudice in Apprehension and Disposition Decisions

Compared to other youths, Negroes and boys whose appearance matched the delinquent stereotype were more frequently stopped and interrogated by patrolmen—often even in the absence of evidence that an offense had been committed[21]—and usually were given more severe dispositions for the same violations. Our data suggest, however, that these selective apprehension and disposition practices resulted not only from the intrusion of long-held prejudices of individual police officers but also from certain job-related experiences of law-enforcement personnel. First, the tendency for police to give more severe dispositions to Negroes and to youths whose appearance corresponded to that which police associated with delinquents partly reflected the fact, observed in this study, that these youths also were much more likely than were other types of boys to exhibit the sort of recalcitrant demeanor which police construed as a sign of the confirmed delinquent. Further, officers assumed, partly on the basis of departmental statistics, that Negroes and juveniles who "look tough" (e.g., who wear chinos, leather jackets, boots, etc.) commit crimes more frequently than do other types of youths.[22] In this sense, the police justified their selective treatment of these youths along epidemiological lines: that is, they were concentrating their attention on those youths whom they believed were most likely to commit delinquent acts. In the words of one highly placed official in the department:

If you know that the bulk of your delinquent problem comes from kids who, say, are from 12 to 14 years of age, when you're out on patrol you are much more likely to be sensitive to the activities of juveniles in this age bracket than older or younger groups. This would be good law enforcement practice. The logic in our case is the same except that our delinquency problem is largely found in the Negro community and it is these youths toward whom we are sensitized.

As regards prejudice per se, eighteen of twenty-seven officers interviewed openly admitted a dislike for Negroes. However, they attributed their dislike to experiences they had, as policemen, with youths from this minority group. The officers reported that Negro boys were much more likely than non-Negroes to "give us a hard time," be unco-operative, and show no remorse for their transgressions. Recurrent exposure to such attitudes among Negro youth, the officers claimed, generated their antipathy toward Negroes. The following excerpt is typical of the views expressed by these officers:

They (Negroes) have no regard for the law or for the police. They just don't seem to give a damn. Few of them are interested in school or getting ahead. The girls start having illegitimate kids before they are 16 years old and the boys are always "out for kicks." Furthermore, many of these kids try to run you down. They say the damnedest things to you and they seem to have absolutely no respect for you as an adult. I admit I am prejudiced now, but frankly I don't think I was when I began police work.

Implications

It is apparent from the findings presented above that the police officers studied in this research were permitted and even encouraged to exercise immense latitude in disposing of the juveniles they encountered. That is, it was within the officers' discretionary authority, except in extreme limiting cases, to decide which juveniles were to come to the attention of the courts and correctional agencies and thereby be identified officially as delinquents. In exercising this discretion policemen were strongly guided by the demeanor of those who were apprehended, a practice which ultimately led, as seen above, to certain youths (particularly Negroes[23] and boys dressed in the style of "toughs") being treated more severely than other juveniles for comparable offenses.

But the relevance of demeanor was not limited only to police disposition practices. Thus, for example, in conjunction with police crime statistics the criterion of demeanor led police to concentrate their surveillance activities in areas frequented or inhabited by Negroes. Further-more, these youths were accosted more often than others by officers on patrol simply because their skin color identified them as potential trouble-makers. These discriminatory practices—and it is important to note that they are discriminatory, even if based on accurate statistical information —may well have self-fulfilling consequences. Thus it is not unlikely that frequent encounters with police, particularly those involving youths innocent of wrongdoing, will increase the hostility of these juveniles toward law-enforcement personnel. It is also not unlikely that the fre-quency of such encounters will in time reduce their significance in the eyes of apprehended juveniles, thereby leading these youths to regard them as "routine." Such responses to police encounters, however, are those which law-enforcement personnel perceive as indicators of the serious delinquent. They thus serve to vindicate and reinforce officers' prejudices, leading to closer surveillance of Negro districts, more fre-quent encounters with Negro youths, and so on in a vicious circle. Moreover, the consequences of this chain of events are reflected in police statistics showing a disproportionately high percentage of Negroes among juvenile offenders, thereby providing "objective" justification for con-centrating police attention on Negro youths.

To a substantial extent, as we have implied earlier, the discretion practiced by juvenile officers is simply an extension of the juvenile-court philosophy, which holds that in making legal decisions regarding juve-niles, more weight should be given to the juvenile's character and life-situation than to his actual offending behavior. The juvenile officer's disposition decisions—and the information he uses as a basis for them— are more akin to the discriminations made by probation officers and other correctional workers than they are to decisions of police officers dealing with non-juvenile offenders. The problem is that such clinical-type decisions are not restrained by mechanisms comparable to the principles of due process and the rules of procedure governing police decisions regarding adult offenders. Consequently, prejudicial practices by police officers can escape notice more easily in their dealings with juveniles than with adults.

The observations made in this study serve to underscore the fact that the official delinquent, as distinguished from the juvenile who simply commits a delinquent act, is the product of a social judgment, in this case a judgment made by the police. He is a delinquent because someone in authority has defined him as one, often on the basis of the public face he has presented to officials rather than of the kind of offense he has committed.

Notes

1) Richard D. Schwartz and Jerome H. Skolnick, "Two Studies of Legal Stigma," *Social Problems*, X (April, 1962), 133–42; Sol Rubin, *Crime and Juvenile Delinquency* (New York: Oceana Publications, 1958); B. F. McSally, "Finding Jobs for Released Offenders," *Federal Probation*, XXIV (June, 1960), 12–17; Harold D. Lasswell and Richard C. Donnelly, "The Continuing Debate over Responsibility: An Introduction to Isolating the Condemnation Sanction," *Yale Law Journal*, LXVIII (April, 1959), 869–99.
2) Richard A. Cloward and Lloyd E. Ohlin, *Delinquency and Opportunity* (Glencoe, Ill.: Free Press, 1960), pp. 124–30.
3) Frank Tannenbaum, *Crime and the Community* (New York: Columbia University Press, 1936), pp. 17–20; Howard S. Becker, *Outsiders: Studies in the Sociology of Deviance* (New York: Free Press of Glencoe, 1963), chaps. i and ii.
4) For a detailed accounting of police discretionary practices, see Joseph Goldstein, "Police Discretion Not to Invoke the Criminal Process: Low Visibility Decisions in the Administration of Justice," *Yale Law Journal*, LXIX (1960), 543–94; Wayne R. LaFave, "The Police and Non-enforcement of the Law—Part I," *Wisconsin Law Review* (January, 1962), pp. 104–37; S. H. Kadish, "Legal Norms and Discretion in the Police and Sentencing Processes," *Harvard Law Review*, LXXV (March, 1962), 904–31.
5) Approximately thirty officers were assigned to the Juvenile Bureau in the department studied. While we had an opportunity to observe all officers in the Bureau during the study, our observations were concentrated on those who had been working in the Bureau for one or two years at least. Although two of the officers in the Juvenile Bureau were Negro, we observed these officers on only a few occasions.
6) Although observations were not confined to specific days or work shifts, more observations were made during evenings and weekends because police activity was greatest during these periods.
7) "Wanted" juveniles usually were placed under arrest or in protective custody, a practice which in effect relieved officers of the responsibility for deciding what to do with these youths.
8) Quoted from a training manual issued by the police department studied in this research.
9) Presumably this also implied that police action with juveniles was to be determined partly by the offenders' need for correctional services.
10) This was reported by beat officers as well as supervisory and administrative personnel of the juvenile bureau.
11) In actual practice, of course, disposition decisions regarding adult offenders also were influenced by many factors extraneous to the offense per se.
12) For example, in dealing with adult violators, officers had no disposition alternative comparable to the reprimand-and-release category, a disposition which contained elements of punishment but did not involve mediation by the court.
13) The concern of officers over possible loss of authority stemmed from their belief that court failure to support arrests by appropriate action would cause policemen to "lose face" in the eyes of juveniles.
14) It is also likely that the possibility of negative publicity resulting from the failure to arrest such violators—particularly if they became involved in further serious crime—brought about strong administrative pressure for their arrest.
15) For example, in the year preceding this research, over 30 per cent of the juveniles involved in burglaries and 12 per cent of the juveniles committing auto theft received dispositions other than arrest.
16) On occasion, officers apprehended youths whom they personally knew to be prior offenders. This did not occur frequently, however, for several reasons. First, approximately 75 per cent of apprehended youths had no prior official

records; second, officers periodically exchanged patrol areas, thus limiting their exposure to, and knowledge about, these areas; and third, patrolmen seldom spent more than three or four years in the juvenile division.

17) While reliable subgroup estimates were impossible to obtain through observation because of the relatively small number of incidents observed, the importance of demeanor in disposition decisions appeared to be much less significant with known prior offenders.

18) Systematic data were collected on police encounters with seventy-six juveniles. In ten of these encounters the police concluded that their suspicions were groundless, and consequently the juveniles involved were exonerated; these ten cases were eliminated from this analysis of demeanor. (The total number of encounters observed was considerably more than seventy-six, but systematic data-collection procedures were not instituted until several months after observations began.)

19) The data used for the classification of demeanor were the written records of observations made by the authors. The classifications were made by an independent judge not associated with this study. In classifying a youth's demeanor as co-operative or unco-operative, particular attention was paid to: (1) the youth's responses to police officers' questions and requests; (2) the respect and deference—or lack of these qualities—shown by the youth toward police officers; and (3) police officers' assessments of the youth's demeanor.

20) Officers' animosity toward recalcitrant or aloof offenders appeared to stem from two sources: moral indignation that these juveniles were self-righteous and indifferent about their transgressions, and resentment that these youths failed to accord police the respect they believed they deserved. Since the patrolmen perceived themselves as honestly and impartially performing a vital community function warranting respect and deference from the community at large, they attributed the lack of respect shown them by these juveniles to the latters' immorality.

21) The clearest evidence for this assertion is provided by the overrepresentation of Negroes among "innocent" juveniles accosted by the police. As noted, of the seventy-six juveniles on whom systematic data were collected, ten were exonerated and released without suspicion. Seven, or two-thirds of these ten "innocent" juveniles were Negro, in contrast to the allegedly "guilty" youths, less than one-third of whom were Negro. The following incident illustrates the operation of this bias: One officer, observing a youth walking along the street, commented that the youth "looks suspicious" and promptly stopped and questioned him. Asked later to explain what aroused his suspicion, the officer explained, "He was a Negro wearing dark glasses at midnight."

22) While police statistics did not permit an analysis of crime rates by appearance, they strongly supported officers' contentions concerning the delinquency rate among Negroes. Of all male juveniles processed by the police department in 1961, for example, 40.2 per cent were Negro and 33.9 per cent were white. These two groups comprised at that time, respectively, about 22.7 per cent and 73.6 per cent of the population in the community studied.

23) An unco-operative demeanor was presented by more than one-third of the Negro youths but by only one-sixth of the white youths encountered by the police in the course of our observations.

CHAPTER FOUR

to insure

The first section of this introduction deals with matters relevant to defining "domestic Tranquility." The issues dealt with include the frequency with which normal activities are interrupted, the degree to which the legitimacy of opposition is challenged, and the amount of violence used to attain desired ends. The second section discusses conditions and practices that help insure the domestic tranquillity. It concentrates on the questions of how the expression of conflict and discontent are managed and of what the reactions to such expressions are in a tranquil society. The final section examines the relationship between domestic tranquillity and two other Preamble goals: union and justice.

What Is Domestic Tranquillity?

There are at least three separate senses in which a society may be said to be tranquil. This section examines these as criteria that may be used to judge the degree of domestic tranquillity prevailing in America. The first of these criteria, the frequency with which there are serious interruptions in normal activities, is defined in terms of the number of people whose normal activities are interrupted, the importance of the interrupted activity, and the availability of effective substitutes. Thus, an industry-wide steel strike is serious in that it interrupts the normal activities of the

domestic Tranquility . . .

hundreds of thousands who work in the industry. Moreover, the seriousness of the strike increases if it persists and disrupts the activities of those other industries which are dependent upon the availability of steel, such as the automotive industry. On the other hand, the interruption of some vital service such as the delivery of food or the operations of medical facilities may be regarded as serious even if only a relatively small number of people are affected. Finally, the seriousness of stopping one activity may be mitigated by the availability of alternate means of accomplishing the goals of that activity. For example, the seriousness of an interruption in rail travel is mitigated when other modes of transportation are available. The degree of domestic tranquillity increases, then, as the degree to which the stability of the society increases, where stability simply means the absence of interruptions of normal activities involving many people or involving services that are vital or irreplaceable.

The second criterion for judging the degree of domestic tranquillity is the frequency with which expressions of conflict and discontent contain challenges to the legitimacy of an opposing position. Such challenges may be designed to reduce the obligation to listen to opposing positions or to deny opponents the right to speak. In some instances, the motives or integrity of the opposing party may be questioned. For example, the honesty of public officials with whom one disagrees may be disputed. Second, the legitimacy of a position may be challenged by claiming that whatever the intent of its supporters, it is not consistent with basic values. The opposing position may be said to be immoral, un-American, or treasonous: a position which cannot or should not be taken by "true and loyal" members of the society, and which is beyond the protection of the usual guarantees of free speech.[1] In any case, it is not the mere presence of disagreements or conflicts which constitutes a breach of the domestic tranquillity: it is the challenge to the legitimacy of the opposition. That is, conflicts and grievances can and do exist in a tranquil society, but when they do, they are expressed in an atmosphere of civility and mutual respect.

A third criterion for judging the degree of domestic tranquillity is the frequency with which force or violence is used illegitimately. That is, the use of force or violence itself is not sufficient to constitute a breach of tranquillity; the tranquillity is breached only when force is used by unauthorized persons or in an unauthorized manner. The tranquillity of the society is not breached, for example, when the state executioner takes a murderer's life, but it is when a murder is committed. On the other hand, not all uses of violence or force by authorized persons need be legitimate. When the police, for example, use excessive and unnecessary force to subdue unruly persons or to prevent a peaceful demonstration, they may be as responsible for breaching the peace as the people they subdue. In short, a tranquil society is a peaceful society in the sense that it is one in which such force as is used is used by authorized persons in the authorized manner. "Violence on the Fanatical Left and Right" by Arnold Forster traces the history of movements in the United States, from the Know-Nothings of the nineteenth century to the Ku Klux Klan and the Black Muslims of the twentieth century, which have threatened the domestic tranquillity by resorting to or advocating the illegitimate use of violence.

The tranquil society is, then, one which is stable, civil, and peaceful in the senses discussed above. It is not necessarily a society from which conflict and discontent are absent. Nor need it be changeless, sterile, and serene.

The tranquil society may be undergoing change and development; it may be beset by loud and continuous argument. However, in the tranquil society, change, development, and argument do not seriously disrupt nor-

---

[1] See Paul B. Horton and Gerald R. Leslie, "Civil Liberties and Subversion," *The Sociology of Social Problems*, 3rd ed. (New York: Appleton-Century-Crofts, 1965), pp. 630–673, for a discussion of problems faced in attempting to set the limits of free speech.

mal activities, do not lead to challenges to the legitimacy of opposing parties, nor to the unauthorized use of force. Stability, civility, and peace persist, not because conflict and discontent, change and argument are absent, but because the prevailing conditions and practices induce their tranquil, rather than untranquil, expression.

Insuring Domestic Tranquillity

Perhaps the prime requisite for insuring domestic tranquillity is providing the means of instituting reforms that actually resolve conflicts or redress the grievances of the discontented.[2] The elaborate mechanisms of labor-management negotiations, for example, generally resolve the existing differences without resort to disruptive strikes.[3] An effective judicial system deals with conflicts and grievances so as to make breaching the domestic tranquillity unnecessary.

The resolution of conflicts and the redress of grievances are further facilitated when existing conditions favor compromise and discourage adamant adherence to a given position. The absence of strong ideological commitments is a condition which favors compromise; only with difficulty can dogmatists be induced to compromise. Thus, while Americans may chide their politicians for being men of expedience and deals rather than of principle and ideals, their being so decreases the likelihood of political strife and civil war. Politicians who can compromise with their opponents need not lead their followers into bitter conflict.

The nature of a society's political system may also affect the willingness to compromise. The American two party system, for example, encourages compromise[4] because the discontented realize that only under one of the two party labels can they hope to share in the political power needed to implement their programs. Thus, even discontents are encouraged to compromise so as to be acceptable to one of the two

[2] Both governmental and nongovernmental systems for the resolution of conflict and the redress of grievances are discussed in William G. Scott, *The Management of Conflict: Appeal Systems in Organizations* (Homewood, Ill.: Irwin, 1965).

[3] For a treatment of techniques of collective bargaining, see Edwin Beal and Edward D. Wickersham, *The Practice of Collective Bargaining* (Homewood, Ill.: Irwin, 1963). For a discussion of the relationship of maintaining tranquillity by collective bargaining and other societal goals, see Bernard Nossiter, "Some Hidden Costs of Industrial Peace," *Annals of the American Academy of Political and Social Science*, CCCXLIII (September, 1962), 104–108.

[4] See Seymour M. Lipset, *Political Man: The Social Bases of Politics* (Garden City, N.Y.: Doubleday Anchor, 1963), pp. 70–82; and Talcott Parsons, "Voting and the Equilibrium of the American Political System," in Eugene Burdick and Arthur Brodbeck (eds.), *American Voting Behavior* (New York: Free Press, 1959), pp. 80–120, for a discussion of the role of America's two party system in maintaining tranquillity.

dominant parties. In addition, the two-party system encourages the dominant parties to accept such compromises as are offered. The division of voters between the parties is usually close and unstable enough so that each must act to gain whatever new support it can and to prevent any increase in the support of the opposition.

A third factor facilitating compromise is the existence of a system of values common to all disputants. People who share a common value system can understand each other more readily than those who do not share values. Where people have the same values, the concerns and discontents of one party are intelligible to the other. Such mutual understanding can often lead to a compromise agreement before resort to untranquil means appears necessary or desirable.

The maintenance of tranquillity does not, however, necessitate that compromises be arrived at, disagreements resolved, and grievances redressed. Other factors may keep a society stable, civil, and peaceful. In discussing these other factors, it is useful to distinguish between those factors that forestall the expression of discontent and disagreement and those that, like the resolution of differences, assume the open expression of feelings and opinions but which keep them from reaching a point where they cause a breach of tranquillity.

The expression of serious discontent is apt to be uncommon where who voice their grievances face the prospect of reprisals. The fear of arrest, of being beaten, of losing a job or one's draft deferment may still the expression of disagreement with those in power. Should threats of reprisals fail to deter the expression of discontent, the first breach of tranquillity may come from those who carry out threats involving unauthorized use of force. For example, the peace of some Southern communities has been broken by the Ku Klux Klan and others who resort to violence to keep Negroes quietly "in their place."

Discontent may, of course, be stilled without resort to reprisals. Ignorance of undesirable conditions works to prevent or mute the expression of discontent with the status quo. Michael Harrington, for example, claims that the lack of contact with or knowledge of the conditions of the poor was a major factor in the failure of liberal members of the middle class to call for a war on poverty in the 1950s.[5] In this sense a society may remain tranquil if there are systematic distortions, whether deliberate or not, in the information which its people receive about conditions within it. Of course, those who live in the undesirable conditions cannot be kept ignorant of them. They may,

[5] Michael Harrington, "The Invisible Land," *The Other America* (New York: Macmillan, 1963), pp. 1–18.

however, believe that their lot, although undesirable, is deserved. Negroes who accept the notion of the inferiority of their race or women who believe in the inferiority of their sex may well tolerate conditions which others in the society would deem undesirable.[6]

Ignorance may even play a role in muting the discontent of those who do regard their lot as both undeserved and undesirable. Ignorance of how to have demands heard and heeded may lead to a resigned silence. Hope that change can be brought about can be undermined by ignorance of how to effect a program for change. Where hope for change is absent, apathy is likely to spread and with apathy, silence.[7]

The interdependence of individuals and organizations in a complex society may also mute expressions of differences. Where people are interdependent, the expression of differences, especially in an untranquil manner, may alienate those upon whom they depend. The South of 1860 could contemplate secession and rebellion since it was not highly dependent on the North for the satisfaction of its needs. However, in the 1960s, secession, even if militarily feasible, would be economic suicide. Compliance with federal school desegregation orders may be tolerated in the South lest needed or desired federal funds are cut off. In time of war or other serious threats, when awareness of one's dependence on others is heightened, labor and management may agree not to press their demands to the point where a strike is inevitable, and rival politicians may mute their disagreements on foreign and even domestic policy.[8]

Despite the existence of means for resolving differences and despite fear, ignorance, or the restraints of interdependence, serious discontent and disagreement often are expressed in a society and can threaten its tranquillity. A society that seeks to be tranquil must, therefore, have means of dealing with expressions of conflicts and grievances that can or do lead to breaches in the domestic tranquillity.

Disagreements can be prevented from leading to serious breaches of the peace by depriving people of the means for violence or by rendering the means they do have ineffective. The use of firearms is under partial

[6] For a discussion of the "oppression" of women, see Ellen Keniston and Kenneth Keniston, "An American Anachronism: The Image of Women and Work," *American Scholar*, XXXIII (Summer, 1964), 355-375. Some means for ending the "oppression" of women are discussed in Alice Rossi's article, "Institutional Levers for Achieving Sex Equality," in Chapter Three.

[7] For a discussion of the relationship between knowing how to make effective protests and reduction of apathy, see Charles E. Silberman, "Power, Personality and Protest," *Crisis in Black and White* (New York: Random House, 1964), pp. 189-223.

[8] The unifying effect of war is discussed by Robert A. Nisbet, *Community and Power* (New York: Oxford University Press, 1962), pp. 38-44.

government regulation.[9] The tear gas of the local police and the superior weapons of the state militia have been sufficient to contain most contemporary outbreaks of violence. It is, of course, neither necessary nor prudent to wait until disagreements have resulted in breaches of the peace before acting to insure tranquillity. Breaches of the peace may be prevented by the use of coöptation, tokenism, and name-calling.

Cooptation, according to the definition in "Coöptation" by Philip Selznick, is "the process of absorbing new elements into the leadership or policy-determining structures of an organization [or society] as a means of averting threats to its stability or existence." For example, putting the leader of a protest group on a city human relations commission or a civilian review board may give him the responsibility of serving as a link between the protesters and the power structure. To the extent that he identifies with his new position or has to defend positions taken by his former opponents and present colleagues, he will try to "put the brakes" on those he once led. An open-class system involves widespread coöptation whereby talented persons and potential leaders of lower-class and minority-group protests become part of the middle-class establishment themselves. They are then often more likely to resist the advances of their former neighbors and to sympathize with their former "betters."[10]

Tokenism is a second technique of dampening conflict before a breach of tranquillity. It involves the granting of relatively minor changes in the hope of heading off more important changes. Integrating swimming pools in the hope of forestalling the integration of schools and neighborhoods is an example. In some cases, the token change is only symbolic. Promises of action or other tokens of good faith may renew the hope of peaceful settlement and deter protesters from disruptive tactics even though no concrete demands have been fulfilled. The prevalence and temptations of tokenism in the handling of racial conflicts are discussed in "The Specter of Conflict" by Lewis M. Killian and Charles Grigg.

Potential conflict may also be muted without any concessions when the protesters and their demands are branded as illegitimate. One contemporary American form of this name-calling approach is to charge that a group is a "communist front" or led by "dupes of the communist conspiracy." Such charges themselves represent a breach in the civility of

[9] For discussions of recent attempts to strengthen federal firearms laws, see Carl Bakal, *The Right to Bear Arms* (New York: McGraw-Hill, 1966); and "Federal Regulation of Firearms Sales," *University of Chicago Law Review*, XXXI (Summer, 1964), 780–790.

[10] For a discussion of the coöpting influence of social mobility in an open-class system, see E. Franklin Frazier, *The Black Bourgeoisie* (Glencoe, Ill.: Free Press, 1947); and C. Wright Mills, *New Men of Power* (New York: Harcourt, Brace, 1948).

public debate; nevertheless, if they are believed, they can deprive a dissenting group of the aid of potential allies and members which it needs to remain viable. Thus, stability and peace may be attained at the cost of a slight breach of civility.

In general, then, the stability, peace, and civility—the domestic tranquillity of a society—can be insured if the prevailing conditions and practices favor the resolution of conflicts, the redress of grievances, and the acceptance of compromise. The domestic tranquillity may also be protected, at least temporarily, by preventing the expression of discontent or sapping the strength of those who do express their discontent.

Tranquillity, Union, and Justice

There is an intimate relationship between the problems of insuring the domestic tranquillity and those of forming a more perfect union and establishing justice. Threats to domestic tranquillity often stem from disagreements over the degree to which present conditions represent a perfect union and a just society. For example, changes in political, economic, and religious aspects of the American union have led many to join organizations of the Radical Right which question the legitimacy of the prevailing American order. The nature of the grievances of the Radical Right is discussed further in "Super-Patriotism Defined" by Richard Schmuck and Mark Chesler.

Similarly, there is a close link between justice and tranquillity; those feeling unjustly treated my seek redress at the cost of tranquillity. Often, it is the distribution of material rewards which is at issue, as it was in the years between the world wars when veterans marched on Washington to demand a bonus from Congress. During that same period, labor and management engaged in many angry, violent battles. Troops were called out to restore order when the veterans marched on Washington, and it was not uncommon for police action to be used to restore peace between labor and management.

The injustices that threaten tranquillity are not, however, confined to the distribution of material goods. The early labor-management disputes, for example, involved not only wages but union demands for more power in determining working conditions. Recently, Negroes have demanded political power as well as more economic opportunities.

The inequalities which cause some to challenge the tranquillity of the society need not even involve anything as objective or external as money and power. They may involve differences in prestige or status. Writers such as Daniel Bell, Seymour Lipset, and Richard Hofstadter suggest that inequalities in status and prestige are associated with extremist protest activities.[11] These protest activities may attract either older families and prestigious figures who have lost status, or new, upwardly mobile lower-middle-class persons.

The link between justice and tranquillity is not simply one in which injustice may lead to threats to the domestic tranquillity. There is also the question of what are the just consequences of having breached the domestic tranquillity. This issue is often raised when a strike disrupts one of the society's vital activities. Typically, the case in point is a strike by school teachers, policemen, nurses, or others engaged in providing vital services. Contemporary America has, however, come to regard strikes in most industries as a worker's right and as such an activity which cannot, in general, be justly punished.[12]

The issue of who has the right to breach the domestic tranquillity extends beyond that of labor-management relationships to that of the relationship between the citizen and the state. Here the question is the right to engage in political protest without punishment or the threat of punishment. America, of course, seeks to protect the right to engage in political protest. However, where the protest takes the form of civil disobedience and threats to the legitimacy of the prevailing order, there are many who believe the right to political protest can justly be curtailed in order to insure the domestic tranquillity. "Democracy and the Problem of Civil Disobedience" by David Spitz discusses issues involved in deciding if political protesters have the right to disobey a law in the course of expressing their position.[13] Those who believe protesters have such a right stand ready to sustain a breach of the domestic tranquillity. For them, establishing justice or perfecting the union may take precedence over insuring stability, civility, and even domestic peace.

[11] See Daniel Bell, "The Dispossessed," Seymour M. Lipset, "The Sources of the Radical Right," Richard Hofstadter, "The Pseudo-Conservative Revolt," in Daniel Bell (ed.), *The Radical Right* (Garden City, N.Y.: Doubleday Anchor, 1964).

[12] A brief history of the acceptance of the right to strike is found in Philip Taft, "The Right to Strike," *Current History*, XLIX (July, 1965), 17–22. The special problems of strikes by public employees are discussed in "Labor Relations in the Public Service," *Harvard Law Review*, LXXV (December, 1961), 391–413; and Stefan Rosenzweig, "The Condon-Wadlin Act Re-examined," *ILR Research*, XI (May, 1965), 3–8.

[13] Other discussions of civil disobedience are found in Carl Cohen, "The Essence and Ethics of Civil Disobedience," *The Nation*, CXCVIII (March 16, 1964), 257–262; M. Liebman, "Civil Disobedience: A Threat to Our Society," *Vital Speeches*, XXX (October 1, 1964), 766–768; R. A. Wassertrom, "The Obligation to Obey the Law," *UCLA Law Review*, X (May, 1963), 780–807; and Robert B. McKay, "The Function of Civil Disobedience," *Current*, LX (June, 1965), 33–37. See also Milton R. Konvitz, "Sit-in Demonstrations and Free Speech," *Expanding Liberties: Freedoms Gains in Postwar America* (New York: Viking, 1966), pp. 267–280.

Violence on the Fanatical Left and Right

༄

Arnold Forster

If violence is the refuge of unreason, then we must never be greatly surprised to find violent tendencies far out on those political extremities of the Left and the Right which have exchanged reason for passion and mystical faith. Extremism of thinking and extremism of action are close to parallel. The "revolution" and the "holy war" are similar fanaticisms in which the impassioned ends necessarily justify any and all means. And history indicates that our Centrist constitutional democracy tends not so much to check as merely to frustrate political unreason, to drive it into the hills or into the dark of night, often increasing its desperation and virulence.

The United States

Tracing the history of violence in the United States—at least with respect to establishing responsibility—is no simple task, violence by its very nature being beyond any simple or reasonable laws of causation. It is, rather, a kind of contagious irresponsibility which allows its advocates to shrug off all blame for specific acts frequently resulting from the emotions they have generated. The leaders of the two main branches of today's Ku Klux Klan (KKK), for example, both have piously disavowed violence and denied using it. One of them, James Venable, leader of the National Knights of the KKK, nonetheless told an Atlanta audience a few years ago that schools should be burned to the ground if necessary to prevent them from being integrated. The other, Robert Shelton, head of the United Klans (the largest of the KKK groups today), has declared:

Reprinted from "Violence on the Fanatical Left and Right," *Annals of the American Academy of Political and Social Science*, 364 (March, 1966), 142–148, by permission of the author and publisher.

"We don't advocate violence. If someone steps on our toes we are going to knock their heads off their shoulders."[1]

Klan leaders denied any part of the bombing of a Baptist church in Birmingham, Alabama, in 1963, which took the lives of four little Negro girls, but a Klan speaker in St. Augustine, Florida, told an assembly of Klansmen:

If they can find those fellows, they ought to pin medals on them. It wasn't no shame they was killed. . . . Why? Because when I go out to kill rattle-snakes, I don't make no difference between little rattlesnakes and big rattle-snakes. . . . I say good for whoever planted the bomb.[2]

And so it goes. The Know-Nothings, the "Wobblies," and the Black Muslims have all disavowed violence at one time or another—it is always someone else stepping on their toes—and yet American history is littered with the heart-breaking reminders of their agitational words spoken on more fiery occasions.

It is, perhaps, an almost automatic reaction to the thought of violence as the weapon of ideological fanatics to think immediately of the Ku Klux Klan. Under various leaderships the hooded terror has been with us for a century now. It provides the classic patterns for our study—the hatred planted and nurtured, the cowardice behind a mask (the covering of cloth or of a crowd), the barbarism of murder, the distrust of this nation's democratic process, or the open contempt for its laws. The Klan is our showcase—but hardly our sole exhibit.

THE NINETEENTH CENTURY

A fiercely emotional superpatriotism shaking America throughout the nineteenth century gave birth to a series of huge political movements whose national platforms—nativist bigotry—inevitably produced precinct-level violence on a wide scale.

The first of these, the Native American party, was an anti-Catholic, anti-immigrant political organization strong in the eastern cities and manufacturing areas in the 1830's and 1840's. Rooted in a long history of prejudices, this party quickly rose to power at the time of an increased Irish immigration, electing a mayor of New York in 1843 and sending several members to Congress. In Philadelphia, in 1844, a series of Native American party street meetings and parades (in which marchers were well armed) led to serious rioting over a period of three months. Two Catholic churches, two parochial schools, and at least a dozen homes owned by Catholics were burned to the ground. Several persons were killed and many injured. The militia, and eventually United States Cavalry and Marine units, had to be called to quell the uprisings. At its national convention in 1845, the Native American party excused the violence as defensive, claiming that Philadelphia mobs had put down the "foreign aggression" of Irish Catholics.

The Native American organization was followed in the 1850's by the Know-Nothings—technically, the Grand Council of the United States of North America—the initial purpose of which was to prevent foreigners and Catholics from holding political office.[3] But the devotees of the new nativism instigated anti-Catholic riots in dozens of American cities. In May 1854, a mob marched on New York's city hall, assaulting everyone who looked Irish. Three months later, St. Louis, Missouri, saw a 48-hour orgy of mob violence in which a dozen persons were killed and fifty or more homes belonging to Irish Catholics were wrecked and looted. In 1855, twenty persons were killed in a two-day riot instigated by Know-Nothings in Louisville.

This was no hate fringe; for when, in the election of 1854, the secret and violent order entered the open political arena (under the name of "the American party"), it elected governors in nine states and placed 104 of its members in the United States House of Representatives—then a body of 234. In 1856, former President Millard Fillmore, running as the Know-Nothing candidate, captured almost a million votes—about one-fifth of the total cast.

Nine years later, in the early months of the Reconstruction, the focus of terror's history moved south as the Negro, with the founding of the first Klan, became the victim. By 1871, the invisible empire had a membership of over half a million, and a Congressional investigation that year uncovered hangings, shootings, whippings, and mutilations in the thousands. In Louisiana alone, two thousand persons had been killed, wounded, or injured in a short few weeks before the election of 1868. The commanding general of federal forces in Texas reported: "Murders of Negroes are so common as to render it impossible to keep accurate accounts of them."[4]

THE EARLY TWENTIETH CENTURY

Between the original KKK and the one that rides today lies the noteworthy history of the "second Klan." With its heyday in the 1920's, this one hit a peak membership of between four and five million and became a major factor on the national political scene, amassing substantial power in the North and West as well as in the South. Once again, it was political power on the barbaric mob level. The *New York World* reported these statistics on Klan activities within a single year (October 1920 to October 1921):

Four killings, one mutilation, one branding with acid, forty-two floggings, twenty-seven tar-and-feather parties, five kidnappings, forty-three persons warned to leave town or otherwise threatened, fourteen communities threatened.[5]

The period of the second Klan and the years immediately preceding World War I—with its war fever, its strikes and draft riots, and its Palmer Raids—constituted an era of heightened emotions and hatreds, one in which the extremist political tempers had short fuses. The enemy —the anarchist, the Red, the capitalist oppressor, the Hun, the Jew, the Papist—was carrying out his plots everywhere and had to be immediately and forcefully clubbed down (if one were viewing from the Right) or overthrown (in the view from the Left). By this time the KKK had added anti-Semitism and anti-Catholicism to its race hatred. And the Communist party had arrived.

It is hardly surprising, in view of the events in Russia in 1917, that the word "violence" became synonymous with the word "communism" in the public mind. According to the "conditions" imposed upon it by the Third International, the American Communist party had to reject democratic parliamentarianism openly in favor of violent revolution. But the Communists in America, even at their peak of influence, were far from realizing their dreams as to size and power, and they were under a tight disciplinary control; as a result of these factors there had been less open violence under their direction, whatever may have been the designs of their foreign mentors.

The Industrial Workers of the World (IWW)—in the turbulent atmosphere of labor disputes—provided a different story. The IWW, the well-known Wobblies, were a union, controlled by hard-core syndicalists, revolutionary socialists who opposed political democracy, teaching that "a struggle must go on until the workers of the world organize as a class, take possession of the earth and the machinery of production and abolish the wage system"—a victory to be won by force. The Wobblies advocated sabotage as a matter of policy. IWW strikes saw violence against non-member workers as well as against public and private property. But as to our focus on "political" movements: these American syndicalists' contempt for the democratic process kept them, as they vainly awaited the Revolution, from achieving or even trying to achieve any degree of political power by the accepted processes of the nation.

Violence swirls about the history and deliberations of the Left. The American Communist party itself had emerged (ultimately, in 1919) from a 1912 debate within the Socialist party on the very question of violence as a social weapon—the Socialist convention voting overwhelmingly to expel anyone "who opposes political action or advocates crime, sabotage or other methods of violence as a weapon of the working class."[6]

Much of the violence involving the Left, however, has resulted from the agitation of its extremist enemies. Super-patriots have indulged in many an orgy of Red-hunting, and the end result has been, as in most such crusades, the justification of violent acts. During the World War I hysteria, a Tulsa newspaper went so far as to advise its readers:

If the IWW . . . gets busy in your neighborhood, kindly take the occasion to decrease the supply of hemp. . . . The first step in the whipping of Germany is to strangle the IWW's. Kill 'em just as you would any other kind of a snake. Don't scotch 'em; kill 'em! And kill 'em dead! It is no time to waste money on trials.[7]

There is little doubt that the extreme Left has welcomed and capitalized on such cries from the other side, and may on occasions have encouraged them in order to foster the persecution image and rally naïve civil libertarians to their side.

The instances of organizational or mob violence in American history always seem, upon reflection, shocking—this, in all probability, because they are so alien to the theory and the usual operation of the American political system with its democratic superstructure, its dynamic usefulness, its protection of enumerated human rights, and its imperfect but nonetheless visible devotion to the values both of order and of change. The turbulence and repressions and the resulting fears that have characterized societies in so much of the world are out of place here.

It is logical, then, that our manifestations of political violence should accompany political doctrines which assail democracy, which deny rights, which despise order, or which resist enlightened change.

It is logical also that the forces of violence themselves seem alien, if not exotic—the Klan, for example, pursuing its nighttime quests in ghostly Inquisitional robes, or the Black Muslims founding their "Nation" in weird, science-fictionalized distortions of Mohammedanism. The second Klan actually reached its climax, in 1940, in a burst of pagan pageantry in which it joined with the German-American Bund, at the Nazis' Camp Nordland in New Jersey, to sing Hitler's marching songs and burn a cross forty feet high.

But even in the most "nativist" of the camps of violence there is

something that might be called "un-American" in the truest sense of that
abused word: an inability to come to terms with the American system
and to take advantage of the unique opportunities which our system
offers for the free expression and propagation of dissent. The most
obvious reason for the links between the espousal of violence and a
contempt for democracy lies in the common tendencies of crusaders and
revolutionaries to value some impersonal abstraction above both the individual's rights and the majority's will. Thus, the industrial units of the
syndicalists or the almost mystical "race" of the Klan, the Nazis, or the
Muslims—or some such ineffable idealization as "God and Country" or
"the Common Man"—is glorified to the denigration of the individual
human person and of society's laws.

While violence ultimately fails—for the very reason that it will not
come to terms with American principles—it is, nevertheless, real, and by
its nature it stimulates fear and heartbreak and deep concern.

MID-TWENTIETH CENTURY

Parallel to the rise of the new Radical Right since 1960, and that of the
new Left subsequently, there has been a sharp increase in the interest
shown in weaponry, military tactics, "self-defense," "riot control," and
the like. Advertisements in gun journals across the country reflect a short
supply of small arms. Much of this interest, certainly, has been stimulated
by the growth of the KKK, by the rise of "guerrilla" bands such as the
Minutemen, and by excited advertisements for weapons in the hate sheets
—publications such as *The Thunderbolt*, distributed by the National
States' Rights Party (NSRP), a Nazilike group with Klan connections
and a passion for military pageantry.

The present era of racist violence in the South began in the late
1950's, when it was highlighted by the dynamiting of a number of
synagogues.[8] Police arrested five suspects, all having connections with the
National States' Rights Party, after a bomb tore apart the temple of a
Reform Jewish congregation in Atlanta in October 1958. The police
investigators had noted close similarities in this bombing to others in
Jacksonville, Miami, Nashville, and Birmingham—patterns indicating a
criminal conspiracy working in several Southern states. The suspects
were never convicted, though the weighty evidence introduced at the
trial of one of the men provided a detailed picture of the religious hatred
and the potential violence in the National States' Rights Party's activities.
In the subsequent renaissance of the KKK, the NSRP has appeared to be
a militant ally of the hooded order.

The current rise of the Klan was heralded by the race riots which rocked Jacksonville, Florida, on "Axe Handle Saturday"—August 27, 1960. Jacksonville was then the target of civil rights "sit-in" demonstrations. From a meeting of the Jacksonville klavern of the Florida Knights of the Ku Klux Klan held earlier that week, a call went out to all Klan units urging them to converge on the city the following Saturday. On that day, local stores reported brisk sales of baseball bats and axe handles. Violence erupted and continued sporadically for several days.

In the three or four years that followed, years of increased activity—and increasing progress—in civil rights, Ku Klux Klan membership climbed into the thousands for the first time in decades. And violence, as usual, has followed upon this growth, the memory of its headlines still fresh: eighteen bomb blasts in Negro churches and homes in McComb, Mississippi, alone during 1964 (Klansmen convicted in at least one case); the bombing of the Birmingham church in which four little Negro girls were killed (Klansmen arrested, freed); the 1964 murder of Negro educator Lemuel Penn (four Georgia Klan members arrested, two tried and acquitted by an all-white jury); the 1965 murder of Mrs. Viola Gregg Liuzzo (three Klan members convicted of violating her civil rights); the murder of three civil rights workers in Philadelphia, Mississippi (six Klansmen among those arrested); weeks of violent racial incidents in St. Augustine, Florida, in 1964, during desegregation efforts by Dr. Martin Luther King (the Klan staging open parades and street harangues on the scene).

And accompanying such recent history have been literally thousands of cross-burnings—the Klan's traditional ritual of terror. As always, however, the hooded "empire" has expressed shocked denials of its responsibility for such outrages. But even without the evidence of its active participation, stand the words of its leaders, the pitchmen whose emotional exhortations are essential for the marshaling of a mob or the poisoning of an individual mind. At about the time the Civil Rights Bill became law in 1964, Klan recruiting posters in Jackson, Mississippi, declared:

> If we don't win in the next eight months, we're all destined for Communist slavery and our wives and daughters will be chattels in Mongolian and African brothels. . . . Absolutely refuse to register or give up arms. . . . Stock up on rifles and shotguns and pistols, all of the standard make, and lots of ammunition. . . . Form an organization with next-door neighbors. . . . Be your own leader of your own household and make it an armed arsenal.

It is not among the white supremacists alone that racial tensions have led to violent talk or violent actions. The Black Muslims—advocates of

Negro supremacy—first came to national attention thirty years ago when they rioted in a Chicago courtroom where one of their members was facing trial on a minor charge.[9] Before the riot squad was called, one police officer was killed and several injured, and the courtroom was wrecked. The Muslims today are urged to refrain from violence, but their seemingly cautious leaders still preach a crude and fantastic racism—that white men, the "blue-eyed devils," are base, inferior, and totally evil—the very hate from which violence springs. And to this race hatred the so-called "Nation of Islam" adds a measure of anti-Christian bigotry, and—like their hooded white counterparts—anti-Semitism.

On the extreme Left, the leader of the Harlem branch of the "Progressive Labor Movement" has been arrested and charged with attempting to use the 1964 riot in New York's ghetto for violent revolutionary purposes.[10] William Epton had stated (according to the testimony of a New York City detective who had infiltrated the movement under orders) that his organization planned to "fight and carry arms" against the police and the National Guard as the spearhead of a proposed Negro rebellion designed to overthrow the government by force and violence. Epton's plans, the detective further testified, called for the mobilization of Harlem residents "block by block" with terrorist bands being trained for guerrilla warfare against the police.

The Progressive Laborites are Marxist extremists who prefer the Peking "line" to that of Moscow—at least insofar as the Red China theorists hold to the necessity of war and violence to accomplish ultimate Communist aims. Testimony such as that of the New York police investigator is hardly surprising in view of such admitted leanings. The antidemocratic Left has advocated war and violence before.

THE JOHN BIRCH SOCIETY

As mentioned earlier, the recent period which has witnessed the resurgence of the Ku Klux Klan, the rise of the armed Minutemen in the hills, and all sorts of stirrings in the various ideological camps has also been the time of an unparalleled growth on the Radical Right. A natural question arises: Where do the organizations of this phenomenon stand—the John Birch Society, particularly—on the matters under consideration? Does the fear-ridden vision of Robert Welch arouse violent thought in his followers? We might ask the same with respect to the written invective of the Birchers' Revilo P. Oliver or the fright-peddling orations of Billy James Hargis.

First, it is important to remember that the Radical Right of the

1960's has been, predominantly, and in the areas of its greatest influence and noise, a middle-class movement—also, a movement with quasi-religious overtones and with a largely suburban membership. Many members of this movement are shocked by the activities of the Klan and feverishly disassociate themselves from such things—despite their own similar, almost hysterical view of current racial problems and their similar fears of an imminent Bolshevik takeover of America.

But, secondly, it is important to realize that many of the manifestations of the Radical Right over recent years display a degree of violence —even if only a small degree—that generally has been considered unthinkable among the "fine, upstanding citizens" which the Birch Society claims to have at its core. Opponents of the Extreme Right have been threatened or harassed with anonymous telephone calls and poison-pen letters. Meetings that could not be controlled or swayed have been disrupted. Those who would not go along with this or that temporary Rightist fanaticism have been intimidated or blackballed. Character has been maligned, dedication insulted, opinions censored. The late Adlai Stevenson was spat upon in Dallas by a follower of the Birchers' General Edwin A. Walker.

Violence must be a state of mind before it can be translated into action. The "nice" suburbanite may never kill a civil rights worker—but the impact of his aroused fury may differ only by degree. What has been produced in the Radical Rightist ideologues is a state of mind *relatively* fevered. The Birch view of the Selma civil rights march ("a horde of termites from all over the country, led by half-crazed ministers . . . in a typical demonstration of Communist activism") would serve to arouse the frenzy of hooded rednecks as well as anything the Klan itself has whipped up. The actions of different persons in response to such propaganda would vary with differing personal factors, but the state of mind is already there.

The California Senate Fact-Finding Subcommittee on Un-American Activities, which always has been noticeably partial to conservative, "anti-Communist" causes, reported, after a 1965 investigation of the John Birch Society, that Robert Welch's organization "has attracted a lunatic fringe that is now assuming serious proportions," and that it has been "beset by an influx of emotionally unstable people, some of whom have been prosecuted in the courts for their hoodlum tactics."[11]

Extremism can and does attract such people, and it can instill similar attitudes in others who had not displayed them previously. At more than one far-right-wing meeting the Birch Society's cry of "Impeach Earl

Warren" has been followed by the suggestion that the United States Chief Justice be hanged or shot rather than impeached—and this suggestion has been met on such occasions with tumultuous cheers.

It is hardly surprising that the members of the John Birch Society, like the KKK, like the IWW, and like all the revolutionaries and Rightist radicals of our history, have disdain for the processes of democracy. The Birchers, too, prefer to operate outside of politics, and their founder and chieftain, Robert Welch, wrote in his famous *Blue Book* that democracy is "a fraud,"[12] and "the worst of all forms of government."[13] Such is the pattern of the state of mind from which violent action tends to arise.

Such action has produced tragic blots on the pages of the American record in all times, but the pages also indicate that when political democracy has been kept strong and dynamic, political violence has ultimately failed. It has ever been thus—and will be again in respect to the current crop of extremists on the Left and Right.

Notes·

1) *Long Island Newsday,* March 27, 1965.
2) Eyewitness account, KKK meeting, St. Augustine, Florida, September 1963. Also, for this and all other references to the KKK: "The Ku Klux Klans—1965," *Facts* (Anti-Defamation League), Vol. 16, No. 3 (May 1965).
3) Gustavus Myers, *History of Bigotry in the United States* (New York: Capricorn Books, 1960), pp. 123 ff.
4) *Ibid.,* p. 216.
5) Samuel Tenenbaum, *Why Men Hate* (Philadelphia: Jewish Book Guild of America, 1947), p. 236 (quoting *New York World*).
6) Irving Howe, *The American Communist Party* (Boston: Beacon Press, 1957), p. 15.
7) John P. Roche, *The Quest for the Dream* (New York: The Macmillan Company, 1963), p. 64 (quoting from the *Tulsa World,* November 9, 1917).
8) "Anti-Semitism in the South," *Facts* (Anti-Defamation League), Vol. 13, No. 4 (October–November 1958).
9) Cf. C. Eric Lincoln, *The Black Muslims in America* (Boston: Beacon Press, 1961).
10) *New York Times,* December 1, 1965, p. 34.
11) "Un-American Activities in California: Thirteenth Report, 1965," California Senate Fact-Finding Subcommittee on Un-American Activities (June 1965), p. 174.
12) Robert Welch, *Blue Book of the John Birch Society,* Fourth Printing (Belmont, Mass.: Author, 1961), p. 159.
13) *Ibid.,* p. xv.

Coöptation

こうか

Philip Selznick

. . . *To risk a definition:* coöptation is the process of absorbing new *elements into the leadership or policy-determining structure of an organization as a means of averting threats to its stability or existence.* . . .

Coöptation tells us something about the process by which an institutional environment impinges itself upon an organization and effects changes in its leadership, structure, or policy. Coöptation may be formal or informal, depending upon the specific problem to be solved.

Formal Coöptation

When there is a need for the organization to publicly absorb new elements, we shall speak of formal coöptation. This involves the establishment of openly avowed and formally ordered relationships. Appointments to official posts are made, contracts are signed, new organizations are established—all signifying participation in the process of decision and administration. There are two general conditions which lead an organization to resort to formal coöptation, though they are closely related:

1) When the legitimacy of the authority of a governing group or agency is called into question. Every group or organization which attempts to exercise control must also attempt to win the consent of the governed. Coercion may be utilized at strategic points, but it is not effective as an enduring instrument. One means of winning consent is to coöpt into the leadership or organization elements which in some way reflect the sentiment or possess the confidence of the relevant public or mass and which will lend respectability or legitimacy to the organs of control and thus reëstablish the stability of formal authority. This device is widely used, and in many different contexts. It is met in colonial

Reprinted from *TVA and the Grassroots* (Berkeley: University of California Press, 1949), pp. 13-15, by permission of the University of California Press.

countries, where the organs of alien control reaffirm their legitimacy by coöpting native leaders into the colonial administration. We find it in the phenomenon of "crisis-patriotism" wherein normally disfranchised groups are temporarily given representation in the councils of government in order to win their solidarity in a time of national stress. Coöptation has been considered by the United States Army in its study of proposals to give enlisted personnel representation in the courts-martial machinery—a clearly adaptive response to stresses made explicit during World War II. The "unity" parties of totalitarian states are another form of coöptation; company unions or some employee representation plans in industry are still another. In each of these examples, the response of formal authority (private or public, in a large organization or a small one) is an attempt to correct a state of imbalance by formal measures. It will be noted, moreover, that what is shared is the responsibility for power rather than power itself.

2) When the need to invite participation is essentially administrative, that is, when the requirements of ordering the activities of a large organization or state make it advisable to establish the forms of self-government. The problem here is not one of decentralizing decision but rather of establishing orderly and reliable mechanisms for reaching a client public or citizenry. This is the "constructive" function of trade unions in great industries where the unions become effective instruments for the elimination of absenteeism or the attainment of other efficiency objectives. This is the function of self-government committees in housing projects or concentration camps, as they become reliable channels for the transmission of managerial directives. Usually, such devices also function to share responsibility and thus to bolster the legitimacy of established authority. Thus any given act of formal coöptation will tend to fulfill both the political function of defending legitimacy and the administrative function of establishing reliable channels for communication and direction.

In general, the use of formal coöptation by a leadership does not envision the transfer of actual power. The forms of participation are emphasized but action is channeled so as to fulfill the administrative functions while preserving the locus of significant decision in the hands of the initiating group. . . .

Informal Coöptation

Coöptation may be, however, a response to the pressure of specific centers of power within the community. This is not primarily a matter of the sense of legitimacy or of a general and diffuse lack of confidence. Legitimacy and confidence may be well established with relation to the general public, yet organized forces which are able to threaten the formal authority may effectively shape its structure and policy. The organization faced with its institutional environment, or the leadership faced with its ranks, must take into account these outside elements. They may be brought into the leadership or policy-determining structure, may be given a place as a recognition of and concession to the resources they can independently command. The representation of interests through administrative constituencies is a typical example of this process. Or, within an organization, individuals upon whom the group is dependent for funds or other resources may insist upon and receive a share in the determination of policy. This type of coöptation is typically expressed in informal terms, for the problem is not one of responding to a state of imbalance with respect to the "people as a whole" but rather one of meeting the pressure of specific individuals or interest groups which are in a position to enforce demands. The latter are interested in the substance of power and not necessarily in its forms. Moreover, an open acknowledgment of capitulation to specific interests may itself undermine the sense of legitimacy of the formal authority within the community. Consequently, there is a positive pressure to refrain from explicit recognition of the relationship established. . . .

Coöptation reflects a state of tension between formal authority and social power. This authority is always embodied in a particular structure and leadership, but social power itself has to do with subjective and objective factors which control the loyalties and potential manipulability of the community. Where the formal authority or leadership reflects real social power, its stability is assured. On the other hand, when it becomes divorced from the sources of social power its continued existence is threatened. This threat may arise from the sheer alienation of sentiment or because other leaderships control the sources of social power. Where a leadership has been accustomed to the assumption that its constituents respond to it as individuals, there may be a rude awakening when organization of those constituents creates nucleuses of strength which are able to effectively demand a sharing of power.

.   .   .

The Specter of Conflict

Lewis M. Killian / Charles Grigg

. . .

It is true that tokenism is "too little and too late." But it is also true that token desegregation will be the dominant pattern until the cultural deficit of the Negro masses is reduced or the majority of Negroes reject integration as a goal, as the Black Muslims would have it. Although many local laws sustaining compulsory, racial segregation survive pending the day they are specifically challenged, segregation is legally dead. Despite the volume of criticism aimed at the U.S. Supreme Court, there has not been enough unified opposition to lead to nullification by constitutional amendment. And such opposition will never develop as long as the Negro bears the burden of compelling compliance and the white power structure is able to find ways to soften the impact of desegregation through tokenism.

The spatial distribution of the Negro population, the cultural deprivation of the Negro masses, and the social organization of the Negro community make it clear that, in the present circumstances, not many Negroes can benefit directly from the Supreme Court's decisions. Only a minority of "qualified," highly motivated individuals will be willing and able to take advantage of the opportunities provided by the new legal principle. Over and over again it has been demonstrated that plans for "voluntary desegregation" either result in token desegregation or, if more than a token number of Negro volunteers appear, in the eventual "re-segregation" of the institution or neighborhood.

To make desegregation compulsory and comprehensive, not voluntary and token, would require major changes in the civil rights laws, in

Reprinted from "The Specter of Conflict," *Racial Crises in America* (Englewood Cliffs, N.J.: Prentice-Hall, 1964), pp. 130–133, by permission of Prentice-Hall, Inc. © 1964.

the judicial application of the principle of equity, and in the role of the federal executive. There is little indication that the American electorate to whom the legislative and executive branches are responsive is likely to demand the resolution of the crisis through compulsory desegregation on a massive scale. Ironically, authoritarian methods would be necessary to bring about rapid desegregation and "racial democracy" in the absence of a legislative mandate. But there is great danger that the use of such methods would at once transform the apathy and complacency of the majority of the white populace into active resistance.

Tokenism as a Continuing Objective

In spite of the increasing volume of denunciations of tokenism by Negro leaders, many of these leaders will continue to fight for the symbolic gains which token desegregation brings. Even tokenism shatters the castelike uniformity of traditional patterns of segregation. It provides the basis of hopes for greater gains in the future. Even Negroes who may not be able to take advantage of token desegregation experience a temporary feeling of victory, although they will soon feel frustrated and impatient again. Getting James Meredith into the University of Mississippi did represent a victory for Negroes, just as failure to keep Autherine Lucy in the University of Alabama constituted a defeat. Negroes will continue to fight for such victories as long as they can—and rejoice in them.

More important, for the Negro leader who cannot accept the "racism in reverse" of the Black Muslims, this is the easiest type of victory to achieve. In spite of the costs and the danger, it is still easier to desegregate a few lunch counters than to raise the level of living of millions of Negroes; to gain the admission of a handful of Negro children to a few white schools than to raise the achievement level of thousands of children still attending segregated schools; to compel the employment of a few white-collar workers in "white" stores than to solve the problem of Negro unemployment. Segregation is the symbol of the pervasive inequality of the Negro in American society, and the symbol is a more accessible target than the basic, underlying inequality. Thus either in response to the pricks of conscience or the desire for prestige, many Negro leaders will continue to lead attacks on the surface manifestations of the Negro's inferior status. They will receive support from many lower-class Negroes, who will derive psychic rewards from the struggle even if the victory brings them no direct gains. They will receive even more enthusiastic support from middle-class Negroes, who are able to take advantage of the gains of token desegregation. Because they are "ready" for desegregation, such middle-class Negroes find the arbitrary racial barriers all the more onerous.

Conflict Over Tokenism

But even when Negro leaders accept the limited objective of tokenism, their relationship with white society and its leaders is fundamentally one of conflict. From the legal standpoint, tokenism consists of granting to the individual citizen rights which are his by virtue of his citizenship and which cannot be withheld on the basis of his group membership. They are *his* rights, not the group's. But it is difficult for the white citizen to perceive the Negro pioneer as an individual claimant when he claims rights that have long been enjoyed only by the white group. When the individual is aided and supported by Negro organizations and his legal claim is described as a "class action," it is even more difficult for the white person to see the Negro claimant as anything but a representative and spearhead of the entire Negro community. The Negro pioneer, no matter how exceptional, stands in the shadow of the culturally deprived Negro community. As long as he does, white Americans will react to the threat of having to accept the Negro lower class along with the pioneer. They will not voluntarily sacrifice their status advantage. They will give it up only when confronted with power that threatens other values.

So the prospect is that most of the Negro's gains will continue to come through conflict. White liberals may regard each token step as a gain for which all Americans should be thankful. But in the context of intergroup relations each of these steps will be a victory for Negroes and a defeat for the dominant white group. But such small, symbolic victories will not signify the termination of the power struggle either in the communities in which they occur or in the larger American society. In spite of temporary victories or temporary defeats, the drive of Negroes for identity will continue for a long time. There will be respites following periods of struggle and stress. Token victories will not eliminate the substratum of dissatisfaction which underlies the Negro's struggle, but they will encourage renewal of the struggle.

.   .   .

Super-Patriotism Defined

Richard Schmuck / Mark Chesler

"*Radical Right*" (Baum, *1962;* Brant, *1962;* Cook, *1962;* Lipset, *1955;* Schlesinger, 1962; Westin, 1962), "Far Right" (Dudman, 1962; Holliday, 1962; Horton, 1961), "Rampageous Right" (Barth, 1962), "Right Winger" (Ellsworth & Harris, 1962), "Rightest" (Holliday, 1962), "Extremist" (Case, 1962; Sherwin, 1963), "Ultras" (Cook, 1962; Suall, 1962), are terms used by a variety of authors to characterize a growing socio-political protest. The term "Super-Patriot" is adopted here because pro-Americanist and anti-foreign sentiments seem to be the dominant and unifying themes of positions taken by organizations and individuals who engage in such protests. Indeed, most of these people are not "rightist" in the economic sense of that term; they typically hold laissez-faire, free enterprise beliefs which are technically rooted in Nineteenth century liberalism (Trow, 1958; Viereck, 1955). However, even these historically liberal concepts were and are associated with patriotic nationalism. It is this nationalistic emphasis which is the most pervasive characteristic of the "rightist" phenomena.

To demonstrate their patriotic feelings, some Super-Patriots identify themselves as "card carrying Americans." They carry a small card with the pledge of allegiance, a picture of the American flag, and their personal signature. On the reverse side, the card notes that the holder is proud to be a Super-Patriot, Conservative, Right Winger and Reactionary. Specifically the card reads:

I am a Super-Patriot—I love my country and those things that made it great.

I am a Conservative—I want to save this country.

Reprinted from "Super-Patriotism Defined" in "On Super-Patriotism: A Definition and Analysis," *Journal of Social Issues*, 19 (April, 1963), 32–38, 46–47, by permission of the authors and publisher.

I am a Right Winger—I advocate that we must lead our country to
the right principles.

I am a Reactionary—I am opposed to anything that has harmed or
will harm my country.

These four statements summarize some prominent perspectives of
Super-Patriotism. First, Super-Patriots exhibit a sincere reverence for
what they conceive to be American principles and traditions. Secondly,
they sincerely wish to save their country from what they see as its
destruction by virtue of governmental actions. Thirdly, Super-Patriots are
convinced that their interpretations of American ideals are the only true
ones; their moralistic speeches and articles reflect this assurance. Finally,
Super-Patriots are opposed to anything that they see as changing America
in a different direction than their own. In this respect, changes away from
conservative political conceptions or committed Americanism are seen as
subversive aids to an International Communist Conspiracy, and are
policies that should be opposed.

Super-Patriots are opposed to recent social changes because most of
them are seen to run counter to their principles. Their pattern of
opposition is especially directed at political, economic, religious and
educational institutions. To be more specific, Super-Patriot speeches and
articles aggressively criticize current policies about one or more of the
following: America's role in international relations, domestic social equality, economic organization, religious orientations, educational philosophy
and practice, and mental health programs. An index for measuring Super-
Patriotism can be generated by using these six areas of concern as a basic
series of dimensions. Table 1 represents an abstraction of these dimensions
expressed by Super-Patriot groups and individuals.

Column one identifies the major areas of concern while column two
summarizes the specific positions advanced by Super-Patriots. Each area
of concern also represents a conservative-liberal controversy in contemporary American politics. *Conservative positions advanced on such
issues, accompanied by a fervent Americanism and the perception that
people who do not accept these positions are Communists or Communist
sympathizers, typifies the Super-Patriot pattern.* These six areas of concern are elaborated here.

1) International Political Change and America's Role

Many Super-Patriots believe that absolutely no compromise or negotiation is possible between Communist countries and the nations of the Free

World. Any such cooperation is seen as aiding Satanic forces in their drive to "enslave" America and destroy Christianity. Further, international organization and nuclear disarmament negotiations are perceived as leading to a loss of national sovereignty and autonomy. In this regard, the activities of the United Nations, the United Nations Educational Scientific and Cultural Organization, as well as citizen groups advocating peace, are suspected of being subversive.

TABLE 1 / *Some Super-Patriot General Concerns and Specific Positions*

I) *Areas of concern*	II) *Specific positions advanced*
1) International political change and America's role	Against loss of national sovereignty Against threat of "enslavement" through International Government Against cooperating with "evil" Communist forces
2) Domestic political change and social equality	For states rights Against egalitarianism Against using "biased" social science to form public policy
3) Economic changes in private and public enterprises	For free enterprise without governmental intervention Against trade with Communist countries Against international trade agreements
4) Religious institutions and social change	Social service is not the mission of the church Not fighting against Communism is sinful For a personalized church and religious system
5) Educational institutions and practice in change	Against permissiveness in schools For training in traditional moral values Against psychological counseling and testing, "brainwashing" & "brainpicking" Against federal influences in schools & curricula
6) Mental health of individuals	Against invasions of privacy Against uses of psychology to analyze political activity Against permissiveness & impulse expression

2) Domestic Political Change and Social Equality

Super-Patriots often oppose federal governmental influence in local and regional affairs. This outlook is manifest particularly in their perception of encroachments on Southern "States Rights." Super-Patriots see local autonomy being threatened, and social science being used as a tool, by the current advocates of desegregation and social equality. Some Super-Patriots explicitly charge that various civil rights organizations are Communist dominated and thereby have conspiratorial intentions to destroy the American way of life.

3) Economic Changes in Private and Public Enterprises

Some Super-Patriots are critical of what they perceive to be dangerous trends in public control over the structure and operation of the American economy. They are especially concerned with governmental encroachments on private production and free enterprise. Several organizations are lobbying to repeal the income tax and to force the government to relinquish all holdings. Super-Patriots are also concerned with the potential loss of American sovereignty resulting from international trade agreements, such as the common market. Loss of the United States' economic independence, and the possibility of supporting Communist economies, is seen as occurring in our trade relations with the Communist nations. Therefore, some Super-Patriots are attempting to boycott goods imported from Communist countries, and are putting pressure on local merchants to curtail stocks of such goods.

4) Religious Institutions and Social Change

Since many Super-Patriots are engaged in protests against the moral trends of the contemporary culture, their charges are often directed at the organized religious institutions as the traditional custodian of societal morality. Super-Patriots are especially critical of those institutions that do not join them in a "Holy Christian War" against the Communists. They are also concerned with the growth in size and complexity of some churches and what they see as the resultant impersonalization of religion. Further, Super-Patriots charge that churches which define part of the religious mission as working to improve social conditions and social problems are aiding the Communist program. Advocates of this "Social Gospel" are seen as provoking internal strife in American society and as seeing the origin of sin in societal conditions rather than in man's nature. Both trends are perceived by Super-Patriots as advancing Communist purposes.[1] One target for these particular charges has been the National Council of Churches, and certain denominations which are seen to be infiltrated by Communists and Communist sympathizers.

5) Changes in Educational Institutions and Practices

The manner in which young people are being educated is a source of concern for some Super-Patriots. They generally charge that our children are not being educated in the basic academic fundamentals. Schools are seen as emphasizing irrelevant social adjustment goals and, in the process, are "brainwashing" children in anti-moral and anti-American values.[2] Furthermore, as noted above with regard to domestic political and economic institutions, Super-Patriots are critical of the role the federal government plays in education. Federal aid is seen as leading to federal and eventually international control of educational curricula and practices. Some Super-Patriots are convinced that Communists and Communist sympathizers have already infiltrated and now direct various educational systems from the elementary grades through post-graduate and adult education programs.

6) Mental Health of Individuals

The focus of a growing number of Super-Patriot charges are federal and community based mental health programs. One of the Super-Patriots' concerns is that liberals, socialists, and communists are using mental health theory and practice as a hidden umbrella from which to exercise thought control. In addition, these programs are seen as teaching "world-mindedness," internationalism, atheism and immorality. Psychiatrists, social workers, and educational counselors are seen as plotting to subvert American moral traditions and replace them with doctrines of atheism, materialism, expressionism and permissiveness. All of these doctrines are viewed as components of international Communism and their proponents are seen as subversive.

Although Super-Patriots are characterized by their opposition to current policies in one or more of the above six areas, such typical concerns constitute only one aspect of the Super-Patriot syndrome. Along with taking some of these positions, Super-Patriots, in contrast to conservatives, view those who disagree with them as Communists, or at least as being sympathetic with the Communist Conspiracy.

The role played by the Communist Conspiracy in providing a focus for these perceptions and positions is evident with further analysis. The Soviet Union's military power and the apparent danger of internal subversion are two issues posed by the prominence of Communism. Because of these circumstances, most Americans believe that Communism actually threatens the security and sovereignty of the nation. However, Super-Patriots are distinctive from most other Americans in that they associate the dangers of Communism with numerous aspects of contemporary domestic life. For instance: mental health programs, seen as leading to invasions of personal privacy and the control of one's mind, are associated with Chinese Communist brainwashing during the Korean War; public housing programs are linked to the Communist emphasis on communal living; and federal supports for racial desegregation are associated with centralized planning and control in Russia. More generally, increasing governmental involvement in regional or local matters is associated with a Marxist-Leninist emphasis on "democratic centralism," public planning, and central governmental control. Sin and immorality are connected to atheism, scientific materialism and the general Communist deemphasis of religion. These latter concepts, in turn, are seen as being associated with psychiatry, social science, and the social service orientations in religious institutions. In short, the Communist Conspiracy is blamed for most of the recent changes in the United States that the Super-Patriots oppose.

The Super-Patriot sees the antithesis of these "Communist" tendencies in the traditional American way of life. He understands America to be "One Nation Under God," committed to strong state governments and local jurisdiction; a free and independent nation where privacy and individualism are fostered, and a place where individual property rights and private belongings are respected. Furthermore, the Super-Patriot sees his country as respecting the sovereignty of other nations and as never having been involved in imperialism or the enslavement of other nations.

Some Super-Patriot organizations promulgate general philosophies embracing many issues and direct their energies on several fronts at once, e.g., the John Birch Society, the Christian Anti-Communism Crusade, the Christian Crusade, the Conservative Society of America, and We, The People. Other groups emphasize only one area of concern and focus on one aspect of the changing American culture, e.g., The Liberty Lobby, Committee to Warn of the Arrival of Communist Merchandise on the Local Business Scene, and the National Health Federation. No group will be categorized as Super-Patriot unless it can be shown that: (1) most of its members see internal subversion occurring in several areas, (2) its leadership or members argue that political liberals are consciously or unconsciously helping the Communists to take over America.

Although it is important to suggest the explicit criteria for Super-Patriotism, it is perhaps equally important to specify the limits of this definition. There are certain groups and individuals that take positions, such as those in Table 1, that are not Super-Patriots. Neither openly

Fascist organizations, e.g., American Nazi Party and National Renaissance Party; nor members of the so-called "lunatic fringe," are included in this definition. Also, it is a mistake to consider growing Super-Patriotism as just a manifestation of mental derangement or illness. Furthermore, most of the conservative politicians of the Republican and Democratic parties are not now Super-Patriots. Senators Goldwater, Dirksen, and Russell, as well as Representatives such as Halleck of Indiana and Meader of Michigan are political conservatives but not Super-Patriots. They may well be very conservative and particularly extreme on certain issues, but it is a mistake to classify them in the same category with Robert Welch, Fred Schwarz, Billy Hargis, and Edwin Walker. These latter four individuals have conservative positions in several of the six areas outlined above. At the same time they advocate fervent Americanism and see internal Communist-Socialist-Liberal collaboration as a powerful subversive force in this country. Indeed, the views of these men typify contemporary Super-Patriotism and distinguish it from both traditional conservatism and native Fascism.

Notes

1) Further documentation of these Super-Patriot perceptions are presented in Roy, 1953; and Sowing Dissension in the Churches, 1961.
2) Further documentation of these Super-Patriot perceptions is presented in Bainbridge, 1952; and Raywid, 1962.

References

Bainbridge, J. "Save Our Schools." *McCall's*, 1952, September.
Barth, A. "Report on the Rampageous Right." *New York Times Magazine*, 1962, April 29, 13, 93–96.
Baum, W. C. "The World of the Radical Right: Implications for Political Behavior." Paper read at American Psychological Association meetings, St. Louis, Missouri, September, 1962.
Bell, D. (Ed.). *The New American Right*, New York: Criterion, 1955.
Benson, E. T. *The Red Carpet*, Derby, Connecticut: Monarch Books, 1963.
Brant, J. "The Anti-Communist Hoax." *The New Republic*, 1962, May 28, 15–19, and June 4, 17–20.
Case, C. "The Politics of the Extremist." *Anti-Defamation League Bulletin*, 1962, January 6.
Cook, F. J. "The Ultras: Aims, Affiliations and Finances of the Radical Right." *The Nation*, 1962, June 30, 68 pp.
Dudman, R. *Men of the Far Right*, New York: Pyramid Books, 1962.
Ellsworth, R. E., and Harris, S. M. *The American Right Wing*, Washington, D.C.: Public Affairs Press, 1962.

First National Directory of "Rightist" Groups, Publications and Some Individuals in the United States (and some foreign countries) (Fourth Ed.), Sausalito, California: The Noontide Press, 1962.

Hoffer, E. *The True Believer,* New York: Harper, 1951.

Holliday, B. "What I Found Inside the John Birch Society." *Detroit Free Press,* 1962, August 12, 13, 14, 15, 16, 17.

Horton, P. "Revivalism on the Far Right." *Reporter Magazine,* 1961, July 20, 25–29.

Lipset, S. M. "The Sources of the 'Radical Right.' " In D. Bell (Ed.), *The New American Right,* New York: Criterion, 1955.

Parsons, T. "Social Strains in America." In D. Bell (Ed.), *The New American Right,* New York: Criterion, 1955.

Raywid, Mary Anne. *The Ax-Grinders,* New York: Macmillan, 1962.

Roy, R. L. *Apostles of Discord,* Boston: Beacon Press, 1953.

Schlesinger, A., Jr. "The Threat of the Radical Right." *New York Times Magazine,* 1962, June 17.

Schwarz, F. C. *You Can Trust the Communists . . . to Be Communists,* Englewood Cliffs, New Jersey: Prentice-Hall, 1960.

Sherwin, M. *The Extremists,* New York: St. Martin's Press, 1963.

Sowing Dissension in the Churches, New York: Department of Christian Social Relations, The National Council of the Protestant Episcopal Church, 1961.

Suall, I. *The American Ultras,* New York: New America, 1962.

Trow, M. A. "Small Businessmen, Political Tolerance and Support for McCarthy." *Amer. J. Sociol.,* 1958, 64.

Viereck, P. "The Revolt against the Elite." In D. Bell (Ed.), *The New American Right,* New York: Criterion, 1955.

Welch, R. *The Blue Book of the John Birch Society,* Belmont, Massachusetts: Author, 1961.

Westin, A. "The Deadly Parallels: Radical Right and Radical Left." *Harper's Magazine,* 1962, April, 25–32.

Democracy and the Problem of Civil Disobedience

David Spitz

IV

Of those who accept democracy as the theoretically or practically best political order, yet contemplate disobedience to the law, two classes of citizens must, I think, be distinguished. One denies the intrinsic merit or rationality of the law itself; the other challenges as well the claim of the particular form of state enacting the law to be called a democracy.

For this latter group, democracy is good but the state is not democratic; hence with respect to the principle of political obligation their attitude toward the political order is not essentially different from that of those who accept the state as democratic but deny that democracy is good. They not only argue, with Aristotle,[1] that a government democratic in form may be oligarchical in fact; they insist further that a careful examination of the American political system discloses it to be formally insufficient as well. From their point of view, the American Senate (based on a quota system that does violence to the principle of popular representation), the Supreme Court (with its power of judicial review), the staggered system of elections (which not infrequently prevents a popular majority from becoming a legal or controlling majority), the involved apparatus that separates and checks powers so as to deadlock no less than to balance them, the amending clause (which puts the Constitution itself beyond the reach of normal majorities)—all these and more (e.g., suffrage restrictions, gerrymandering, and the like) are but devices to hinder and at times effectively to block the translation of

Reprinted from "Democracy and the Problem of Civil Disobedience," *American Political Science Review*, 48 (June, 1954), 396–402, by permission of the author and The American Political Science Association.

public opinion into public policy. Even the sacred rules of the game may be changed by the group in power when those rules no longer operate to that group's advantage. This is amply evidenced by the history of the Supreme Court with respect, for example, to the Fourteenth Amendment.

Knowing these things (or feeling this way), a citizen confronted by what he conceives to be a morally reprehensible law (or an action under that law) has difficulty in accepting the argument that he should express his disapproval not through civil disobedience but through the regular legal and political channels available to him. In his view, it is simply not true that these legal and political channels *are* available to him, that is, available in the way that democracy ideally requires. Such a citizen might agree that all human contrivances are imperfect. He might admit, too, that it is great folly, if not fanaticism, to insist on the perfectibility of political institutions regardless of consequences. Nevertheless, if it is not simply to evoke his blind acquiescence, a democratic system must above all be democratic; it must embody to a major degree elements of that just political order which it purportedly represents. If it falls so far short of this ideal as to foreclose any real possibility of correcting legislative evils by (say) normal majorities, if the political mechanism obstructs public opinion by institutionalizing various forms of minority control, it is in fact not a democracy at all. It is a perverted form of democratic government and, as such, it is bound to rely on unjust laws.[2]

To the extent that there is substance in this view—in the sense that the indictment of institutional arrangements is sound—men committed to democracy are under no moral obligation to obey "undemocratic" laws. Those who place a different weight on the shortcomings of the system may deplore their judgment in this regard, but if the shortcomings are serious and real they cannot in democracy's name be asked to give absolute obedience to a less-than-democratic (and to this degree un-democratic) system. Like the good churchgoers of Concord who were taken ill when Thoreau asked them also to read the Bible, protagonists of the system might well be discomfited and silenced when confronted, for instance, by a Negro suffering political and educational discrimination in one of our states, or an interned Nisei, who to justify an act of civil disobedience asks but a single question: "Is this the content of democracy?"

V

We come, finally, to those democrats who accept the system as essentially democratic and who are prepared, on the whole, to obey the laws. They understand that government by consent means consent not to each particular law but to the entire system of order itself, and ultimately to the idea of justice which that system represents. For the sake of the greater good secured by that system through its government and its laws, they accept specific enactments which they otherwise disapprove. They obey not necessarily because they think that the law is right, but because they think it right to obey the law.[3]

For this reason they reject the individualistic ethics of a Protagoras, who would justify disobedience to the law provided you can get away with it, or of a Harold Laski or of a Thoreau, who would demand of each law that it provide "moral adequacy,"[4] or of other legal and political theorists who would measure the obligation of a citizen to the law in terms of the degree to which it serves some other end. If a man's loyalty is to the system, then obedience cannot be determined solely by immediate approbation. He cannot attempt to evaluate the law simply in terms of its expressed content;[5] nor can he separate laws from their cumulative total effect on the assumption that disobedience to a particular law leaves unaffected the system of law. Very few laws are accepted unanimously, and if the considerable number of citizens who dislike a law are literally free to disobey it, the state and the social order can hardly be expected to survive. A plea for total disobedience, or for the right of total disobedience, logically entails not a state at all but anarchy.

Does it follow that the citizen who admits his obligation to obey the laws must obey *all* laws *always?* Is one who rejects the extreme individualism of a Laski compelled to accept the extreme absolutism of a Hegel,[6] or the near-absolutism of a Hobbes[7] or of a John Dickinson, who join with Socrates of the *Crito* in entering an affirmative answer? If a law is disobeyed, they tell us, the social order will collapse. In their view, each law is an integral part of a coherent, corporate body of law, which in turn sustains society. Consequently, disobedience to a law is a challenge to sovereignty itself. As Dickinson put it: "It is not a question of a bare conflict between the individual and the sovereign; the conflict must be regarded as rather between the individual and all that the sovereign stands for." In disobeying the sovereign we bring "dominantly into the foreground the large issue of the desirability of preserving public authority and civil society itself." In disobeying the sovereign we strike at just this essential method of civil society.[8]

This is a plausible argument. It avoids the individualistic fallacy by emphasizing the need for order and the role of law in maintaining that order. But it is not without fallacies of its own. What holds society together, for example, is not simply law (and perhaps not even law) but the customs and moral codes, the sentiments, of the people. The classic formulation of T. H. Green still applies: it is not the state that produces cohesive will; it is will that creates and sustains the state.[9] Political loyalties and political obligations do not exclude other loyalties and other obligations, and it is the meaning of democracy that it does not seek to command a monopoly of man's allegiances. Democracy seeks to root its fundamental unity not in the power of the state but in the sense of common interest that sustains but does not obliterate the vital differences among men.[10] So long as these differences are admitted, with respect not simply to things that do not matter much but to things that touch the very heart of the existing order as well,[11] the democratic state can find its essential solidarity not in the structure of law but in the minds of men.

Nor does the absolutist position rest on solid ground when it assumes that all laws form a coherent unity, so that disobedience to a particular law necessarily involves the destruction of the entire system of law. Evasion of the law is a normal concomitant of all legal systems, and it is doubtful that the existence of jails constitutes sufficient proof of the breakdown of the system. We are all familiar with the propensity of people not in jails to disobey laws that inconvenience them—e.g., traffic regulations, income tax laws, and prohibitions on gambling and on the traffic in liquor and women. Police and other political officials do not enforce all laws equally and at times they conspire with people who seek to disobey them. Governments too evade or disobey the law—witness the oft-cited examples of Southern states that have largely ignored the Fourteenth and Fifteenth Amendments to the American Constitution; of the many Congresses that have failed to apply the constitutional provision (Sec. 2, Amend. XIV) requiring that the representation of such states in the House of Representatives be reduced; and of the refusal of the Congress in 1920 to carry out the required reapportionment of the House of Representatives. Despite these and other acts of disobedience, the system of law has not, I think, disappeared. Clearly, *some* laws are not essential to the maintenance of the social order.

If, therefore, the state is not equivalent to the whole of the social order, and if all laws are not integrated into a single coherent unity, disobedience to a particular law need not imply an attempt to overthrow the political system or the social order itself. To Dickinson's charge that the conflict is between the individual and all that the sovereign stands for, we must reply: the conflict is also between the sovereign and all that the individual stands for. It may even, in fact, be between the actual sovereign and all that the ideal sovereign stands for. In these two points, I believe, we can find a sufficient justification for *some* acts of civil disobedience.

Consider, first, what is involved when the state demands that an individual obey not his conscience but the law. In a general sense, it appears to ask only that he recognize the necessity of compromise if men are to live together. But when the issue is joined so that men question the justice of the terms on which they are asked to live together, the state requires far more: it demands nothing less than that he submit to a civil theology.[12] For if action contrary to conscience is immoral, the state by insisting that the individual follow not his conscience but a command of the state contrary to his conscience thereby insists that he act immorally. Since the state will not admit that its command is immoral, it must—if it is to vindicate its claim to obedience—argue that the judgment of the individual conscience is wrong, and that by acting instead according to the state's judgment of what is right the individual will realize his true morality, his true freedom. There are many who still take seriously this teaching of Rousseau, Hegel, and Bosanquet. Nevertheless, the notion that the state embodies our real will, our true morality, our true freedom, as against our actual will, which is said to represent a false morality, is incompatible with the democratic principle. For democracy, if I understand it correctly, stands above all else for a method whereby men can resolve peacefully which of competing moralities shall temporarily prevail. It cannot—if it is to remain a democracy—maintain that it has discovered the true morality which shall henceforth bind all men. Yet when the government of a democratic state demands of a citizen that he surrender his conscience to the state—as it demanded of Jehovah's Witnesses that they (or their children) salute the flag—it in effect demands that he submit to the true morality. From this point of view, imprisonment for civil disobedience becomes, paradoxically, a prolonged appeal to the prisoner's conscience, detention being but a means of permitting his conscience time in which to adjust,[13] after the state has by putting him in prison already denied the validity of his conscience.

To escape this dilemma democracy must deny the theological sanction. It cannot assume what Eric Voegelin suggests the Oxford political philosophers have assumed: namely, that by the mystery of incarnation the principles of right political order have become historical flesh more perfectly in their country than anywhere else at any time.[14] It must recognize that the political order is not perfect and that the laws are not always just. It must affirm no more than that a law is law not because it is absolutely good or right but because a legal majority has decreed it.

Democracy would, of course, insist that it is right for the majority to have this power, and that men should respect this right of the majority as a necessary condition of democracy. But if it is true that the majority may act wrongly—i.e., affront on intrinsic or instrumental grounds the notion of justice held by a dissenting individual or minority—such insistence leads to the paradoxical principle that while the system and the laws that institutionalize that system are just, particular laws emanating from the system may be wrong and therefore unjust. A just system may produce unjust laws.

Now the Aristotelian question—whether a good man can always be a good citizen—has traditionally formed the basis for the problem of political obligation. But if there is validity to the conception of citizenship that I have argued here, the mark of the good citizen—at least in a democracy—is not loyalty to the laws but loyalty to the system, to the principle of democracy itself. The good citizen is obligated not to the sovereign but to all that the sovereign stands for.[15] Consequently, law can command his allegiance not because it is law but because it serves something that is good, because it respects the system of democracy and the purposes for which the democratic state exists.[16] If he obeys simply because it is law, he worships means, not ends; and this is surely a perversion of purpose.

When, therefore, a government holding office and trust under that system so acts—whether directly through its laws or indirectly through non-legal sanctions and the cultivation of a climate of opinion characterized by suspicion and fear—as to deny or to threaten the integrity of the system itself, it creates a situation in which men loyal to democracy may be compelled to defend it against the laws.

It has been urged, not perhaps without reason, that such defense should look first to the democratic processes of persuasion and election.[17] But where it is precisely these processes that the laws attack, where the incursions of government are upon freedom of opinion and the elements of democratic procedure, this may well prove a vain hope. Men are not without warrant in saying today what men have all too often had to say before: the times are "out of joint." Once again, this is a moment when the ordinary rules of decency are to some men in power apparently unknown, when some men cloaked in the sanctity of the law seek to exorcise the spirit of free inquiry.[18] Under such circumstances, it may well be that obedience to democracy can best, and perhaps only, be served by disobedience to the laws. It may well be that men of moral sensitivity and courage will have to say, with Thoreau: "They are the lovers of law and order who observe the law when the government breaks it."[19]

✧

Notes

1) *Politics*, 1292b.
2) There is substantial though not complete truth in Aristotle's dictum that "a well-formed government will have good laws, a bad one, bad ones." *Ibid.*, 1282b.
3) See R. M. MacIver, *The Modern State* (London, 1926), p. 154. This is not to argue that reason is the only, or the decisive, factor in leading men to obey laws which they regard as unjust. Habit, indolence, deference, fear, and the like, are in most cases the crucial determinants of obedience. See James Bryce, *Studies in History and Jurisprudence* (New York, 1901), pp. 467 ff., and R. M. MacIver, *The Web of Government* (New York, 1947), pp. 73–81.
4) "My problem," Laski wrote to Holmes, "is to take away from the state the superior morality with which we have invested its activities and give them [*sic*] back to the individual conscience." Mark de Wolfe Howe (ed.), *Holmes-Laski Letters* (Cambridge, Mass., 1953), Vol. 1, p. 23. See further his *Authority in the Modern State* (New Haven, 1919), Ch. 1, especially pp. 43, 46, 55; *A Grammar of Politics*, 4th ed. (London, 1938), Part I; and *Studies in Law and Politics* (New Haven, 1932), Ch. 11. See also Thoreau: "Must the citizen ever for a moment, or in the least degree, resign his conscience to the legislator? Why has every man a conscience, then? I think that we should be men first, and subjects afterward. It is not desirable to cultivate a respect for the law, as much as for the right. The only obligation which I have a right to assume is to do at any time what I think right." Thoreau, "Civil Disobedience," pp. 636–37.
5) This is convincingly demonstrated in Felix S. Cohen, *Ethical Systems and Legal Ideals* (New York, 1933), pp. 62–65.
6) There is, however, a certain ambiguity in Hegel's absolutism, stemming from his apparent insistence that Antigone in refusing to obey the law of the state was both right and wrong. Cf. Georg W. F. Hegel, *The Phenomenology of Mind*, trans, J. B. Baillie, 2 vols. (New York, 1910), Vol. 2, pp. 453 ff., and Georg W. F. Hegel, *Philosophy of Right*, trans. T. M. Knox (Oxford, 1942), pp. 3–10, 100, 114–15, 165–73, and the relevant translator's notes on pp. 299, 301, and 351. Hegel's subordination of the state (the highest reality within the realm of right) to philosophical truth (the highest reality within the whole system) is emphasized in Herbert Marcuse, *Reason and Revolution* (New York, 1941), p. 178.
7) For Hobbes' denial that political obligation requires an absolute obedience to all laws, see for example *De Cive*, VI, 13; VIII, 1; and XV, 18.
8) "A Working Theory of Sovereignty," *Political Science Quarterly*, XLIII (March, 1928), 32–63.
9) See also Elijah Jordan, *Theory of Legislation; An Essay on the Dynamics of Public Mind* (Chicago, 1952).
10) Cf. MacIver, *The Modern State*, p. 482; Dorothy Fosdick, *What is Liberty?* (New York, 1939), p. 128; and the writer's *Patterns of Anti-Democratic Thought*, pp. 204–6, 247–48.
11) As Mr. Justice Jackson so aptly put it in *West Virginia State Board of Education* v. *Barnette*, 319 U.S. 624, 642 (1943). See also the interesting argument of Charles R. Nixon, "Freedom vs. Unity: A Problem in the Theory of Civil Liberty," *Political Science Quarterly*, Vol. 68, pp. 70–88 (March, 1953).

12) This, indeed, is what Lincoln frankly urged in his address in 1838 on "The Perpetuation of Our Political Institutions": "Let every American, every lover of liberty, every well wisher to his prosperity, swear by the blood of the Revolution, never to violate in the least particular, the laws of the country; and never to tolerate their violation by others. . . . let every man remember that to violate the law, is to trample on the blood of his father, and to tear the character of his own, and his children's liberty. Let reverence for the laws, be breathed by every American mother, to the lisping babe, that prattles on her lap—let it be taught in schools, in seminaries, and in colleges; let it be written in primers, spelling books, and in Almanacs;—let it be preached from the pulpit, proclaimed in legislative halls, and enforced in courts of justice. And, in short, let it become the *political religion* of the nation; and let the old and the young, the rich and the poor, the grave and the gay, of all sexes and tongues, and colors and conditions, sacrifice unceasingly upon its altars." *Abraham Lincoln: His Speeches and Writings*, ed. Roy P. Basler (Cleveland, 1946), pp. 80–81.

13) In employing here a modified phrase from Professor Julius Stone, *The Province and Function of Law* (Sydney, Australia, 1950), p. 228, I do not mean to associate him with the doctrine in the text.

14) Eric Voegelin, "The Oxford Political Philosophers," *The Philosophical Quarterly*, Vol. 3, pp. 97–114, at p. 100 (April, 1953).

15) This is not, perhaps, inconsistent with Aristotle who, while he defines a citizen as "one who obeys the magistrate" (*Politics*, 1277a), also affirms that the one care common to all the citizens—that which *describes* a citizen—is "the safety of the community" (*ibid.*, 1276b).

16) Despite certain phrases in which Professor Ernest Barker seems to argue that obedience to the law is the highest political obligation (*Principles of Social and Political Theory* [Oxford, 1951], p. 194), I take his general position to be in accord with the proposition affirmed here: that it is the state, not the law, which merits that obedience. Clearly, he concurs with the further judgment that since the state is less than society, obedience to law must be subordinate to obedience to right, the highest moral obligation. *Ibid.*, pp. 193, 221 ff.

17) So Lincoln in the address cited earlier (note 12, above, Basler, p. 81): ". . . bad laws, if they exist, should be replaced as soon as possible, still while they continue in force, for the sake of example, they should be religiously observed."

18) It is well to recall the insight of Spinoza: "All men are born ignorant, and before they can learn the right way of life and acquire the habit of virtue, the greater part of their life . . . has passed away." Spinoza, *Tractatus Theologico-Politicus*, trans. R. H. M. Elwes, Ch. 16.

19) "Slavery in Massachusetts," in *op. cit.*, p. 669. Compare the principles and grounds of justifiable disobedience in Franz L. Neumann, "On the Limits of Justifiable Disobedience," in *Conflict of Loyalties*, ed. R. M. MacIver (New York, 1952), pp. 49–56.

CHAPTER FIVE

〜〆〆〆

to provide for

The problem of providing for America's common defense involves preventing or at least minimizing harm caused by the actions of other nations. More specific conceptions of the common defense vary according to their resolution of two related problems: (1) identifying what is to be defended or protected; and (2) distinguishing defensive from offensive uses of military forces. Both problems are discussed in the first section of this introduction. The second section discusses various means of providing for the common defense. The final section deals with the relationship between providing for the common defense and the attainment of other Preamble goals.

What Is the Common Defense?

As indicated above, one of the problems encountered in specifying what the common defense consists of is that of identifying what is to be protected or defended.[1] The article "Defense of What?" by Robert C. Angell notes that the first component of a common defense is the pro-

---

[1] For a treatment of some of the problems of specifying what is to be defended, see Arnold Wolfers, " 'National Security' as an Ambiguous Symbol," *Political Science Quarterly*, LXVII (December, 1952), 481–502; and Lynn H. Miller, "The Contemporary Significance of the Doctrine of Just War," *World Politics*, XVI (January, 1964), 254–286.

the common defence . . .

tection of the physical safety of people and property. But the common defense need not be equated with or limited to merely providing physical safety. Defense of America's sovereignty may be of equal or greater importance. An America which lost much of its people or property in a nuclear holocaust, but thereby avoided foreign domination, might be regarded as having provided for its common defense, while one which secured its physical safety at the cost of its sovereignty need not be.

Angell goes on to note that America may seek to defend not only itself but other societies as well and may even seek to protect certain relationships among nations. These relationships may either be cooperative ones, such as those which constitute Angell's picture of the minimum acceptable world order, or they may be the more antagonistic relations of a military balance of power. In pursuit of the latter, the United States might resist an attempt to arm one side of a conflict such as the one between the Arab nations and Israel, or to preserve its own relative military power by preventing the arming of nations hostile to it, such as Cuba. Finally, America's common defense may be thought of as including the protection of a position of influence or prestige among some or all nations. The Monroe Doctrine, for example, has been interpreted by some as a commitment to preserve American influence in the Western Hemisphere. The great expense of participation in the "space race" can be viewed as helping provide for the common defense in that it preserves American prestige. In short, the common defense may be seen as requiring the protection of such tangibles as physical property as well as such intangibles as international power and prestige.

The second problem encountered in specifying what constitutes the common defense is that of distinguishing between defensive and offensive uses of military forces.[2] It is clear that the use of military force following an attack to resist and repel the attacker is defensive in nature. It is not clear, however, just what constitutes an attack on the United States; nor is it clear that all defensive uses of military force must follow an attack or that all reactions to an attack are defensive.

In the era when America's interests were largely confined within its own borders and those of its territories, an "attack" referred to the destruction of American life or property. Attacks on even friendly nations were not equated with attacks on the United States. Loss of American life and property, not that of potential allies, provoked American entry into World Wars I and II. However, as America's interests have extended beyond its own borders, attacks on some other countries have become equated with attacks on America. Defense now implies a commitment to defend nations in Europe and Asia even before American territory and life are destroyed. Moreover, "attack" is no longer equated with invasion in the classical sense of troops crossing borders. Attempts by a local population to overthrow their government may be regarded as an attack on American interests if they are aided by enemy (Communist) countries or led by persons (Communists) opposed to American interests in that nation. Such "attacks" preceded American armed intervention in the Dominican Republic in 1965, and in Vietnam. In short, "an attack on America" no longer has the clear and simple meaning of armed assault on its territory or population.

Whatever one's definition of an attack on America, however, defensive use of military force need not be confined to reactions to actual attacks. The deployment of troops so as to be able to retaliate in the event of attack may be regarded as defensive even though it is not a response to an actual attack. Moreover, such actions may be considered defensive even though they anger, threaten, or otherwise offend a potential opponent. World War I began after a series of "defensive" troop mobilizations

[2] For a discussion of American policy on the use of force, see Robert W. Tucker, *The Just War: A Study in Contemporary American Doctrine* (Baltimore: Johns Hopkins Press, 1960).

and maneuvers. Nevertheless, the United States and the Soviet Union each claims the presence of their troops on foreign European soil and the deployment of their missile-carrying submarines are defensive because they are not intended to be used before the other side attacks.

The pre-emptive strike is another use of military force which is considered by some as defensive even though it precedes, rather than follows, an actual attack. A pre-emptive strike is an attack on an enemy in the hope of destroying its ability to carry out a planned offensive. One need not, after all, wait to be shot at to plead self-defense if somebody already has pointed a gun at his head and has sworn to use it. Stopping the Japanese on their way to Pearl Harbor could well have been regarded as an act of self-defense and not of offense. In general, the justification of a pre-emptive attack relies heavily on the imminence of planned enemy attack. But the certainty of attack in the more distant future may also be used in an attempt to justify such action. Those who believe it is certain that Communist China will use nuclear weapons once it develops the capacity to deliver them, may call for a pre-emptive attack on its testing grounds as an act of self-defense. In any event, where defensive actions are said to include those which precede an actual attack, the line between defense and offense is blurred. Deployment of troops on foreign soil or in international waters and pre-emptive strikes occupy the blurred region as well.

The line between defense and offense is also blurred by the fact that not all reactions to an attacker need be regarded as defensive. Where the reaction involves not only withstanding and repelling the attack, but advancing other interests as well, the response may not be regarded as defensive. The acquisition of former Spanish territories after the Spanish-American War casts doubt on the defensive nature of American involvement. Similarly, an American attempt to maintain control of Vietnamese territory after the signing of a peace treaty would cast doubt on the defensive nature of American involvement in Vietnam.

Providing for the Common Defense

The various tangible and intangible American interests may be defended in a variety of ways:[3] through the proper use of military power;[4] or by

[3] For discussions of various ways in which a nation's interest may be defended, see Norman J. Padelford and George A. Lincoln, "Instruments and Patterns of Foreign Policy," *The Dynamics of International Politics* (New York: Macmillan, 1962), pp. 339–646; and Davis Bobrow (ed.), *Components of Defense Policy* (Chicago: Rand McNally, 1965).

[4] American military defense policy and needs are discussed in Roswell Gilpatric, "Our Defense Needs: The Long View," *Foreign Affairs*, XLII (April,

taking advantage of opportunities for negotiation provided by participation in the United Nations.[5] Economic resources may be manipulated to keep potential enemies from needed resources and to help neutral nations attain essential resources so as to convert them to allies or keep them unaligned.[6] Finally, insofar as nations are sensitive to the opinions of their own and of other people and insofar as these opinions lead to action, the ideology and propaganda which shape opinion must be taken into account as America seeks protection from other nations. In short, successful manipulation of force, deals, goods, and ideas contributes to the common defense. But whatever the specific factors involved in providing for the common defense, the general process involves minimizing the likelihood of hostile actions on the part of foreign powers and reducing the effect of any hostile actions which do occur.

Raising the cost of hostile foreign actions is an obvious means of making such activity unlikely. American defense policy is based largely on its ability to rain more destruction upon a potential attacker than he is willing to tolerate.[7] The destruction of property or the loss of life, however, are not the only costs which may deter an attack on American interests. Loss of important economic trade may deter hostile actions. For example, American trade with Eastern European countries helps create a situation in which the threat of stopping such trade may deter some

1964), 366–378; Robert A. Goldwin (ed.), *America Armed* (Chicago: Rand McNally, 1963); Hans J. Morgenthau, "The Four Paradoxes of Nuclear Strategy," *American Political Science Review*, LVIII (March, 1964), 23–35; and Gordon Turner, "Classic and Modern Strategic Concepts," in Gordon Turner and R. D. Challener (eds.), *National Security in the Nuclear Age* (New York: Praeger, 1960), pp. 3–30.

For treatment of the nonviolent alternatives to military defense, see William R. Miller, *Non-violence: A Christian Interpretation* (New York: Associated Press, 1964), pp. 97–130; and Gene Sharp, "'The Political Equivalent of War'—Civilian Defense," *International Conciliation*, DLV (November, 1965), 1–67.

[5] See Lincoln Bloomfield, "The UN and National Security," *Foreign Affairs*, XXXVI (July, 1958), 597–610; and Lincoln Bloomfield, "Peacekeeping and Peacemaking," *Foreign Affairs*, XLIV (July, 1966), 671–687.

[6] See Robert A. Goldwin (ed.), *Why Foreign Aid?* (Chicago: Rand McNally, 1963); Hans J. Morgenthau, "A Political Theory of Foreign Aid," *American Political Science Review*, LVI (January, 1962), 301–309; Henry S. Reuss, "The United States Foreign Aid Program: An Appraisal," *Annals of the American Academy of Political and Social Science*, CCCXXXVI (July, 1961), 23–29; and Charles C. Abbott, "Economic Penetration and Power Politics," in David S. McLellan, William C. Olson, and Fred A. Sonderman (eds.), *The Theory and Practice of International Relations* (Englewood Cliffs, N.J.: Prentice-Hall, 1960), pp. 250–258.

[7] For further treatment of the question of defense by deterrence, see Bernard Brodie, "The Anatomy of Deterrence," *World Politics*, XI (June, 1954), 13–28; Malcolm W. Hoag, "On Stability in Deterrent Races," in Morton Kaplan (ed.), *The Revolution in World Politics* (New York: Wiley, 1962), pp. 388–410; and Thomas W. Milburn, "What Constitutes Effective U.S. Deterrence?" in D. J. Hekhuis, C. S. McClintock, and A. L. Burns (eds.), *International Stability: Military, Economic and Political Dimensions* (New York: Wiley, 1964), pp. 174–186.

hostile actions directed at America. Dependence on American aid has probably kept some Latin American and Asian regimes from being openly hostile to America's interests.

A second means of providing for the common defense is by preventing a potential enemy from becoming strong enough to challenge American interests. Such is the aim of the American refusal to trade with Communist China and the attempts to induce others to cease such trade. Moreover, the struggle in Southeast Asia can be seen as a struggle to prevent the resources of that area from coming under Chinese control. Denying China the goods it can obtain in trade and denying it the resources of neighboring countries may weaken any Chinese threat to American interests.

A third means for decreasing the probability of hostility is to avoid giving a cause or excuse for it. Policies of isolation and neutrality have been urged on Americans through much of their history in the hope of keeping free of international conflicts. Similar policies have helped Sweden and Switzerland avoid involvement in two world wars. Moreover, the attempt to avoid conflicts need not be absolute. The United States does not generally shy from conflicts with the Soviet Union, yet, in 1956 it chose not to intervene in the Hungarian revolt. In 1965, both countries sought United Nations action in Kashmir rather than risk the consequences of involvement and direct confrontation. Finally, the avoidance of conflicts may require or involve controlling allies more than it does controlling oneself. For example, America has sought to keep Nationalist Chinese forces on Formosa from invading the Mainland.

A fourth means of reducing the likelihood of hostility is that of providing the means and incentives for the peaceful resolution of conflicts. The American border with Canada can be left unarmed because such means and incentives do exist and thus Canadian-American differences do not threaten the common defense. The ideological and historical ties between the United States and Western Europe, similarly, mean that differences lead to negotiation and not attack. The United Nations was founded in the hope that it would provide means for peaceful resolution of international conflicts sufficiently effective to render armed hostility unnecessary and relatively unattractive.[8]

[8] Defense through peaceful conflict resolution and the creation of a world order are discussed in Amitai Etzioni, "Prerequisites of a World Community," in Robert K. Merton and Robert A. Nisbet (eds.), *Contemporary Social Problems* (New York: Harcourt, Brace & World, 1966), pp. 751–761; Richard N. Gardner, *In Pursuit of World Order: U.S. Foreign Policy and International Organizations* (New York: Praeger, 1964); "Conditions of a World Order," *Daedalus*, Vol. XCV (Spring, 1966); and Arthur I. Waskow, *Keeping the World Disarmed* (Santa Barbara, Cal.: Center for the Study of Democratic Institutions, 1965). For a discussion of the more specific

America's common defense, then, may be provided for in one or more of four general ways. A potential enemy may: (1) be induced to see that an attack is not worth it; (2) be prevented from becoming strong enough to attack; (3) be deprived of a cause or excuse for hostile actions; and (4) be provided with peaceful alternatives for attaining desired ends.

The Common Defense and Other Goals

The means that America uses to provide for its common defense can greatly affect its ability to maintain its desired form of political union, to promote the general welfare, and to secure the blessings of liberty for its members.

One of America's distinguishing characteristics has been its stress on the supremacy of civilian interests over military interests. However, as Marc Pilisuk and Thomas Hayden argue, in "Is There a Military-Industrial Complex which Prevents Peace?," there is reason to question whether American life is presently dominated by civilian or military concerns. There is also reason to wonder if civilian leaders can meaningfully use the power over military decisions which the Constitution sought to give them.[9] The Constitution gives the civilian leaders in Congress the power to decide against whom to declare war.[10] However, a congressional declaration of war need not precede the commitment of troops to combat. No declaration of war preceded the use of troops in Korea, their use in South Vietnam, and the bombing of North Vietnam. Indeed, in some instances, a congressional declaration of war cannot be made meaningfully. War is declared by one nation against another, yet the United States has committed troops in Vietnam, where the enemy is not a formally constituted government or nation; accordingly, no declaration of war can be made by Congress.[11]

---

question of disarmament and arms control, see "Arms Control," *Daedalus*, Vol. LXXXIX (Fall, 1960); and Evan Luard, "Conventional Disarmament," *World Politics*, XVI (January, 1964), 189–204.

[9] The problem of maintaining civilian control of the military in contemporary America is treated in D. W. Brogan, "The United States: Civilian and Military Power," in Michael Howard (ed.), *Soldiers and Governments* (Bloomington: Indiana University Press, 1959), pp. 167–185; Gene M. Lyons, "The New Civil-Military Relations," *American Political Science Review*, LV (March, 1961), 53–67; and R. J. Mosen, Jr., and M. W. Cannon, "The Military Bureaucracy," *The Makers of Public Policy* (New York: McGraw-Hill, 1965), pp. 258–290.

[10] See Arlen J. Large, "Who Declares War?" *The Wall Street Journal* (February 23, 1967), for a brief discussion of the history of Congress' exercise of its power to declare war.

[11] Under Secretary of State Nicholas deB. Katzenbach, in testimony before the Senate Foreign Relations Committee, has gone so far as to state that with respect to

Moreover, American involvement in undeclared wars not only commits troops without a direct act of Congress, it restricts congressional control over military expenditures. It is difficult for a congressman to deny funds to men in battle; such a vote would not only challenge the prestige of the President who committed the troops, but would indicate to the families of men killed in action that they had died in vain. Congressional votes on funds to continue an ongoing conflict are usually merely rubber stamps.

Further alteration and erosion of congressional control over military expenditures stems from the complexity of modern military weapon systems. Often a congressman must simply take the experts' word that the system is worth the money. Moreover, in an America that is constantly at war, albeit a cold war, voting against an expenditure sought by the military leaves one open to the charge of weakening overall defenses and thereby giving aid and comfort to the enemy.

These conditions lead to a situation wherein Congress often finds that it does not have effective control over the disposition of American troops nor over the expenditure of funds for military use.[12] It is also possible that the President cannot or does not use his power as commander-in-chief to overrule decisions made on essentially military grounds. For example, President Kennedy reportedly did not follow his own best judgment and cancel the Bay of Pigs invasion. He chose instead not to so challenge the military experts who planned the attack. As he becomes more confident in his office, of course, the civilian head-of-state becomes a more effective military commander-in-chief.[13] The United States, however, may have a new president every four years who is similarly reluctant to challenge the plans leading military experts made before he assumed office. Moreover, the military may gain the crucial voice in presidential decisions on international matters even where their plans do not antedate the president's inauguration. He need only believe, as the rhetoric of the cold war dictates, that military action is of

America's involvement in Vietnam, "the expression of declaring a war is one that has become outmoded . . ." See *The New York Times,* August 18, 1967.

[12] Congress' role in forming and checking military policy is discussed in Samuel P. Huntington, "Separation of Powers and the Cold War," *The Soldier and the State: The Theory and Politics of Civil-Military Relations* (Cambridge: Harvard University Press, 1957), pp. 171–195; Edward L. Katzenbach, *The Separation of Power and National Security* (New York: Harper & Row, 1960); Edward A. Kolodziej, "Congress and Foreign Policy: Through the Looking Glass," *Virginia Quarterly Review,* XLII (Winter, 1966), 12–27; and Edward A. Kolodziej, *The Uncommon Defense and Congress: 1945–1963* (Columbus: Ohio State University Press, 1966).

[13] For an account of the decisions on the Bay of Pigs, see Arthur Schlesinger, Jr., *A Thousand Days* (Boston: Houghton Mifflin, 1965).

fundamental importance and generally more effective than other means of treating disputes.[14]

Meeting the demands of providing for the common defense may affect the nature of the American union not only through changes in the balance of power within government, but by hampering the informed and open debate essential to the preservation of democratic institutions. Such debate may not be compatible with national military security.[15] It is, after all, impossible to inform the American people of various options under consideration without simultaneously informing their enemies. Thus, the electorate was not properly informed when, during the 1960 presidential campaign, Richard Nixon chose not to tell the people that an armed invasion of Cuba was planned. His opponent, John F. Kennedy, had publicly suggested that such an operation be undertaken.[16] Whatever the effect Nixon's decision had on his chances of being elected, it is clear the electorate made its decision without full and accurate knowledge of his position on the issue. Moreover, the requirements of military security may not only result in uninformed or misinformed debate, it can restrict the freedom of debate itself. Some opinions may be regarded as beyond the range of legitimacy and acceptability because they divide the nation in time of crisis or aid enemy propaganda.[17]

The exigencies of the cold war and the nature of modern armaments have, then, affected the nature of the American political union. The problem of meeting the requirements of military defense has also raised the question of the relative priority of cold war demands and the

[14] Charles W. Tait claims such militaristic thinking already rules the civilian State Department in his "Whatever Happened to the State Department?" *The Nation,* CCI (September 13, 1965), 137–141.

[15] Gabriel Almond, "Public Opinion and National Security Policy," *Public Opinion Quarterly,* XX (Summer, 1956), 371–378, discusses how the gravity, difficulty, and secrecy surrounding issues relating to defense hamper debate.

[16] For an account of this incident, see Theodore White, *The Making of a President: 1960* (New York: Atheneum, 1961).

[17] Demonstrations against government policy and action with respect to Vietnam have been so regarded by many. *The New York Times,* October 19, 1965, reports "the President was dismayed by the demonstrations [against the war in Vietnam] and had given his full endorsement to the Justice Department investigation of possible communist infiltration of the antidraft movement." The *Times* report continued: "According to his aides, Mr. Johnson believes that once the communists are persuaded that the protesters represent a sizable segment of American opinion they will be encouraged to fight harder." See also "The Politics of Protest During War," *Current,* LXVI (December, 1965), 51–54. We do not wish to imply that the restriction of free speech can never be justified. The justification of such restrictions depends, in large measure, on the degree to which the nation is actually threatened, and how effectively the restriction minimizes the threat in question. Nor do we wish to imply that the stresses, preparation for, and conduct of a war, whether hot or cold, have no positive effects. Some positive effects are discussed in Robert A. Nisbet, *Community and Power* (New York: Oxford University Press, 1962), pp. 38–42.

promotion of the general welfare, discussed by Senator J. William Fulbright in "The Cold War in American Life."[18]

The most obvious occasion for treating the question of the relative priorities of the common defense and the general welfare are the yearly debates over the federal budget. In any given year, it is difficult, if not impossible, to provide the funds needed to best conduct both the cold war and a war on poverty. However, decisions which require balancing the needs for defense and welfare are not restricted to those involving the allocation of economic resources. Such decisions also involve the use of human resources. Just as a dollar spent on weapons is not one spent on schools, a man fighting in Vietnam is not home to pursue a college career. The issue of allowing a man to further his education rather than joining the military can be just as pressing and important as that of how to divide tax money between the production of weapons and public works. Draft laws and budgets both reflect American thinking about the relative priority of the demands of specific civilian and military undertakings. The selection "Student Deferment in Selective Service" by Merriam H. Trytten discusses the effect of the drafting of college students on the general welfare.[19]

The means of providing for the common defense may, then, affect the welfare of the American people and the nature of the union in which they participate. The means themselves may be designed to affect the cost, capabilities, and causes of attacks on American interests and the availability of peaceful means of resolving international conflicts. Finally, selecting means for providing for the common defense may be influenced by what is to be defended and by what is regarded as distinguishing defensive from offensive reactions to attack.

[18] See also Seymour Melman, *Our Depleted Society* (New York: Holt, Rinehart & Winston, 1965).

[19] See also John C. Esty, Jr., "Fallacies of the Draft," and Norman S. Paul, "Military Manpower Policies," in Garth S. Mangnum (ed.), *The Manpower Revolution* (Garden City, N.Y.: Doubleday, 1965), pp. 280–287, and 287–303, respectively; Hanson W. Baldwin, "The Draft Is Here to Stay, But It Should Be Changed," *The New York Times Magazine*, November 20, 1966, pp. 48ff.; Eli Ginzberg, "The Case for a Lottery," *The Public Interest*, V (Fall, 1966), 83–89; and Morris Janowitz, "The Case for a National Service System," *The Public Interest*, V (Fall, 1966), 90–109.

Defense of What?

Robert C. Angell

*In times so fraught with peril to all mankind as ours, it is well to re-*examine fundamental assumptions. Most Americans are convinced that they know quite well what we are defending. But have they thought the question through? Have they taken into account the new context within which it is posed today?

When any of us asks himself, "What are we defending?" the first thing that springs to mind is the national territory. This reaction doubt-less goes back to countless generations of agricultural forebears who cherished their acres almost as much as they cherished their children. Can there be anything more obvious than that no one has the right to wrest from us the land from which we draw our sustenance? Although the attachment to territory is still very strong, especially locally or region-ally, it is perhaps less so than it once was. The decline in the farm population and the movement of urban families from one location to another, by weakening our attachment to real estate, have perhaps led us to cherish less the national territory. Even though a Californian would certainly bridle at any suggestion that a border area of his state be ceded to Mexico, would he object if Texas were asked to make a similar sacrifice? We were able to bring ourselves to move the natives of the Bikini atoll to a new island. If there were some good reason why Americans and Canadians should trade islands in the St. Lawrence or swap equal tracts in Montana and Manitoba (thus creating salients across the 49th parallel), would we really mind very much, provided the families were resettled equitably?

Although territory certainly remains an element of what we are defending, it seems likely that this is so mainly because land is closely

---

Abridged from "Defense of What?" *Journal of Conflict Resolution*, 6 (June, 1962), 116–124, by permission of the author and The University of Michigan. Copyright 1962 by the University of Michigan.

associated with the web of social life that has been woven on it. It has become symbolic of that web. I remember the words of a French woman, married to an American officer at the close of World War I and long resident in this country: "I cannot bear to think of being buried anywhere but in the soil of France." What I think she was saying was that she could not bear to be cut off permanently from her French cultural roots. And so it is for all who have grown up in a particular way of life and learned to love it.

But precisely what do we mean when we say "the American way of life"? Of all the forms and patterns of our daily round, which are the essential ones, which the inconsequential? Or, to invert the order, which could we let go without a tear, which would we fight to defend?

In another place[1] I have suggested that there are three classes of constants in American life—constants from conviction, from external pressure, and from utility. It is not in point to discuss the last two classes; it is the constants from conviction that I believe exemplify the essentials of our way of life and therefore stand for what we are defending.

The constants from conviction are the precipitations of such typically American common values as equal opportunity, humanitarianism, and technological progress. They are perhaps best described by the term institutions. The frame of our government, with its democratic control and its checks and balances, is perhaps most central. Our free system of public education is only a little less so. Nor can we conceive the good life without monogamous families with an equalitarian relation between husband and wife and a recognition of the moral worth of children. There is no established church, but our system fully protects the right of citizens to found churches and worship according to their convictions. In the economy, it is not altogether clear what deserves to be called institutional and what does not. Laissez-faire capitalism has already been greatly altered and yet we are far from being socialists. Perhaps on this matter we may say that we want to work out the problems in our own way, and that we are defending our right to do so.

＊　　＊　　＊

So far we have discussed what we are defending only in terms of our national territory and the way of life built upon it. It is obvious that today we do not defend only what lies within this compass. There are two wider circles of life that we defend. One of them is best expressed by the phrase "our bloc." The other does not have such a convenient identity. It may be described by the awkward phrase: "a world order we can live with." I will take up each of these in turn.

Even if we limit our bloc to the nations with which we have treaties that will bring us to their aid if they are attacked, it is apparent that what we are defending is far from a homogeneous group of societies. As a matter of fact, our allies fall into two quite distinct categories. One of these consists of nations with whom we feel a real affinity because their way of life is very like ours. Culturally, we have much in common with them. In this category are the members of the British Commonwealth that are members of the North Atlantic Treaty Organization or the Southeast Asia Treaty Organization—Canada, Britain, Australia, and New Zealand; democratic European nations—Iceland, Norway, Denmark, West Germany, Belgium, France, Italy, and Greece; and another member of the Southeast Asia Treaty Organization, the Philippines. The second category contains a much more varied group of nations, some of which are strange bedfellows. South Korea, Turkey, Thailand, and Iran are not fully democratic in their political processes, but Pakistan, Portugal, Spain, and Nationalist China are either outright dictatorships or one-party states. Japan is more acceptable to us politically, but its culture is very different.

When we ask how it happens that the second group of nations is in our bloc, the reason is unmistakable: they represent a crucial resource in the struggle against international Communism. When including them in what we are defending we have not demanded that their central values and institutions be closely similar to ours. We have been willing to throw the cloak of our protection around them for the simple reason that we wish to contain Communism within its present borders. In order to accomplish this result we are willing to overlook profound cultural differences. Some have argued that we should not collaborate with countries like Portugal and Spain, but this objection has carried little weight with our policy-makers.

In passing, it is interesting to note that most of the nations of the second group are very distant from the United States and very close to the Soviet-Chinese heartland. This gives a vivid demonstration of the radically increased power of modern weapons. For the first time in history, states feel that they can effectively deter attacks upon allies that live closer to the potential enemy than to themselves.

If by some magic of diplomacy the threat of war between the Soviet-Chinese coalition and ourselves were to be removed, it is a sure prediction that we would be less inclined to remain allied to nations in the second category than in the first. The first group represents both principles of social organization that we believe in and religious traditions with which we have much in common. One or the other of these ties is lacking for all the nations of the second group.

The heterogeneity of the bloc proves clearly that we can live, if need be, with those of quite different conceptions of the good life from ours. This fact becomes very significant when we pass to the examination of the third circle that I mentioned—the world order we can live with.

It is a great error to assume, as many do, that the two great blocs of our time operate in a sort of vacuum or perhaps float in a colorless medium. Actually, an elaborate web of relationships is being woven among the peoples of the world and the two blocs are entangled in the web. We cannot be content merely to have a strong nation and a strong bloc. We must also be concerned with the nature of the enveloping web. We must identify the texture that will be satisfactory to us, and try to see that it comes into being. To change the figure, there is live and growing tissue around us, interstitial tissue if you will, which is spreading and becoming stronger every year.

.   .   .

In order that there may be no mistake about what I am saying, let me put it baldly. We are going to be more and more enmeshed in social organization of world-wide scope. The nature of that organization will be fateful for our own way of life. It will affect the meaning of existence for our citizens. It behooves us therefore to be vitally concerned about its nature as it develops. We must try to fix upon clear preferences for its characteristics, preferences that reflect the feasible as well as the desirable. Since much of the web that we will prefer has not yet been woven we shall be defending, in part at least, not an actuality but a vision.

It would be only natural to visualize this world that we can live with as an extension of our own society. But in this direction lies frustration. There are many nations that do not admire our way of life and have no intention of acquiescing in making the world a blown-up facsimile of this country. The interstitial tissue which will gradually develop will reflect the very small common denominator that there is in the various cultures of the world. Many principles that we believe in ardently will not be expressed in that tissue. They will, as it were, have been compromised out.

In view of this situation the only feasible course is to make minimum demands upon the world order, not the maximum ones that politicians, backed by superpatriots, make in the heat of international controversies or presidential elections. We must stop thinking, to paraphrase an oft-quoted remark, that what is good for the United States is good for the world. To take a less imperialistic view requires that we distinguish sharply between our own system of life and the world's system. Perhaps our trouble is that we leapt too quickly from isolationism to world-mindedness. In making the jump, we hardly realized that we were operating at a new level to which many of our traditional practices and values were unsuited. We must never cease being concerned about the nature of the growing intersocietal tissue, but our concern should take the form of insisting only upon that minimum of characteristics that will allow us and others like us to live happily and creatively on this shrunken globe.

Why is it so important to make only minimal demands? It is important because to be more ambitious is to invite hostility, increase tensions, and thwart our own hope to be a leader in constructing a viable world order. There are too many other peoples in the world with too many different orientations to life for us to monopolize the creative process of nourishing the interstitial tissue. We have lost much ground in the world already because of the blindness of American travelers to this truth. We can not afford to lose more.

It should not be so very difficult for us to take this stance. After all, we have admitted to our bloc nations with which we have little in common. If we can make minimum demands upon our allies, surely we can learn to make minimum demands upon the world order.

Of course what we do others must do also. Neither the Soviet Union, nor Communist China, nor India, nor Britain, nor France can make more than minimal demands. But if they all follow this course, there is real hope that the world can move along the tortuous path to a peaceful world order.

Now what precisely is meant by minimum American demands? What should we insist upon and what should we forgo? It seems to me that a minimal world-we-can-live-with would have two chief characteristics: (1) strengthened political means for preventing the conflicts among nations from erupting into war; and (2) an agreed program for fostering the development of more intersocietal linkages.

Under the first head fall the twin immediate necessities of movement toward disarmament and a strengthened United Nations. It is obvious that nuclear deterrence, even if roughly balanced, is too risky a policy to live with any longer than is absolutely necessary. The United States Program for General and Complete Disarmament offered by President Kennedy to the United Nations Assembly on September 25, 1961 gives an admirable starting point for negotiating a disarmament agreement. This document voices our demand for a United Nations Peace Force to be built up as national armaments decline. In order to develop further other peace-keeping activities of the United Nations we should probably demand a revision of the Charter to make more realistic the representation in the Assembly. Some such scheme of weighted voting as is set forth in the Clark-Sohn proposals would seem essential to give the great powers confidence in the proceedings of the organization. Continuing emphasis on the development of international law and expanded use of the International Court of Justice would be other features of a world-we-can-live-with. To this end, the repeal of our own Connally amendment is urgent.

The second characteristic of a minimal world-we-can-live-with, an agreed program for fostering more intersocietal linkages, is less discussed than are movements toward disarmament and the strengthening of the United Nations, but in the long run is equally important. The value differences in the world are so great, particularly between the Western bloc and the Communist bloc, that some means of lessening them must be found if we are ultimately to have a world rule of law. An enforceable legal system requires more threads of world-wide common value than presently exist. Such threads are most likely to appear as by-products of working together in common enterprises.

A cumulative process of increasing the number and strength of intersocietal linkages would have three main features: (1) the immediate intensive search for those areas in which national values are already sufficiently compatible to make feasible the broadening of existing international relationships, the enlargement of the functions of existing international organizations, and the establishment of new relations and organizations; (2) the full participation of all the key nations in the enlarged structural network thus brought into being; and (3) constant study of the changing attitudes and orientations resulting from this broadened participation to discover opportunities for extending the structural network still further.

The theory that lies back of this suggestion is simple: cooperation on tasks of mutual concern tends to breed trust. The more fully present possibilities for joint undertakings are exploited, the more trust will be created; and the more trust is created, the more it will be possible to set up new undertakings. Hence, the process is cumulative. Matters that are now so fraught with conflict as to be untouchable will gradually seem more amenable to collaboration as the climate changes because of the successful carrying through of mutually satisfactory undertakings in other fields.

If such a process is to succeed, it is obvious that two alternatives must be avoided. Too great hesitancy to embark upon joint enterprises will give a minimum basis for the development of trust, and hence the cumulation of confidence and of structure resulting therefrom will be inordinately slow. On the other hand, too great optimism about what can be done will breed failure and disillusion. The whole process would then be interrupted. These dangers are so great that it will take a combination of careful social science analysis and political wisdom to steer between Scylla and Charybdis.

The Specialized Agencies of the United Nations already give impressive evidence of international cooperation. Important as these are, however, they have two limitations—they are universal and they are governmental. Conditions are almost certainly ripe for many joint ventures among some, but not all, countries, and with private persons and organizations as participants as well as governments.

Since the Cold War between the Communist bloc and the West is the greatest present threat to peace, structure that will bridge this value gap is what is most direly needed. Trade, travel, sport, scholarly contact, communication and exchange, and the interchange of musical and dramatic talent are the principal forms of cooperation today. Only one of these, scholarly contact, communication and exchange, gives real opportunity for persons from the two sides to work together over a period of time to achieve a joint result. The planning and holding of world congresses in scholarly fields gives great opportunities for friendly collaboration. The International Geophysical Year was the high water mark so far for cooperation in substantive research. It affords a model that might be followed in other fields with beneficial results.

If the theory here put forward is sound, the United States should be asking for a thorough canvass of the present possibilities of this kind. In the realm of science, there might be joint expeditions to Antarctica, joint investigation of the ocean deeps and of outer space, and joint meteorological projects beyond participation in the World Meteorological Organization. If it proved to be feasible, a joint attack on the world population problem, involving both biological and social science, would be of great importance.

Nothing is more global than questions of communication and transportation. At present, there is the setting of standards through the International Telecommunications Union and the International Civil Aviation Organization, but there may be further possibilities for joint action that might be considered. One in particular that has been suggested is the establishment by the United States and the Soviet Union of a network of communication satellites that will reflect messages back to any point on the earth and would be available for the use of all peoples.

A possibility, for which the time may not be ripe, is that the United States and the Soviet Union set up joint development projects in underdeveloped countries. Certainly nothing would be a more dramatic demonstration of their willingness to collaborate.

Disarmament is a special case because of its urgency. Although a joint study commission made up of natural and social scientists from both sides might seem to come under the head of risky adventures that might lead to disillusion, the tremendous benefits that might flow from such an enterprise may make it worth the risk. At all events, it should be carefully studied.

Although I have emphasized the need for the United States and the Soviet Union to take the initiative in building more intersocietal structure between the two blocs, there would of course be hope in new world-wide projects and organizations so long as both sides participated wholeheartedly in them. A United Nations university is one project of this type that has been repeatedly suggested. Since the ideological split between Western and Communist blocs would be the most difficult obstacle to be overcome in such an undertaking, Russian and American collaboration would be a *sine qua non*. In all cases there should be insistence that no new elements of structure be developed unless there is sufficient value consensus to make them good risks. Thus, all parties are protected against innovations that would be unacceptable to them.

If intersocietal linkages of the kinds we have discussed could be multiplied, both trust and greater ability to appreciate the values of the opposing group should increase. This should lead to opportunities for rational discussion of some of the really important problems on which the two blocs are divided. In international trade, there are the difficulties where private trading enterprises of the West meet the government monopolies of the Communist bloc; the tensions that arise from exchange controls; the disruptions caused by "dumping" of surpluses abroad; and the question of repaying foreign investors after properties have been nationalized. There are also many problems in the political field to which new approaches might become possible. Cross-national radio propaganda, including international slander, is one. Another is freedom of travel, seen from the viewpoint both of domestic restrictions on the travel of citizens abroad, and restrictions on incoming foreign nationals. Closely related is the freedom of expression and organization for those sympathetic to foreign ideologies.

If such problems could be rationally discussed, there would be a chance of finding principles for their solution to which all could agree. By this means the world rule of law would be brought nearer. Thus, if the immediate peace-keeping problems could be solved by political means, the long-run-value problems might be solved by jurisprudential means.

The answer to the question with which we started falls, then, into three parts. We are defending our own way of life, the bloc which is helping us defend that way of life, and a crescive world order in which there are effective peace-keeping agencies and wide support for processes leading toward the minimum of value consensus needed for a world rule of law.

Note

1) "The Structure of United States Society, and Politics," (Lasswell and Cleveland, 1962, ch. 15).

Reference

Lasswell, Harold D. and Cleveland, Harlan (eds.). *The Ethic of Power: the Interplay of Religion, Philosophy and Politics.* New York: Harper & Bros., 1962.

Is There a Military-Industrial Complex which Prevents Peace?

Marc Pilisuk / Thomas Hayden

. . .

The New Concern

*Not since the 30's has there been such a rash of attention to military-*industrial power as there is today. Then, as now, the President himself raised the spectre of improper military influence. FDR, on the eve of a Senate investigation of the munitions industry, said flatly that the arms race was a "grave menace . . . due in no small measure to the un-controlled activities of the manufacturers and merchants of the engines of destruction and it must be met by the concerted action of the people of all nations." (Raymond, 1964, p. 262; also Congressional Quarterly Weekly Report, 6, 1964, pp. 265–278.) While Dwight Eisenhower did not sound as militant as Roosevelt, and while he never adopted FDR's 1932 campaign pledge to "take the profits out of war," he did resume a popular tradition with his warning about the "unwarranted influence" of the military-industrial complex. It may be a significant measure of the times that one President could make such warnings in his very first campaign for office, while the other couched it among several other going-away remarks.

The 30's serve as a prelude to the 60's, too, in the area of congres-sional investigation of militarism. Then it was Senator Gerald P. Nye investigating the fabulous World War I profits of U.S. Steel and Her-cules Powder and discovering, with horror, the instrumental role of

Abridged from "Is There a Military-Industrial Complex which Prevents Peace?" *Journal of Social Issues*, 21 (July, 1965), 68–117, by permission of the authors and publisher. The original article is reproduced with minor modification in an anthology on social problems, *The Triple Revolution: Social Problems in Depth*, edited by Marc Pilisuk and Robert Perrucci (Boston: Little, Brown, 1967 forthcoming).

munitions-makers and other commercial interests in beginning the war. Nye revealed, for example, that the American ambassador in London informed President Wilson in 1917 that probably "the only way of maintaining our pre-eminent trade position and averting a panic is by declaring war on Germany" (Raymond, p. 264). As Roosevelt was more aggressive than Eisenhower, so also were Nye, Borah and other popular Senators more aggressive than their present counterparts in the 60's. But, nevertheless, similar issues are now being raised in congressional committees. The most shocking of these may be found in the hearings of Senator John McClellen's committee on *Pyramiding of Profits and Costs in the Missile Procurement Program*. This report pointed out the likely danger that the government "can be placed in the unenviable position of reluctant acquiescence to the demands and conditions set by the contractor," and that "profits were pyramided on other profits without any relationship at all to the effort being expended by those making the profit." In what might have been front page scandal in any area but national defense, the committee documented two mechanisms by which millions upon millions of dollars of excess profit have been reaped by the defense industries. The mechanisms are: a) claiming profits on work subcontracted to other firms (which in turn subcontract portions of their work to others and charge a profit on the sub-subcontracted work, too), and b) overestimating the subcontracting costs (on incentive type contracts) thereby reaping huge profit rates by undercutting the original estimates. However, the contrast with the 30's is clear; Senator McClellen only wants to improve the efficiency of what he calls "these necessary monopolies." (U.S. Senate, Committee on Government Operations, report of the Permanent Subcommittee on Investigations, *Pyramiding of Profits and Costs in the Missile Procurement Program*, March 31, 1964.) A more far-reaching investigation, under the direction of Senator Clark, deals with the convertibility of the defense empire to civilian job-creating tasks. He claims that 1) the new defense emphasis on electronics and on research and development, and the monopolization of defense by a few companies and geographic areas, considerably reduces the potential effect of defense as an economic stabilizer; and 2) that certain firms, especially those in the aerospace industry, are suffering an over-capacity crisis that spurs them to insist on more missiles than the nation needs. (U.S. Senate, Committee on Labor and Public Welfare, report of the Subcommittee on Employment and Manpower, *Convertibility of Space and Defense Resources to Civilian Needs: A Search for New Employment Potentials*, 88th Congress, 2d Session, 1964.) Senator Clark's hearings, too, are mild in contrast to the 30's. Even milder, however, was the recent survey report of Senator Hubert Humphrey, who says it is "nonsense" to believe American industry is opposed to disarmament. (U.S. Senate, Committee on Senate Foreign Relations, Subcommittee on Disarmament, *The Economic Impact of Arms Control Agreements*, Congressional Record, October 5, 1962, pp. 2139–2194.)

Another measure of interest in military-industrial power is the number of popular and technical books dealing with the subject. In the 30's, the widely read books were Davenport's *Zaharoff, High Priest of War*, Engelbrecht and Haneghen's *Merchants of Death* and Selde's *Iron, Blood and Profits*. Two decades then passed before the work of C. Wright Mills began to attract broad attention to the subject of organized militarism. Including Mills' pioneering books, there have been at least 21 major books published in this area during the past several years. Many of them are by journalists (Cook, Coffin, Raymond, Swomley, Wise and Ross); some by economists (Benoit, Boulding, Melman, Peck, Perlo, Scherer); sociologists (Etzioni, Horowitz, Janowitz, Mills); political scientists (Meisel, Rogow); novelists (Bailey, Burdick, Knebel, Sutton); and at least one physical scientist (Lapp).

Whatever the objective referent, if any, of a "military-industrial complex" may be, it is undeniable that the concept occupies an important role in the political consciousness of many persons, on a scale without precedent since the 30's. It is a telling fact that the new literature, with the exceptions of Mills, Cook and Perlo, still lacks the bite of the old, and that the proposed solutions are quite "modest." In the 30's a typical popular solution, proposed by the Nye Committee but never implemented, was the nationalization of the munitions industries. By the 60's the reverse has happened; most military research, development, and production is done by private companies subsidized by the Federal government. The loci of military-political-industrial cooperation are so pervasive and frequent that it becomes a hair-splitting task to identify specifically any "merchants of death." Also, the scale of potential destruction has so increased, the nature of warfare strategy so changed, and the existence of the military in peacetime so accepted, that it seems quaint to associate defense contractors with bloody hands. Furthermore, the assumed threat of communist expansion has become the ultimate justification of the post-war military buildup, whereas in the past such buildups could be attributed more clearly to industrial profit and power motives. Probably reasons such as these explain both the long silence and the modest character of the current resurgence in discussion of these matters.

But these reasons account partially for the inadequacy of analysis as well. The question, "Does there exist a military-industrial complex which prevents peace?" at first seems debatable in straightforward yes-or-no terms. Indeed, it might have been answerable in the 20's or 30's but not in the post-war period. When there is permanent intermingling and coordination among military, industrial, and governmental elites, and whenever greater war-preparedness can be justified by reference to the communist movement, it becomes a much "stickier" question. Because it is sticky, the easiest conclusion to support is that a "complex" simply does not exist as an omnipresent obstacle to policy change. Indeed, this belief has become the accepted norm for "informed" discussion of interests vested in the perpetuation of military preparedness. The next most easily supported conclusion would be that we have become trapped in the hell-fires of militarism by a sinister but concealed elite of military-industrial leaders, which through its puppets, pulls the strings on every major policy decision. This latter theory is non-conformist, radical, and smacks too closely of classical conspiracy theory to be palatable to most scholars. Indeed, the dominant attitude (explicit or tacit) in most of the new literature is that there exists no military-industrial complex capable of preventing peace. It is claimed that the military-industrial complex operates as a sub-group within the limits of an essentially civilian society. In this view the complex is seen as making an interest-conscious equation of its own interests with those of the nation as a whole. But, it is argued, this tendency of power aggrandizement is checked by countervailing interest blocks in the society. Moreover, the "complex" is not seen as having a corrosive effect on democratic processes; even if it is conceded that military and technological expertise or well-financed public relations give the "complex" unusual privilege and visibility, this is no different, in principle, from certain other influential groups, all of which are limited by the web of constraints but comprise a pluralist society. Usually, it is added that the internal differences in the "complex" such as differences among the separate services or between the military and the industrial procurement sectors, tend to restrict further its ability to impose a policy "line" on the United States. . . .

.   .   .

None of these denials of irresponsible military-industrial power marshal very significant evidence to support their views. There are examples given of specific conflicts between civilian and military groups which were lost by the military (e.g., the dropping of General Walker, the refusal to be first to break the moratorium on testing). There are examples given of heated divisions between the services over what military strategy should be pursued (the arguments over conventional warfare in the late 50's and the more recent RS 70 controversy). There are sociological studies which reveal underlying diversities within single corporations, between competing corporations, and within the demographic and institutional character of each branch of the armed services.[1] And, throughout, there are citations of American pluralism as an automatic check system against any elite group.[2]

At a more general level, these fragments of evidence point toward three grounds for denying that a military-industrial complex prevents peace:

1) it is held that the *scope* of decisions made by any interest group is quite narrow and cannot be said to govern anything so broad as foreign policy.
2) it is held that the "complex" is not *monolithic, not self-conscious,* and *not coordinated,* the presumed attributes of a ruling elite.
3) it is held that the military-industrial complex does not wield power if the term "power" is defined as the ability to realize its will even against the resistance of others and regardless of external conditions.

These formulations, to repeat, are made neither explicitly nor consistently in the new literature. But they crystallize the basic questions about definition which the new literature raises. Moreover, they are quite definitely the major contentions made by academic criticisms of power elite theory. The more widely read of these academic critics include Daniel Bell, Robert Dahl, and Talcott Parsons. Since their critiques are mainly directed at the work of C. Wright Mills, it is with Mills that we will begin to analyze the theories which claim there *is* a military-industrial complex blocking peace.

The Thesis of Elite Control

Mills is by far the most formidable exponent of the theory of a power elite. In his view, the period in America since World War II has been dominated by the ascendance of corporation and military elites to positions of institutional power. These "commanding heights" allow them to exercise control over the trends of the business cycle and international relations. The Cold War set the conditions which legitimize this ascendance, and the decline and incorporation of significant left-liberal movements, such as the CIO, symbolizes the end of opposition forces. The power elite monopolizes sovereignty, in that political initiative and control stem mainly from the top hierarchical levels of position and influence. Through the communications system the elite facilitates the growth of a politically indifferent mass society below the powerful institutions. This, according to the Mills argument, would explain why an observer finds widespread apathy. Only a small minority believes in actual participation in the larger decisions which affect their existence and only the ritual forms of "popular democracy" are practiced by the vast majority. Mills' argument addresses itself to the terms of the three basic issues we have designated, i.e., scope of decision power, awareness of common interest, and the definition of power exerted.

By *scope*, we are referring to the sphere of society over which an elite is presumed to exercise power. Mills argues that the scope of this elite is general, embracing all the decisions which in any way could be called vital (slump and boom, peace and war, etc.). He does not argue that *each* decision is directly determined, but rather that the political alternatives from which the "Deciders" choose are shaped and limited by the elite through its possession of all the large-scale institutions. By this kind of argument, Mills avoids the need to demonstrate how his elite is at work during each decision. He speaks instead in terms of institutions and resources. But the problem is that his basic evidence is of a rather negative kind. No major decisions have been made for 20 years contrary to the policies of anti-communism and corporate or military aggrandizement: *therefore* a power elite must be prevailing. Mills might have improved his claims about the scope of elite decisions by analyzing a series of actual decisions in terms of the premises which were *not* debated. This could point to the mechanisms (implicit or explicit) which led to the exclusion of these premises from debate. By this and other means he might have found more satisfying evidence of the common, though perhaps tacit, presuppositions of seemingly disparate institutions. He then might have developed a framework analyzing "scope" on different levels. The scope of the Joint Chiefs of Staff, for instance, could be seen as limited, while at the same time the Joint Chiefs could be placed in a larger elite context having larger scope. Whether this could be shown awaits research of this kind. Until it is done, however, Mills' theory of scope remains open to attack, but, conversely, is not subject to refutation.

Mills' theory also eludes the traditional requirements for inferring monolithic structure, i.e., consciousness of elite status, and coordination. The modern tradition of viewing elites in this way began with Mosca's *The Ruling Class* in a period when family units and inheritance systems were the basic means of conferring power. Mills departs from this influential tradition precisely because of his emphasis on institutions at the basic elements. If the military, political, and economic *institutional orders* involve a high coincidence of interest, then the groups composing the institutional orders need not be monolithic, conscious, and coordinated, yet still they can exercise elite power.[3] This means specifically that a military-industrial complex could exist as an expression of a certain fixed ideology (reflecting common institutional needs), yet be "composed" of an endless shuffle of specific groups. For instance, our tables show 82 companies have dropped out of the list of 100 top defense contractors, and only 36 "durables" have remained on the list in the years since 1940. In terms of industry, the percentage of contracts going to the automobile industry dropped from 25 percent in World War II to 4 percent in the missile age. At the same time, the aircraft companies went from 34 to 54 percent of all contracts, and the electronics industry from 9 to 28 percent (Peck and Scherer, 1962). Mills' most central argument is that this ebb-and-flow is not necessarily evidence for the pluralists. His stress is on the unities which underlie the procession of competition and change. The decision to change the technology of warfare was one which enabled one group to "overcome" another in an overall system to which both are fundamentally committed. Moreover, the decision issued from the laboratories and planning boards of the defense establishment and only superficially involved any role for public opinion. The case studies of weapons development by Peck and Scherer, in which politics is described as a marginal ritual, would certainly buttress Mills' point of view.

Making this institution analysis enables Mills to make interesting comments on his human actors. The integration of institutions means that hundreds of individuals become familiar with several roles: General, politician, lobbyist, defense contractor. These men are the power elite, but they need not know it. They conspire, but conspiracy is not absolutely essential to their maintenance. They mix together easily, but can remain in power even if they are mostly anonymous to each other. They make decisions, big and small, sometimes with the knowledge of others and sometimes not, which ultimately control all the significant action and resources of society.

Where this approach tends to fall short, is in its unclarity about how discontinuities arise. Is the military-industrial complex a feature of American society which can disappear and still leave the general social structure intact? Horst Brand has suggested a tension between financial companies and the defense industries because of the relatively few investment markets created by defense (1962). Others are beginning to challenge the traditional view that defense spending stimulates high demand and employment. Their claim is that the concentration of contracts in a few states, the monopolization of defense and space industry by the largest 75 or 100 corporations, the low multiplier effect of the new weapons, the declining numbers of blue-collar workers required, and other factors, make the defense economy more of a drag than a stimulant (Melman et al., 1963; Etzioni, 1964). Mills died before these trends became the subject of debate, but he might have pioneered in discussion of them if his analytic categories had differentiated more finely between various industries and interest groups in his power elite. His emphasis was almost entirely on the "need" for a "permanent war economy" just when that need was being questioned even among his elite.

However, this failure does not necessarily undermine the rest of Mills' analysis. His institutional analysis is still the best means of identifying a complex without calling it monolithic, conscious and coordinated. Had he differentiated more exactly he might have been able to describe various degrees of commitment to an arms race, a rightist ideology constricting the arena of meaningful debate, and other characteristics of a complex. This task remains to be done, and will be discussed at a later point.

Where Mills' theory is most awkward is in his assertions that the elite can, and does, make its decisions against the will of others and regardless of external conditions. This way of looking at power is inherited by Mills, and much of modern sociology, directly from Max Weber. What is attributed to the elite is a rather fantastic quality: literal omnipotence. Conversely, any group that is *not* able to realize its will even against the resistance of others is only "influential" but not an elite. Mills attempts to defend this viewpoint but, in essence, modifies it. He says he is describing a tendency, not a finalized state of affairs. This is a helpful device in explaining cracks in the monolith—for instance, the inability of the elite to establish a full corporate state against the will of small businessmen. However, it does not change the ultimate argument—that the power elite cannot become more than a tendency, cannot realize its actual self, unless it takes on the quality of omnipotence.

When power is defined as this kind of dominance, it is easily open to critical dispute. The conception of power depicts a vital and complex social system as essentially static, as having within it a set of stable governing components, with precharted interests which infiltrate and control every outpost of decision-authority. Thereby, internal accommodation is made necessary and significant change, aside from growth, becomes impossible. This conception goes beyond the idea of social or economic determinism. In fact, it defines a "closed social system." A "closed system" may be a dramatic image, but it is a forced one as well. Its defender sees events such as the rise of the labor movement essentially as a means of rationalizing modern capitalism. But true or false as this may be, did not the labor movement also constitute a "collective will" which the elite could not resist? An accommodation was reached, probably more on the side of capital than labor, but the very term "accommodation" implies the existence of more than one independent will. On a world scale, this becomes even more obvious. Certainly the rise of communism has not been through the will of capitalists, and Mills would be the first to agree. Nor does the elite fully control technological development; surely the process of invention has some independent, even if minor, place in the process of social change.

Mills' definition of power as dominance ironically serves the pluralist argument, rather than countering it. When power is defined so extremely, it becomes rather easy to claim that such power is curbed in the contemporary United States. The pluralists can say that Mills has conjured up a bogeyman to explain his own failure to realize his will. This is indeed what has been done in review after review of Mills' writings. A leading pluralist thinker, Edward Shils, says that Mills was too much influenced by Trotsky and Kafka:

> Power, although concentrated, is not so concentrated so powerful, or so permeative as Professor Mills seems to believe. . . . There have been years in Western history, e.g. in Germany during the last years of the Weimar Republic and under the Nazis when reality approximated this picture more closely. . . . But as a picture of Western societies, and not just as an ideal type of extreme possibilities which might be realized if so much else that is vital were lacking, it will not do (Shils, 1961).

But is Mills' definition the only suitable one here? If it is, then the pluralists have won the debate. But if there is a way to designate an irresponsible elite without giving it omnipotence, then the debate may be recast at least.

.   .   .

Revising the Criteria for Inferring Power

After finding fault with so many books and divergent viewpoints, the most obvious conclusion is that current social theory is currently deficient in its explanation of power. We concur with one of Mills' severest critics, Daniel Bell, who at least agrees with Mills that most current analysis concentrates on the "intermediate sectors," e.g., parties, interest groups, formal structures, without attempting to view the underlying system of "renewable power independent of any momentary group of actors" (Bell, 1964). However, we have indicated that the only formidable analysis of the underlying system of renewable power, that of Mills, has profound shortcomings because of its definition of power. Therefore, before we can offer an answer of our own to the question, "Is there a military-industrial complex which blocks peace?", it is imperative to return to the question of power itself in American society.

We have agreed essentially with the pluralist claim that ruling-group models do not "fit" the American structure. We have classified Mills' model as that of a ruling-group because of his Weberian definition of power, but we have noted also that Mills successfully went beyond two traps common to elite theories, *viz.*, that the elite is total in the scope of its decisions, and that the elite is a coordinated monolith.

But we perhaps have not stressed sufficiently that the alternative case for pluralism is inadequate in its claim to describe the historical dynamics of American society. The point of our dissent from pluralism is over the doctrine of "counter-vailing power." This is the modern version of Adam Smith's economics and of the Madisonian or Federalism theory of checks-and-balances, adapted to the new circumstances of large-scale organization. Its evidence is composed of self-serving incidents and a faith in semi-mystical resources. For instance, in the sphere of political economy, it is argued that oligopoly contains automatic checking mechanisms against undue corporate growth, and that additionally, the factors of "public opinion" and "corporate conscience" are built-in limiting forces.[4] We believe that evidence in the field, however, suggests that oligopoly is a means of stabilizing an industrial sphere either through tacit agreements to follow price leadership or rigged agreements in the case of custom-made goods; that "public opinion" tends much more to be manipulated and apathetic than independently critical; that "corporate conscience" is less suitable as a description than Reagan's terms, "corporate arrogance."

To take the more immediate example of the military sphere, the pluralist claim is that the military is subordinate to broader, civilian interests. The first problem with the statement is the ambiguity of "civilian." Is it clear that military men are more "militaristic" than civilian men? To say so would be to deny the increasing trend of "white-collar militarism." The top strategists in the Department of Defense, the Central Intelligence Agency and the key advisory positions often are Ph.D.'s. In fact, "civilians" including McGeorge Bundy, Robert Kennedy, James Rostow and Robert McNamara are mainly responsible for the development of the only remaining "heroic" form of combat: counter-insurgency operations in the jungles of the underdeveloped countries. If "militarism"[5] has permeated this deeply into the "civilian" sphere, then the distinction between the terms becomes largely nominal. Meisel's description is imaginative and alluring:

> What we still honor with the name of peace is only the domestic aspect of a world-wide industrial mobilization let up at intervals by the explosions of a shooting war. . . . The industrial revolution in its class-struggle aspect is becoming externalized, projected upon the industrial field, that it is being relegated, so to speak, from barricade to barracks. . . . The armies, navies, and air forces of our time [are] the embodiment of the industrial revolution in its aggressive form (Meisel, 1962, pp. 157–158).

While the more traditional military men have not taken kindly to the takeover of military planning by civilian professors, the takeover has, none-the-less, gone far. More than 300 universities and non-profit research institutions supply civilian personnel to, and seek contracts from, the Department of Defense. Approximately half of these institutions were created specifically to do specialized strategic research. Probably the most influential of the lot of these civilian centers is the Rand Corporation.

Consistent with its Air Force origins, Rand's civilian army of almost 1,000 professional researchers and supporting personnel derives most of its support from Air Force Project Rand Studies. Rand charges the Air Force six percent of the estimated cost of the contracts which the Air Force farms out to private industry as a result of work done at Rand. This brings the Air Force contribution to Rand to over 80 percent where it has been for the past few years. When a large Ford Foundation Grant permitted Rand's reorganization in May of 1948, the organization was granted virtual autonomy from the Air Force and from Douglas Aviation which were its original parents. Such autonomy seemed necessary both to draw independent intellectuals into the establishment and to promote the image of objectivity in its research. The charter establishes a non-profit corporation to "further and promote scientific, educational and charitable purposes, all for the public welfare and security of the United States of America." The actual measure of Rand autonomy should not be taken solely from its dependence upon Air Force money. In actual practice, Rand scholars have differed with the Air Force and on issues quite important to the Air Force. The turns of the cold war strategies from massive retaliation through finite deterrence and limited war, through counterforce, and on into controlled response had never, until 1961 and 1962 involved major reductions in any type of weaponry other than the post Korean War automotive cutbacks. Automotives were, however, a largely civilian market industry. The first place where the strategic innovations served not only to rationalize existing weaponry (in the more specialized defense industry) or to call for accelerated development in additional areas, but also to call for "cost effectiveness" or cutting back in a favored weapon area, came at the expense of the Air Force. In short order the Skybolt and the RS 70 met their demise. For a time, Harvard economist Charles Hitch (then with Rand, now Defense Department comptroller) and perhaps the entire battalion of systems analysts at Rand were personally unpopular with Air Force brass. The Air Force was particularly incensed over the inclination and ability of Rand personnel to consult directly with the Defense Department and bypass the Air Force. Rand, incidentally, maintains a permanent Washington office which facilitates such confrontation. This is not exactly what Air Force spokesmen intend when they see Rand serving the function of giving "prestige type support for favored Air Force proposals to the Department of Defense and the Congress" (Friedman, 1963). The controversy shows that there is obviously no monolithic influence in defense policy. It shows also that civilian and military factions are involved and that, in this instance, even the combined influential interests of traditional Air Force leaders and industrial aircraft contractors could not hold sway over the civilian analysts. The case also illustrates the weakness of the pluralist argument. The controversy, involving sums of money exceeding the total requested for President Johnson's war on poverty, did not threaten to starve either the Air Force or the aircraft industries. Indeed, it was a controversy among family members all sharing the same source of income and the same assumptions regarding the need for maximal military strength in the cold war. While Rand scientists played the role of civilian efficiency experts in this particular controversy, Rand experts have clearly played the role of military expansionists in civilian clothing at other times. Albert Wohlstetter and Herbert Dinerstein, Rand experts on military strategy and Soviet policy, deserve major credits for the creation of the mythical "missile gap" and for the equally unreal-preemptive war strategy for the Soviet Union during the period from Sputnik, in October of 1957, until the issue of inadequate military preparedness helped bring the New Frontier to Washington. Among the possible consequences of the U.S. missile buildup to overcome the mythical gap may well have been the Soviet resumption of nuclear tests in defiance of the moratorium, an act which completed a rung of the spiralling arms race which in turn nourishes all factions, civilian and military, who are engaged in military preparedness. We do not wish to labor the point that Rand experts have, at times, allowed the assumptions of their own ideology to form the basis of their rational analyses of Soviet capability and intentions. The point we wish to stress here is merely that the apparent flourishing of such civilian agencies as Rand (it earned over 20 million dollars in 1962 with all the earnings going into expansion and has already spawned the non-profit Systems Development Corporation with annual earnings exceeding 50 million dollars) is no reflection of countervailing power. The doctrine of controlled response under which the RS 70 fell was one which served the general aspirations of each of the separate services; of the Polaris and Minuteman stabile deterrent factions, of the brushfire or limited war proponents, guerrilla war and paramilitary operations advocates, and of the counterforce adherents. It is a doctrine of versatility intended to leave the widest range of military options for retaliation and escalation in U.S. hands. It can hardly be claimed as victory against military thought. The fighting may have been intense but the area of consensus between military and civilian factions was great.

The process of "civilianizing" the military is not restricted to the level of attitudes but extends to the arena of social interaction. Traditionally, the military has been a semi-caste quite apart from the mainstream of American life. But that changed with World War II; as Mills points out:

> Unless the military sat in on corporate decisions, they would not be sure that their programs would be carried out; and unless the corporation chieftains knew something of the war plans, they could not plan war production . . . the very organization of the economics of war made for the coincidence of interest and the political mingling among economic and military chiefs (Mills, 1965, p. 212).

One relatively early statement (January, 1944), by Charles E. Wilson, shows that the intermeshing of military and industrial leaders was, at least on the part of some, a self-conscious and policy-oriented enterprise. Wilson proposed a permanent war economy led by the Commander in Chief, and the War Department in cooperation with an industrial partner whose response and cooperation must be free from such political accusations as the "merchants of death" label. The program would not be a creature of emergency but rather an interminable measure to eliminate emergencies. "The role of Congress," Wilson added, "is limited to voting the funds" (Swomley, 1959). . . .

· · ·

The same kind of planning requirements for modern war forced an overlapping of politicians with military and businessmen. There too, the very nature of world war, and especially cold war, integrated military, political and economic concepts of strategy, making the military officer much more than a cog. A variety of recent studies demonstrate the outcome of these developments. The 1959 hearings and survey by the House Armed Services Subcommittee disclosed that over 1400 retired officers with the rank of major or higher (including 261 of general or flag rank) were in the employ of the top 100 defense contractors (Hébert Subcommittee of the House Armed Services Committee, 1959). Coffin listed 74 Senators and Representatives with continuing status in the armed forces (Coffin, 1964). By 1957, 200 active (not reserve) generals or admirals were on assignment to "non-military" departments of the government or to international or interservice agencies. An added 1300 colonels or naval officers of comparable rank, and 6000 lower grade officers were similarly assigned (Swomley, 1959). Janowitz studied an historical sample of over 760 generals and admirals, administered questionnaires to about 600 current Pentagon staff officers, and interviewed 113 career officers. He found an "elite in transition" toward civilian and managerial habits: 1) the basis of authority and discipline is changing from authoritarian domination to greater reliance on manipulation, persuasion and group consensus; 2) the skill differential between civilians and soldiers is narrowing because of the need for technical specialties in the military; 3) officers are being recruited from a broader status and class base, reflecting the demand for more specialists; 4) the source of prestige recognition is shifting from military circles to the public at large; 5) this growth makes the officer define himself more and more as a political, rather than a technical, person with concerns about national security concepts and affairs (Janowitz, 1960, pp. 3–16, 442–452). These trends clearly demonstrate that the traditional American separation of military and civilian is outmoded. The new, blurred reality has not been successfully defined.

The main point here is that the pluralist argument relies on "countervailing forces" which are more mythical than real. The Wise and Ross book shows indisputably that at least during certain instances the Executive is not countervailing the CIA. Moreover, who is countervailing the "military-civilian" Executive centered in the Pentagon and the White House? What Knorr sees as a "peacefare state" countervailing the "wårfare state" is merely its white-collar brother. The symbolic figure of the Arms Control and Disarmament Agency demonstrates this reality vividly. One side of the ACDA figure is a diplomat with tie and attaché case; the other side is a warrior dedicated to the pursuit of stabilizing control measures which might assure national advantages in a never ending cold war.

ACDA's narrow conception of its own role is as much a function of its internal quest for respectability as it is a matter of the prerogatives given it by a reluctant Congress. It has sought respectability not only in its apparent choice of essentially technical questions for study but also in its manner of study. One favored study technique is to collapse large socially significant questions into several questions answerable by short-term studies and suited for study by the grossly oversimplified techniques of policy appraisal employed by those same operations research corporations which serve, and live upon, defense contracts. These organizations have traditionally produced quick answers embedded in rationalistic models which ring with scientism and jargon. *Strategy and Conscience*, a powerfully written book by Anatol Rapoport, documents the manner in which the rationalist models employed in such strategic studies frequently conceal (often unknowingly) gross assumptions of the nature of the cold war. The point here is that if these are the same assumptions which necessitate a high level of military preparedness, then it matters little whether the studies are commissioned by civilian or military authorities.

Consensus

All that countervailing power refers to is the relationship between groups who fundamentally accept "the American system" but who compete for advantages within it. The corporate executive wants higher profits, the laborer a higher wage. The President wants the final word on military strategies, the Chairman of the Joint Chiefs does not trust him with it. Boeing wants the contract, but General Dynamics is closer at the time to the Navy Secretary and the President, and so on: what is prevented by countervailing forces is the dominance of society by a group or clique or a party. But this process suggests a profoundly important point; that *the constant pattern in American society is the rise and fall of temporarily-irresponsible groups.* By temporary we mean that, outside of the largest industrial conglomerates,[6] the groups which wield significant power to influence policy decisions are not guaranteed stability. By irresponsible we mean that there are many activities within their scope which are essentially unaccountable in the democratic process. These groups are too uneven to be described with the shorthand term "class." Their personnel have many different characteristics (compare IBM executives and the Southern Dixiecrats) and their needs as groups are different enough to cause endless fights as, for example, small vs. big business. No one group or coalition of several groups can tyrannize the rest as is demonstrated, for example, in the changing status of the major financial groups, particu-

TABLE 1 / *Social Characteristics of American Elites*

Elite	Nativity % foreign born	Rural-urban % urban born[a]	Religion % Protestant	Education % college grads.
Military	2%	30–40%[c]	90	73–98%[c]
Economic	6	65	85	61
Political	2	48	81	91
Diplomatic	4	66	60	81
U.S. adult males	7[b]	42[d]	65	7[b]

[a] Towns of 2,500 or more. [b] 30 years of age and older.
[c] Taking the services separately. [d] 1910 U.S. population.

NOTE: The majority of foreign-born and second-generation come from Northwestern Europe. The proportion of foreign-born from these areas is significantly lower for the general male population.

The difference between "political" and "diplomatic" and "economic" indicated that Congress, in the 1950's was more conservative—especially in its small business and non-integrationist attitudes—than the federal executive or the corporation leaders. The sharp difference between "military" and the rest lumps military policymakers with lower level personnel, thus underemphasizing the new trend cited by Janowitz.

larly the fast-rising Bank of America which has been built from the financial needs of the previously-neglected small consumer.

However, it is clear that these groups exist within consensus relationships of a more general and durable kind than their conflict relationships. This is true, first of all, of their social characteristics. The tables which follow combine data from Suzanne Keller's compilation of military, economic, political and diplomatic elite survey materials in *Beyond the Ruling Class* (1963) and from an exhaustive study of American elites contained in Warner, et al., *The American Federal Executive* (1963). Data on elites vary slightly from study to study because of varying operational definitions of the elite population. However, the data selected here are fairly representative and refer exclusively to studies with major data collected within the decade of the fifties. (See Tables pp. 296–298.)

The relevant continuities represented in this data suggest an educated elite with an emphasis upon Protestant and business-oriented origins. Moreover, the data suggest inbreeding with business orientation in backgrounds likely to have been at least maintained, if not augmented, through marriage. The consistencies suggest orientations not unlike those which are to be found in examination of editorial content of major business newspapers and weeklies and in more directly sampled assessments of elite opinions.[7]

The second evidence of consensus relationships, besides attitude and background data indicating a pro-business sympathy, would come from an examination of the *practice* of decision-making. By analysis of such

TABLE 2 / Father's Occupation

	Civilian federal executives	Military executives	Business leaders	Total U.S. male pop. 1930
Unskilled laborer	4%	2%	5%	33%
Skilled labor	17	12	10	15
White-collar (clerk or sales)	9	9	8	12
Foreman	5	5	3	2
Business owner	15	19	26	7
Business executive	15	15	23	3
Professional	19	18	14	4
Farm owner or manager	14	9	8	16
Farm tenant or worker	1	1	1	6
Other	1	1	2	2

actual behavior we can understand which consensus attitudes are reflected in decision-making. Here, in retrospect, it is possible to discover the value and assumptions which are defended recurrently. This is at least a rough means of finding the boundaries of consensus relations. Often these boundaries are invisible because of the very infrequency with which they are tested. What are visible most of the time are the parameters of conflict relationships among different groups. These conflict relationships constitute the ingredients of experience which give individuals or groups their uniqueness and varieties, while the consensus relations constitute the common underpinnings of behavior. The tendency in social science has been to study decision-making in order to study group differences; we need to study decision-making also to understand group commonalities.

Were such studies done, our hypothesis would be that certain "core beliefs" are continuously unquestioned. One of these, undoubtedly, would be that efficacy is preferable to principle in foreign affairs. In practice, this means that violence is preferable to non-violence as a means of defense. A second is that private property is preferable to collective property. A third assumption is that the particular form of constitutional government, which is practiced within the United States is preferable to any other system of government. We refer to the preferred mode as limited parliamentary democracy, a system in which institutionalized forms of direct representation are carefully retained but with fundamental limitations placed upon the prerogatives of governing. Specifically included among the areas of limitation are many matters encroaching upon corporation property and state hegemony. While adherence to this

Table 3 / *Business and Executive Origins of Wives of Elites*

Occupation	Political executives		Foreign-service executives		Military executives		Civilian federal executives		Business leaders	
	FATHER	SPOUSE'S FATHER	FATHER	SPOUSE'S FATHER	FATHER	SPOUSE'S FATHER	FATHER	SPOUSE'S FATHER	FATHER	SPOUSE'S FATHER
Minor executive	10%	10%	11%	11%	15%	12%	11%	11%	11%	7%
Major executive	6	5	9	9	5	7	4	4	15	8
Business owner	21	25	19	24	19	22	20	23	26	28
Professional	24	19	25	23	18	19	19	16	14	15
Military executive					9	11				

form of government is conceivably the strongest of the domestic "core values," at least among business elites, it is probably the least strongly held of the three on the international scene. American relations with, and assistance for, authoritarian and semi-feudal regimes occurs exactly in those areas where the recipient regime is evaluated primarily upon the two former assumptions and given rather extensive leeway on the latter one.

The implications of these "core beliefs" for the social system are immense, for they justify the maintenance of our largest institutional structures: the military, the corporate economy, and a system of partisan politics which protects the concept of limited democracy. These institutions, in turn, may be seen as current agencies of the more basic social structure. We use the term "social structure" as Robert S. Lynd does as the stratification of people identified according to kinship, sex, age, division of labor, race, religion, or other factors which differentiate them in terms of role, status, access to resources, and power. According to Lynd:

> This structure established durable relations that hold groups of people together for certain purposes and separate them for others. Such social structures may persist over many generations. Its continuance depends upon its ability to cope with historical changes that involve absorption of new groupings and relations of men without fudamental change in the structure of the society of a kind that involves major transfer of power (Lynd, 1959).

The "renewable basis of power" in America at the present time underlies those institutional orders linked in consensus relationships: military defense of private property and parliamentary democracy. These institutional orders are not permanently secure, by definition. Their maintenance involves a continuous coping with new conditions, such as technological innovation and with the inherent instabilities of a social structure which arbitrarily classifies persons by role, status, access to resources, and power. The myriad groups composing these orders are even less secure because of their weak ability to command "coping resources," e.g., the service branches are less stable than the institution of the military, particular companies are less stable than the institutions of corporate property, political parties are less stable than the institution of parliamentary government.

In the United States there is no ruling group. Nor is there any easily discernible ruling institutional order, so meshed have the separate sources of elite power become. But there is a social structure which is organized to create and protect power centers with only partial accountability. In this definition of power we are avoiding the Weber-Mills meaning of *omnipotence* and the contrary pluralist definition of power as consistently *diffuse*. We are describing the current system as one of overall "minimal accountability" and "minimal consent." We mean that the role of democratic review, based on genuine popular consent, is made marginal and reactive. Elite groups are minimally accountable to publics and have a substantial, though by no means maximum, freedom to shape popular attitudes. The reverse of our system would be one in which democratic participation would be the orienting demand around which the social structure is organized.

Some will counter this case by saying that we are measuring "reality" against an "ideal," a technique which permits the conclusion that the social structure is undemocratic according to its distance from our utopian values. This is a convenient apology for the present system, of course. We think it possible, at least in theory, to develop measures of the undemocratic in democratic conditions, and place given social structures along a continuum. These measures, in rough form, might include such variables as economic security, education, legal guarantees, access to information, and participatory control over systems of economy, government, and jurisprudence.

The reasons for our concern with democratic process in an article questioning the power of a purported military-industrial complex are twofold. First, just as scientific method both legitimizes and promotes change in the world of knowledge, democratic method legitimizes and promotes change in the world of social institutions. Every society, regardless of how democratic, protects its core institutions in a web of widely shared values. But if the core institutions should be dictated by the requisites of military preparedness, then restrictions on the democratic process, i.e., restrictions in either mass opinion exchange (as by voluntary or imposed news management) or in decision-making bodies (as by selection of participants in a manner guaranteeing exclusion of certain positions), then such restrictions would be critical obstacles to peace.

Second, certain elements of democratic process are inimical to features of militarily oriented society, and the absence of these elements offers one type of evidence for a military-industrial complex even in the absence of a ruling elite. Secretary of Defense Robert McNamara made the point amply clear in his testimony in 1961 before the Senate Armed Services Committee:

Why should we tell Russia that the Zeus development may not be satisfactory? What we ought to be saying is that we have the most perfect anti-

ICBM system that the human mind will ever devise. Instead the public domain is already full of statements that the Zeus may not be satisfactory, that it has deficiencies. I think it is absurd to release that level of information (Military Procurement Authorization Fiscal Year 1962).

Under subsequent questioning McNamara attempted to clarify his statement that he only wished to delude Russian, not American, citizens about U.S. might. Just how this might be done was not explained.

A long established tradition exists for "executive privilege" which permits the President to refuse to release information when, in his opinion, it would be damaging to the national interest. Under modern conditions responsibility for handling information of a strategic nature is shared among military, industrial, and executive agencies. The discretion regarding when to withhold what information must also be shared. Moreover, the existence of a perpetual danger makes the justification, "in this time of national crisis" suitable to every occasion in which secrecy must be justified. McNamara's statement cited above referred not to a crisis in Cuba or Viet Nam but rather to the perpetual state of cold war crisis. And since the decision about what is to be released and when, is subject to just such management the media became dependent upon the agencies for timely leaks and major stories. This not only adds an aura of omniscience to the agencies, but gives these same agencies the power to reward "good" journalists and punish the critical ones.

The issues involved in the question of news management involve more than the elements of control available to the President, the State Department, the Department of Defense, the Central Intelligence Agency, the Atomic Energy Commission or any of the major prime contractors of defense contracts. Outright control of news flow is probably less pervasive than voluntary acquiescence to the objectives of these prominent institutions of our society. Nobody has to tell the wire services when to release a story on the bearded dictator of our hemisphere or the purported brutality of Ho Chi Minh. A frequent model, the personified devil image of an enemy, has become a press tradition. In addition to a sizeable quantity of radio and television programming and spot time purchased directly by the Pentagon, an amount of service, valued at $6 million by *Variety,* is donated annually by the networks and by public relations agencies for various military shows (Swomley, 1959). Again, the pluralistic shell of an independent press or broadcasting media is left hollow by the absence of a countervailing social force of any significant power.

The absence of a countervailing force for peace cannot, we have claimed, be demonstrated by an absence of conflicting interests among powerful sectors of American society. Indeed, such conflicts are ever-present examples of American pluralism. Demonstrating the absence of a discussion of the shared premises, among the most potent sectors of society, would go far in highlighting the area of forced or acquiescent consensus. But even the absence of debate could not complete the case unless we can show how the accepted premises are inconsistent with requisites of a viable peace-time social system. It is to this question: of the compatibility of the unquestioned assumptions of American society with conditions of peace, that we now turn. The "core beliefs" which we listed as unchallenged by any potent locus of institutionalized power are:

a) Efficacy is preferable to principle in foreign affairs (thus military means are chosen over non-violent means);
b) Private property is preferable to public property; and
c) Limited parliamentary democracy is preferable to any other system of government.

What characteristics of a continuing world system devoid of military conflict fly in the face of these assumptions?

We identify three conditions for enduring peace which clash with one or more of the core beliefs. These are: 1) the requirements for programming an orderly transition and the subsequent maintenance of a non-defense economy within a highly automated and relatively affluent society; 2) the conditions for peaceful settlement of internal disputes within underdeveloped countries and between alien nations and commercial interests; and 3) the conditions under which disparities in living standards between have and have-not nations can be handled with minimum violence.

If one pools available projections regarding the offset programs, especially regional and local offset programs, necessary to maintain economic well-being in the face of disarmament in this country, the programs will highlight two important features. One is the lag time in industrial conversion. The second is the need for coordination in the timing and spacing of programs. One cannot reinvest in new home building in an area which has just been deserted by its major industry and left a ghost town. The short-term and long-term offset values of new hospitals and educational facilities will differ in the building and the utilization stages and regional offset programs have demonstrable inter-regional effects (Reiner, 1964). Plans requiring worker mobility on a large scale will require a central bank for storing job information and a smooth system for its dissemination. Such coordination will require a degree of centralization of controls beyond the realm which our assumption regarding primacy of private property would permit.

Gross intransigence can be expected on this issue. Shortly after Sperry Rand on Long Island was forced to make major cutbacks of its professional and engineering staff to adapt to the termination of certain defense contracts, the union approached Sperry's management with the prospect of collaborating in efforts to commence contingency plans for diversification. The response, by Carl A. Frische, President of Sperry Gyroscope, a division of Sperry Rand, remains a classic. There must be no "government-controlled mechanisms under the hood of the economy." He suggested, with regard to such planning, that "we let Russia continue with that." (*Long Island Sunday Press*, February 23, 1964.) Sperry is an old-timer in defense production. Its board of directors average several years older than the more avant garde board of directors of, say, General Dynamics. But the prospect of contingency planning will be no more warmly welcomed in the newer aeroframe industry (which is only 60% convertible to needs of a peace-time society), (McDonagh and Zimmerman, 1964). Private planning, by an individual firm for its own future does occur, but, without coordinated plans, the time forecast for market conditions remains smaller than the lag time for major retooling. A lag time of from six to ten years would not be atypical before plans by a somewhat over-specialized defense contractor could result in retooling for production in a peace-time market. In the meantime, technological innovations, governmental fiscal or regulatory policies, shifts in consumer preferences, or the decisions by other firms to enter that same market could well make the market vanish. Moreover, the example of defense firms which have attempted even the smaller step toward diversification presents a picture which has not been entirely promising (Fearon and Hook, 1964). Indeed, one of several reasons for the failures in this endeavor has been that marketing skills necessary to compete in a private enterprise economy have been lost by those industrial giants who have been managing with a sales force of one or two retired generals to deal with the firm's only customer. Even if the path of successful conversion by some firms were to serve as the model for all individual attempts, the collective result would be poor. To avoid a financially disastrous glutting of limited markets some coordinated planning will be needed.

The intransigence regarding public or collaborative planning occurs against a backdrop of a soon-to-be increasing army of unemployed youth and aged, as well as regional armies of unemployed victims of automation. Whether one thinks of work in traditional job market terms or as anything worthwhile that a person can do with his life, work (and some means of livelihood) will have to be found for these people. There is much work to be done in community services, education, public health, and recreation, but this is people work, not product work. The lack of a countervailing force prevents the major reallocation of human and economic resources from the sector defined as preferable by the most potent institutions of society. One point must be stressed. We are not saying that limited planning to cushion the impact of arms reduction is impossible. Indeed, it is going on and with the apparent blessing of the Department of Defense (Barber, 1963). We are saying that the type of accommodation needed by a cutback of $9 billion in R & D and $16 billion in military procurement requires a type of preparation not consistent with the unchallenged assumptions.

Even the existence of facilities for coordinated planning does not, to be sure, guarantee the success of such planning. Bureaucratic institutions, designed as they may be for coordination and control, do set up internal resistance to the very coordination they seek to achieve. The mechanisms for handling these bureaucratic intransigencies usually rely upon such techniques as bringing participants into the process of formulating the decisions which will affect their own behavior. We can conceive of no system of coordinated conversion planning which could function without full and motivated cooperation from the major corporations, the larger unions, and representatives of smaller business and industry. Unfortunately, it is just as difficult to conceive of a system which would assure this necessary level of participation and cooperation. This same argument cuts deeper still when we speak of the millions of separate individuals in the "other America" whose lives would be increasingly "administered" with the type of centralized planning needed to offset a defense economy. The job assignment which requires moving, the vocational retraining program, the development of housing projects to meet minimal standards, educational enrichment programs, all of the programs which are conceived by middle-class white America for racially mixed low income groups, face the same difficulty in execution of plans. Without direct participation in the formulation of the programs, the target populations are less likely to participate in the programs and more likely to continue feelings of alienation from the social system which looks upon them as an unfortunate problem rather than as contributing members. Considering the need for active participation in real decisions, every step of coordinated planning carries with it the responsibility for an equal step in the direction of participatory democracy. This means that the voice of the unemployed urban worker may have to be heard, not only on city council meetings which discuss policy on the control of rats in his dwelling, but also on decisions about where a particular major corporation will be relocated and where the major resource allocations of the country will be invested. That such decision participation would run counter to the consensus on the items of limited parliamentary democracy and private property is exactly the point we wish to make.

Just as the theoretical offset plans can be traced to the sources of power with which they conflict, so too can the theoretical plans for international governing and peace-keeping operations be shown to conflict with the unquestioned beliefs. U.S. consent to international jurisdiction in the settlement of claims deriving from the nationalization of American overseas holdings or the removal of U.S. military installations is almost inconceivable. Moreover, the mode of American relations to less-developed countries is so much a part of the operations of those American institutions which base their existence upon interminable conflict with Communism that the contingency in which the U.S. might have to face the question of international jurisdiction in these areas seems unreal. Offers to mediate, with Cuba by Mexico, with North Viet Nam by France, are bluntly rejected. Acceptance of such offers would have called into question not one but all three of the assumptions in the core system. International jurisdictional authority could institutionalize a means to call the beliefs into question. It is for this reason (but perhaps most directly because of our preference for forceful means) that American preoccupation in those negotiations regarding the extension of international control which have taken place, deal almost exclusively with controls in the area of weaponry and police operations and not at all in the areas of political or social justice.[8]

The acceptance of complete international authority even in the area of weaponry poses certain inconsistencies with the preferred "core beliefs." Non-violent settlement of Asian-African area conflicts would be slow and ineffective in protecting American interests. The elimination, however, of military preparedness, both for projected crises and for their potential escalation, requires a faith in alternate means of resolution. The phasing of the American plan for general and complete disarmament is one which says in effect: prove that the alternatives are as efficient as our arms in protection of our interests and then we disarm. In the short term, however, the effectiveness of force always looks greater.

The state of world peace contains certain conditions imposed by the fact that people now compare themselves with persons who have more of the benefits of industrialization than they themselves. Such comparative reference groups serve to increase the demand for rapid change. While modern communications heighten the pressures imposed by such comparisons, the actual disparities revealed in comparison speak for violence. Population growth rates, often as high as three percent, promise population doubling within a single generation in countries least able to provide for their members. The absolute number of illiterates as well as the absolute number of persons starving is greater now than ever before in history. Foreign aid barely offsets the disparity between declining prices paid for the prime commodities exported by underdeveloped countries and rising prices paid for the finished products imported into these countries (Horowitz, 1962). All schemes for tight centralized planning employed by these countries to accrue and disperse scarce capital by rational means are blocked by the unchallenged assumptions on private property and limited parliamentary democracy. A recent restatement of the principle came in the report of General Lucius Clay's committee on foreign aid. The report stated that the U.S. should not assist foreign governments "in projects establishing government owned industrial and commercial enterprises which compete with existing private endeavors." When Congressman Broomfield's amendment on foreign aid resulted in cancellation of a U.S. promise to India to build a steel mill in Bokaro, Broomfield stated the case succinctly: "The main issue is private enterprise vs. state socialism." (*The Atlantic*, September, 1964, p. 6.) Moreover, preference for forceful solutions assures that the capital now invested in preparedness will not be allocated in a gross way to the needs of underdeveloped countries. Instead, the manifest crises periodically erupting in violence justify further the need for reliance upon military preparedness.

We agree fully with an analysis by Lowi (1964) distinguishing types of decisions for which elite-like forces seem to appear and hold control (redistributive) and other types in which pluralist powers battle for their respective interests (distributive). In the latter type the pie is large and the fights are over who gets how much. Factional strife within and among military industrial and political forces in our country are largely of this nature. In redistributive decisions, the factions coalesce, for the pie itself is threatened. We have been arguing that the transition to peace is a process of redistributive decision.

Is there, then, a military-industrial complex which prevents peace? The answer is inextricably imbedded into the mainstream of American institutions and mores. Our concept is not that American society contains a ruling military-industrial complex. Our concept is more nearly that American society *is* a military-industrial complex. It can accommodate a wide range of factional interests from those concerned with the production or utilization of a particular weapon to those enraptured with the mystique of optimal global strategies. It can accommodate those with rabid desires to advance toward the brink and into limitless intensification of the arms race. It can even accommodate those who wish either to prevent war or to limit the destructiveness of war through the gradual achievement of arms control and disarmament agreements. What it cannot accommodate is the type of radical departures needed to produce enduring peace.

The requirements of a social system geared to peace, as well as the requirements for making a transition to such a social system, share a pattern of resource distribution which is different from the one the world now has. Moreover, these requirements for peace are, in significant measure, inconsistent with constraints set by the more enduring convergencies among power structures in the United States. The same is true whether one speaks of allocation of material or of intellectual resources. Both are geared to the protection of the premises rather than to avenues of change. We are not saying that war is inevitable or that the changes cannot be made. We are saying that the American political, military, and industrial system operates with certain built-in stabilizers which resist a change in the system. If there is to be peace, as opposed to detente or temporary absence of war, marked changes will be needed. . . .

·   ·   ·

Notes

1) See Janowitz for a good sociological study of interservice differences.
2) For the thesis that a "peacefare state" counterweighs the "warfare state," see Klaus Knorr's review of Fred J. Cook in the *Journal of Conflict Resolution*, *VII*, 4 (December, 1963). The "pluralist position," which usually is that the social system has semi-automatic checking mechanisms against tyranny, appears as basic in discussion not only of the military, but of economics and politics as well. See Robert Dahl, *Who Governs?*; J. K. Galbraith, *American Capitalism*; Seymour Martin Lipset, *Political Man*; Talcott Parsons, *The Social System*.
3) See James H. Meisel, *The Myth of the Ruling Class*, for the best available discussion of this innovation in theorizing about elites.
4) For this argument, see A. A. Berle, *The Twentieth Century Capitalist Revolution* and J. K. Galbraith, *American Capitalism*. For sound criticisms, but without sound alternatives, see Mills' and Perlo's books. Also see Michael Reagan, *The Managed Economy* (1963) and Berland Nossiter, *The Mythmakers* (1964) for other refutations of the counter-vailing power thesis.
5) We are defining the term as "primary reliance on coercive means, particularly violence or the threat of violence, to deal with social problems."
6) The term used in recent hearings by Senator Philip A. Hart refers to industrial organizations like Textron, which have holdings in every major sector of American industry.

7) For some interesting work bearing upon the attitudes of business and military elites see (Angell, 1964; Bauer et al., 1963; Eells and Walton, 1961; and Singer, 1964).
8) An objective account of the major negotiations related to disarmament which have taken place may be found in Frye (1963).

References

Angell, Robert C. "A Study of Social Values: Content Analysis of Elite Media." *The Journal of Conflict Resolution, VIII,* 1964, 4, 329–85.
Bank Holding Companies: Scope of Operations and Stock Ownership. Committee on Banking and Currency. Washington: U.S. Government Printing Office, 1963.
Barber, Arthur. "Some Industrial Aspects of Arms Control." *The Journal of Conflict Resolution, VII,* 1963, 3, 491–95.
Bauer, Raymond A., Pool, I., and Dexter, L. *American Business and Public Policy.* New York: Atherton, 1963.
Bell, Daniel. *The End of Ideology.* Glencoe, Illinois: Free Press, 1959.
Benoit, Emile, and Boulding, K. E. (Eds.). *Disarmament and the Economy.* New York: Harper, 1963.
Berle, Adolph A. *The Twentieth Century Capitalist Revolution.* New York: Harcourt, 1954.
Bluestone, Irving. "Problems of the Worker in Industrial Conversion." *The Journal of Conflict Resolution, VII,* 1963, 3, 495–502.
Brand, Horst. "Disarmament and American Capitalism." *Dissent,* Summer, 1962, 236–51.
Burdick, Eugene, and Wheeler, H. *Fail-safe.* New York: McGraw-Hill, 1962.
Burton, John. *Peace Theory.* New York: Knopf, 1962.
Cartwright, Dorwin. "Power: A Neglected Variable in Social Psychology." In Cartwright, D. (Ed.). *Studies in Social Power.* Ann Arbor: Research Center for Group Dynamics, 1959.
Catton, Bruce. *The War Lords of Washington.* New York: Harcourt, 1948.
Coffin, Tristram. *The Passion of the Hawks.* New York: Macmillan, 1964.
Cohen, Bernard C. *The Press and Foreign Policy.* Princeton: Princeton University Press, 1963.
Convertibility of Space and Defense Resources to Civilian Needs. Subcommittee on Employment and Manpower. 88th Congress, 2d Session, Vol. 2. Washington: U.S. Government Printing Office, 1964.
Cook, Fred J. "The Coming Politics of Disarmament." *The Nation,* February 6, 1963.
———. *The Warfare State.* New York: Macmillan, 1962.
Dahl, Robert A. *A Modern Political Analysis.* Englewood Cliffs, New Jersey: Prentice-Hall, 1963.
———. *Who Governs?* New Haven: Yale University Press, 1961.
Dillon, W. *Little Brother Is Watching.* Boston: Houghton Mifflin, 1962.
Economic Impacts of Disarmament. U.S. Arms Control and Disarmament Agency. Economic Series 1. Washington: U.S. Government Printing Office, 1962.
Eells, Richard, and Walton, C. *Conceptual Foundations of Business.* Homewood, Illinois: Irwin Press, 1961.
Etzioni, Amitai. *The Hard Way to Peace.* New York: Collier, 1962.
———. *The Moon-Doggle.* Garden City, New York: Doubleday, 1964.
Fearon, H. E., and Hook, R. C., Jr. "The Shift from Military to Industrial Markets." *Business Topics,* Winter, 1964, 43–52.
Feingold, Eugene, and Hayden, Thomas. "What Happened to Democracy?" *New University Thought,* Summer, 1964, 1, 39–48.
Fisher, Roger (Ed.). *International Conflict and Behavioral Science.* New York: Basic Books, 1964.

Fishman, Leslie. "A Note on Disarmament and Effective Demand." *The Journal of Political Economy*, LXX, 1962, 2, 183–186.
Foreign Assistance Act of 1964. Committee on Foreign Affairs. Hearings, 88th Congress, 2nd Session, Parts VI and VII. Washington: U.S. Government Printing Office, 1964.
Friedman, S. "The Rand Corporation and Our Policy Makers." *Atlantic Monthly*, September, 1963, 61–68.
Frye, Wm. R. "Characteristics of Recent Arms-Control Proposals and Agreements." In Brennan, D. G. (Ed.). *Arms Control, Disarmament, and National Security*. New York: Braziller, 1963.
Galbraith, J. K. *American Capitalism*. Boston: Houghton Mifflin, 1956.
———. "Poverty among Nations." *The Atlantic Monthly*, October, 1962, 47–53.
Gans, Herbert J. "Some Proposals for Government Policy in an Automating Society." *The Correspondent*, 30, January–February, 1964, 74–82.
Government Information Plans and Policies. Subcommittee on Government Operations. Hearings, 88th Congress, 1st Session, Parts I–V. Washington: U.S. Government Printing Office, 1963.
Green, Philip. "Alternative to Overkill: Dream and Reality." *Bulletin of the Atomic Scientists*, November, 1963, 23–26.
Hayakawa, S. J. "Formula for Peace: Listening." *N.Y. Times Magazine*, July 31, 1961.
Horowitz, David. "World Economic Disparities: the Haves and the Have-Nots. Santa Barbara: Center for Study of Democratic Institutions, 1962.
Horowitz, I. L. *The War Game: Studies of the New Civilian Militarists*. New York: Ballantine, 1963.
Humphrey, Hubert H. *The Economic Impact of Arms Control Agreements*. Congressional Record, October 5, 1962, 2139–94.
Impact of Military Supply and Service Activities on the Economy. Report to the Joint Economic Committee. 88th Congress, 2nd Session. Washington: U.S. Government Printing Office, 1963.
Isard, Walter, and Schooler, E. W. "An Economic Analysis of Local and Regional Impacts of Reduction of Military Expenditures." *Papers Vol. 1, 1964, Peace Research Society International*. Chicago Conference, 1963.
Janowitz, Morris. "Military Elites and the Study of War." *The Journal of Conflict Resolution, I*, 1957, 1, 9–18.
———. *The Professional Soldier*. Glencoe, Illinois: Free Press, 1960.
Keller, Suzanne. *Beyond the Ruling Class*. New York: Random House, 1963.
Knebel, Fletcher, and Bailey, C. *Seven Days in May*. New York: Harper, 1962.
Knorr, Klaus. "Warfare and Peacefare States and the Acts of Transition." *The Journal of Conflict Resolution, VII*, 1963, 4, 754–762.
Lapp, Ralph E. *Kill and Overkill*. New York: Basic Books, 1962.
Larson, Arthur. *The Internation Rule of Law*. A Report to the Committee on Research for Peace. Program of Research No. 3. Institute for International Order, 1961.
Lasswell, Harold. *Politics: Who Gets What, When & How*. New York: Meridian, 1958.
Lipset, Seymour M. *Political Man*. Garden City, New York: Doubleday, 1959.
Long Island Sunday Press, The, February 23, 1964.
Lowi, Theodore J. "American Business, Public Policy, Case-Studies, and Political Theory," *World Politics*, July, 1964, 676–715.
Lumer, Hyman. *War Economy and Crisis*. New York: International Publishers, 1954.
Lynd, Robert S., and Merrill, Helen. *Middletown*. New York: Harcourt, 1959.
Mannheim, Karl. *Freedom, Power, and Democratic Planning*. London: Routledge and Kegan Paul, 1956.
McDonagh, James J., and Zimmerman, Steven M. "A Program for Civilian Diversifications of the Airplane Industry." In *Convertibility of Space and Defense*

Resources to Civilian Needs. Senate Subcommittee on Employment and Manpower. 88th Congress. Washington: U.S. Government Printing Office, 1964.

McNamara, Robert S. Remarks of the Secretary of Defense before the Economic Club of New York. Department of Defense Office of Public Affairs. Washington, November 18, 1963.

Meisel, James H. *The Fall of the Republic.* Ann Arbor: University of Michigan Press, 1962.

———. *The Myth of the Ruling Class.* Ann Arbor: University of Michigan Press, 1958.

Melman, Seymour (Ed.). *A Strategy for American Security.* New York: Lee Offset, 1963.

———. *The Peace Race.* New York: Braziller, 1962.

Merbaum, R. Rand. "Technocrats and Power." *New University Thought,* December–January, 1963–64, 45–57.

Michael, Donald. *Cybernation: the Silent Conquest.* Santa Barbara: Center for the Study of Democratic Institutions, 1962.

Milbrath, L. W. *The Washington Lobbyists.* Chicago: Rand McNally, 1963.

Military Posture and Authorizing Appropriations for Aircraft, Missiles, and Naval Vessels. Hearings No. 36, 88th Congress, 2nd Session. Washington: U.S. Government Printing Office, 1964.

Military Procurement Authorization Fiscal Year 1962. Senate Committee on Armed Services. Hearings, 87th Congress, 1st Session. Washington: U.S. Government Printing Office, 1961.

Mills, C. Wright. *The Causes of World War III.* New York: Simon and Schuster, 1958.

———. *The Power Elite.* New York: Oxford University Press, 1959.

Minnis, Jack. "The Care and Feeding of Power Structures." *New University Thought,* 4, Summer, 1964, 1, 73–79.

Nossiter, Berland. *The Mythmakers: An Essay on Power and Wealth.* Boston: Houghton Mifflin, 1964.

Osgood, Charles E. *An Alternative to War or Surrender.* Urbana: University of Illinois Press, 1962.

Parsons, Talcott. *Structure and Process in Modern Societies.* Glencoe, Illinois: Free Press, 1959.

———. *The Social System.* Glencoe, Illinois: Free Press, 1951.

Paul, J., and Laulicht, J. "'Leaders' and Voters' Attitudes on Defense and Disarmament." *In Your Opinion,* V. 1, Clarkson, Ontario: Canadian Peace Research Inst., 1963.

Peck, M. J., and Scherer, F. M. *The Weapons Acquisition Process.* Cambridge: Harvard University Press, 1962.

Perlo, Victor. *Militarism and Industry.* New York: International Publishers, 1963.

Piel, Gerard. "Consumers of Abundance." Santa Barbara: Center for the Study of Democratic Institutions, 1961.

Pilisuk, Marc. "Dominance of the Military." *Science,* January 18, 1963, 247–48.

———. "The Poor and the War on Poverty." *The Correspondent,* Summer, 1965.

Pyramiding of Profits and Costs in the Missile Procurement Program. Senate Committee on Government Operations. Hearings, 87th Congress, 2nd Session, Parts 1, 2, and 3. Washington: U.S. Government Printing Office, 1962.

Pyramiding of Profits and Costs in the Missile Procurement Program. 88th Congress, 2nd Session, Report No. 970. Washington: U.S. Government Printing Office, 1964.

Rapoport, Anatol. *Fights, Games, and Debates.* Ann Arbor: University of Michigan Press, 1960.

———. *Strategy and Conscience.* New York: Harper, 1964.

Raymond, Jack. *Power at the Pentagon.* New York: Harper, 1964.

Reagan, Michael. *The Managed Economy.* New York: Oxford University Press, 1963.

Reiner, Thomas. "Spatial Criteria to Offset Military Cutbacks." Paper presented at the University of Chicago Peace Research Conference, November 18, 1964.

"Report on the World Today." *Atlantic Monthly*, September, 1964, 4–8.
Rogow, Arnold A. *James Forrestal*. New York: Macmillan, 1963.
Satellite Communications, 1964 (Part 1). Committee on Government Operations, Hearings, 88th Congress, 2nd Session. Washington: U.S. Government Printing Office, 1964.
Scherer, Frederick. *The Weapons Acquisition Process: Economic Incentives*. Cambridge: Harvard Business School, 1964.
Shils, Edward. "Professor Mills on the Calling of Sociology." *World Politics*, XIII, 1961, 4.
Singer, J. David. "A Study of Foreign Policy Attitudes." *The Journal of Conflict Resolution*, VIII, 1964, 4, 424–85.
———. *Deterrence, Arms Control and Disarmament*. Columbus: Ohio State University Press, 1962.
———. (Ed.). "Weapons Management in World Politics." *The Journal of Conflict Resolution*, VII, 3, and *Journal of Arms Control*, 1, 4.
Stachey, John. *On the Prevention of War*. New York: St. Martin's Press, 1963.
Strauss, Lewis L. *Men and Decisions*. Garden City, New York: Doubleday, 1962.
Sutton, Jefferson. *The Missile Lords*. New York: Dell, 1963.
Swomley, J. M., Jr. "The Growing Power of the Military." *The Progressive*, January, 1959.
———. *The Military Establishment*. Boston: Beacon Press, 1964.
Toward Full Employment: Proposals for a Comprehensive Employment and Manpower Policy in the U.S. A Report of the Committee on Labor and Public Welfare, United States Senate. Washington: U.S. Government Printing Office, 1964.
Toward World Peace: A Summary of U.S. Disarmament Efforts Past and Present. U.S. Arms Control and Disarmament Agency Publication 10. Washington: U.S. Government Printing Office, 1964.
Warner, Wm. Floyd, and Abegglen, J. D. *Big Business Leaders in America*. New York: Harper, 1955.
———, Van Riper, P. P., Martin, N. H., and Collins, O. F. *The American Federal Executive*. New Haven: Yale University Press, 1963.
Watson-Watt, Sir Robert. *Man's Means to His End*. London: Heinemann, 1962.
Westin, Alan. "Anti-Communism and the Corporations." *Commentary Magazine*, December, 1963, 479–87.
Wise, David, and Ross, Thomas. *The Invisible Government*. New York: Random House, 1964.
Wright, Quincy, Evans, Wm., and Deutsch, Morton (Eds.). *Preventing World War III: Some Proposals*. New York: Simon and Schuster, 1962.

The Cold War in American Life

⚜

J. William Fulbright

The Constitution of the United States, in the words of its preamble, was established, among other reasons, in order to "provide for the common defense, promote the general welfare, and secure the blessings of liberty." In the past generation the emphasis of our public policy has been heavily weighted on measures for the common defense to the considerable neglect of programs for promoting the liberty and welfare of our people. The reason for this, of course, has been the exacting demands of two World Wars and an intractable cold war, which have wrought vast changes in the character of American life.

Of all the changes in American life wrought by the cold war, the most important by far, in my opinion, has been the massive diversion of energy and resources from the creative pursuits of civilized society to the conduct of a costly and interminable struggle for world power. We have been compelled, or have felt ourselves compelled, to reverse the traditional order of our national priorities, relegating individual and community life to places on the scale below the enormously expensive military and space activities that constitute our program of national security.

This of course is not the only change in American life brought about by the cold war. There have been many others, some most welcome and constructive. Directly or indirectly, the world struggle with communism has stimulated economic and industrial expansion, accelerated the pace of intellectual inquiry and scientific discovery, broken the shell of American isolation and greatly increased public knowledge and awareness of the world outside the United States. At the same time, the continuing world conflict has cast a shadow on the tone of American life by introducing a strand of apprehension and tension into a national style which has traditionally been one of buoyant optimism. The continuing and incon-

Reprinted from *Congressional Record*, 110 (April 7, 1964), 7093–7097.

clusive struggle, new in American experience, has in Walt Rostow's words, "imposed a sense of limitation on the Nation's old image of itself, a limitation which has been accepted with greater or less maturity and which has touched the Nation's domestic life at many points with elements of escapism, with a tendency to search for scapegoats, with simple worry, and with much thoughtful, responsive effort as well."[1]

Overriding all these changes, however, good and bad, has been the massive diversion of wealth and talent from individual and community life to the increasingly complex and costly effort to maintain a minimum level of national security in a world in which no nation can be immune from the threat of sudden catastrophe. We have had to turn away from our hopes in order to concentrate on our fears and the result has been accumulating neglect of those things which bring happiness and beauty and fulfillment into our lives. The "public happiness," in August Heckscher's term, has become a luxury to be postponed to some distant day when the dangers that now beset us will have disappeared.

This, I think, is the real meaning of the cold war in American life. It has consumed money and time and talent that could otherwise be used to build schools and homes and hospitals, to remove the blight of ugliness that is spreading over the cities and highways of America, and to overcome the poverty and hopelessness that afflict the lives of one-fifth of the people in an otherwise affluent society. It has put a high premium on avoiding innovation at home because new programs involve controversy as well as expense and it is felt that we cannot afford domestic divisions at a time when external challenges require us to maintain the highest possible degree of national unity. Far more pervasively than the United Nations or the "Atlantic community" could ever do, the cold war has encroached upon our sovereignty; it has given the Russians the major voice in determining what proportion of our Federal budget must be allocated to the military and what proportion, therefore, cannot be made available for domestic social and economic projects. This is the price that we have been paying for the cold war and it has been a high price indeed.

At least as striking as the inversion of priorities which the cold war has enforced upon American life is the readiness with which the American people have consented to defer programs for their welfare and happiness in favor of costly military and space programs. Indeed, if the Congress accurately reflects the temper of the country, then the American people are not only willing, they are eager, to sacrifice education and urban renewal and public health programs—to say nothing of foreign aid—to the requirements of the Armed Forces and the space agency. There is indeed a most striking paradox in the fact that military budgets of over $50 billion are adopted by the Congress after only perfunctory debate, while domestic education and welfare programs involving sums which are mere fractions of the military budget are painstakingly examined and then either considerably reduced or rejected outright. I sometimes suspect that in its zeal for armaments at the expense of education and welfare the Congress tends to overrepresent those of our citizens who are extraordinarily agitated about national security and extraordinarily vigorous about making their agitation known.

It may be that the people and their representatives are making a carefully reasoned sacrifice of welfare to security. It may be, but I doubt it. The sacrifice is made so eagerly as to cause one to suspect that it is fairly painless, that indeed the American people prefer military rockets to public schools and flights to the moon to urban renewal. In a perverse way, we have grown rather attached to the cold war. It occupies us with a stirring and seemingly clear and simple challenge from outside and diverts us from problems here at home which many Americans would ·rather not try to solve, some because they find domestic problems tedious and pedestrian, others because they genuinely believe these problems to be personal rather than public, others because they are unwilling to be drawn into an abrasive national debate as to whether poverty, unemployment, and inadequate education are in fact national rather than local or individual concerns.

The cold war, it seems clear, is an excuse as well as a genuine cause for the diversion of our energies from domestic well-being to external security. We have been preoccupied with foreign affairs for 25 years, and while striking progress has been made in certain areas of our national life, the agenda of neglect has grown steadily longer. We can no longer afford to defer problems of slums and crime and poverty and inadequate education until some more tranquil time in the future. These problems have become urgent if not intolerable in an affluent society. It is entirely reasonable to defer domestic programs in time of an all-out national effort such as World War II, but in the present cold war it is not reasonable to defer our domestic needs until more tranquil times, for the simple reason that there may be no more tranquil times in this generation or in this century . . . we must turn some part of our thoughts and our creative energies away from the cold war that has engaged them for so long back in on America itself. If we do this, and then let nature take its course, we may find that the most vital resources of our Nation, for its public happiness and its security as well, remain locked within our own frontiers, in our cities and in our countryside, in our work and in our leisure, in the hearts and minds of our people.

Note

1) W. W. Rostow, *The United States in the World Arena* (New York: Harper & Bros., 1960), p. 451.

Student Deferment in Selective Service

Merriam H. Trytten

The problem of maintaining college and university training while the nation is in a condition of partial mobilization is difficult and complex. It is a problem which touches a great majority of the American people and hence is affected by waves of public reaction. It involves the military services directly because it relates to competing demands for youth. It touches deeply the future of the nation because what we do with our youth today will determine the kind of people we have tomorrow, and thus will affect our strength in technology, our culture, our social organization, our economy, and in a special way our military power.

As a nation we are peculiarly unready for the solution of this problem, because the values which must be taken into account have never before needed to be weighed and balanced against other values related to national welfare in a conscious effort to fashion national policy. Our educational establishment has grown out of a remarkable public consciousness of the value of education. The people of the United States have always approved steps to develop and improve our great educational system and have been willing to give of their private resources to establish and maintain great schools and universities. They have done this, not so much because of a general understanding that the products of higher education become essential factors in our national strength, as because the people of America seek to improve opportunities for their youth.

War crises which previously in our history interfered with education came so suddenly and ended so quickly that the issue did not have time to become acute. Because of long eras of peace prior to World War I and

Reprinted from *Student Deferment in Selective Service: A Vital Factor in National Security* (Minneapolis: University of Minnesota Press, 1952), pp. 3-5, 43-45, by permission of the University of Minnesota. Copyright 1952 University of Minnesota.

World War II, when the youth of the land could pursue education without interruption, we entered those conflicts with resources of highly trained scientists, engineers, linguists, and specialists in the human sciences and the healing arts sufficient to meet the needs of the crisis. World War II did eventually interfere with education, but the effect was not dramatic and can only be sensed by those close to the problem. The problem of education has in the past seemed always to take care of itself.

The problem of military manpower mobilization, on the other hand, has always needed attention at the national level. It is for this reason that national manpower policies have focused largely on the procurement of military manpower, with only minor attention given to other manpower needs.

The public, used to thinking of education in terms of personal opportunity and privilege and not in terms of national needs, has not been conscious of the extent to which all the activities of the nation depend on the product of higher education. Yet there is today scarcely an activity which contributes to the national health, safety, or welfare that does not rest squarely upon the knowledge and skill of specialists trained to high levels of competence in colleges and universities. And military defense itself is peculiarly dependent on the specialized personnel of the nation, whether serving in uniform or not.

For the first time in our history, then, it is necessary to weigh these values and to determine what arrangements can be made to provide for our military manpower needs while at the same time making sure that the necessary number of specialists shall emerge from institutions of higher education to fill the hard core of other national needs.

The issue is sharp because the age group which is traditionally in college is the very age group which bears liability for military service. Congress has, by law, placed military liability upon young men from eighteen and a half to twenty-six years of age, and this is precisely the age span of the typical college-university student in undergraduate and graduate training.

Policies relating to the procurement of military manpower must necessarily affect the processes of higher education more than any other aspect of our national life. Since our civilization and its defense both depend to an extraordinary and unprecedented degree on our supply of persons with special knowledge and skills which require long training, and since our educational processes are the means to pump new supplies of such personnel into the activities of the nation, the effects of mobilization policies on these processes can and probably will be great. Policies which are not based on careful and full consideration of these basic facts could be destructive of the values in our civilization which we prize—could even destroy our strength to defend those values.

.   .   .

Our civilization depends on a continued flow of trained personnel in all the many fields of special competence which make up the complex pattern of our society. We could not maintain our social and economic structure without doctors, lawyers, engineers, economists, teachers, and the like. In some fields such as engineering and the sciences, the effect of even a temporary cessation of the flow of college-trained specialists would be felt very soon on both our economy and its defense. And in all fields such a cessation would quickly result in appreciable lack of vigor in the many activities our specialists carry forward. We cannot afford, in order just to make a gesture toward surface equality, to sacrifice the future development of our society by an action which in the event of full-scale war would be futile—or, worse, dangerously wasteful of much-needed skills.

Because the present situation is actually a partial mobilization in peacetime, a time of preparation for an uncertain and indefinite future, the policies we adopt now may be with us for years and may gradually shape the course of our national thinking and mold the culture of the United States decades hence. This fact makes it exceedingly dangerous to attempt to name essential curriculums as a criterion for student defer-ment.

We cannot foresee the future. We cannot know what the relative roles of the natural sciences, the social sciences, and the humanities will be in that future. We cannot guess what area of knowledge or narrow portion of an area of knowledge, seemingly esoteric and useless in practical matters today, may become of basic and vital importance in the future. And until we can know these things, until we can develop omnis-cience and clairvoyance about developments to come, we must cling fast to across-the-board student deferment—that is, to deferment of the scholastically promising individual regardless of the field of knowledge he chooses to specialize in.

True, the purpose of naming essential areas of study would be to serve immediate needs, but the effects of such an action would not stop with the present. By its influence on the thinking and the career choices of young people, it would quickly change the scope and direction of all higher education and subsequently the entire pattern of our culture. Yet who among us is wise enough or mighty enough to say that our civilization shall go forward in this direction and not in that? No government or government official has a right to take the awful responsibility of saying to American youth: "This curriculum or branch of study is important, that one is not."

In an all-out mobilization to meet the threat of immediate warfare against a powerful enemy, we might have to take that tremendous risk for the sake of present survival. But in our current situation there can be no justification for even contemplating it.

There is no doubt a strong temptation for the person faced with the pressing task of finding men to fill a local draft quota to say, in considering students who have qualified for deferment: "This one should be deferred, yes; an engineer will be useful. This one, no; we can get along without a philosopher." But let that person, let all of us, beware. To guess wrong in this matter might well be to dig the very pitfall in which, a decade or a generation hence, we may drop to destruction.

. . .

to promote the

The general welfare of a society is intimately related to the welfare or well-being of the individuals in it. The general welfare, however, is not simply the sum of the welfare of individuals. It is not necessarily promoted if, for example, the aggregate welfare increases because the rich get richer faster than the poor get poorer. The distribution of individual welfare, how many have how much (or how little), must be taken into account as well as how much there is overall.

The problem of evaluating the general welfare is discussed further in the first of this introduction's two sections which examines the steps taken when judging whether the general welfare has been promoted, retarded, or left unchanged. The second section discusses problems encountered in promoting the general welfare.

Evaluating the General Welfare

Three steps must be taken if the general welfare is to be adequately evaluated. First, the components of individual welfare or well-being must be identified so that their aggregate and distribution can be determined. Second, the measures to be used in determining the aggregate and distribution of individual welfare must be selected. Third, standards must be established for comparing the state of the general welfare at one time

general Welfare...

with that at another so that decisions can be made as to whether the general welfare has been promoted, retarded, or left unchanged.

There is, of course, much variation from person to person and from one historical period to another with respect to the first step in evaluating the general welfare, the identification of the specific components of individual well-being. For example, such things as indoor plumbing and telephones once thought luxuries have now become necessities of life. Whatever the differences concerning the specific components of individual welfare, however, there is some consensus as to what its major components are: these include sustenance, physical comforts, leisure, prestige, mental health, and personal contentment.[1] Assessing the aggregate and distribution of these components comprises the second step in evaluating the general welfare.

Assessments reflecting the aggregate of sustenance, physical comforts, and leisure can be more or less readily made. For example, the gross amount of food, calories, or vitamins consumed can be regarded as a

---

[1] This list of components of individual welfare is adapted from the list of "rewards a society has at its disposal," presented in Kingsley Davis and Wilbert E. Moore, "Some Principles of Stratification," *American Sociological Review*, X (April, 1945), 242–249. Davis and Moore speak of "things that contribute to sustenance and comfort, . . . to humor and diversion and . . . to self respect and ego expansion" (p. 243).

reflection of the aggregate state of individual sustenance. Similarly, the amount of clothes and the number of adequately heated homes reflect the aggregate physical comfort; the number of man-hours spent on vacations, on golf courses, and at sports arenas can be used to assess the aggregate state of American leisure.

There are, then, measures which could be used to evaluate the aggregate welfare insofar as sustenance, physical comfort, and leisure are concerned. However, it is not possible to speak meaningfully of the total amount of prestige, mental health, or personal contentment enjoyed by all individuals in the United States. The prestige, health, and contentment of two individuals, like the climate of two cities, cannot be added.[2] Nevertheless, it is possible to compare the prestige, health, and contentment of individuals, just as one can compare the climates of different cities, and to determine the distribution of individual welfare with respect to such components. For example, the number or per cent who are regarded as having a very high, or very low degree of a given component can be determined, as can the per cent who fall above or below some given level of well-being. Thus, if the distribution rather than the total is considered it is possible to compare the general welfare of America at two points in time with respect to prestige, mental health, and personal contentment. Using such a method, the general welfare might be said to have been promoted if more people hold jobs with excellent prestige or if fewer hold jobs with poor prestige. Increases in the per cent of people who have an adequate diet and a satisfactory place to live may be said to reflect the promotion of the general level of sustenance and physical comfort; while an increase in the per cent who own swimming pools, camping equipment, or other recreation equipment can be regarded as a sign that the distribution of leisure has improved.

Setting the standards for comparing the state of the general welfare at two points in time is the third step in determining whether the general welfare has been promoted, retarded, or left unchanged. The most difficult problem encountered in comparing measures of the general welfare taken at different times involves balancing losses in one area with gains in another. For example, an increase in aggregate material wealth

[2] Measures of prestige, mental health, and personal contentment are taken on ordinal scales. That is, individuals are ranked as being first, second, third, and so on rather than given numbered values, such as one, two, three. Numbers such as one, two, and three form an interval or ratio scale and can be added, but ordinal values cannot. For a further discussion of various kinds of measurement scales and their properties, see Virginia L. Senders, *Measurement and Statistics* (New York: Oxford University Press, 1958), Chaps. 2–8.

and physical comfort accompanied by an increase in the per cent of mentally ill may represent an increase in the general welfare according to some and a decrease according to others. Difficulties also result from a lack of agreement on whether there can be "too much of a good thing." An increase in the amount of food consumed might denote a decline in the general welfare if it means that more people are overweight. Similarly, it can be argued that great amounts of leisure merely indicate laziness and unproductivity, that too much contentment undermines ambition and drive. For those who value productivity and ambition there can be too much leisure and too much contentment just as there can be too much food. Thus, while Americans may agree on what the components of individual welfare are and on how to measure their aggregate and distribution, they may not agree on whether a given change in one or a combination of measures indicates that the general welfare has been promoted.[3]

Promoting the General Welfare

The problem of promoting the general welfare encompasses three related subproblems: (1) What principles are to guide the production of goods and the provision of services which constitute a basis for individual welfare? (2) What principles are to guide the distribution of goods and services among the members of society? (3) What specific measures, if any, are to be undertaken to improve the lot of those not benefited by the general mechanisms for creating and distributing goods and services? In other words, promoting the general welfare involves both creating the means for providing the greatest good for the greatest number and deciding what, if anything, is to be done with respect to those not among the great number so benefited.

As indicated in the earlier discussion of America's economic union in the introduction to Chapter Two, the goods and services which provide the basis for the welfare of individual Americans are made available by both public and private enterprise. The exact division of labor between these two sectors of the economy has, of course, varied over time. Education, once primarily a private enterprise, is now generally in the public sphere. Medical services and old age insurance, once entirely private matters, are now both partially provided by the Social Security

[3] For alternate views on how to assess the general welfare, see Bertram W. Gross, "The Social State of the Union," *Trans-action*, III (November–December, 1965), 14–17; and Raymond A. Bauer (ed.), *Social Indicators* (Cambridge: The M.I.T. Press, 1966).

system of the public sector.[4] In any case, as John Kenneth Galbraith asserts, in "The Social Balance and the Investment Balance," the principles that govern the production of goods and services by private enterprise do not govern their provision by government. Private enterprise is basically governed by the rules of the economic marketplace—profit, supply, and demand.[5] For example, economic supply and demand basically govern how many cars are produced and bought and insures that the steel and manpower needed in their manufacture is made available. However, the market does not guarantee that there will be sufficient roads for the cars to move over nor that there will be laws and police to help make their use safe. Roads, laws, and police are provided by government, and the availability of public goods and services is governed basically by politics, not economics. Public services and public funds result directly from voting and taxation, not buying and selling.

The distribution of goods and services provided by public and private enterprise is, like their production, governed by two different principles.[6] Most goods and services are distributed on the basis of individual willingness and ability to pay for them. However, some goods and services are distributed on the basis of need. The protection of the police and fire departments, for example, are supplied to those who need them. Typically their services cannot be bought, although one may pay for alternate means of protection.

While the principles of distribution by need and distribution by payment both prevail, it is clear that the latter is by far the dominant rule. Therefore, the means by which individuals obtain the money to pay for what they desire plays a crucial role in the distribution of goods and ser-

---

[4] For discussions of the relative advantages and disadvantages of public and private action in meeting health needs, see Marvin Bressler (ed.), "Meeting Health Needs by Social Action," *Annals of the American Academy of Political and Social Science*, CCCXXXVII (September, 1961), 1–145; Roul Tunley, *The American Health Scandal* (New York: Harper & Row, 1966); and Russell Dynes, A. C. Clark, S. Dinitz, and I. Ishino, "Medical Care: Individual or Organizational Problem," in *Social Problems: Dissensus and Deviation in an Industrial Society* (New York: Oxford University Press, 1964), pp. 224–254.

A brief history of Social Security is found in Evaline M. Burns, "Social Security in Evolution: Towards What?" *Social Service Review*, XXXIX (June, 1965), 129–140.

[5] There are, of course, many private organizations concerned with the general welfare, or some specific aspect of it, not governed directly by the profit motive. These include private philanthropic foundations, churches, settlement houses, and the many voluntary clubs and associations. Private philanthropy is discussed in Richard Carter, *The Gentle Legions* (Garden City, N.Y.: Doubleday, 1961); and Richard Eells, *Corporation Giving in a Free Society* (New York: Harper & Row, 1956).

[6] Henry M. Pachter, "Three Economic Models: Capitalism, Welfare-State and Socialism," *Dissent*, XI (Spring, 1964), 173–188, discusses the role of the principles of distribution by need and by payment in different economic systems.

vices among the members of American society. In general, money is distributed according to the contribution made to the productivity of the society either by working or by investing capital. For most, the job is the main link to income. However, while the job-income link has sufficed in the past, in the future, at least some income, as Robert Theobald argues in "The Background to the Guaranteed-Income Concept" may have to be guaranteed to all whether or not they work.[7]

Whatever the future holds, it is clear that America's reliance on the job-income link and its mixed system of public and private enterprise has been instrumental in raising the general welfare, or at least the general material welfare, to unprecedented heights. However, increases in the general welfare have not eliminated all discomfort and despair. One of the central domestic questions in twentieth-century American life is what to do about promoting the welfare of the disadvantaged members of society. In "Strategies in the War on Poverty," Fritz Machlup describes and evaluates several specific approaches to helping one segment of the disadvantaged, the financially impoverished.[8] We discuss three general questions raised by specific programs to help the underprivileged.

One of the first problems which must be dealt with before establishing a program to help the disadvantaged is to determine who is entitled to the benefits of such a program.[9] The state of need is one basis for evaluating applicants. Medical services, for example, could be offered to all who are mentally or physically ill. Similarly, whoever lives below some agreed upon standard of living might be given financial aid. (Of course, as Machlup's article notes, gaining agreement on standards of objective need is itself a difficult problem.) Criteria other than need may also be considered. Social Security benefits, for example, are not available to all elderly people who need extra income, but only to those who held

[7] For further discussion, see the essays in Robert Theobald (ed.), *The Guaranteed Income: Next Step in the Economic Evolution?* (Garden City, N.Y.: Doubleday, 1966); and *Technology and the American Economy*, No. 0-788-561 (Washington: U.S. Government Printing Office, 1966). The latter is a report of the National Commission on Technology calling for a guaranteed annual income.

[8] Poverty, and how to deal with it, is discussed in Louis Ferman, J. Kornbluh, and A. Haber (eds.), *Poverty in America* (Ann Arbor: University of Michigan Press, 1965); Margaret S. Gordon (ed.), *Poverty in America* (San Francisco: Chandler, 1965); Hanna H. Meissner (ed.), *Poverty in the Affluent Society* (New York: Harper & Row, 1966); Frank Riessman, J. Cohen, and A. Pearl (eds.), *Mental Health of the Poor* (New York: Free Press, 1964); Robert E. Will and Harold G. Vatter (eds.), *Poverty in Affluence* (New York: Harcourt, Brace & World, 1965).

[9] For a discussion of the historical arguments over who, if anybody, should receive welfare aid, see Sidney Fine, *Laissez Faire and the General-Welfare State* (Ann Arbor: University of Michigan Press, 1956); and Harold Wilensky and Charles Lebeaux, *Industrial Society and Social Welfare* (New York: Russell Sage Foundation, 1958).

jobs covered by the Social Security Law for the required length of time. Furthermore, people, regardless of their need, who have not taken steps to help themselves by seeking work may be deemed ineligible for aid. In short, criteria defining need may be supplemented or replaced by criteria defining who *deserves* or has earned the right to aid. Since there is no guarantee that the most needy are also deserving, the benefits of a given program may not go to those who most need it.[10]

In some instances, the continued application of rules defining the deserving clientele may result in perpetuating rather than eliminating dependency on the program. For example, it is common practice to restrict occupancy in government housing projects to those with incomes below some established amount. Should a family succeed in raising its income above the stated dividing line, they are evicted. However, the rents for privately owned facilities are often so much higher than they are in such projects that the raise in family income does not cover the increased rent. This situation may result in there being little economic incentive to strive for increased income. Further, since those who do "make it" are forced to leave the project, it contains few models of success to prove to other project families· that one of them can earn a decent wage.[11]

A second problem encountered in establishing a welfare program is that of determining the level of benefits to be offered. One aspect of this problem is whether to render benefits less desirable than what one may get through his own efforts. Some argue that if participation in a program is extremely attractive, the society may find itself helping rather than being helped by potentially useful members. The result would be to lower rather than raise the general welfare. However, it should be noted that certain minimal standards of living are provided the mentally ill and the criminal without creating a serious threat that vast numbers will feign illness or break the law merely to get a place to live and three square meals a day. The loss of freedom and the stigma of being an inmate in a mental hospital or prison may be sufficient to deter malingerers. Similarly, the material gains of being on relief may not outweigh the stigma of receiving "charity."[12] Where there are social barriers to seeking aid, the

[10] Martin Rein discusses the failure to help the most needy in "The Strange Case of Public Dependency," *Trans-action*, II (March–April, 1965), 16–23.

[11] See Michael Harrington, "Old Slums, New Slums," *The Other America* (New York: Macmillan, 1963), pp. 139–157; and Herbert J. Gans, "The Failure of Urban Renewal," *Commentary*, XXXIX (April, 1965), 29–37.

[12] See W. Cohen, W. Haber, and E. Mueller, *The Impact of Unemployment in the 1958 Recession*, prepared for consideration by the Senate Subcommittee on Unemployment (Ann Arbor: Survey Research Center, 1960); and Earl L. Koos, "Why Slum Families Don't Seek Help," in Harry C. Bredemeier and Jackson Toby (eds.),

probability of losing the services of potential contributors to society is lowered. However, these same social barriers may prevent those who need help from seeking it. The confidence, dignity, and hope of those already receiving aid may be severely damaged and their chances of rehabilitation lowered if participation in the program stigmatizes them. A man on relief may give up looking for a job if he comes to believe that being on relief is a sign that he is "no good for anything." An ex-mental patient may suffer a relapse because people will not accept or befriend him.

A third problem encountered in attempts to help the disadvantaged is to determine whether or not it is possible to provide means for them to join or rejoin the ranks of the "advantaged." Where the disadvantage is biological, there is often great hope that dependency on the program may be terminated or minimized. The diabetic, the blind, and the amputee can be helped to lead normal or near-normal lives. However, in the realm of socioeconomic handicaps, the means for rehabilitation are not easily found. In a sense, what is needed is a modern equivalent of the Homestead Act of the 1860s which provided to all who asked the means of earning a livelihood—160 farmable acres. The equivalent in a modern, complex, and industrialized society, however, is not immediately apparent. Perhaps this equivalent is the better education provided by the GI Bill after World War II; perhaps the skills one can learn in the Job Corps; perhaps the political skills learned in a community action program; or perhaps the creation of new and needed jobs which use the particular talents of some of the disadvantaged.[13]

In sum, the problems encountered in promoting the general welfare are those encountered in evaluating the aggregate and distribution of individual welfare and in devising the means of improving them. The former problems include those of deciding what the constituents of individual welfare are, and of creating the measures and standards for evaluating the general welfare. The latter problems, the problems of promoting the general welfare, include devising means for providing the greatest good for the greatest number and deciding what, if anything, is to be done with respect to those not among the great number so benefited.

Social Problems in America: Costs and Casualties in an Acquisitive Society (New York: Wiley, 1960), pp. 208–212.
    [13] See Arthur Pearl and Frank Riessman, *New Careers for the Poor* (New York: Free Press, 1965), on the possibility of creating jobs to fit the skills of the poor; and O. R. Gursslin and J. L. Roach, "Some Issues in Training the Unemployed," *Social Problems*, XII (Summer, 1964), 86–98, on the problems of training the poor to fit available jobs.

The Social Balance and the
Investment Balance

⌒⌒

John Kenneth Galbraith

The Social Balance

. . .

11

In the production of goods within the private economy it has long been recognized that a tolerably close relationship must be maintained between the production of various kinds of products. The output of steel and oil and machine tools is related to the production of automobiles. Investment in transportation must keep abreast of the output of goods to be transported. The supply of power must be abreast of the growth of industries requiring it. The existence of these relationships—coefficients to the economist—has made possible the construction of the input-output table which shows how changes in the production in one industry will increase or diminish the demands on other industries. To this table, and more especially to its ingenious author, Professor Wassily Leontief, the world is indebted for one of its most important of modern insights into economic relationships. If expansion in one part of the economy were not matched by the requisite expansion in other parts—were the need for balance not respected—then bottlenecks and shortages, speculative hoarding of scarce supplies, and sharply increasing costs would ensue. Fortunately in peacetime the market system operates easily and effectively to maintain this balance, and this together with the existence of stocks and some flexibility in the coefficients as a result of substitution, insures that no serious difficulties will arise. We are reminded of the existence of the

Reprinted from *The Affluent Society* (Boston: Houghton Mifflin, 1958), pp. 253–261, 266–269, 270–277, by permission of the author and Houghton Mifflin Company.

problem only by noticing how serious it is for those countries—Poland or, in a somewhat different form, India—which seek to solve the problem by planned measures and with a much smaller supply of resources.

Just as there must be balance in what a community produces, so there must also be balance in what the community consumes. An increase in the use of one product creates, ineluctably, a requirement for others. If we are to consume more automobiles, we must have more gasoline. There must be more insurance as well as more space on which to operate them. Beyond a certain point more and better food appears to mean increased need for medical services. This is the certain result of the increased consumption of tobacco and alcohol. More vacations require more hotels and more fishing rods. And so forth. With rare exceptions—shortages of doctors are an exception which suggests the rule—this balance is also maintained quite effortlessly so far as goods for private sale and consumption are concerned. The price system plus a rounded condition of opulence is again the agency.

However, the relationships we are here discussing are not confined to the private economy. They operate comprehensively over the whole span of private and public services. As surely as an increase in the output of automobiles puts new demands on the steel industry so, also, it places new demands on public services. Similarly, every increase in the consumption of private goods will normally mean some facilitating or protective step by the state. In all cases if these services are not forthcoming, the consequences will be in some degree ill. It will be convenient to have a term which suggests a satisfactory relationship between the supply of privately produced goods and services and those of the state, and we may call it social balance.

The problem of social balance is ubiquitous, and frequently it is obtrusive. As noted, an increase in the consumption of automobiles requires a facilitating supply of streets, highways, traffic control, and parking space. The protective services of the police and the highway patrols must also be available, as must those of the hospitals. Although the need for balance here is extraordinarily clear, our use of privately produced vehicles has, on occasion, got far out of line with the supply of the related public services. The result has been hideous road congestion, an annual massacre of impressive proportions, and chronic colitis in the cities. As on the ground, so also in the air. Planes collide with disquieting consequences for those within when the public provision for air traffic control fails to keep pace with private use of the airways.

But the auto and the airplane, versus the space to use them, are merely an exceptionally visible example of a requirement that is pervasive. The more goods people procure, the more packages they discard and the more trash that must be carried away. If the appropriate sanitation services are not provided, the counterpart of increasing opulence will be deepening filth. The greater the wealth the thicker will be the dirt. This indubitably describes a tendency of our time. As more goods are produced and owned, the greater are the opportunities for fraud and the more property that must be protected. If the provision of public law enforcement services do not keep pace, the counterpart of increased well-being will, we may be certain, be increased crime.

The city of Los Angeles, in modern times, is a near-classic study in the problem of social balance. Magnificently efficient factories and oil refineries, a lavish supply of automobiles, a vast consumption of handsomely packaged products, coupled with the absence of a municipal trash collection service which forced the use of home incinerators, made the air nearly unbreathable for an appreciable part of each year. Air pollution could be controlled only by a complex and highly developed set of public services—by better knowledge stemming from more research, better policing, a municipal trash collection service, and possibly the assertion of the priority of clean air over the production of goods. These were long in coming. The agony of a city without usable air was the result.

The issue of social balance can be identified in many other current problems. Thus an aspect of increasing private production is the appearance of an extraordinary number of things which lay claim to the interest of the young. Motion pictures, television, automobiles, and the vast opportunities which go with the mobility, together with such less enchanting merchandise as narcotics, comic books, and pornographia, are all included in an advancing gross national product. The child of a less opulent as well as a technologically more primitive age had far fewer such diversions. The red schoolhouse is remembered mainly because it had a paramount position in the lives of those who attended it that no modern school can hope to attain.

In a well-run and well-regulated community, with a sound school system, good recreational opportunities, and a good police force—in short a community where public services have kept pace with private production—the diversionary forces operating on the modern juvenile may do no great damage. Television and the violent mores of Hollywood and Madison Avenue must contend with the intellectual discipline of the school. The social, athletic, dramatic, and like attractions of the school also claim the attention of the child. These, together with the other recreational opportunities of the community, minimize the tendency to delinquency. Experiments with violence and immorality are checked by an effective law enforcement system before they become epidemic.

In a community where public services have failed to keep abreast of private consumption things are very different. Here, in an atmosphere of private opulence and public squalor, the private goods have full sway. Schools do not compete with television and the movies. The dubious heroes of the latter, not Miss Jones, become the idols of the young. The hot rod and the wild ride take the place of more sedentary sports for which there are inadequate facilities or provision. Comic books, alcohol, narcotics, and switchblade knives are, as noted, part of the increased flow of goods, and there is nothing to dispute their enjoyment. There is an ample supply of private wealth to be appropriated and not much to be feared from the police. An austere community is free from temptation. It can be austere in its public services. Not so a rich one.

Moreover, in a society which sets large store by production, and which has highly effective machinery for synthesizing private wants, there are strong pressures to have as many wage earners in the family as possible. As always all social behavior is part of a piece. If both parents are engaged in private production, the burden on the public services is further increased. Children, in effect, become the charge of the community for an appreciable part of the time. If the services of the community do not keep pace, this will be another source of disorder.

Residential housing also illustrates the problem of the social balance, although in a somewhat complex form. Few would wish to contend that, in the lower or even the middle income brackets, Americans are munificently supplied with housing. A great many families would like better located or merely more houseroom, and no advertising is necessary to persuade them of their wish. And the provision of housing is in the private domain. At first glance at least, the line we draw between private and public seems not to be preventing a satisfactory allocation of resources to housing.

On closer examination, however, the problem turns out to be not greatly different from that of education. It is improbable that the housing industry is greatly more incompetent or inefficient in the United States than in those countries—Scandinavia, Holland, or (for the most part) England—where slums have been largely eliminated and where *minimum* standards of cleanliness and comfort are well above our own. As the experience of these countries shows, and as we have also been learning, the housing industry functions well only in combination with a large, complex, and costly array of public services. These include land purchase and clearance for redevelopment; good neighborhood and city planning, and effective and well-enforced zoning; a variety of financing and other aids to the housebuilder and owner; publicly supported research and architectural services for an industry which, by its nature, is equipped to do little on its own; and a considerable amount of direct or assisted public construction for families in the lowest income brackets. The quality of the housing depends not on the industry, which is given, but on what is invested in these supplements and supports.

III

The case for social balance has, so far, been put negatively. Failure to keep public services in minimal relation to private production and use of goods is a cause of social disorder or impairs economic performance. The matter may now be put affirmatively. By failing to exploit the opportunity to expand public production we are missing opportunities for enjoyment which otherwise we might have had. Presumably a community can be as well rewarded by buying better schools or better parks as by buying bigger automobiles. By concentrating on the latter rather than the former it is failing to maximize its satisfactions. As with schools in the community, so with public services over the country at large. It is scarcely sensible that we should satisfy our wants in private goods with reckless abundance, while in the case of public goods, on the evidence of the eye, we practice extreme self-denial. So, far from systematically exploiting the opportunities to derive use and pleasure from these services, we do not supply what would keep us out of trouble.

The conventional wisdom holds that the community, large or small, makes a decision as to how much it will devote to its public services. This decision is arrived at by democratic process. Subject to the imperfections and uncertainties of democracy, people decide how much of their private income and goods they will surrender in order to have public services of which they are in greater need. Thus there is a balance, however rough, in the enjoyments to be had from private goods and services and those rendered by public authority.

It will be obvious, however, that this view depends on the notion of independently determined consumer wants. In such a world one could with some reason defend the doctrine that the consumer, as a voter, makes an independent choice between public and private goods. But given the dependence effect—given that consumer wants are created by the process by which they are satisfied—the consumer makes no such choice. He is subject to the forces of advertising and emulation by which production creates its own demand. Advertising operates exclusively, and emulation mainly, on behalf of privately produced goods and services.[1] Since management and emulative effects operate on behalf of private production, public services will have an inherent tendency to lag behind. Automobile demand which is expensively synthesized will inevitably have a much larger claim on income than parks or public health or even roads where no such influence operates. The engines of mass communication, in their highest state of development, assail the eyes and ears of the community on behalf of more beer but not of more schools. Even in the conventional wisdom it will scarcely be contended that this leads to an equal choice between the two.

The competition is especially unequal for new products and services. Every corner of the public psyche is canvassed by some of the nation's most talented citizens to see if the desire for some merchantable product can be cultivated. No similar process operates on behalf of the non-merchantable services of the state. Indeed, while we take the cultivation of new private wants for granted we would be measurably shocked to see it applied to public services. The scientist or engineer or advertising man who devotes himself to developing a new carburetor, cleanser, or depilatory for which the public recognizes no need and will feel none until an advertising campaign arouses it, is one of the valued members of our society. A politician or a public servant who dreams up a new public service is a wastrel. Few public offenses are more reprehensible.

So much for the influences which operate on the decision between public and private production. The calm decision between public and private consumption pictured by the conventional wisdom is, in fact, a remarkable example of the error which arises from viewing social behavior out of context. The inherent tendency will always be for public services to fall behind private production. We have here the first of the causes of social imbalance.

.   .   .

VI

A feature of the years immediately following World War II was a remarkable attack on the notion of expanding and improving public services. During the depression years such services had been elaborated and improved partly in order to fill some small part of the vacuum left by the shrinkage of private production. During the war years the role of government was vastly expanded. After that came the reaction. Much of it, unquestionably, was motivated by a desire to rehabilitate the prestige of private production and therewith of producers. No doubt some who joined the attack hoped, at least tacitly, that it might be possible to sidestep the truce on taxation vis-à-vis equality by having less taxation of all kinds. For a time the notion that our public services had somehow become inflated and excessive was all but axiomatic. Even liberal politicians did not seriously protest. They found it necessary to aver that they were in favor of public economy too.

In this discussion a certain mystique was attributed to the satisfaction of privately supplied wants. A community decision to have a new school means that the individual surrenders the necessary amount, willy-nilly, in his taxes. But if he is left with that income, he is a free man. He can decide between a better car or a television set. This was advanced with some solemnity as an argument for the TV set. The difficulty is that this argument leaves the community with no way of preferring the school. All private wants, where the individual can choose, are inherently superior to all public desires which must be paid for by taxation and with an inevitable component of compulsion.

The cost of public services was also held to be a desolating burden on private production, although this was at a time when the private production was burgeoning. Urgent warnings were issued of the unfavorable effects of taxation on investment—"I don't know of a surer way of killing off the incentive to invest than by imposing taxes which are regarded by people as punitive."[2] This was at a time when the inflationary effect of a very high level of investment was causing concern. The same individuals who were warning about the inimical effects of taxes were strongly advocating a monetary policy designed to reduce investment. However, an understanding of our economic discourse requires an appreciation of one of its basic rules: men of high position are allowed, by a special act of grace, to accommodate their reasoning to the answer they need. Logic is only required in those of lesser rank.

Finally it was argued, with no little vigor, that expanding government posed a grave threat to individual liberties. "Where distinction and rank is achieved almost exclusively by becoming a civil servant of the state . . . it is too much to expect that many will long prefer freedom to security."[3]

With time this attack on public services has somewhat subsided. The disorder associated with social imbalance has become visible even if the need for balance between private and public services is still imperfectly appreciated.

Freedom also seemed to be surviving. Perhaps it was realized that all organized activity requires concessions by the individual to the group.

This is true of the policeman who joins the police force, the teacher who gets a job at the high school, and the executive who makes his way up the hierarchy of Du Pont. If there are differences between public and private organization, they are of kind rather than of degree. As this is written the pendulum has in fact swung back. Our liberties are now menaced by the conformity exacted by the large corporation and its impulse to create, for its own purposes, the organization man. This danger we may also survive.

Nonetheless, the postwar onslaught on the public services left a lasting imprint. To suggest that we canvass our public wants to see where happiness can be improved by more and better services has a sharply radical tone. Even public services to avoid disorder must be defended. By contrast the man who devises a nostrum for a nonexistent need and then successfully promotes both remains one of nature's noblemen.

The Investment Balance

I

Social balance relates to the goods and services we consume. There is an allied problem in the way we commit the resources that are available for investment in the economy. The same forces which bring us our plenitude of private goods and leave us poverty-stricken in our public services also act to distort the distribution of investment as between ordinary material capital and what we may denote as the personal capital of the country. This distortion has far-reaching effects. One of them is to impair the production of private goods themselves. The situation will be seen in sharpest focus if we pursue the latter point. It is not, however, the only or, indeed, the most important consequence.

Economic growth—the expansion of economic output—requires an increase in the quantity of the productive plant and equipment of the country or in its quality or, as in the usual case, in both. This is fully agreed. The increase in quantity is capital formation. The increase in quality is what we call technological advance.

In the earliest stages of economic development, from which so many of our economic attitudes are derived, the simple and sufficient way of getting more growth was to have more saving and therefore more material capital. Entrepreneurial talent was needed but, at least in western countries, it was almost invariably, if not invariably, forthcoming. To perform this function required some education. But, as the example of any number of great entrepreneurs from Commodore Vanderbilt to Henry Ford made clear, the education could be exiguous and often was.

The existence of an educated and literate body of workers was desirable but by no means essential. Some of the greatest industrial enterprises in the United States in the past were manned principally by men who could speak no English. Most important of all, in all the earlier stages of development there was no close and predictable correlation between the supply of educated men and the nature of their training and the rate of technological innovation. Inventions were more often the result of brilliant flashes of insight than the product of long prepared training and development. The Industrial Revolution in England was ushered in by the invention of the flying shuttle by John Kay, the spinning jenny by James Hargreaves, the spinning frame (presumptively) by Richard Arkwright and, of course, by James Watt's steam engine. These represented vast improvements in the capital which was being put to industrial use. But only in the case of Watt could the innovation be related to previous education and preparation. Kay and Hargreaves were simply weavers with a mechanical turn of mind. Arkwright had been apprenticed as a boy as a barber and a wigmaker and was barely literate.

However, with the development of a great and complex industrial plant, and even more with the development of a great and sophisticated body of basic science and of experience in its application, all this has been changed. In addition to the entrepreneurs (and perhaps one should add the accountants and clerks) who were more or less automatically forthcoming, modern economic activity now requires a great number of trained and qualified people. Investment in human beings is, *prima facie*, as important as investment in material capital. The one, in its modern complexity, depends on the other.

What is more important, the *improvement* in capital—technological advance—is now almost wholly dependent on investment in education, training, and scientific opportunity for individuals. One branch of the conventional wisdom clings nostalgically to the conviction that brilliant, isolated, and intuitive inventions are still a principal instrument of technological progress and can occur anywhere and to anyone.[4] Benjamin Franklin is the sacred archetype of the American genius and nothing may be done to disturb his position. But in the unromantic fact, innovation has become a highly organized enterprise. The extent of the result is predictably related to the quality and quantity of the resources being applied to it. These resources are men and women. Their quality and quantity depends on the extent of the investment in their education, training, and opportunity. They are the source of technological change. Without them investment in material capital will still bring growth, but it will be the inefficient growth that is combined with technological stagnation.

I I

We come now to the nub of the problem. Investment in material capital is distributed to the various claimant industries by the market. If earnings are high (at the margin) in the oil industry and low in the textile business, it is to the oil industry that capital will flow. This allocation by the market works, it would appear, with tolerable efficiency. Among the recognized crimes of economics, any interference with the "free flow" of capital has a very high standing.

But while this flow operates as between different material claimants on investment funds, it operates only with manifest uncertainty and inefficiency as between material and personal capital. Nearly all of the investment in individuals is in the public domain. And virtually all of it is outside the market system. It is the state which, through primary and secondary schools, and through the colleges and universities, makes the largest investment in individuals. And where, as in the case of private colleges and universities, the state is not directly involved, the amount of the investment is not directly related to the eventual pay-out in production. Investment in refineries being higher than in textile mills, the refineries will draw investment funds. But engineers to design the re-fineries may be even more important—in effect yield a higher return. And the highest return of all may come from the scientist who makes a marked improvement in the refining process. These are not imaginative possibilities but common probabilities. Yet the high return to scientific and technical training does not cause the funds to move from material capital to such investment. There is no likely flow from the building of the refineries to the education of the scientists. Here, at the most critical point in the vaunted process of investment resource allocation, is an impediment of towering importance. Characteristically, however, it has received little comment. It is not, like the tariff or monopoly, one of the classic barriers to capital movement. Hence it did not get a foothold in economics in the last century and, accordingly, under the intellectual grandfather clause which has such sway in the science it has no real standing now.

There can be no question of the importance of the impediment. Investment in individuals is in the public domain; this investment has become increasingly essential with the advance of science and tech-nology; and there is no machinery for automatically allocating resources as between material and human investment. But this is not all. As we have seen in earlier chapters, there is active discrimination against the invest-ment in the public domain and hence in any part of it. The investment in the refinery is an unmitigated good. It adds to our stock of wealth. It is a categorical achievement. But the training of the scientists and engineers who will run the refinery, improve its economic efficiency, and possibly in the end replace it with something better is not a categorical good. The money so invested is not regarded with approval. On the contrary, it is widely regarded as a burden. Many will judge the magnitude of the achievement in this area by the smallness of the investment. Others will hold this investment in abeyance while arguing the ancient issue of equality. So incredible is the provision for such investment that a considerable part will have to be begged. Even the prestige of the word investment itself is not regularly accorded to these outlays. A century ago, when educational outlays were not intimately related to production, men sensibly confined the word investment to the increases in capital which brought a later increase in product. Education was a consumer outlay. The popular usage has never been revised.[5]

Could it be legally arranged that youngsters were sorted out at an early age, possibly by their test score in mathematics, and the promising then be indentured for life to a particular corporation, the flow of investment into human development might soon be placed on a rough parity with that into material capital. Firms would perceive the need for investing in their scientific and engineering stock much as major league baseball clubs have learned the wisdom of investing in their farm teams. Under ideal arrangements any surplus talent could be marketed. The cost of unsuccessfully trying to educate the inevitable errors of selection would be either written off or partially retrieved by using the individuals as salesmen. Under such a system, which as noted would unfortunately involve the elimination of the liberty of the individuals in question, it is fairly certain that investment in human beings would rise and at a rapid rate.

But so long as free choice remains, such investment must remain largely a public function. The individual, since he is only at the beginning of earning power, cannot himself make any appreciable part of the investment. Whether his parents can and will be willing to do so is a highly accidental matter. His future employer can hardly be expected to invest in an asset that may materialize in the plant of a competitor or another industry. At most he will, as now, distribute scholarships and fellowships in the hope of ultimately influencing the choice of those in whom the investment is nearly complete. This has no appreciable effect on the total of the investment in people. It is a scalping operation. It does, however, suggest the store which is set by the resulting assets.

III

Human development, in other words, is what economists have long termed an external economy. Its benefits accrue to all firms; it is not sufficiently specific to any one to be bought and paid for by it.

What is true of human development is also true of one of its principal fruits. That is scientific research. A society which sets for itself the goal of increasing its supply of goods will tend, inevitably, to identify all innovation with additions to, changes in, or increases in its stock of goods. It will assume, accordingly, that most research will be induced and rewarded by the market.

Much will be. Under the proper circumstances—firms must be of adequate size in the industry, and certain other conditions must be met[6]—we may expect our economy to do a superior job of inventing, developing, and redesigning consumers' goods and improving their process of manufacture. Nor is there reason to doubt that similar attention will be given, under equally favorable circumstances, to the capital goods industries which support this consumers' goods consumption. Much of this achievement will impress us only so long as we do not inquire how the demand for the products so developed is contrived and sustained. If we do we are bound to observe that much of the research effort—as in the automobile industry—is devoted to discovering changes that can be advertised. The research program will be built around the need to devise "selling points" and "advertising pegs" or to accelerate "planned obsolescence." All this suggests that the incentive will be to allocate research resources to what, in some sense, are the least important things. The quantity is more impressive than the way it is allocated. Still one would not wish to suggest that the American economy is delinquent in the attention it devotes to change and improvement in consumers' goods. Clearly it is not.

These incentives, however, operate over but a small part of total scientific and research activity and, indeed, over but a small part that is potentially applicable to the production of goods. Thus a very large amount of highly useful research cannot be specialized to or be sustained by any marketable product. This is most obviously true of much so-called basic research. But it is also true of a large amount of applied effort. The modern air transport is the stepchild of the military airplane. It would never have sustained the underlying research and development endeavor on its own. The same is true in even greater degree of the nonmilitary uses of nuclear energy. There are numerous other cases.

It is because military considerations have induced a large allocation of resources to research that this problem is, on the whole, less striking than that of investment in personal resources. Although the research must be in the public domain, military urgency has helped to offset this blight. There is little comfort for man in the circumstances which have induced this allocation of resources or from the resulting weapons. But it has catalyzed a great deal of important scientific innovation and development. Far more significant research lies back of the effort to exceed the speed of sound than lies back of even the best new soap. It may well be more significant for industry itself. In any event the rate of technical progress in American industry in recent decades would have been markedly slower had it not been for militarily inspired and for this reason publicly-supported research.

·   ·   ·

Notes

1) Emulation does operate between communities. A new school or a new highway in one community does exert pressure on others to remain abreast. However, as compared with the pervasive effects of emulation in extending the demand for privately produced consumer's goods there will be agreement, I think, that this intercommunity effect is probably small.
2) Arthur F. Burns, Chairman of the President's Council of Economic Advisers, *U. S. News & World Report*, May 6, 1955.
3) F. A. Hayek, *The Road to Serfdom* (London: George Routledge & Sons, 1944), p. 98.
4) Cf. for example the article by G. Warren Nutter, "Monopoly, Bigness and Progress," in *Journal of Political Économy*, December 1956.
5) Since this was written and under the impact of Soviet scientific achievements there has been considerable discussion of our lag in *investment* in scientific education. However, this is being treated as a kind of aberration, and not as a fundamental flaw in our machinery of resource allocation.
6) Cf. *American Capitalism*, pp. 84–94 (2d ed.).

The Background to the Guaranteed-
Income Concept

Robert Theobald

Social critics often claim that the present need for economic and social reform stems from past failures in economic and social policy. There is, of course, much merit in this contention. It is, however, far more realistic to perceive present problems as resulting not from failures but from the extraordinary success of Western societies in fulfilling their drive for ever-greater mastery over nature and, in particular, developing the productive potential that today makes it possible to provide every individual in the rich countries with a decent standard of living while requiring a decreasing amount of toil from the vast majority of the population.[1]

The economic history of the past two hundred years may perhaps most properly be couched—to paraphrase H. G. Wells—in terms of a race between increasing production based on ever more complex and sophisticated technology and man's cultural inventiveness in devising and gaining acceptance of new methods of distributing and using this increasing production. It is surprising, therefore, that the mainstream of economics has only recently become concerned with the problems of balancing the available production with the rights of individuals and institutions to obtain this production. Throughout the nineteenth century it was rather generally accepted by economists that production and purchasing power—effective supply and potential demand—would automatically stay in balance. This assumption, called Say's law after its originator, dominated economic analysis until the great slump of the 1930s.

Innovations in techniques of distributing rights to resources have not, therefore, been based until recent years upon theoretical analysis but rather on pragmatic adjustments to the need to be able to sell what could be produced or to obtain the labor force required for the production of quality goods. The lack of a theoretical basis for changes in techniques of distributing income inevitably led to widespread controversy about the impact and implications of each new measure designed to raise purchasing power or attract workers. Thus Ford's five-dollar day, rapid growth in consumer credit and advertising, social security, and unemployment compensation were, in the past, just as controversial as the guaranteed income is today.

The motivation of Ford in introducing the five-dollar day early in the twentieth century and thus doubling the wages of his workers is still far from clear. Some interpreters argue that his main aim was to increase the number of people who could afford to buy the cars that he was turning out in ever greater numbers. Some have concluded that he was motivated by a desire to obtain a more highly skilled and stable labor force, and some believe he wished to increase the welfare of his workers. It would certainly be unprofitable to re-evaluate Ford's motives at this point in time. It would be equally unprofitable to examine in this essay the implications of the fact that the pattern of income distribution that has resulted from Ford's initiative cannot be reasonably explained in terms of existing economic theory—and indeed destroys its validity.[2] It is important to recognize here only that Ford did introduce a mechanism that made it possible for the wages and salaries of workers to rise in parallel with production. This mechanism has been the chief factor responsible for ensuring that American purchasing power has kept in reasonable balance with American productive power during the last fifty years—with, of course, the exception of the Great Depression.

Two major developments in methods of distributing and using production occurred in the twenties. First, widespread use of consumer credit developed—people were allowed to purchase *before* they had earned the required funds. Second, manufacturers and distributors widened the range and scope of selling activities designed to cultivate new tastes. Despite these efforts, however, potential supply was so far ahead of effective demand by 1929 that the economy collapsed.

It was the Great Depression, which followed this collapse, that led economists to become deeply concerned with the problem of maintaining purchasing power. The change in the thrust of economic analysis is generally and correctly attributed to John Maynard Keynes's book *The General Theory of Employment, Interest and Money*. Nevertheless, it must be noted that there is a good deal of evidence suggesting that the brute facts of the Depression forced politicians to move in the direction of increasing purchasing power before a full economic justification for this step had been found—and indeed even while a large proportion of the economic profession was still opposing this step and calling for decreases in government expenditure. Thus social security and the make-work schemes of the thirties were conceived as a response to social unrest rather than justified on economic grounds as a means of ending the recession through increasing demand.

It is also important to recognize that present developments in economic theorizing, which are generally believed to be an extension of Keynesian analysis, do not adequately reflect the spirit of Keynesian thought—as opposed to his technical conclusions. Keynes's main contribution to theory came when he proved that it was possible for unemployment to persist over long periods because effective demand would not necessarily rise as fast as potential supply. Modern economic theorists grasped this insight and set to work to devise policies that would lead to a sufficiently rapid increase in effective demand to balance increases in potential supply and thus ensure minimum unemployment. However, this is not the *only* policy proposal that can be derived from an interpretation of Keynesian analysis: society could equally well decide that it no longer wished to channel the quasi-totality of its efforts toward the goal of full employment but rather desired to seek a new social order that would allow us to take full advantage of the potential of emerging abundance and our ability to eliminate toil.

Keynes himself quite clearly hoped for the second development, arguing that

> when the accumulation of wealth is no longer of high social importance, there will be great changes in the code of morals. We shall be able to rid ourselves of many of the pseudo-moral principles which have hag-ridden us for two hundred years, by which we have exalted some of the most distasteful of human qualities into the position of the highest values. We shall be able to afford to dare to assess the money-motive at its true value. . . . All kinds of social customs and economic practices affecting the distribution of wealth and its rewards and penalties which we now maintain at all costs, however distasteful and unjust they may be in themselves . . . we shall then be free, at last, to discard.[3]

It is quite clear, therefore, that although present policy is justified on the basis of Keynesian analysis, Keynes would, in present conditions, reject many of the policy prescriptions being advanced, for he would hold that they perpetuated the worst of the values of the industrial age.

What methods have economists proposed to ensure that potential supply and effective demand would stay in balance? The first step toward this goal, which was accomplished around the end of the Second World War in almost all Western countries, was the passage of legislation pledging the efforts of governments to ensure that supply and demand would remain in balance and thus provide jobs for all: in the United States this was accomplished by the Employment Act of 1946.

This commitment to a full employment policy through balancing supply and demand has deepened in all Western countries in the years since the Second World War. The United States has undoubtedly been the last country to understand the full implications of this policy approach, but the first five years of the sixties have marked its final acceptance. It is now generally believed, not only by economists but by the vast majority of businessmen, that it is the responsibility of the government to ensure that the economy remains in balance—that the government should aim to balance the economy rather than to balance the budget. . . . the government has now essentially taken a commitment to "guarantee the national income" by ensuring that rights to all available productive resources are distributed.

The difference between this approach to the government's responsibility and that current in the nineteenth century, when it was believed that government damaged the operation of the economy whenever it intervened, is so vast as to need no stressing. Unfortunately, economic theory has not yet re-examined all the implications of the shift in approach. For example, if the government is deeply involved in guaranteeing the national income of the whole country, and if, as is inevitable, its interventions affect the pattern of income distribution, what goals should it adopt? Another facet of this problem results from the fact that a large number of people are unable to earn their living because they are too old, too young, too mentally or physically ill. How should they be provided with incomes and what amount of resources should they receive? Economics has few, if any, answers to these and similar questions.

The problem of providing incomes to those who are too old, too young, or too sick to hold a job is already urgent and is certain to become more so in coming years because of the inevitable shifts in patterns of age distribution. This reality is already causing the emergence of a new consensus that cuts across party lines and interest groups. This consensus is based on a belief that the government has already taken an implied commitment to provide a minimum level of income to all individuals, but that the present mosaic of measures designed to ensure this result is both excessively complex and unduly costly. It is argued that it would there-fore be desirable to introduce a single plan that would meet the implied commitment of government as simply and cheaply as possible through the introduction of a guaranteed income floor for all those who either cannot, or should not, earn their living through holding a job.

There should be no need to justify payments to the physically and mentally ill: they cannot work and society should surely provide for them. Some justification, however, is often felt to be required for more adequate payments to the old, for one of the most sanctified of our work myths is that older people both could and should have saved enough to provide for their old age. This is, of course, merely a cynical fiction. Those who are old today worked in an era when their income was necessarily far lower than is paid for jobs demanding a comparable level of skills and application today. They needed to spend a large proportion of their income just to cover their expenses, including the education of their children. They were therefore able to save very little, if anything, whether directly or through insurance schemes. Today's labor force, however, would not be enjoying its present level of income without their hard work and that of earlier generations who had even less to show for their toil. Any fair distribution of the nation's resources should ensure that old people be allowed to share in the wealth they created. Their labor was, in fact, wealth, and it was invested in the national economy at a time when its value was at a premium. Today this group should be collecting their "earned interest."

It will, perhaps, help to put this question in perspective if we recognize that most of those presently being paid social security benefits are receiving more than the actuarial value of their contributions: i.e., they did not pay in enough money to cover the benefits they are receiving. Continuing expansion of the social security system makes it almost certain that it will not become actuarily sound at any point in the future. Thus we have already accepted, on a practical basis, that the old are entitled to a more adequate income than would be theirs on an insurance basis. The next step is to bring the logic of this position into the open and see what more needs to be done.

The question of income distribution among the young poses equally serious problems, for we have not yet been willing to accept the fact that we have extended the principle of parental support of the young far beyond the breaking point. In an agricultural or even an early industrial society, a child was wealth. After a few years of care, the child added to the family income rather than subtracted from it. In addition, the younger generation was expected to support their parents as they grew old. There was, thus, a rough balance between the economic responsibility of the parents and that of the children.

Let us contrast this with the situation today. Because of the demands of the new world in which we live, a child should be educated at least until he is twenty-one and perhaps until he is twenty-five or thirty. Despite the growing number of loans, grants, and scholarships, it is still a fundamental assumption of our society that the primary economic responsibility for the education and support of the child lies with the parent. However, the parent receives little financial return, for by the time the child leaves the educational process he is generally married and feels little obligation for the economic support of his parents. Parents should no longer be expected to underwrite the lengthy educational process that the future society requires of today's and tomorrow's young people. We must recognize that the student is already "working" as relevantly as the man in the factory or the office.

While the idea that we must find new ways of providing income to those who cannot, or should not, hold a job has received increasing support in recent years, the wider concept that *everybody* should receive a guaranteed income as a matter of right is still highly controversial. The proposal for a universal guaranteed income can be justified on the ground . . . that most types of structured[4] jobs will be taken over, within a relatively brief period, by advanced machinery. This will necessarily be true because, in addition to the often substantial direct economic savings from the use of automatic machinery, machinery also appears more attractive than men for a wide range of noneconomic reasons. Machine systems do not get tired, they can carry out a particular task with a continued precision that cannot be demanded or expected of a human work force; they are incapable of immorality, they do not lie, steal, cheat, or goof off; they do not claim that their rights as human beings are being violated by factory work practices; they are not class-conscious; above all, they are not vocal in their criticism of management and they do not go on strike.

In the relatively near future, therefore, those who need to expand their plant to meet created demand will prefer to buy machines rather than to hire men: the machines they buy will be produced predominantly by other machines. The new machines purchased will be so much more efficient than earlier machinery that large numbers of existing firms using older machinery and thus employing many men will be forced to close down: they will be too inefficient to compete.

The process can be summarized as follows: created demand will lead to purchases of highly efficient and productive machine systems that need few men to control them: i.e., to the installation of cybernation. Thus, in the relatively near future, a policy of forcing rapid growth in demand in order to increase employment opportunities will actually lead to the opposite result: it will raise unemployment rather than lower it.

The conclusion that massive unemployment is inevitable is still rejected by most economists and policy-makers, who argue that increases in demand brought about, if necessary, by federal intervention to balance the economy can *always* be large enough to ensure that all the available labor will be used. Unfortunately, however, there is no economic theory of contemporary evidence to support this conclusion. The neoclassical theorizing of the last part of the nineteenth century and the beginning of the twentieth assumed that men and machines would cooperate with each other; today, however, they are competitive. Keynes, who is presently used as the justification for the assertion that demand and supply can be kept in balance, and jobs provided for all, should not be used for this purpose because he excluded from his analysis those very factors that now threaten massive unemployment. "We take as given the existing skill and quantity of available labor, the existing quality and quantity of available equipment, the existing technique. This does not mean that we assume these facts to be constant, but merely that in this place and context, we are not considering or taking into account the effects and consequences of changes in them."[5]

In effect, therefore, economists have no valid theoretical structure to support their contention that unemployment can be avoided by increases in demand. To the non-economist, such a statement will necessarily be shocking, but it is unfortunately valid. Economists, like many social scientists, have generally been far more concerned about theoretical rigor within a given pattern of assumptions than about the validity of the assumptions themselves; the development of theory has proceeded despite the ever decreasing relevance of the assumptions on which it is based. Economic predictions about unemployment rates will not be valid until the analysis from which they are drawn is based on a new and more relevant set of assumptions.

As minimum unemployment cannot be achieved in coming years, fundamental change in the socioeconomic system will be absolutely essential. As we have already seen, our present system is postulated on the belief that every individual who desires a job will be able to find one and that the jobs thus obtained will pay well enough to enable the individual to live with dignity. I am convinced that if we desire to maintain freedom, a guaranteed income will necessarily have to be introduced. In addition, during the period of transition from a scarcity to an abundance socioeconomy, we will have to consider the whole problem of income maintenance for those whose income level is above the minimum income floor in order to allow them to update their education and to minimize hardship when individuals lose their jobs because of further increases in technological sophistication. Although neither this essay nor this book can deal with the issue of income maintenance, it is necessary to stress that the need for an income maintenance program is just as great as the need for a guaranteed income floor.[6]

The economic controversy is not, however, the most important one. Just as Keynes foresaw that the issue of scarcity was not the long-run problem of mankind, he warned us against placing too much emphasis on strictly economic analysis: "Do not let us overestimate the importance of the economic problem, or sacrifice to its supposed necessities other matters of greater and more permanent significance."[7] The real question raised by the coming of cybernation is not whether we *can* provide jobs for everybody, but whether we *should* provide jobs for everybody: the question we need to examine is whether our present policy of providing income rights on the basis of job-holding is the best way to ensure that the urgent work of society will be accomplished.

Most economists, as well as government, management, and union leaders claim that the type of work that now needs to be done and will need to be done in the future can, and should, be turned into jobs for which a wage or salary can then be paid. This is the assumption that is explicitly challenged by those who support the guaranteed income. Job-holding within the increasingly bureaucratic structures whose growth can be expected, given the continuation of the present socioeconomic system, would certainly not be conducive to the self-development of the individual. In addition, and even more importantly, the lack of flexibility inherent in bureaucratic structures makes them unsuitable forms of organization for acting upon, or even perceiving, developments that would benefit the socioeconomic system.

. . . many individuals are perfectly capable of perceiving what needs to be done to develop themselves and their society and that these individuals would act upon this perception if they had the funds that would free them from the necessity of holding a job. A parallel is often made with the ownership of capital: it is claimed that the possession of capital has not led to a general decline in individual and social responsibility and that there is therefore no reason why a guaranteed income should lead to a decline in individual and social responsibility. Comparisons with the dole are rejected; it is suggested that the dole results in degradation partly because it is seen by its recipients as "charity" rather than as a right, and partly because the techniques of distribution used in many areas of the country inevitably sap self-respect and initiative.

For society at large, and especially for those creative individuals now shackled by the absence of a guaranteed source of income, the situation would seem to be analogous to that which obtained at the time of the introduction of limited liability in the nineteenth century. Limited liability was introduced to encourage risk-taking by those investing in companies. The concept of a joint venture was replaced by the concept that a stockholder's liability for company debts no longer put a lien on his total wealth but only on the amount he invested in the company. Limited liability was a precondition for the taking of risks: it did not ensure innovation or risk-taking, but it did make them possible, thus allowing the economy and society to benefit from the self-interested acts of individuals.

A guaranteed income provides the individual with the ability to do what he personally feels to be important. This will allow risk-taking and innovation in areas where the existing and emerging needs of society are not being met by an otherwise efficiently functioning free-enterprise system. The guaranteed income is not mediated through the offices of any other individual or organization within the market system and therefore does not bring with it built-in pressures for the recipient to continue doing what is already being done through the market system.

The guaranteed income therefore involves a major shift in rights and obligations. Today we demand of an individual that he find a job, but we then provide him with the right to "pursue happiness." Tomorrow we will provide him with the right to receive enough resources to live with dignity, and we will demand of him that he develop himself and his society.

The guaranteed-income proposal is based on the fundamental American belief in the right and the ability of the individual to decide what he wishes and ought to do. This is surely the basic meaning of the phrase "private enterprise": that the individual should have the right to obtain enough resources to do what he believes to be important. In the past, the individual could go into business for himself and thus obtain resources. Today all the evidence shows that neither the self-employed businessman nor the small company can compete with the large corporation. The ideal of private enterprise can, therefore, be preserved only if the guaranteed income is introduced.

The guaranteed income will, in fact, lead to the revival of "private enterprise." Once the guaranteed income is available, we can anticipate the organization of what I have called "consentives": productive groups formed by individuals who will come together on a voluntary basis simply because they wish to do so. The goods produced by these consentives will not compete with mass-produced goods available from cybernated firms. The consentive will normally produce the "custom-designed" goods that have been vanishing within the present economy. The consentive would sell in competition with firms paying wages, but its prices would normally be lower because it would need to cover only the costs of materials and other required supplies. Wages and salaries would not need to be met out of income, as the consentive members would be receiving a guaranteed income. The consentive would be market-oriented but not market-supported.

We can anticipate that small market-supported firms will be enabled to survive by transforming themselves into market-oriented consentives. The opposite process will occur as consentives that make significant profits automatically turn into market-supported firms.[8] Thus the guaranteed income would help to bring about a reversal of the present trend toward similarity in type of goods and services, inflexibility in methods of production, and uniformity in productive organization.

At the present time we are committed as a society to the idea that we can and should provide jobs for all. This goal is no longer valid, and we should therefore provide everybody with an absolute right to a guaranteed income. This will, of course, mean that there will be far more unemployment in the future than there is today. We will, however, come to perceive unemployment as favorable rather than unfavorable. The individual and the society fear unemployment today for two reasons: first, because it usually involves the receipt of an inadequate income; second, because it threatens cessation of all activity that seems meaningful and indeed encourages antisocial activities. Once we have provided adequate incomes to all and have introduced the new policies required to develop each individual's potential, unemployment—which will then be redefined as the condition of *not* holding a job—will be seen to be highly desirable, for it will provide the individual with freedom to develop himself and his society.

Notes

1) It is, of course, true that those in the developing countries cannot be provided with a decent standard of living today. But this does not mean, as many argue, that the rich countries should produce everything they can and deliver it to the poor. We should have learned by now that excessive aid can be just as dangerous

as too little. We must accept the bitter fact that poverty in the poor countries—opposed to the rich—cannot be abolished in the near future. We must also recognize that we still have no strategy for the elimination of poverty in the underdeveloped countries. For an examination of this subject see: Robert Theobald, "Needed: A New Development Strategy," *International Development Review*, March, 1964.

2) Economic theory claims that each factor of production—land, labor, and capital—will be paid in accordance with its marginal (additional) contribution to production. Throughout the twentieth century, most of the increase in production has resulted from increased sophistication of equipment (i.e. capital) rather than through the harder work or the greater knowledge of the average worker. Thus most of the increase in production should, on the basis of theory, have gone to capital. This does not mean that we should distribute rights to resources by widening the ownership of capital—the proposal made by Lewis Kelso and Mortimer Adler. Rather we need a revision of theory on the basis of the new realities of a cybernated era.

3) J. M. Keynes, *Essays in Persuasion* (New York: Harcourt, Brace and Company, 1932), pp. 369–370, "Economic Possibilities for Our Grandchildren."

4) A structured job is one in which the decision-making rules can be set out in advance. While computer theorists agree that the computer can, by definition, take over all structured jobs, they still disagree on the proportion of jobs on the factory floor and in the office which can eventually be structured. Everybody agrees, however, that the process of replacement of men by machines is only beginning.

5) J. M. Keynes, *The General Theory of Employment, Interest and Money* (New York: Harcourt, Brace and Company, 1936), p. 243.

6) Proposals for both a guaranteed income and income maintenance are set out in Part II and the Appendix of my book *Free Men and Free Markets* (Garden City, N.Y.: Doubleday & Company, Inc., 1965).

7) Keynes, *Essays in Persuasion*, p. 373.

8) For a description of these processes see *Free Men and Free Markets*, Chapter 9.

Strategies in the War on Poverty

cᴀ⁀ᴀ᷄

Fritz Machlup

If I counted correctly, 33 speakers have preceded me on the platform at this conference. Some have spoken at the same time, in different rooms. Thus, if anybody in this audience has listened to as many as he could, he has heard what 15 experts had to say on the subject of poverty and poverty abolition in the United States. Coming at the tail end of this gabfest, I cannot reasonably be expected to say anything strikingly original. Indeed, the only way to be original at this conference would be to deny either the existence of poverty or the possibility of conquering it. Perhaps I was expected to do just that. When I received the invitation to make the concluding speech at this conference, I wondered why I was chosen for this spot. One of the hypotheses that occurred to me was that I was chosen because I have the reputation of being one of the few surviving individuals of an almost extinct species: an economist with value judgments firmly based on 19th century liberalism, or what most Americans now wrongly call "conservatism."

If this hunch is correct, and I *was* chosen as the anchor man because I might add a conservative counterpoint to a symphony of largely interventionist voices, I am afraid it will be only to a limited extent that I can satisfy the expectations behind that choice. For I do recognize that poverty exists in the United States. I do not believe that a policy of *laissez-faire* would eliminate it, and I favor certain government interventions to combat it. Perhaps, however, my old-fashioned liberalism will still show in some collateral judgments and proposals, and thus I will not let you down completely.

Who Is Poor?

The question—"Who is Poor?"—calls for two different tasks: first, who is defined as poor, and second, who, on the basis of the chosen definition, are the types and kinds of people that compose the class regarded as the poor. The first question is one of convention or reasonable judgment; the second question calls for statistical fact-finding, for a descriptive inquiry, which may suggest some of the causes of poverty and perhaps also the directions of attacking it.

The definition of poverty is usually stated in terms of income and property available for meeting some "minimum" measure of consumption. An operational definition requires a numerical "poverty line" to be drawn, separating the poor from the non-poor. There are basically at least five ways of drawing such a line:

1) One might agree on a fixed consumption standard in terms of dollars of unchanged purchasing power; but if one had done this in a distant past, without later adjustments, poverty would have been eliminated several times over.

2) One might agree on a fixed place in the size distribution of income, for example, the lowest decile or quintile; but if this were done, poverty could never be eliminated or even reduced, for there will always be a lowest decile or quintile, no matter how well-off those in such positions may become.

3) One might agree on a standard, fixed as a percentage of the average or median income of the nation or community, for example, at one-third or one-half of the average or median; but in this case poverty could be reduced only if and as the earning power of the lowest-income recipients rose faster than that of the average or median earners—which we have no strong reason to expect. (Assume that the poor consist largely of aged or otherwise unemployable; why should their incomes increase at a faster rate than those of workers of average productivity?)

4) One might agree on a standard set at one time but rising annually at a rate fixed as a percentage of the rate of growth of the average or median income of the nation or community; for example, the standard would be increased by one-half the rate at which national income per head had increased since the time of the original stipulation. (The relation of the relative uplift of the poverty standard to the relative growth of average income was called, by

Theodore W. Schultz, the "society's income-elasticity of demand for services to the poor.")

5) One might agree periodically to adjust the standard of poor living to the standard of average living according to the social sentiment of the time, which could be more charitable or less charitable than it had been earlier but would most likely be increasingly generous; the upward adjustment of the poverty line would probably be between those indicated by methods 3 and 4.

Economic historians may find out what poverty lines were drawn or proposed at various times in various countries and compare them with estimates of average or median incomes (per family, household, or head) at these times and places. This might reveal some regularity in the relative differences between the poor and the average or median. (I understand that such a study has been made for New York City.) One should not expect, however, such regularity to be anything but rough, since the judgments about "subsistence levels" differ widely at any one time. For the United States today, some would reduce the poverty line to $2,000 per year for a family of four, others would raise it above the $3,000 proposed by the Council of Economic Advisers.

One-third, One-eighth, One-fifth

In the mid-1930's we used to speak of the ill-fed, ill-housed, and ill-clad, and we referred to them as the "underprivileged *third*." If the household budget that marked this poverty line had remained unchanged, merely being adjusted for the price changes of the last 30 years, we would be able to speak today only of the "underprivileged *eighth*." But we have adjusted the poverty line to a rising standard of living; as real national income per head increased, we have lifted the poverty line, if only by a smaller percentage. With the higher standard of poor living, we are invited—by the President's Council of Economic Advisers—to admit one-*fifth* of the household units to the class of the poor.

One may, of course, quarrel with the proposal of the $3,000 standard.[1] It fails to take account of the number of children in the family and, in concentrating on annual income, it disregards accumulated savings or property as well as the possibility of borrowing against future income. Of the $3,000 budget, regarded as the poverty line for a family, some $800 was taken to be the need for housing. Yet, 40 per cent of the poor households in 1962 had some equity in houses and therefore could meet part of their budget without drawing on current cash income. But I must stop haggling, lest you think I am a heartless reactionary.

War on Poverty

Only a relatively rich society can expect to wage a successful war against poverty. Where almost all the people are poor, the incomes of the few rich are not sufficient to alleviate poverty significantly by redistribution or to reduce poverty significantly through services raising the productivity of the poor.

In an affluent society, *redistributive, remedial,* and *preventive* measures are possible. Where as little as two or three per cent of the national income would suffice to supplement all low incomes and bring them up above the poverty line, poverty can undoubtedly be eliminated. This is especially easy to accomplish where society has been wasting financial and productive resources on useless programs and thus can achieve its purpose simply by putting good programs in the place of bad ones.

The United States is in this position and, hence, can win its war against poverty. We cannot, of course, do this in a *Blitzkrieg,* within a few weeks, but we can do it within a few years if we go about it in the right way.

Before one can reasonably examine the potential effectiveness of anti-poverty measures, one must examine the major characteristics of the poor. This has been done in several statistical studies, and we know now quite well that the chances of being poor are especially high for the aged, the disabled, the nonwhite, the uneducated, the families without male breadwinners, the Southern farmers. If a family suffers from several of these misfortunes at the same time—say, a family headed by an uneducated nonwhite farmer in the South—its chance of being poor becomes almost a certainty.

This does not mean that poverty can be eliminated in the shortest time if government tackles first the problem of those groups in which the incidence of poverty is highest. Assume, for example, a particular group in the country has an incidence of poverty of 75 per cent. To concentrate on this group may be called for on several grounds, but even the most effective measures can do little for the elimination of poverty in the nation if the particular group is very small. If this group represents, say, only 2 or 3 per cent of all the poor, complete elimination of poverty in that group would reduce poverty in the country by only 2 or 3 per cent. In the evaluation of a program to reduce poverty in the nation both criteria must therefore be observed: how high is the *incidence* of poverty in a group for which certain measures are designed, and how large is the *share* of that group in the entire population of the poor.

Three Main Problems

If I may step back a little further from the statistical record presented by several investigators, I find it convenient to distinguish three main problems.

1) the problem of substandard earnings of employed persons;
2) the problem of unemployment of persons in the labor force; and
3) the problem of zero-earnings of persons not in the labor force.

This breakdown has the advantage of logical consistency: the member of the first group is in the labor force and has a job—but it pays too little; the member of the second group is in the labor force—but has no job; the member of the third group is not even in the labor force. This breakdown also helps us understand why some measures cannot solve all three problems. Higher unemployment benefits, for example, can help neither the first nor the third of these groups. Nor can full-employment policies help those who are permanently outside the labor force. (Let me mention that 39 per cent of all poor families in 1963 were headed by persons not in the labor force.) On the other hand, direct assistance to the poor, say, through cash payments, can help all three groups, although this may not be regarded as adequately remedial or preventive.

It may be useful to describe various types of measures that have been adopted or proposed to deal with poverty, that is, to relieve, to remedy, or to prevent poverty.

Distinctions

The usual distinction between *redistributive measures* and *measures increasing the earning power of the poor* misses some essential points. First of all, if the cost of measures to increase the earning power of the poor is paid by the rich, these measures are also redistributive; the difference singled out for attention is, evidently, whether the redistribution takes the form of transfer payments and/or relief in kind, supplementing the income earned by the poor, *or* of paying for actions that raise the market value produced, and hence the income earned, by the poor. Secondly, the usual distinction indiscriminately puts into the second category—raising the earning power—two economically different measures: those which really increase the *productive capacity* of the poor and those which merely raise, by subsidies or restrictions, the *market prices* of the products made with the labor of the poor. "Earning power" can be raised in both ways, but subsidies and other price supports must not be confused with increased efficiency.

To take account of these differences we should distinguish the following categories: (1) income supplements (relief, direct assistance), (2) income increases through indirect subsidies and restrictive and protective measures, (3) income increases through better use of the productive capacities of the people, (4) income increases through improvements of their productive capacities, and (5) income increases through measures to raise the aggregate demand for labor by means of general monetary expansion. Some of these categories should be further subdivided in order to bring out significant differences in approach. I believe that a catalogue of types of measures adopted or proposed in the war against poverty will help our discussion.

TYPES OF ADOPTED OR PROPOSED MEASURES
AGAINST POVERTY

A) *Direct Assistance*
   1) in kind—housing, food, clothing, medical care
   2) in cash—
      (a) for particular occupations
      (b) for particular industries
      (c) for particular age groups
      (d) for disabled or handicapped persons
      (e) for the "poor" regardless of group
      (f) for low-income recipients without property (negative tax)

B) *Indirect Assistance through Subsidies or Protection to Particular Industries, Occupations, or Regions*
      (a) through price supports
      (b) through limitations of domestic competition (entry, minimum prices, etc.)
      (c) through limitations of foreign competition (tariffs, quotas, etc.)
      (d) through cash subsidies of various sorts

C) *Abolition of Discriminatory Exclusions from Jobs* (i.e., preventing discrimination on account of age, sex, race, color, nationality, ethnic origin, religion, and so forth)

D) *Abolition of Restrictive Laws and Practices Which Reduce Employment Opportunities* (especially for low-grade labor), including the abolition of
   1) (a) legal minimum wages
       (b) trade-union minimum wages
       (c) conventional minimum wages (employers' inhibitions)
   2) regressive employment taxes, pension contributions, and other deductions from wages
   3) restrictions of access to better jobs (direct barriers or wage contracts limiting the amount of labor demanded)

E) *Raising the Productivity of Low-Grade Labor* (both of poorly paid or of unemployed)
   1) Provision of complementary facilities (roads, factories in distress areas; loans to farmers and small business)
   2) Better job information, loans and assistance in moving
   3) Increasing skills (employability) through adult education, training, retraining

F) *Raising the Productivity of Future Recruits to the Labor Force*
   1) Family-planning assistance
   2) Prenatal and postnatal care
   3) Adding years of schooling (especially at ages 3 to 6)
   4) Preventing dropouts from school
   5) Accelerating and improving school programs
   6) Job corps for dropouts and high-school graduates
   7) Work experience for new entrants into the labor force
   8) Work-study programs in higher education
   9) Aid to education on all levels

G) *Increasing Aggregate Demand through Monetary Expansion*—especially
   1) Increased government spending
   2) Reduced taxes
   3) Increased credit availability to business and consumers

General Appraisal

Measures of types A and B in this catalogue are direct and indirect assistance; the measures of type B are likely to involve inefficiencies in the allocation of productive resources. Types C and D are measures which lead to a better use of available human resources, by making jobs available that do not exist at present (for example, jobs for unskilled, low-quality labor) and by making *better* jobs available to persons now forced to work below their productive capacity. Types E and F are measures designed to raise the productivity of our manpower—type E the productivity of persons now in the labor force, type F of persons joining the labor force in the future. Type G is not a specific measure against poverty, but rather a remedy in the nature of a cure-all. Let me note that many economists question its effectiveness in the long run, even if they recognize that it may work well for short periods. We shall have more to say about all seven strategies in the war on poverty.

There is only one way to appraise a program intelligently: to examine its benefits (to ask, especially, whether it is likely to achieve the results intended) and to examine its costs (both the directly measurable and those that are concealed as unintended and undesirable side-effects). If one of two measures which can achieve an intended result has more unintended, undesirable side-effects than the other, it ought to be rejected.

Direct Assistance

Measures of Type A, direct assistance to the poor, are, as a rule, the most immediately effective and involve the lowest cost—provided they are not discriminatory, and really go to the poor, not to others. This proviso is usually not satisfied in the case of *assistance in kind*. It is in the nature of housing programs, medical care programs, etc., that they are discriminatory and indiscriminate at the same time: discriminatory in the sense that they do not benefit all poor groups, and indiscriminate in the sense that they benefit many that are not poor and need no help. Some of the programs may degenerate into rackets.

Cash assistance can perhaps be more easily identified and controlled. But, if certain groups are politically powerful, they may attain favored positions at the expense of the rest, including the really poor. This is notorious in the case of assistance to particular industries, which always starts with appeals that the members of the industry are intolerably poor, but usually ends up with a rich flow of cash into well-lined pockets. As a prototype, we may refer to our farm program: it is true that many, perhaps most, of the 3,500,000 farmers in the United States are poor; but it is also true that 80 per cent of the direct and indirect assistance under that program goes to 1,000,000 farmers with an average income of almost $10,000 a year, and that only the remaining 20 per cent of the assistance goes to the 2,500,000 poorer farmers.

The only really efficient cash-assistance programs are the ones that help *only* the poor and help *all* the poor, regardless of industry and of occupation. Assistance for the poor farmer should be given, not because he is a farmer, but only because he is poor. For administrative reasons, the proposal of the "negative income tax" is probably the most efficient of all such programs. Just as we use the system of exemptions—$600 per person—to free families with low incomes from all income tax obligations, we may under the proposed system make persons whose income is farther below these exemptions eligible to receive payments from the Internal Revenue Service. They would receive checks from the Government just as those who have overpaid their income tax receive checks as refunds. Perhaps their asset holdings could be taken into account—because we may not wish that wealthy people whose annual income may be negative, counting losses from capital transactions, get a bonus—though the total amount of such negative tax payments to the wealthy may be negligible.

Indirect Assistance

Measures of Type B are ordinarily stupid or wicked, from the point of view of economic welfare, and are almost certainly wasteful. They cost the nation much more than they benefit those whom they favor and, since the beneficiaries include many nonpoor, the cost to the nation is a multiple of the benefit to the poor. Thus, if the producers and workers in any line of production, be it in agriculture or in the manufacturing of watch movements or bicycles, obtain an increase in their "earning power," this is achieved by making their products scarcer (more expensive) to domestic consumers and by using productive resources less efficiently than it would be possible. While virtually nothing good can be said about subsidization or protection to particular industries, the case for particular depressed geographic areas is not entirely open and shut. *Ex ante* some persuasive arguments in terms of deviations of social from private benefits and costs can be made for area development or rehabilitation—but *ex post* things usually look disappointing. Experience, on balance, has not been good.

Abolishing Discrimination

Type C measures would get high marks from this professor if their cost—in resources and in individual freedoms—is not excessive. Since the costs may be only temporary, but the benefits permanent, the net yield of a breakdown of discriminatory barriers may be very high. If the barriers can be removed by noncoercive measures, by using incentives rather than police force, even the temporary cost can be reduced. But one should also bear in mind that the cost of inaction or delayed action against discrimination may be high—indeed, terribly high—in resources, freedoms, and even in blood. Some well-meaning defenders of civil liberties in the battle for civil rights, and of personal freedoms in the battle for nondiscrimination, should note that it is wiser to hold one's nose and take distasteful medicine than to die in upholding the principle of nonintervention.

Abolishing Restraints on Job Opportunities

In explaining my position regarding measures of Type D, I shall probably arouse the anger of many allies in the war against poverty, especially the noneconomists in the field of labor economics. For they often believe that restrictive laws and practices which set a floor under the wage rates of various categories of labor, especially under the pay for the lowest grades of labor, are measures against poverty. I submit that, on the contrary, the *abolition* of these restrictions would be among the effective measures in the war against poverty.

To explain this, I may resort to an analogy. Assume there are two types of coal of different caloric content; in a free market, high-calory coal will fetch a higher price, corresponding to the difference in technical efficiency. Assume now that, for reasons good or bad, a minimum price is fixed, raising the price for the poorer coal. The reduction of the price difference will undoubtedly reduce the demand for the low-grade coal, and some portion of the supply will remain unused. The chief beneficiaries will be the producers of the high-calory coal. Similarly, if there are two types of labor, wage differentials in a free labor market would reflect differences in productivity. If a minimum wage is fixed, raising the rate for the lower-grade labor, the wage differential is reduced, the demand for the low-grade labor decreases, and some portion of it remains unemployed. While those finding employment are paid better, the jobless earn nothing at all. Their potential product is lost to society and their potential earnings are lost to the poor.

Minimum wages, although demanded in the name of helping the poor, in effect create more unemployment and more poverty. Perhaps they can be regarded as examples of the notorious attitude of the well-to-do man who, facing a poor beggar at the door of his house, says to his butler: "He breaks my heart, throw him out!" In a more realistic interpretation, the minimum-wage constraint is an example of restraint of competition, since, in reducing the employability of low-grade workers, it shelters nonpoor workers against competition from poor workers.

My argument is not directed at legal minimum wages alone. Even if there were no such laws, and no trade union contracts either, there still might be minimum wages by social convention. Employers, ordinarily, prefer paying higher wages for higher-grade labor to employing low-grade labor at very low wages, because it is bad public relations to pay less than a "living wage." Businessmen do not want to be known as employers of labor at substandard pay. These inhibitions restrict employment of poor labor and thus contribute to unemployment and poverty. Society stands to gain by the disappearance of such inhibitions. If very low wages paid to poor labor leave these workers too poor, society can supplement their family earnings by means of a negative income tax. This is not a recommendation of subsidies paid to the employers of substandard labor, but only of income supplements paid to poor families. Subsidies would lead to inefficient uses of labor; moreover, where families include several wage earners, such subsidies might accrue to nonpoor families. Hence we conclude: income supplements to the poor—yes; subsidies to their employers—no.

The second item under D refers to regressive deductions from wages and regressive taxes on the employment of cheap labor. Social-security contributions, falling more heavily on low-paid labor than on well-paid labor, may be the unintended product of thoughtless legislators, but in any event they operate to reduce the earnings and the employment of poor workers. The abolition of such provisions in the laws would be a measure reducing poverty.

The third item under D is of greater significance. It refers to existing restrictions on the access to better-paid jobs, forcing many more workers to compete for jobs of lower grade than would be the case if more could be employed as skilled labor. The restrictions are of two sorts: (1) direct barriers through apprenticeship rules in various crafts, limited admission into trade unions, and similar exclusions, and (2) indirect barriers through wage contracts between unions and employers making labor costs so high that the amount of labor demanded is smaller than the amount of labor available.

Indirect barriers are rarely understood. Just as price-fixing businessmen often wrongly assume that the demand for their products is completely inelastic, so the wage-fixing trade-union officers believe that the number of jobs is "given," regardless of the cost of labor. This is a tragic error; in fact, practically every collective wage contract eliminates jobs. The workers thus excluded from better-paying employment are compelled to join less qualified workers in the market for jobs requiring lesser skills. If wage rates are similarly fixed for these jobs, increasing numbers of workers are pushed into markets for unskilled labor. The supply of labor in these markets is then far greater than it would be with unrestricted access to the better jobs.

It may be impossible to produce testable estimates of the number of jobs eliminated by restrictions of these sorts, but few trained economists will deny that the problem may be of serious magnitude. The responsibility for the reduction of job opportunities cannot even approximately be divided between a minimum wage setting an absolute floor for labor of any sort, and contractual wage rates for certain kinds of labor in particular industries. Given the latter, with the resulting reduction in the number of well-paying jobs, the minimum wage could be assigned most of the blame for unemployment. However, if none of the wages for higher grades of labor were fixed above competitive levels, and if, therefore, many more people could obtain better jobs and would not flood the market for low-grade labor, the employment-reducing effect of the minimum wage at the present level might be insignificant. A strong emphasis on the minimum wage as a cause of unemployment and poverty is justified only on the assumption that a successful attack on contractual wage fixing is probably out of the question.

A Digression on an Apparent Paradox

In my appraisal of various policies I endorsed the proposal of a negative income tax for the poor but condemned the adopted practice of setting minimum wages. The negative income tax, by providing "transfer incomes" to persons without earned incomes, would probably reduce the eagerness of some of these persons to seek or accept work. Is it not inconsistent to approve of a plan that would induce some people to remain idle, and to reject a widely approved device of preventing people from working for less than a "decent" rate of pay? Both these schemes reduce the total amount of work performed, and their different evaluation may look paradoxical.

The paradox is only apparent, for there is an essential difference between the two schemes. To offer a "social minimum" for no work is to increase the choices of some persons: the very lazy ones may prefer to enjoy leisure and collect the negative tax rather than work and earn an income. To forbid work for less than a "minimum wage" is to reduce the choices of some persons: the very unskilled ones might prefer to work for low wages rather than remain idle because payments of such wages is prohibited. In other words, the social minimum (the negative income tax) may increase voluntary leisure; the minimum wage increases involuntary idleness. Voluntary leisure is a "good," while forced idleness is an evil.

Raising the Productivity of Labor

Labor can be made more employable by lowering its price or by raising its productivity. There are essentially three ways of doing the latter: to give it better tools and facilities, to move it to places and occupations in which it can do better than where it is now, and to increase its physical and mental performance. The first of these types of measures involves investment in physical capital, the third, investment in "human capital." All investment, of course, is risky: the return is uncertain and it is easy to make mistakes.

The provision of complementary facilities in the form of highways, factories, and modern equipment by the government or with financial aid from the government is advocated especially for the development or rehabilitation of distress areas. We must keep in mind that capital is not abundant and greater allocations to one area imply smaller allocations to others. The only justification for such reshuffling is that the return, counting all benefits, is thereby increased. Advance calculations often contain serious fallacies and wrong estimates; and even where everything looks all right, the actual outcome is ordinarily far less favorable than what had been anticipated. This is not an argument against all regional investment programs, but a warning that many projects have been wasteful from their very conception and even more of them have been both wasteful and ineffective in their execution.

Whereas the record of programs of bringing productive facilities to areas of surplus labor has been discouraging, experience with programs of facilitating the movement of surplus labor to regions and occupations where it can be more efficiently employed has been good. Better information about job opportunities is a prerequisite for the improved use of labor, and the provision of loans or other assistance in moving may be necessary if the information is to be used to full advantage.

Investment in human capital in the form of improved skills may pay off handsomely if the right techniques are used. The proposed programs under this heading emphasize training, retraining, and general adult education. Some programs, providing specialized vocational training, have been quite ineffective because they trained people for nonexisting jobs. Other programs, for example, improving the reading and writing abilities of quasi-illiterates, have had very good results. By and large, the enthusiasm with which some local and national programs have been launched merits approval and ought not to be doused with excessive skepticism.

Raising the Productivity of Future Workers

Programs designed to raise the productivity of *present* members of the labor force who are unemployable at the minimum wage or whose earning capacity is too low to put them above the poverty line, are *remedial* strategies in the war on poverty. In contrast, programs designed to raise the productivity of *future* recruits to the labor force are *preventive*. Viewed as investment in human capital, these programs are more long-term in character, but their return is not for that matter more uncertain. The point is, rather, that the flow of income produced by retraining a person of age 40 or so is surely of shorter duration than the flow of income produced by improved education of the young. To raise the lifetime earnings of future members of the labor force is an opportunity for a social investment with a high yield.

This does not mean that all projects under this heading are equally promising. The most meritorious seem to be (1) family-planning assistance, (2) prenatal and postnatal care, and (3) schooling for children at ages 3 to 5.

The incidence of poverty is very high among large families, especially if the poverty line is redrawn to take account of nutritive adequacy. Since children in oversized families are more likely to be undernourished and undereducated, planned parenthood, in avoiding excessive numbers of neglected children, can reduce the percentage of substandard members in the labor force of the future.

Mental retardation is responsible for a large share of the number of those whose earning power is small or nil. Prenatal and postnatal care can do much to reduce the incidence of mental deficiency.

Adding a few years of schooling has been proposed by many as a measure for raising the productivity of the next generation. Many school reformers, however, propose to add the years at the wrong end, at ages 15 to 18 instead of 3 to 6. Schooling ought to be provided at the earliest age, when systematic mental stimulation can still do something to increase the capacity of the mind. Children thus prepared will be able to absorb much more of what they are taught later.

Programs to prevent dropouts from school are rather useless under the present system. Many of those who leave school at ages 15 or 16, insufficiently prepared for work, would not be much better prepared if forced or persuaded to stay in school for another two or three years.

They will only be bored, resentful, hateful, rebellious against a society that keeps them against their will from a more active, more useful life. As Michael Harrington said yesterday, these dropouts know that school cannot do anything for them any more and they have enough sense to get out. It is a shame that so many virtuous educators and educationalists do not have enough sense to know how little they can help the would-be dropout by chaining him to the school bench. If schooling started at ages 3 or 4, there would be fewer wanting to quit school at age 14 or 15, and those who quit would be better prepared than if they stayed in school until 18 under the present system.

Acceleration and other improvements of school programs rank high in my list of promising measures. I said "acceleration and *other* improvements," because I contend that acceleration is *per se* one of the most potent improvements of education. Compression of the curriculum, requiring more concentrated learning, develops better working habits as well as better-trained minds. Perhaps I may refer you to my book on *The Production and Distribution of Knowledge in the United States*, in which I argued this case.

I am inclined to endorse the plans for "job corps" for dropouts and high-school graduates, and the plans to provide work experience for new entrants into the labor force. We do not know yet whether the hopes of the proponents will be fulfilled, at least in part, but again these are projects attractive to people inspired by a will to help others without taking excessive amounts of public funds. I am sympathetic with the enthusiasm that fills the job corps workers, and I want them to succeed.

All in all, I regard measures to raise the productivity of future recruits to the labor force as promising strategies in the war on poverty.

Increasing Aggregate Demand

Some very excellent economists argue that the most powerful policy against poverty is to create enough "effective demand" to secure "full employment" and a faster growth rate. Increased aggregate demand for goods and services is easily translated into demand for more labor of all sorts, and this means more employment as well as higher earnings of the employed.

Advocates of more spending by private business and consumers favor either a monetary policy of increasing the availability of credit or a fiscal policy of tax reduction. Advocates of more spending by government favor a fiscal policy of enlarged budgets. Opponents of the strategy of "spending one's way out of unemployment and poverty" are suspicious of a tendency to regard the creation of effective demand as a cureall and fearful of possible inflationary effects, and sometimes also neurotically fearful of the increase in the public debt.

Real deficiencies in effective demand undoubtedly call for compensatory increases in spending. Such deficiencies may be viewed as absolute reductions in total spending or as reductions relative to the size of the labor force (or, alternatively, total population). It has become fashionable, however, to diagnose all lapses from full employment as demand deficiency and/or to prescribe demand creation as the therapy for every case of unemployment. Many of those who quarrel about whether, or to what extent, unemployment is due to "structural causes" or to "demand deficiency" overlook that structural unemployment may be cured by demand creation and that demand deficiency may be offset by structural adjustments. (The demand for labor, as for anything else, is elastic with respect to changes in both relative prices and aggregate income.) The more reasonable participants in the controversy, however, do not deny either the existence of "structural causes" of unemployment or the possibility of reducing unemployment through "structural adjustments," but they hold that reductions in wage rates cannot be arranged whereas increases in spending can be arranged quite easily. This is a straightforward policy recommendation without a cloak of pseudo-scientific analysis.

Some want to rely on demand creation as the sole strategy in the war on poverty. Professor Harry Johnson is a protagonist of this view:

> The key to the solution of the poverty problem . . . is not to try to educate and train the poor up to the point where someone will find them employable at a decent wage, but to raise demand so as to make labor scarce enough for it to be privately profitable to find a way of making the poor employable at a decent wage.

> But in the absence of a policy of raising the demand for labor to the stretching point, ad hoc policies for remedying poverty by piecemeal assaults on particular poverty-associated characteristics are likely to prove both ineffective and expensive.

This position is objectionable on several grounds:

1) Increases in the demand for labor "to the stretching point" will cause continuous increases in wage rates; employment will increase only as long as wage rates lag behind the increase in spending; but in advanced industrial countries this lag may become very short, zero, or even negative (in the sense that wages will rise faster than demand).

2) Even before the policy of monetary expansion becomes ineffective in reducing unemployment, political forces are likely to lead to its discontinuance, with the result that unemployment will vary "cyclically" without being reduced in the long run.

3) The increase in consumer prices effected by the creation of monetary demand for goods and services will reduce the purchasing power of the dollar and make the low incomes of the poor still less adequate.

4) Even if the policy of creating effective demand were to succeed in more than temporary increases in the rate of employment and in continual increases in the real incomes of the employed, it still could not be the sole weapon in combating poverty. For it would do nothing to relieve the poverty of families with no member in the labor force—and this means 39 per cent of all poor families. (As a matter of fact, higher consumer prices would make them still poorer.)

On the fourth point, a qualification is called for regarding persons who are outside the labor force only because they have given up hope of finding employment, but would rejoin the labor force when jobs became easier to find. This possibility would not exist for the disabled, the aged, the women with small children, and hence the qualification may be relatively insignificant.

If I reject full-employment policy through demand creation as the sole anti-poverty measure, this should not stigmatize me as a "deflationist." I have no doubt that the fiscal and monetary policies of the United States were unduly restrictive at times and that more expansionary policies during these periods would have helped to reduce poverty.

No Single Strategy

The conclusion of my evaluation of policies is clear: the war on poverty cannot be won with a single strategy but must be fought on several fronts and with several strategies. Some of the policies adopted are actually harmful and ought to be abolished; some of the policies proposed but never tried look quite promising and ought to be adopted; and some of the policies initiated may prove useful and ought to be continued.

The war on poverty is of course not without cost, and all measures should be subjected to judicious cost-benefit analyses. In such analyses a strict distinction must be made between the adoption of a new project *in lieu* of an existing one and the adoption of a new project *on top* of the existing ones. There may be a huge difference in the respective findings, since the substitution of a better project for a weak one may have a great payoff, whereas the addition of even an excellent project to all existing ones may run into the difficulties of rapidly increasing costs. Since among the existing programs there are some rather ineffectual ones with high costs and low benefits, new projects in lieu of others stand a chance for a high mark in even a very strict examination. Some of the programs proposed in the war on poverty may have a net yield for the nation of really spectacular magnitude *if* their adoption can be linked with the abolition of some of the existing programs of support and protection for particular groups.

Note

1) For a severe criticism of this standard, see Rose D. Friedman, *Poverty: Definition and Perspective* (Washington: American Enterprise Institute, 1965). Using the same general principles as were used in the studies on which the Council of Economic Advisers based the poverty line of $3,000, Mrs. Friedman computes a set of poverty lines, stating the "income levels at which households of different size achieve adequate nutrition" at 1962 prices. These are $1,295, $1,785, $2,195, $2,550, $2,855, and $3,155 for nonfarm households with 2, 3, 4, 5, 6, and 7 or more persons, respectively (p. 25). On this basis, only one-tenth of the households is poor. Yet, according to Mrs. Friedman, the difference "results neither from a different basic criterion of adequate nutrition nor from the use of different data. The high estimate by the Council results from the crudity of its analysis" (p. 46).

to secure the

In general terms, the blessings of liberty are twofold, consisting of the *freedom from* constraint and oppression and the *freedom to* develop and mature.[1] The nature of the constraints and oppression from which Americans wish to be free are discussed in the first section of this introduction. Some of the undesired constraints and oppression stem from sources outside of the individual and some from sources within him. The directions in which Americans want the freedom to develop are also discussed. Special attention is given to conceptions of the character of mature relationships to work and leisure and to one's fellowman. The second section turns to the problem of securing the blessings of liberty; it examines factors which help determine which, if any, of the blessings of liberty can be secured in contemporary America. Attention is focused upon the role played by the social environment in freeing the individual from constraints and in encouraging him to develop.

The Blessings of Liberty

To many Americans the primary blessing of liberty is the freedom from the constraints and oppression which governments can visit upon indi-

---

[1] The distinction between "the freedom from" and "the freedom to" is based upon that made in Erich Fromm, *The Escape from Freedom* (New York: Farrar and Rinehart, 1941), see especially Chaps. 1, 2, 4, and 7.

Blessings of Liberty . . .

viduals. For example, they regard the absence of religious and political oppression as among the main benefits of living in a free society. In particular, freedom from penalties and prison terms imposed by government because of an individual's religion or politics is generally regarded as a primary blessing of liberty. Government is not, however, the only source of constraint and oppression; traditionalism and psychological barriers also engender constraint.

A man who can only do as his forefathers did is no more free than one who can only do as his government decrees. The stifling of departures from the ways of the past can be as oppressive as the punishment of deviations from the party or government line. By and large Americans have rejected traditionalism in favor of the judging of an idea or practice on its pragmatic merits. The resulting freedom from tradition is another of the blessings of liberty which Americans seek to secure.

Americans also wish to be free from their own personal anxieties and insecurity, their fears and prejudices. They recognize, as psychologists and psychiatrists have discovered, that a man's choice can be constrained by his own unwillingness or inability to consider an alternative. The insecure man who fears the responsibilities which a promotion will bring may have no more real freedom of occupational choice than one who is told by government or tradition to "keep in his (rightful, lowly) place."

Similarly, persons who do not know of an alternative to their present practices or who are too prejudiced to give it serious consideration are just as constrained from taking that alternative as people warned not to do so.

The blessings of liberty are not only defined in terms of what the individual is to be free from, they are also defined in terms of what one is free to develop and mature into. American views on what constitutes maturity have greatly changed within the last several decades as America itself has changed from a society dominated by individual entrepreneurs, with their philosophy of economic, political, and social laissez-faire, to one characterized by the corporate bureaucrat and the regulated economy of the welfare state.[2] The essential differences between the two conceptions of maturity lie in their views of man's relationship to work and leisure and to his fellowman.[3]

The older conception of the fully developed or mature man is that of a person who regards the degree of success he attains at work as the true measure of his personal merit. He is a man who constantly seeks to develop his work-related talents and to live up to his own high standards of performance. He is more concerned with achievements on the job than with the comforts he can secure for himself and his family. Productivity is valued more than consumption. Relaxation and leisure activities are viewed as necessary evils to be kept at a minimum. They merely distract one from his work. Competition and exploitation are regarded as more basic and more prevalent than cooperation and nurturance, and relations to others are based on their instrumental value or utility. Moreover, human needs and emotions are seen either as tools to be used or obstacles to be overcome as the individual strives to live up to his standards of performance. Independent, individual thought and labor are expected to be more fruitful than the work of a committee; dependence on others is avoided in favor of self-reliance. Within the older conception, the chief blessing of liberty is the freedom to become an effective, independent, and self-reliant member of the world of work—the world of business and finance.[4]

---

[2] Some observers contend that the change from entrepreneurial to bureaucratic capitalism not only accompanied but influenced changes in the conceptions of maturity. See, for example, Daniel R. Miller and Guy E. Swanson, *The Changing American Parent* (New York: Wiley, 1958).

[3] It should be noted that the "individual" generally referred to in the discussions of what constitutes the mature person is a white male of the middle or upper-middle class. Members of other groups may, however, be judged by these standards and be expected to live up to them as well as by special codes developed by or for them.

[4] The description of the older conception of maturity is based on the accounts of the character of the "inner-directed man," "the adherent to the Protestant Ethic,"

The newer conception of the fully developed or mature man is that of a person who regards his ability to perform and enjoy leisure activities as much a reflection of his personal qualities as success at work. He seeks both to play well and to "make it" on the job. His job is viewed as an expedient: the means by which one earns the money to finance family and leisure activities. The comforts he and his family secure yield as much satisfaction as does success on the job. Consumption is on a par with productivity. Leisure time is jealously guarded against the intrusions of the office. Cooperation or teamwork is regarded as basic to all human endeavor. Moreover, the social context is seen as giving meaning and value to the actions of individuals—social interaction provides the cues for understanding what he has done. What is proper or valued in one social situation is known to be improper or undesirable in another. One charges his employer for his services, but not his family. The act which is regarded as courageous resistance in one setting is foolish obstinacy in another. Alone, man is thought to be insecure, lost in the ambiguity of a varied and changing social world. Where possible, isolation is avoided in favor of interaction. Within the newer conception, the blessings of liberty include the freedom to develop into a well-rounded person, effective at work, at play, and in the home, and the freedom to develop the social relations which give meaning to life.[5] "Neo-Freudian Views of Maturity and Bureaucratic Norms" by Rosabeth Moss Kanter examines the similarities between two versions of the newer conception of maturity, namely, the popularized interpretation of the neo-Freudian view of man and the view of man encouraged by bureaucratic norms. "The Hang-Loose Ethic" by J. L. Simmons and Barry Winograd examines another variant of the newer conception of maturity.

Securing the Blessings of Liberty

The problem of securing the blessings of liberty has two components: first, the conditions which free the individual from constraints and oppression must be secured; and second, conditions must be created which encourage the individual to take advantage of the absence of barriers to further his own development and maturation.

---

and the "individuated-entrepreneur" in, respectively, David Riesman, Nathan Glazer, and Reuel Denney, *The Lonely Crowd* (Garden City, N.Y.: Doubleday, 1955); William H. Whyte, *The Organization Man* (Garden City, N.Y.: Doubleday, 1957); and Miller and Swanson, *op. cit.*

[5] The description of the newer conception of maturity is based on the accounts of the "other-directed man," "the organization man," and the "welfare-bureaucrat" in, respectively, Riesman, Glazer, and Denney, *op. cit.*; Whyte, *op. cit.*; and Miller and Swanson, *op. cit.*

374 ≈ *To Secure the Blessings of Liberty*

There are, as indicated in the first section, essentially three shackles that free men seek to avoid: the shackles of government control, of tradition, and of their own personal inadequacies. The factors which help Americans to avoid each of these limits on their freedom will be examined in turn.

The main source of the individual American's protection against oppression by government is, of course, the preservation of democracy —the preservation of the power of the electorate to remove the leaders of government from office. Should the persons in office become oppressive, they can be removed from power at the next election and thus deprived of the means to oppress. Moreover, knowledge of the power of the electorate deters officials from taking an oppressive action lest it lose them votes needed to remain in power. Thus, democratic elections provide both a means to end tyranny and a way to prevent it.

The preservation of the power of the electorate, in turn, is dependent upon the continued existence of social pluralism. Pluralism exists in a society to the extent that power is divided among a number of relatively autonomous groups or social organizations.

The existence of social pluralism helps preserve the power of the electorate in several ways. First, powerful organizations help like-minded individuals to influence and even resist the power of government. They can do this between elections,[6] thus mitigating any tendency toward oppression before it gets so strong that the next election is canceled, as it has been in other countries. Second, the existence of a plurality of powerful groups makes it possible to oppose those in power by making it possible for those out of office to find alternate sources of support and by encouraging the dissemination of information and opinion upon which to base an opposition campaign. In short, pluralism helps prevent one party "elections" from becoming the dominant American practice. Other ways in which social pluralism helps preserve democracy are discussed in "Why Pluralism Is Necessary" by Robert A. Dahl and Charles Lindbloom.

[6] The role of strong, secondary organizations in preserving a pluralistic political community is discussed by Riesman, Glazer, and Denney, *op. cit.*, pp. 246–251 and 254–258, who refer to the power of "veto groups." C. Wright Mills, *The Power Elite* (New York: Oxford University Press, 1956), questions the ability of contemporary veto or power groups to protect the individual from government. The positions taken by Riesman, Glazer, and Denney and by Mills are compared in William Kornhauser, "'Power Elite' or 'Veto Groups,'" in Richard L. Simpson and Ida H. Simpson (eds.), *Social Organization and Behavior* (New York: Wiley, 1964), pp. 199–208. See also V. O. Key, *Politics, Parties and Pressure Groups*, 5th ed. (New York: Crowell, 1964), from which the selection in Chapter Two is taken. The article by Pilisuk and Hayden in Chapter Five challenges the differing positions of Mills and Riesman, Glazer and Denney.

Pluralism is not, however, a perfect guarantor of democracy. Indeed, as Joseph R. Gusfield argues, in "Mass Society and Extremist Politics," under certain conditions it may induce some groups to abandon democratic procedures and to threaten democracy itself.[7] Such threats may be counterbalanced, as Gusfield suggests, by the impact of the mass culture of contemporary America.

In any event, the individual American is protected from governmental constraint and oppression not only by democracy, but by the prevailing system of law. Within that system, the individual who can demonstrate that government actions with respect to his case are illegal can prevent their occurrence and reassert his freedom from their constraining or oppressive influence. Anti-government pickets who show that the police had no right to stop their demonstration become free from a constraint on their right to express their views. Similarly, the property owner who proves that the government has no grounds on which to condemn his house is free from that threat to his home. In short, a system of law that binds and regulates the actions of government frees the individual from the constraints and oppression which the forbidden actions might visit upon him.[8]

American law also protects the individual from government action by guarding his right to privacy. The law regulates and limits the means by which government can discover what it is an individual has done. Without such knowledge the government cannot harass those who oppose it. Totalitarian regimes, on the other hand, unhampered by a concern for the individual's right to privacy, often establish elaborate systems for monitoring the private acts and conversations of its citizens. In the past, these systems have relied heavily on human informers, even to the point of asking children to inform on their parents. However, with the development of a myriad of electronic listening devices, the reliance on human informers may diminish. Technological developments have, or may soon, come to a point where it is possible for government officials to monitor virtually everything one does. With the availability of listening devices, the main source of an individual's ability to maintain his privacy may, ironically, stem mainly from the adherence of government and

---

[7] Using the terms in the Preamble, Gusfield's argument is that, under certain conditions, a pluralistic system encourages or causes some groups to breach the civility or tranquillity of the society and thus threatens the democratic political union which secures the blessings of liberty.

[8] A history of the attempts of one group, The American Civil Liberties Union, to extend individual freedom by applying the law to governmental action is found in Charles Markmann, *The Noblest Cry* (New York: St. Martin's Press, 1965). See also Milton R. Konvitz, *Expanding Liberties: Freedom's Gain in Postwar America* (New York: Viking, 1966).

others to rules which define certain areas as off limits to them. Where "bugging" devices are readily available, a man's home is no more assuredly private than a booth in a restaurant. As in the restaurant, the privacy of an individual's conversations will then depend more on the reluctance of others to listen in than on any inability to do so.[9]

The individual can be free from the constraints and oppression of government where democratic elections prevail and where there is a system of law to protect him from arbitrary governmental action and to ensure his privacy. However, the free individual is also free from the tethers of tradition and the shackles of his own inadequacies.

The American freedom from traditionalism stems, first, from the high value which is placed on individualism. The individual is freed from having to follow the ways of the past because he is urged to be as different and unique as he wishes to be. The stress on individualism, in turn, has its roots in the religious and philosophical history of the country: in the Protestantism of its founders and their acceptance of the arguments of Locke and Rousseau. Paradoxically, the American freedom from traditionalism stems from its traditional support of individualism.

The rapid pace of technological and industrial development has also contributed to freedom from traditionalism. Such change has served to convince many that change in all areas of life is inevitable and even desirable; that blind adherence to the way of the past is impractical and self-defeating.

Freedom from one's own inadequacies, like freedom from government oppression and the yoke of traditionalism, has its sources in the social environment. The limitations of ignorance can be overcome if others can teach one what is known. Prejudice may vanish when social experience provides neither evidence for its validity nor support for its acceptance. Insecurity, which feeds on fear of the unknown, can be removed in an ordered and predictable social world. Science and religion help create such a world. In addition, where anxiety reflects a belief that harm cannot be prevented, alliance with powerful individuals and groups may encourage faith that the worst will not happen.

The social environment, then, may free the individual from internal

---

[9] The right to privacy and the threats to it posed by modern technology are discussed by Alan F. Westin, "Surveillance, Privacy and the Free Society," address presented at the Annual Meetings of the American Political Science Association, Washington, D.C., September, 1965, and summarized under the title "Is Privacy a Condition of Freedom?" *Current*, LXV (November, 1965), 14–16. See also "Privacy," *Law and Contemporary Problems*, XXXI (Spring, 1966), 251–435; and Alan F. Westin, "Science, Privacy and Freedom: Issues and Proposals for the 1970's; Part I—The Current Impact of Surveillance on Privacy," *Columbia Law Review*, LXVI (June, 1966), 1003–1050.

and external constraints. It may also encourage him to take advantage of his opportunity to develop and mature. As Marvin E. Olsen suggests, in "The Mature Society: Personal Autonomy and Social Responsibility," the existence of an elaborate division of labor in a society encourages its individual members to be concerned with the course of their personal development. An elaborate division of labor also increases the possibility that a person can choose a role in society which fits his own unique needs since the roles available are so numerous and so varied. Nevertheless, an elaborate division of labor is a mixed blessing. The resulting complexity of modern life and the increased reliance upon specialists to interpret that complexity may rob the individual of his sense of having a personal understanding of the world around him. The existence of many equally attractive lines of development may force the individual who is making a choice to painfully doubt and re-examine the standards and values which guide his selection. The increasing automation and fragmentation of work may deprive the individual of a sense of personal responsibility for the fruits of his labor. Thus, the same complex division of labor which induces the individual to be concerned with his own development and which makes it possible for him to develop his unique talents may also induce a degree of confusion, doubt, and alienation which threatens his development.[10] In either case, the social environment proves to be a powerful influence over the use an individual makes of the *freedom to* develop created by the *freedom from* the shackles of government and tradition.

[10] See Eric Josephson and Mary Josephson (eds.), *Man Alone: Alienation in Modern Society* (New York: Dell, 1962).

Neo-Freudian Views of Maturity and Bureaucratic Norms

ᴄ⟋⟍ᴐ

Rosabeth Moss Kanter

Two trends, the popularization of neo-Freudianism and the bureauc-
ratization of society, provide the basis for a definition of psychological
maturity in contemporary America. That is, individual behavior can be
judged both by the popularized version of neo-Freudianism[1] and the
norms of bureaucratic organizations.[2] Furthermore, there are important
similarities between the goals and standards outlined by the neo-Freudians, Horney, Fromm and Sullivan, and those encouraged by the norms
of bureaucratic organizations. The aim of this paper is to indicate these
similarities.

The first similarity between popularized neo-Freudianism and
bureaucratic norms is that both place a high value on rational or non-
emotional behavior. Indeed, in a general sense, the neo-Freudian view
holds rationality to be the goal of human development. That is, it holds
that the mature man is one who knows and controls the unconscious
impulses which impede his effective action. Similarly, the bureaucrat
seeks to overcome irrationality through knowing and controlling the
anxieties, hostilities and affectual involvements which threaten his effectiveness. The bureaucratic structure, as Merton put it, "is one which
approaches the complete elimination of personalized relationships and
nonrational considerations [such as] hostility, anxiety [and] affectual
involvements. . . ."[3]

Second, popularized neo-Freudianism and the norms of bureaucratic
organizations both regard social, rather than individual, factors as the root
causes of human failure. The neo-Freudians have translated the basic
antagonism between man's natural impulses and the requirements of

---

This article was prepared especially for this book.

civilized life posited by Freud[4] into the responsibility of society for producing mature men. It is society's duty, according to popularized neo-Freudianism, to replace man's unconscious antisocial impulses (which are no fault of his own) with civilized social tendencies. Society can work in the interests of man, and it is society's responsibility to do so. To paraphrase a common observation, there are no intentionally bad people, only bad socializing agents. "Society has failed the neurotic, never vice versa."[5] Fromm even suggests that societies be considered unhealthy, rather than the people in them.[6] Individual neurosis might, he suggests, be a "socially patterned defect."[7] Personal accountability is thereby diminished. Society, not the individual, is the basic source of a man's neuroses or failures.

Bureaucratic norms also shift responsibility for failure from the individual to the social organization. For example, the norms call for the use of standardized tests as the basis for assigning people to positions. Thus, failure in role performance becomes attributable to a mistaken assignment by the organization rather than the personal fault of the deficient individual. In addition, bureaucratic organizations take a statistical rather than a personal view of failure. They presume that there will be a certain number of imperfect goods manufactured and a certain turnover rate. Moreover, these "failures" are seen as being inherent in the nature of the organization and not the fault of particular individuals. Furthermore, bureaucracy limits personal accountability by providing clearly defined rules and routines. Mistakes can be attributed to defects in the rules such as a failure to take a given contingency into account. The rules, not the individual, are at fault. In general, individual behavior in a bureaucratic organization is regarded as a function of the setting in which one works, just as the behavior of people in general is explained by the culture and social structure into which they are born. The individual is not completely responsible for his actions, and that, according to the popular version of neo-Freudianism, is as it should be.

Third, both neo-Freudianism and the norms of bureaucratic organizations de-value and de-emphasize competition. In the neo-Freudian view, interpersonal conflict, especially that stemming from competition and rivalry, is at the root of many neuroses. According to Horney, for example, individual competition leads to the diffuse hostile tension and fear of failure often found in the neurotic.[8] The neurotic "constantly measures himself against others."[9] He wishes to be exceptional and superior, seeking his own success at the expense of others.[10] Moreover, even the victor may be anxious since there is always the possibility that someone more skilled than he will appear and triumph over him.[11]

Bureaucratic organizations also view the noncompetitive man more positively than the competitive one. The smooth running of the organization is enhanced by team-work. Loyalty to the system is stressed above individual rivalry. As Merton writes,

> bureaucratic . . . functionaries have a sense of a common destiny for all those who work together. They share interests, especially since there is relatively little competition in so far as promotion is in terms of seniority. In-group aggression is thus minimized and this arrangement is therefore conceived to be positively functional for the bureaucracy.[12]

Thus, competition is undesirable for the bureaucracy and unhealthy according to the neo-Freudians.

Fourth, popularized neo-Freudianism and the norms of bureaucratic organizations both emphasize security. According to the neo-Freudians, man can only function as a "calm, complacent adult" when he knows that his world will stay fairly constant and predictable.[13] The bureaucracy is similarly built on security, on the fixity of procedure and the constancy of stimuli and response. Furthermore, the bureaucracy eliminates uncertainty and insecurity by such mechanisms as the routinization of promotion, by the institutions of tenure and seniority and by generally fixed wages or salaries which are not affected by fluctuations of the market nor precisely determined by individual performance.

Finally, the control of anxiety is a central concern both to the neo-Freudians and the bureaucrat. Horney terms anxiety the "dynamic center of neurosis."[14] Sullivan writes,

> I believe it fairly safe to say that anybody and everybody devotes much of his lifetime and a great deal of his energy . . . to avoiding more anxiety than he already has and, if possible to getting rid of some of this anxiety.[15]

Moreover, the conditions which, in the popular neo-Freudian view, produce anxiety are precisely the conditions which are largely eliminated in bureaucratic organizations. They are uncertainty, mystery, coercion and peer conflict. Yet, it is just these factors which are largely eliminated by the bureaucratic stress on clear rules for decision-making, fixity of procedure, constancy of stimuli, a rational scientific world-view, non-coercive means of social control, narrowing of personal accountability and interpersonal harmony.

Thus, the man attuned to the bureaucracy should be seen as healthy, mature and well-adjusted by the neo-Freudians. He is a man who avoids the trauma of competition and uncertainty; a man who prefers togetherness and the security of routine. Neo-Freudianism and the norms of bureaucratic organizations are not only similar, they can be mutually reinforcing. Neo-Freudianism, in the hands of its popularizers, can justify and guide accommodation to the bureacracy. The demands of the bureaucracy can make popularized neo-Freudianism an attractive rationale for what one has to do anyway. The conception of the mature man advanced by the neo-Freudians, that is, a rational, secure, cooperative and non-anxious person, is similarly the ideal bureaucrat. Both neo-Freudianism and bureaucracy seek to free man from uncertainty, from the fear of failure and from the tensions of competition. However, both may obtain freedom from these psychological pressures only to subject man to the social pressures of the bureaucratic society.

Notes

1) What is here called popularized neo-Freudianism is called the "Freudian ethic" by Richard T. LaPiere in *The Freudian Ethic* (New York: Duell, Sloan & Pearce, 1959). However, the term "Freudian" is something of a misnomer, since Freud's own writings maintain a skepticism about the ability of society to meet individual needs (see Philip Rieff, *Freud: The Mind of the Moralist* [New York: Viking, 1959]). The neo-Freudians have muted this skepticism. Furthermore, Freud shows a fundamental ambivalence toward work and authority which does not coincide with an approval of increasing bureaucratization (see David Riesman, *Selected Essays from Individualism Reconsidered* [Garden City, N.Y.: Doubleday Anchor, 1955], pp. 174–302). The views of the neo-Freudians, on the other hand, can be seen as supporting an acceptance of increasing bureaucratization, as pointed out in Herbert Marcuse, *Eros and Civilization, A Philosophical Inquiry into Freud* (New York: Vintage Books, 1962), pp. 217–251.
   Further, it should be noted that neo-Freudianism has undergone changes in the process of becoming a popular viewpoint. Thus, its originators, Horney, Fromm and Sullivan, might not completely agree with the popular interpretations of their work.
2) The norms of bureaucracy discussed here apply primarily to the middle and lower levels of bureaucratic organizations. Some of the statements made here would not be true of the upper levels of bureaucracy, as is noted by Daniel R. Miller and Guy E. Swanson, *The Changing American Parent* (New York: Wiley, 1958). For a discussion of the norms of the ideal-typical bureaucracy, see "Bureaucracy," in Hans Gerth and C. Wright Mills (eds. and trans.), *From Max Weber: Essays in Sociology* (New York: Oxford University Press, 1958), pp. 196–244.
3) Robert K. Merton, "Bureaucratic Structure and Personality," *Social Theory and Social Structure* (2d ed.; Glencoe: Free Press, 1957), p. 196.
4) Sigmund Freud, *Civilization and Its Discontents*, trans. James Strachey (New York: Norton, 1962).
5) LaPiere, *op. cit.*, p. 53.
6) Erich Fromm, *The Sane Society* (New York: Holt, Rinehart & Winston, 1955).
7) *Ibid.*, p. 15.
8) Karen Horney, *The Neurotic Personality of Our Time* (New York: Norton, 1957), p. 284.
9) *Ibid.*, p. 188.

10) *Ibid.,* p. 192.
11) *Ibid.,* p. 207.
12) Merton, *op. cit.,* p. 201.
13) LaPiere, *op. cit.,* p. 92.
14) Horney, *op. cit.,* p. 41.
15) Harry Stack Sullivan, *Interpersonal Theory of Psychiatry* (New York: Norton, 1953).

The Hang-Loose Ethic

∽

J. L. Simmons / Barry Winograd

A barefooted man with a beard and a surplus Navy jacket that had "Love Is" written on the back of it was walking down the main street of a small midwestern city, digging the sunlight and thinking that the heat was really pleasant when you got into it. A group of high school kids rode by him in a car and began shouting to him. "Hey beatnik." "Hey, you're high man." "What color's your dingy?" And, from one of the less imaginative boys, "Why don't you go fly a kite?"

The man looked up musingly, jaywalked across the street to a dime store, bought a kite and some luminous paint and two thousand feet of string. He took them to his battered car and drove around the adjacent suburbs for awhile, rounding up kids to fly the kite with him. Some parents looked him over and scurried their kids away, shaking their heads about the invasion of perverts; others looked into his face and saw nothing evil there, so consented. They drove to the top of a hill over-looking the town, painted the kite with bright psychedelic colors, sent it up and flew it all afternoon. Toward sunset, they cut loose the string and watched their *objet d'art* disappear into the aerial world above them.

The thing about this story is that the young man didn't turn upon his assailants and by opposing them become their likes. Nor did he go into a fetal crouch over a beer, pitying himself as a sensitive and misunder-stood soul (which he is) and condemning the society which trains even its children to put down the unusual. He transcended the harassment, rather than succumbing to it by being roused to self-pity or anger.

The emerging ethic is hang-loose in a number of senses, but, its deep-running feature is that things once taken for granted as God-given or

Reprinted from "The Hang-Loose Ethic," *It's Happening: A Portrait of the Youth Scene Today* (Santa Barbara, Cal.: Marc-Laird, 1966), pp. 6–20, by permission of the authors and Marc-Laird Publications.

American Constitution-given—those basic premises about the world and the way it works—are no longer taken for granted or given automatic allegiance. In other words, many Americans are hanging a bit loose from traditional Americana.

This new ethos is still in the process of forming and emerging; the adherents themselves are mostly unaware of the credo they are participating in making and are already living by. For instance, if you went up to many of the likely young people about town and said, "Say, are you an adherent of the hang-loose ethic?", many of them would look at you oddly and wonder what the hell you were talking about.

Well, if this thing is still so amorphous and you can only speculate about it, and the supposed followers are hardly even aware of it, why bother?

Because we want to see what lies beneath the legion of different concrete happenings. A society can be portrayed in a number of different ways and each gives a different picture of what the society is. It can be done by sketching the material objects, the streets, the buildings, the childhood and adult toys. It can be done by describing the typical behavior, the activities, the rituals, the average life-course of an ordinary member. It can also be done by trying to ferret out the underlying ideology or ethos, which comes forth in a thousand and one different ways and which is the wellspring from which flows the other things, the toys, the scenes, the lives, the typical attitudes and responses. Our attempt to ferret out the ideology behind the happenings is an attempt, then, to dive beneath the trappings and veneers down to the basic world view of the people who are making them happen.

At first glance, it might seem as if the hang-loose ethic is the absence of any morality, that it rejects every ideology, that the followers have no rudder and no star except the swift gratification of all impulses. At a second glance it appears only as a bewildering melange of scenes in various locales. But upon closer examination, one can see that it does embody some values and some guiding principles which, although still ill-formed and vaguely expressed, shape the attitudes and actions of the followers. However, to convey a fuller picture of this ethos, we must sketch the previous American ethics from which it emerged.

Europeans and Americans of the past few centuries have been characterized by most writers as human beings who subscribed to and lived by what is called the Protestant Ethic. This Protestant Ethic was a way of life and a view of life which stressed the more somber virtues, like the quiet good feeling of a hard day's work well done, the idea that the good man always more than earned his pay, and a kind of fierce pragmatism in which the hard and fast, here and now, seeable, touchable, aspects of reality were the only things given the name of reality.

Another thing about the Protestant Ethic was a kind of positive moderatism. Moderation wasn't just a safe course between extremes; moderation was an optimum, positive, good in-and-of-itself thing. Moderation was raised almost to a first principle of ethics. It was a mandate on how to conduct your life.

Anything which veered very far from this somber dignity in oneself and one's accumulations was thought of as bad and suspect. We will see, for example, when we discuss "tripping" that whereas most of the world has regarded exceptional behavior that strays beyond the mundane with an awe combining wonder and terror, in the Western world the wonder has until very recently dropped away and it was suppressed as altogether dangerous. Western man neglected what other times and places made a good deal of, the positive aspects which exceptional experiences might have.

This moderatism carried over into virtually every aspect of the lives of the people. Even in religion and young love, anything smacking too much of mysticism was suspect. The West has relied mostly upon dogma rather than experience in its religious institutions and, despite our hungry romanticism, most of our marriages and other sexual liaisons have been made largely by arrangement.

This Protestant Ethic seems to have characterized the majority of our forefathers although there was always a "lunatic" fringe and a subterranean stratum composed of those at the bottom of the social ladder and of outsiders. And, like all people everywhere, the adherents didn't entirely live up to their own ideals. But, the Protestants ran the schools and the courts and the country and the fringe was contained and circumscribed, largely kept at the fringe.

Then, as the decades passed and we moved into the present century, America began to undergo a secularization which involved not only a dwindling of the force of religion but also a dwindling of the force of the work ethic and the rather stiff personal code which surrounded it. Particularly in the mushrooming urban areas after the Second World War, something grew up which William F. Whyte termed "the Social Ethic."

The Social Ethic (or perhaps more aptly, the Sociable Ethic) was a kind of jocular, benign, superficial, "we're all in the same boat," goodwill. But it shared many things with the Protestant Ethic from which it evolved under the impact of modern times. It was still taken for granted that getting ahead in the Establishment was the thing to do, and that the accumulation of material wealth was a good thing in and of itself. Whyte used the "organization man" living in the new suburbs as his prototypic example and he made a good argument that this was tending to become the overweening American ethos. Work and play, family and politics, each of these were supposed to be a good thing, a fun thing, a comfortable thing. The Sociable Ethic was a secularization of the Protestant ideology combined with a feeling of comfort and goodwill which is easy to generate in a luxuriant society such as ours.

Risk is minimized in the Sociable Ethic. All parties join in a collusion which reduces the chance of great failure and great success once you've been hooked into the system. Of course, there were some dark counter-themes in this portrait: those thirty percent of the people who were not in any real sense beneficiaries of the luxuriant system. And it certainly was not a comfortable place for them—it was as Baldwin has suggested, another country. This didn't just mean the Negro of the South; it also included most Northern Negroes, the uneducated, the abysmally poor, those who lacked the skills to sell themselves, to make themselves an attractive enough package to get recruited into the system.

But the majority of Americans were in it and were doing fairly well. And the continuities with the earlier ethic remained. There still existed a kind of blandness, a real distrust for the exceptional and the bizarre, and there still remained a real distrust for doing something, let's say, "just for kicks." We had in the fifties almost the Utopian culmination of the principle of moderation. Moderate in politics, moderate in work—not too much because it doesn't really pay, not too little because you might get dropped. Moderate in family which involved a kind of thing where you were moderately attached to your spouse and children and moderately concerned with their welfare and you were moderately unfaithful and moderately blasphemous. But you also gave a moderate allegiance to your family and your company and your country.

This was not a picture window nightmare. Most of those involved were probably moderately comfortable and moderately happy.

Does this mean that these people were apathetic and uninvolved, just going through some motions?

No. They were moderately involved in many things. They cried a little and they cared a little and they strove a little and were proud a little and ashamed a little. You see, these people were veterans of hard times; a world depression which was tough, a world war which was tough, an uncertain time afterwards which was tough. And so at last they arrived in their ranch houses and they could afford cocktails on the way home without much worrying about the price. It was, in a sense, the indulgence of a dream, the dream of building an affluent society. Because in the fifties that's exactly what we had—fantastically affluent compared with anything that had ever existed before.

Certainly, there were a few hot social movements and protests about the thirty percent who weren't "in." But, we must realize that in most times and countries it's been 90% or 98%. So only thirty percent left out is pretty damn good and something brand new in history. And the first scattered appearance of the beats and the freedom cats must not obscure the fact that the vast majority were (moderately) good Americans in the small sense of not rocking any boats.

Yet even as the sociable ideology was crystallizing and taking hold and Eisenhower was virtually proclaiming moderation the cornerstone of our national policy, a new kind of feeling was beginning to stir across the land—a feeling which had many ties with the past but which was also new.

Although there were precursors in the late fifties when Ginsberg was telling people he'd seen the best minds of his generation driven mad, and hip talk (and an inevitable bit of the philosophy behind it) was being picked up by teenagers, the hang-loose ethos really belongs to the sixties because this is the decade in which it is emerging and spreading throughout our society.

When we search for the "philosophy" which is the common denominator running through the variety of happenings—the implicit code of values pushing those involved toward some things and away from other things—some of the characteristics of this yet crystallizing view can be discerned.

One of the fundamental characteristics of the hang-loose ethic is that it is *irreverent*. It repudiates, or at least questions, such cornerstones of conventional society as Christianity, "my country right or wrong," the sanctity of marriage and premarital chastity, civil obedience, the accumulation of wealth, the right and even competence of parents, the schools, and the government to head and make decisions for everyone—in sum, the Establishment. This irreverence is probably what most arouses the ire and condemnation of the populace. Not only are the mainstream institutions and values violated, but their very legitimacy is challenged and this has heaped insult upon moral injury in the eyes of the rank and file.

Sin, as the violation of sacred beliefs and practices, is nothing new and most of us have had at least a few shamefully delightful adventures somewhere along the way. But what is qualitatively new is that the very truth and moral validity of so many notions and practices, long cherished in our country, are being challenged. When caught by parents or authorities, youths are no longer hanging their heads in shame. Instead, they are asserting the rightness, at least for themselves, of what they're doing. And they are asking what right do their elders have to put them down?

And not infrequently the irreverence takes a form which goes beyond this openly aggressive challenging. An increasing number of happeners have reached a level of disrespect so thoroughgoing that they don't even bother to "push their cause." Not only have they dropped their defensive posture, but their own assertiveness has become quiet, even urbane, in its detachment and indifference toward the "other morality." This withdrawal has aroused some of the greatest resentment and opposition since it is perhaps the gravest affront to an established ethic not to be taken seriously. To be defied is one thing; to be simply ignored and dismissed out of hand is something else. The spread of this more fullblown irreverence testifies to the fact that a good many happeners are managing to set up a life that is relatively independent of conventional society.

Another basic aspect of the hang-loose ethic is a diffuse and pervasive *humanism* which puts great store upon the value of human beings and human life. Adherents don't necessarily proclaim the rationality of men or their inherent "goodness," but they do claim that people are precious and that their full development is perhaps the most worthwhile of all things.

Killing is a heinous violation of this ethos and so is any action which puts others down, except under extreme circumstances. The most approved method of defense and retaliation is to turn one's oppressors onto the good life they're condemning and to help them resolve hangups which prevent this from happening. If this fails, one may attempt to "blow their minds," to shock their preconceptions and prejudices in some way and hence force them to open their eyes, to re-evaluate, and hopefully to grow. The happeners refuse under most circumstances to employ the weapons of their adversaries because they feel that by so doing they would merely become like them. Instead, they try to transform their adversaries into fellows. The only really endorsed aggression is to try and force your enemies to become your friends. Only in extreme cases is putting down—the main strategy of the Establishment—even partly acceptable.

Ideally, the happeners do not fill the role of modern missionaries, though their practice in conversation and contact reminds one of historical attempts at persuasion and conversion. When approaching others, they welcome acceptance as well as adoption, but this does not imply that happeners resemble the adventurous, pioneering missionaries of established religions or ideologies. The few actual organizations existing in the happening world are there, first, to serve their "constituents" and, second, to espouse and inform.

This humanism, combined as it is with irreverence, produces a passive resistance toward the Establishment and the persuasive efforts of straights, rather than an active rebellion. The happeners are more transcendent than antagonistic; more indifferent and benevolently contemptuous than negative and bitter. Bitterness does occur over concrete immediate cases of harassment or "for your own good" busts, commitments, and putdowns. But it fades rather quickly again into the more general mood of simple wariness. The mood is not grim, although there is a diffuse paranoia toward the established social order which waxes and wanes as the scene gets hot and cools down again.

Another basic aspect of the hang-loose ethic is the pursuit of *experience* both as a thing in itself and as a means of learning and growing. The idea is that a great variety and depth of experience is beneficial and not at all harmful as long as you can handle it. This entails a heightened attention to the present ongoing moment and far less concern with the past or future. It also involves a mistrust of dogmas and principles which tend to obscure the richness of life. For this reason, they also often reject the categorizing and generalizing which is so rampant in our educational system. Within the drug scenes, for instance, there is full awareness that LSD-25 can trigger "bad trips," for some people. But, again the fact of experience alone, whether guided officially by researchers or informally by "guides," overrides the application of a generalized rule about the possible detrimental effects of such drugs.

This courting of raw experience is what gives many people the impression that those participating in the happenings are without any morals whatsoever; that they are selfishly pursuing swift gratification of their impulses. And it is true that the unabashed seeking of experiences will frequently lead the seeker to violate what other people consider proper. But such judgments are one-sided. Although they see that swingers are breaking standards, they entirely miss the point that swingers are following another, different set of standards; so that arguments between the camps are in reality debates between conflicting ideologies.

As part and parcel of the importance placed on directly experiencing oneself and the world, we find that *spontaneity*, the ability to groove with whatever is currently happening, is a highly valued personal trait. Spontaneity enables the person to give himself up to the existential here and now without dragging along poses and hangups and without playing investment games in hopes of possible future returns. The purest example of spontaneity is the jazz musician as he stands up and blows a cascade of swinging sounds.

Another facet of the hang-loose ethic is an untutored and unpretentious *tolerance*. Do whatever you want to as long as you don't step on other people while doing it. A girl is free to wet her pants or play with herself openly while she's up on an acid trip and no one will think less of her for it. A man can stand and stare at roadside grass blowing in the wind and no one will accuse him of being the village idiot. If you like something that I don't like, that's fine, that's your bag; just don't bring me down.

The swingers, when you come down to it, are anarchists in the fullest sense. They chafe at virtually all restrictions because they see most every restriction that modern man has devised as a limitation on directions people can travel and grow. They feel that the irony of contemporary society is that the very restrictions necessary to curb an immature populace prevent that same populace from becoming mature enough to live without restrictions, just as a girdle weakens the muscles it supports.

Even clothes are regarded by some as mostly a nuisance and swingers have led the whole Western world toward simplicity and ease in styles and makeup. And over weekends and vacations, small groups will often go up together to back country retreats where whoever wants to can run around naked.

Without the fuss or the self-righteousness so common among Establishment liberals, the happeners have come closer to integrating the races, religions, and the sexes than any other group one can think of. A fierce equality is practiced among them, which is appreciative of differences in backgrounds and temperaments. Equality and tolerance aren't abject attempts to make people feel comfortable or wanted; they are dispositions that permit things and relationships to just happen without deliberate forethought and planning. In most happening circles, a Negro is not the recipient of conscious liberal acceptance, but an individual in and of himself who may or may not be a "good" person. Acceptance and participation is based more on how the individual presents himself within the context of the scene, not by preconceived and nurtured stereotypes about the way he is expected to be.

One's past is not held against one and one's reputation is not spoiled by the fact that one might have served time in a prison or mental institution, had an abortion, or perhaps a homosexual affair.

This doesn't mean that the swingers will indiscriminately associate with anyone. Like everybody else, they choose their friends, their lovers, their acquaintances and the people they avoid by how well they get along with one another and enjoy doing things together. But they are less down on the people they don't choose to associate with than others generally are.

But the tolerance stops if somebody is stepping on other people. For instance, if a guy shows up in a particular scene and starts tooling around with other people's minds or bum tripping them just for his own kicks, several people are likely to get together and elect themselves to deal with him by busting *his* mind. And such a guy can quickly be shut out of virtually the entire happenings in that specific scene.

The ideal person in the hang-loose view embodies traits that are difficult to combine. Being as spontaneous as a child yet being sophisticated and worldwise; being fully self-expressive yet being always in control of oneself. This is the ambiguity of being cool. Being able to dig the ongoing present as it unfolds yet being able to get things done and maintain a competent life of fulfilled commitments and involvements. Being hang-loose from any constraining orthodoxy, yet being courageous enough to follow your own path wherever it may lead and whatever the travails it plunges you into.

The heroes are those who have managed to swing in some eminent way especially if they did so in spite of tough conditions. The distinguished outsiders of history, avant-garde artists, the leaders of unpopular social movements. The list of admirable people would include figures such as Aldous Huxley, Allen Ginsberg, Gandhi, John F. Kennedy, Fidel Castro, Alpert and Leary, and Bob Dylan. But such people are not so much heroes in the ordinary sense because, although they are much admired, they are not so much worshipped, and because they are critically discussed as well as fondly quoted.

The fact that swingers operate at least partly outside the Establishment and often even outside the law produces a certain admiration and sympathy among them for other categories of alienated and disaffiliated people, such as the Negroes, the poor, the mentally disturbed, the delinquent, the sexual deviant, and the peoples of under-developed countries. They do not necessarily approve of what these people do, but they do see them as victims of Establishments.

These sympathies, coupled with their tolerance and opposition to restrictiveness lead the happeners to take a "liberal" stand on almost every question and issue, from welfare measures to disarmament, to the legalization of pot and abortions, to racial integration and civil liberties generally, to recognition of Red China and negotiations with the Viet Cong, to sexual permissiveness and progressive education, to socialized medicine and the exploration of space.

But most of them are not self-conscious "liberals." They take these stands for granted as the only reasonable and sensible ones, but they usually don't work within organized political parties to bring them about and they are not very happy with the compromising Establishment liberals who do. They support such men as Governor Brown, Clark Kerr and Bobby Kennedy only as the best of the poor choices available, all of whom are really more alike than different, and none of whom are really worth a good God damn.

But they are not pro-Communist either, although sympathetic toward revolutionaries in under-developed countries. They see Communism as at least as odious and repressive as the societies of the West and probably a good deal more so.

The hang-loose people are not joiners; indeed this is one of their defining attributes. They tend to shy away from any kind of conventional ideologies or fanaticisms, seeing them as unfree compulsions and obsessions rather than noble dedications. They regard those who are too intensely and doggedly involved in even such highly approved causes as integration and peace, a little askance and happeners will sometimes describe their own past involvements in these movements as something of a psychological hangup.

The villains in the hang-loose view are people and social forces which put other people down and hang them up, which teach people to be stolid and dignified rather than swinging, self-righteous, and moralistic rather than responsible, dutiful rather than devoted. Those who, for the sake of some ideology, will set fire to other peoples' kids; who, for the sake of some ideology, will slap their own children into becoming something less than they might have been. The villains are those who pass their own hangups onto those around them and thus propagate a sickness, "for your own good."

This seems to be the still amorphous and emerging ethos which is the basis of the happenings we're concerned with. Admirable in some ways, perhaps a bit idealistic and innocent and even silly in others, still in the process of forming and changing, and creating many problems for everyone. And perhaps as inevitable, given current conditions, as the spring winds which stir its adherents.

And it is a set of ideals which, like all people, the adherents are not able to live up to. Sometimes when things get uptight, they betray themselves and each other. Sometimes, they can't resist selling out for a better package deal. Sometimes, despite their utterances they can become as provincial and arrogant as any tribesman who thinks he has the monopoly on truth. And sometimes they are driven by other motives to cheat and exploit one another. But such shortcomings are panhuman and can be leveled at any group including the United States Senate or the medical profession. And this should not obscure the fact that ideals are a potent social force which have a major hand in making people what they are. Ideals, aside from having a part in making individual attitudes, attachments and adjustments, also serve to categorize people as runners along certain tracks of life. What is today called deviant is tomorrow only eccentric. What harps upon and tortures the older ethics and ideologies, can eventually become an accepted, if not generally followed, belief system.

Like all ideologies, this ethos is sometimes used as a rationalization and justification. Irresponsibility can be excused as freedom. Apathy can be called being cool. Lack of dependability can be called spontaneity and so can boorishness and sloth. And virtually any behavior can be justified on the grounds that it is experience and will lead in some way to personal growth.

But then pointing out these blindspots may be a pot calling a kettle black for all ideologies are so misused and the misuse doesn't destroy the fact that they are also faithfully followed.

.　　.　　.

Why Pluralism Is Necessary

⌐⌐

Robert A. Dahl / Charles Lindbloom

Reasoning from what they conceived to be the experience of very small, face-to-face organizations, many people have been blinded to the importance of social pluralism in large societies. Early democratic ideologues like Rousseau were downright hostile to social pluralism; and no doubt this is one of the reasons political parties and caucuses initially seemed reprehensible to many observers. From thinking about small face-to-face organizations, Rousseau could regard the individual himself as the unit; he could plausibly argue that subgroup loyalties were unnecessary as a protection against the community and undesirable as a threat to agreement. Hence the idea of a society composed of "factions" is the very opposite of most utopias.[1] That Rousseau, like most utopians, had precious little empirical information to go on permitted him to slur over the powerful subgroup loyalties operating even in most small organizations—for example, the strength of "family" loyalties in small egalitarian tribes.[2]

Why is some degree of social pluralism a necessary condition for polyarchy,* at least in the modern nation-state? Whatever the case may be in small organizations, in large areas some degree of social pluralism is necessary to polyarchy, for in at least five ways it limits the capacity of officeholders to extend their control over ordinary citizens.

First, social pluralism means the existence of social organizations, organizational loyalties, organizational leaders; in union there is strength. A lone citizen speaking only for himself can often be intimidated by officials; but a spokesman for a body of citizens is less easily cowed. If the official has sanctions, so does the organization leader: publicity, votes, and even the threat of resistance. And besides there is a kind of psychological

  * The term "polyarchy" may be regarded as a synonym for "democracy." [Editor's note.]

multiplier effect to organization membership; the knowledge that one is not alone often helps reinforce one's courage and determination. (Refugees from totalitarian rule report that one of the most unnerving features of totalitarian society is the feeling of loneliness in the individual who may secretly be opposed to the regime.) Then, too, organization leaders are likely to have more status than ordinary citizens; they are more likely to move easily in official circles, to command the respect and deference of officials.

Second, social pluralism facilitates competition by insuring the existence of rival leaders with differing loyalties and support. Thus the possibility that officeholders will become uncontrollable is reduced; for officeholders are only one group of leaders, or, more likely, themselves consist of many competing leaders. To wipe out other leaders, revolutionaries must first possess the loyalty and support of more people than they are likely to win over in a pluralistic society; diversified organizational loyalties inhibit this kind of loyalty.

Third, social pluralism facilitates the rise of political leaders whose main skill is negotiating settlements among conflicting social organizations. Thus the whole cast of the political elites is modified by pluralism; the fanatic, the Messianic type, the leader whose aim is to consolidate the supremacy of some small group tend to trip themselves up on the barrier of groups and group loyalties. The Federalists, concerned with maintaining the domination of eastern financial and commercial interests, were unable to compete with the Jeffersonian alliance; they died out as a party. All important American politicians have been excellent negotiators of group alliances, from Jefferson and Jackson to Roosevelt and Truman. Nor is it any different in England: Peel, Disraeli, Gladstone, Asquith, Lloyd George, Baldwin, Churchill, Attlee all show to a marked degree the capacity to ride herd on an unwieldy political alliance. Much of the energy of political elites is expended simply in the effort to hold the alliance together. Incautious moves to extend one's control may bring about defections to the other side.

Fourth, social pluralism increases the probability that one is simultaneously a member of more than one social organization; hence action by a leader against what seems to be an enemy organization may in fact strike against his own alliance. In Jackson's day this phenomenon existed in almost laboratory purity. One might be a resident of the Ohio Valley and therefore tied to the South by the need to keep open the Mississippi, but increasingly tied to the Northeast by railroads and canals. Of Connecticut stock, he might have married a girl whose parents came out of Virginia and Tennessee. A Congregationalist, he may have had little sympathy with the popishness of southern Episcopalianism. A grain grower, he lobbied for railways and canals to transport his products to the East. His children may have moved west—or gone east for their education. Thus during this period, until slavery in the western territories became a fundamentally divisive issue after 1850, the diversity of memberships characteristic of any particular individual made it necessary for political leaders to proceed cautiously in a spirit of moderation and compromise. Purists may find the results distressingly untidy; but one result was to force American political leaders to perfect the art of working out not merely an agreement among members of their own alliance but also an agreement with the opposition. Henry Clay and Stephen Douglas are only extreme examples of the political craft as it must be practiced in a pluralistic society.

Fifth, social pluralism has some important consequences for information and communication. It increases the probability that alternative sources of information not under direct government control will be technically available to citizens. It is true, of course, that many citizens expose themselves to information that confirms their own norms and those of the group.[3] But as we said earlier, effective criticism of policy or political leaders is a somewhat specialized function; and those who specialize in criticism and communication *can* make use of alternative sources of information.

Communication of politically relevant information in a large and heterogeneous polyarchy like the United States is an exceedingly complex matter, and any simplified description of it is likely to be wrong. One aspect of the process, however, is undoubtedly the way in which group leaders in a pluralistic society act as a focus of information, criticism, and communication. The group leader is the sensitive point of contact: with members of his own group, with other leaders at his own level, with higher leaders. A variety of leaders sensitive to the desires of non-leaders in their group, the limits of their own control, the coöperativeness of allied group leaders, and the responsiveness of more powerful leaders bring their specialized influence to bear on other leaders in behalf of group goals, and at the same time restrain their own group within the bounds set by the leaders' frequently more realistic calculations of what is possible. Hence, a great deal of politically relevant communication is of a specialized kind, moving up, down, and across a complex chain of leaders.

In these ways social pluralism develops a complex distribution of control. It does not eliminate hierarchical organizations but it makes polyarchal government possible. Ordinary citizens control their immediate leaders and are controlled by them. These leaders in turn control other leaders and are controlled by them. Hence, a society of reciprocal relationships exists to control government policy. A national political alliance is therefore a vast and slightly shaky enterprise, not a monolith but a pile of billiard balls held together with a poor grade of paste.

.   .   .

Notes

1) "Il n'y a guère de dissidents dans les sociétés utopiennes. Pas ou peu d'opposition, de partis qui se combattent." Raymond Ruyer, *L'Utopie et les utopies*, Presses Universitaires de France, Paris, 1950, p. 44.
2) Cf. Richard Thurnwald, *Werden, Wandel und Gestaltung von Staat und Kultur*, in *Die Menschliche Gesellschaft*, Vierter Band, Walter de Gruyter and Co., Berlin and Leipzig, 1945, pp. 14 et seq.
3) Many studies of communication have confirmed this fact; cf., for example, Paul Lazarsfeld, Bernard Berelson, and Hazel Gaudet, *The People's Choice*, Duell, Sloan and Pearce, New York, 1944.

Mass Society and Extremist Politics

Joseph R. Gusfield

A dominant stream of thought in current political sociology explains many contemporary anti-democratic movements as products of a distinctive social organization—Mass Society. Writers who utilize this approach have maintained that modern, Western societies increasingly show characteristics of mass organization which sharply differ from the features of such societies in the nineteenth and earlier centuries. Mass societies, in this view, demonstrate a form of politics in which traditional sociological concepts, such as class or culture, are not relevant to an understanding of the sources, genesis, or careers of extremist, anti-democratic political movements. Mass politics is the form of political action unique to mass societies. As modern democratic societies become mass societies, we may then anticipate that political crises are likely to generate extremist, anti-democratic responses. Leading advocates of this theory of "mass politics," in whole or part, are Hannah Arendt, Erich Fromm, Karl Mannheim, William Kornhauser, Robert Nisbet, and Philip Selznick.[1] This paper is a critical analysis of this approach and a reformulation of some of the relations between mass societies and political action.

There are two major contentions in this paper. The first is a criticism of the assumptions about democratic politics underlying the theory of mass politics. The second is a reformulated theory of the relation between mass society and political extremism in contemporary, democratic societies.

It is our first contention that implicit in the theory of mass politics is an idealized conception of the pluralistic social and political system held necessary for the maintenance of democratic institutions. This conception is idealized in that it fails to give adequate weight to barriers which

Reprinted from "Mass Society and Extremist Politics," *American Sociological Review*, 27 (February, 1962), 19-30, by permission of the author and The American Sociological Association.

conflicts of interest offer to political harmony and compromise under any political structure.

Our second contention is that the elements of mass societies viewed with alarm by mass politics theorists in actuality contain positive connotations for the maintenance of democratic political institutions. Mass communications, bureaucratic institutions, and equalitarianism have implications which strengthen pluralistic political structures. Extremist politics may be expected in modern societies as a response of those adversely affected by the changes towards a mass society and most insulated from mass institutions. Contrary to the theory of mass politics traditional concepts of political sociology *are* adequate to the analysis of extremism.

It must be made clear that our major interest in this paper is in the explanation of anti-democratic movements as they develop within historically democratic societies. This excludes consideration of authoritarian regimes in traditional societies or the development of anti-democratic movements in developing economies under the impact of intensive social and economic change.[2] Our interest is confined to those writers who explain such modern extremist movements as Fascism, Communism, or McCarthyism by reference to characteristics of mass society. These represent one variant of mass society theory, but an influential one.[3]

Mass Society and the Theory of Mass Politics

Mass Society analysts view modern social systems as significantly different from non-industrial and earlier societies. Whatever the differences among individual writers, there is a common core of description in the term "mass society" which suggests the attenuation of primary and local associations and groups. Impersonal, bureaucratized relationships in large-scale organizations have replaced the informal systems of loyalty in small groups and local affiliations. Equalitarian conditions and ideologies have weakened systems of political and social authority characteristic of stratified communities. Technological innovations have made possible a high degree of standardization, both of products and ideas. The elongation of the chain of organizational command has enhanced the possibilities of oligarchic control as local groups are less viable, hence less resistant to control. The emphasis is upon the breakdown of immediate relationships and differentiations so that the population is now more homogeneous but also less sharply identified and affiliated with distinctive social groups. It is in this sense that the theorist of mass society views the traditional categories of sociological analysis—family, class, community, ethnic identity, etc.—as having lost significance in mass societies. The mass is masslike: shapeless, structureless, undifferentiated. Mass politics trace the implications of this loss of differentiation for the bonds of loyalty to democratic political institutions.

Exponents of mass politics viewpoints have described modern Western, industrial societies as ones in which persons lack attachment to primary and secondary associations. "The chief characteristic of the massman," Hannah Arendt has written, "is not brutality and backwardness, but his isolation and lack of normal social relationships."[4] Political extremism, manifested in anti-democratic movements, is seen as a result of the *structural* and *psychological* consequences for political loyalty or disattachment to democratic procedures and aims.

Supporters of this view hold that structural characteristics of bureaucratization and equality undermine the functions of secondary and primary associations in inculcating values and in transmitting political norms. In mass society, such theories maintain, secondary associations of school, church, community or union, operate in a large-scale fashion. Rank-and-file identification with the organizational elite is diminished as the member's associational life is peripheral and tangential. The high mobility rates and standardized life styles destroy economic class as an important source of motivation and interest in political events. Institutions functioning under conditions of mass society do not touch the character and the personal values of those exposed to them. Being solely instrumental means, the major associations and institutions of the society cannot act as agencies through which values are inculcated. Because of this, the political elites of the society cannot mediate political decisions to the acceptance of the rank-and-file. Such political "untouchables" are described by Selznick when he writes, "He has lost the meaning provided by the articulated social structure to which he belonged."[5]

In previous centuries the lack of integration of rank-and-file members of the society into political institutions was a matter of little political consequence. Mass societies, however, are politically equalitarian. The development of large aggregates of persons unattached to democratic political structures and norms is significant because such groups are capable of spontaneous development unguided by the norms of democratic society. The diminished role of intermediate structures—both institutions and specific political associations—leaves the person unattached and capable of being reunited into a new group. "A strong intermediate structure consists of stable and independent groups which represent diverse and frequently conflicting interests."[6] In mass society, however, the representative nature of these groups (classes, ethnic

groups, regions, etc.) is undermined. Both because participation is peripheral and because political elites are limited in authority, mass societies are
less able to control the values and political aspirations of citizens.

To the structural disintegration of society there is added the personal
disorganization of the individual. The psychological consequences of mass
society are described in terms of the feeling of detachment. The key
word here is alienation, "a mode of experience in which the person
experiences himself as an alien."[7] Whether the emphasis of the writer is
on estrangement from work, the normlessness of contemporary culture
or the powerless feeling of the individual in large-scale organizations,
mass conditions are described as producing feelings of *malaise* and insecurity.

The alienation of the individual in modern societies is the psychological statement of detachment. It describes a condition in which the
person is not involved in or committed to primary or secondary groups.
It adds to this the description of the person as someone with positive,
unfulfilled needs for identity, affection, and assurance.

In both its structural and psychological elements the theory of mass
politics states that political alienation—the disattachment of the person
from political institutions—is a function of the disintegrating influences
of mass society on the ties of sentiment and loyalty to specific groups
which characterized the social structure of democracies in an earlier
historical period. Without attachment to primary or to intermediate
structures, the individual has no bond to national political institutions
which commands his loyalty to its political norms.

Pluralistic and Extremist Politics

In the emphasis on a transition from an earlier historical period to a
modern, mass society the theories here considered have suggested that
political democracy functioned relatively unimpeded under non-mass
conditions. It is imperative then that we examine the type of political
structure from which mass politics is seen as differing. Political extremism
is so defined in contradistinction to pluralistic politics. The mass theorist
sees pluralistic politics as impaired under current social conditions. As a
corollary pluralistic structure is implicitly posited as an essential condition for democratic politics.

The theory of a balance of power among a plurality of groups has
been the dominant analytical tool of American political scientists.[8] Its
classic defense has been presented in Hamilton and Madison's *The*

Federalist Papers. The theory presupposes a society of many and diverse social groups. The political institutions force each group to moderate and compromise their interests in the interplay of party, secondary association, and locality. In the pluralist conception of the citizen, each person is integrated into politics in his capacity as member of some segment of the society—worker or manager, city or country dweller, Southerner or Northerner, immigrant or native, white or black. The units of politics are thus organized groups built upon the sentiments and interests of persons in their affiliations with specific primary associations which occupy positions and perform specific functions within the major institutions.

Pluralistic politics involves certain "rules of the game" by which political conflict is carried on. These "rules of the game," part of the definition of politics as an institution, are adhered to by the participants. Chief among tenets of democratic politics is acceptance of opposing forces into the political process on the same terms as those binding on one's own group. This acceptance supplies the necessity for political compromise and conciliation. If all groups possess some political power and are admitted into the political process, bargaining and negotiation are the chief modes of political conflict. Violence is ruled out as a possible way of solving social or economic conflicts.

It is essential to this process that each group be willing to accept the total or partial defeat of its aims and accept the total or partial achievement of the aims of its opponents. Compromise includes the ability to settle for less than full victory. This "realistic" orientation is achieved in an atmosphere governed by rational calculation of interests. It is most negated when objectives have become correlated with considerations of honor and when compromise, negotiation, and defeat are suffused with connotations of dishonor.

Political extremism occurs when movements advocate violation of the democratic, pluralist "rules of the game." Shils suggests a distinction between pluralistic and ideological politics which emphasizes the disattachment of the extremist from self-limiting and rationally calculative aspects of pluralism:

> Extremism consists in going to an extreme in zealous attachment to a particular value, e.g., private property, ethnic homogeneity, or status equality. . . . The extremist must be deeply alienated from the complex of rules which keep the strivings for various values in restraint and balance. An extremist group is an alienated group. . . . Its hostility is incompatible with that freedom from intense emotion which pluralistic politics needs for its prosperity. . . . The focus of the extremists attention on one or a few completely fulfilled values and his impatience with compromise when a

plurality of values, never internally consistent, have to be reconciled with each other makes the extremist feel that he is worlds apart from the compromising moderates.[9]

This distinction between pluralist and extremist politics differs, as others have pointed out,[10] from traditional distinctions between Right and Left, Conservative, Liberal and Radical, and reform and revolution. It is a distinction between styles and not between contents. It is in this sense that extremism is alienated from the institutions of democratic politics. It denies the legitimacy of democratic political institutions as devices for mediating conflict. Extremist style refuses to accept the possible or probable outcomes of whole or partial defeat. Total victory is too important in the hierarchy of values to permit of compromise.

In several ways, then, the extremist breaks with the normative patterns of pluralist political behavior: (1) *He attempts to close the political process to opposing forces*: Politics is held to be the legitimate area of conflict for some, but not for all groups. Both Fascism and Communism have made this a cornerstone of the political structure as well as a tenet of their movements.

(2) *He attempts to carry on social and economic conflicts outside of political institutions*: The confinement of conflict to politics marks a cardinal principle of democratic politics. Violence, intimidation and fraud are excluded as means of achieving group ends.

(3) *He impairs the culture of democratic discussion*: An emphasis is placed on the value of uniform opinions and behavior. The criteria of rational calculation of interests is replaced by intensive appeals to sentiment and symbolism. This strain in McCarthyism captured the attention of those concerned with extremism in politics. It is only in this sense that membership and participation in extremist movements seems authoritarian. The extremist style has little appreciation of dissent and schism in the total society.

The extremist movement is marked by the low degree of commitment to the values of procedure in democratic institutions. Pluralist norms enforce tolerance, barter, and the inclusion of opponents as joint members of the same social system. Extremist resentment against democratic politics is not that of indifference but that of intensive conviction. It is the thoroughly moralistic attitude which marks the extremist and distinguishes him from the slightly cynical pluralist.

As we have sketched it so far, political extremism is found in one or both forms: an increased attachment to a single, over-riding value or a weakened attachment to the norms of pluralist politics. In either case, the extremist is alienated from the *existing* democratic order.[11]

The theorists of mass politics visualize extremist movements as consequences of weakened attachments to political institutions and persons resulting from the breakdown in functioning of primary and secondary associations in mass societies. Without a sense of affiliation to specific interest groups, the citizen has no way to develop a frame of reference for political events. Intermediate secondary associations cannot touch him sufficiently to act as forces limiting intensity of opposition and resentment of rival political claims. Political figures become distrusted and democratic institutions no longer legitimate sources of social control. In Kornhauser's words:

> . . . intermediate groups help to protect elites by functioning as channels through which popular participation in the larger society (especially in the national elites) may be directed and restrained.[12]

The mass theorist goes a step further and suggests that such detachment from democratic political institutions leaves the individual susceptible to political participation in extremist channels. The socially alienated individual is not only politically alienated; he is also more likely to become the extremist activist than is the member of a structured interest group. He is no longer limited in his attack on rivals by the controls of a structured pluralistic society. His resentments against opposing groups and against the existing institutions themselves need not be confined to the calculative, instrumental style of democratic politics. The mass man is a passionate supporter of ideology.

Lack of control mechanisms regulating the political attitudes and behavior of mass citizenry furthers the extremist character of participation in politics. It enables the person to project destructive impulses into the political arena. Mannheim, for example, maintained that in traditional societies collective impulses and wishes are absorbed by smaller groups and directed toward group aims. The social disintegration of modern society, he felt, set such impulses free to seek integration around some new object, often a symbol or a leader.[13]

The attenuation of local and primary associations and mediating secondary interest groups and associations, is, in the theory of mass politics, the source of the extremism frequent in contemporary mass societies. As a system of analysis this view finds that traditional concepts of class and status aims are limited ways of characterizing political movements. As a philosophy of politics, the theory adds up to a defense of the virtues of a pluralistic political system. The transition from a pluralistic society to a mass society is implicitly and explicitly bemoaned. For this reason, the analysis of pluralist assumptions is central to our discussion.

Pluralistic Sources of Political Extremism

The theory of mass politics assumes that a pluralistic social structure diminishes the possibilities that political action will take extremist directions. Conflicts and demands for change will occur but will be moderated by adherence to the style of democratic institutions. An analysis of this assumption, however, shows that extremism both *can* and often *does* occur within pluralistic structures. There are at least four situations in which pluralism either invites or fails to forestall behavior outside the range of democratic norms for the mediation of conflicts:

(1) *Disenfranchised classes*: Change often brings new groups into formation or increases the demands of old ones. In any case, at any given time, some groups are excluded from the political process. Often it is not in the interest of some or most of the included groups to accept new political forces. Excluded groups must either function outside of the political "game" or force their way into it. The militancy of the American Negro in the South today is of this nature. Compromise and legality are not relevant political alternatives unless a group is within the political structures in the first place.

(2) *Doomed and defeated classes*: The theory of democratic politics has never developed a satisfactory answer to the problem: When is compromise to be rejected? When is political defeat not an acceptable alternative to violence and other breaks with pluralist procedure? The facts of the American Civil War and of the Algerian crisis in contemporary France illustrate the thesis that well-structured groups, with channels of representation in parliamentary bodies, are far from willing to accept defeat of important aims through parliamentary procedures. Robert Dahl sees this as a serious impediment in democratic theory. Referring to the election of Abraham Lincoln in 1860, Dahl writes:

> Thus any election interpreted as a clear-cut victory for one side was almost certain to be so intolerable to the other that it would refuse to accept the outcome. . . . Where each side is large and regards the victory of the other as a fundamental threat to some very highly ranked values, it is reasonable to expect serious difficulties in the continued operation of a (pluralistic) system.[14]

This is apt to be the case under conditions of social or economic change which gravely threaten a previous position of power and supremacy. To such "doomed classes,"[15] the future looks far less inviting than the past. A radical reorganization of society, might be a solution to their problem but such a reorganization against politically ascendent forces is precisely what the moderating elements in the structure of political balance operate against. Recent discussions of the plight of the "old middle classes" in American life have stressed the indignation of these groups at their loss of power and status.[16] It is not a failure to "belong" that lies at the source of their alienation and possible "right-wing radicalism." Their response is touched off by the contents of the social changes to which they react.

(3) *Public opinion and the imbalance of competing interests*: The theory of democratic politics as a balance between competing interests often ignores the important role played by the neutral, non-competing elements in the political process. A great many groups without specific interests in a particular issue nevertheless have power to effect governmental decisions. Such decisions are made with a concern for the general climate of opinion toward an issue. Whether the "public" is friendly or hostile is an important element in an interest group's decision to pursue its aims within or without the political process. As Murray Edelman has pointed out, labor will pursue its goals through economic processes (strikes, bargaining, etc.) when the political climate is hostile.[17] Recourse to non-political means is not ruled out by the existence of pluralistic machinery.

(4) *Development of periodic crisis*: Mass politics theory generally recognizes economic and military crisis as an essential "trigger" to extremist movements. Because pluralistic politics is oriented toward compromises between groups, it is less open to long-run considerations. This is especially the case in issues of foreign policy. Unless there is some consensual basis other than group interest, elites must "sell" policy in terms communicable to specific classes and interests. Even assuming a diffusion of power in the form of what Riesman calls "veto groups,"[18] a hiatus develops between long-run perspectives of governmental leaders and the short-run perspectives of intermediate associations and their constituencies. The result is often a stalemate and an immobilism which enables problems to develop into major crises. One instance of this is contained in LaPalombara's analysis of French and Italian politics in the post-war years.[19] He explains greater cohesion and agreement within the Italian moderate parties than among the French as a consequence of differences in the power of the Communist Party in each of the countries. Italian moderates were forced into agreement by fear.

While there has not been any serious fear in France that PCF could come peacefully to power, this reassuring assessment has been denied the democratic party leaders in Italy. . . . They have not been able to permit themselves the capricious inaction in which the French Center Party Leaders have indulged over the last decade.[20]

Inability of political elites to deal with crisis is itself one strong source of mass alienation from a political institution. Third parties have fared better at the polls in the United States during periods of economic depression than during periods of prosperity.[21] As Lipset has pointed out, there is a direct correlation between levels of economic well-being and the existence of democratic political systems.[22] Prosperous countries may avoid problems which threaten political stability in less affluent nations.

In each of these four situations, extremist politics is developed and conducted by well-structured groups, representing discrete and organized parts of the social structure, acting to secure goals related to group needs. While such groups are alienated from the existing political institutions they are not socially disintegrated or unrelated to the society and its political system. They function within a pluralist framework in which their values receive short shrift. Failure to recognize that pluralist assumptions cannot alone sustain political institutions is at the root of the implicit ideology of the theorist of mass politics.

The Pluralist Ideology

The sanguine view of political balance at the base of mass politics theory reveals a repetition of the ideological bias of nineteenth century liberalism —the assumption that there is a natural harmony of interests which sustains the social and political system. Occurrences of sharp conflict are therefore indicative of disruptions in the *form* of social arrangements. There is nothing in the *content* of interests and beliefs which makes compromise improbable. Mannheim reflects this ideology in a passage in *Man and Society* in which he suggests that experience in trade unions and in other associations trains participants for planning on a societal basis: "He is gradually realizing that by resigning partial advantages he helps to save the social and economic system and thereby also his own interests."[23]

The belief that participation in the primary and secondary associations of the society will moderate conflict arises from this ideological commitment to pluralist politics. It leads the mass politics theorist to identify political defeat with social alienation, to view extremist movements as actions of disattached persons, unrelated to specific social bases or pursuing interests of a discrete social base. Because of this tendency, the mass politics approach has felt traditional political analysis to be deficient.

It is *not* true that attachment to intermediate structures insures attachment to the larger national institutions and structures. As a society undergoes change, it is likely that specific groups will be adversely affected by economic or social change. Similarly, some groups may develop new aspirations and objectives. In both cases they may come to feel that the existent political order is insufficient to command their allegiance. A shifting balance of forces is, however, not the same phenomenon as the breakup of an associational structure, the shattering of a class, or the decline of primary group support. It is even reasonable to maintain that an external threat to a group promotes its sense of solidarity and aids in the development of group identity and organization.[24] Attachment to intermediate structures may indeed promote a shared sense of alienation of the group from the total political order. The more informal organization the group possesses the more likely is it that politically extremist sentiments can be communicated and legitimated. In playing the game of politics, it is not only important whether or not one is permitted to play, but also whether one is winning or not. This problem is not solved by the degree of access which the group has to political association.

The point can be made through an analysis of a frequently used study of McCarthyist attitudes, which mass politics theorists have used as support for their position. Trow's study of Bennington, Vermont found a disproportionate amount of support for Senator McCarthy among small businessmen, especially those holding the nineteenth century liberal hostility to both big business and labor unions.[25] In explaining his findings, Trow maintains that not only are small businessmen "resentful of a world that continually offends their deepest values" but equally important is the fact that they have little voice or representation in political institutions, such as the major parties. Granting the rather dubious assumption that small business has little place in the current constellation of political and ideological forces in the United States, the picture of disaffection portrayed in Trow's study is a classic picture of a well-organized economic group losing out in the process of social and economic change. This type of disaffection is readily analyzed in terms of class and status conflict. If mass movements are not to be understood in traditional forms of political analysis, they must be shown to be unrelated to analysis in terms of group interests and discrete social bases. This would involve more than the traditional view that social change produces disaffection among groups adversely exposed to it.

The assumption of a natural harmony of interests gives rise to another failing of the mass politics approach. This is the lack of concern for the development of consensus around the norms of democratic politics. If it is assumed that representation of interests assures harmony, then the problem of achieving moral sentiments supportive of the political institution becomes meaningless. However, such moral sentiments *are* essential; otherwise, the source of moderate politics, of commitment to the political process *per se* is missing. When the values at stake are intensely held and the constellation of political forces is adverse to a group, there is nothing in pluralistic theory which suggests a source of loyalty to moderateness. Oscar Gass has expressed this in excellent fashion:

> I know that Democracy is a technique for reaching agreement, but it in turn rests upon a measure of agreement. It is, of course, formally true that, if only you agree on the technique of getting decisions, you don't have to agree on the outcome. But that is merely like saying that people can ride on the same bus even if they wish to get off at different places. The places must not be *too* different—or else they have to set a value on riding beyond that of getting to their destinations.[26]

A pluralistic system can be maintained only if the conflict of interest groups is balanced to some extent by cohesive elements in the cultural and social system which moderate the intensity of conflicts and which provide loyalties to maintenance of a defined area in which politics is conducted under pluralistic rules.[27] The ideology of pluralism has become a defense of moderateness, and an attack on political activism. Yet pluralist structure enhances activist sentiments.

Mass Culture and Political Cohesion

Contrary to mass politics theory, conditions of mass societies are not necessarily detrimental to sentiments supporting pluralistic politics. In fact the opposite appears to be the case. Certain conditions of modern, mass societies function to increase cohesion and consensus around norms of pluralist politics.

Mass politics approaches have emphasized bureaucratization, equalitarianism, and technological integration as forces weakening past mediating structures. It must also be pointed out that the same forces operate to incorporate persons into a larger national culture and social system. While mediating structures and local units may be weakened, direct attachment to the total society is enhanced. In Shils' phrase, "The new society is a mass society precisely in the sense that the mass of the population has become incorporated into *society*."[28]

Conditions of mass society develop a homogeneous set of cultural experiences for members. Technological forces have led to an economy and a means of communication which can absorb all the citizens in common. As this has occurred, the autonomy of the local community has given way to a national politics, a national economy and a national culture. In an era of high mass consumption, the equalization of incomes and the style-setting influence of a national market have promoted a more homogeneous standard of living. In the use of commodities and of leisure, as well as in high rates of social mobility, class lines are becoming blurred. In this society, major social institutions operate in similar fashion upon all communities and within most classes. School, church, medicine, family and politics are increasingly open to the influence and control of centrally-trained professionals and their organizations. The consequences of such homogenizing forces are the development of a national mass culture and a national society. In this society, common sentiments increasingly cut across the social segments of class, region, and other sub-cultural units. In this sense mass society is a new social system.

These features of mass society, of course, are recognized in the theories considered above. Where we differ, however, is in stressing these as positive agencies of social integration, rather than only as devices which weaken earlier units of social life. The theories of mass politics suggest only one possible relationship between mass societies and political extremism. In the remainder of this paper we wish to suggest another relationship, one in which the trend toward mass society provides opportunities for strengthening the attachments of the individuals to institutions which accept diversity and support political balance. The conditions of mass society, we suggest, mitigate against political extremism because they operate against the isolation of differentiated sub-cultures from which strong ideological attachments can develop. At the same time, they provide conditions which promote acceptance of innovations.

(1) *They provide sources of direct attachment to supra-local institutions.* It has become something of an axiom in electoral behavior studies that interest and participation is at its highest in national rather than local elections. In a mass society, the individual is oriented toward a national culture and stratification system. Mass culture is carried through national systems of communications and education which may be, and often are, in conflict with local groups. Lack of attachment to local agencies, kinship units and secondary associations by no means implies a lack of attachment to standards, tastes and values of the mass culture. The same is true in respect to political participation. As the range of areas affected by local decisions grows smaller, the orientation of the individual to national political units grows more significant. Studies of cosmopolitan and local

types indicate that the individual may be marginal within his local environment but very much committed to structures of occupational, educational and political organization at levels above that of the local community.[29]

(2) *Mass culture enhances the possibilities of substantive consensus.* We have argued above that although cultural and class diversity provides a resistant force against oligarchic controls, it may also develop intensive attachments to particular aims which prevent the compromise and toleration presupposed by political pluralism. Indeed, pluralistic politics is hard to reconcile with intensity of conviction and a moralistic approach to politics. Insofar as mass societies create homogeneous experience for a population, there is an increased possibility of consensus on substantive issues. Will Herberg's[30] thesis of a growing uniformity in American religions is a case in point. Similarity of education, consumer products, income and communications is also associated with similarity in morals and, to some extent, interests. The issues open to political conflict are then limited and less apt to arouse intense opposition. While this may mean a diminution in ideological commitments and controversy, it is hardly the same thing as production of extremist activism. Indeed, those who are critical of contemporary American society for its presumed conformist tendencies are often dismayed at the disappearance of activism, utopian thought and radical attitudes, all of which are also forms of extremism, alienation and discontent.

(3) *Mass culture can, and often does, shore up the support for consensus on procedural norms of pluralistic politics.* Because they include multiple sub-cultures, mass institutions are open to the influence of numerous social segments in ways in which local and class institutions are not. Further, mass culture is more apt to be influenced by norms of cosmopolitan and nationalized groups than local and sub-cultural units. Within American society today, the norms of pluralist styles in politics find more response at the national than at the local levels. Efforts to censor artistic and educational experiments and dissent are more frequent at the local than at the national levels of education and communications. The development of a mass educational system, with a high degree of equalitarian recruitment, has been a distinctive aid to the acceptance of civil liberties sentiment.[31]

(4) *Mass culture diminishes the intensity of social conflicts by evening out the impact of major social and cultural changes.* Major social changes are frequently disruptive and focus on dimensions which involve clashes between attackers and defenders of tradition. This is particularly true in areas of cultural conflict—religion, morality or race relations are

examples. The appearance of mass communications and educational agencies diminishes the degree to which the population is differentially exposed to a new set of norms. This is seen in the current desegregation crisis in the South. Opposition to a national culture of race relations is found most intensively among those most localistic, least educated, least urban, least exposed to mass media, and least integrated into the national economy.[32] Mass media, the extension of education and professionalization tend to equate the rates at which different classes and regions are exposed to changing standards.

(5) *Mass society increases the linkages between groups and minimizes the possibilities of "superimposition."* The concept of a pluralistic social system often fails to differentiate between two types of segmentation.[33] In one, which we will call "linked pluralism," there are multiple groups but membership in one often cuts across membership in others. A situation of linked pluralism, for example, would be one in which many Catholics are lower-class and many are middle-class while Protestants are similarly represented in each class. Both Catholics and Protestants are "linked" as members of the same social class. "Superimposed" segmentation occurs when membership in one group also implies membership in another. If most Catholics were lower-class and most Protestants were middle-class, then class and religion would be superimposed. It is fairly evident that intense social conflicts are maximized under conditions of superimposition and minimized under conditions of linked pluralism. In the example used, superimposition would mean that religious conflicts tended to be class conflicts as well.

The conditions of mass society tend to increase linked forms of pluralism and to minimize superimposed forms of pluralism. Perhaps the most salient aspect of this is a result of equalitarianism and mobility. When groups are not frozen by rigid stratification into a specific occupational and class position, such social categories as religion, race, residence, and community play less of a role as devices isolating one part of society from another.

It follows from this analysis that there are two major ways in which extremist movements may develop within the framework of contemporary mass societies. In one case, we are dealing with the general problem of reactions to social and economic change already discussed above in reference to "doomed classes" and to groups previously excluded from the political process. The transition from pluralistic structure to mass society is most keenly felt as loss and deprivation by those whose social and economic position is threatened by the development of bureaucratic organization, equalitarian social structure and mass culture. The attention given to the status loss and economic hardship of the "old middle classes" as the society becomes more consumption-oriented, more organizationally structured and more technically professionalized provides one strand of evidence in what Lipset has called the "extremism of the Center."[34] Riesman has expressed the same idea of reaction to change in characterological terms in saying:

> . . . his own life experience is often disappointing; he is deprived of a feeling of competence and place. Even this would not be so bad if the world made sense, if he could apply to what goes on his internalized standards of judgment, but as it is, neither his character nor his work is rewarded. In that situation he tends to turn both on himself . . . and on the world.[35]

The other case exists when groups are isolated from the major institutions and cultural streams of mass society. Localized groups are less open to the impact of the mass agencies. The less educated, the lowest income levels, the least protected minorities, the most fundamentalist in religion are least oriented to the rhythm of modernity with which so much of mass influence is carried. In this case, it is those least "caught up" in the historical currents of transition that are most likely to be immune from the moderating influences of mass culture. To cite such groups as products *of* mass society is misleading.

Carried to a logical extreme, the mass society becomes a political community in which bland tolerance and uniform ideas are the rule. Carried to its logical extreme, pluralistic societies are likely to generate either disintegrating conflict or stalemate. It is fruitless, however, to push typologies to their logical extremes. An empirical sociology must be concerned with the interaction between mass and pluralistic conditions. Elements of one model interact with elements of the other, sometimes as figure, sometimes as ground. De Tocqueville pointed out that one of the characteristics of American political institutions was the moderation of popular government by a leaven of aristocratic rule. He viewed the Supreme Court power of review as one such instance of balance.[36]

Mass conditions are thus likely to present many features which are not only consistent with a pluralistic theory of politics but even enhance such features. Rather than providing a source of extremist movements they are just as likely to mitigate the development of opposition and to increase the degree of toleration for dissent. Whether variety and controversy are likely to develop under the dominance of mass conditions is another question. However, those who seek to understand the conditions of stable, democratic institutions are mistaken in dispensing with traditional concepts and in emphasizing mass society as a demonic villain.

ℰ─⫘─э

Notes

1) The following relevant writings embody the theory of mass politics: Hannah Arendt, *The Origins of Totalitarianism*, New York: Harcourt, Brace and Co., 1954; Erich Fromm, *Escape from Freedom*, New York: Rinehart, 1945; Karl Mannheim, *Man and Society in an Age of Reconstruction*, London: Routledge and Kegan Paul, 1940; William Kornhauser, *The Politics of Mass Society*, Glencoe, Ill.: The Free Press, 1959; Robert Nisbet, *The Quest for Community*, New York: Oxford University Press, 1953; Philip Selznick, *The Organizational Weapon*, New York: McGraw-Hill, 1952.

2) See the discussion of the political effects of social and economic change in Western and non-Western societies in William Kornhauser, *op. cit.*, Chs. 7, 8.

3) We have confined our analysis here to theorists who find mass societies an explanatory tool in analyzing the rise of contemporary anti-democratic movements. Other writers have also described modern society as mass-like and have evaluated it in negative terms. This latter group, however, has not viewed political extremism as a likely consequence of mass conditions. Writers such as David Riesman, in *The Lonely Crowd*, and C. Wright Mills, in *The Power Elite*, have emphasized developing trends toward conformity and passivity rather than toward militance and activism. Still another stream in mass society writings is represented by E. A. Shils. He agrees that modern society is, by reason of mass conditions, best described as qualitatively different from earlier Western societies. This stream of writings, however, denies the disorganizing and overconforming consequences stressed by the other views. See the positive acceptance of mass society in Edward A. Shils, "Mass Society and Its Culture," *Daedalus*, 89 (Spring, 1960), pp. 288–314.

4) Hannah Arendt, *op. cit.*, p. 310.

5) Philip Selznick, *op. cit.*, p. 283.

6) William Kornhauser, *op. cit.*, p. 78.

7) Erich Fromm, *The Sane Society*, New York: Rinehart, 1955, p. 120.

8) The best descriptions of this process in contemporary political science are probably David Truman, *The Governmental Process*, New York: A. A. Knopf, 1951, and V. O. Key, *Parties, Politics and Pressure Groups*, New York: Thomas Y. Crowley, 1947.

9) Edward A. Shils, *The Torment of Secrecy*, Glencoe, Ill.: The Free Press, 1955, p. 231. In similar vein, Nathan Leites introduces his study of French politics by a statement exempting the Communists and the "extreme right" from his discussion. He reasons that their style in politics is distinctly different from the "national" groups of the Center. In the period of post-war politics which he studied, "the extremes entered but little in 'the game' so that the patterns of political calculation used in parliament had little reference to their behavior." Nathan Leites, *On the Game of Politics in France*, Stanford, Calif.: Stanford University Press, 1959, p. 1.

10) Milton Rokeach, *The Open and Closed Mind*, New York: Basic Books, 1960, Ch. 3; Edward A. Shils, "Authoritarianism—Right and Left," in R. Christie and M. Jahoda, editors, *Studies in the Scope and Method of 'The Authoritarian Personality,'* Glencoe, Ill.: The Free Press, 1954.

11) It should be emphasized that the degree of commitment of democratic populations to its political institutions is a relative matter. Many studies of attitudes toward civil liberties show a great gap between the acceptance of civil liberties among a minority of educated and participating citizens and the rank and file, especially among the lower-income and lesser educated. In this case, political extremism represents less an alienation *from* political institutions than it does the advent of increased political democracy. For studies of civil liberties see Samuel Stouffer, *Communism, Conformity and Civil Liberties*, Garden City, N.Y.: Doubleday, 1955; Seymour Lipset, "Democracy and Working-Class

Authoritarianism," in *Political Man*, Garden City, N.Y.: Doubleday, 1960, pp. 97–130; and Raymond Mack, "Do We Really Believe in the Bill of Rights?," *Social Problems*, 3 (April, 1956), pp. 264–269.

12) William Kornhauser, *op. cit.*, p. 77.

13) Karl Mannheim, *op. cit.*, p. 62.

14) Robert Dahl, *A Preface to Democratic Theory*, Chicago: The University of Chicago Press, 1956, pp. 97–98.

15) The term is used by Franz Neumann in "Notes on the Theory of Dictatorship," in *The Democratic and the Authoritarian State*, Glencoe, Ill.: The Free Press, 1957, p. 251.

16) See the articles by Richard Hofstadter and by Seymour M. Lipset in Daniel Bell, editor, *The New American Right*, New York: Criterion Books, 1955. For a fuller treatment of this theme see Seymour M. Lipset, "Social Stratification and Right-Wing Extremism," *British Journal of Sociology*, 10 (December, 1959), pp. 1–32.

17) Murray Edelman, "Government's Balance of Power in Labor-Management Relations," *Labor Law Journal*, 2 (January, 1951), pp. 31–35. This point is also discussed in C. Wright Mills, *The Power Elite*, New York: Oxford University Press, 1957, pp. 246–248.

18) David Riesman, *The Lonely Crowd*, New Haven: Yale University Press, 1950, pp. 242–255.

19) Joseph LaPalombara, "Political Party Systems and Crisis Government: French and Italian Contrasts," *Midwest Journal of Political Science*, 11 (May, 1958), pp. 117–139.

20) *Ibid.*, p. 133.

21) Murray and Susan Stedman, *Discontent at the Polls*, New York: Columbia University Press, 1950, Ch. 8.

22) Seymour M. Lipset, "Economic Development and Democracy," in *Political Man*, *op. cit.*, pp. 45–76.

23) Karl Mannheim, *op. cit.*, p. 70. For discussions of the assumption of a natural harmony of interests see the analysis of sociological thought in C. Wright Mills, *op. cit.*, Ch. 11; Werner Stark, "Christian Thought in Social Theory," in *Social Theory and Christian Thought*, London: Routledge and Kegan Paul, 1959; Ralf Dahrendorf, *Class and Class Conflict in Industrial Society*, Stanford, Calif.: Stanford University Press, 1958.

24) See the discussions of this factor in the history of labor movements in Sidney and Beatrice Webb, *History of Trade Unionism*, New York: Longmans, Green and Co., 1920, Ch. 1, and in Selig Perlman, *Theory of the Labor Movement*, New York: Augustus M. Kelly, 1928, Ch. 5.

25) Martin Trow, "Small Business, Political Tolerance, and Support for McCarthy," *American Journal of Sociology*, 64 (November, 1958), pp. 270–281.

26) Oscar Gass, "Socialism and Democracy," *Commentary*, 29 (June, 1960), p. 574.

27) For an especially illuminating statement of this view, see Adolf Lowe, *The Price of Liberty*, Day-to-Day Pamphlets, No. 36, London: Hogarth Press, 1937. Also see Edward A. Shils and M. Young, "The Meaning of the Coronation," *Sociological Review*, series 1 (1953), pp. 63–81. Political consensus as a focus of sociological study is a central theme in Seymour M. Lipset, "Political Sociology" in Robert K. Merton, Leonard Broom, and Leonard S. Cottrell, Jr., editors, *Sociology Today*, New York: Basic Books, 1959.

28) Edward A. Shils, "Mass Society and Its Culture," *op. cit.*, p. 288.

29) Robert K. Merton, "Patterns of Influence," in Paul Lazersfeld and Frank Stanton, editors, *Communications Research, 1948–49*, New York: Harper and Bros., 1949, pp. 180–219; Alvin W. Gouldner, "Cosmopolitans and Locals," *Administrative Science Quarterly*, 2 (December, 1957 and March, 1958), pp. 281–306, 444–480.

30) Will Herberg, *Protestant, Catholic, Jew*, Garden City, N.Y.: Doubleday Anchor Books, 1955.

31) Studies of tolerance and authoritarianism have repeatedly shown a direct relation between amount of education and tolerance for political diversity. See

Martin Trow, *op. cit.*, and the summarization of many studies in Seymour M. Lipset, "Working-Class Authoritarianism," *Political Man, op. cit.*

32) Melvin Tumin, *Desegregation,* Princeton, N.J.: Princeton University Press, 1958.

33) This distinction and the terms "pluralistic" and "superimposed" are used in Ralf Dahrendorf, *op. cit.*, pp. 213–218.

34) Seymour M. Lipset, *Political Man, op. cit.*, pp. 131–134, 173–176.

35) David Riesman, *op. cit.*, also see Joseph Gusfield, "Social Structure and Moral Reform," *American Journal of Sociology,* 61 (November, 1955), pp. 221–232.

36) Alexis de Tocqueville, *Democracy in America,* New York and London: Oxford University Press, 1947, pp. 493–499.

The Mature Society: Personal Autonomy and Social Responsibility

Marvin E. Olsen

The quest for personal autonomy within a framework of social responsi-
bility is not unique to our era. In fact, it is as old as mankind itself, and
might well be termed the "basic human dilemma."

On the one hand, the individual human being is always dependent on
other people, and hence by his very nature is committed to a social life
with his fellow men. The utter helplessness of the new-born infant is only
the most obvious form of human dependency; throughout our lives we
continually rely on others for the satisfaction of countless physical,
mental, emotional, and social needs. All the knowledge we possess, as well
as our total personality structure, must be learned from other people. Hell
is not physical torture, Sartre suggests in his play *No Exit*, but simply
aloneness. Recent psychological studies of the destructive psychological
effects of extreme social isolation fully support his basic contention.
Finally, no human society of any kind could exist without the constant
interaction and cooperation of large numbers of individuals.

On the other hand, however, human existence is a continual effort to
increase independence of thought and action. Not only in childhood, but
throughout his entire life, the individual is growing and developing—
always reaching for the goal of greater personal autonomy. Life is a never-
ending process of "becoming," to use Gordon Allport's[1] term. On a
much broader scale, the entire sweep of human history, from "cave man"
to "space man," may be seen as man's struggle to free himself from the
bonds of his natural environment and his own ignorance.

Three important generalizations are immediately apparent from this

Reprinted from "The Mature Society: Personal Autonomy and Social Responsibility," *Michigan Quarterly Review*, 3 (July, 1964), 148–159, by permission of the
author and *The Michigan Quarterly Review*.

brief introductory sketch: First, there is certainly no short, simple answer to the dilemma of personal autonomy versus social responsibility. Mankind has wrestled with this eternal problem since the earliest moments of reflective thought, and the perpetually changing conditions of human life will undoubtedly continue to give rise to myriads of new variations on the basic theme. There can never be a "new synthesis" which will permanently resolve the question. By examining and analyzing the issue, however, we may gain new perspectives which will broaden our understanding of this challenge which we all face.

The second generalization is that neither side of the coin—autonomy or responsibility—is satisfactory or desirable by itself. No matter how necessary either condition may be for the effective functioning of individuals or societies, a one-sided solution inevitably invites disaster. The effects of both Hobbes' chaotic "war of all against all" and Huxley's "brave new world" would be to rob man of his essential humanity. The only possible answer to the predicament is some combination of both elements, fused together in a fashion suitable for the given historic context, but flexible enough to change with a changing social world.

Finally, the autonomy-responsibility dilemma is not limited to the problem of the relationship of the individual to his society. Rather, it is a generic question which pertains to all levels of human action. From this viewpoint, the plight of two spouses quarrelling over their family budget is basically the same as two nations debating over the control of nuclear weapons. In these and all other cases of social interaction and organization, the perpetual question of "individual rights" versus "obligations to others" can never be escaped. The terms "individual" and "society" in this paper are intended only as illustrative, and not limiting, cases.

Thus far we have followed the common usage of referring to autonomy and responsibility as two horns of a dilemma, which suggests that to some extent they are incompatible, and can only be satisfied at each other's expense. If it were actually a case of the individual *versus* society, the solution to the quandary would be theoretically quite clear. We should simply put the two conditions of autonomy and responsibility on an analytic "scale" to determine their exact "balancing point," and then apply this "golden mean" to actual situations. Unfortunately, life is never this simple.

The main point I wish to make in this essay is that conditions of autonomy and responsibility do not confront mankind with a dilemma to be resolved through compromise, as is commonly assumed. On the contrary, we should speak of them as a paradox. *Personal autonomy and social responsibility can be mutually reinforcing,* so that an increase in one condition may also produce an increase in the other. The rest of this paper will attempt to explain and illustrate this seemingly self-contradictory proposition by drawing on several contemporary theories and descriptions of social organization.

'What is meant by "social organization"? In bare outline, the idea is as follows: Man is a social creature; he cannot exist alone. In order to satisfy their countless needs—ranging from food and sex to emotional security and intellectual stimulation—individuals are forced to relate their actions to each other. They form social groups in order to join efforts toward securing common goals. Many such cooperative ventures prove fruitless, and are sooner or later abandoned. Some groups do succeed in achieving some of their goals, though, and hence prove satisfying to their members. In order to maintain and perpetuate these collective efforts, the members organize their relationships into certain patterned forms. (This process is often unintended and unplanned, but it can also be purposefully directed.) Furthermore, group members, through symbolic communication, come to identify themselves with the other members and with the organized social relationships which comprise the group. When this happens, individuals are willing to take action to defend the organization from both internal or external disruptions.

These social structures—or organized patterns of social relationships—are "real" in that they have observable effects on their members. If social relationships are to be organized and perpetuated, the actions of the individual members must be controlled so as to make social interaction stable and predictable. Rules of behavior, or social norms, are therefore created by the group and applied to all members. If one wishes to remain a member of the group, he must act in accordance with these group norms. To enforce social norms, two basic types of social controls are established: External controls consist of social sanctions, or rewards and punishments, which are applied by agents of the group to deviant members. Much more efficient is internal social control, in which members are taught (often in early childhood) to value the group norms and to want to abide by them without external sanctions. When norms are internalized in this manner, the social organization not only increases its influence over its members, but it also gains greater cohesion and stability.

Thus far we have been describing social organization as it occurs in relatively small, informal groups. As the population of a group and its accumulated body of knowledge (or culture) increase in size, the social structure of the group almost invariably becomes more complex. Individual members begin to specialize in particular types of activities, and to assume formally designated social roles. (Some role playing occurs in all groups, especially along age and sex lines, but in more complex organizations the number of specialized roles increases rapidly.) Numerous role expectations in turn impose an even greater number of social demands on the group members. Furthermore, increasing division of labor necessitates a more formally organized social structure. If multitudes of specialized activities are to be coordinated and integrated so as to achieve over-all group goals, individuals must be assigned to specified positions in the social structure, and some form of centralized controlling body, or government, must be established. This requires an even greater elaboration of social duties and obligations, with a corresponding spiralling of social responsibilities on group members.

In capsule form, this picture of social organization indicates that organized and controlled group activities are absolutely necessary for the satisfaction of human needs. If groups are to achieve their goals and satisfy their members, these members must take upon themselves many kinds of social responsibilities, including adherence to social norms, performance of role expectations, and assumption of functional obligations. Responsibility is inherent in social life!

A fundamental generalization about contemporary societies on which virtually all social scientists agree is that social organization is constantly becoming more and more complex. The combined pressures of increasing populations and rapidly growing bodies of technical and scientific knowledge are inevitably leading to greater specialization of functions and elaboration of structures. This trend is most evident in Western societies today, but its seeds can be seen sprouting throughout the world.

Elaborate division of labor and complex social organization is most often noted in business and industrial activities, but it also occurs in virtually every other area of human endeavor. If any group experiencing functional differentiation is to remain integrated and productive, it must develop a formalized social structure; specialization without coordination and direction creates chaos. For this reason we witness in all realms of social activity today the accelerating growth of myriads of complex, bureaucratic organizations. Big government, big cities, big business, big labor, big military, big universities, big churches, *ad infinitum*, surround us on all sides. This is not to say that small, intimate groups have vanished from the scene. The family is certainly a very dynamic institution in today's society, and most individuals also belong to many informal neighborhood, friendship, and special-interest groups. But all of these "primary groups," as sociologists call them, are essentially icing on the cake of complex organization.

Formal organizations can take several different basic forms, according to whether they are built around affectual ties, established traditions, fealty obligations, charismatic influences, or rational conceptions. A second universal generalization of social science, however, is that increasingly one of these forms—rational-legal bureaucracy—is coming to dominate almost all types of formal groups. Organized according to rational principles and held together through legal bonds, a bureaucracy can normally achieve its goals much more effectively than any other type of structure, despite its many well-known functional deficiencies. No matter where one looks, from the local PTA to the United Nations, bureaucratic organizational forms predominate. The frequency with which observers of the current social scene note this vast trend toward larger and more complex bureaucratic organizations needs no elaboration here; William H. Whyte's[2] recent debunking of the "organization man" is only one instance of a vast sea of literature which attempts to describe this dramatic process.

The central importance of this dominant trend for our consideration of autonomy and responsibility is quite plain: Social responsibility is inherent in all aspects of social life, but as social organization becomes increasingly complex and bureaucratic, the demands made on individuals by their social environment mount astronomically. Things we take for granted, such as our responsibility to be at work at 8 A.M. and to remain there until 5 P.M., are anathemas to members of simpler peasant societies when they are recruited into a factory for the first time.

What does this seemingly irreversible trend toward large, complex, bureaucratic organization in all spheres of social life mean for the individual member of such a society? More pointedly, what is the future of personal autonomy in "Organizational Society"? The answers given to this question by most contemporary social theorists share one common feature—gloomy pessimism. They see the individual slowly and reluctantly, but nevertheless inevitably, surrendering larger and larger portions of his personal freedom to a monolithic society. The individual eventually becomes nothing but a numbered cog in a vast, impersonal, mechanical organization, and has no choice but to conform to what others (either superiors or peers, or both) demand of him. The result of mass conformity, say these critics, is "dehumanization" of the individual—mankind exists, but man does not. Not only is choice among available actions lost, but also the awareness of the possibility of choice. The individual is left without an identity of his own.

Within this community of despair two fairly distinct schools of thought can be identified:

1.) The older and more traditional picture of the loss of individual freedom to organized society is quite straightforward. Any time an individual joins a group he relinquishes part of his personal freedom to the group, and allows it to control some of his actions. It follows, then, that the larger and more complex the scale of social organization, the more social responsibilities an individual will acquire, and the less autonomy he will retain. The end result of this process is a world in which each person's actions are largely predetermined, and individuals are conditioned to cheerfully carry out whatever tasks are assigned to them. As a corollary to this position, many social philosophers—ranging from Plato to Ortega y Gasset[3]—have stressed the importance of exempting a small elite group from the demands made on the other members of the society. The function of this elite group is to guide and direct the rest of the population, and hence keep the social system functioning smoothly and make human civilization possible. More recently, however, other observers have pointed out that an isolated elite is not necessary to keep a society functioning. Once a full-scale bureaucratic structure is established, they say, it continues to virtually "run itself," regardless of what individuals wish or do. This is the process which Whyte[4] is describing when he warns of the pervasiveness of "the organization."

Regardless of whether one adopts the "elitist" or the "bureaucratic" side of this picture, the result is the same for the vast majority of the population. Mankind is forced to conform to some type of superior authority. The name most commonly given to this type of society, in which the people are virtual slaves to a central controlling authority, be it an elite group or an impersonal bureaucracy or some combination of the two, is *totalitarian society*. The dominant feature of a fully developed totalitarian society is that the governing body exercises absolute and unrestricted control over almost all aspects of human life. To skeptics who scoff at the possibility of ever maintaining complete control over all human actions, these prophets of doom merely point to the remarkable "success" of Nazism and Communism despite their crude techniques. It could very well happen here, they add.

2.) In recent years, a second conception of "Organizational Society" has been developed by a number of social and political theorists. As in the first case, they also see loss of individualism and surrender to conformity as the result of the growth of complex social organization. The crucial difference, however, lies in the direction of this conformity and the nature of the standards to which one conforms. Instead of obeying orders from above, people slavishly seek to abide by the demands of their peers.

The result is a *mass society* of socially isolated or "atomized" individuals. The only guides for behavior are the expectations of an amorphous "they," as perpetuated by mass culture. Control by the masses can be even more destructive of individual autonomy than is control by a centralized authority, these commentators suggest, since the person does not even know who is dominating him. David Riesman's[5] sketch of the "other-directed" individual is the prototype of this "mass man," while C. Wright Mills'[6] description of the "personality market" among white collar workers gives an idea of the effects of mass society on the individual.

To explain how complex social organization produces mass society, these theorists utilize the concept of alienation. As Marx[7] first suggested, there is a vast social distance between the functioning of huge organizations such as capitalistic industries and the highly specialized and routinized everyday experiences of their members. The individual can see no relationship between the particular activities he performs and the attainment of goals by the larger organization. He feels utterly powerless to influence his social world in any way, and this in turn leads to a feeling that life is meaningless. Mills[8] and William Kornhauser,[9] among other contemporary writers, have argued that this condition exists not only in industry, but also in large bureaucracies, in urban metropolises, in national politics, and in all other spheres of life dominated by complex social organization. Modern urban-industrial man, they assert, is denied the sense of "community" which gave purpose and meaning to life in simpler societies. Estranged from a society which is too big and too complex for him, the individual soon begins to lose confidence in his more personal social relationships, and finally even in himself. Contemporary man, alienated from his values, his society, his friends, and from himself, is defenseless against the demands of the anonymous masses. Indeed, he actively seeks out the expectations of mass culture, in a futile attempt to find meaning for his life. The "tyranny of the majority" reigns supreme, in de Tocqueville's[10] words. Writers in this vein merely point to current social trends in the United States; if we are not already a mass society, they say, we soon shall be one.

Although these theories of totalitarian and mass societies differ in many details, there is no reason why they should be incompatible. In fact, to the extent that they are combined, as in the writings of Erich Fromm,[11] their effects on the individual are mutually reinforcing. Certainly there would be very little room for personal autonomy in a society totally dominated by a powerful elite group working through a centralized bureaucratic structure which allowed no effective or meaningful participation by the masses of the people, but kept them satiated with the mental pabulum of mass culture.

Thus far we have struck a uniformly pessimistic note concerning the possibilities for individual autonomy in both present and future societies. We have purposefully given considerable attention to these theories of despair because they dominate so much thinking in contemporary social science. Furthermore, there is certainly no denying the possibility that one or both of these predictions could easily come true, however reprehensible the results might be. But is there no way out of this seemingly unavoidable trend toward increasing limitations on individual freedom? Must social responsibility inevitably wipe out personal autonomy?

This is a question of vital concern to many intellectuals in America. They are aware of the possibilities of our becoming either a totalitarian or a mass society, and they are urgently searching for a means of stemming the tide before it is too late. Most of these "solutions of desperation" can be grouped into two broad categories, which Winston White[12] has labeled the "moralistic" and the "reform" approaches.

Moralists tend to hold the individual responsible for any conditions of mass servitude or conformity that may occur. Loss of personal autonomy, they say, is caused by the weakening of basic individualistic values. This situation is often attributed to a preoccupation with science and technology, so that concern for instrumental means undermines commitments to more enduring humanistic values. These writers do not deny the existence or power of complex social organizations, but they hold that it is the individual's responsibility to recognize this power and to "assert himself against it."[13] To be capable of such resistance, they suggest, the individual must be transformed into a new kind of person. Thus Riesman[14] holds out the possibility of combining "inner-directed" and "other-directed" character types into what he terms "autonomous man." This kind of individual possesses a self-awareness that enables him to carry out those social responsibilities which are functionally necessary, while at the same time remaining free to choose when and how to conform to society and when to assert his unique identity. Quite similar is Fromm's[15] "spontaneously creative" individual who is capable of transforming necessary instrumental actions into creative and meaningful activities which in themselves have value for the person. Needless to say, these ideas appear to offer the perfect solution to our problem—until one asks how they can be achieved in practice. The moralists offer us an ultimate goal, but not a specific plan of action.

Reformers, on the other hand, place the blame for loss of autonomy on the structure of society, not on the individual. If basic individualistic values have been weakened, they say, it is because unsatisfactory social conditions are inhibiting personal growth and development. The individual is essentially a product of his social environment, so that his values will reflect whatever social forces play upon him. The solution to the problem of over-conformity offered by the reformers therefore involves social change. What is needed is a vast, interlocking network of "mediating groups" to fill the structural gap between the individual's personal world of primary relationships and the realm of complex bureaucracies and total societies. These "intermediate groups" are large enough and powerful enough to give the individual member a sense of control over his social destiny and of meaning to his life. At the same time, they are small enough to allow him to retain his unique identity. The prototype of such a mediating group is the special-interest, voluntary association—ranging in size and function from stamp collectors' clubs to labor unions. It is of crucial importance, however, that there be a great many such groups in a society, and that they have overlapping memberships. In this way they can act as checks and balances on each other's power, so that no one group comes to dominate completely the lives of its members, while at the same time they mutually reinforce each other's activities. This idea of the role of intermediate groups in preserving personal autonomy has a long history in social theory, extending from de Tocqueville[16] to Émile Durkheim[17] to William Kornhauser.[18] The reformers without doubt give us a definite plan of action, but their suggestions lack the contribution offered by the moralists—a long-range goal.

It is my contention that although both the moralists and the reformers offer many valuable ideas which should not be ignored, both schools of thought are nevertheless committing a grave oversight. As mentioned previously, most of these writers are looking for "solutions" to the "problem" of loss of autonomy. That is, they have accepted the thesis that increasing social organization inevitably produces greater social control over individuals, and hence reduces personal freedom. This process is seen as a non-problematic phenomenon which perhaps may be limited and re-directed, but which cannot be reversed. This is not to say that increasing social organization could not result in either a totalitarian or a mass society; both forms of complete social conformity are distinct possibilities, given the present drift of world affairs. But we must not overlook a third type of society which could also result from the basic trend toward greater complexity of social organization. Unlike the first two models, it magnifies personal autonomy as well as social responsibility. It, too, is only a possibility for the future—and perhaps not a very likely possibility—but it should not be dismissed on these grounds. I shall call this third model a *mature society*,[19] although social maturity is implied only in relation to the present, and not in any absolute sense. Furthermore, as a conceptual model, or "pure type," it does not represent any real society, although it can serve as an ideal by which actual societies may be evaluated.

To describe this concept of the mature society, we must squarely face the seemingly paradoxical question of how individual freedom can be expanded in a world of increasing social responsibilities. First of all, we must guard against making two common logical errors. One of these is "zero-sum" thinking, to borrow a term from game theory. This approach assumes that there is a fixed quantity of choices available in a situation, so that a gain on one side must result in a loss on the other. While many games, both parlor and serious, do operate on this principle, there is no basis for assuming that it must also apply to the functioning of all social life. Increased social demands may, but do not necessarily, result in decreased personal freedom. In fact, there is no logical reason why both conditions could not increase simultaneously.

The second logical error to be avoided can be called the fallacy of "uncritical induction." Even though a particular relationship between two variables does exist in several specific instances, this is no basis for automatically assuming that it is a general rule applicable to all situations. There may be many other cases which flatly contradict the generalization. Thus, even if the growing complexity of social organization does impose greater social responsibility on individuals in some areas of life, this is no reason for assuming that personal autonomy in a general sense is being surrendered. We may be gaining much more than we are losing.

The next step after noting these two logical pitfalls is to examine the concept of autonomy in greater detail. The dictionary synonyms of "independent" and "self-governing" are inadequate when the term is applied to the totality of human life. Taken too literally, such definitions could lead one to the conclusion that an amoeba is the most autonomous form of animal life, since its actions are minimally dependent on other animals. The concept of human freedom has a long history of intellectual debate and development, which can briefly be summarized in the form of five conditions which must be met before personal autonomy is possible. (1) As emphasized by German philosophers beginning with the Reformation, the individual must be aware of, and committed to, some transcendent values and principles with which he can judge passing historical events. Only in this manner can man escape the fate of all other creatures of being entirely bound to their immediate existence. (2) Thinkers of the

Enlightenment added to this idea the necessity of possessing adequate rational and scientific knowledge to enable the individual to express his ideas in action, and thus bring the world more in line with his ideals. (3) Liberal political theorists, of whom Locke is the best example, have argued that the individual must also be freed from constraining external restraints on his activities, so that it is realistically possible for him to take action to reach his goals. (4) More recent philosophers, beginning with Hegel and Marx, have pointed out that action by the individual can only be successful to the extent that his social world is ordered or organized in such a way that instrumental activities will result in desired ends. (5) Finally, contemporary psychologists from Freud to Fromm have added the observation that the individual will still be incapable of acting in an autonomous manner unless he has achieved sufficient personality development to be able to take on the burdens of independent action without relying on dominating external support. Taken together these ideas suggest that the autonomous individual must have meaningful values and goals, adequate practical knowledge, freedom of action, an ordered social environment, and a high level of personal integration. All these conditions, I suggest, are not only fully possible in a world of complex social organization, but actually require a very elaborate degree of societal development for their fullest expression.

How can a mature society provide these prerequisites for autonomy? A discussion of four major characteristics of mature societies will provide an answer to this question. The first of these characteristics is elaborate functional specialization, or division of labor, which we have already seen is an inevitable factor in the growth of complex social organization. Individuals will be required to play a wide range of quite diversified social roles. Without doubt this will increase a person's burden of social responsibilities, since he must become familiar with many different role expectations. But as Durkheim[20] and Talcott Parsons[21] have pointed out, it also results in greater opportunities for individual freedom of action. Most role definitions do not minutely prescribe required behavior, but rather provide only broad outlines of obligations and privileges for the individual. Within these guidelines there is normally extensive room for personal modifications and variations. And as the number of roles in a social system increases, the rigidity of the role definitions normally declines. Therefore, if the person is limited to playing a few traditional roles, such as in most primitive societies, it is very difficult for him to escape the "cake of custom" which controls so much of his life. With a high degree of division of labor, on the other hand, the individual gains greater flexibility to select the particular roles which he wants to occupy and to play them as he desires. He is released from many of the bonds of ascribed social characteristics such as age, sex, race, and family, and can pursue social positions which are based on individual achievement. Of course, the person may choose to bind himself to customs and traditions —for example, to "carry on the business just as Dad would have wanted" —but at least the possibility of choice of action does exist. This opportunity for the individual to select and play social roles which are compatible with his particular temperament, personality, interests, and talents, is absolutely necessary if he is to achieve autonomy of action.

Second, a trend toward more complex social organization can also produce increased structural differentiation, or diversification of groups and social institutions. Because social roles involve reciprocal behavior, they must always be interrelated within social structures. And the more specialized the roles, the more diversified are the structures which they comprise. In most simple societies one type of group—usually the extended family—performs all of the major social functions, including economic, political, religious, educational, welfare, socialization, affectual, and defense activities. This arrangement works fairly well in a society of 200 people, but with 200 million people it would prove disastrous for personal freedom. The family in such a society would become such a dominant social institution that it would control the entire lives of its members. The modern example of attempted structural unity is the totalitarian society, in which all social functions are controlled by the central government. By contrast, in a structurally differentiated society there is a proliferation of limited, but relatively independent, social groups. In this type of social structure, each person has greater opportunities to participate effectively in groups oriented toward his particular values and goals. At the same time, no one group is strong enough to gain complete domination over all his activities.

We have already encountered this idea of structural differentiation in the suggestion by the "reformers" that a network of overlapping intermediate groups such as voluntary associations is a necessary protection against the emergence of mass or totalitarian society. We are incorporating their proposal of social pluralism into our picture of a mature society, not in the form of a "solution to a problem," but rather as a basic and essential element of the total social structure. Not only does structural differentiation provide meaningful opportunities for individual freedom of action, but it also immensely strengthens the integration and stability of the total society, with a corresponding decline in the possibility of social chaos. Finally, the point must be emphasized that the maintenance of social pluralism in a society is never automatic; it must always be carefully guarded.

A third major characteristic of a mature society is routinization of normal functioning. Any social system must somehow deal with a number of basic problems, or functional imperatives, if it is to survive for long. These include acquiring and training new members, procuring resources and transforming and distributing them to meet the needs of the members, maintaining order so that social interaction can take place with a minimum of disruption, protecting the system against threatening forces, preserving its knowledge and values, and directing and coordinating its overall functioning. In groups that are relatively new, inexperienced, or simply organized, many of these requirements are often handled on an *ad hoc* basis. Unfortunately, many of these "spur of the moment" solutions are inefficient or completely ineffective. Moreover, the members are forced to spend a great deal of their time, efforts, and resources dealing with these basic problems, so that the life of the group frequently centers around the struggle for group survival. A more adequate way of satisfying these functional imperatives is obviously to establish organized, stable social structures which are specifically designed to handle such requirements. Each specialized subsystem can anticipate, plan for, and more effectively solve its particular problems. Thus a complex society with well developed social institutions is much more stable and durable than is a simple folk society which lacks this degree of social organization.

Functional routinization also has consequences for the individual. On the one hand, a society with a high degree of functional complexity does require much social responsibility on the part of its members. But at the same time it also frees the individual from having to devote all his time and efforts to basic subsistence tasks. Whereas the primitive hunter must devote practically his entire life to the job of finding enough food to stay alive, a typical worker in a highly industrialized society can earn in eight hours of work enough money to very adequately feed his entire family for a week. And with increased automation this ratio of work to consumption will decline even more markedly. Or to take another example, most of us in this society rarely have to worry about protecting our homes from fire and theft; as long as we meet our responsibility of paying city taxes, we know that police and fire departments will handle these problems for us.

In more general terms, we are saying that with the growth of complex social organization, problems that previously had to be solved at each occurrence and at great expense to the individual can now be handled relatively automatically through established, routinized procedures. Social life thus becomes more predictable and rewarding. Personal choice is restricted in some areas, but the total autonomy of the individual is greatly enhanced. He is freed from many of the mundane burdens of staying alive, and is given the time and resources to devote himself to more personal endeavors. Complex social organization, and its consequent routinization of some areas of life, actually increases the total number of possible activities and choices within the system. Consequently, the number of choices gained by the individual through this process can be much greater than the number relinquished to the social order. Once again, though, this outcome is never inevitable. For instance, a rigid stratification system which assigned a large portion of the population to menial servitude for the benefit of a small elite would certainly deprive many people of any meaningful autonomy.[22]

The final characteristic of our model of a mature society—encouragement of creativity—is a direct result of functional routinization. Complex social organization gives the individual many opportunities for non-sustenance activities, but what will he do with this free time? Conceivably, he could choose to spend it all amusing himself, or in a drunken stupor. The quality of the choices made by the individual—whether or not they add to the development of both his personality and the society—is largely shaped by his social and cultural environment. If his society does not give him the opportunity, motivation, and education necessary to make wise decisions and seek valuable goals, his personal freedom will be hollow and meaningless. In Fromm's[23] terms, the individual must have "freedom to" participate in creative activities as well as "freedom from" external restraints. The results of turning people loose from prescribed social relationships without also providing them with the skills necessary to use their freedom include such phenomena as feelings of apathy and alienation, perpetual attempts to escape via the mass media, support for strong authoritarian social movements, socially deviant behavior, mental illness, and even suicide. To say that society must shape these more personal activities of the individual does not imply that once again personal autonomy is lost; the ultimate choice of creative activities must remain with the individual. But if his freedom of decision is to have any real meaning, appropriate social conditions must exist to guide him in worthwhile directions.

A mature society can encourage individual creativity by providing these social conditions that make possible and probable the upgrading of human activity to higher levels of achievement. It is a curious fact of human existence that our collective problems are never eliminated. As a society develops various social institutions to "solve," or routinize, old problems, these social arrangements themselves raise many new questions of a higher order for the society to face. Modern society may have solved the problem of maintaining sustenance, but a primitive group would never face the issues of technological unemployment. Utopia, it appears, is never attained by arresting the process of social evolution at any given stage. Life is a continual series of challenges; as we meet and conquer one hurdle, we are inextricably led down the path toward other more demanding challenges which call forth in us even higher levels of performance.

This process of continual social evolution provides many opportunities and demands for the full development of individual abilities. Standards and expectations for personalities and behaviors are upgraded in the face of rising challenges. The person is encouraged and taught to improve the quality of his cognitive, esthetic, and moral knowledge and judgments. Not only is he freed from giving full attention to his basic biological needs, but he is led to develop to their fullest extent those capabilities which are uniquely human and expressive of his highest potential. In short, social evolution provides the foundation and encouragement for the growth of individual creativity. Furthermore, as more and more members of a society achieve "freedom to" participate in creative activities, there is a general growth in both the quantity and the quality of the cultural heritage.

On the other hand, the members of a society might at any time choose to endure rather than attempt to solve present problems, and hence effectively halt the process of social development. Social, cultural, and personality growth will occur only if individuals continually face toward the future rather than the past, and are always willing to confront increasingly demanding challenges. To encourage such attitudes, the society must possess a body of transcendent and enduring values which will serve as goals and guides in all social activities. At this point, then, we must include the suggestions of the "moralists" in our model of a mature society. As with the reformers, we are using these ideas not as "solutions of desperation," but rather as essential elements of the total picture of a mature society. The main emphasis of the moralists, it will be remembered, is on the necessity for strengthening basic values within the individual, so as to better equip him to meet the demands of a complex society. They are insisting that we not lose sight of the elementary truth that the ultimate worth of any society, no matter how mature it may be, lies in its contribution to human betterment. At the same time, a society is only as strong as the social relationships among the individuals who

432 ≈ *To Secure the Blessings of Liberty*

comprise it, and these in turn depend ultimately on the values which shape and guide human action. If socially mature values—such as the importance and dignity of the individual, the right of freedom of thought and action, and the necessity of always considering the consequences of our behavior for other people—are not institutionalized in the functioning of a society and internalized within most of its members, that society may well become nothing but an elaborate prison which confines and destroys its inmates.

As a means of integrating our thoughts up to this point, let us review the five criteria for personal freedom discussed earlier, to see if our model of a mature society has fulfilled all of them. These five requirements were meaningful values and goals, adequate functional knowledge, freedom of action, an ordered social environment, and a high level of personal integration. The first characteristic of a mature society—elaborate division of labor—facilitates the growth of knowledge in all fields of endeavor by freeing individuals from ascribed positions and customs and allowing them to specialize in those roles to which they are best suited and in which they can make the greatest contribution to society. The second characteristic—increased structural differentiation—ensures freedom of individual action by distributing social influence and power among a variety of relatively independent groups which hold each other in check while at the same time giving expression to all shades of opinion and interest. The third characteristic—functional routinization—provides an ordered and stable social environment by establishing definite procedures for dealing with the everyday problems of individual and societal maintenance, so that these factors do not dominate people's lives. The final characteristic of a mature society—encouragement of creativity— makes possible the upgrading of human activity and the development of higher levels of personality integration by providing opportunities and stimulation for the growth of human creativity, which in turn also preserves and strengthens basic values and goals of personal autonomy. It is for these reasons, then, that I propose the concept of the mature society as a model of a social system which integrates personal freedom and autonomy with complex social organization and responsibility, so that each supports and reinforces the other. The individual's potential for personal autonomy is a direct consequence of his interdependence with others in society. Our basic paradox of autonomy *and* responsibility is thus resolved.

As a concluding note, we should stress again a point which has been mentioned repeatedly throughout our discussion of the mature society.

The trend toward increasingly complex social organization which we are witnessing today can lead toward several different types of future societies. Unfortunately, the two types which are the least desirable from the point of view of individual freedom—totalitarian and mass societies—are perhaps the easiest paths to follow, since blind inertia alone will provide much pressure in both of these directions. On the other hand, the model of a mature society presented in this essay offers probably the most difficult goal of all for societal development. There is nothing inherent in complex social organization which insures inevitable evolution toward more mature forms of social life. In fact, there are so many hazards and pitfalls along this path that we should ask if it is even possible for any society to approach the goal of social maturity, however relative that goal may be. My answer to this question is that relative social maturity is indeed possible, though never inevitable, if certain pre-conditions are continually met.

First, the society must develop techniques for controlling and directing social change. Any society with a high degree of social organization is bound to experience many structural and functional strains; the extreme complexity of the system virtually prohibits perfect harmony among all its parts, and there will be unlimited opportunities for real conditions to depart radically from ideal conceptions. The result of these strains will be continuous and extensive social change within the society. Although this change does produce many problems for the system, it is not undesirable in itself, since only in this manner can the society keep moving along the never-ending path toward greater social maturity. However, sheer exhaustion from dealing with perpetual strains and changes can also cause a social system to disintegrate. If a society is to successfully overcome the challenges and problems which are inevitable in human social life, it must develop some skill in handling social change, so that progress can be achieved with a minimum amount of disruption to the system.

Second, the society and its individual members must always be guided in their actions by fundamental humanistic values. We must never lose sight of the fact that in all social life the individual person is an end in himself, and not merely a means to some other goal. Not only are these basic values an essential element of the mature society, as we saw previously, but they also play a crucial role in leading us toward that goal. The path toward increasing social maturity is easily lost; a depression or would-be demigod can often lead a society astray, as seen in Germany in the 1930's. This path can be successfully followed only if these humanistic values continually light the way and guide our struggles. These values cannot be hollow slogans and rituals, but must be built into the structure and functioning of all social institutions, and deeply internalized by most individuals.

The third pre-condition for the attainment of a mature society is deceptively simple—a great deal of purposeful and dedicated human effort. Certainly no degree of social maturity throughout a whole society can be attained in even a few years. We must be content to do the best we can today, and then look to succeeding generations for the fruition of our efforts. To give in to frustration, bitterness, and despair at the slowness of the process is only to admit defeat. The struggle can be eased somewhat, though, if we can learn to avoid blind, impetuous actions. To the extent that we rationally direct our social activities through objective analysis and purposeful planning, they are much more likely to achieve permanent and meaningful results. In short, the mature society will never just occur, but we can create it if we are willing to put forth the necessary effort.

The ultimate question is this: Will mankind come to understand the paradox of its own existence—that humanity fulfills its destiny only to the extent that both personal autonomy and social responsibility are maximized—before it is too late for us to choose our own path to the future?

Notes

1) Allport, Gordon, *Becoming* (New Haven, Yale University Press, 1955).
2) Whyte, William H., *The Organization Man* (Garden City, Doubleday and Co., 1956).
3) Ortega y Gasset, José, *The Revolt of the Masses*, anonymous translation (New York, Mentor Books, 1950).
4) Whyte, *op. cit.*
5) Riesman, David, with Reuel Denney and Nathan Glazer, *The Lonely Crowd* (New Haven, Yale University Press, 1950).
6) Mills, C. Wright, *White Collar* (New York, Oxford University Press, 1951).
7) Marx, Karl, *Economic and Philosophic Manuscripts of 1844* (London, Lawrence and Wishart, 1959).
8) Mills, *op. cit.*
9) Kornhauser, William, *The Politics of Mass Society* (Glencoe, The Free Press, 1959).
10) Tocqueville, Alexis de, *Democracy in America*, 2 vols. (New York, Alfred A. Knopf, 1957).
11) Fromm, Erich, *Escape from Freedom* (New York, Rinehart and Co., 1941).
12) White, Winston, *Beyond Conformity* (Glencoe, The Free Press, 1961).
13) Whyte, *op. cit.*, p. 14.
14) Riesman, *op. cit.*
15) Fromm, *op. cit.*

16) Tocqueville, *op. cit.*

17) Durkheim, Émile, *The Division of Labor in Society*, translated by George Simpson (Glencoe, The Free Press, 1949).

18) Kornhauser, *op. cit.*

19) This term is mine, but I am indebted to Winston White, *op. cit.* and Talcott Parsons for several of the ideas presented in the following discussion. See Parsons and White, "The Link Between Character and Society," in *Culture and Social Character*, edited by Seymour M. Lipset and Leo Lowenthal (Glencoe, The Free Press, 1961), pp. 89–135.

20) Durkheim, *op. cit.*

21) Parsons and White, *op. cit.*

22) From this observation it could be argued that a mature society also requires relative homogeneity of social status, with a minimum of social distance between the lowest and the highest status levels. Furthermore, there should be no sharp boundaries between any two status levels, so that social mobility can easily occur. Such a condition of relative status equality and open mobility is being approached in the U. S. today.

23) Fromm, *op. cit.*

to ourselves

Each generation of Americans relates to its posterity in three ways. First, each generation leaves behind a legacy of accomplishments and unfinished business which shapes the world in which its posterity will live. Second, each generation seeks to commit those that follow it to the continuing tasks of clarifying and striving for the Preamble goals. Third, each generation affects the supply of resources available to future generations.

This introduction looks first at the legacy the present generation of Americans in leaving to its posterity, the commitments it seeks to generate in them, and the resources it works to leave for them; it then turns to the problems of planning and shaping the future in which America's posterity will live.

The Present American Generation and Its Posterity

The present American generation leaves to its posterity a mixed legacy, one of great accomplishments, many from its own inheritance, coupled with much unfinished business. Full membership in "We the People" is increasingly regarded as open to all who are born in the United States. There is also a growing agreement to limit the ranks of the foreign-born eligible to become American citizens through immigration restrictions.

and our Posterity . . .

Yet, the questions of how all are to attain full membership in the society and of how, if at all, to control the natural growth of population are far from settled. The basic structure of the American union, with powers divided between public and private spheres and among state and federal agencies, is well formed, although adjustment to the growth of federal power is uneasy and incomplete. A system of justice through law is firmly established, but there are questions as to how well it serves the poor, how far to extend the rights of the criminal, and how to control the discretion of the police.

The society is basically tranquil, although threatened from both the right and the left. The United States is prepared to defend itself against military attack, but a true peace eludes it. Moreover, the possibility that military views and interests will subvert the traditional dominance of the civilian remains a constant threat. The general welfare has reached unprecedented heights, but not all share in it. Better means of coordinating private and public endeavors are needed, as are more effective antipoverty programs. Finally, the blessings of liberty are secure in that democracy, law, and the mixture of pluralistic and mass society characteristics free most individuals *from* most constraint. However, many wonder whether the present social and technological environment helps or hinders those who strive to use their freedom *to* develop their personalities and talents.[1]

Whatever its legacy, however, the present generation would not have fulfilled its responsibilities to posterity if it did not also generate a commitment in the next generation to continue to clarify and strive for the Preamble goals, and if it did not create or conserve the resources needed to implement that commitment. As in any pluralistic community, and as reflected throughout this volume, this task is complicated by disagreement over just what should be transmitted. Some would be content to pass on only a generalized understanding of the Preamble goals without also transmitting any particular ideology or program detailing how they are to be achieved. They would prefer to encourage each generation to adopt the specific ideas and programs best suited to the particulars of their own time. Other Americans would commit posterity to a set of means as well as a set of goals. They would have posterity seek not only to promote the general welfare, but to do so within the framework of a capitalistic system. They may also wish that their posterity continue to defend the United States but not resort to aggressive or preemptive warfare, and that America forever search for justice, but always with a strong regard for due process of law. And there are some who would be specific with respect to one goal but not another.

No matter how posterity comes to define the Preamble goals and to strive for them, it will need certain resources if it is to persevere.[2] The responsibility of the present generation is to help insure that those resources are available. In the past, the availability of resources was guaranteed by their sheer abundance in unexplored and undeveloped areas of the nation. The young had only to "go west" to find the resources they and their country needed. However, in present-day America, deliberate and systematic efforts are required to guarantee the availability of resources to posterity. Future generations will need fresh air and clean water, but unless steps are taken to reduce and prevent pollution, they will become unusable. Similarly, only proper conservation programs will guarantee a supply of lumber for building materials and pulp. The supply of some resources has to be replenished, and finite sources of energy as coal and oil will have to be substituted for someday.

[1] For an alternate view of the unfinished business which the next generation will face, see Donald N. Michael, *The Next Generation* (New York: Random House, 1965).

[2] The future resource needs of the United States are discussed in Harrison Brown, James Bonner, and John Weir, *The Next Hundred Years* (New York: Viking, 1957); and Hans Landsberg, Leonard Fischman, and Joseph Fisher, *Resources in America's Future: Patterns of Requirements and Availabilities, 1960–2000* (Baltimore: Johns Hopkins Press, 1963).

Steps taken now can help future Americans make better use of alternate sources of energy such as the sun and the atom.

The supply of knowledgeable and skilled manpower also must be continually replenished. The present generation has the responsibility to teach its youth how to understand and cope with the society in which they will live, but the pace of social and technological change may render obsolete many of the lessons the present generation can teach. Fortunately, youth can be taught how to acquire new knowledge and skills on its own. Indeed, lessons on learning to learn or on how to adapt to change could prove to be most valuable in a future where social and technological development will be commonplace. Some of the other problems and changes which await the schools that seek to train the next generation are discussed in "Education in the Next Generation" by Donald N. Michael.[3]

Finally, above and beyond the obligation to conserve or replenish the human and material resources which posterity will need, there is the obligation to preserve life itself: the obligation to avoid a nuclear holocaust which will render the world virtually uninhabitable and America's posterity a dream (or nightmare).

Planning and Shaping the Future

Each American family is charged with the responsibility of planning and shaping the future of its own progeny or posterity. Each family helps shape the future behavior of its offspring through its practices during the crucial years of childhood. Each transmits its own interpretation of the Preamble goals. Finally, within the limits of its own finances and foresight, each family protects the future of its own children through savings, insurance, and other investments.

But the family is not alone in these endeavors. The child is also influenced by his school and his peer group, and possibly by such groups as the Scouts and the Y's. Youth-oriented political organizations such as the Students for a Democratic Society, Young Democrats, Young Republicans, and Young Americans for Freedom seek to induce youth to help perpetuate one or another frankly partisan interpretation of American goals. And beyond the efforts of groups and organizations explicitly and specifically concerned with youth, lie the efforts of government, science,

[3] For other views on the problems facing the American educational system, see Martin Trow, "Two Problems in American Public Education," in Howard S. Becker (ed.), *Social Problems: A Modern Approach* (New York: Wiley, 1966), pp. 76–116; Burton Clark, *Educating the Expert Society* (San Francisco: Chandler, 1962), pp. 280–291; and Paul Goodman, "Compulsory Mis-education," *Compulsory Mis-education and the Community of Scholars* (New York: Vintage Books, 1964), pp. 1–154.

and industry, to protect and shape the future through intelligent planning.

The planning efforts of government have been limited by two characteristically American beliefs: first that human nature and collective life are rendered so unpredictable by man's Free Will that meaningful planning is not feasible, and second that the existence of an extensive and detailed plan will induce public officials to coerce private citizens to meet the demands set forth by the plan.[4] Nevertheless, Americans have come, albeit begrudgingly and with much hesitance, to accept limited government planning in certain areas, namely those involving natural resources, defense, the economy, and the development of cities.

Governmental efforts to help conserve natural resources extend back to 1891 when Congress passed the Forest Reserve Act giving the President the power to set aside timber lands. The greatest expansion of governmental conservation efforts, however, was made during the administrations of Theodore Roosevelt and Franklin Roosevelt. The federal government now has programs to help conserve soil, forests, wildlife, water-power, mineral resources, and fuel deposits. More recently, efforts have been made to protect America's supply of fresh air and clean water from the polluting effects of the activities of private industry, local government, and private citizens.[5]

While the commitment to plan for the conservation of natural resources has roots in the nineteenth century, extensive peacetime defense planning is a relatively recent development (post-World War II). Prior to the cold war, the United States habitually began the great bulk of planning and preparation of its defenses after fighting had begun. In the present era, however, billions of dollars and millions of men are engaged in providing for future defenses even in the absence of overt military aggression. Initially, cold war defense plans concentrated on the establishment of alliances and on the deterrence of nuclear attack. More recently, the plans have been extended to include preparations for involvement in limited "brush-fire wars," with only the token assistance of American

[4] Criticisms of governmental planning are made in Benjamin F. Young, *Social Planning in the United States: The Road to Collectivism* (New York: Pageant Press, 1960). Factors encouraging support for planning are discussed in William O. Stanley, "The Collapse of Automatic Adjustment," in Warren G. Bennis, Kenneth Benne, and Robert Chin (eds.), *The Planning of Change* (New York: Holt, Rinehart & Winston, 1961), pp. 28–34; and Robert E. Lane, "The Decline of Politics and Ideology in a Knowledgeable Society," *American Sociological Review*, XXXI (October, 1966), 649–662.

[5] Conservation efforts in the United States are reviewed in David C. Coyle, *Conservation: An American Story of Conflict and Accomplishment* (New Brunswick, N.J.: Rutgers University Press, 1957); Guy-Harold Smith, *Conservation of Natural Resources*, 3rd ed. (New York: Wiley, 1965); and Stewart Udall, *The Quiet Crisis* (New York: Holt, Rinehart & Winston, 1963).

allies. Furthermore, in a parallel development, plans to protect Europe against the Soviet Union and against Communist-inspired subversion have been supplemented by plans to defend Asia against China and Communist-assisted "wars of national liberation."[6]

The government has also recently made efforts to plan for its economic future, to insure its vitality in the years ahead. Since the Great Depression of the 1930s, the government has worked to avoid the extremes of boom and bust, of inflation and deflation, which have plagued the economy in the past. The level of government spending and taxation are now set with a realization that they affect at least the immediate economic picture. An increase in spending or a drop in taxes may create inflationary pressures, while a decrease in spending or a rise in taxes may create deflationary pressures.[7]

Of course, governmental economic planning in the United States is not as detailed and extensive as in Communist nations; nor is it coordinated. Usually the plans seek to affect the factors upon which decisions are based rather than to order or require specific decisions. For example, interest rates may be raised to discourage the making of loans, but loans are not forbidden. Congress, the President, and such agencies as the Federal Reserve Board and the Securities and Exchange Commission each play more or less autonomous roles. Still, the very existence of any economic planning, even if lacking in detail and coordination, reflects a departure from the abhorrence of planning inherent in the laissez-faire economics of America's past.

While planning in the areas of conservation, defense, and the economy is primarily the result of efforts by the federal government, planning in the cities is more a matter for local governments. Urban planning presently concentrates on providing the physical facilities needed by individuals and organizations to carry out their own purposes. It concentrates on construction programs to provide homes, shopping centers, and recreational facilities with a transportation system to link them so people can use them as they wish.[8] There are, as yet, few explicit attempts to

---

[6] See Roswell Gilpatric, "Our Defense Needs: The Long View," *Foreign Affairs*, XLII (April, 1964), 336–378.

[7] See E. L. Dale, Jr., "Another Look at the New Economics," *The New York Times Magazine*, September 18, 1966, pp. 50ff.; Alvin Hansen, *The American Economy* (New York: McGraw-Hill, 1957); and Arthur F. Burns, *The Management of Prosperity* (New York: Columbia University Press, 1966) for discussions of the impact of taxing and speeding programs on the economy.

[8] See Alan Altschuler, *The City Planning Process* (Ithaca, N.Y.: Cornell University Press, 1965); and F. Stuart Chapin, Jr., *Urban Land Use Planning* (Urbana: University of Illinois Press, 1965), for discussions of urban planning in the United States. See also Melvin M. Webber, "The Prospects for Policies Planning," and Harvey S. Perloff, "Social Planning in the Metropolis," in Leonard J. Duhl (ed.),

plan and shape the goals of the community and of its individual members.[9] Some of the difficulties entailed by attempts at such planning are reviewed in "Social Planning, Social Planners, and Planned Societies" by John W. Dyckman. Planning by local governments concentrates on improving extant communities and rarely calls for the creation of entirely new communities as did the plans for Reston, Virginia and Irvine, California.[10]

Other efforts to shape the future are being made by the private agencies of science and industry. Scientists constantly seek to extend the future resources of man; new elements and chemicals are created and new materials devised. In the future, man will have available metals far stronger and fabrics far more delicate than any provided by nature. Labor-saving devices, from the sewing machine to the computer, free people to make better use of their own personal and mental resources.[11] Science has extended resources to combat disease after disease, from smallpox to polio. Present-day researchers look forward to the conquest of the threats posed by cancer, heart disease, and other illnesses.

Industrial organizations play a role in shaping the future by supporting much of the research which enables science to extend man's resources. Industry also plans for the expansion of physical plants and the introduction of more efficient means of production. Further, new product lines are carefully considered and plans made for introducing them. Research and development have become integral parts of modern, large-scale industry.

The future, then, is of concern not only to families and youth-oriented organizations, but to government, science, and industry. No matter who is concerned, intelligent action with respect to the future has two basic ingredients: the determination of the available alternatives; and the establishment of the priority and importance of each of the goals to be attained. That is, intelligent efforts to plan or shape the future call for knowing both what is possible and what is desired.

It is extremely difficult to discover precisely what alternatives lie

---

The Urban Condition (New York: Basic Books, 1963), pp. 311–318, and 319–330, respectively.

[9] Possible goals for community life and the city planning appropriate to it are discussed in Paul Goodman and Percival Goodman, *Communitas: Ways of Livelihood and Means of Living* (New York: Vintage Books, 1960).

[10] See Edmund K. Faltermayer, "We Can Cope with the Coming Suburban Explosion," *Fortune*, LXXIV (September, 1966), 147–151, 187–190, and especially p. 188 for comments on "new towns."

[11] See George S. Counts, "The Impact of Technological Change," in Bennis, Benne, and Chin, *op. cit.*, pp. 20–28.

ahead. Almost certainly, nobody living in the 1760s could have foreseen that the United States would be a nation torn by civil war in the 1860s. Nor is it likely that anybody living in the 1860s could have foreseen with accuracy the character of life in the United States of the 1960s. However, plans need not be made for a century to come. They may only cover a generation or even only half a decade and the shorter the time span, the more accurate the prediction can be. Moreover, within a relatively short time span, predictions and plans can readily take into account developments already underway. For example, supersonic passenger planes and electric automobiles will, no doubt, be among the means of travel available to future generations. Their development has already begun and their advantages are obvious. Similarly, it can be confidently predicted that Americans will soon make wide use of automation and computers. They have already begun to do so.[12] One may even, as John Friedmann and John Miller do in the selection "The Urban Field," predict the general character of the cities of the future based on trends and developments already underway.[13] Finally, the development of the sciences, especially of the social sciences, will help predict the future by discovering the factors which have the greatest impact on the course of events and by uncovering such regularities as the affairs of man and his environment exhibit. Of course, the "scientific laws" of human affairs may never enable predictions as accurate as those based on the laws of physics or astronomy. Nevertheless, they may permit sufficient accuracy to render some intelligent planning feasible. Even with a complete picture of the possible alternatives, however, no plan can be intelligently drawn unless the priority and importance of each desired goal has been established.[14]

In general, the alternative leading to the goal with the highest priority is to be chosen from among incompatible alternatives. For example, where justice and tranquillity cannot both be attained, the path to justice is to be taken if it has the higher priority. Similarly, knowing the importance of a given goal helps to determine if the costs of taking

[12] The present and future effects of automation on society are discussed in John T. Dunlop (ed.), *Automation and Technological Change* (Englewood Cliffs, N.J.: Prentice-Hall, 1962); Paul Einzing, *Economic Consequences of Automation* (New York: Norton, 1957); William Francois, *Automation: Industrialization Comes of Age* (New York: Collier Books, 1964); and Charles E. Silberman (ed.), *The Myths of Automation* (New York: Harper & Row, 1966).

[13] See also John C. Bollens and Henry J. Schmandt, "The Shape of the Future," in *The Metropolis: Its People, Politics and Economic Life* (New York: Harper & Row, 1965), pp. 577–598.

[14] The role of setting the priorities of goals in the process of planning is discussed in Leonard A. Lecht (ed.), *Goals, Priorities and Dollars: The Next Decade* (New York: Free Press, 1966), pp. 1–12, 17–27.

the path leading to it are justifiable. For example, military defense is regarded as important enough to many Americans to justify a very great cost in money and lives in order to provide for it.

Until Americans come not only to clarify what their goals are, but to specify the priority and importance of each, no amount of knowledge and foresight will complete the task of planning for posterity. Until their meanings, priorities, and importance are established, difficulty and controversy will surround the efforts of

We the People of the United States, . . . to form a more perfect Union, establish Justice, insure domestic Tranquility, provide for the common defence, promote the general Welfare, and secure the Blessings of Liberty to ourselves and our Posterity. . . .

Perhaps this is as it should be. Surely, it is as it has been in a society where plural and differing values are considered legitimate.

It has been the aim of this book to identify the difficulties and to specify the vital problems which continually have been, and will be, encountered in attempts to master the problems of meanings and means—the problems of defining and implementing the goals to which the Preamble commits America.

Education in the Next Generation

Donald N. Michael

Changing Perspectives

Only gradually, and chiefly at the occupationally elite level of society, will it become evident that the educational requirements for productive and meaningful lives will require profound changes in the procedures, substance, and spirit of the educative processes, beginning at least as early as the primary grades and continuing throughout life. Values and behavior that emphasize and comfortably mesh commitment to task; flexibility in learning, unlearning, and relearning; constructive attitudes toward and effective use of more hours of leisure, and so on, cannot be taught just at the college level, or probably even as late as high school; and they cannot be taught by teachers who do not share these values. They probably must be learned in childhood and then modified throughout life as an active learning experience.

On a national scale this deep change in the philosophy and content of education can only come gradually as the appropriate influential institutions develop sufficient sense of where they should go and what needs to be done to get there. More research will be necessary to determine what needs to be done and which of the many ways explored are the most effective and economical. These studies will be evaluated and re-evaluated, if only because there will be partisan argument about their meanings. Then the results, good, bad, and indifferent, will have to be understood and accepted by those who must act on them to alter the complex institutions of teaching. This will require changes in the viewpoints of Congress, state legislatures, teachers' colleges and schools of education, public school systems, PTA's, taxpayers, and, not least, the teacher. After this the changes will have to be applied. Still later, the products will begin to move into the adult world.

Then, too, various powerful and vocal groups will slow the rate of the inevitable and necessary commitment of truly large-scale Federal Government investments for educational support. In the words of the Carnegie Corporation:

> Race, religion, federal "control" of education, division of the spoils among the states, the purposes for which aid should be given—each of these issues has figured as an effective deterrent to passage since the beginning of federal aid legislation. But whereas in the past one issue, or a combination of two or three, has been sufficient to block legislation, now *all* of them are involved in the controversy, which leads . . . [to] . . . an extremely dim view of the possibilities of early passage of general aid.[1]

Gradual, erratic, disparate as these changes in education will be, they nevertheless will be great over the next twenty years.

Elementary School and High School Developments

More intensive experiments will be conducted to determine better ways to use live teachers, team teaching, and teachers' aides; programed and self-paced instruction and audio-visual aids. The results will be applied gradually in more primary and secondary schools, particularly those whose student bodies are relatively privileged. To the extent that these methods for learning depend on self-starting and self-sustaining motives, they will be more easily and successfully applied to these privileged youth. Then, too, such experiments need strong support from parents, teachers, and school administrations. Generally, these conditions are more likely to be found in the wealthier communities where parents, by virtue of their socioeconomic position, are more likely to have favorable attitudes toward teaching experiments and toward providing their children with the best opportunity to compete successfully for college acceptance. As a rule, too, the more imaginative and experimental teachers and administrators will find their way to these better schools because of their superior working environments, higher pay, and greater status.

In the better primary and secondary schools the more talented students will be increasingly allowed to blur the boundaries between school years by dealing with subject matter according to their ability rather than by age or grade. Until programed instruction is used and administered more imaginatively, and until teaching and administrative staffs have physical resources and personal commitment sufficient to deal with the coming school population explosion better than they deal with today's situation, self-paced study at least for the superior student (including such as advanced placement and honors programs) and team teaching are likely to be the two most widespread changes instituted within and among schools.

Another change will grow from the likelihood that all school levels from primary through university will move toward a twelve-month operation. Greater variety of subject matter and increasing numbers of students will encourage this change. Vacations for some students (particularly the preprofessionals) will be shortened, and not all students and teachers will have their vacations at the same time. Staggered vacations will both ease the teacher's work load and permit a more even distribution of demand on increasingly overloaded recreational facilities. It will also encourage a more even distribution over the year of the (longer) vacation periods of working parents.

The significance of the junior high school and its future trend seems to be summed up by Margaret Mead:

> The junior high school has become a forcing ground for inappropriate and socially maladjusted attitudes in both boys and girls, laying the basis for hostility to females on the boys' part and, on the girls' part, grasping pressure toward marriage combined with contempt for males. Although these deficiencies of the junior high school are widely recognized, the attractiveness of using new junior high schools as a quick solution to the population pressures on the school system makes it probable that the evils of the junior high school will increase rather than decrease during the next decade.[2]

At the same time, it is likely that more school systems will experiment with graded or ungraded arrangements which eliminate the junior high. The shortage of good teachers who are willing to teach junior high, more flexible teaching and administrative schemes, and the problems Mead emphasizes will add incentives to try other arrangements.

Programed Instruction

The potential flexibility and utility of programed instruction seems very great indeed, and it is being used and will be used imaginatively and fruitfully.[3] However, little of this potential is likely to be exploited to the fullest during the next decade or so. Wilbur Schramm, in his summary of the present and foreseeable state of programed instruction, has this to say:

> a) Although the research gives us little reason to be satisfied with the theories and the standards of today's programing, and every reason to believe

that it will be possible some day to make programs vastly more effective than today's programs, nevertheless programed instruction shows signs of hardening, partly under commercial pressure, into a fixed and mechanical technology, with theories and procedures taken for granted.

b) Although programed instruction has within it the potential to turn the attention of education and educational research more intensively and productively than ever before to the processes by which humans learn, there is very little sign that it is being used productively to test theories of human learning or theories of cognitive process, or to enlighten the teacher concerning the process by which she teaches.

c) Although programed instruction is essentially a revolutionary device, in that it has the potential to help free man from some of his bondage—the waste of human resources where there are no teachers or where people cannot go to school; the waste of time and talent where all students are locked into the same pace, and all teachers into the same routine; the tyranny of tradition which permits the study of a certain topic to begin only at a certain age, and expects a student to accomplish only so much as a questionable test of his ability says he can do; and the inadequacy of outmoded and inadequate curricula—despite this, programed instruction is very slow to rise to such a revolutionary potential.[4]

Thus, unless otherwise noted, subsequent discussions of the role of teaching machines and programed instruction assume that, for a number of years at least, their popular application, with notable exceptions, will be to facilitate a relatively pedestrian level of factual learning and as an adjunct to today's typical modes of educational administration.

Of course, experiments with programed learning, teaching machines, and related aids are and will be conducted in run-of-the-mill and deprived schools in the hope that these devices will overcome the limits imposed on live teachers working with large classes. Funds for such experiments will be progressively easier to find, but it will take time to train staffs to teach effectively by these means, to gain the active support of parents, and to generate motives in the students which will be rewarded by the fact of learning correctly. (Doubtless, studies focused on expanding the variety of motives that teaching machines can stimulate and reward will be under way.) But unless the government and the educational establishment make an all-out effort to provide funds and direction for changing the school system as a whole, the rate of introduction of these methods will be slowest in precisely those schools whose students have relatively the most to gain through the substitution of good programed learning for overworked or mediocre teachers.

Possibly by the 1970's the situation will have reached a sufficiently critical state for the government to take the lead on the required scale. By then, the educational gap between the well educated and comparatively poorly educated will be serious and obvious, made so by growing and unmet demands for people capable of working with exceedingly complex ideas and situations, which the next decade will produce in abundance, and by decline in opportunities for well-paying, high-status jobs for those with only a mediocre education, to say nothing of the desperate plight of those with little or no education.

. . .

Organizational Trends at the College Level

Because they face the same problems as the primary and secondary schools, colleges will only gradually make important improvements, and these will be uneven. Nevitt Sanford, editor of *The American College,* puts it this way:

> The American college, and American institutions of higher learning generally, are embedded in our culture and in our society. They are expressive of persistent trends, and persistent conflicts, in the American value system, and they have a diversity of important functions in society. This means that fundamental or widespread change in the colleges can come about only when there is a shift of emphasis in our general system of values or when there is a change in our general societal processes.[5]

In the next twenty years higher education will be struggling with problems parallel to those facing the nation. Most important, the colleges and universities face an enormous population explosion. According to the Office of Education, the 4,200,000 students enrolled in the fall of 1962 are projected to increase by 24 per cent by 1965, by 67 per cent by 1970, and by 111 per cent by 1975! And these projections do not fully consider the potential enrollment of older adults returning in growing numbers for refresher courses, degrees, and for sheer intellectual and aesthetic stimulation during their increasing leisure time.[6]

Housing problems will themselves be enormous; Dr. Ernest V. Hollis, Director of College and University Administration in the Department of Health, Education and Welfare, estimates that two to three billion dollars will be needed annually for plant and equipment.

Administrative problems and experiments in administration will increase as more and more schools try to deal with a heterogeneous community of youth, many from backgrounds totally unfamiliar with the idea of higher learning and traditional university values. A growing portion of students will be well past the age of consent, many will be married, and many of the older students will be unsympathetic to rules designed to enforce the university's role *in loco parentis*.

Decentralization of administration and social control by dividing the student body into "houses" or "colleges" is one trend likely to gain in popularity. Another trend already well under way is the proliferation of satellite universities and junior colleges intended to absorb the less intellectually endowed and less career-focused students. The demand for school administrators will increase greatly. But in the absence of an adequate supply of good ones, and even in their presence, the ubiquitous computer will take on more and more of the paper work. In the days of the small college or university "individual student attention" was the minimum standard to which the administration aspired. However, the population explosion will make dim indeed the chances for implementing this standard. Under the combined impact of impracticability and the pressure to deal efficiently with paper work, the tendency will be to organize the administration of large universities around the rationalized procedures the computers make possible.

As the university population grows and becomes more heterogeneous, the university's ability to fulfill its role *in loco parentis* will lessen, and in some places disappear altogether. The rules in the books may become more explicit and precise for a few years, but enforcing them will become too tedious. Moreover, as parents come to see the large university as in reality a rather large community, with many of the more unsavory characteristics of the world outside the home, they will come less and less to expect the large university to substitute for themselves. Gradually, then, the large university or college will lose its protective role and the student will come to it expecting to be an autonomous individual, as he has been in most European universities.

However, European institutions of higher learning have had smaller student populations than ours do, and students came to them with a more intellectual and less socially oriented set of expectations about themselves and university life. Clearly, there will be emotional adjustments to be worked out in the big university environment as immature youths, in the midst of trying to find out who they are, are exposed to new ideas and to youths and older people from different backgrounds who espouse and live by many different values. For the emotionally secure student, this environment will be rich and stimulating. For the less secure youth, the sheer size and drive of the system may well push him into encapsulating himself among his own kind, thereby stripping the university experience of much enrichment beyond what he learns applicable to getting a job, or a spouse, or making "contacts." It is not impossible that married students will become mentors to the unmarried, and older students to the younger, married or single. By and large, the peer group will be the single most potent source of guidance. If the group is inspired by contact with ideas and a live teacher to spark real intellectual and emotional growth, this will be the chief mechanism available at large universities for learning and insight. For the great majority of the students, "higher education" probably will not add much more than it does now to their wisdom or deeper understanding.

Not all colleges and universities will be so big that they will face the problems and opportunities just speculated on. There will be a growing number of smaller satellite and independent two- and four-year colleges. Moreover, many of the better smaller colleges will restrict enrollment to about present levels. By keeping enrollments small these colleges will be able to skim off the best applicants. On the other hand, many of the applications to the two-year colleges and satellite institutions will be from those not acceptable at the central colleges; these institutions will be more likely to get the less desirable students and have less experienced and less talented faculties. Whether the latter trend is expressed this clearly will depend in part on how satisfied good students and good faculty will be with the environment of the big university. It is possible that later there may be a migration of better students and faculty away from the big institutions, analogous to the migration to the suburbs. This may be especially true in the humanities and the fine arts where large central physical facilities and laboratories are not prerequisites for training or original contributions as they are (and will be even more) in the natural and social sciences.

Moreover, the smaller institution will be able to continue to act *in loco parentis* and those students and their parents who prefer this relationship will seek out such institutions, even if the quality of the faculty and plant are not as imposing as those of the biggest universities.

Teaching Methods at the College Level

Like primary and secondary schools, colleges will be pressed to develop and use audio-visual and related machines to improve the quality and amount of learning per unit time and to lessen the human teaching load as the student population increases. Both reasons will be influential, but the better institutions will emphasize the first, and the bigger or poorer schools, the second. The efflorescence of junior colleges and training schools will especially encourage this trend. There will not be enough good teachers to go around. Salaries offered in these schools will not be competitive with those of the richer schools; many classes will be too large for a good teacher to be truly effective; and much of their subject matter will be of the sort that can be relatively easily programed. These schools will have little choice but to amplify the quality and quantity of their staff by using audio-visual aids and teaching-machine programs.

As the college population grows, less and less of it will have opportunities for personal exposure to great live teachers, or even very much to mediocre ones (though vicarious exposure to great teachers will increase through closed-circuit TV and films). To be sure, this is already frequently the case as classes become larger and teachers more preoccupied with research. But with the increasing use of machine teachers and machine graders, attitudes toward the purposes of teaching and learning may be deeply affected. Important differences in perspective may develop between the viewpoints of those chiefly exposed to the facts-and-methods teaching machines and those relatively few also regularly exposed to the give-and-take of good live teachers.

Already the trend at each educational level is for only the most promising students to be truly exposed to an intimate teacher-student relationship. More and more, the relatively few good teachers will arrange their time and attention to mold and inspire the most interested and creative students through the give-and-take of conversations and essays involving the continuous, constructive "intellectual midwifery" that (insofar as we know) only live teachers can provide. The vast remainder of the student body will learn in good part, but not exclusively, from closed-circuit television, films, and teaching machines, and will be tested automatically as well. Whether programed instruction will be able to provide the special influence of a good live teacher remains to be discovered. But the research needed is certain to take long and the implementation of any positive findings, still longer. Meanwhile, the growing size of the student body will increase the pressures to provide whatever education can be offered most of them via more primitive programs and machines.

Quality of Education at All Levels

Over all, the difference in quality of education for average students will diminish and will average up rather than down, at least for factual learning—and, perhaps, for something more than that, if the number of better qualified instructors increases rapidly enough and as carefully planned teaching films and TV are used more broadly. But the difference between the learning experience of the ordinary student and the extraordinary one will be great.

However, it will become easier in future years to pay for a "higher" education. More and more subsidies will be available for both students and institutions. Two conditions are likely to stimulate the pace of giving: the continuing shortage of skilled people and the economic necessity to keep not-yet-skilled young people out of the competitive labor market. Support will be in the form of loans, outright gifts, and gifts contingent on occupational or service commitment to the fund's source, as is now the case with those receiving an advanced education at the expense of the military services and with those institutions doing contract research for the government and industry.

On balance, the next years will very likely see the beginnings of a pre-elite comprised of students who receive a special education at each level, which in turn will prepare them better than average students for special education at the next level. This has, of course, always been so to some extent. Education programs geared to the capabilities and career plans of students are already a trend, as evidenced by multiple "track" high schools and by two-year colleges which emphasize subjects congruent with the needs of local industry. But this trend will become more widespread and more urgent as the needs and standards for superior intellectual ability become ever higher in order to keep up with burgeoning social and technical problems and the exotic techniques available for trying to deal with them. This is not to say that the "elitist" trend will not be fought; it will be politically touchy indeed. Many schools will reject the elitist approach, and many will hide their compliance with it by hiring additional mediocre teachers to give the impression that all students receive equal attention. And, too, these students won't be defined as an "elite." Instead, they will more likely be described as especially dedicated and endowed potential "social servants" who, by virtue of their willingness to forego the pleasures of leisure, are to be compensated by a more intensive education which will also make them better social servants. The chances are good that a growing sense of the threat to social survival from growing social complexity will encourage this tendency to attend most solicitously to the most promising.

Over the next two decades all of these factors are likely to contribute to a state of mind in many adults and young people that unless one is highly talented, the "natural" way to learn is chiefly by depersonalized means. In large parts of the population it will also reinforce the view that the chief purpose of education is to provide the prerequisites for a well-paying job. Both views will be consonant with the general state of mind embracing or submitting to increasing rationalization.

Occupation-Oriented Education at All Levels

Primary and secondary school training for work and for style of living [for] would-be professionals, skilled technicians, and the unskilled will become more differentiated and focused than is now the case.

By and large, the most accomplished of the professionals (which increasingly will include management) will for the next two decades tend to work long hours, be time-oriented, require a deep and broad background in their fields, and need a lifelong ability to absorb fresh intellectual material. The youth aiming for such a career will begin to prepare for it early in life—certainly in high school, in most cases probably in primary school—if he is to compete successfully for access to the advanced education needed for professional success. Even though there will be more centers of higher education, the chances are that relatively few of these will be perceived as providing the best training and, at least in the physical sciences, probably only relatively few will be able to provide first-rate training. Top faculties in many of the most demanding and demanded professions will continue to be relatively scarce, as will be basic but costly equipment. The preprofessional student will also have to make a career choice in a broad but specific area (e.g., law vs. social science vs. physics) earlier than those not aspiring to a profession. He will be a "grind" in school rather than a seeker after "personal" experiences. Generally, he will feel more anxiety and be subject to more restraints on his time and activities which, compared to other youths, will hem him in and more intensively channel his activities. And if the youth has the talent, especially if he is a boy, he will be under increasing pressures to choose such a way of life in the national interest.

The technician (and more skilled jobs will become technical jobs as both standards and techniques become more demanding) will often, but not always, work shorter hours than the professional; be trained at a specialty; frequently expect to change specialty two or three times in his working life; and possess the social and psychological capabilities for learning a new specialty and for moving to another place to practice it. Since he will be well paid, he will also need training and values to make additional leisure time a rewarding social and private experience.

For many technical tasks it will not be necessary to be as time-bound in outlook as the professional. Thus the student will be more casual about when he selects or is selected for education emphasizing job training; he will not have to make his general career choice as early or irrevocably as the preprofessional. He will be able to "play around" more throughout most of his schooling and, very possibly, his school hours will be fewer than the preprofessional's. He may also have more time to study non-vocationally oriented topics.

The unskilled will be unskilled because he will be relatively poorly educated, poorly motivated, and poorly incorporated into the values and behavior of the society of the intellect toward which we are headed. Thus he will also be poorly paid, whether he works short or long hours. A disproportionately large portion of the unskilled work force will be nonwhite, especially Negro, at least for the next two decades, simply because a disproportionately large portion of the nonwhite population will continue to receive education inadequate for more demanding jobs.

Not everybody will fall neatly into one of these three categories, of course, and the numbers in each category will not increase all at once. In particular, those planning creative careers in the fine arts and humanities will probably be exposed to and follow teachers and values very similar to those which now characterize these activities. The growing popularity of the fine arts and the growing number of potential artists will put greater strains on student-centered methods of teaching, and no doubt improvements will be introduced which use machines in ways similar to those now used in language teaching. But no great social forces applied through the formal educational system will drive the arts in the direction of mediocrity or mass production.

The humanities will also continue free from undue pressure, though much of what is now taught in the large lecture hall will increasingly be taught by machine and film, and often taught much more effectively and vividly by these methods than by good scholars who are poor teachers. The proportion of younger students majoring in the liberal arts or taking many courses in them will probably decrease in the years ahead as the requirements for well-paying jobs demand more hours devoted to technical subjects. But the proportion of older people using their increased leisure time to study the fine arts and humanities will increase, in part because neither they nor the subjects will be oriented toward work.

Nevertheless, the three occupational categories described above will become sufficiently large and sufficiently important and different in social function and personal value so that those who follow these three paths will be exposed to different educations, each gradually evolving into different emphases in substance and values. These trends toward educational differentiation will parallel another type of differentiation which, by and large, will tend to reinforce the type of schooling characteristic of these three categories. Primary and secondary schools will continue to be good, mediocre, and bad depending on the economics, politics, and related factors associated with their geographic and ethnic location. The good schools will become better, being most responsive to the precursors of change and most able to take advantage of new methods to make the best of the changes anticipated. The mediocre schools, generally speaking, will improve, but not so much and not so all-inclusively, being subject to forces limiting foresight and funds and having to service many more students. The poor schools will probably become "relatively" poorer compared to the others—at least until the alienation and unemployment spawned by them produces a national crisis. But for some time yet, much will tend to work against these schools, including public indifference and frequently hostility, as well as the impotence and misdirected motivations of the students and their families.

.   .   .

Guidance Counseling

There will be increasing emphasis on vocational guidance for both privileged and underprivileged youth, but adequate guidance will be difficult to provide and will for many years be least effective where most needed. Unless there are major changes in present operating conditions, qualified guidance personnel with the wide-ranging knowledge and (most important) with the influence to affect school curriculum planning will be in short supply for many years. It is estimated that only about three fifths of the recommended number of high school counselors. There are twice as many men as women counselors in secondary schools, a ratio which takes on special importance in the light of needed changes in occupations and avocations for women.[7]

Guidance will be especially important for technicians' jobs, since these will be the jobs most subject to change in a rapidly changing technology. Counselors will need detailed information about occupational opportunities two or ten years ahead and about anticipated labor markets abroad. But . . . it will be several more years, at least, before such information *may* be forthcoming.

Then, too, effective vocational guidance should be based on statistical knowledge about the characteristics of those who fail or succeed in particular occupations. But in the years ahead, job requirements and working conditions will change greatly—so greatly that different personal characteristics will be required in many jobs which may appear not to have changed because they will still carry the same old labels. (As a case in point, the frequent first-priority requirement today is that a scientist be able to get along on a team; in the old pattern, the scientist frequently was better off if he preferred to work alone.)

To counsel well requires knowledge about both candidate and job. But, increasingly the counselor is unlikely to have any real feel for the environment or spirit of the new occupations. Moreover, the high rate of technological change and rapid growth of specialized skills will mean that job types, variety, and qualifications will be changing relatively rapidly, especially in the skilled technical area. Such jobs will go to the less privileged and more average youth, but this group will be the most difficult for the counselor to reach in the more overcrowded, under-staffed schools—which are also likely to be the least well organized to adjust their programs in the light of anticipated job changes.

Private enterprise and unions will probably contribute substantially to career guidance, as they now do through their in-service education programs. In this way, their own future needs will be well served.

Education for Values and Perspectives

In the years ahead there will be growing debate about the purposes of schooling beyond education for jobs or the national interest, and about how to educate to realize these purposes. Most fundamental will be the continuing and growing debate about the proper role of education in inculcating values and behavior appropriate to each of the occupational categories described above in a rapidly changing, complex, and contra-dictory world. Over the next twenty years this debate about the proper values for youth—who when they grow up will live in a world quite different from the world their elders know and can understand—will be carried on by parents and leaders, most of them trained by the past. It will be an intense debate and a partisan one, since we will continue to be unclear about the kind of world we want and what education we wish to emphasize for those ends. Unless we choose the garrison state as our preferred means for seeking preferred ends, this confusion will probably increase as our world becomes more complex. (For example, of renewed importance will probably be such issues as the virtues of saving and conserving versus those of spending and using up. On this and other issues, it will probably be socially desirable that different segments of the youth population hold different viewpoints when they become adults. These will be more fully subscribed to if they are cultivated during childhood and adolescence.) Implicit in the debate will be very difficult questions about the processes involved in teaching and changing values. For, although the understanding of the motivational and learning processes operating in the school context is considerable, it is still practically limited and will continue to be so until subtle studies providing additional understanding have been completed and evaluated.

At any rate, it is highly likely that, whatever else is involved, changing student perspectives will require teachers whose values are also appropriate to tomorrow's world. However, in general, primary and secondary school teachers for at least the next decade will continue to be recruited from backgrounds that stress lower-middle-class values of good behavior, "fitting in," political neutralism or conservatism, nationalism, reservations about alternative life styles, and conventional means for obtaining economic security.[8] They do not notably stress commitment to task, craftsmanship, independence, integrity, spontaneity, wide-ranging social and cultural tolerance and experiment, and attitudes encouraging the expectation of occupational changes. Thus, to considerable extent, the debate is likely to be an abstract one for most schools and students for many years.

One major focus of this debate will have to do with the extent and content of education for leisure and avocations. Conventional viewpoints on the virtues of work and pressures to remove educational "frills" in order to speed up the production of skillful workers will vie with the economic necessity to train youth in techniques for the voracious consumption of leisure-time products and to keep as many young people as possible out of the competitive work force. Stress on the need to teach the virtues of and means for the "creative" and "productive" use of leisure will increase, too.

As time goes on, this debate will be paralleled by many experiments in education for leisure—some specifically focused, some attempting to combine leisure and work. Margaret Mead suggests:

It should be possible to develop a new kind of vacation center which would provide for individuals of different ages—alone or as members of family groups—previews and test experiences of things they might do if they wished. Such a center would be a place where one could try out under expert tutelage the possibility of learning a new language, or dressmaking, or mechanics, or short story writing, or philosophy; it could provide the novice or the slightly trained student with two weeks of carefully planned laboratory experience in well-equipped, modern laboratories, with test experience in a field related to one in which the individual already had a growing interest—marine biology for the student who had some grounding in general biology, food chemistry for the student who had an elementary knowledge of general chemistry, and so on.[9]

Experiments such as the one Mead describes will involve education of the "how to do it" and "how to do it well" variety for all age levels, as well as the inculcation of values emphasizing the virtues of nonwork. But students who will have the most time free for leisure will be mostly from social backgrounds that are (so far, at least) little interested in the creative use of leisure and are made uncomfortable in the absence of the self-respect and preoccupation that derive from a job which takes up much of their time. These students are likely to be in the less experimental, less imaginative schools. Yet, in effect, the debate will be about just these schools. Even assuming that social pressures and the inclinations of school boards and parents favor such experiments, it is far from clear that teaching leisure-oriented values in school environments comprised of teachers, administrators, and plant-oriented toward operational efficiency and the production of workers is possible. While debate and experiments are very likely to increase, it is unlikely that by 1980 the formal educational system will be able to deal with leisure on the scale or with the emphasis that the topic deserves.

For all the reasons discussed above—the need for nation-wide occupational retraining and updating, the need to educate for more meaningful leisure hours, the economic necessity to keep unskilled young people out of the competitive labor force, earlier retirement, the increasing numbers of older adults seeking more education—it will gradually come to be recognized that, for either work or leisure, education can no longer be something essentially completed halfway through a person's third decade, at the latest. Erratically and unevenly during the next twenty years, we will experiment with and begin to establish a multilevel educational system which will encourage those of any age to continue their education for both work and leisure from wherever they left off to wherever their abilities permit them to go.[10] But we begin from a very low level and have a long way to go.

The most damning single fact about higher education today is that among nearly 2,500 accredited and unaccredited institutions there seem to be fewer than half a dozen radical experiments dedicated to testing new conceptions of what college life, and hence adult life, are capable of becoming. Unless not only the scholars and teachers and administrators who launch new ventures, but the parents and philanthropists who support them, all show more courage and imagination in the next decade than they have in the past, the fruits of universal higher education are likely to taste rather tinny.[11]

∽⊃

Notes

1) Carnegie Corporation of New York, "Education and Politics," *Quarterly*, January 1963, Vol. XI, No. 1.
2) Mead, Margaret, "Problems of the Late Adolescent and Young Adult," *Golden Anniversary White House Conference on Children and Youth.* Department of Health, Education and Welfare. Washington, D.C., 1960, p. 3.
3) Mechner, Francis, and Donald A. Cook, "Behavioral Technology and Manpower Development." New York: Basic Systems Incorporated, 1964.
4) Schramm, Wilbur, *Programed Instruction Today and Tomorrow.* New York: Fund for the Advancement of Education, 1962, pp. 37–38.
5) Sanford, Nevitt, ed., *The American College: A Psychological and Social Interpretation of the Higher Learning.* New York: John Wiley & Sons, 1962, p. 17.
6) Hechinger, Fred M., "Education: A New Pattern—Colleges Face Dramatic Changes in Student Population," *New York Times,* September 16, 1962.
7) Westervelt, Esther, *The Recruitment and Training of Education/Vocational Counselors of Girls and Women* (mimeo.), President's Commission on the Status of Women. Washington, D.C., March 14, 1963.
8) Friedenberg, Edgar Z., *The Vanishing Adolescent.* New York: Dell Publishing Co., 1962.
9) Mead, Margaret, "Outdoor Recreation in the Context of Emerging American Cultural Values: Background Considerations," in *Trends in American Living and Outdoor Recreation,* Outdoor Recreation Resources Review Commission Study Report 22, Washington, D.C., 1962, p. 24.
10) Mead, Margaret, "Thinking Ahead: Why is Education Obsolete?" *Harvard Business Review,* Vol. 36, No. 6, p. 23.
11) Jencks, Christopher, "The Next Thirty Years in the Colleges," *Harper's,* October 1961, p. 128.

References

Bailey, Stephen K., Richard T. Frost, Paul E. Marsh, and Robert C. Wood, *Schoolmen and Politics, A Study of State Aid to Education in the Northeast,* Vol. 1 of The Economics and Politics of Public Education. Syracuse, N.Y.: Syracuse University Press, 1962.

Bowles, Frank H., "Patterns of Dominance and Choice," *College Board Review,* No. 38, Spring 1959, pp. 5–10.

Bricks and Mortarboards—A Report on College Planning and Building, Educational Facilities Laboratories, Inc. New York: Ford Foundation, 1964.

Bruner, Jerome S., *The Process of Education.* Cambridge, Mass.: Harvard University Press, 1962.

David, Henry, ed., *Education and Manpower.* New York: Columbia University Press, 1960.

De Grazia, Alfred, ed., "The New Educational Technology," *The American Behavioral Scientist,* Vol. VI, No. 3, Trenton, N.J., November 1962.

Drucker, Peter, "Education in the New Technology," *Think,* Vol. 28, No. 6, June 1962, pp. 3–5.

"Education in the Age of Science," *Daedalus,* Gerald Holton, ed., American Academy of Arts and Sciences, Winter 1959.

Evans, Luther H., and George E. Arnstein, eds., *Automation and the Challenge to Education.* Washington, D.C.: National Education Association, 1962.

Jacobs, P. E., *Changing Values in College.* New York: Harper & Row, 1957.

Jencks, Christopher, "Slums and Schools," Parts I and II, *The New Republic,* Vol. 147, No. 10 and 11, September 10, 1962, pp. 19–22, and No. 12, September 17, 1962, pp. 13–16.

Kimball, Solon T., and James E. McClellan, *Education and the New America.* New York: Random House, Inc., 1962.

Martin, Roscoe C., *Government and the Suburban School,* Vol. 2 of The Economics and Politics of Public Education. Syracuse, N.Y.: Syracuse University Press, 1962.

Mayer, Martin, *The Schools.* New York: Harper & Row, 1961.

Munger, Frank J., and Richard R. Fenno, Jr., *National Politics and Federal Aid to Education,* Vol. 3 of The Economics and Politics of Public Education. Syracuse, N.Y.: Syracuse University Press, 1962.

Rivlin, Alice M., *The Role of the Federal Government in Financing Higher Education.* Washington, D.C.: The Brookings Institution, 1961.

Sexton, Patricia Cayo, *Education and Income: Inequalities in Our Public Schools.* New York: Viking Press, 1961.

Sufrin, Sidney C., *Issues in Federal Aid to Education,* Vol. 4 of The Economics and Politics of Public Education. Syracuse, N.Y.: Syracuse University Press, 1962.

Tannenbaum, Abraham J., *Adolescent Attitudes toward Academic Brilliance.* New York: Bureau of Publications, Teachers College, Columbia University, 1962.

Wrenn, C. Gilbert, *The Counselor in a Changing World.* Washington, D.C.: American Personnel and Guidance Association, 1962.

Social Planning, Social Planners, and Planned Societies

John W. Dyckman

Social planning is a belated and tentative response of American planners to functional lag. Physical planning, particularly of cities, has been accepted as a legitimate activity at the governmental level for more than half a century. Economic planning, though partial and inconstant, has been an established part of the governmental scene since the 1930's. Social planning, on the other hand, has been openly recognized only more recently, and then it has proceeded under a cover of confusion which has prevented public debate on its scope and its intentions.

For the most part, social planning in the USA is defensive, and arises from the crises which are spun off as by-products of action programs of government. Public intervention in urban development and renewal, for example, has cast up problems of relocation which are so intertwined in the fabric of social life of the affected communities that "social" planners are called upon for relief.

At the same time, the residual issues of the affluent society are so clearly social issues that earlier concerns of physical and economic planning have in some cases given way to priorities for direct planning of social outcomes. The Poverty Program, for example, recognizes that the problem of poverty is not merely a problem of economics, but is also a problem of the culture of poverty which can be addressed only by direct social action. Juvenile delinquency, mental health, and a range of other social ills are, in the view of the behavioral scientists who examine them, more than economic problems. Indeed, there are many who argue that a

Reprinted from "Social Planning, Social Planners, and Planned Societies," *American Institute of Planners Journal*, 32 (March, 1966), 66–76, by permission of the author and publisher.

planned economy cannot eliminate these problems. The presence of social pathology alongside planning then becomes an argument against an excessively "materialistic" view of society. Paradoxically, opponents of the excessive economic determinism often attributed to Marxism are cast in the role of advocates of increasing planning in the social sphere.

Other types of social planning have been made necessary by rejection of the "planned society" of socialist economists. The whole complex of welfare services which have grown up in the United States were traditionally, and still remain, devices to compensate for the wastage and breakage in a competitive, individual-serving, industrial society. They have existed to cushion the blow of this competitive struggle for those so disadvantaged as to be unable to compete effectively. The traditional social services, both privately and publicly provided, are ad hoc solutions for specific problems. They have not, until recently, drawn upon a common context or comprehensive planning outlook.

The notion of coordinated social services, of planned cooperation between agencies, is relatively recent in the field of social welfare and social work. But even where such coordinating councils exist in cities or metropolitan areas, their planning is roughly advisory (except for determinations which enter into the division of the Community Chest) and lacks measures of progress which would guide the allocative decisions. Even more important, the social goals which planning would presumably help to advance are vague and are often stated so as to obscure rather than to adjudicate differences between the goals of the independent agencies.

As a result, there is a great deal of remedial social action, and some social planning in the United States, but this goes on in the absence of even a schematic societal plan which will guide the individual plans of the operating agencies. Societal planning in the United States is principally hortatory, as in the National Goals Reports issued during the Eisenhower Administration.

Some of the most thoughtful work on the meaning of social planning in the American context was instituted several years ago under the direction of Everett Reimer for the Puerto Rican Planning Board. Reimer, assisted by Janet Reiner, commissioned thoughtful papers by Herbert Gans, Abraham Kaplan, and other consultants, and produced many useful internal memoranda. In one of these papers Gans clearly distinguished "societal planning" from "social programs." The former is much more difficult to treat, since it entails some specification of the goals of the society, while the latter are farther along in the "means" end of the means-ends continuum. Gans developed a paradigm for locating programs and actions in this framework which is an excellent statement for orientation to the problem of social planning in the context of the remedial actions of social agencies traditional in the United States.[1]

Let us extend this line of reasoning, and take *social planning* to mean the effort to plan for the fate of a whole society. This view emphasizes the interdependence of activities and the shared consequences of program actions. It recognizes that there may be unplanned consequences of planned actions, and that these may deserve attention equal to that given the programs themselves. Much of the concern with social planning among city planners in the United States stems from the unplanned social dislocations and stresses that follow upon public programs such as re-development. In a comparable vein, the interest in social planning in developing economies arises from similar stresses that follow upon planned economic development. Indeed, the former draws heavily on the literature developed in the latter, and both have made liberal use of studies developed in crisis situations such as bombings, floods, and depor-tations. The problems of disrupted working class urban neighborhoods described by Gans and others are in one perspective a pale copy of the disruptions and strains on social goals of political realization, social justice, and cultural self-expression which have accompanied pursuit of the goal of economic development in preindustrial societies.

When societal goals are advanced by unilateral programs of service agencies, unexpected or perverse results may emerge. Thus the goals of economic justice may dictate an emphasis on low-cost meritorious con-sumer goods such as housing, and the goals of social justice may indicate that the housing should be placed in neighborhoods as favored as those claimed by higher income groups, but the actual programs for achieving these goals may make for outcomes that disturb the harmonious relations between groups, aggravate class tension, and encourage some forms of antisocial actions. Programs of economic development have almost in-evitably favored certain classes whose cooperation was vital to the program, to the relative disadvantage of others. More specifically, these programs have been concerned with incentives necessary to realization of the goals, such as high rewards to entrepreneurs, which may have been paid for by relatively disadvantaged groups. One can proliferate examples of this kind, both in economic development and in urban renewal. These examples dramatize the need for a true social planning framework in which to evaluate the social consequences of individual programs.

To clarify these relations, we might distinguish three operational meanings of *social planning*, and three levels of action.

1) At the societal planning level, social planning means the selection of the social goals of the nation or state, and the setting of targets for their achievement. It requires a ranking of these goals, and assessment of the cost (in terms of other objectives) of achieving them, and judgments of the feasibility of such programs.

2) Social planning, in a closely related meaning, involves the application of social values and action criteria to the assessment of programs undertaken in the pursuit of economic or political goals. Thus, it can mean the testing of the consequences—in terms of intergroup or interpersonal relations—of everything from broad economic development programs to specific redevelopment projects.

3) Social planning can mean specifically "social" programming arising from the broad social goals of the community. The traditional welfare activities of public and private agencies have been the principal focus of such planning in the United States. The coordination of programming for and by the multitude of caretaker agencies that have grown up in our free enterprise economy is a popular task for this type of social planning.

Much of the discussion of social planning, and the identification of activities under this label, belongs in the third category. It is my contention that this category has developed in a variety of directions without an adequately specified set of objectives at the first and second levels. This view is independent of considerations of the planned society, though subsequent discussion will make clear that the latter are not irrelevant to it.

Social planning has long been treacherous ground for the city planner because of the ever present danger that the expert determination of need might degenerate into the imposition of class or professional prejudices upon a resistant clientele. Social planning, in the sense of determination of the social needs of a community or a group within the community is torn between the desire to require certain levels of consumption of merit goods on the one hand, and the recognition of the legitimacy of individual choice on the other. Many social planners assert that their interest is in the maximization of opportunity, or freedom of choice. But as a practical matter, no society has found a feasible way of maximizing choice for all groups or individuals at all times. For the exercise of one man's choice is a limitation on the freedom of choice of another.

It is not surprising that social planning has often turned away from goals, in the direction of means. For one thing, it is firmly in the tradition of modern clinical psychology, and the positivism of sociology, to accept individually determined ends as legitimate, and to emphasize means of realizing these ends. But it is a matter of some subtlety, worthy to challenge the professional social actionist, or clinical caretaker, to emphasize the manipulation of behavior, rather than the alteration of goals of behavior. Let us consider some of the problems encountered in these tasks.

Finding Appropriate Remedies: Diagnosis of the Client

Remedial social planning is necessary in our society because the major forces shaping our lives are unplanned. Social planning has come to the fore because we have been unable to predict, control, or shape the repercussions of technological change or of our planned programs. Because we do not plan our technology, but allow it to follow opportunistic lines, we do not control the repercussions of its development. These repercussions cast up many of the persistent social problems of our times, such as the sharp segregation of the poor, the aged, and the minorities in the cities; the left-behind regions of economic depression; the unemployable cadres of displaced workers; and the great gaps in educational attainment. In many respects, the advanced technological societies need therapeutic social planning as badly as the countries experiencing the stresses of early technological change. For example, urban renewal, which was embraced avidly by liberals and city planners in 1949 at passage of the Housing Act, has proven a specific source of embarrassment and friction to liberal politicians for fifteen years. It is the realization of this fact that has created the call for a Domestic Peace Corps in the United States.

These problems have traditionally been easier to identify in the newly developing economies. One might swiftly recognize the particular problems raised for Puerto Rican planning by a host of world and hemispheric developments: the emergence of a new stage in world industrialization; the extension of the urban life style and the obliteration of differences between city and country in the most industrially developed nations; the sharpening of differences between the "educated" and "uneducated"; the development of new technological advances in transportation and communication. Until a Michael Harrington, or some other prophet, calls attention to the lags in our perception, we are likely to miss the similar phenomena which take place in societies starting from a more favored base. It is the merit of urban renewal that it called attention to problems of the city, to implications of public intervention in the city, and to undeveloped perspectives in city planning.

Further, the issue of relocation in urban redevelopment emphasizes the interdependence of the social fabric of communities. It has underlined the reality that one cannot intervene in any important portion of this web without disrupting the structure and entangling himself in the consequences.

But the urban renewal issue is complicated by the complexity of modern government and its ingrown bureaucracy in response to technological pressures operating through the inexorable drive of organizational efficiency. In the course of this transformation of government, many of the more purely "social" concerns, which were adequately handled in the days when political community and social community were identical, have disappeared in the larger governmental apparatus. As a result, the need for social planning is one symptomatic side effect of the organizational conquest of government. This bureaucratization is present at all levels—the distance between the local communities and city government is evident at a public hearing in a major city on the subject of a freeway location or a redevelopment proposal—though it is most intense at the federal level, where the bureaucracies are relatively rationalized and professionalized. Because we have not been conscious of the organizational and technological revolutions in our modern life, we approach the discovery of disparities between local community feeling and bureaucratic objectives with indignation. Truly effective social planning, even in a limited therapeutic sense, would need to deal more self-consciously with the relation between local social objectives and larger organizational requirements.

It is largely this sense of bureaucratic distance, which exists between city planners and citizens, almost equally with practitioners of welfare services and their clients, that has led to the social planning emphasis on *client analysis*. Presumably, by detailed sociological analysis of the client population, akin to the market analysis conducted by firms seeking outlets for their products, social planning can be equipped to overcome this bureaucratic disability. Client analysis has drawn upon, and has developed, substantial insights into the aspirations and motives of the target populations. Presumably, client analysis will also help uncover and recognize the interest of groups who are disenfranchised of power, and whose real aspirations would rarely be reflected in public programs. This more dynamic, or even revolutionary, aspect of client analysis has been widely stressed by social planners operating in minority group areas. It may be likened to a caretaker variant of the civil rights position that the society must do some things to help disadvantaged groups which have not yet been discovered by the disadvantaged groups themselves. In the advertising analogy, client analysis thus leads to taste-making, as well as taste-serving.

In this latter formulation, the client analysis position strikes a responsive note in the ideology of city planners, who have commonly felt that the citizens of the megapolitan world must be saved from themselves. In the social planning context, the inarticulate disadvantaged are saved from a temporary ignorance of their own best interests in order that they can more effectively express those interests over time.

The client analysis position, however, has one great advantage over that of traditional city planning. It explicitly identifies these interests, and neither subsumes them in vague categories of public interest, nor freely ascribes the prejudices of the bureaucracy to the long-run best interest of the poor. Client analysis, moreover, begins from the presupposition that many of the bureaucratic standards will be ill-suited to serve the real client population. Nevertheless, one cannot escape the reality that social planning with client analysis merely substitutes market research for the operations of the market. That is, client analysis notwithstanding, social planning is the antithesis of laissez-faire.

Social planning, in fact, cannot escape the ire of the conservatives by adopting some of the instruments of the market. Indeed, the violence of objections to the rent supplements included in last year's Housing Bill is evidence that indirectness and subtlety in social programs, which place a greater premium on planning than on direct action, may be more deeply resented by opponents of the programs' purposes. One is reminded that the late Senator Bricker belabored his compatriot Senator from Ohio, Robert Taft, for introducing the "Trojan Horse" of private redevelopment into the publicly subsidized 1949 Housing Act. There is no particular ground for believing that social planning and market mechanisms make public spending any more palatable to enemies of the programs. The very informational requirements of social planning may make the priests of that planning more suspect of hoarding secrets.

Caretakers and Long-Run Client Interests

Most social planners have at least a modified "caretaker" orientation. In his statement on "Meeting Human Needs" in *Goals for Americans*, the report of the President's Commission in 1960, James P. Dixon, Jr. wrote, "[society] can develop ways by which people can meet their own needs more readily and fruitfully, and it can develop ways by which society as a whole can meet needs that would otherwise be unmet. There are individuals who will not meet their own needs, and others who cannot."[2] The caretaker responsibility presumably extends to those who will not as well as those who cannot. Few societies take a wholly permissive view towards freedom of choice. In addition to the collective goods which we make available for the use of all citizens, from national defense to national parks, there are public programs encouraging the consumption of certain goods and services, and discouraging others. Economists recognize that societies encourage the consumption of the "merit" goods and discourage the consumption of demerit goods. Thus we exempt certain foods from sales taxes and place punitive taxes on alcohol, tobacco, and other products, and severely restrict the use of narcotics.

Americans have been understandably wary of social planning, since these responsibilities place the planners in the role of caretakers of "safety," "health," and "morals." The technological competence of highly organized government is today so great that there is widespread suspicion and apprehension about government power. We are afraid of the information handling capabilities which modern technology has placed at the disposal of government, for the "disutopians" have warned us of the threat to liberty which may lurk in such power. We all tend to be slightly apprehensive about the governmental capacity for storing information about the individual and recalling it by means of his social security number, zip code, or other identification. These fears may be legitimate even when it is recognized that the information technology is itself morally indifferent, and can be used with equal effect for widely approved and undesirable social purposes. The issue of what is "desirable" is an openly divisive one. Humanists have never been reluctant to prescribe remedies for fellow humans, but a central problem of democratic planning, as Davidoff and Reiner have emphasized, is that of preserving an adequate area of individual choice in the face of expert judgments of the "good."[3]

This issue is a persistent stumbling block in all social planning programs aimed at overcoming some of the undesirable consequences of our great technical efficiency. The Poverty Program is split, from the very start, on disagreement over the meaning of poverty. The traditional libertarian nineteenth century economists argue that the problem of poverty is one of inadequate income, and the provision of that income will eliminate the poverty. Some of the contemporary liberals argue the contrary, maintaining that there is a culture of poverty independent of income which cannot be redressed by simple money payments. The choice of a measurement of poverty engages this issue. A "market basket" approach as contrasted with an income level approach commits one to a definition of poverty in terms of merit goods, and required consumption, rather than income payment. In short, it takes some of the choice away from the poor, and refers the determination to an objective standard.

In social planning, the caretaker issue directly confronts choice. The case of planning for mental health, for example, is fraught with instances of value conflict. Even at the margin, where relatively clear-cut issues of community interest can be adduced, there are few clear-cut policy directions. Take the control of dischargees from mental hygiene programs. It serves the cause of effective treatment to continue the contact with the patient over a period of time. To maintain this contact normally requires a legal hold on the patient. But it is a matter of great administrative delicacy to decide when the imposition of that hold, usually by court order, is genuinely "protective," and when it is a violation of the patient's civil liberties.

In such cases, the welfare economics rule, crudely paraphrased, would be to restrain the patient only when the marginal social benefit from the continuing contact exceeds the marginal social cost of diminishing individual liberty. In practice, the probability of relapse once removed from contact is the decisive "factual" input. When the social cost of relapse, weighted by the probability of relapse once the patient is removed from contact, exceeds the social cost of deprivation of liberty multiplied by the probability of such deprivation in enforced contact, the restraint is justified. Clearly, administrators may be divided on their relative valuation of the social damage of the behavior of the mentally ill and of freedom to come and go at will. But it is sometimes overlooked that the social sciences, on which such calculus is dependent for its "factual" inputs, are often equally at variance over the behavioral probabilities. As Hans Morgenthau once observed, social sciences are not only uncertain about the nature of causes, given effects, but are also uncertain about the evaluation of the effects, given the causes.

The problem of choice is therefore shifted uncomfortably to the social planner. He finds that he must have a theory of long-run client interests. If he is to engage in this perilous activity, he cannot afford the luxury of positivist detachment. He will not be handed a ready-made packet of goals in the form of a set of well-ordered preference functions, and the task of discerning "latent" goals will take great patience and much free interpretation. The enterprise of social planning has always been facilitated by strong ideology. At the least, it requires determined leadership.

Social Planning and Social Leadership

If the democratic ideals of decentralized decision and individual choice are to be pursued concurrently with the officially defined community goals of health and welfare, including increased consumption of meritorious goods and services, extraordinary efforts must be made to bulwark the choosing processes of the disadvantaged with vast amounts of technical information, political leverage, and economic means. In particular, it may be necessary for the poor and disadvantaged to have their own planners. This realization is quickly forced upon those who hold uncompromisingly democratic goals, and who become engaged in the action processes. For example, Paul Davidoff has on various occasions urged that planners take up the role of advocates for the disadvantaged.[4]

The problem is closely analogous to that of foreign aid. In making grants or loans to undeveloped nations, the donors are always faced with the difficult task of insuring efficient use of the funds, without imposing imperialistic controls. The difficulties in such action may account for the predilection in Soviet aid programs for concrete development projects, rather than outright grants. If the projects chosen are popular, some of this difficulty can be avoided. Presumably, if federal programs followed indigenous market choice rather than bureaucratic determination of merit, they would provide freedom schools, key club memberships, and cut-rate Cadillacs rather than public housing, Job Corps camps, and school lunches. It would then be up to local planners, working in the community as advocates, to both extend the impact of the actual choices of the community, and to reshape the choice, by dramatizing the relations between means and ends.

Taken seriously programs like the rent subsidy provisions of the present Housing Act, which are aimed at encouraging the consumption of merit goods, entail a basic reeducation of consumers. Indeed, real incomes measured by consumer satisfaction, may not go up in the short run under such programs even if the objective level of consumption is raised. (In the case of relocation of slum dwellers in housing estates in England, Ireland, and elsewhere, there is even some evidence that the objective level of living has at times declined slightly with the increased consumption of a particular merit good, housing.)

The closer one gets to the community level, and the closer to the client, the more acute are these problems of individual liberty and choice. The main problem of social planning at the national level is to establish social goals which are attainable, or at least approachable, which can be given some hierarchical ordering, and which can be programmed. National planners should use program guides, standards, and other bureaucratic controls sparingly, lest they make demands on localities which are unreasonable in this sense.

At the local level, where these goals are to be implemented, the democratic ideal would hold out the opportunity for citizens to participate in defining the operational form of their goals. In practice, however, there is a tendency toward organizational efficiency which requires each local agency action to be measured against the operating rules of output which are established by the national bureaucracies. While planning as an activity is independent of the issue of centralization, the same organizational forces that make for planning push for the efficiencies realizable by central control. What is more, the planners are often impatient with the delays, losses, and frictional costs imposed by decentralized administration. The conduct of the Antipoverty Program is an example of such costs, and the uneasiness which these arouse in the planners.

Social Planning and Administrative Efficiency

The Great Society is determined to be The Efficient Society, not content to provide butter with its guns, but bent on having the most Bang for the Buck and the smoothest spreading, high-score product in Dairyland. The success of economic thinking in the Defense Department's planning and the great growth of efficiency analysis techniques supported by government contract effort have encouraged governmental planners to apply performance tests to social welfare programs as well as to military procurement. The city planning profession, which has long vacillated between social utopianism and managerial efficiency aims, now must increasingly accommodate to the imposition of the latter by the administering federal bureaucracies. Local social planning has barely begun to digest the implications of this trend.

The drive for evaluation of the effectiveness of social service programs is eminently reasonable. In the absence of well articulated national social goals, individual program progress is difficult to measure; in a society only recently concerned with defining more subtle measures of social progress than income and employment some confusion of direction is to be expected. The presence of established bureaucracies poised to soak up the new program funds does not reassure the operations analyst. After all, what percentage of applicants to the U.S. Employment Service are placed in jobs by that service? What percentage of referrals to Mental Health clinics are successfully treated? Existing welfare agencies tend to be audited in terms of operations performed, not results achieved. Senator

Ribicoff's recent observation that federal agencies may lack the competence to administer the new social programs enacted by Congress is only half the picture; Congress has failed to give clearly the direction of results expected from these programs. Administrative audits may be premature until these purposes are clarified. There is even a danger that too-hasty efficiency measures will impede the development of these goals, for the latter must be defined by the interactions between the clients and the supply agencies.

Since a prime goal of administration is efficiency, and since individuals may be legitimately indifferent to the efficiency of the system or organization, individual behavior is a friction to be overcome in administration. Resistance to the imposition of preference rankings from above is a fundamental democratic tenet, but it is almost inevitably in conflict with programs planned by experts, whether social planners or physical planners. Efficiency-minded physical planners become impatient at the economic and engineering inefficiencies produced by obdurate human behavior, and the social planners, since the origins of the settlement house movement, have marvelled at the capacities of the poor for resisting "self-betterment."

Robert Moses, one of the more impatient of planners, recently gave vent to this common annoyance, commenting on an engineering feasibility report for a proposed Long Island Sound crossing which he favors. Since the feasibility depends, to some extent, on the ability of the planners to persuade people to use the crossing at times other than summer months and week-ends, Mr. Moses complained that "the usual short season, dependent on the opening and closing of schools, and occasional mid-summer peak loads due to silly, gregarious travel hours, are the despair and curse of those who operate our seashore." The stickiness of this behavior puzzled Mr. Moses, for he continued, "as to hourly schedules, why should motorized lemmings instinctively crawl in huge armies to cast themselves into the sea just at high noon, instead of staggering their arrivals? Why can't they listen to radio and other mechanical instruction? Why must a driver behave like an ant, and if he must, why isn't he an obedient ant?"[5]

The administrative, or management, sciences differ in their approach to planning, depending on the scope and degree of control exercised by the management. More centralized management leans to a "hard" style, with decentralized or democratic management styles featuring a "soft" approach. The mnemonic public administration acronym POSDOORB (plan, organize, staff, direct, coordinate, report, budget) is appropriate to the hard style, while its counterpart DECOCOMO (decide, communicate, coordinate, motivate) is more representative of the soft. The soft style in administrative planning does not ask why man is not an obedient ant, it assumes that strict obedience is not feasible, and that manipulation of the actor's motives will be necessary to achieve the desired performance. But both POSDOORB and DECOCOMO are "top-down" procedures, as the words "direct" and "decide" reveal. The ends, in either case, are given.

The Community Action Committees set up by the Office of Economic Opportunity in its "Poverty Program" wish to have a hand in setting these ends. They wish to exploit the "maximum feasible participation" phrase in the enabling legislation to take a major part in the direction of the program. The Bureau of the Budget, guardian of administrative efficiency and witting or unwitting ally of the established big-city political machinery, has moved to curb the power of the clients in policy-making. Administrative efficiency and mass democracy have often been in conflict; Veblen's Engineers could not leave the conduct of the economy to so anarchic a mechanism as the Price System. Elites and the electorate are constantly in tension, both about the proper ends of the society and the appropriate forms of participation in decision-making.

Social Planning and Radical Reform

Proponents of social planning in the United States are impeded from developing a coherent plan of action by the ideological strictures of the society in which they operate. Our pragmatic, conservative, democratic ideology holds that *one*, the structure of power cannot be changed from below, and *two*, behavior and taste cannot be changed from above. Under the first, not only are revolutionary *means* excluded, but radical ends are ruled out as well. By the canons of presupposition *two*, democracies must resist the imposition of preferences upon the weak by the strong. Despite welfare economists' demonstration that aggregation of individual values into a community value function is greatly facilitated by acceptance of the preference of authority as the preference of the group (the dictatorship case) this convenience is denied social planners.

Given these limitations, social planning is split, with its left wing rejecting presupposition *one* and accepting *two;* an administrative right accepting *one* but altering *two;* and a political right accepting both *one* and *two* and insisting on confining operations within the alternatives of the status quo. Only the last mentioned has no crisis of legitimation. Radical social planners bent on changing the distribution of power and available actions to maximize individual choice and administrative social planners accepting the power distribution and attempting to secure behavior of the wards to conform to the tastes of their guardians are both pushing for social change. The left wishes substantial redistribution so that its clients will be allowed to transform themselves (along lines of their choosing) while the administrative right wants the clients to transform themselves so that the whole game will work more smoothly, even if the chief beneficiaries of smoother functioning prove to be the more powerful. Examples of these ideal types are not hard to find in city planning.

The task of the radical social planners is difficult. Society is less tolerant of those who would tamper with the goals than of those who would alter the means, and its organized apparatus is especially uneasy at efforts to incorporate machinery for regularly changing the goals, through radical indulgence of free choice, even when the rhetoric of the social planners uses venerated slogans. The experience of Mobilization For Youth in New York is evidence that revolutionary programs guided by social planners are not likely to be treated by the custodians of civil order with the degree of indulgence sometimes accorded illegal sit-ins. Mobilization For Youth, moreover, was challenging the local governmental administration more directly than it was threatening some vague "power structure." This was true even when it supported tenant movements, for the slum landlords' "power" is vested in their relations with local political figures rather than in connections with financial and economic powers.

In comments at the workshop on "Centrally Planned Change" two years ago, John R. Seeley expressed the fear that the federal involvement in traditional local social planning would create a more formidable bureaucratic administrative barrier to the "grass roots" choice school of social planning. Observing that "a number of the executive departments of the federal government have moved into a species of planning and plan-forcing on a scale so massive as to constitute almost a new force in American life, and, incidentally, to render peripheral and probably powerless the previous incumbents of 'the social planning activity,'" he went on to cite Karl Mannheim as labelling "correctly the major danger on which would turn the fate of planning as between the dictatorial and democratic varieties. The former fate would be sealed if planning fell into the hands of the bureaucracies."[6] But the dilemma for social planning leadership is clearly not "bureaucracy or grass roots," but "what bureaucracy?" In a society in which the "establishment" has vast bureaucratic, rationalizing, technically competent apparatus at its disposal, can a more tolerant, permissive, choice-maximizing movement succeed in redistributing power? And if the radical social planners are allowed to keep presupposition *two* on condition that they give up their opposition to *one*, that is, that they retain democratic choice at the price of foregoing revolutionary redistribution, will they not become the leaders of the lost, the counselors of despair?

This tension in the leadership condition of the radical social planners in the American ghetto slums has been bared by the anarchic outbreaks of Harlem last summer and Los Angeles this year. The democratic social planner resists being made a recruitment officer for the Establishment. He wants the client to be taken on his own terms, to be taken seriously as an arbiter of his own values. He may even attempt to protect indigenous forms and life styles when they are illegal. But he has no revolutionary role or power. In a direct confrontation of authority and the frustrated aspirations of his clients, he has no function, for he cannot relinquish or curb his doctrine of self-determination—that would mean rejection of position *two*—and he cannot speedup the transfer of power.

Social Planning, Social Science, and Societal Goals

At best, our contemporary social planning can achieve some coordination of welfare agency efforts, some limited participation by community groups in welfare planning, and a readiness to be measured against such goals as the discerning savants of our society can muster. Positive social science, which is steadfastly descriptive, and determined to be value-free, can play an important diagnostic role, but without the informing graces of ideology it is remarkably mute on prescription. Social scientists tell us of the plight of the bottom fifth of our society, of the obstacles to social mobility, of the frustrating flight of meaningful work, of intergenerational transmission of dependency, and even of the private grasp of public decision, but they leave program to the reformers and ideologues. Ideologically sustained societal planning, as the socialist experiments show, virtually dispenses with social science.[7]

The ideological socialists are steadfast in their commitment to equity principles, though in practice efficiency considerations of economic development may be allowed to supersede these as "temporary" expedients. The utilitarian postulates of the economic-efficiency administrative analysts are regarded by social critics as convenient oversimplifications. As a nation we have slipped into a program of broad social reform which involves the organization of our economy, of the space organization of our cities, and even of interpersonal relations, without benefit of societal planning. At the same time our social scientists have compiled some of the best social statistics in the world, and have supported these with unexcelled social analysis and a great deal of partial social theory. At the local community level we are on the verge of comprehensive social accounts.[8]

We are now in an increasingly good position to measure the impact of public programs on their various clients, to establish the benefits and costs of programs, and to measure, in limited terms, the efficiency of public actions, thanks to a host of social studies, social measurements, and social accounts. Our social intelligence system is·potentially powerful. Some, like Seeley, fear that this power will be manipulated by the planner-bureaucrats. Others feel, somewhat wryly, that the bureaucrats will keep this knowledge from being mobilized for social action. The "broad citizen involvement and participation" sought in community social planning is frustrated by the lack of basic social democracy. Without this involvement, the political legitimacy of social planning is open to challenge, for we have no consensus on a national social program to guide the community effort.

In any event, the social democracy which is a precondition to collective social planning in a political democracy depends on social gains which will be engineered, for the most part, from Washington. The achievement of economic democracy, the securing of equality in civil rights, the abolition of gross regional differences in education, and other major social gains will be forged by federal power, or not at all. But the societal plan which will set the targets against which all the ad hoc programs will be measured does not exist.

If such national social planning were to be instituted in the USA, substantial reorganization and improvement of our social data might be required. It is obvious, for example, that the relation of economic planning to social planning requires a national manpower policy, and that the latter, in turn, requires a national manpower budget with great regional and local detail. The material for such a budget is abundantly available, but the policy—which would require the setting of targets on full employment, local and regional labor force mobility, and similar matters —is not available to organize the data.

Social science can inform policy directly, as well as contribute to social accounting. The findings of social scientists have influenced the highest councils in the land, as the wholesale citation of Myrdal's *American Dilemma* by the Supreme Court in its civil rights decisions showed, and the revival of brain-trusting style in the executive branch is now graced by richer social science material than was available to the New Deal. At times it seems we have fallen back on "objective" social science findings because our political ideology offers so few positive guides to social reconstruction. Thus a program which might be openly embraced in other countries out of commitment to an ideology might be introduced in the USA under the seemingly nonarbitrary cloak of social "science." There is a danger in this process, for it could lead to the tyrannical "scientism" predicted by intellectual opponents of planning.

More likely, however, it would lead to much ad hoc social planning. For the social scientists cannot supplant the goal-making role of ideology, or relieve the political decision makers of their responsibility for setting the public preference scale and the targets to be embodied in a societal plan. The protection of the citizen against administrative abuses, the biases of planners, the condescension of caretakers, and all arbitrariness in social planning depends upon the open articulation of coherent national social goals, and the public acceptance of social planning targets. The Poverty Program, Appalachia Bill, aid to education, and other "Great Society" Acts need a national social accounting against which to be measured. Even more, they need a national social plan which articulates policy, and target dates, for achieving minimum levels of income and consumption, direction and amount of redistribution of population, reduction of intergenerational dependency, equalization of education, and a host of other social goals.

ᏋᏆᎧ

Notes

1) Herbert Gans, "Memorandum," an unpublished paper of the Puerto Rican Planning Board.
2) James P. Dixon, Jr., "Meeting Human Needs," *Goals for Americans*, The Report of the President's Commission on National Goals (Englewood Cliffs, N.J.: Prentice-Hall, 1960), p. 249.
3) P. Davidoff and T. Reiner, "A Choice Theory of Planning," *Journal of the American Institute of Planners*, XXVIII (May, 1962), 103–115.
4) Good statements of the Davidoff position may be found in: Paul Davidoff, "The Role of the City Planner in Social Planning," *Proceedings of the American Institute of Planners, 1964 Annual Conference*, pp. 125–131, and, "Advocacy and Pluralism in Planning," *Journal of the American Institute of Planners*, XXX (November, 1964), 331–338.
5) Remarks by Robert Moses on the proposed Long Island Sound Crossing, Triborough Bridge Authority, 1965.
6) John R. Seeley, "Central Planning: Prologue to a Critique," *Centrally Planned Change: Prospects and Concepts*, ed. Robert Morris (New York: National Association of Social Workers, 1964), p. 58.
7) A well-documented case for this conclusion appears in a yet-unpublished paper on Soviet Social Science prepared by Peter R. Senn for the Annual Meeting of the American Association for the Advancement of Science at Berkeley, December, 1965.
8) See Harvey Perloff, "New Directions in Social Planning," *Journal of the American Institute of Planners*, XXXI (November, 1965), 297–303.

The Urban Field

✑

John Friedmann / John Miller

In Search of a New Image

There has been a growing dissatisfaction with the historical concept of
the city. Don Martindale, in his brilliant introduction to Max Weber's
essay, *The City*, has composed a fitting epitaph:

> The modern city is losing its external and formal structure. Internally it is
> in a state of decay while the new community represented by the nation every-
> where grows at its expense. The age of the city seems to be at an end.[1]

If this is so from a sociological standpoint, it is equally true from the
perspective of a physical planner. Various concepts have been put forward in the endeavor to capture the expanding scale of urban life.
Metropolitan region, spread city, megalopolis, ecumenopolis . . . each
attempt to redefine the new reality has led to a broader spatial conception. Behind these efforts lies an awareness of the constantly widening
patterns of interaction in an urbanizing world.

Modern utopian constructs have been equally intent on fitting city
concepts to the possibilities created by our communications-based society. Clarence Stein's *Regional City* is a constellation of moderately sized
communities separated by great open spaces and bound closely together
by highways.[2] Frank Lloyd Wright's *Broadacre City* represents a complete melding of the urban and rural worlds that, without pronounced
centers, would uniformly dissolve throughout a region.[3] Both these
constructs see the city as an essentially unlimited form of human settlement, capable of infinite expansion.

None of the new concepts, however, has been completely successful.
The Bureau of the Census has had to shift the meaning of metropolitan
region from "metropolitan district" to "standard metropolitan area" to

Reprinted from "The Urban Field," *American Institute of Planners Journal*, 31
(November, 1965), 312–320, by permission of the authors and publisher.

"standard metropolitan statistical area" in order to keep pace with our improved understanding of what constitutes the fundamental ecological area of urban life, and it is once more reexamining the question.[4]

The much looser conception of *spread-city* has been applied only to the New York region, but no attempt has been made to generalize from it to other urban areas.[5] Jean Gottmann's *megalopolis* appears as a geographic place name for the chain of metropolitan giants along the Boston-Washington axis.[6] Although later writers have taken it as a generic term for contiguous metropolitan regions, the concept, lacking precision as well as generality, has frequently been misapplied. One writer has gone so far as to extend its meaning to the entire region from Phoenix to Minneapolis.[7] His Midwest Central Megalopolis is a geographic and conceptual absurdity. Finally, C. A. Doxiadis' *ecumenopolis* is no concept at all but a poetic vision.[8]

Planners therefore, are left in a quandary. "Modern metropolitan trends," wrote the late Catherine Bauer Wurster, "have destroyed the traditional concept of urban structure, and there is no new image to take its place."[9] Yet none would question the need for such an image, if only to serve as the conceptual basis for organizing our strategies for urban development. Our hope in this paper is to meet this great need, suggesting an image of the new *polis* that will be adequate to the tasks that face the nation in the decades ahead.

The Enlarged Scale of Urban Life

It has become increasingly possible to interpret the spatial structure of the United States in ways that will emphasize a pattern consisting of *one*, metropolitan areas and *two*, the inter-metropolitan periphery. Except for thinly populated parts of the American interior, the inter-metropolitan periphery includes all areas that intervene among metropolitan regions that are, as it were, the reverse image of the trend towards large scale concentrated settlement that has persisted in this country for over half a century. Like a devil's mirror, much of it has developed a socio-economic profile that perversely reflects the very opposite of metropolitan virility.

Economically, the inter-metropolitan periphery includes most of the areas that have been declared eligible for federal area redevelopment assistance. This is illustrated in Map 1, which shows the geographic extent of substandard income and high unemployment areas relative to the urbanized regions of the United States.[10] Situated almost entirely outside the normal reach of the larger cities, these areas are shown to be clearly peripheral. They have a disproportionately large share of low-growth and declining industries and a correspondingly antiquated economic structure. Nevertheless, one-fifth of the American people are living in these regions of economic distress.

Demographically, the inter-metropolitan periphery has been subject to a long-term, continuous decline. This trend reflects the movement of people to cities, especially to the large metropolitan concentrations. Although the smaller cities on the periphery have to some extent bene-fitted from migration, their gains have been less, on the average, than for all urban areas.[11] In addition, migration from economically depressed regions has been highly selective, so that the age distribution of the remaining population has become polarized around the very young and very old. In Appalachia, for example, the two million people who left the region during the 1950's were, for the most part, drawn from the productive age groups from 18 to 64. At the same time, the population over 65 years old increased by nearly one-third.[12] In some areas, re-corded death rates now actually exceed birth rates.[13]

Socially, the standard indices of education and health are substan-tially lower along the periphery than in metropolitan areas. The quality of public services has deteriorated (though their *per capita* cost has increased), the housing stock is older, and the level of educational attain-ment is significantly below the average for metropolitan America. Rapid and selective outmigration, a declining economic base, the burden of an aging population, and low incomes have rendered many peripheral com-munities helpless in their desire to adapt to changing circumstances in the outside world. The remaining population is frequently short both on civic leadership and hope. They can neither grasp the scope of the events that have overtaken them nor are they capable of responding creatively to the new situations.[14]

Politically, many peripheral areas have lost their ability to act. They are fragmented, disorganized, and without effective economic leverage. The Area Redevelopment Administration has for a number of years been at work in these regions on a county by county basis (itself a fragmented strategy) and now the Appalachia program has been launched amidst much fanfare. Yet, since neither of these programs has adequately recog-nized the relationship between metropolitan cores and their peripheries, their scale, though ambitious, has been dwarfed by the extent of the social and economic problems of the periphery.

The emergence in large sections of the country of the inter-metro-politan periphery as a major problem area has been the direct result of the concentration of people and activities around closely contiguous metro-politan cores. Growth in and around these cores has drawn off the productive population, economic activities, and investment capital of the periphery, but the forces of urbanization are now in the process of reversing this trend.[15]

Looking ahead to the next generation, we foresee a new scale of urban living that will extend far beyond existing metropolitan cores and penetrate deeply into the periphery. Relations of dominance and dependency will be transcended. The older established centers, together with the inter-metropolitan peripheries that envelop them, will constitute the new ecological unit of America's post-industrial society that will replace traditional concepts of the city and metropolis. This basic element of the emerging spatial order we shall call the *urban field*.

The urban field may be viewed as an enlargement of the space for urban living that extends far beyond the boundaries of existing metropolitan areas—defined primarily in terms of commuting to a central city of "metropolitan" size—into the open landscape of the periphery. This change to a larger scale of urban life is already underway, encouraged by changes in technology, economics, and preferred social behavior. Eventually the urban field may even come to be acknowledged as a community of *shared* interests, although these .interests may be more strongly oriented to specific functions than to area. They will be shared because to a large extent they will overlap and complement each other within a specific locational matrix. Because urban fields will be large, with populations of upwards of one million, their social and cultural life will form a rich and varied pattern capable of satisfying most human aspirations within a local setting.

It is no longer possible to regard the city as purely an artifact, or a political entity, or a configuration of population densities. All of these are outmoded constructs that recall a time when one could trace a sharp dividing line between town and countryside, rural and urban man. From a sociological and, indeed, an economic standpoint, what is properly urban and properly rural can no longer be distinguished. The United States is becoming a thoroughly urbanized society, perhaps the first such society in history. The corresponding view of the city is no longer of a physical entity, but of a pattern of point locations and connecting flows of people, information, money, and commodities. This new understanding of the city has been incorporated into the census concept of a Standard Metropolitan Statistical Area and has since been widely accepted as a basis for public and private decisions.

The idea of an urban field is similarly based on the criterion of interdependency. It represents a fusion of metropolitan spaces and non-metropolitan peripheral spaces centered upon core areas (SMSA's) of at

MAP I / *ARA Designated Eligible Areas*

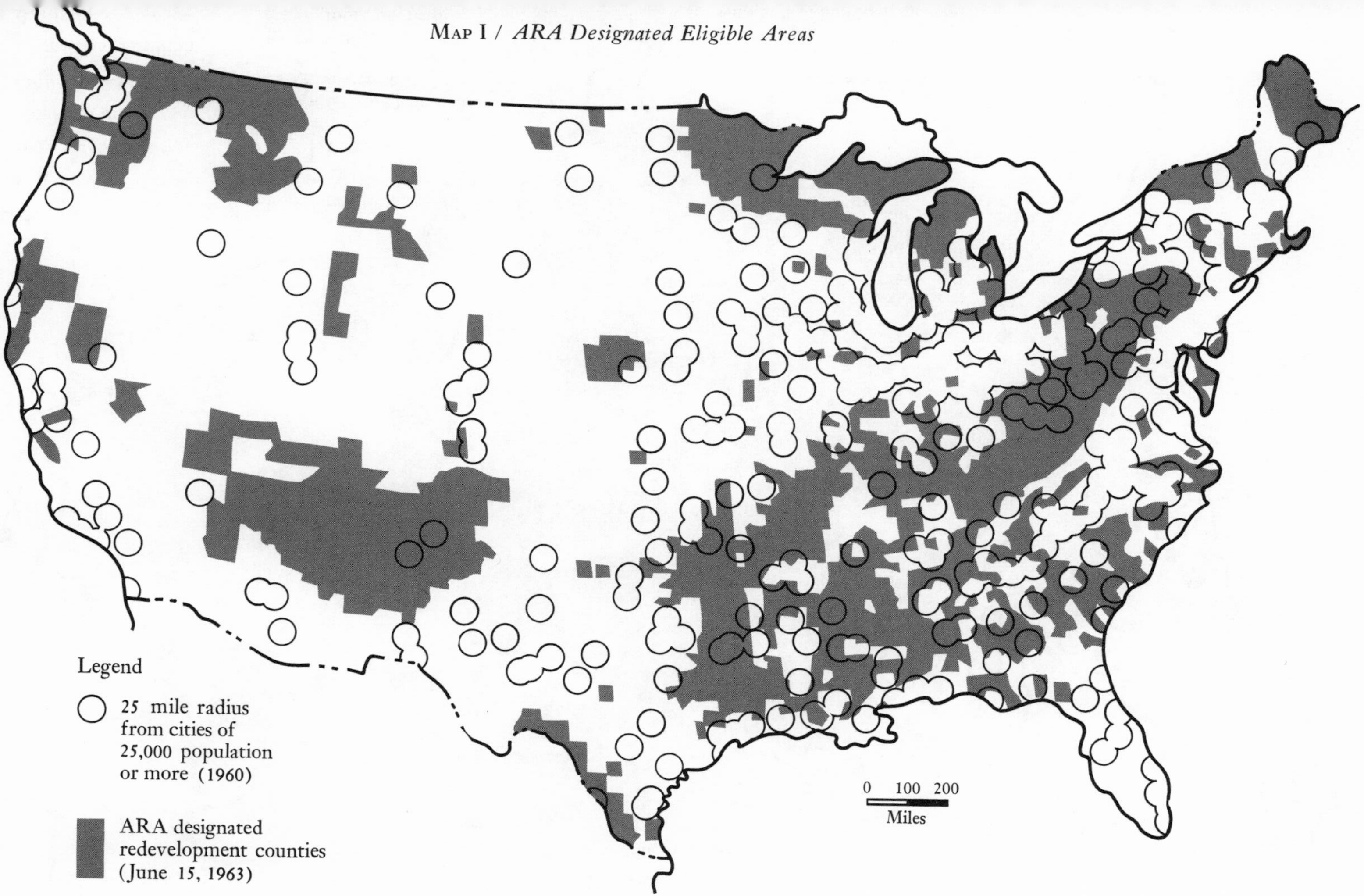

Legend

◯ 25 mile radius
from cities of
25,000 population
or more (1960)

▨ ARA designated
redevelopment counties
(June 15, 1963)

0 100 200
Miles

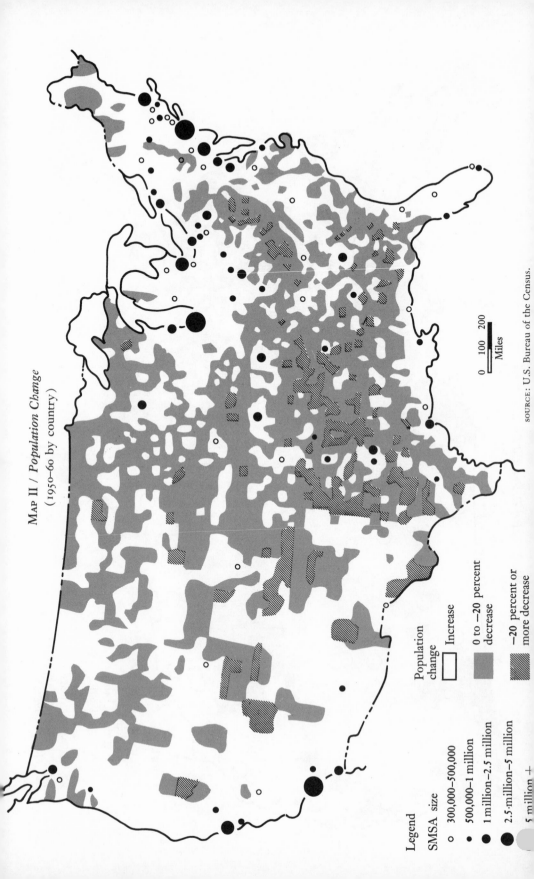

MAP II / *Population Change*
(1950–60 by country)

SOURCE: U.S. Bureau of the Census.

0   100   200

Miles

Population
change

☐ Increase

▨ 0 to –20 percent
   decrease

▨ –20 percent or
   more decrease

Legend

SMSA size

○ 300,000–500,000

• 500,000–1 million

● 1 million–2.5 million

⬤ 2.5 million–5 million

⬤ 5 million +

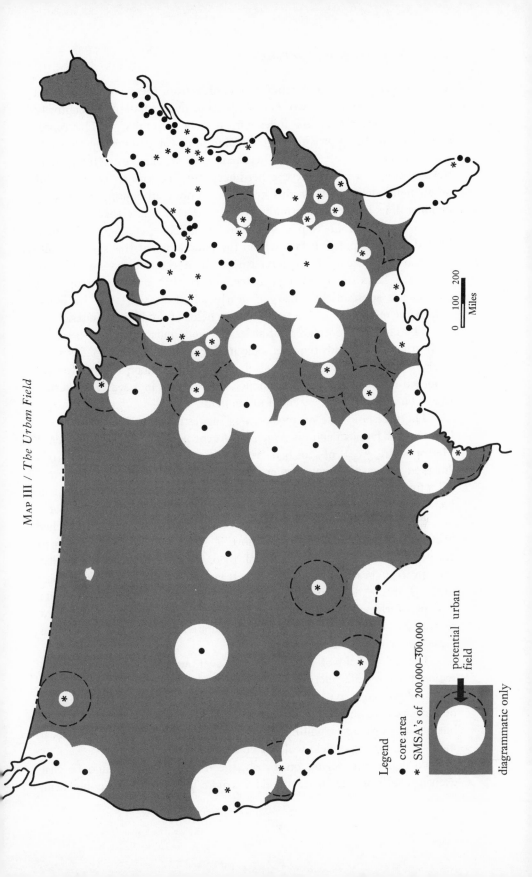

Map III / The Urban Field

Legend

• core area

* SMSA's of 200,000–300,000

⌀ potential urban field

diagrammatic only

0   100   200
Miles

least 300,000 people and extending outwards from these core areas for a distance equivalent to two hours' driving over modern throughway systems (approximately 100 miles with present technology). This represents not only an approximate geographic limit for commuting to a job, but also the limit of intensive weekend and seasonal use (by ground transportation) of the present periphery for recreation. A system of urban fields delineated by this criterion without attempting to draw a dividing line between metropolitan cores that are less than 200 miles apart is presented in Map 3. Between 85 and 90 percent of the total United States population falls within the boundaries of this system while less than 35 percent of the total land area of the country is included. These are facts of signal importance, for as the area of metropolitan influence is substantially enlarged nearly all of us will soon be living within one or another of the 70-odd urban fields of the United States.[16]

The choice of core areas of at least 300,000 inhabitants as a basis for delineating urban fields requires some justification. Karl Fox, for instance, recommends a reduction of central city size to 25,000 or less for his proposed set of Functional Economic Areas which, in a sense, is alternative to our concept of a system of urban fields.[17]

The threshold size of 300,000 was suggested to us by the work of Otis Dudley Duncan and his associates. According to Duncan, a Standard Metropolitan Area of 300,000 people in the United States in 1950 "marked a transition point where distinctively 'metropolitan' characteristics first begin to appear. Adequately to describe the base of the 'urban hierarchy'—consisting of almost all urban centers smaller than this size— one would have to shift the emphasis from 'metropolitanism' to other principles of functional differentiation."[18] Although the SMA's of 1950 are not equivalent to the SMSA's of 1960, the two concepts are similar enough to suggest the possibility of a transfer of Duncan's threshold size to the SMSA. An additional consideration was the expectation that core regions of this size and larger will continue to expand over the next several decades and will consequently generate a vast demand for various uses of inter-metropolitan space.

The urban field of the future, however, will be a far less focused region than today's metropolitan area. The present dominance of the metropolitan core will become attenuated as economic activities are decentralized to smaller cities within the field or into the open country, but because proximity will continue to account for a good deal of local interaction, the urban field will be a coherent region.

To define this region on a map, the main criterion should be that exchange relations *within* each field are more intensive than among them, during the course of an entire year. The calculation of this measure on an annual basis instead of at a single point in time is important because some of the functional relationships among subareas may be subject to seasonal variations. The enjoyment of summer and winter recreation areas is the outstanding example of this phenomenon. These areas should be allocated to that realm whose population makes the most intensive use of them.

It is important to recollect what this projected geographic expansion of urban living space will accomplish. First, it will turn the resources of the inter-metropolitan periphery to important uses by existing metropolitan populations; second, as the periphery becomes absorbed into the urban field, it will be eliminated as a distinctive problem area. The remaining parts of the United States will either remain in low density agrarian uses or revert to wilderness for the enjoyment of distant populations.

Forces Underlying the Emergence of Urban Fields

Our case for the urban field rests on two propositions. The first is that the future growth of population in the United States will take place almost exclusively within the areas we have defined as urban fields. The second is that within each urban field substantial centrifugal forces will propel the settlement of population and the location of activities from existing metropolitan centers into the present periphery.

CONTINUED POPULATION CONCENTRATION IN URBAN FIELDS

One of the clearest national trends of the past few decades has been that of increasing demographic concentration. Most of the discussion, however, has emphasized the pulling together of people in metropolitan and coastal regions. It has been less well publicized that the great majority of counties that lost population during the 1950's are predominantly rural and lie outside the boundaries of any urban realm. The gains, as Map 2 clearly demonstrates, have occurred almost entirely within these boundaries, though not exclusively in metropolitan counties. We have no reason to expect this trend to be reversed during the coming generation.

In 1960, an estimated 150 million Americans lived in potential urban fields. We have projected their number to more than double the present number by the year 2000. This increase of 150 to 180 million will have to be accommodated within roughly the same area that we have provisionally delimited. The question arises as to where, within a given field,

this population will be living. In approaching this question, we are
mindful of the New York Metropolitan Region Study which for 1985
foresees as many people living in the "outer ring" as in the central core.
This "outer ring" extends as far as 100 miles from New York City and is
not today part of the daily life of the metropolis.[19] Elaborating on this
startling projection, Raymond Vernon writes that employment and population trends

> cast doubt on any image of the Region as a giant cluster of human activity
> held together by a great nub of jobs at the center. Instead . . . [they afford] a
> picture of a Region in which the centripetal pull is weakening. This, in turn,
> means a further modification of the oversimplified picture of the Region as a
> ring of bedroom communities in the suburbs emptying out their inhabitants
> every morning to the central city. Incomplete and misleading as this picture is
> today, it promises to be even more misleading in the decades ahead. . . . And
> the chronic complaint of the outlying areas that they lack an "economic base"
> may continue to lose some of its realism and force.[20]

Vernon has foreshadowed the appearance of an urban field that
would have New York City as its core. What are the forces, then, which
suggest this occupancy of the periphery by people and activities, not only
for New York, but for all other core regions in the United States? And
what specific forms will it assume?

CENTRIFUGAL FORCES: RESOURCES OF THE PERIPHERY

The main pull, we submit, is the increasing attractiveness of the
periphery to metropolitan populations. It has space, it has scenery, and it
contains communities that remain from earlier periods of settlement and
preserve a measure of historical integrity and interest.

Demand for these resources will be generated by three main trends:
increasing real income, increasing leisure, and increasing mobility. Although these trends are familiar, brief discussion of them will help to
suggest their cumulative impact.

The President's Council of Economic Advisors estimates that output
per man-hour may undergo a threefold expansion by the year 2000.[21]
Holding constant both working hours and labor force participation rates,
this would raise average family income (in today's prices) to approximately $18,000. Although there is every reason to expect that part of the
potential gains in income will be taken in the form of greater leisure
through a combination of shorter working hours, longer vacations, later
entry into the labor force, and earlier retirement, the prospective rise in
wealth is still very substantial. If present patterns of consumption are any

guide, we can expect a good share of this new wealth to be devoted to the purchase of space, privacy, travel, education, culture, and various forms of recreative leisure.

The present allocation of leisure time is distributed among numerous activities. The Stanford Research Institute reports that already 50 million Americans are actively participating in amateur art activity; that 32 million are musicians, and 15 million are painters, sculptors, and sketchers. There are more piano players than fishermen, as many painters as hunters, and more theater goers than boaters, skiers, golfers, and skin-divers combined.[22]

The United States Department of Health, Education and Welfare has published statistics showing that new museums, including aquariums and zoos, are being established at the rate of one every three days, and that one-third of all existing museums in the country have been opened since 1950.[23] Other cultural activities have shown equally phenomenal gains. For instance, there are now 1400 symphony orchestras in the United States, compared to only 100 in 1920.

These new cultural facilities are more mobile, more intimate, and more dispersed than their predecessors. They are different from the grand centers of high culture left in our central cores by the nineteenth century cultural ideology.

Participation in outdoor sports is likewise on an impressive scale. In 1964, there were an estimated 38 million boaters, 20 million campers, 7 million skiers, and an equal number of golfers. Skiing enthusiasts alone have jumped by 600 percent during the past ten years. And attendance in official park and forest areas has been rising at a cumulative annual rate of about 10 percent.

With increasing leisure time available, the prospects for the future show no abatement in these activities. For the mass of the people, nearly two-thirds of their waking hours will be essentially in free, unstructured time.[24] It is therefore not surprising that the Outdoor Recreation Resources Review Commission has predicted a tripling in the overall demand for recreation by the year 2000.[25] For the hedonistic leisure society we are becoming, this estimate may indeed be a conservative one.

The combined trends in income and leisure are bound to arouse great popular interest in the periphery, but their full effect will be transmitted through the increased mobility which our technology affords.

The gradual lifting of constraints which during the industrial era packed jobs and people into tightly confined urban spaces will encourage what Jean Gottmann has called the "quasi-colloidal dispersion" of activities throughout the urban field. Impending communications technologies suggest the possibility of relaxing the need for physical proximity in distribution, marketing, information services, and decision-making.

A few examples may be cited. Computers which keep business inventories and send information on replenishment items over TV or telephone are now technically feasible. They may also be used to alert suppliers to periodically recurring needs for product service. In retailing, a major revolution is in the making, as videophones have been developed that can transmit images of products and convert these images on signal into photographic reproductions. The use of coded cards to send information, order items, and transfer funds by telephone has already passed the laboratory stage and no doubt will soon be introduced on the market.

Transport technology continues to advance toward greater speed and versatility. Supersonic and short-distance jets, automated highways, and rail transport which moves at several hundred miles an hour through densely built-up regions, are expected to pass from drawing board to commercial application within ten to twenty years. The result will be a further shrinkage of the transportation surface and vastly increased accessibility on a national scale no less than within each urban field.

One effect of increased accessibility especially worthy of note is the estimated 3.5 to 7.5 million acres which will be opened up for urban

TABLE 1 / *Uses of the Inter-metropolitan Periphery*

Recreation	*Institutions*
camps	boarding schools
parks	junior colleges
forests	universities
wilderness areas	museums
nature sanctuaries	cultural centers
resorts	scientific research stations
outdoor sport areas	conference centers
quietist retreats	hospitals
	sanatoria
	government administrative offices

Communities	*Economic activities*
holiday communities	agro-business
retirement communities	space-extensive manufacturing plants
vacation villages	research and communications-based industries
art colonies	mail order houses
diversified "new towns"	warehouses
historical communities	insurance companies
second home areas	jet airports

development when the federal interstate highway program is completed. This land newly available for urbanization will represent a major resource to the national economy.

The combined effects of greater income, leisure, and mobility will be felt, by virtue of these arguments, primarily on the present periphery of metropolitan regions, as demand for the use of its resources are vastly intensified. Some of these uses are shown in Table 1. They are distinctly urban in character. And they remind us of Lewis Mumford's prophetic vision of the "Invisible City."

Gone is primitive local monopoly through isolation: gone is the metropolitan monopoly through seizure and exploitation. . . . The ideal mission of the city is to further (a) process of cultural circulation and diffusion; and this will restore to many now subordinate urban centers a variety of activities that were once drained away for the exclusive benefit of the great city.[26]

Emerging Life Styles of the Urban Field

The projected incorporation of the periphery into the urban realm will be accompanied by significant changes in American patterns of living. On the whole, we expect that these changes will be evaluated favorably. Derogatory slogans, such as "sprawl" and "scatteration," bandied about in ideological campaigns, will have to be discarded in any serious search for what it means to live on the new scale. Although not all the consequences can be foreseen now, a few merit closer attention. We shall restrict our comment to only three of them: a wider life space on the average, a wider choice of living environments, and a wider community of interests.

1) *A wider life space.* The effective life space of an individual includes all the geographic areas within which his life unfolds. It includes his home and its immediate vicinity; his place of work or schooling; the places in which he does his shopping and engages in leisure activities; the more distant places to which he travels for business, recreation, or learning; the residence areas of the friends and relatives he visits; and the connecting paths over which he travels to reach his destination.

It is possible to map these spaces for individuals—distinguished by age, sex, and socio-economic status—as well as for entire communities. These maps would show which areas of the total available space are actually being used by different parts of the population as well as the intensity of their use. An important feature of these maps would be data relating to the percentage of the individual's total annual time spent at different localities and travelling over various routes. A further distinction with regard to the seasonability of use could be made.

Such maps for an urban field would reveal greatly expanded and more complexly structured systems of life spaces for the total population compared to existing patterns. The higher speeds, greater versatility, and lower costs expected in transportation and communication during the next few decades will encourage a dispersion of people and activities throughout the urban field and a further thinning out of metropolitan core areas on an unsurpassed scale. Technological innovations will make it possible to substitute mobility for location. The strong likelihood that this will occur is suggested by foreseeable changes in patterns which underlie the location decisions of families and firms.

For individual families, locational decisions will be increasingly influenced by larger incomes that will permit the purchase of more space, more privacy, and more transportation; by a growing concern with the qualitative aspects of life, especially with the quality of the physical environment; by the gradual relaxation of the puritanical distinction between work and play, especially among professional and business elite groups; and by the desire for an environment that will permit a richer family life. All of these forces will tend to render the inter-metropolitan periphery more attractive as a place to live, and help to tie it more closely into the expanding urban field.

The location of business firms will encounter fewer economic constraints within the urban field than at present. This is especially true for the new kinds of service activities—professional, managerial, research- and communications-based—which are the leading edge of a post-industrial society. Urban infrastructure and services will be nearly ubiquitous throughout the urban field; the pressing need for physical propinquity among firms is declining; and the expansion and improvement of transport and communication services will tend to make regional as well as national markets equally accessible. If only those economic factors that operate generally throughout a given field are taken into account, thereby excluding local subsidies or differences in local tax structure, which provide only small and temporary advantages, it is possible to assert that firms may locate nearly at random throughout the field, subject only to the constraint of labor force distribution. Location of the labor force will then become a primary determinant in business location decisions, with the result that firms will be attracted in increasing numbers into what is now the inter-metropolitan periphery. Firms as well as families will substitute mobility and machine-interposed communications for location.

2) *A wider choice of living environments both for resident and non-resident use and more frequent interchange among environments.* The urban field offers a heterogeneous landscape, consisting of metropolitan

cores, small towns, and varied open spaces.[27] Within it, a wide variety of living environments may be sought and created. There is nothing rigid or predetermined about the physical form of the field: rather, it may be viewed as a mosaic of different forms and micro-environments which coexist within a common communications framework without intruding spatially on each other.

For the family, the urban field offers a far greater choice of living environments than do the old metropolitan areas. Alternatives include country and in-town living, perhaps combined, through a steep increase in the frequency of second homes for year-round use; single family dwellings and apartment towers; dense metropolitan clusters and open countryside; new towns and towns with an historical tradition; and functionally specialized communities.

No part within the urban field is isolated from another. There is rather an easy-going interchange among all the parts, encouraged not only by the wider distribution of population but also by the larger amounts of time available for the pursuit of leisure. All areas are located no further than two hours' driving distance from old metropolitan cores. And although these cores will lose much of their present importance to the people of the field as functions are decentralized, they will continue for at least a few more decades to attract many people to the activities that are traditionally carried out within them, such as major educational and governmental institutions, famous museums, outstanding music, artistic, and sport events. Many cultural facilities, however, will be dispersed throughout the realm and many metropolitan services will become available at any point within it through extended distribution systems. At the same time, easy access to other urban fields can be provided through a regional system of airports capable of handling short-distance jets and vertical take-off craft. High-speed rail transport may be a significant means for inter-realm travel in some parts of the country, such as the "Northeast Corridor."

3) *A wider community of interests.* The already noted increase in the effective life space of the population suggests that each person will have interests in happenings over a larger segment of the field than at present. In the course of a year, he may actively participate in the life of a number of spatially defined local communities. As a result, he is likely to be less concerned with the fate of the community where he resides and more with activities that may be scattered throughout the field but are closest to his interests, leading to a stronger identification on his part with the realm as a whole at the cost of a declining interest in purely local affairs. (In some places, this loss may be offset by the smaller size of his

resident community which would encourage more active participation in problem-solving.) We foresee continuation of the present trend toward a cosmopolitanization of values, attitudes, and behavior, with politically relevant behavior organized principally along functional lines, and with the governing of local communities (places) passing increasingly into the hands of professionals.

Implications for Public Policy

In the preceding sections of this essay, we have speculated openly about the future. The urban field would emerge as a normal consequence of the forces that are currently operating on the space economy of the United States. Its designation as an ecological unit, however, is purely conceptual: it is only one of the many spatial patterns that might have been recognized. Specifically, its choice was dictated by our belief in the utility of the urban field as an appropriate region for planning. The vastly enlarged scale of urban living we envisage for the future holds clear implications for public action. We shall comment on only two of these: actions to reinforce existing trends toward the incorporation of the inter-metropolitan periphery into the urban field and actions that will assure the environmental integrity of all activities within the field.

1) *Reinforcement of existing trends.* We have portrayed the emergence of the urban field in approving language. We might have spoken out, as others have, against the rootlessness of modern man, the loss of community, and the misfortune of urban sprawl. Our words, however, were carefully selected; they represent our conviction that there is, indeed, a social good to be obtained from the substitution of mobility for location. Not only is the urban field the living environment most consistent with the aims of a wealthy leisure society, it will also help to reverse the steady deterioration of the periphery; and this we see as a major social objective. There are losses as well as gains to be incurred by allowing the expansion of metropolis into the periphery, but we believe the gains will outweigh the losses. Political considerations strengthen this judgment: it would be difficult in the extreme to change the direction of existing trends and squeeze an urban population to be doubled in size within the next thirty years into the confines of existing metropolitan areas. We conclude that public policy should in this instance "cooperate with the inevitable" and support the penetration of the inter-metropolitan periphery by forms of urban life.

Governments can exercise two modes of influence to hasten the arrival of urban fields: the first is the location of government-financed investments; the second is information. The former is perhaps the more persuasive in the long view. There is a singular opportunity for planning on the scale of urban fields in the design of regional highway and railroad systems, in the location and design of regional airports, in the siting of regional colleges and government-sponsored research institutions, in the distribution of administrative offices, and in the designation and development of public land reserves for recreation. Somewhat less direct controls over location can be used in connection with subsidy programs for the acquisition of second homes as well as for the building of retirement communities and new towns.

To contribute to the emergence of urban fields, determination of public and private locations should occur within an adequate framework of information. The potential reality of the urban field should be captured in statistical series and maps. As a first step, the boundaries of the realm must be empirically ascertained on the basis of careful studies of daily, weekly, and seasonal flow patterns and tested against a gravity model. It is clear that the boundaries so delimited for statistical purposes will be shifting over time as the region begins to be more fully developed, transportation technology advances, and the inevitable phenomenon of zones transitional to adjacent fields is better understood. Once the region has been roughly defined, its present uses and potential assets should be investigated and evaluated against the changing pattern of metropolitan demands, with particular attention to the trends of change in spatial structure. These investigations would culminate in a general regional development plan as a guide to location decisions. The plan which, like all good plans, would need to be constantly in elaboration, would suggest broad land use patterns as well as desirable new investments, public and private. The final step would involve the establishment of an information and monitoring system for the realm to maintain close watch over regional changes as they occur.

2) *Assuring environmental integrity.* If the urban field is to be developed as a meaningful living environment, it is essential that its manifold uses do not encroach upon each other and in the process destroy its most valuable assets: open space, scenic attractiveness, and historical tradition. Indiscriminate metropolitan growth should be minimized; new towns should be selected with attention to the total pattern of land uses and the evolving distribution of population, activities, and transportation. Cultural institutions should be so located as to reinforce other forms of recreation, present and contemplated. Areas for agricultural production

should be set aside, not only for economic reasons, but also to provide a richer visual and environmental experience to the inhabitants of the urban field.

Assuring an appropriate environmental setting for each activity (or bundle of activities) in the field will involve something more than the judicious application of traditional land use controls, though no doubt these will be necessary. It will require forthright programs of area development and resource conservation, including the preservation of old townscapes and the more outstanding features of the rural landscape.

A suggestion for this type of program is provided by experience in France. "Throughout France, the fast-spreading ownership of automobiles is making it possible to restore and maintain the rural villages that are so much a part of her charm. A national inventory of abandoned houses is published, and liberal government credits are given to purchasers who restore them. In recent years, thousands of old country homes have become summer houses for city people. Whole villages have come to life again."[28] Much can be done at the national or state level to encourage the repossession of the inter-metropolitan periphery in view of the varied uses proposed for it within the urban field.

The institutional basis for developmental planning in the urban field will have to face up to new constraints that will limit social decision-making. These include the multiplication of governments (not 1400 as in New York but perhaps 4000!), overlapping jurisdictions and responsibilities, the increasing functional rather than spatial orientation of interests among the population, the gradual loosening of communal ties, the fuzziness of field boundaries, lagging citizen response to the enlarged scale of living, and the extension of urban fields into adjacent states as well as the continuing conflicts of values (public versus private, conservationist versus expansionary, traditionalist versus modern, residential versus productive). No easy rationalization of the planning process is possible under these conditions nor, perhaps, is it desirable. If metropolitan-wide planning is only now coming into being—decades after the "discovery" of the metropolitan region as the new urban scale, and just when this scale is about to be replaced by the even broader concept of the urban realm—it seems futile to argue for the exclusiveness of the urban field as a planning unit. Field planning will have to coexist with other forms. Primary responsibility for the development of urban fields will unquestionably come to rest with the states; but this is only a beginning. The federal government will have a role to play as important as that of local governments, while interstate and intercommunity cooperation in developmental planning will become much more common than it is at present. The coordination of these different levels of planning presents a major problem that must be solved through both formal and informal methods of program cooperation. The formulation of a regional development plan in joint consultation with all the relevant parties will be necessary to provide the common framework for decisions.

A Challenge of Mounting Urgency

It would indeed be a pity if our era were to fail in taking advantage of the great opportunities which the dynamism and tensions of our society are creating for building a new urban culture. The expansionary forces that suggest the possibility of urban fields are irreversible; what we make of them is our choice. They could well terminate in the desecration of the urban landscape, in a grey formlessness, the spoliation of resources. In place of designing an environment for exuberant living, we could acquiesce in the gradual attrition of life by neglecting to take the appropriate measures now. The pattern of the urban field will elude easy perception by the eye and will be difficult to rationalize in terms of a Euclidean geometry. It will be a large complex pattern which, unlike the traditional city, will no longer be directly accessible to the senses. We might think of it rather as a time-space continuum that must first be reduced to a meaningful abstract model before it will submit to being managed as a whole. Such models are not yet in sight. But the challenge to search for them confronts the planning profession with mounting urgency.

Notes

1) Max Weber, *The City* (Glencoe, Illinois: The Free Press, 1958), p. 62.
2) Clarence S. Stein, "A Regional Pattern for Dispersal," *Architectural Record*, CXXXVI (September, 1964), 205–206.
3) Frank Lloyd Wright, *The Living City* (New York: Horizon Press, Inc., 1958).
4) The review is being conducted by the Social Science Research Council Committee on Areas for Social and Economic Statistics.
5) *Christian Science Monitor*, November 14, 1964, p. 3.
6) Jean Gottmann, *Megalopolis* (New York: The Twentieth Century Fund, Inc., 1961).
7) Herman C. Berkman, *Our Urban Plant: Essays in Urban Affairs* (Madison, Wisconsin: The University of Wisconsin Extension, 1964), pp. 4–5.
8) The final stage in the hierarchy of living spaces. Cf., for example, "The Ekistic Grid," *Ekistics*, XIX (March, 1965), 210.
9) Catherine Bauer Wurster, "The Form and Structure of the Future Urban Complex," in Lowdon Wingo, Jr., ed., *Cities and Space*. Published for Re-

sources for the Future, Inc. (Baltimore: The Johns Hopkins Press, 1963), p. 73.

10) ARA eligibility criteria are rather complicated. They are fully stated in U.S. Department of Commerce, Area Redevelopment Administration, *Summary List of Redevelopment Areas and Eligible Areas, Public Works Acceleration Act,* October 1, 1964 (Washington: U.S. Government Printing Office, 1964), p. 2.

11) Ray M. Northam, "Declining Urban Centers in the United States: 1950–1960," *Annals of the Association of American Geographers,* LIII (March, 1963), 50–59.

12) Appalachian Regional Commission, *Appalachia* (Washington: U.S. Government Printing Office, 1964).

13) U.S. Department of Agriculture, Economic Research Service, *Recent Population Trends in the United States with Emphasis on Rural Areas,* Agricultural Economic Report No. 23 (Washington: U.S. Government Printing Office, 1963), pp. 24–25.

14) Harry M. Caudill has documented this physical and social deterioration of declining inter-metropolitan peripheral areas in his able study of eastern Kentucky, *Night Comes to the Cumberlands* (Boston: Little, Brown & Company, 1962). See especially Chapter Twenty: "The Scene Today," pp. 325–351. Evidence that this is not an isolated phenomenon exists for other inter-metropolitan peripheral areas. The New York *Times,* March 21, 1965, reports that "hundreds of Texas towns and smaller cities that once drew incomes from agriculture are finding few farmers left today to trade in their stores and banks. Massive depopulation has been the rule." Only where aggressive local leadership in a few communities has grasped opportunities in regional and national markets has the decline been decelerated. According to the University of Texas Bureau of Business Research, regional and national corporations are not attracted to invest in these communities. Disintegration of morale, physical facilities, and the economic climate was also characteristic of large parts of the inter-metropolitan periphery of Western Massachusetts within the dynamic "megalopolis" described by Gottmann. A regional study of this area by M.I.T. students elicited a general expression of disintegrating community through the comments of local citizens. "People feel," as one citizen volunteered, "it is a second rate town. Young people get it from their parents." "The people move out, leave their houses vacant, and after awhile they look dingy." "We are in a rut. We have an inferiority complex." "Young people don't plan to stay." "Look at those vacancies on main street. It's depressing." "The people who should be leading just are not." "Leadership. Business people think it is a thankless job—don't want any part of it."

15) The Economic Research Service of the U.S. Department of Agriculture in a study of the effects of metropolitan growth trends on rural counties asserts that "the existence of a large, dense, and growing urban population in a region tends to create conditions of population growth in rural counties of the same region. This is true not only because an ever-larger number of the rural counties are within commuting range of urban centers, but also because more distant counties are affected by the accession of businesses or residents who do not need frequent commutation to the city but whose work or choice of residence is related to the city—especially the large metropolitan city. These are counties beyond 'exurbia' which the geographer Wilbur Zelinsky has referred to as the 'urban penumbra.'" *Op. cit.,* p. 14.

16) It is significant to note that if all present SMSA's of between 200,000 and 300,000 people were to reach the critical threshold size of 300,000 during the next generation, only a small expansion of the area now included in urban realms would occur. Most of these centers are located within or close to the edge of an existing urban realm and are thus encompassed by the boundaries we have provisionally defined.

17) For his most recent statement, see Karl Fox, "Programs for Economic Growth

in Non-Metropolitan Areas," paper prepared for the Third Conference on Regional Accounts, Miami Beach, Florida, November 19–21, 1964.

18) Otis D. Duncan, W. Richard Scott, Stanley Lieberson, Beverly Duncan, and Hal H. Winsborough, *Metropolis and Region*. Published for Resources for the Future, Inc. (Baltimore: The Johns Hopkins Press, 1960), p. 275.

19) The Core (New York City's four major boroughs and Hudson County) total population in 1985 is estimated by Vernon to be 7,810,000, a decline of almost half a million from the 1955 population. The Outer Ring (90 minutes from Manhattan to up to 30 miles beyond that) total is given to be 7,809,000, an increase of over 300 percent. Raymond Vernon, *Metropolis 1985* (Cambridge, Massachusetts: Harvard University Press, 1960), p. 221.

20) *Ibid.*, p. 224.

21) President's Council of Economic Advisers, *1964 Annual Report*, as reported in *Christian Science Monitor*, January 28, 1965.

22) As reported by Ralph Lazarus, "An 'Age of Fulfillment,'" in *Christian Science Monitor*, February 6, 1964.

23) As reported by Josephine Ripley, "U.S. Cultural Crescendo," in *Christian Science Monitor*, January 1, 1965.

24) The National Planning Association has projected an average work week of only 30 hours for the year 2000.

25) Outdoor Recreation Resources Review Commission, *Action for Outdoor Recreation for America* (Washington: Citizen's Committee for the ORRRC Report, 1964), p. 8.

26) Lewis Mumford, *The City in History* (New York: Harcourt, Brace & World, Inc., 1961), p. 564.

27) It will be recalled that the definition of an urban field is based on a metropolitan center of at least 300,000 inhabitants. From this it follows that an urban field may include within its perimeter smaller metropolitan areas as well as "satellite" cities of varying size up to the size of the metropolitan core area.

28) Archie Robertson, "Europe Moves to the Suburbs," *The Lamp*, XLVII (Spring, 1965), 29.

Bibliography

Bibliography

BIBLIOGRAPHY

INTRODUCTION *The Preamble and American Social Problems*

BECKER, HOWARD S., ed. *Social Problems: A Modern Approach.* New York: Wiley, 1966.
BERNARD, JESSE. *American Community Behavior,* 2nd ed. New York: Holt, Rinehart & Winston, 1962.
BREDEMEIER, HARRY C., and JACKSON TOBY, eds. *Social Problems in America: Costs and Casualties in an Acquisitive Society.* New York: Wiley, 1960.
CUBER, JOHN F., WILLIAM F. KENKEL, and ROBERT A. HARPER. *Problems of American Society: Values in Conflict,* 4th ed. New York: Holt, Rinehart & Winston, 1964.
DYNES, RUSSELL R., ALFRED C. CLARKE, SIMON DINITZ, and IWAO ISHINO. *Social Problems: Dissensus and Deviation in an Industrial Society.* New York: Oxford University Press, 1964.
HORTON, JOHN B. "Order and Conflict Theories of Social Problems as Competing Ideologies," *American Journal of Sociology,* LXXI (May, 1966), 701–714.
HORTON, PAUL B., and GERALD R. LESLIE. *The Sociology of Social Problems,* 3rd ed. New York: Appleton-Century-Crofts, 1965.
LERNER, MAX. *America as a Civilization.* New York: Simon and Schuster, 1957.
MARTINDALE, DON. *American Society.* Princeton, N.J.: Van Nostrand, 1960.
MERTON, ROBERT K., and ROBERT A. NISBET, eds. *Contemporary Social Problems,* 2nd ed. New York: Harcourt, Brace & World, 1966.
TOCQUEVILLE, ALEXIS DE. *Democracy in America,* 2 vols. New York: Vintage Books, 1954.
TUMIN, MELVIN. "The Functionalist Approach to Social Problems," *Social Problems,* XII (Spring, 1965), 379–388.
WILLIAMS, ROBIN M., JR. *American Society: A Sociological Interpretation,* 2nd ed. New York: Knopf, 1965.

CHAPTER ONE *We the People of the United States*

BROOM, LEONARD, and NORVAL D. GLEN. *Transformation of the Negro American.* New York: Harper & Row, 1965.
CLAGUE, EWAN. "Democratic Trends and Their Significance," in Hoke S. Simpson, ed., *The Changing American Population.* New York: Institute of Life Insurance, 1962, pp. 1–10.
CLARK, KENNETH B. *Dark Ghetto: Dilemmas of Social Power.* New York: Harper & Row, 1965.
DAY, LINCOLN, and ALICE T. DAY. *Too Many Americans.* Boston: Houghton Mifflin, 1964.
ELKINS, STANLEY M. *Slavery: A Problem in American Institutional and Intellectual Life.* New York: Grosset & Dunlap, 1963.

FREEDMAN, RONALD, ed. *Population: The Vital Revolution.* Garden City, N.Y.: Doubleday Anchor Books, 1964.

GENDELL, MURRAY, and HANS L. ZETTERBERG, eds. *A Sociological Almanac for the United States.* New York: Bedminster Press, 1961.

GLAZER, NATHAN. "The People of America," *The Nation,* CCI (September 20, 1965), 137–141.

GORDON, MILTON M. *Assimilation in American Life.* New York: Oxford University Press, 1964.

GUTTMACHER, ALAN F. "Fertility Rights in America," *Current,* LVIII (April, 1965), 30–32.

HANDLIN, OSCAR. *Race and Nationality in American Life.* Boston: Little, Brown, 1957.

HAUSER, PHILIP. *Population Perspectives.* New Brunswick, N.J.: Rutgers University Press, 1960.

HUGHES, EVERETT C., and HELEN M. HUGHES. *Where People Meet: Racial and Ethnic Frontiers.* Glencoe, Ill.: Free Press, 1952.

HUTCHINSON, E. P., ed. "The New Immigration," *The Annals of the American Academy of Political and Social Science,* CCCLXIII (September, 1966), 1–149.

"Immigration," *Law and Contemporary Problems,* XXI (Spring, 1956), 211–426.

KENNEDY, JOHN F. *A Nation of Immigrants.* New York: Harper & Row, 1964.

MARDEN, CHARLES F. *Minorities in American Society.* New York: American Book, 1952.

OGBURN, WILLIAM F., and OTIS DUDLEY DUNCAN. "City Size as a Sociological Variable," in Ernest W. Burgess and Donald J. Bogue, eds., *Contributions to Urban Sociology.* Chicago: University of Chicago Press, 1964, pp. 129–147.

PETERSEN, WILLIAM. *Population.* New York: Macmillan, 1961.

——. "The 'Scientific' Basis of Our Immigration Policy," in William Petersen and David Matza, eds., *Social Controversy.* Belmont, Cal.: Wadsworth, 1963, pp. 197–205.

ROSE, PETER I. *They and We.* New York: Random House, 1964.

ROSSI, ALICE S. "Abortion Laws and Their Victims," *Trans-action,* III (September-October, 1966), 7–12.

SCHUR, EDWIN. "Abortion," in *Crimes Without Victims: Deviant Behavior and Public Policy.* Englewood Cliffs, N.J.: Prentice-Hall, 1965.

SIMPSON, GEORGE E., and J. Milton Yinger. *Racial and Cultural Minorities,* 3rd ed. New York: Harper & Row, 1965.

SULLOWY, ALAN W. "The Legal and Political Aspects of Population Control in the United States," *Law and Contemporary Problems,* XXV (Summer, 1960), 593–613.

TOMLINSON, RALPH. *Population Dynamics: Causes and Consequences of World Demographic Changes.* New York: Random House, 1965.

U.S. BUREAU OF THE CENSUS. *Americans at Mid-Decade.* Washington, D.C.: Government Printing Office, Series P-23, No. 16, 1966.

VANDER ZANDEN, JAMES. *American Minority Relations: The Sociology of Race and Ethnic Groups.* New York: Ronald Press, 1963.

WATTENBERG, BEN J., and RICHARD M. SCAMMON. *This U.S.A.: An Unexpected Portrait of 194,067,296 Americans Drawn from the Census.* Garden City, N.Y.: Doubleday, 1965.

WAY, H. FRANK, JR. "Birth Control: A New Consensus," in Judson R. Landis, ed., *Current Perspectives on Social Problems.* Belmont, Cal.: Wadsworth, 1966, pp. 147–150.

WRONG, DENNIS H. *Population and Society,* 3rd ed. New York: Random House, 1964.

CHAPTER TWO *To Form a More Perfect Union*

ADAMS, WALTER. *The Structure of American Industry.* New York: Macmillan, 1961.

BERLE, ADOLPH A., JR. *Power Without Property.* New York: Harcourt, Brace, 1959.

———. "Property, Production and Revolution," *Columbia Law Review*, LXV (January, 1965), 1-20.

BIDWELL, CHARLES E. "Values, Norms and the Integration of Complex Social Systems," *Sociological Quarterly*, VII (Spring, 1966), 119-136.

BLAKE, JUDITH, and KINGSLEY DAVIS. "Norms, Values and Sanctions," in Robert E. L. Faris, ed., *Handbook of Modern Sociology*. Chicago: Rand McNally, 1964, pp. 456-484.

BODO, JOHN R. "The Pastor and Social Conflict," in Robert Lee and Martin E. Marty, eds., *Religion and Social Conflict*. New York: Oxford University Press, 1964, pp. 158-172.

BUNZEL, JOHN H. *The American Small Businessman*. New York: Knopf, 1962.

CHEIT, EARL F., ed. *The Business Establishment*. New York: Wiley, 1964.

COMMAGER, HENRY STEELE. "To Form a Much Less Perfect Union," *New York Times Magazine* (May 3, 1964), pp. 16ff.

D'ANTONIO, WILLIAM V. "Community Leadership in an Economic Crisis: Testing Ground for Ideological Cleavage," *American Journal of Sociology*, LXXI (May, 1966), 688-700.

ELAZAR, DANIEL J. *The American Partnership*. Chicago: University of Chicago Press, 1962.

FREEDMAN, RONALD, AMOS H. HAWLEY, WERNER S. LANDECKER, GERHARD E. LENSKI, and HORACE M. MINER. "Normative Integration" and "Functional Integration," in *Principles of Sociology*. 2nd ed. New York: Holt, Rinehart & Winston, 1956, pp. 170-230.

GRODZINS, MORTON. *The Loyal and the Disloyal*. Chicago: University of Chicago Press, 1956.

HANSEN, ALVIN. *The American Economy*. New York: McGraw-Hill, 1957.

HARRISS, C. LOWELL. *The American Economy: Principles, Practices and Policies*. Homewood, Ill.: Richard Irwin, 1953.

LANDECKER, WERNER S. "Types of Integration and Their Measurement," *American Journal of Sociology*, LVI (January, 1951), 332-340.

LITTELL, FRANKLIN HAMLIN. *From State Church to Pluralism: A Protestant Interpretation of Religion in American History*. Garden City, N.Y.: Doubleday Anchor, 1962.

MARNELL, WILLIAM H. *The First Amendment: The History of Religious Freedom in America*. Garden City, N.Y.: Doubleday Anchor, 1964.

MARTIN, ROSCOE C. *The Cities and the Federal System*. New York: Atherton, 1965.

McCONNELL, GRANT. *Private Power and American Democracy*. New York: Knopf, 1966.

MOORE, WILBERT E., and MELVIN TUMIN. "Some Social Functions of Ignorance," *American Sociological Review*, XIV (December, 1949), 787-795.

MOTT, PAUL E. "Some Sources of Integration," and "The Family as an Integrating Influence," in *The Organization of Society*. Englewood Cliffs, N.J.: Prentice-Hall, 1965, pp. 278-304.

REYNOLDS, HARRY W., ed. "Intergovernmental Relations in the United States," *Annals of the American Academy of Political and Social Science*, CCCLIX (May, 1965), 1-156.

TRUMAN, DAVID B. *The Governmental Process: Political Interests and Public Opinion*. New York: Knopf, 1955.

WILLIAMS, ROBIN M., JR. "The Integration of American Society," in *American Society*, 2nd ed. New York: Knopf, 1960, pp. 541-575.

ZEIGLER, HARMON. *Interest Groups in American Society*. Englewood Cliffs, N.J.: Prentice-Hall, 1964.

CHAPTER THREE   *To Establish Justice*

BEDAU, HUGO ADAM, ed. *The Death Penalty in America*. Garden City, N.Y.: Doubleday Anchor, 1964.

BENDIX, REINHARD, and SEYMOUR MARTIN LIPSET, eds. *Class, Status and Power*, 2nd ed. New York: Free Press, 1966.

Bordua, David J. *The Police.* New York: Wiley, 1966.

Brandt, Richard B., ed. *Social Justice:* Englewood Cliffs, N.J.: Prentice-Hall, 1962.

Carlin, Jerome E. *Lawyer's Ethics: A Survey of the New York City Bar.* New York: Russell Sage Foundation, 1966.

"Criminal Responsibility," *Issues in Criminology,* I (Fall, 1965), 1–178.

Dougherty, Richard. "The Case for the Cop," *Harpers,* CCCXXVIII (April, 1964), 129–133.

Evan, William M. "Public and Private Legal Systems," in William M. Evan, ed., *Law and Sociology: Exploratory Essays.* New York: Free Press, 1962, pp. 165–184.

Freed, Daniel J., and Patricia M. Wald. *Bail in the United States: 1964.* New York: Vera Foundation, 1964.

"The Future of Imprisonment in a Free Society," *Key Issues: A Journal of Controversial Issues in Criminology,* II (1965), 4–112.

Gellhorn, Walter. "Police Review Boards: Hoax or Hope?" *The Columbia University Forum,* IX (Summer, 1966), 5–10.

Ginsberg, Morris. *On Justice in Society.* Ithaca, N.Y.: Cornell University Press, 1965.

Goldfarb, Ronald. *Ransom: A Critique of the American Bail System.* New York: Harper & Row, 1965.

Goldstein, Joseph. "Police Discretion Not to Invoke the Criminal Process: Low-Visibility Decision in the Administration of Justice," *The Yale Law Review,* LXIX (March, 1960), 543–594.

Kalven, Harry, Jr., and Hans Zeisel. *The American Jury.* Boston: Little, Brown, 1966.

Kenniston, Ellen, and Kenneth Kenniston. "An American Anachronism: The Image of Women and Work," *American Scholar,* XXXIII (Summer, 1964), 355–375.

Lasswell, Harold D., and Richard G. Donnelly. "The Continuing Debate Over Responsibility: An Introduction to Isolating the Condemnation Sanction," *The Yale Law Review,* LXVIII (April, 1959), 869–899.

Lenski, Gerhard E. *Power and Privilege.* New York: McGraw-Hill, 1966.

Lipset, Seymour Martin, and Reinhard Bendix. *Social Mobility in an Industrial Society.* Berkeley: University of California Press, 1959.

Mayhew, Leon. "Law and Equal Opportunity." Unpublished dissertation, Harvard University, 1963.

Mead, Margaret, and Frances Bagley Kaplan, eds. *American Women: The Report of the President's Commission on the Status of Women and Other Publications of the Commission.* New York: Scribners, 1965.

Nagel, Stuart S. "The Tipped Scales of American Justice," *Trans-action,* III (May–June, 1966), 3–9.

Parmenter, Tom, ed. "The Credibility of American Justice," *Trans-action,* IV (July–August, 1967), 6–48.

Parsons, Talcott. "The Law and Social Control," in William M. Evan, ed., *Law and Sociology: Exploratory Essays.* New York: Free Press, 1962, pp. 56–72.

Reiss, Ira L., ed. "The Sexual Renaissance in America," *Journal of Social Issues,* XXII (April, 1966), 1–137.

Schur, Edwin M. *Crimes Without Victims.* Englewood Cliffs, N.J.: Prentice-Hall, 1965.

Simon, Rita James. *The American Jury: The Defense of Insanity.* Boston: Little Brown, 1967.

Skolnick, Jerome. *Justice Without Trial.* New York: Wiley, 1966.

"A Symposium on the Supreme Court and the Police: 1966," *Journal of Criminal Law, Criminology and Police Science,* LVII (September, 1966), 238–311.

Waelder, Robert. "The Concept of Justice: The Quest for an Absolutely Just Society," *Journal of Criminal Law, Criminology and Police Science,* LVII (March, 1966), 1–6.

Wechsler, Herbert. "Culpability and Crime: The Treatment of *Mens Rea* in the Model Penal Code," *Annals of the American Academy of Political and Social Science,* CCCXXXIX (January, 1962), 25–41.

WILSON, EVERETT K. "Class Differences in the Transmission of Culture," in *Sociology: Rules, Roles and Relationships.* Homewood, Ill.: Dorsey, 1966, pp. 181–226.

WRONG, DENNIS H. "The Functional Theory of Stratification," *American Sociological Review,* XXIV (December, 1959), 772–783.

ZEISEL, HANS, HARRY KALVEN, JR., and BERNARD BUCHOLZ. *Delays in Court.* Boston: Little, Brown, 1959.

CHAPTER FOUR *To Insure the Domestic Tranquility*

BAKAL, CARL. *The Right to Bear Arms.* New York: McGraw-Hill, 1966.

BEAL, EDWIN, and EDWARD D. WICKERSHAM. *The Practice of Collective Bargaining.* Homewood, Ill.: Richard D. Irwin, 1963.

BELL, DANIEL, ed. *The Radical Right.* New York: Doubleday Anchor, 1964.

COHEN, C. "The Essence and Ethics of Civil Disobedience," *The Nation,* CXCVIII (March 16, 1964), 257–262.

EDELMAN, JACOB MURRAY. "Symbols and Political Quiescence," in *The Symbolic Uses of Politics.* Urbana: University of Illinois Press, 1964, pp. 22–43.

"Federal Regulation of Firearm Sales," *University of Chicago Law Review,* XXXI (Summer, 1964), 780–790.

GAMSON, WILLIAM A. "Rancorous Conflict in Community Politics," *American Sociological Review,* XXXI (February, 1966), 71–80.

HAMMOND, PHILIP E., and ROBERT MITCHELL. "Segmentation of Radicalism: The Case of the Protestant Campus Ministry," *American Journal of Sociology,* LXXI (September, 1965), 133–143.

HORTON, PAUL B., and GERALD R. LESLIE. "Civil Liberties and Subversion," in *The Sociology of Social Problems,* 3rd ed. New York: Appleton-Century-Crofts, 1965, pp. 630–673.

LIEBERMAN, M. "Teachers' Strikes: An Analysis of the Issues," *Harvard Educational Review,* XXXVI (Winter, 1956), 36–69.

LIPSET, SEYMOUR MARTIN. "Social Conflict, Legitimacy and Democracy," in *Political Man.* Garden City, N.Y.: Doubleday Anchor, 1959, pp. 77–86.

LYND, STAUGHTON, ed. *Nonviolence in America: A Documentary History.* Indianapolis: Bobbs-Merrill, 1966.

NOSSITER, BERNARD. "Some Hidden Costs of Industrial Peace," *Annals of the American Academy of Political and Social Science,* CCCXLIII (September, 1963), 105–108.

PARSONS, TALCOTT. " 'Voting' and the Equilibrium of the American Political System," in Eugene Burdick and Arthur Brodbeck, eds., *American Voting Behavior.* Glencoe, Ill.: Free Press, 1959, pp. 80–120.

PROSHANSKY, HAROLD M., and RICHARD I. EVANS, eds. "America's Political Extremism in the 1960's," *Journal of Social Issues,* XIX (April, 1963), 1–131.

SCOTT, WILLIAM G. *The Management of Conflict: Appeal Systems in Organizations.* Homewood, Ill.: Irwin and Dorsey, 1965.

WASSERTROM, R. A. "The Obligation to Obey the Law," *UCLA Law Review,* X (May, 1963), 780–807.

WOLFGANG, MARVIN E., ed. "Patterns of Violence," *Annals of the American Academy of Political and Social Science,* CCCLXIV (March, 1966), 1–157.

CHAPTER FIVE *To Provide for the Common Defence*

ALMOND, GABRIEL. "Public Opinion and National Security Policy," *Public Opinion Quarterly,* XX (Summer, 1956), 371–378.

ARON, RAYMOND. *Peace and War: A Theory of International Relations,* translated by Richard Howard and Annette Baker Fox. New York: Doubleday, 1967.

BALDWIN, HANSON W. "The Draft Is Here to Stay, But It Should Be Changed," *New York Times Magazine* (November 20, 1966), pp. 48ff.

BENOIT, EMILE, and KENNETH BOULDING, eds. *Disarmament and the Economy.* New York: Harper & Row, 1963.

BLOOMFIELD, LINCOLN. "Peacekeeping and Peacemaking," *Foreign Affairs*, XLIV (July, 1966), 671–687.
——. "The UN and National Security," *Foreign Affairs*, XXXVI (July, 1958), 597–610.
BOBROW, DAVIS. *Components of Defense Policy.* Chicago: Rand McNally 1965.
BOULDING, KENNETH. *Conflict and Defense.* New York: Harper & Row, 1961.
BRODIE, BERNARD. "The Anatomy of Deterrence," *World Politics*, XI (January, 1959), 13–28.
BROGAN, D. W. "The United States: Civilian and Military Power," in Michael Howard, ed., *Soldiers and Governments.* Bloomington: Indiana University Press, 1959, pp. 167–185.
CHAPMAN, BRUCE K. *The Wrong Man in Uniform.* New York: Trident Press, 1967.
COOK, FRED J. *The Warfare State.* New York: Macmillan, 1962.
ETZIONI, AMITAI. *Winning Without War.* Garden City, N.Y.: Doubleday Anchor, 1965.
GARDNER, RICHARD N. *In Pursuit of World Order: U.S. Foreign Policy and International Organizations.* New York: Praeger, 1964.
GILPATRIC, ROSWELL. "Our Defense Needs: The Long View," *Foreign Affairs*, XLII (April, 1964), 366–378.
GOLDWIN, ROBERT A., ed. *America Armed.* Chicago: Rand McNally, 1963.
——. *Why Foreign Aid?* Chicago: Rand McNally, 1963.
HOAG, MALCOLM W. "On Stability in Deterrent Races," in Morton Kaplan, ed., *The Revolution in World Politics.* New York: Wiley, 1962, pp. 388–410.
HOROWITZ, IRVING L. *The War Games: Studies of the New Civilian Militarists.* New York: Ballantine Books, 1963.
HUNTINGTON, SAMUEL P. *The Soldier and the State.* Cambridge, Mass.: Harvard University Press, 1957.
KAHN, HERMAN. "The Arms Race and Some of Its Hazards," *Daedalus*, LXXXIX (Fall, 1960), 744–780.
KATZENBACH, EDWARD L. *The Separation of Power and National Security.* New York: Harper & Row, 1960.
KOLODZIEJ, EDWARD A. *The Uncommon Defense and Congress: 1945–1963.* Columbus, Ohio: Ohio State University Press, 1966.
LEVINE, ROBERT A. *The Arms Debate.* Cambridge, Mass.: Harvard University Press, 1963.
LUARD, EVAN. "Conventional Disarmament," *World Politics*, XVI (January, 1964), 189–204.
LYONS, GENE M. "The New Civil-Military Relations," *American Political Science Review*, LV (March, 1961), 53–67.
MELMAN, SEYMOUR. *Our Depleted Society.* New York: Holt, Rinehart & Winston, 1965.
MILLER, LYNN H. "The Contemporary Significance of the Doctrine of Just War," *World Politics*, XVI (January, 1964), 254–286.
MILLER, WILLIAM R. "Nonviolent National Defense," in *Nonviolence: A Christian Interpretation.* New York: Associated Press, 1964, pp. 97–118.
MILLS, C. WRIGHT. "The Warlords" and "The Military Ascendancy" in *The Power Elite.* New York: Galaxy Books, 1959, pp. 171–224.
MORGENTHAU, HANS. "The Four Paradoxes of Nuclear Strategy," *American Political Science Review*, LVIII (March, 1964), 23–35.
——. "A Political Theory of Foreign Aid," *American Political Science Review*, LVI (January, 1962), 301–309.
OSGOOD, ROBERT E. *Limited War: The Challenge to American Strategy.* Chicago: University of Chicago Press, 1957.
SCHELLING, THOMAS C. "The Role of Deterrence in Total Disarmament," *Foreign Affairs*, XL (April, 1962), 392–406.
——. *The Strategy of Conflict.* Cambridge, Mass.: Harvard University Press, 1960.

SHARP, GENE. "The Political Equivalent of War–Civilian Defense," *International Conciliation*, DLV (November, 1965), 1–67.

TUCKER, ROBERT W. *The Just War: A Study in Contemporary American Doctrine*. Baltimore: Johns Hopkins Press, 1960.

WASKOW, ARTHUR I. *The Limits of Defense*. Garden City, N.Y.: Doubleday, 1962.

WOLFERS, ARNOLD. "'National Security' as an Ambiguous Symbol," *Political Science Quarterly*, LXVII (December, 1952), 481–502.

CHAPTER SIX *To Promote the General Welfare*

BAUER, RAYMOND, ed. *Social Indicators: A First Approach*. Cambridge, Mass.: M.I.T. Press, 1966.

BECK, BERNARD. "Welfare as a Moral Category," *Social Problems*, XIV (Winter, 1967), 258–277.

BURNS, EVELINE. "Social Security in Evolution: Towards What?" *Social Science Review*, XXXIX (June, 1965), 129–140.

CARTER, RICHARD. *The Gentle Legions*. Garden City, N.Y.: Doubleday, 1961.

EELLS, RICHARD. *Corporation Giving in a Free Society*. New York: Harper & Row, 1956.

FERMAN, LOUIS, J. KORNBLUH, and A. HABER, eds. *Poverty in America*. Ann Arbor: University of Michigan Press, 1965.

FINE, SIDNEY. *Laissez Faire and the General-Welfare State*. Ann Arbor: University of Michigan Press, 1956.

GANS, HERBERT. "The Failure of Urban Renewal," *Commentary*, XXXIX (April, 1965), 29–37.

GILBERT, CHARLES E. "Policy-Making in Public Welfare: The 1967 Amendments," *Political Science Quarterly*, LXXXI (June, 1966), 196–224.

GORDON, MARGARET S., ed. *Poverty in America*. San Francisco: Chandler, 1965.

GREER, SCOTT. *Urban Renewal and American Cities*. Indianapolis: Bobbs-Merrill, 1965.

GURSSLIN, O. R., and J. L. ROACH. "Some Issues in Training the Unemployed," *Social Problems*, XII (Summer, 1964), 86–98.

HARRINGTON, MICHAEL. *The Other America*. New York: Macmillan, 1963.

———. "The Politics of Poverty," *Dissent*, XII (Autumn, 1965), 412–430.

KOOS, EARL L. *Families in Trouble*. New York: Kings Crown Press, 1946.

MARSH, DAVID C. *The Future of the Welfare State*. Baltimore: Penguin Books, 1964.

MEISSNER, HANNA, ed. *Poverty in the Affluent Society*. New York: Harper & Row, 1966.

MILLER, S. M. "The Politics of Poverty," *Dissent*, XI (Spring, 1964), 210–219.

MUSOLF, LLOYD D. *Government and the Economy: Promoting the General Welfare*. Chicago: Scott, Foresman, 1965.

MYRDAL, GUNNAR. *Challenge to Affluence*. New York: Vintage Books, 1965.

PACHTER, HENRY M. "Three Economic Models: Capitalism, Welfare-State and Socialism," *Dissent*, XI (Spring, 1964), 173–188.

PEARL, ARTHUR, and FRANK RIESSMAN, *New Careers for the Poor*. New York: Free Press, 1965.

REIN, MARTIN. "The Strange Case of Public Dependency," *Trans-action*, II (March-April, 1965), 16–23.

RIESSMAN, FRANK, JEROME COHEN, and ARTHUR PEARL. *The Mental Health of the Poor*. New York: Free Press, 1964.

Technology and the American Economy. Washington, D.C.: Government Printing Office, 0-788-561, 1966.

THEOBALD, ROBERT, ed. *The Guaranteed Income: Next Step in the Economic Evolution?* Garden City, N.Y: Doubleday, 1966.

WILENSKY, HAROLD, and CHARLES LEBEAUX. *Industrial Society and Social Welfare*. New York: Russell Sage, 1958.

WILL, ROBERT E., and HAROLD G. VATTER, eds. *Poverty in Affluence*. New York: Harcourt, Brace & World, 1965.

CHAPTER SEVEN   *To Secure the Blessings of Liberty*

ARENDT, HANNAH. *The Origins of Totalitarianism.* New York: Meridan Books, 1958.

CAHN, EDMOND. *The Predicament of Democratic Man.* New York: Delta Books, 1962.

FRIEDRICH, CARL, ed. *Totalitarianism.* New York: Grosset & Dunlap, 1964.

FROMM, ERICH. *The Escape from Freedom.* New York: Farrar and Rinehart, 1941.

JOSEPHSON, ERIC, and MARY JOSEPHSON. *Man Alone: Alienation in Modern Society.* New York: Dell, 1962.

KONVITZ, MILTON R. *Expanding Liberties.* New York: Viking, 1966.

KORNHAUSER, WILLIAM. *The Politics of the Mass Society.* Glencoe, Ill.: Free Press, 1959.

LEE, ALFRED MCCLUNG. *Multivalent Man.* New York: Braziller, 1966.

LIPSET, SEYMOUR MARTIN, and LEO LOWENTHAL. *Culture and Personality.* Glencoe, Ill.: Free Press, 1961.

MARKMANN, CHARLES. *The Noblest Cry.* New York: St. Martins Press, 1965.

MILLER, DANIEL R., and GUY E. SWANSON. *The Changing American Parent.* New York: Wiley, 1958.

NISBET, ROBERT A. *Community and Power.* New York: Galaxy Books, 1962.

PRESTHUS, ROBERT. *The Organizational Society.* New York: Random House, 1962.

RIESMAN, DAVID, NATHAN GLAZER, and REUEL DENNEY. *The Lonely Crowd.* Garden City, N.Y.: Doubleday Anchor, 1961.

WESTIN, ALAN F. *Science, Privacy and Freedom.* New York: Atheneum, 1967.

———. "Science, Privacy and Freedom: Issues and Proposals for the 1970's: Part I—The Current Impact of Surveillance on Privacy," *Columbia Law Review,* LXVI (June, 1966), 1003–1050.

WHITE, WINSTON. *Beyond Conformity.* Glencoe, Ill.: Free Press, 1961.

WHYTE, WILLIAM. *The Organization Man.* Garden City, N.Y.: Doubleday Anchor, 1957.

CHAPTER EIGHT   *To Ourselves and Our Posterity*

ALTSCHULER, ALAN. *The City Planning Process.* Ithaca, N.Y.: Cornell University Press, 1965.

BENNIS, WARREN G., KENNETH BENNE, and ROBERT CHIN, eds. *The Planning of Change.* New York: Holt, Rinehart & Winston, 1961.

BOLLENS, JOHN, and HENRY SCHMANDT. "The Shape of the Future," in *The Metropolis: Its People, Politics and Economic Life.* New York: Harper & Row, 1965, pp. 577–598.

BROWN, HARRISON, JAMES BONNER, and JOHN WEIR. *The Next Hundred Years.* New York: Viking, 1957.

BURNS, ARTHUR F. *The Management of Prosperity.* New York: Columbia University Press, 1966.

CHAPIN, F. STUART, JR. *Urban Land Use Planning.* Urbana: University of Illinois Press, 1965.

CLARK, BURTON R. *Educating the Expert Society.* San Francisco: Chandler, 1962.

COYLE, DAVID C. *Conservation: An American Story of Conflict and Accomplishment.* New Brunswick, N.J.: Rutgers University Press, 1957.

GOODMAN, PAUL. *Compulsory Mis-Education and the Community of Scholars.* New York: Vintage Books, 1964.

———. *Growing Up Absurd.* New York: Vintage Books, 1960.

GREENSTEIN, FRED I. *Children and Politics.* New Haven, Conn.: Yale University Press, 1965.

HEILBRONER, ROBERT L. *The Future as History.* New York: Grove, 1961.

LANDSBERG, HANS, LEONARD FISHMAN, and JOSEPH FISHER. *Resources in America's Future: Patterns of Requirements and Availabilities, 1960–2000.* Baltimore: Johns Hopkins Press, 1963.

LECHT, LEONARD, ed. *Goals, Priorities and Dollars: The Next Decade.* New York: Free Press, 1966.

LIEBERMAN, MYRON. *The Future of Public Education.* Chicago: University of Chicago Press, 1960.

MICHAEL, DONALD. *The Next Generation.* New York: Random House, 1965.

OGBURN, WILLIAM F. *On Culture and Social Change.* Chicago: University of Chicago Press, 1964.

PERLOFF, HARVEY S. "Social Planning in the Metropolis," in Leonard J. Duhl, ed., *The Urban Condition.* New York: Basic Books, 1963, pp. 319–330.

PETERSEN, WILLIAM. "On Some Meanings of 'Planning,'" *Journal of the American Institute of Planners,* XXXII (May, 1966), 130–142.

REISS, ALBERT J., JR., ed. *Schools in a Changing Society.* New York: Free Press, 1965.

RODWIN, LLOYD, ed. *The Future Metropolis.* New York: Braziller, 1961.

SIGEL, ROBERTA, ed. "Political Socialization: Its Role in the Political Process," *Annals of the American Academy of Political and Social Science,* CCCLXI (September, 1965), 1–129.

SMITH, GUY-HAROLD. *Conservation of Natural Resources,* 3rd ed. New York: Wiley, 1965.

"Toward the Year 2000: Work in Progress," *Daedalus,* XCVI (Summer, 1967), 639–988.

UDALL, STUART L. *The Quiet Crisis.* New York: Holt, Rinehart & Winston, 1963.

YOUNG, BENJAMIN F. *Social Planning in the United States: The Road to Collectivism.* New York: Pageant Press, 1960.

"Youth: Change and Challenge," *Daedalus,* LXXXIX (Winter, 1962), 3–237.

Indexes

AUTHOR INDEX

SUBJECT INDEX

A

Affluence
  moderation in, 386–387
  and war on poverty, 355
AFL-CIO, and Negroes, 70–71
Alcoholism, 140
Algerian crisis, 405
Alienation, 402, 406, 407, 423
American Civil War, 405
American Law Institute, 187
American society
  civilian vs. military interests, 268–271, 301–307
  countervailing power doctrine, 290–307
  and the hang-loose ethic, 383–393
  means of social control, 82–84
  religious vs. secular culture, 127–135, 385
  role of women, 142, 161–178
  as a social organization, 12–17, 299–300, 419–434
  thesis of elite control, 285–289
  value systems of, 86–94
American way of life
  definition of, 273
  effect of the cold war, 312–315
  in international relations, 275–276
  the open-class society, 148–149

and religion, 134
and super-patriotism, 148–149, 245–251
system of justice, 143–149
in the urban field, 491–494
values of business elites, 297–299
Amish sect, 80–81
Anglo-conformity
  defined, 41–46
  as a value, 14–15
Appalachia, poverty in, 478, 481
Area Redevelopment Administration, 481
Arms Control and Disarmament Agency, 294–295
Assimilation
  behavioral, 55–56
  of Negroes, 58
  of religious groups, 56
  social individualism vs. minority organization, 65–66
  structural, 55–56
  theories of, 39–59
Automation
  effect on labor force, 30
  and Negro unemployment, 64
  and the unions, 70
  See also Cybernation
Autonomy
  and the guaranteed income, 348–349